DOING PEACE THE RIGHTS WAY

Essays in International Law and Relations in Honour of Louise Arbour

Edited by
Fannie Lafontaine
François Larocque

intersentia
Cambridge – Antwerp – Chicago

Intersentia Ltd
Sheraton House | Castle Park
Cambridge | CB3 0AX | United Kingdom
Tel.: +44 1223 370 170 | Fax: +44 1223 370 169
Email: mail@intersentia.co.uk
www.intersentia.com | www.intersentia.co.uk

Distribution for the UK and Ireland:
NBN International
Airport Business Centre, 10 Thornbury Road
Plymouth, PL6 7PP
United Kingdom
Tel.: +44 1752 202 301 | Fax: +44 1752 202 331
Email: orders@nbninternational.com

Distribution for Europe and all other countries:
Intersentia Publishing nv
Groenstraat 31
2640 Mortsel
Belgium
Tel.: +32 3 680 15 50 | Fax: +32 3 658 71 21
Email: mail@intersentia.be

Distribution for the USA and Canada:
Independent Publishers Group
Order Department
814 North Franklin Street
Chicago, IL 60610
USA
Tel.: +1 800 888 4741 (toll free) | Fax: +1 312 337 5985
Email: orders@ipgbook.com

Doing Peace the Rights Way. Essays in International Law and Relations in Honour of Louise Arbour

ISBN 978-1-78068-354-6
D/2019/7849/6
NUR 824

GPRC
Guaranteed
Peer Reviewed
Content

British Library Cataloguing in Publication Data. A catalogue record for this book is available from the British Library.

FOREWORD

Lasting peace on Earth remains one of humankind's most earnest aspirations. As our population grows and our collective impact on this "pale blue dot" (to borrow Carl Sagan's imagery) is felt with increasing urgency, human societies must strive continuously to find new paths toward prosperous and peaceful coexistence. The manner in which we rise together to meet the ongoing challenges of our time – war, terrorism, environmental degradation, inequality and oppression – will ultimately determine the future of our species. It is only through multilateralism, dialogue and coordinated action that we can one day achieve the peaceful planet that our poets have imagined and that our children dearly deserve.

The edifice of this fairer, more peaceful world must be built on the pillars of security, inclusive development, the rule of law and respect for human rights. Together, these pillars mutually reinforce one another, all while remaining ends unto themselves. They also provide the United Nations with its *raison d'être*, grounded in the spirit of the UN Charter and the Universal Declaration of Human Rights. No country can develop in the long term without security and stability, nor can one remain stable without inclusive development that lifts up the people and ensures their welfare. But these must in turn be based on the rule of law and respect for human rights. An edifice of peace and prosperity is always weakened when public power is left unchecked and human dignity is forfeited for security or profit.

In a thought-provoking examination of these themes comes this new collection of texts: *Doing Peace the Rights Way*. Dedicated to Louise Arbour, it explores an impressive variety of issues and perspectives on the enforcement of human rights and the pursuit of peace. Throughout the various posts that she has held during her remarkable career, Louise Arbour has always championed the cause of human rights, framing her analyses and arguments to applicable law, urging nations to cooperate and unite by complying with their international human rights obligations. I came to see this first hand when I nominated her to serve as UN High Commissioner for Human Rights during my tenure as Secretary-General.

The chapters in this collection of essays, written by leaders from various fields who interacted with Louise Arbour at different times of her life, touch on themes she cares about. They touch on themes I care about. They touch on themes we all care – or should care – about. Louise Arbour's life's work powerfully illustrates how the rule of law is essential to the building of a fairer, more peaceful world. This book is a tribute to the outstanding contribution she has made toward that goal and an authoritative companion to our efforts to realize the noblest of humanity's collective ideals.

Kofi A. Annan
May 2017, Geneva

DOING PEACE THE RIGHTS WAY

CONTENTS

LIST OF CONTRIBUTORS

Tity Agbahey holds degrees in criminal law and criminology and works at Amnesty International's Regional Office in Dakar, Senegal. Prior to that, she was the Africa Programme Associate at Girls Not Brides, a global partnership of over 500 civil society organizations committed to ending child marriage and enabling girls to fulfil their potential. She was previously a member of UNICEF Paris' advocacy team and has worked as a Junior Research Fellow in the Dakar office of the Institute for Security Studies (ISS) in the conflict prevention and risk analysis division. As part of her work, she conducted policy-oriented research on human security issues in Nigeria and the Mano River Union region. She is a member of WATHI, a participative and multidisciplinary citizen think tank on West African issues.

Philip Alston is John Norton Pomeroy Professor of Law at New York University School of Law. He has taught at the European University Institute, the Australian National University, Harvard Law School and the Fletcher School of Law and Diplomacy. He co-founded both the European and the Australian and New Zealand societies of international law and was Editor-in-Chief of the European Journal of International Law. He served as UN Special Rapporteur on extreme poverty and human rights; UN Special Rapporteur on extrajudicial execution; Member of the Independent International Commission on Kyrgyzstan; UN Group of Experts on Darfur; Special Adviser to the UN High Commissioner for Human Rights on the Millennium Development Goals; UN Committee on Economic, Social, and Cultural Rights (chairperson and rapporteur); and Senior Legal Adviser on children's rights at UNICEF.

Natasha Bakht is Associate Professor of Law at the University of Ottawa, Canada. Her research interests are generally in the area of law, culture and minority rights and specifically at the intersection of religious freedom and women's equality. She has written extensively in the area of religious arbitration and assisted in Canadian judicial education on issues of religion, culture and diversity. Her writings on the rights of niqab-wearing women were cited by the Supreme Court of Canada. She clerked for Justice Louise Arbour at the Supreme Court of Canada and was an active member of the Law Program Committee of the Women's Legal Education and Action Fund. She is the current English Language Editor of the Canadian Journal of Women and the Law (CJWL). She is also an Indian contemporary dancer and choreographer.

Camille Marquis Bissonnette is a doctoral candidate in International Law at Université Laval, Quebec City, Canada. She is the Coordinator of the Canada Research Chair on International Criminal Justice and Fundamental Rights. Her thesis deals with the impact of the indeterminacy of the word "terrorism" on the protection of the person in international law. She is co-editor of the academic blog *Quid Justitiae*. She completed a Master of Laws at the Academy of International Humanitarian Law and Human Rights in Geneva, which also led to her articling at the United Nations International Law Commission.

Andrew Clapham is Professor of Public International Law at the Graduate Institute of International and Development Studies, Geneva. He was the first Director of the Geneva Academy of International Humanitarian Law and Human Rights. Prior to joining the Institute, he was the Representative of Amnesty International at the United Nations in New York. He served as Special Adviser on Corporate Responsibility to High Commissioner for Human Rights Mary Robinson, and Adviser on International Humanitarian Law to Sergio Vieira de Mello, Special Representative of the UN Secretary-General in Iraq. He is an Associate Member of Matrix Chambers. He was recently appointed by the Human Rights Council's President to be a member of the Commission on Human Rights in South Sudan.

Luc Côté has been a criminal law attorney for nearly 30 years, with a particular focus on international criminal law, and is an expert on transitional justice. He served as Senior Legal Adviser with the UN International Criminal Tribunal for Rwanda and Chief of Prosecutions for the Special Court for Sierra Leone. He was Executive Director of the UN Independent Special Commission of Inquiry for Timor-Leste, led the UN mapping exercise on the Democratic Republic of Congo (DRC), served on the Independent International Commission of Inquiry for Kyrgyzstan, coordinated the program to support the rule of law for the UN Mission in Haiti and was appointed to the international team of experts on the situation in the Kasai regions of the DRC.

Pablo Espiniella is a Human Rights Expert currently working at the Office of the Director of the Division of Field Operations and Technical Cooperation, Office of the United Nations High Commissioner for Human Rights (OHCHR). Previously, he was OHCHR Deputy Regional Representative for South East-Asia in Bangkok and OHCHR Deputy Regional Representative for Europe in Brussels. He has undertaken numerous human rights monitoring missions and short deployments to Timor Leste, Myanmar, Nepal, Tunisia and Guatemala. He has been the assistant to numerous UN Special Rapporteurs including migrant rights, internally displaced persons, indigenous peoples, extrajudicial or summary executions, and worked in the Secretariat of the Human Rights Committee. Through these experiences and his academic work, he has provided legal advice on the advancement of protection and promotion of migrant rights, in particular migrant children. His experience outside of the Office of the High Commissioner includes two years with the World Bank. He has a PhD in International Law and Human Rights with a Doctoral Thesis focused on the legal protection of article 3 of the Convention on the Rights of the Child in the case of unaccompanied migrant children.

Fabrizio Hochschild is UN Assistant Secretary-General for Strategic Coordination. He previously served as Deputy Special Representative for the UN Multidimensional Integrated Stabilization Mission in the Central African Republic; Deputy to the UN Secretary-General's Special Adviser for the Summit on Addressing Large Movements of Refugees and Migrants; UN Resident Coordinator, Humanitarian Coordinator and Resident Representative of the UN Development Programme in Colombia; Director of the Field Personnel Division in the United Nations Department of Field Support; and Chief of Field Operations and Technical Cooperation in the Office of the High Commissioner for Human Rights. He has worked in the Office of the United Nations High Commissioner for Refugees, the UN Relief and Works Agency for Palestinian Refugees and in the Office for the Coordination of Humanitarian Affairs, with Postings in Sudan, Jerusalem, Bosnia & Herzegovina, Geneva, New York, Timor-Leste, Serbia and Tanzania.

Hina Jilani has over 30 years' experience as a lawyer and civil society activist in Pakistan. She specializes in human rights litigation on behalf of women, children, minorities and prisoners. Along with her sister, the late Asma Jahangir, she co-founded Pakistan's first all-female legal practice in 1980. She is a co-founder of the Human Rights Commission of Pakistan and the Women's Action Forum, as well as the founder of Pakistan's first legal aid center in 1986. She has collaborated with the UN Center for Human Rights, the Carter Center and the UN Conference on Women. She served as the UN Special Representative of the Secretary General on Human Rights Defenders, Member of the UN International Fact-Finding Commission on Darfur, and Member of the Eminent Jurists Panel on Terrorism, Counter-Terrorism and Human Rights. She was recently appointed President of the World Organisation Against Torture.

Alana Klein is an Associate Professor at McGill University's Faculty of Law, where she is co-convener of the McGill Research Group in Health and Law. She teaches and researches in the areas of criminal law, health law, and human and constitutional rights. Current research, funded by FQRSC, SSHRC and CIHR, focuses on harm reduction and on the roles of marginalized groups in shaping and informing law and governance. She received a J.S.D. from Columbia Law School in 2011, and earned LL.B. and BCL degrees from McGill University's Faculty of Law in 2002. Prior to joining McGill's Faculty of Law, she was a law clerk to Justice Louise Arbour of the Supreme Court of Canada, a senior policy analyst with the Canadian HIV/AIDS Legal Network, and a member of the Ontario Human Rights Commission.

Fannie Lafontaine is a lawyer, Professor at the Faculty of Law at Université Laval and holder of the Canada Research Chair on International Criminal Justice and Human Rights. She directs the SSHRC-funded Canadian Partnership for International Justice and co-directs the International Criminal and Humanitarian Law Clinic, which she founded. She is the author of the book *Prosecuting Genocide, Crimes Against Humanity and War Crimes in Canadian Courts* and of many other publications in Canadian and international law and relations. Before joining Université Laval, she worked at the Office of the UN High Commissioner for Human Rights, on the International Commission of Inquiry on Darfur, at the Supreme Court of Canada as a clerk for Louise Arbour, in NGOs and at a large Canadian law firm. She continues to advise human rights organizations and, more recently, serves as the independent civilian auditor of an investigation into criminal acts alleged to have been committed by members of different police forces against members of First Nations in Quebec.

François Larocque is a lawyer, Professor and holder of the Canadian Francophonie Research Chair in Language Rights at the University of Ottawa Faculty of Law. Prior to his academic appointment, he clerked at both the Court of Appeal for Ontario and at the Supreme Court of Canada for Justice Louise Arbour. He completed his doctoral research at the University of Cambridge (Trinity College) under the joint supervision of Professors James Crawford and Philip Allott on the jurisdiction of national courts in civil proceedings for serious violations of international law. He has published numerous books and articles on transnational human rights litigation and language rights and practices law in these areas as well, and has appeared before all levels of court in Canada in several precedent-setting cases.

Tim McCormack is Dean of Law at the University of Tasmania Law School, an honorary Professorial Fellow at Melbourne Law School, Special Adviser on International Humanitarian Law to the Prosecutor of the International Criminal Court in The Hague and Fellow of the Australian Academy of Law. Tim was the Charles H Stockton Distinguished Scholar-in-Residence at the US Naval War College in Newport, Rhode Island (2015–16), a member of the International Group of Experts for Tallinn Manual 2.0 on the International Law Applicable to Cyber Operations (2015–17), an international observer for Phase II of the Turkel Commission to Enquire into Israel's Procedures for Investigating Allegations of Violations of the Law of Armed Conflict (2011–13) and *amicus curiae* on International Law matters for the trial of Slobodan Milošević (2002–06).

Lisa N. Oldring is Senior Adviser on Human Rights and Security Policies with the Office of the United Nations High Commissioner for Human Rights in

Geneva. She has been the principal author of UN reports on human rights and counter-terrorism; global surveillance practices and the right to privacy; the use of force; and other related issues. She has served with the UN as legal advisor to international commissions of inquiry on Darfur and on Lebanon, and as a human rights officer in Rwanda. She has also served as Special Advisor to Mary Robinson, based in New York, and to the first UN Special Rapporteur on the right to health.

Kim Pate is a Canadian Senator. She was the Executive Director of the Canadian Association of Elizabeth Fry Societies (CAEFS) from January 1992 until her appointment to the Senate in November 2016. She has dedicated her career to working in and around the legal and penal systems of Canada, with and on behalf of some of the most marginalized, victimized, criminalized and institutionalized – particularly imprisoned youth, men and women. She is widely credited as the driving force behind the Inquiry into Certain Events at the Prison for Women in Kingston, headed by Louise Arbour. During the inquiry, she supported women as they aired their experiences and was a critical resource and witness in the inquiry itself. She graduated from Dalhousie Law School in 1984 with honours in the Clinical Law Programme and has completed postgraduate work in the area of forensic mental health. She taught at the law faculties at the University of Ottawa, Dalhousie University and the University of Saskatchewan respectively.

Antonia Potter Prentice is co-managing partner of Athena, which provides specialist advice, policy analysis and project management on peace and security issues. She is also Director of Alliance 2015, a global network of humanitarian and development organizations. Previously she served as Senior Manager on Mediation Support, Gender and Inclusion for the Crisis Management Initiative (CMI); Senior Adviser to the European Institute for Peace; interim Senior Gender Adviser to the Joint Peace Fund for Myanmar; Adviser to UN Women and the Office of the Special Envoy of the UN Secretary General to the Yemen peace process; Senior Advisor to the Dialogue Advisory Group; Senior Associate to the European Peacebuilding Liaison Office; and Project Manager and Senior Adviser for the Centre for Humanitarian Dialogue (HD) project, 'Women at the Peace Table – Asia Pacific'. She was Country Director for Oxfam GB in Indonesia.

Mona Rishmawi is Chief of the Rule of Law, Equality and Non-Discrimination Branch at the Office of the UN High Commissioner for Human Rights. She served as the OHCHR Legal Adviser and the Coordinator of the Rule of Law and Democracy Unit, and as the Executive Director of the UN International Commission of Inquiry on Darfur. She served as Senior Policy Adviser to UN High Commissioners for Human Rights Mary Robinson and Sérgio Vieira de Mello; UN Independent Expert on the Situation of Human Rights in Somalia;

and Director of the Centre for the Independence of Judges and Lawyers of the International Commission of Jurists (ICJ) in Geneva. She practiced law from 1981–91 in the West Bank and was a senior member of the human rights organization Al-Haq, which she also directed from 1990–91. She holds an LLM from Columbia Law School.

William Schabas is Professor of International Law at Middlesex University, London; Professor of International Criminal Law and Human Rights at Leiden University; and Emeritus Professor of Human Rights Law at the National University of Ireland Galway. He is the author of more than twenty books dealing with international human rights law and has published more than 350 articles in academic journals, principally in the fields of international human rights law and international criminal law. His writings have been translated into Russian, German, Spanish, Portuguese, Chinese, Japanese, Arabic, Persian, Turkish, Nepali and Albanian. He has served on the Sierra Leone Truth and Reconciliation Commission. He has worked as a consultant on capital punishment for the UN Office of Drugs and Crime, and drafted the 2010 and 2015 reports of the Secretary-General on the status of the death penalty.

J. **Michael Spratt** is a partner at the criminal law firm Abergel Goldstein & Partners, Ottawa. Mr. Spratt was called to the Bar in 2005 after graduating law school at Dalhousie University and articling in Toronto at the criminal law firm Hicks Block Adams. He has appeared in the Supreme Court of Canada and all levels of court in Ontario. He frequently appears as an expert witness before Canada's House of Commons and the Senate, providing evidence on criminal law policy. He is an award-winning blogger and has a podcast, *The Docket*, which he co-hosts with his spouse Emilie Taman, daughter of Louise Arbour. He has served as a Director of the Criminal Lawyers' Association and Treasurer and Vice-President of the Defence Counsel Association of Ottawa. He has been a guest instructor at the University of Ottawa law school, Carleton University and Algonquin College, and frequently presents at legal conferences.

James K. Stewart is Deputy Prosecutor at the International Criminal Court. Prior to joining the Office of the Prosecutor (OTP) of the ICC in 2012, Mr. Stewart worked as General Counsel in the Crown Law Office within the Ministry of the Attorney General, Toronto. Before this, he served as Senior Trial Attorney in the OTP at the International Criminal Tribunal for Rwanda (ICTR); as Chief of Prosecutions in the OTP at the International Criminal Tribunal for the former Yugoslavia (ICTY); and as Senior Appeals Counsel and then Chief of the Appeals and Legal Advisory Division in the OTP at the ICTR. He also served with the Office of the Ombudsman as a legal officer for two years. He is bilingual in English and French, graduated from the Faculty of Law at the University of Toronto and was called to the Ontario Bar.

Gilles Olakounlé Yabi is the founder of WATHI, a West Africa Citizen Think Tank based in Senegal. He spent seven years as Senior Political Analyst and later as Project Director for the West Africa Project of the International Crisis Group, a think tank dedicated to conflict prevention and resolution. He holds a PhD in Development Economics from the University of Clermont-Ferrand, France, and has also worked as a journalist for the weekly magazine *Jeune Afrique*.

INTRODUCTION

This *festschrift* honours the remarkable career of Louise Arbour and the indelible impact she has had and continues to have on the development of international law and institutions as Prosecutor for the International Criminal Tribunals for Rwanda and the former Yugoslavia (1996–1999), United Nations High Commissioner for Human Rights (2004–2008), CEO of the International Crisis Group (2009–2014) and Special Representative of the UN Secretary-General for International Migration (2017–present). She rose to the top rungs of the Canadian legal profession, shaping the law first as an academic and then as a judge, eventually sitting on its highest bench, the Supreme Court of Canada. Of course, Louise's career is not over. Truth be told, we doubt it will ever really be over. This collection of essays is thus not meant as an *au revoir* or as a celebration of past achievements. She would hate that, and we know her far too well to even consider indulging in nostalgia or panegyrics. Rather, this book is meant as a tribute, which comes at no particularly striking moment, to salute the ongoing contributions of this admired and influential woman, jurist and thought leader. It is also one of the only recognitions we could offer that would stand out in the vast constellation of prestigious prizes and awards she has received over the years!

Louise Arbour is a leader on issues of conflict prevention and resolution, criminal justice, human rights and migration, to name but a few, and her vision often sets the standard. In each of the positions she has held, she has worked with fierce determination and great intelligence to unprecedented effect, and always with a view of advancing the rule of law and respect for human rights. She once said: "Nothing happens without people. Nothing lasts without institutions. Nothing lives without people reinventing institutions."[1] This uncompromising belief in the human potential to change things for the better has not only been the drive behind her initiatives and successes, but also a true source of inspiration for the countless individuals who have gravitated in her orbit along the years.

The contributors to this collective work are all leading experts on the international stage or in their national jurisdictions and they have interacted closely with Louise Arbour in the course of her extraordinary career. The chapters in this collection focus on a broad range of international and national problems, norms and institutions, in recognition of the breadth and depth of

1 Louise Arbour, "Convocation Address" (2001) 26 *Queen's LJ* 569 at 570.

Louise's influence in a variety of areas. Those chapters that deal principally with Canadian law often do so on a comparative basis with other jurisdictions, showing the universal resonance and challenges of human rights and law enforcement. The authors challenge longstanding assumptions and bring fresh ideas to ongoing debates that lie at the core of global debates. A common thread running through the individual contributions is the interaction between justice and peace, between human rights and conflict, and between law and politics in both the international and domestic spheres. Another common thread is the passion and dedication that ground the contributors' choice of topics, which all closely or tangentially link to Arbour's work and interests along the years.

The book opens with a foreword by the late Kofi Annan, former Secretary-General of the United Nations and Nobel Peace Prize Laureate, who appointed Louise as United Nations High Commissioner for Human Rights and who was closely involved with her in some of the greatest battles for peace and human rights in the United Nations' recent history. Mr. Annan passed away on 18 August 2018 as this book was in the final process of publication. His words and *hommage* to Louise, written a few months ago and published now that he has left us, resound with unequalled power and are felt with the greatest of emotions. On the day of his passing, Louise commented: *"C'est un homme qui a représenté et qui continue de représenter des valeurs qui sont en perte de vitesse dans le monde actuel. Des valeurs de paix, de justice, de compassion, d'humanité."*[2] As his foreword eloquently shows, this respect and admiration was reciprocal. We are grateful that Mr. Annan added his voice to this *festschrift*.

The book is separated into three main parts that imperfectly group together contributions that relate to some of Louise Arbour's great interests throughout her career. Part I, entitled "Of Freedom and Equality," covers issues such as the human rights obligations and accountability of non-state actors, and the role of civil society in promoting the rule of law; the right to truth; the links between terrorism and corruption and inequality; socio-economic rights; the war on drugs; and the rights of children in a migration context.

Andrew Clapham writes on the human rights obligations of non-state actors, accepting from the outset that these obligations indeed exist, despite the unsettled appearance of the question in the legal literature. Non-state actors are indeed held accountable in different ways, though the extent of their obligations is invariably contextual, turning on their legal capacity and commitments. Clapham illustrates his claim by discussing the legal and attitudinal developments

2 "This is a man who has embodied and continues to embody values that are losing ground in today's world. Values of peace, justice, compassion, humanity." Radio-Canada, "Les hommages pleuvent après la mort de Kofi Annan", 18 August 2018, available at: https://ici.radio-canada.ca/nouvelle/1118760/kofi-annan-mort-80-ans-secretaire-general-onu.

that have emerged with respect to armed groups, such as ISIS, and multinational corporations.

William Schabas' chapter on the right to truth is a thoughtful reflection on that norm's conceptual ancestry, content and current position within the mainstream human rights framework. Though it is often framed as a personal right belonging to individual victims of crime and their families, the right to truth also possesses a collective dimension and broad social function by requiring the establishment of a credible historical record on which national healing, reconciliation and peace can be based. A related question is the temporal scope of the right and whether it applies in equal measure to recent and more ancient historical events.

Tity Agbahey and Gilles Olakounlé Yabi present a thoughtful history and analysis of the social, economic and political contexts that contributed to the rise of Boko Haram in Nigeria, highlighting that country's continuing struggles with corruption and inequality.

Alana Klein canvasses a number of creative approaches toward the realization of social and economic rights developed in human rights scholarship and practice since the turn of the millennium. These approaches are aimed at overcoming the capacity and legitimacy concerns that are typically alleged in relation to the adjudication of social and economic rights relative to civil and political rights, while also responding to a deeper skepticism about the relationship between legal and human rights practice more broadly and progressive social change.

Examining the experience of her native Pakistan, Hina Jilani reflects on the role civil society can play in ensuring respect for human rights and the rule of law. She makes a powerful case on that front by highlighting the positive results that were obtained through public interest litigation and popular mobilization in the fight against bonded labor and violence against women. The human rights success stories, if they are to be replicated, require, among other elements, an engaged citizenry and an independent judiciary.

J. Michael Spratt's chapter is an indictment of Canada's so-called war on drugs and its harmful effects on thousands of Canadians. Referencing reports from the Global Commission on Drug Policy that have yet to find much traction in Canada, Spratt describes and critiques that country's evolving drug policy, from prohibition to safe injection sites and the legalization of marijuana.

Pablo Espiniella looks at the complex situation of unaccompanied or separated children in the context of large mixed movements of people, undoubtedly one of the greatest human rights protection challenges of our time. He provides a thorough review of the applicable international legal rules, digging into the sometimes damaging interaction between migration policies and child protection frameworks, exploring crucial issues such as age determination processes in light of the central concept of the best interest of the child.

Part II, entitled "Of Peace and Justice," contemplates the challenges that arise in contemporary criminal justice at both the international and national levels; human rights fact-finding; national security and human rights; civil accountability for gross human rights violations; and the laws of war.

In his chapter, the International Criminal Court's Deputy-Prosecutor James K. Stewart discusses both the theoretical function and real-world impact of the International Criminal Court in deterring or preventing international crimes. Social science evidence measuring the efficacy of international criminal liability regimes in reducing violence and enhancing protection for human rights is still scarce. The Office of the Prosecutor, for its part, is bound to adhere to the Rome Statute's underlying rationale of deterrence and crime prevention, even if the results on the ground prove to be imperfect.

In her chapter, Mona Rishmawi sets out a four-part taxonomy of the various types of human rights fact-finding during times of raging conflict. It is a useful primer on the topic that explains the normative framework and various applicable legal regimes, in addition to practical considerations such as the use of third-party contractors and witness protection.

Lisa N. Oldring offers a thought-provoking look at what she calls "the normalization of exceptional measures in the context of national security." Policies and practices that were once considered extraordinary in liberal democratic societies, such as the extended or indefinite detention of individuals without charge, the use of secretive judicial processes, mass surveillance of individuals' communications without warrant and targeted killings, are adopted in response to real or perceived security threats and are no longer exceptional. She examines the shift toward the normalization of exceptional measures and reflects on how legitimate security concerns can be accommodated within a rule of law framework.

Fannie Lafontaine, the co-editor of this book, critically assesses the Canadian approach to war criminals present on its territory in light of comparative experiences in other states and of the international law framework related to states' responsibility in the fight against impunity for international crimes. She explains the historical context of the Canadian approach, delves into the dilemmas that states must face when confronted with the presence of foreign war criminals, and proposes a reflection on what could be called 'alternative universal justice', which would recognize the impossibility of prosecuting all potential suspects of international crimes present on the territory of a third state, while taking into account fundamental principles of accountability, satisfaction and reparation.

In his chapter, Luc Côté explores the legal, political and institutional challenges that face all international criminal prosecutors. From Nuremberg to the International Criminal Court, international prosecutors play a unique and difficult role in a system that is at once consensual (international law) and coercive (criminal law). He explains the institutional and normative safeguards that are and must be put in place to ensure the independence and impartiality of the prosecutor, and discusses the various challenges faced by the individuals occupying the position and the successes and failures in upholding these fundamental values.

In his chapter, François Larocque, the other co-editor of this book, describes the current infelicitous state of an international law that fails to recognize the jurisdiction of national courts in civil proceedings for extraterritorial torture and upholds the immunity and impunity of governments that violate the peremptory norms that prohibit torture.

In an extensive survey, Tim McCormack reflects on the challenges to international humanitarian law since the 1990s and those that have emerged in the twenty-first century. He argues that in a complex global environment, characterized by the absence of a comprehensive international criminal justice system (despite the International Criminal Court), variegated efforts to prohibit indiscriminate weapons of war and increasingly devastating technologically driven threats – the international community must imperatively reaffirm its commitment to humanitarianism and to the fundamental ideals of international humanitarian law.

Part III, entitled "Of Women and Leadership," offers discussions on individual and institutional leadership, on women's human rights, and on their role and potential in peace-making.

Fabrizio Hochschild's chapter on moral courage (which he distinguishes from physical courage) is a thought-provoking reflection on the qualities of leadership that have occasionally been exemplified within the United Nations (notably by Louise Arbour). Weaving lesser-known anecdotes and inspiring quotes from UN leaders, he states a powerful case for the need, now more than ever, for courageous women and men to be at the helm of our international institutions.

Philip Alston addresses the question of whether the World Bank should engage with human rights and, if so, why and how. With a lucid analysis, he describes how human rights are approached differently depending on which aspect of the World Bank's multifaceted work is involved, in the areas of legal policy, public relations, policy analysis, operations and safeguards. He knowledgably explores the historical aversion of the institution towards human rights and offers compelling arguments as to why a new approach to human rights is needed for this leading institution, what it would change and what it could look like.

Antonia Potter Prentice and Camille Marquis Bissonnette assess the impact of UN Security Council Resolution 1325 (2000) on women's representation in peace negotiations. They expertly delve into the reasons why women should be involved in peace-making, explaining what UNSCR 1325 was intended to do, before looking at its achievements and shortcomings. Their recommendations to fast-track the implementation and impact of UNSCR 1325 with regard to women's participation in peace-making are grounded in a profound reflection on the transformational power of UNSCR 1325, and on the risks associated with the existing status quo in the context of the current proliferation of armed conflicts, violent extremism and their massive and indiscriminate impact on society, civilians and social institutions.

In her chapter, Kim Pate explores why women – particularly indigenous women and those with disabling mental health issues – constitute Canada's fastest-growing prison population. She exposes the systemic causes and alarming significance of this trend, but also describes potential solutions involving both public policy and law reform.

Using France and Canada as examples, Natasha Bakht deconstructs the arguments that are regularly put forth by western democracies that attempt to prohibit face veils or the niqab in the name of secularism or equality. In so doing, she illuminatingly highlights the voices of niqab-wearing women who challenge stereotypes that link agentic choices with oppression.

The Appendix first contains a 2014 interview that the *Ottawa Law Review* conducted with Louise Arbour. It traces her career and enters into lesser-known biographical details about the different paths she chose, or that chose her, at different intersections of her professional journey. Her remarkable sense of humour and self-mockery transpire throughout the interview. "Why am I so often moved to very different things? … I think it's pretty obvious that what I like and crave is that period of uncertainty – that kind of learning curve. It's very clear: I really like that phase where I don't really get it … It's just that I seem to have this irresistible attraction to taking on something for which I'm entirely unqualified". How many internationally renowned jurists and leaders could answer a question on their career path with such humility and wit? Louise Arbour has always been inclined to take on new challenges, filling her suitcase along the way with experience and knowledge that would then allow her to bring fresh perspectives and new ideas on the next journey.

As the great Québécois poet Gilles Vigneault once said: "La violence, c'est un manque de vocabulaire."[3] Citing him at a convocation address while receiving one of her innumerable honorary doctorates, Louise Arbour said: "I believe that education and knowledge offer us the ability to develop a vocabulary for expressing ourselves without violence. But the richness of that vocabulary will mean nothing without the courage to speak it out loud."[4] Louise has always found and used the right words with great talent to fiercely and restlessly fight against oppression and abuse. Her language is unswerving, frank, just, accessible and fearless. Her messages of justice, dignity and equality speak truth to power

3 Editors' translation: "Violence is a lack of vocabulary."

4 Arbour, "Convocation Address," *supra* note 1.

without complacency, with prudent optimism and irresistible conviction. They are weaved with stories, metaphors and humour, the recognizable hallmarks of all her speeches and writings.

We therefore include in this book a bibliography of Louise Arbour's own words, through a selection of speeches and writings produced at different times in her career, most of which are freely available. They cover different topics – laws of war, self-determination and conflict resolution, the responsibility to protect, economic and social rights, transitional justice, international criminal justice, the rule of law, human rights in the fight against terrorism and migration. The exercise of curating her thoughts and words was excruciatingly difficult. To ensure that this book remains affordable and thus accessible to a greater number of readers, we set aside (for now) the goal of publishing her complete works and opted more modestly for a fairly representative sample of her writings on a broad range of issues that were of great importance to her. Of course, the chosen texts are all intellectually challenging and stimulating, but they are also that rarest of things in the world of high-level policy and law – great fun to read.

We close this book with a tribute to Asma Jahangir, one of the most courageous and noble human rights defenders this world has known, who passed away on 11 February 2018. Asma had very special words for her friend Louise, which we are privileged to be able to share.

Louise Arbour once dared to name some "essential truths of our age," which are that: "Peace without justice is unsustainable. Security without human rights is illusory. Force without humanity is impermissible. Life without the protection of law is unacceptable."[5] Few have so convincingly strived to balance these truths to attain justice and peace more than Louise. *Doing Peace the Rights Way* is our tribute to this unchallengeable truth.

Fannie Lafontaine and François Larocque

5 Louise Arbour, "Dedications" in L. Sadat and M.P. Scharf (eds), *The Theory and Practice of International Criminal Law Essays in Honor of M. Cherif Bassiouni* (Leiden: Martinus Nijhoff, 2008).

PART I

OF FREEDOM AND EQUALITY

HUMAN RIGHTS OBLIGATIONS FOR NON-STATE ACTORS

Where Are We Now?

Andrew CLAPHAM

The organizers of this volume had suggested that I write something in Louise Arbour's honour with the "provisional" title: "Human Rights Obligations of Non-State Actors: Are We There Yet?" This reveals, I suppose, that in some quarters it is inevitable that international law and human rights practice will evolve in a progressive way so that armed groups and others will eventually have human rights obligations attached to them. At another level, the proposed title reveals that those of us who have been whining about this topic, for some years now, might be thought by some to be annoying back-seat children pestering the grown-ups, the up-front parents in the driving seats of the serious business of inter-state relations and proper international human rights law.

My premise, in this short piece, is that the issue of the human rights obligations of non-state actors is more complex than the question of how far we have come along the road toward an ultimate consensus as to the existence of international responsibilities. I will argue that non-state actors do already have international human rights obligations (the lack of academic consensus notwithstanding) and that there are several routes by which they can already be held accountable. I will also suggest that the extent of their obligations depends on what kind of non-state actor they are, the context in which they are operating, and any relevant promises made by them. In other words, the scope of their obligations depends on their capacity, context, and commitments.

In a 2005 speech on combating economic social and cultural rights violations, as part of the struggle against torture, Louise Arbour, as United Nations (UN) High Commissioner for Human Rights, focused on accountability, and in that vein highlighted the adoption of the Optional Protocol to deal with individual complaints about violations of the International Covenant on Economic Social and Cultural Rights. She then pointed out: "The growing recognition that the private sector has responsibilities to respect human rights is also welcome. But means of holding States and non-State actors accountable for their actions in relation to human rights are still wanting."[1] In what follows we will explore what sort of growing recognition we are now talking about, and how far we have come in terms of the means of holding non-state actors accountable.

1. WHAT DO WE MEAN BY NON-STATE ACTORS?

Different people mean different things when they speak about non-state actors. In the passage above, Louise Arbour was referring to large companies providing essential services, such as water, education, and health care. In the context of armed conflict, displacement and peace negotiations, we may furthermore be speaking about mercenaries, private security companies, peace-keepers, armed rebel groups, or even authorities representing a people with a recognized struggle for self-determination. Beyond essential services and armed conflict, we may be speaking about large extraction companies and their attendant security contractors, enterprises in the garment industry, the pharmaceutical industry, and financial institutions, including entities such as the International Monetary Fund and the World Bank. Less obvious as potential bearers of human rights obligations is the sector made up of non-governmental and civil society organizations. Lastly we should mention religious organizations and political parties. The human rights responsibilities attaching to each context have generated considerable scholarship in the last few years with a greater theorization of the topic.[2] In the following pages we will confine ourselves to looking at selected developments concerning just two types of non-state actors: armed groups and private companies.

---

1 Keynote address to the International Conference organized by the World Organisation against Torture, 4 October 2005.

2 L. Cameron and V. Chetail, *Privatizing War: Private Military and Security Companies under Public International Law* (Cambridge: Cambridge University Press, 2013); K. M. L. Larsen, *The Human Rights Treaty Obligations of Peacekeepers* (Cambridge: Cambridge University Press, 2012); K. Fortin, *The Accountability of Armed Groups under Human Rights Law* (Oxford, Oxford University Press, 2017); K. Mastorodimos, *Armed*

2. THE STATE OF THE DEBATE

Arguments over the appropriateness of extending human rights obligations to non-state actors have rumbled on for decades. Discussions over the need to avoid granting recognition to armed groups, or diluting attention on the state by attaching human rights obligating to corporations, take place in multiple fora, but the ultimate contemporary opposition to an extension of human rights law into the non-state sector remains, in my experience, fueled by two factors: first, a fear that human rights law will lose its specificity and heritage if it is extended to the acts of rebels/terrorists/criminals; and second, concern that legal developments could lead to new forms of liability for corporations which would leave them vulnerable to lawsuits beyond the control of their home states. We will consider first developments concerning armed groups, and will then turn to corporations.

2.1. ARMED GROUPS

Where are we now then with regard to armed non-state actors? For years, non-governmental organizations (NGOs) and some governmental legal departments insisted that armed opposition groups were not bound by human rights law, but were only bound by international humanitarian law. From the non-governmental side, there was a sense that they should follow "the notion of human rights as traditionally understood", holding armed groups to human rights standards ran the risk of being accused of imposing alien values, and that impartiality would be compromised if one questioned the methods used to achieve statehood,

---

Non-state Actors in International Humanitarian and Human Rights Law: Foundation and Framework of Obligations, and Rules on Accountability (Farnham: Ashgate, 2016); G. Nystuen, A. Follesdal and O. Mestad (eds), *Human Rights, Corporate Complicity and Disinvestment* (Cambridge: Cambridge University Press, 2011); J. G. Ruggie, *Just Business: Multinational Corporations and Human Rights* (New York: W.W. Norton, 2013); D. J. Karp, *Responsibility for Human Rights: Transnational Corporations in Imperfect States* (Cambridge: Cambridge University Press, 2014); S. Deva and D. Bilchitz (eds), *Human Rights Obligations of Business: Beyond the Corporate Responsibility to Respect?* (Cambridge: Cambridge University Press, 2013); J. P. Bohoslavsky and J. L. Èerniè (eds), *Making Sovereign Financing and Human Rights Work* (Oxford: Hart, 2014); W. Van Genugten, *The World Bank Group, the IMF and Human Rights* (Cambridge: Intersentia, 2015); S. Fujita, *The World Bank, Asian Development Bank and Human Rights Developing Standards of Transparency, Participation and Accountability* (Cheltenham: Edward Elgar, 2013); A. McBeth, *International Economic Actors and Human Rights* (Abingdon: Routledge, 2010); I. Cismas, *Religious Actors and International Law* (Oxford: Oxford University Press, 2014); T. Wood, "Extending International Human Rights Obligations to Political Parties" 2(3) *Cambridge Journal of International and Comparative Law* (2013) 1–21; T. Wood, "Reinforcing Participatory Governance Through International Human Rights Obligations of Political Parties" 28 *Harvard Human Rights Journal* (2015) 145–200.

especially where armed groups were seeking to overthrow oppression.[3] From the governmental side, beyond the formulaic assertion that only states are bound by human rights treaties, there was a fear that not only would human rights obligations imply recognition, legitimacy and subjectivity under international law, but also that governments dealing with insurgents would distort the debate at the Human Rights Commission (as it then was). Governments engaged in counter-insurgency would shift the focus from their own records onto the acts of the "terrorists" now also to be known as human rights violators. Imposing human rights obligations on armed non-state actors was seen as a cunning plan to let states off the hook.

Today this has radically changed. NGOs have found it was impossible to report on country situations without documenting the effect that armed groups have had on the enjoyment of human rights. Given that many of the concerns could not be presented as violations of the law of armed conflict, the human rights framework has been extended by NGOs to the activity of certain armed non-state actors.[4] At the same time, UN Commissions of Inquiry and Special Rapporteurs found themselves confronted with the need for balanced reporting and started addressing human rights concerns to armed non-state actors in the situations under consideration.[5] Most recently, states have been confronted with the need to hold special sessions of the UN Human Rights Council to address the atrocities being committed by so-called "Islamic State" (ISIS) and the armed group "Boko Haram".

Moreover, non-governmental organizations and some parts of the UN have started to engage with armed groups over their human rights responsibilities in order to alleviate the suffering of those affected by their activities.[6] In some circles it is even being suggested that armed groups should be more involved in

---

3 See e.g. N. Rodley, "Can armed opposition groups violate human rights?" in K. E. Mahoney and P. Mahoney (eds), *Human Rights in the Twenty-First Century* (Dordrecht: Nijhoff, 1993) 297–318 at 317; however, see now N. Rodley, "Non-state actors and human rights" in S. Sheeran and N. Rodley (eds), *Routledge Handbook of International Human Rights Law* (Abingdon: Routledge, 2013) 523–44.

4 For references, see A. Clapham, "Focusing on armed non-state actors" in A. Clapham and P. Gaeta (eds), *The Oxford Handbook of International Law in Armed Conflict* (Oxford: Oxford University Press, 2014) 766–810, at 802–805; and more recently Amnesty International, *"Strangling Necks" Abductions, Torture and Summary Killings of Palestinians by Hamas Forces during the 2014 Gaza/Israel Conflict*, MDE 21/1643/2015, esp. at 35–37, which separates out human rights law, international criminal law and international humanitarian law. That Amnesty International considers Hamas bound by human rights law is nevertheless clear: "Hamas and the Palestinian national reconciliation government created in June 2014 both have obligations under international human rights law that, to date, they have failed to meet in response to the serious human rights abuses detailed in this report" (at 37).

5 Clapham, "Focusing on armed non-state actors", *supra* note 4 at 793–799.

6 G. McHugh and M. Bessler, *Humanitarian Negotiations with Armed Groups: A Manual for Practitioners, and Guidelines on Humanitarian Negotiations with Armed Groups* (New York: United Nations, 2006).

designing the international standards to which they are to be held accountable.[7] We may now be entering a period when some observers may feel the question is no longer "are we there yet?", but rather "have we gone too far?" Some already suggest that the focus on state accountability is slipping away, as hours and hours are spent condemning the human rights violations being committed by such armed groups.

I would suggest that the answer to the question "have we gone too far?" must be: it depends. I would suggest that it is not appropriate to debate in the abstract whether or not we should be speaking about the responsibilities of non-state actors. Everything is context-specific. A report on Syria today cannot ignore the violations committed by all shades of armed groups. The Human Rights Council could not expect a report on the Gaza war of 2014, which did not address the issue of the *behaviour* of armed groups operating in Gaza. A result which focused purely on the state of Israel would not only be accused of partiality, it would also fail to help the readers and the community of states to understand the situation and ensure full accountability.

At this stage, many human rights diplomats and lawyers start to protest that human rights law should apply to the state, while the armed groups should be judged according to international humanitarian law. This avoids distorting human rights law, they would say, and applies appropriate criteria for armed conflict situations. But I have three objections to such an argument. First, in many cases the threshold for the application of international humanitarian law has not been reached (or states and other actors deny for political reasons that there is any such armed conflict). To fail to address the human rights obligations of the armed group at that point is to miss an opportunity to inform the international community and perhaps even alter the *behaviour* of the groups themselves. It is worth noting that at the start of the Syria catastrophe, the UN Human Rights Council's Commission of Inquiry considered that the threshold for the application of armed conflict had not been reached. Faced with the prospect of not reporting at all on the behaviour of the armed groups, they asserted that such groups were bound by peremptory rules of international law (*ius cogens*), and that the Free Syrian Army had in any event committed to respect human rights:

> The commission carefully reviewed the information gathered on the operations and activities to date of FSA groups. In this regard, the commission notes that, at a minimum, human rights obligations constituting peremptory international law (*ius cogens*) bind States, individuals and non-State collective entities, including

---

7 M. Sassòli, "Involving organized armed groups in the development of the law?" in International Institute of Humanitarian Law, *Non-state Actors and International Humanitarian Law. Organized Armed Groups: A Challenge for the 21st Century* (Milan: Franco Angeli, 2010) 213–221.

> armed groups. Acts violating *ius cogens* – for instance, torture or enforced disappearances – can never be justified.
>
> FSA leaders abroad also assured the commission that the FSA was committed to conducting its operations in accordance with human rights and international law. They requested guidance in shaping rules of engagement consistent with this undertaking. The FSA leadership indicated to the commission that commanders in the field currently made their own rules of engagement in accordance with the training received in the Syrian Armed Forces.[8]

Second, even if the law of armed conflict does apply, it does not cover a number of serious issues of concern in today's conflicts. International humanitarian law does not traditionally cover how an armed group treats its own forces (there are well-known cases of severe punishments and torture being meted out), nor would it cover the treatment of deserters or discrimination with regard to issues relating to health care and education. Although Louise Arbour may not have specifically addressed the economic social and cultural rights of those under the control of an armed group,[9] had she stayed on as High Commissioner, she would have faced the prospect of commenting on situations such as Mali, where armed groups were in control of territory and were denying the human rights of those under their control. The 2013 Report of the High Commissioner (by now Navi Pillay) went further than the lists of *ius cogens* norms mentioned above. It catalogued a series of human rights violations committed by the armed groups, including: extrajudicial and summary executions; torture and other cruel, inhuman, or degrading treatment; arbitrary arrests and detentions; recruitment of child soldiers; sexual abuse; attacks on property; violations of freedom of expression and of the right to information; violations of the right to education; violations of the right to health; violations of cultural rights; and violations of the right to freedom of religion.[10]

Third, human rights bodies and organizations may have mandates restricted to human rights law. To deny them the chance to report on both sides, on the grounds that this is better dealt with by a parallel branch of international law outside their mandate, could unnecessarily jeopardize their effectiveness. This is all the more dramatic as international humanitarian law has no equivalent accountability mechanisms and the default mechanism is the international criminal prosecution of individuals. Needless to say, prosecutions are no substitute for human rights reporting; they focus on the individual and not

---

8 UN Doc. A/HRC/19/69, 22 February 2012, §§106–107.

9 But see on the importance of focusing on economic, social and cultural rights L. Arbour, "Economic and Social Justice for Societies in Transition" 40 *International Journal of Law and Politics* (2007) 1–27.

10 Report of the United Nations High Commissioner for Human Rights on the Situation of Human Rights in Mali, UN Doc. A/HRC/22/33, 7 January 2013.

the group. Prosecution requires that the individual is alive, captured and fit to stand trial. There are only limited jurisdictions where such prosecutions can take place, and the thresholds for prosecuting war crimes may require proof beyond reasonable doubt of intent or recklessness, as well as proof of complex facts to constitute the elements of the relevant international crimes.[11]

At this point in the argument, those still debating the appropriateness of applying human rights law to armed groups sometimes concede that human rights reporting can address the behaviour of armed groups, but that one can only refer to human rights "abuses" being committed by such groups, and one should reserve the expression human rights "violations" for states. I fail to comprehend the logic of this. Presumably the group is being held accountable under customary international law, the rules of *ius cogens*, a unilateral commitment, or some other human rights obligation that is filtered through national law. What does it mean to speak of abuses? If these are not violations of the law, they must be merely transgressions of some moral code. Is it seriously being considered that the UN should explain that Israel has violated international law, but that Hamas and relevant armed groups have only behaved immorally (in human rights terms), and that the two types of human rights transgression cannot be compared? Does Syria violate human rights, while the self-styled "Islamic state" merely abuses them? Of course, one can compare the two under war crimes law, but, as explained above, that is a separate issue, and in many situations how an armed group treats the population it dominates is not covered by international war crimes law, as the group is not bound by the international law of occupation, nor does its treatment of the population come under the rules for the conduct of hostilities.[12]

In fact, in an essay entitled "Where Are We Now?", we should relate that at least one commission of inquiry has reported on an armed group violating a human rights treaty as such. The Commission of Inquiry on Syria concluded in 2013 that: "Anti-Government armed groups are also responsible for using children under the age of 18 in hostilities in violation of the CRC-OPAC [Optional Protocol to the Convention on the Rights of the Child], which by its terms applies to non-State actors." The summary also makes the same point: "Both Government-affiliated militia and anti-Government armed groups were found to have violated the Optional Protocol to the Convention on the Rights of

11 See e.g. K. Dörmann, L. Doswald-Beck and R. Kolb, *Elements of War Crimes under the Rome Statute of the International Criminal Court: Sources and Commentary* (Cambridge: Cambridge University Press, 2003); and T. Rodenhäuser, "Beyond state crimes: Non-state entities and crimes against humanity" 27 *Leiden Journal of International Law* (2014) 913–928.

12 See generally Article 8 of the Statute of the International Criminal Court, and Chapters 1, 2, 21, 31, 36, 67, 69 and 70 of A. Clapham, P. Gaeta and M. Sassòli (eds), *The 1949 Geneva Conventions: A Commentary* (Oxford: Oxford University Press, 2015).

the Child on the involvement of children in armed conflict, to which the Syrian Arab Republic is a party."[13]

Despite occasional drafting dramas at the Human Rights Council where government lawyers scrub up resolutions replacing the word "violation" with "abuse", nearly all speeches and statements at the UN refer to human rights violations being committed by armed groups. And indeed many resolutions leave no doubt that the UN human rights body is condemning human rights violations committed by armed groups. Consider, for example, the Human Rights Council's Resolution on ISIS in Iraq, which makes no reference to any acts by the state of Iraq, leaving no doubt that the condemnations are limited to the acts of the armed group, but confusingly refers to "systematic violations and abuses." In paragraph 1, the UN Human Rights Council:

> *Condemns* in the strongest possible terms the systematic violations and abuses of human rights and violations of international humanitarian law resulting from the terrorist acts committed by the so-called Islamic State in Iraq and the Levant and associated groups taking place since 10 June 2014 in several provinces of Iraq, which may amount to war crimes and crimes against humanity, and strongly condemns in particular all violence against persons based on their religious or ethnic affiliation, as well as violence against women and children.[14]

A subsequent report prepared by Ben Emmerson, the Special Rapporteur on the protection of human rights while countering terrorism, not only details the human rights violations committed by ISIS, but also addresses the doctrinal debate head-on:

> Some still argue that human rights, as a body of law, can only bind States, and cannot or should not apply to non-State armed groups. However, as the Special Rapporteur has previously highlighted in other contexts, a central tenet of international human rights law is that it must keep pace with a changing world. Human rights apply at all times, inherently belong to individuals and are key to individual dignity. Increasingly, non-State armed groups control parts of territories in which populations live. This is the case with ISIL, which now controls large swathes of territory in which millions of individuals live; it has declared itself a "State", and runs both a civil and a military administration, including the establishment of a "court" system. The threshold for

---

13 Report of the Commission of Inquiry on Syria, n 83, para 44 and p 2. For a discussion on the application of multilateral treaties to armed groups, see Clapham, "Focusing on armed non-state actors", *supra* note 4 at 772–779; see also J. K. Kleffner's analytical pieces: "The applicability of international humanitarian law to organized armed groups" 93 *IRRC* (2011) 443–461 and "The collective accountability of organized armed groups for system crimes" in A. Nollkaemper and H. van der Wilt (eds), *System Criminality in International Law* (Cambridge: Cambridge University Press, 2009) 238–269. Most recently, see D. Murray, *Human Rights Obligations of Non-state Armed Groups* (Oxford: Hart, 2016); and K. Fortin, *The Accountability of Armed Groups under Human Rights Law* supra note 1.

14 A/HRC/RES/S-22/1, 1 September 2014.

> ISIL to be bound by human rights obligations has clearly been met. This means, at a minimum, that ISIL is bound under international law to respect core human rights obligations, such as the right to life, the absolute prohibition of torture, cruel, inhuman and degrading treatment, the prohibition of slavery and the prohibition of enforced disappearance, as well as the right to freedom of thought, conscience and religion.
>
> In addition, where ISIL engages in violations that are unrelated to the conflict and not direct consequences of it, the governing legal framework should be international human rights law. In practice, this means that ISIL is legally bound to respect freedom of expression, freedom of assembly and freedom of movement. These rights should be protected without discrimination on any of the grounds prohibited by international law. The right to a fair trial should also be guaranteed. In areas of substantive overlap between international human rights and international humanitarian law, the principles that provide assistance in determining which framework is applicable are those of *lex specialis* and effective control: the more effective control ISIL has over a territory or individuals, the greater is the extent to which human rights law will constitute the appropriate legal framework.[15]

Human rights commissions of inquiry have so far avoided the violations/abuses dichotomy and have sought instead to ground human rights obligations in the theory of *ius cogens*, the fact of control of territory suggesting inherited obligations from the government that has been displaced, through references to the commitments undertaken by the armed group, or simply leaving aside the theory and pointing to the effects on the population.[16] Recommendations are made simultaneously to states and armed groups with no obvious distinction. It would clearly be absurd to suggest that states are under international legal obligations and armed groups are simply being appealed to on a moral plane. Let us consider the latest reasoning and recommendations from the Commission of Inquiry on Gaza (2015):

> 44. In the past, the Palestinian Authority, which exercises its powers in the Occupied Palestinian Territory pursuant to the various Israeli-Palestinian agreements, has declared its commitment to respect international human rights law in a number of public undertakings. These undertakings by the Palestinian Authority, the Palestinian Liberation Organisation and the Palestinian Legislative Council (PLC) have included assurances, decrees and declarations and various agreements under the Oslo Accords signed with Israel, which stated that both parties would exercise their powers and responsibilities with "due regard to internationally accepted norms and principles of human rights and the rule of law." The Palestinian Basic Law also contains a number of articles protecting human rights as well as a commitment to abide by major human

15 A/HRC/29/51, 16 June 2015, at paras 30–31 (footnotes omitted).

16 For a detailed analysis with regard to Syria, see T. Rodenhäuser, "International legal obligations of armed opposition groups in Syria" 2 *International Review of Law* (2015) 1–16.

rights instruments. The setting up of the Palestinian Independent Commission for Citizens' Rights in 1993 through a Presidential Decree also indicates a commitment by the Palestinian Authority to be bound by human rights.

45. With respect to the authorities in Gaza, it is worth recalling that non-State actors that exercise government-like functions and control over a territory are obliged to respect human rights norms when their conduct affects the human rights of the individuals under their control.[17] Moreover, Hamas has indicated that it "is determined ... to promote the rule of law, the respect for the judiciary, the separation of powers, the respect for human rights, the equality among citizens; to fight all forms of discrimination; to protect public liberties, including the freedom of the press and opinion ...". Hamas has also confirmed its commitment to "respect ... public liberties; to strengthen the establishment of democracy; to protect human rights ... and its respect for international law and international humanitarian law insofar as they conform with our character, customs and original traditions" [other footnotes omitted].[18]

The Commission here is separating out three different types of non-state actors: the Palestinian Authority (to the extent that it has separate obligations from the State of Palestine as a party to the relevant human rights treaties), Hamas and non-state actors with control of territory in Gaza. The recommendations are addressed to Israel, to the State of Palestine, and then to the non-state actors. These are tailored to the particular violations. With regard to the treatment of collaborators, the Commission called "upon the authorities in Gaza and Palestinian armed groups: ... (b) To take measures to prevent extrajudicial executions and eradicate torture, cruel, inhuman and degrading treatment; to cooperate with national investigations aimed to bring those responsible for violations of international law to justice; and to combat the stigma faced by families of alleged collaborators."[19] The report addresses the behaviour of the

17 The footnote in the original reads: "A/HRC/10/22, para. 21. Also by way of example, in the joint report on Lebanon and Israel, a group of four Special Rapporteurs concluded that: 'Although Hezbollah, a non-State actor, cannot become a party to these human rights treaties, it remains subject to the demand of the international community, first expressed in the Universal Declaration of Human Rights, that every organ of society respect and promote human rights ... It is especially appropriate and feasible to call for an armed group to respect human rights norms when it exercises significant control over territory and population and has an identifiable political structure,' Report of the Special Rapporteur on extrajudicial, summary or arbitrary executions, Philip Alston; the Special Rapporteur on the right of everyone to the enjoyment of the highest attainable standard of physical and mental health, Paul Hunt; the Representative of the Secretary-General on human rights of internally displaced persons, Walter Kälin; and the Special Rapporteur on adequate housing as a component of the right to an adequate standard of living, Miloon Kothari (A/HRC/2/7), para. 19."

18 Report of the detailed findings of the independent commission of inquiry established pursuant to Human Rights Council Resolution S-21/1, UN Doc. A/HRC/29/CRP.4, 24 June 2015.

19 Ibid at para 683.

armed groups in human right terms speaking of extrajudicial executions. The Commission nevertheless suggests that international human rights law applies due to the failure of the authorities in Gaza (not the State of Palestine) to protect the population from such extrajudicial executions:

> The commission is of the view that inmates were transferred out of the prison and summarily executed with the apparent knowledge of the local authorities in Gaza, in violation of their obligation to protect the right to life and security of those in their custody. These extrajudicial executions, many of which were carried out in public, constitute a violation of both international humanitarian law and international human rights law.[20]

No state seems to have objected to this legal analysis.

Obligations are argued to flow from the exercise of government like functions, control over territory, and commitments entered into. I would suggest that one can only complain about the failure of an armed group to protect the population from other armed groups or private persons where it has not only a legal obligation to do so, but also the *capacity* to prevent and punish those unauthorized armed groups or individuals operating in its sphere of influence.

Let us leave the realm of legal theory, which in the end seems to be of very little influence in this field, and focus instead on the policy reasons for addressing human rights concerns to armed groups. Here, again, context matters. Not all groups will be receptive to human rights overtures or criticism. But interesting work is being done into which sorts of groups are indeed ready to engage and why. Perhaps the simplest conclusion we can draw is that those groups seeking to find international respectability, and a governance role for the people they represent, will indeed be ready to change their behaviour to curry international favour. And such international favour can be seen to lead to success.[21] We can add to this that many armed groups claim to have taken up arms in response to human rights violations; I have found that today many groups would see their struggle as grounded in a need to secure human rights. Human rights monitors are working with this logic rather than against it. To send the message that one need only respect those rights once one succeeds in becoming the government (in charge of a state duly admitted to the international community) would be perverse indeed.

---

20 Ibid at para 501.

21 See M. L. Gross, *The Ethics of Insurgency: A Critical Guide to Just Guerrilla Warfare* (New York: Cambridge University Press, 2015) esp. at 73 and 279; for detailed studies with a typology of groups and their incentives, see J. M. Weinstein, *Inside Rebellion: The Politics of Insurgent Violence* (Cambridge: Cambridge University Press, 2007); A. Bellal and S. Casey-Maslen, *Rules of Engagement: Promoting the Protection of Civilians through Dialogue with Armed Non-state Actors* (Geneva: Geneva Academy of International Humanitarian Law and Human Rights, 2011).

In one particular area, the protection of children in armed conflict, the Security Council has stepped in, not only to condemn violations by armed groups, but also to threaten targeted sanctions against those who refuse to cooperate to bring an end to such violations.[22] The Security Council has over the last decade addressed armed non-state actors directly (using the expressions "all parties" and "factions" or referring directly to the groups by name) and has called on them to respect international humanitarian law and human rights. In 2011 it condemned "human rights violations perpetrated by the FPR" (*Front populaire pour le redressement*) in the Central African Republic,[23] and called on the UN Integrated Peacebuilding Office in the Central African Republic "to report on human rights violations perpetrated by armed groups particularly against children and women."[24]

Reports by the UN Secretary-General to the Security Council on certain country situations now list the non-state actors concerned, and whether or not they are involved in any of six categories of "grave violations" committed against children:

(a) killing or maiming of children;
(b) recruiting or using child soldiers;
(c) attacks against schools or hospitals;
(d) rape or other grave sexual violence against children;
(e) abduction of children;
(f) denial of humanitarian access for children.

The UN Secretary-General's initial report explains that these violations are based on international norms and commitments that have been made by the parties to the conflict, as well as national laws and peace agreements.[25] Subsequent reports on various country situations have detailed the "grave violations of children's rights" committed by the non-state actors concerned. These reports dedicate as much, if not more, space to the violations committed by the non-state actors as they do to addressing the states concerned. Although the focus started with recruitment, the Security Council has now requested the

22 S. Kandiah Thompson, "Children and Armed Conflict" in J. Genser and B. Stagno Ugarte (eds), *The United Nations Security Council in the Age of Human Rights* (Cambridge: Cambridge University Press, 2014) 98–120; A. Constantineides, "Human Rights Obligations and Accountability of Armed Opposition Groups: The Practice of the UN Security Council" 4 *Human Rights and International Legal Discourse* (2010) 89–110.

23 Resolution 2031 (2011) para 13; see also Resolution 2088 (2013) para 13.

24 Resolution 1882 (2031) 14.

25 UN Doc. S/2005/72; for a look at some of the legal background to these categories, see *The Six Grave Violations against Children During Armed Conflict: The Legal Foundation*, Working Paper No. 1, Office of the Special Representative of the Secretary-General for Children and Armed Conflict (2009, updated 2013).

Secretary-General to include in his reports "those parties to armed conflict that engage, in contravention of applicable international law, in patterns of killing and maiming of children and/or rape and other sexual violence against children, in situations of armed conflict."[26]

While the focus seems to be on violations of applicable law in situations of armed conflict, this work is not restricted to the applications of international humanitarian law. The question of the criteria for a group to be considered a party to an armed conflict is not carefully examined. The universal standard applied by the Security Council seems to apply outside the strict framework of international humanitarian law, and resolutions reproduce the framework of the six grave violations when condemning armed groups.[27] The Secretary-General's reports are complemented by the work of the Special Representative of the Secretary-General, whose work not only feeds into the reports to the Security Council, but also relies on country visits, engaging with non-state actors and facilitating commitments by those armed groups. The Special Representative's reports and activities have covered groups that were not recognized as parties to a conflict by the states concerned. Furthermore, the Special Representative has developed a methodology based on commitments by the armed non-state actor rather than a strict application of humanitarian law to a party to a conflict. Rather than focusing on international criminal law prosecutions for individuals, the Council lists the groups and the types of grave violations they have committed. Recent reports list over 50 armed groups as having committed grave violations against children. The Secretary-General's reports use underlining for those groups that "have been in the annexes for at least five years and are therefore considered persistent perpetrators."[28] When it comes to these reports, references to "abuse" are usually limited to sexual, psychological, physical or verbal abuse; no linguistic distinction is drawn between grave violations committed by the state and the armed groups with which they are in conflict. In a review of the last 20 years the UN informed the Security Council that the work on children in armed conflict had led to "The signing of 25 action plans with parties to conflict towards ending violations against children. More than one third of such plans have resulted in the successful delisting of a party".[29] Action plans can be signed both by governments and armed groups, and progress is monitored and encouraged by the Special Representative of the Secretary-General for Children in Armed Conflict.[30]

---

26 Resolution 1882 (2009).

27 See e.g. Resolution 2139 (2014) para 1.

28 For recent reports, see "Children and armed conflict: Report of the Secretary-General", A/69/926–S/2015/409, 5 June 2015; A/70/836-S/2016/360, 20 April 2016.

29 Concept Note S/2016/662, 29 July 2016, at 2.

30 See e.g. "Annual report of the Special Representative of the Secretary-General for Children and Armed Conflict, Leila Zerrougui", A/HRC/34/44, 22 December 2016.

The disconnect between, on the one hand, the work of the UN's reports into grave violations committed by armed groups and, on the other hand, the dogmatic doctrinal distinction between abuses and violations is likely to continue in the short term. In practical terms, it currently makes no difference whether groups are politically condemned for abuses or violations, and both government forces and armed groups can be listed as "persistent perpetrators". Nevertheless, one should be aware that at some stage there will be issues that arise before a court of law, armed groups may be sued for violations of international law,[31] and those who aid and abet them (such as corporations) may similarly be sued for damages. Claiming that such groups have committed no violation of international law, but have merely abused human rights, may allow both types of non-state actor off the hook.

2.2. CORPORATIONS

In 2013, the US Supreme Court handed down its opinion in the case of *Kiobel et al v Shell*.[32] The Supreme Court had asked the following question: "Whether corporations are immune from tort liability for violations of the law of nations such as torture, extrajudicial executions or genocide, as the court of appeals decisions provides, or if corporations may be sued in the same manner as any other private party defendant under the ATS [Alien Tort Statute] for such egregious violations, as the Eleventh Circuit has explicitly held."[33] In the end, the Court chose not to explicitly answer this question, but affirmed the judgment below based on its answer to a second question on which it had asked for re-argument, namely: "Whether and under what circumstances the Alien Tort Statute … allows courts to recognize a cause of action for violations of the law of nations occurring within the territory of a sovereign other than the United States."[34] This means that the US courts remain divided on the abstract question of whether a corporation can violate the law of nations in the context of a claim under the Alien Tort Statute. For the present purposes, it is enough to remark that, so far, the idea that a corporation has human rights obligations under international law has not been authoritatively rejected by the US Supreme Court (even though it had the opportunity to do so). What the Court did do was to limit the scope of the Alien Tort Statute by relying on the presumption against the extraterritorial application of legislation, and demanding that claims

---

31 Consider the litigation in the United States against the Palestinian Authority for an act of torture: *Mohamad et al. v. Palestinian Authority et al.* 566 US _ (2012). While in this case the cause of action was precluded due to the statute being limited to individuals as defendants, the Alien Tort Statute is not so limited.

32 569 US _ (2013), 17 April 2013.

33 Certiorari granted 17 October 2011.

34 Order of 5 March 2012.

demonstrate a nexus with the United States. The nexus has to be more than "mere corporate presence"; the opinion concludes that "where the claims touch and concern the territory of the United States, they must do so with sufficient force to displace the presumption against extraterritorial application."[35] The question of corporate obligations under customary international law was nevertheless extensively debated in court, even if it makes no appearance in the judgment.

On 28 February 2012, during the oral hearings at the Supreme Court, the Counsel for Shell posed and answered the Court's question in the following way: "is there any source in customary international law throughout the world that holds corporations liable for the human rights offenses alleged here? And the answer is there is none." At this point she was interrupted by Justice Breyer, who went on to say:

> you can have a principle that applies even though there isn't a case. And the principle that here would apply is what I said, Pirates, Incorporated. Do you think in the 18th century if they brought Pirates, Incorporated, and we get all their gold, and Blackbeard gets up and he says, oh, it isn't me; it's the corporation – do you think that they would have then said: Oh, I see, it's a corporation. Good-bye. Go home.[36]

One can hear the laughter quite clearly on the audio file. Our interest, however, is not really the prospects of litigation against corporations under this particular statute, but rather the argumentation used today to affirm or deny the idea that corporations have binding obligations under international human rights law. The forum for this debate has now shifted from the Federal Courts of the United States to the UN Human Rights Council. In July 2015, the Open-Ended Intergovernmental Working Group on Transnational Corporations and Other Business Enterprises with Respect to Human Rights held its first meeting to discuss the "content, scope, nature and form" of a future international instrument.[37] This process is likely to be slow-moving and so far looks unlikely to develop our understanding of the existing human rights obligations of

---

35 Slip Opinion at p 14. See also the concurring opinions for an approach which looks to the nationality of the parties to the dispute and the need to avoid the United States becoming a safe haven for torturers and other "common enemies of mankind." For detailed consideration of the judgment, see the symposium on "*Kiobel and After*" in the *Journal of International Criminal Justice* (2014) at 529–614.

36 At p 25 of the transcript.

37 See the reports of the working group, A/HRC/31/50, 5 February 2016; A/HRC/34/47, 4 January 2017, and Resolution A/HRC/RES/26/9, 26 June 2014. See also D. Cassell and A. Ramasastry "Options for a treaty on business and human rights: Prepared for the American Bar Association, Center for Human Rights, and the Law Society of England and Wales"; and International Commission of Jurists "Needs and options for a new international instrument in the field of business and human rights" (ICJ, Geneva, 2014). For a running set of blogs on this development, see <http://business-humanrights.org/en/debate-the-treaty>; and O. De Schutter, "Towards a New Treaty on Business and Human Rights" 1 *Business and Human Rights Journal* (2015) 41–67.

corporations. The mindset is still dominated by past human rights treaties, limiting the field of vision to creating a set of positive obligations for those states that would eventually become parties to the treaty. But our interest in the present contribution is the obligations of the companies themselves.

In 2005, the year of Louise Arbour's speech referred to above, the UN appointed John Ruggie to identify and clarify the relevant human rights standards for corporate responsibility and accountability. In 2011, the resulting Guiding Principles were endorsed by the Human Rights Council, and rest on a protect, respect and remedy framework with three pillars:

- the state's duty to protect against human rights abuses by third parties, including business enterprises, through appropriate policies, regulation and adjudication;
- an independent corporate responsibility to respect human rights, which means that business enterprises should act with due diligence to avoid infringing upon the rights of others, and to address adverse impacts with which they are involved;
- the need for greater access by victims to effective remedy, both judicial and non-judicial.

In Ruggie's words: "Simply, put: states must protect; companies must respect; and those who are harmed must have redress."[38] Paragraph 12 in the UN Guiding Principles on Business and Human Rights states:

> The responsibility of business enterprises to respect human rights refers to internationally recognized human rights – understood, at a minimum, as those expressed in the International Bill of Human Rights and the principles concerning fundamental rights set out in the International Labour Organization's Declaration on Fundamental Principles and Rights at Work.

But the imperative that companies have responsibilities and "must respect human rights" is conceived in this context as a moral (less than legal) demand. The Commentary to the UN Guiding Principles makes clear that legal obligations are found elsewhere: "The responsibility of business enterprises to respect human rights is distinct from issues of legal liability and enforcement, which remain defined largely by national law provisions in relevant jurisdictions."[39] Is this as far as we have come? Is this the end of the road for legal obligations for corporations under international law? I think not. The Ruggie reports and the

---

38 J. G. Ruggie, *Just Business: Multinational Corporations and Human Rights* (New York: W. W. Norton, 2013) at xx–xxi.

39 A/HRC/17/31, 21 March 2011, at 14.

subsequent debate only scratch the surface of the issue of corporate international human rights obligations. I should like here to highlight recent developments in three fields: first, international criminal law; second, international investment law; and third, contract law in the context of the International Code of Conduct for Private Security Service Providers.

2.2.1. International Criminal Responsibility for Corporations

The debate over the reach of international criminal law is well known and need not be rehearsed here.[40] On leaving his mandate, John Ruggie stated that his research suggested "that national jurisdictions have divergent interpretations of the applicability to business enterprises of international standards prohibiting gross human rights abuses, potentially amounting to the level of international crimes."[41] Let us consider three recent developments in this regard.

The first is a new treaty, adopted by the African Union in 2014, which adds a criminal chamber to the African Court of Justice and Human Rights, and does so in a way that makes clear that corporations can be prosecuted for certain international crimes in this new Chamber.[42] For the members of the African Union at least, there is now no doubt as to the applicability of international criminal law to corporations.[43]

So far, all the attention has focused on the provision in the new treaty (a Protocol to amend the Statute of the African Court of Justice and Human Rights) which relates to immunities from the jurisdiction of this proposed new international Criminal Chamber. The Court will not be able to prosecute "any serving AU Head of State or Government, or anybody acting or entitled to act in such capacity, or other senior state officials based on their functions, during their tenure of office."[44] But let us leave that issue to one side and look at the innovations introduced by this Protocol. In particular, let us highlight that it allows for the prosecution of corporations and other legal persons. The prospect of international prosecutions of corporations allows us to sharpen our

---

40 See further J. G. Stewart, "The Turn to Corporate Criminal Liability for International Crimes: Transcending the Alien Tort Statute" 47 *New York University Journal of International Law and Politics* (2014) 121–206; J. Kyriakakis, "Prosecuting Corporations for International Crimes: The Role for Domestic Criminal Law" in L. May and Z. Hoskins (eds), *International Criminal Law and Philosophy* (Cambridge University Press, 2010) 108–137.

41 "Recommendations on follow-up to the Mandate", 11 February 2011; for more discussion, see J. Kyriakakis, "Developments in international criminal law and the case of business involvement in international crimes" 94(887) *International Review of the Red Cross* (2012) 981–1005.

42 STC/Legal/Min/7(I) Rev. 1, 15 May 2014.

43 For research on the war crimes of pillage and plunder as they apply to corporations, see J. G. Stewart, *Corporate War Crimes: Prosecuting the Pillage of Natural Resources* (New York: Open Society Institute, 2011).

44 Article 46A bis.

focus on what factors will need to be further elaborated. As is well known, the tricky question of corporate knowledge has bedevilled national suits against corporations that rely on violations of international criminal law. Here the new Protocol resolves the issues of how to tackle corporate intention, attribution and corporate knowledge. Article 46A states in part:

> 2. Corporate intention to commit an offence may be established by proof that it was the policy of the corporation to do the act which constituted the offence.
>
> 3. A policy may be attributed to a corporation where it provides the most reasonable explanation of the conduct of that corporation.
>
> 4. Corporate knowledge of the commission of an offence may be established by proof that the actual or constructive knowledge of the relevant information was possessed within the corporation.
>
> 5. Knowledge may be possessed within a corporation even though the relevant information is divided between corporate personnel.

Whether or not the new Criminal Chamber is quickly established, we are now a step closer to designing procedures for *national* prosecutions of corporations for international crimes. Considering that this new international jurisdiction will be complementary to national jurisdictions, in the same way that the International Criminal Court (ICC) allows for inadmissibility of certain cases that are properly pursued at the national level, one has to assume that national legislation will be drafted to ensure that cases can be prosecuted at the national level. This will have to go beyond the existing legislation related to the ICC, not only because of the new possibility of corporate criminal responsibility, but also because the list of crimes, including the list of war crimes, has been considerably extended. The headings are:

1) Genocide
2) Crimes against Humanity
3) War Crimes
4) The Crime of Unconstitutional Change of Government
5) Piracy
6) Terrorism
7) Mercenarism
8) Corruption
9) Money Laundering
10) Trafficking in Persons
11) Trafficking in Drugs
12) Trafficking in Hazardous Wastes
13) Illicit Exploitation of Natural Resources
14) The Crime of Aggression.

The Protocol contains definitions for each of these crimes.

We have now come a long way from the assumption that international legal principles do not apply to corporations, or that if they do, this would be limited to "certain war crimes and crimes against humanity."[45] I expect some will dismiss this development as "a regional anomaly", but companies (of whatever nationality) operating in Africa will have to consider that they could in the future be prosecuted for these crimes, and that their behaviour will be judged against these norms. In sum, we now have an international treaty, adopted by states, that assumes or creates international obligations for corporations, and proposes that they be held accountable for any violations of these obligations in courts of law.

The second development is centred at the Special Tribunal for Lebanon. On 2 October 2014, the Appeals Panel ruled that a corporation could be prosecuted for contempt of court before this international criminal tribunal. The Panel drew two interesting conclusions: the first with regard to human rights law and the second with regard to criminal law. Having reviewed developments in human rights law, in particular at the UN Human Rights Council and the UN Human Rights Committee, the Panel concluded "that the current international standards on human rights allow for interpreting the term 'person' to include legal entities for the purposes of Rule 60 *bis* [their contempt jurisdiction]."[46] With regard to criminal law, it examined a number of developments at the national level, as well as treaties that refer to corporate criminal responsibility, and concluded that "corporate criminal liability is on the verge of attaining, at the very least, the status of a general principle of law applicable under international law."[47] Interestingly, the dissenting judge does not wish to be read as disputing the general conclusions about the direction of human rights law, only the applicability of the majority's reasoning in the context of the wording of the Statute of the Special Tribunal. Perhaps just as significant is the policy reasoning that the majority revealed in three paragraphs that is refreshingly honest in such a context. As the decision is still relatively unknown, I will take the liberty of reproducing the paragraphs here:

> 82. In this discussion, we simply cannot ignore the reality that many corporations today wield far more power, influence and reach than any one person. Whilst that was not always the case in the past, it is certainly true of the world we presently inhabit. Such characteristics can be, and often are, a force for the positive development of the societies in which they reside. However, wielding such great power and influence entails great responsibility. Regrettably, modern history is replete with examples

45 See E/CN.4/2006/97 at para 60.

46 *New TV Karma Mohamed Tashin Al Khayat* Decision on Interlocutory Appeal Concerning Personal Jurisdiction in Contempt proceedings, STL-14-05/PT/AP/AR126.1, 2 October 2014 at para 60. It should be noted that ruling has now been rejected by the Contempt Judge in a related proceeding: STL-14-06/PT/CJ, 6 November 2014.

47 Ibid at para 67.

where great harm has been caused by corporations with the advantages that result from the recognition of their status as legal persons.

> 83. In such a scenario, there can exist circumstances where the Tribunal may be unable, due to the complexity of corporate structures, internal operating processes, and the aggregate effect of the actions of many individuals, to identify and apprehend the most responsible natural persons within a corporation. Similarly, the prosecution of natural persons, rather than the legal persons that they serve, would fail to underline and punish corporate cultures that condone and in some cases encourage illegal behaviour. Punishing only natural persons in such circumstances would be a poor response where the need for accountability lies beyond any one person. In other words, the prosecution and punishment of legal persons pursues different aims and interests than the punishment of natural persons alone. Without the ability to address such considerations, the authority of the Tribunal to deal with contempt and obstruction of justice could be impeded. It would potentially lead to unacceptable impunity for criminal actions and effectively yield control over the Tribunal's proceedings to unaccountable legal entities.
>
> 84. Therefore, it would be contrary to the interests of justice, in our view, to shield legal persons when Rule 60 *bis* does not restrict our inherent power to punish contemptuous acts. No person, natural or legal, should be placed above the law or be allowed to operate outside of the rule of law.

The third development relates to crimes against humanity. The Drafting Committee of the International Law Commission (ILC) recently provisionally adopted a text which confirms that corporations can commit crimes against humanity. In the context of the ILC's Draft Articles on Crimes against Humanity, the following paragraph was adopted as draft article 6(7):

> Subject to the provisions of its national law, each State shall take measures, where appropriate, to establish the liability of legal persons for the offences referred to in this draft article. Subject to the legal principles of the State, such liability of legal persons may be criminal, civil or administrative.[48]

The draft article quoted above is significant because it clarifies that the norm contained in the expression crimes against humanity can be violated by a private corporation and not only by an individual or a state. The fact that national liability may take various forms should not distract us from the bigger conceptual clarification that a non-state actor can commit what are often known as massive human rights violations. It is perhaps worth recalling for those who would seek to distinguish as fundamentally different international criminal law and human rights that the ILC's original 1991 Draft Code of Crimes against the Peace and Security of Mankind contained the precursor to an eventual modern definition

48 Draft article 6(7), A/CN.4/L.892, 26 May 2017 and see the commentary in the ILC's Annual Report 2016 UN Doc A/71/10 at 262–265.

of crimes against humanity; at that time they labelled such crimes: "Systematic or mass violations of human rights."[49]

2.2.2. The Promise of International Investment Law

For some time, scholars have remarked how the rights of an investor to trigger international dispute settlement proceedings against a state could suggest enhanced subjectivity or personality for corporations on the international plane, and that arbitrators may take human rights law into account under the terms of the relevant investment treaty or contract.[50] This may be true, but it takes us no further down the road to corporate accountability under international law. The proceedings are designed to hold states, not corporations, accountable.[51] But this may be changing. Some states, fearing the punitive suits that investors are capable of mounting against regulations that are argued to fall foul of the "fair and equitable treatment" standard, may be ready as slates to counterclaim that the investor has violated international human rights law. Alternatively, arbitrators may take corporate behaviour into account when considering the public policy (*ordre public*) aspects of the dispute.[52] Although investment disputes look set to remain affairs where the investor triggers the arbitration, the prospect of losing a counterclaim, or being precluded from claiming on public policy grounds, in effect means that human rights obligations do apply to corporate investors. This would apply in particular to those investors considering at some point resorting to the investor-state dispute mechanisms provided for in the relevant bilateral treaties, and whose awards would be enforced though multilateral treaties, such as the New York Convention on the Recognition and Enforcement of Foreign Arbitral Awards (1958).[53]

---

49 Yearbook of the International Law Commission (1991) Volume II Part 2, A/CN.4/SER.A/1991/Add.l (Part 2) at 96 (Article 21).

50 J. E. Alvarez, "Are corporations 'subjects' of international law" 9 *Santa Clara Journal of International Law* (2011) 1–35; B. Simma, "Foreign investment arbitration: A place for human rights?" 60 *ICLQ* (2011) 573–596; P.-M. Dupuy, E.-U. Petersmann and F. Francioni (eds), *Human Rights in International Investment Law and Arbitration* (Oxford: Oxford University Press, 2009).

51 For background on the issues, see S. Pahis, *Bilateral Investment Treaties and International Human Rights Law: Harmonization through Interpretation* (Geneva: ICJ, 2011); Simma, "Foreign investment arbitration", *supra* note 50.

52 Dupuy, P.-M. and J. E. Viñuales, "Human rights and investment disciplines: Integration in progress" in M. Bungenberg, J. Griebel, S. Hobe and A. Reinisch (eds), *International Investment Law* (Baden Baden: Nomos, 2012) 1739–1767.

53 Even those scholars most opposed to the extension of human rights law to bind non-state actors seem to admit that the Convention on the Settlement of Investment Disputes between States and Nationals of Other States (1965) provides "limited evidence that international law has vested direct responsibility in [business enterprises]." Rodley, "Non-state actors and human rights", *supra* note 3 at 539 fn 81. However, it is clear that investment disputes do not really focus on the human rights obligations of investors (see S. R. Ratner, *The Thin Justice of*

One particular development I should like to highlight is the publication of the *Model Text for the Indian Bilateral Investment Treaty*. This text allows for counterclaims brought by the state against an investor, for example, for a breach of the law relating to human rights.[54] Whether one sees this as an international arbitration over respect for national law or a signal to international investors that the human rights framework is now applicable to their activities, the direction of travel is becoming clearer.[55] Corporations may find themselves judged in an international arbitration for failing to respect human rights. Reparations for their human rights violations could be set against any award to the investor for compensation derived from the violations of the investment treaty.

3. THE INTERNATIONAL CODE OF CONDUCT FOR PRIVATE SECURITY SERVICE PROVIDERS

This new Code of Conduct and its accompanying Charter for the creation of an oversight mechanism and Association represent a shift away from the state-centred approach toward the development of a framework that addresses corporations and their human rights obligations directly. The Code defines the obligations of private security companies, and has been signed by over 700 companies. This is not the place to examine the arrangements for certification, monitoring and oversight established by the newly created Association. The point I should like to highlight is that the Code was written to be legally binding, and not as a soft, aspirational and open-ended document.[56] The idea is that the Code should be incorporated as part of any contract between the private

International Law: A Moral Reckoning of the Law of Nations (Oxford: Oxford University Press, 2015) at 349–379), even if one could argue that an investor abusing child labour would find that any damages that might otherwise be awarded could be "non-compensable" (see C. Lo, "Normative and operational linkages between human rights law and BITs – Building a firmer status of human rights in investor-state arbitration" 8(1) *Contemporary Asia Arbitration Journal* 1–28 at 16).

54 See Articles 14.2(i)(b) and 12.1(v). Article 12.2 is also of interest: "Investors and their Investments shall strive, through their management policies and practices, to contribute to the development objectives of the Host State. In particular, Investors and their Investments should recognise the rights, traditions and customs of local communities and indigenous peoples of the Host State and carry out their operations with respect and regard for such rights, traditions and customs."

55 Another recent development is the award in *Urbaser S.A. et al v Argentina*, 8 December 2017, where the idea is accepted that companies have international human rights obligations to abstain from certain actions (esp at para 1210) where the award refers to the situation where "an obligation to abstain, like a prohibition to commit acts violating human rights would be at stake." The award continues: "Such an obligation can be of immediate application, not only upon States, but equally to individuals and other private parties."

56 For a commentary, see S. Jerbi, *The International Code of Conduct for Private Security Service Providers: Academy Briefing 4* (Geneva: Geneva Academy of International Humanitarian Law and Human Rights, 2013).

security company (the contractor) and the client. In this way, a violation of the Code becomes not just an instance that can be brought to public attention by civil society, and a warning to future clients; a violation of the code can be a violation of the terms of the contract, with all that this implies in contract law. To the extent that contractors/private security companies include in their contracts clauses that allow for the settlement of disputes through arbitration, we find here a similar dynamic to that we encountered when consider counterclaims in international investment law.

4. FINAL THOUGHTS ON CORPORATIONS

The refrain "human rights are none of our business" is fading fast. Businesses now face their human rights responsibilities in multiple contexts beyond investment disputes. Businesses may be precluded from gaining access to export credit guarantees,[57] they may face disinvestment from ethical shareholders including sovereign wealth funds,[58] or they may find themselves on the receiving end of a complaint about human rights lodged with a National Contact Point operating within the context of the Organisation for Economic Co-operation and Development (OECD).[59]

At a more theoretical level, it is becoming clearer that corporations may be persons for the purposes of prosecutions for international crimes (including human rights crimes such as torture, crimes against humanity, and enforced disappearances). We should also not rule out the idea that human rights law as such can bind corporations not only at the national level, but also under international law. We saw that, with regard to armed groups, a UN Commission of Inquiry has already applied the terms of the Optional Protocol on the Involvement of Children in Armed Conflict to an armed group. The idea that a human rights treaty could be binding on a third party is not that new,[60] and with regard to issues such as corporate liability for pollution, the idea of obligations for corporate non-state actors seems unexceptional.[61] As far back

57 See, for example, OECD Doc. TAD/ECG(2012)5, 28 June 2012, Recommendation of the Council on Common Approaches for Officially Supported Export Credits and Environmental and Social Due Diligence.

58 See G. Nystuen, A. Follesdal and O. Mestad (eds), *Human Rights, Corporate Complicity and Disinvestment* (Cambridge: Cambridge University Press, 2011) 222–239.

59 For a critical review of such procedures, see C. Daniel, J. Wilde-Ramsing, K. Genovese and V. Sandjojo, *Remedy Remains Rare* (Amsterdam: OECD Watch, 2015); and more generally the information at <http://oecdwatch.org>.

60 For an early suggestion, see T. Meron, *Human Rights in Internal Strife: Their International Protection* (Cambridge: Grotius, 1987) at 33–40.

61 H. H. Koh, "Separating Myth from Reality about Corporate Responsibility Litigation" 7 *Journal of International Economic Law* 2 (2004) 263–274.

as 1972, the UN Security Council adopted a resolution whereby it called on states whose corporations were operating in Namibia "to use all available means to ensure that such nationals and corporations conform, in their policies of hiring Namibian workers, to the basic provisions of the Universal Declaration of Human Rights."[62] So far, the UN human rights treaty bodies have tended to concentrate on the obligations of the States Parties to the treaties, rather than explaining what is actually expected of the non-state actors themselves, but a new direction may be heralded by two more recent developments. The first is a General Comment prepared by the UN Committee on the Rights of the Child. The Committee recognized that:

> duties and responsibilities to respect the rights of children extend in practice beyond the State and State-controlled services and institutions and apply to private actors and business enterprises. Therefore, all businesses must meet their responsibilities regarding children's rights and States must ensure they do so. In addition, business enterprises should not undermine the States' ability to meet their obligations towards children under the Convention and the Optional Protocols thereto.[63]

The second concerns the new General Recommendation on gender-based violence against women adopted by the UN Committee on the Elimination of Discrimination against Women, which tackles, under the heading "non-state actors", the violence perpetrated by both corporations and armed groups (defined in a wide sense as "rebel forces, gangs, paramilitary groups, etc."). Having explained in some detail the due diligence obligations of the state with regard to preventing and punishing such violence, the Committee asserts: "In addition, both international humanitarian law and human rights law have recognised the direct obligations of non-State actors, including as parties to an armed conflict, in specific circumstances. These include the prohibition of torture, which is part of customary international law and has become a peremptory norm *(jus cogens)*".[64]

---

62 Resolution 310 (1972) at para 5; see also E. Schwelb, "The International Convention on the Elimination of All Forms of Racial Discrimination" 15 *ICLQ* (1966) 996–1068. I am grateful to William Schabas for bringing to my attention this example of the Security Council expecting corporations to conform to the Universal Declaration.

63 General Comment 16 (2013) on state obligations regarding the impact of the business sector on children's rights, at para 8. For a detailed look at this, see P. Gerber, J. Kyriakakis and K. O'Byrne, "General Comment 16 on state obligations regarding the impact of the business sector on children's rights: What is its standing, meaning and effect?" 14 *Melbourne Journal of International Law* (2013) 1–36.

64 General Recommendation 35 (2017) on gender-based violence against women, updating general recommendation No. 19, at para 25.

5. CONCLUDING REMARKS

When Louise Arbour welcomed the growing recognition that "the private sector has responsibilities to respect human rights", she probably had in mind large water companies, private health-care facilities and a range of employers whose impact on human rights is obvious. At the time, this would have been a rather progressive position, but today the statement seems less exceptional because many who would resist the extension of human rights obligation to the private sector understand a "responsibility" to be something less than a legal obligation. Whichever side of that debate one comes down on, the fact is that corporations may today find themselves judged according to human rights standards in multiple contexts, including with regard to: contracts including human rights provisions; ethical investment; export credit guarantees; and investment disputes. Nevertheless, Arbour's assessment still rings true. The means of holding non-state actors accountable are still "wanting."

What was perhaps less evident ten years ago was that the UN (including the Security Council) would now be focused on grave violations committed by armed groups such as ISIS. Nor could one have imagined that the atrocities committed by such groups would defy the strained constructions which suggest that their acts are mere "abuses" or "impairments to the enjoyment" of human rights. At the time of writing, it had been recently reported that ISIS had executed 19 women for refusing to become sex slaves.[65] Those women's human rights were surely violated. The everyday indignities meted out by ISIS to those in its power are being described in multiple quarters as human rights violations. A reading of international law that would deny that ISIS has perpetrated any violations of international human rights law seems unsustainable today. The human rights movement is now increasingly forced to focus on the gruesome violent oppression meted out by a surprising array of brutal non-state actors. This is where we are now.

---

65 "Isis executes 19 women in Mosul 'for refusing to take part in sexual jihad,'" *The Independent*, 9 August 2015.

THE RIGHT TO TRUTH

When Does it Begin?

William SCHABAS OC MRIA

In 2006, the Office of the High Commissioner for Human Rights published a report on the right to truth. The report concluded that "[t]he right to the truth about gross human rights violations and serious violations of humanitarian law is an inalienable and autonomous right," noting its recognition by several treaties and international instruments, as well as in national, regional and international jurisprudence and resolutions of universal and regional organizations.[1] Although initially understood largely as a right belonging to the family members of victims of enforced disappearance, the report noted that it was of broader application in terms of subject matter and, moreover, that "society has the right to know the truth about past events concerning the perpetration of heinous crimes, as well as the circumstances and the reasons for which aberrant crimes came to be committed, so that such events do not reoccur in the future."[2] The right to truth was closely associated with the broader theme of accountability for serious violations of human rights. Presenting the report to the newly formed Human Rights Council in September 2006, High Commissioner Louise Arbour said: "Our study clarifies the concept of the right to the truth by providing

1 Study on the right to the truth, UN Doc. E/CN.4/2006/91, para. 55.
2 Ibid, para. 55.

a detailed and rigorous analysis of several elements of this right, such as its legal and historical bases, its material scope, content and nature."[3]

There is a close relationship between the "right to truth" and issues of justice, impunity and international criminal justice. The "right to truth" is often presented as being an entitlement of victims and their families. Nevertheless, early formulations of a right to truth also focused on the broader collective dimension of the right. In 1986, the Inter-American Commission on Human Rights observed that "every society has the inalienable right to know the truth about past events, as well as the motives and circumstances in which aberrant crimes came to be committed, in order to prevent repetition of such acts in the future."[4] This aspect of the "right to truth" was also highlighted in the 1997 report of Louis Joinet to the Sub-Commission on the Protection and Promotion of Human Rights:

> This is not simply the right of any individual victim or his nearest and dearest to know what happened, a right to the truth. The right to know is also a collective right, drawing upon history to prevent violations from recurring in the future. Its corollary is a "duty to remember" on the part of the State: to be forearmed against the perversions of history that go under the names of revisionism or negationism, for the history of its oppression is part of a people's national heritage and as such must be preserved. These, then, are the main objectives of the right to know as a collective right.[5]

Joinet listed the "right to truth" as Principle 1 in the Set of Principles for the Protection and Promotion of Human Rights through Action to Combat Impunity, where it was presented as a right of a "people" rather than of individuals:

> Every people has the inalienable right to know the truth about past events and about the circumstances and reasons which led, through the consistent pattern of gross violations of human rights, to the perpetration of aberrant crimes. Full and effective exercise of the right to the truth is essential to avoid any recurrence of such acts in the future.[6]

In the French version, he wrote: "Chaque peuple a le droit inaliénable ..." Principle 2, entitled "The Duty to Remember," stated:

> A people's knowledge of the history of their oppression is part of their heritage and, as such, shall be preserved by appropriate measures in fulfilment of the State's duty to remember. Such measures shall be aimed at preserving the collective memory from

---

3 Address by Ms Louise Arbour, UN High Commissioner for Human Rights on the occasion of the 2nd Session of the Human Rights Council, 26 September 2006.

4 Inter-American Commission on Human Rights, Annual Report, 1985–1986, OEA/Ser.L/V/II.68, Doc. 8 rev. 1, p. 193.

5 Final report prepared by Mr Joinet pursuant to Sub-Commission Decision 1996/119, UN Doc. E/CN.4/Sub.2/1997/20/Rev.1, para. 17.

6 Ibid, Annex II, Principle 1.

> extinction and, in particular, at guarding against the development of revisionist and negationist arguments.[7]

Principle 5 required that states should "ensure the preservation of, and access to, archives concerning violations of human rights and humanitarian law."[8]

The updated Principles, prepared by Diane Orentlicher in 2005, made some minor changes to the text of Joinet's first principle:

> Every people has the inalienable right to know the truth about past events concerning the perpetration of heinous crimes and about the circumstances and reasons that led, through massive or systematic violations, to the perpetration of those crimes. Full and effective exercise of the right to the truth provides a vital safeguard against the recurrence of violations.[9]

Diane Orentlicher reformulated the text about "[a] people's knowledge of the history of its oppression" and the importance of archives, saying that this was "part of its heritage and, as such, must be ensured by appropriate measures in fulfilment of the State's duty to preserve archives and other evidence concerning violations of human rights and humanitarian law and to facilitate knowledge of those violations."[10]

The first Human Rights Council resolution on the right to truth declared that "the public and individuals are entitled to have access, to the fullest extent practicable, to information regarding the actions and decision-making processes of their Government, within the framework of each State's domestic legal system."[11] Furthermore: "States should preserve archives and other evidence concerning gross violations of human rights and serious violations of international humanitarian law."[12] The Resolution requested the Office of the High Commissioner for Human Rights to prepare a comprehensive study of the question, "including, in particular, practices relating to archives and records concerning gross violations of human rights with a view to create guidelines on protecting archives and records concerning gross human rights violations."[13]

Following the presentation of the Report of the Office of the High Commissioner, the Human Rights Council adopted a resolution that highlighted "the importance of preserving historic memory related to gross human rights violations and serious violations of international humanitarian law through the

7 Ibid, Principle 2.

8 Ibid, Principle 5.

9 Updated set of principles for the protection and promotion of human rights through action to combat impunity, E/CN.4/2005/102/Add.1, Principle 2.

10 Ibid, Principle 3.

11 Right to the truth, UN Doc. A/HRC/RES/9/11, PP 14.

12 Ibid, PP 15.

13 Ibid, PP 7.

conservation of archives and other documents related to those violations."[14] Subsequently, the Human Rights Council noted a report on the subject by the Office of the High Commissioner that pointed to the importance of ensuring "that all archives pertaining to human rights are preserved and protected, and to enact legislation that declares that the nation's documentary heritage is to be retained and preserved, and creates the framework for managing State records from their creation to destruction or preservation."[15] The General Assembly has justified the protection of archives as a measure necessary to "facilitate knowledge" of gross violations of human rights and serious violations of international humanitarian law.[16]

1. THE "PROCEDURAL RIGHT TO TRUTH" AT THE EUROPEAN COURT OF HUMAN RIGHTS

Not much attention has been given to where the right to truth sits within the recognized framework of human rights. Louis Joinet's early discussion of the question did not point to specific provisions of the Universal Declaration of Human Rights or the treaties. Nevertheless, his remarks were placed in a discussion of impunity where two fundamental rights – the right to life and the prohibition of cruel, inhuman or degrading treatment – are of particular importance. In this context, the European Court of Human Rights has developed the notion of a "procedural dimension" to these rights.[17] Accordingly, there is an obligation upon the state to investigate violations of these fundamental rights, even if it is not itself responsible for them as a perpetrator. The procedural obligation of the right to life, set out in Article 2 of the European Convention on Human Rights, has been held to be "separate and autonomous" from the substantive obligation.[18]

According to the European Court of Human Rights, the procedural obligation entitles victims, their families and heirs to know the truth about circumstances associated with a violation of the right to life, especially when this is linked to a large-scale or massive violation of fundamental rights. For example, it has stressed the importance of this "in the event of widespread use of lethal force against the civilian population during anti-Government demonstrations preceding the transition from a totalitarian regime to a more democratic system."[19]

---

14 Right to the truth, UN Doc. A/HRC/RES/12/12, PP 20. See also Right to the truth, UN Doc. A/HC/RES/21/7, PP 20.

15 Right to the truth, UN Doc. A/HRC/RES/21/7, PP 20, OP 10.

16 Right to the truth, UN Doc. A/RES/68/165, para. 13.

17 *McCann and Others v. United Kingdom*, 27 September 1995, §§157–164, Series A no. 324.

18 *Šilih v. Slovenia* [GC], no. 71463/01, §159, 9 April 2009.

19 *Association "21 December 1989" and Others v. Romania*, nos. 33810/07 and 18817/08, §106, 24 May 2011.

Although the issue arises in the context of individual rights, there is some authority in the Court's jurisprudence for the recognition of a broader collective or social dimension to this right to know the truth. In one decision, the Court framed the importance of an investigation into events in light not only of the rights of the individual applicants, but also "in view also of the importance to Romanian society of knowing the truth about the events of December 1989."[20]

In *El Masri v. The "Former Yugoslav Republic of Macedonia,"* where government complicity in "extraordinary renditions" by the Central Intelligence Agency was involved, the Grand Chamber of the European Court of Human Rights underscored "the great importance of the present case not only for the applicant and his family, but also for other victims of similar crimes and the general public, who had the right to know what had happened."[21] In a concurring opinion in that case, several judges noted that the right to truth was implicit in the European Convention, in particular within the procedural obligation of Articles 2 (right to life) and 3 (prohibition of torture and inhuman or degrading treatment or punishment), although they argued that it was best approached from the perspective of Article 13 (right to a remedy). They wrote:

> In practice, the search for the truth is the objective purpose of the obligation to carry out an investigation and the raison d'être of the related quality requirements (transparency, diligence, independence, access, disclosure of results and scrutiny). For society in general, the desire to ascertain the truth plays a part in strengthening confidence in public institutions and hence the rule of law. For those concerned – the victims' families and close friends – establishing the true facts and securing an acknowledgment of serious breaches of human rights and humanitarian law constitute forms of redress that are just as important as compensation, and sometimes even more so. Ultimately, the wall of silence and the cloak of secrecy prevent these people from making any sense of what they have experienced and are the greatest obstacles to their recovery.[22]

Another decision of the European Court, referring to the killings by soldiers during the conflict in Northern Ireland, insisted upon the importance of a "reasoned decision available to reassure a concerned public that the rule of law had been respected."[23] Granting an application based upon Article 3 of the European Convention, a Chamber of the European Court said it appreciated the fact that descendants of the Polish officers murdered at Katyń had "suffered a double trauma: not only had their relatives perished in the war but they were not allowed, for political reasons, to learn the truth about what had happened

20 Ibid, §130. See also *Şandru and Others v. Romania*, no. 22465/03, §79, 8 December 2009.

21 *El Masri v. "The Former Yugoslav Republic of Macedonia"* [GC], no. 39630/09, §191, ECHR 2012.

22 Ibid, Joint Concurring Opinion of Judges Tulkens, Speilmann, Sicilianos and Keller, §6.

23 *Kelly and Others v. United Kingdom*, no. 30054/96, §118, 4 May 2001.

and forced to accept the distortion of historical fact by the Soviet and Polish Communist authorities for more than fifty years."[24]

If there is such a broad, collective, historical dimension to the right to truth, when does it actually begin? This is an issue that does not arise, or at least not in the same way, as long as the right to truth is confined to the victims themselves or to their next of kin. From the perspective of individual victims, the right presumably exists only as long as they or their offspring are themselves alive.[25] Perhaps the right can even be transmitted to one or more succeeding generations. But when the right is associated with the "people's knowledge of the history of its oppression" and when it is "aimed at preserving the collective memory from extinction" because it is "a collective right, drawing upon history to prevent violations from recurring in the future," can there be any logical basis for a temporal limitation on its scope?

2. THE SPANISH CIVIL WAR AND THE SPECIAL RAPPORTEUR ON TRUTH

The Special Rapporteur on the promotion of truth, justice, reparation and guarantees of non-recurrence, a mandate established by the Human Rights Council in 2011, confronted some of these issues, but only indirectly, in his 2014 report on a mission to Spain. Pablo de Greiff welcomed efforts at the removal of symbols or monuments exalting the military uprising, the Civil War and Franco's dictatorship.[26] Noting the importance of the teaching of history, he urged that it be "approached as a system of investigation rather than a mechanism for simply preserving data [that] can train citizens in habits of analysis and critical reasoning."[27] He discussed a number of measures under consideration as means of elucidating the truth about Spain's history, including oral history projects, a possible truth commission and access to archival materials. He was of course focusing his attention on the Spanish Civil War of 1936–1939, a conflict that took place prior to Spain's membership of the United Nations (UN) and, indeed, prior to the existence of the UN. Moreover, this was well before the modern recognition in international law of fundamental human rights, including the right to life and the prohibition of ill-treatment.

---

24 *Janowiec and Others v. Russia*, nos. 55508/07 and 29520/09, §156, 16 April 2012.

25 In right to life cases, under some circumstances, the European Court of Human Rights will sometimes give standing to the next of kin where the victim is no longer alive: *Fairfield and Others v. United Kingdom* (dec.), no. 24790/04, 8 March 2005.

26 Report of the Special Rapporteur on the promotion of truth, justice, reparation and guarantees of non-recurrence, Pablo de Greiff, UN Doc. A/HRC/27/56/Add.1, paras. 27–33.

27 Ibid, para. 34.

Whether UN human rights mechanisms have the authority to examine issues relating to the Spanish Civil War is an issue that has also arisen before other bodies. In its report to the Committee on Enforced Disappearances, Spain explained that following its ratification of the International Convention for the Protection of All Persons from Enforced Disappearance, "certain organizations – associations and non-governmental organizations (NGOs) which may or may not have consultative status – have raised the issue of its applicability to enforced disappearances alleged to have taken place during the civil war and under the Franco regime and the need to abrogate or declare inapplicable the Amnesty Act (No. 46/1977) of 15 October." Spain invoked Article 35(1) of the Convention, which declares the Committee to be competent "solely in respect of enforced disappearances which commenced after the entry into force of this Convention."[28] Recently, the Working Group on Enforced or Involuntary Disappearance has also considered Spanish cases relating to the Civil War. Spain did not object to the Working Group's authority to inquire into these cases.[29] Previously, however, it seems that the Working Group declined to consider disappearances that occurred prior to the creation of the UN in 1945.[30] In any event, enforced disappearance has special features because of its continuous nature,[31] something that cannot be said about a violation of the right to life or the prohibition of ill-treatment.

The Special Rapporteur on the promotion of truth did not speak to whether he had "jurisdiction" over the Spanish Civil War and fascist Spain. Like the Working Group on Enforced or Involuntary Disappearances, his mandate says nothing specific about its temporal scope. Moreover, if an unresolved disappearance is a continuing violation, surely the same can be said about a partial or incomplete truth. The closest authority for the Special Rapporteur appears to be operative paragraph 1(b) of the relevant resolution: "To gather relevant information on national situations, including on normative frameworks, national practices and experiences, such as truth and reconciliation commissions and other mechanisms, relating to the promotion of truth, justice, reparation and guarantees of non-recurrence in addressing gross violations of human rights and serious violations of international humanitarian law, and to study trends, developments and challenges and to make recommendations thereon."[32]

---

28 Reports of States Parties pursuant to Article 29, paragraph 1, of the Convention due in 2012, Spain, UN Doc. CED/C/ESP/1, paras. 3–4.

29 Report of the Working Group on Enforced or Involuntary Disappearances, UN Doc. A/HRC/13/31, paras. 479–502.

30 Report of the Working Group on Enforced or Involuntary Disappearances, UN Doc. E/CN.4/2003/70, para. 247.

31 See the General Comment on Enforced Disappearance as a Continuous Crime of the Working Group on Enforced or Involuntary Disappearances, UN Doc. A/HRC/16/48.

32 Special Rapporteur on the promotion of truth, justice, reparation and guarantees of non-recurrence, UN Doc. A/HRC/RES/18/7, OP 1(b).

If this passage is read literally, he is on reasonably solid ground. But if his mandate applies to the distant past, then can this also be said about the other special procedures? Would there not be strenuous opposition within the Human Rights Council and the General Assembly if the Special Rapporteur on extrajudicial, summary or arbitrary executions were to investigate lynchings in the United States prior to the Second World War or if the Special Rapporteur on torture were to inquire into the colonial practices of Britain, France, Belgium and the Netherlands in the 1930s? Moreover, if the Special Rapporteur on the promotion of truth can inquire into the Spanish Civil War and its aftermath, can there be any logical reason why he could not also, within the context of his mandate, address issues of historical truth surrounding the Armenian genocide of 1915, the Irish famine of the 1840s, the transatlantic slave trade of the sixteenth, seventeenth and eighteenth centuries, the St Bartholomew's Day Massacre of 1572 and the rape of the Sabine women of 750 BCE?

3. KATYŃ AT THE EUROPEAN COURT

Despite this seemingly inexorable drive within evolving human rights law and practice to peer into the past, some recent judgments also suggest that there is a certain reluctance to do so. In the Polish case concerning the refusal of Russia to release documents on the Katyń massacre, the Russian judge sitting in a seven-judge Chamber penned an ominous dissent, stating that the European Convention on Human Rights had "arisen out of a bloody chapter of European history in the twentieth century," but that it was drafted as part of a process of reconstructing post-war Europe and "not with the intention of delving into that black chapter."[33] His approach seems to have been largely confirmed by the majority of the Grand Chamber of the Court in a judgment overturning the finding of the Chamber that there had been a violation of Article 3 of the European Convention (prohibiting inhuman or degrading treatment). In *Janowiec and Others v. Russia*, the Grand Chamber held that the procedural obligation associated with the right to life, entitling victims to demand that governments conduct proper inquiries into allegations of violations, cannot operate prior to 4 November 1950, the date on which the European Convention on Human Rights was adopted.

It is well established in case law that from the moment that the European Convention enters into force for any given state, there is an obligation upon the state party to "secure to everyone" the rights and freedoms set out in Section I of the Convention. Beginning with this "critical date," all of the state's acts and omissions "not only must conform to the Convention but are also undoubtedly

---

33 *Janowiec and Others v. Russia*, nos. 55508/07 and 29520/09, Joint Concurring Opinion of Judges Kovler and Yudkivska, 16 April 2012.

subject to review by the Convention institutions."[34] The corollary to this is rooted in the presumption that international treaties do not operate retroactively unless a different intention appears from the treaty or is otherwise established, something confirmed in Article 28 of the Vienna Convention on the Law of Treaties. Consequently, the treaty provisions "do not bind a party in relation to any act or fact which took place or any situation which ceased to exist before the date of the entry into force of the treaty with respect to that party."[35] According to the European Court, "the Convention imposes no specific obligation on the Contracting States to provide redress for wrongs or damage caused prior to that date."[36] The Grand Chamber has stated that this principle is "beyond dispute."[37]

The European Convention entered into force on 3 September 1953 following the deposit of the tenth ratification by a Member State of the Council of Europe, as provided for by Article 59(3) of the Convention. For states that have ratified or acceded to the Convention subsequent to that date, the Convention enters into force on the date of deposit of its instrument of ratification or accession with the Secretary-General of the Council of Europe, pursuant to Article 59(4). However, exceptionally the Court may take into account facts that took place prior to the "critical date" in considering the procedural obligation associated with certain fundamental rights, notably those in Articles 2 and 3 of the Convention. Where a substantive violation of the right to life has taken place before the "critical date," the Convention may nevertheless apply to the duty of the state party to conduct an investigation and to ensure that measures of accountability exist. In disappearance cases, even if the body has been found, "[t]his only casts light on one aspect of the fate of the missing person and the obligation to account for the disappearance and death, as well as to identify and prosecute any perpetrator of unlawful acts in that connection, will generally remain."[38]

Following divergences in the case law of the Chambers of the European Court,[39] in 2009 the Grand Chamber confronted the temporal jurisdiction issue with respect to the procedural obligation in a case dealing with medical malpractice. It recognized a procedural obligation pursuant to Article 2 of the

34 *Yağcı and Sargın v. Turkey*, 8 June 1995, §41, Series A no. 319-A; *Broniowski v. Poland* [GC] (dec.), no. 31443/96, §§74 *et seq*., ECHR 2002-X.

35 Vienna Convention on the Law of Treaties, (1980) 1155 UNTS 331, art. 28. See also Draft Articles on Responsibility of States for Internationally Wrongful Acts, UN Doc. A/56/10, art. 13.

36 *Kopecký v. Slovakia* [GC], no. 44912/98, §38, ECHR 2004-IX.

37 *Varnava and Others v. Turkey* [GC], nos. 16064/90, 16065/90, 16066/90, 16068/90, 16069/90, 16070/90, 16071/90, 16072/90 and 16073/90, §130, ECHR 2009; *Blečić v. Croatia* [GC], no. 59532/00, §70, ECHR 2006-III.

38 *Palić v. Bosnia and Herzegovina*, no. 4704/04, §46, 15 February 2011.

39 *Moldovan and Others and Rostaş and Others v. Romania* (dec.), nos. 41138/98 and 64320/01, 13 March 2001. Followed: *Moldovan and Others v. Romania (No. 2)*, nos. 41138/98 and 64320/01, §102, ECHR 2005-VII (extracts); *Kholodov and Kholodova v. Russia* (dec.), no. 30651/05, 14 September 2006; *Bălăşoiu v. Romania* (dec.), no. 37424/97, 2 September 2003.

Convention, even if the actual killing took place prior to the entry into force of the Convention for the respondent state. By 15 votes to two, the Grand Chamber held that "the procedural obligation to carry out an effective investigation under Article 2 has evolved into a separate and autonomous duty" that constitutes "a detachable obligation arising out of Article 2 capable of binding the State even when the death took place before the critical date."[40] Nevertheless, the Court said that "having regard to the principle of legal certainty," this extension of the temporal jurisdiction of the Court was "not open-ended."[41] The Grand Chamber explained the limitations it was placing on the procedural obligation:

> 162. First, it is clear that, where the death occurred before the critical date, only procedural acts and/or omissions occurring after that date can fall within the Court's temporal jurisdiction.
>
> 163. Second, there must exist a genuine connection between the death and the entry into force of the Convention in respect of the respondent State for the procedural obligations imposed by Article 2 to come into effect. Thus a significant proportion of the procedural steps required by this provision – which include not only an effective investigation into the death of the person concerned but also the institution of appropriate proceedings for the purpose of determining the cause of the death and holding those responsible to account – will have been or ought to have been carried out after the critical date. However, the Court would not exclude that in certain circumstances the connection could also be based on the need to ensure that the guarantees and the underlying values of the Convention are protected in a real and effective manner.[42]

In this way, the Grand Chamber established an exception within an exception. The Court could only exercise jurisdiction with respect to a violation of the procedural obligation contained in Article 2 if a "significant proportion of the procedural steps" had been undertaken after the "critical date." However, this requirement could be waived if "certain circumstances" required the Court "to ensure that the guarantees and the underlying values of the Convention are protected in a real and effective manner." This "underlying values" exception has sometimes been called the "humanitarian clause."[43]

---

40 *Šilih v. Slovenia* [GC], no. 71463/01, §159, 9 April 2009. See E. Bjorge, "Right for the Wrong Reasons: *Šilih v. Slovenia* and Jurisdiction *Ratione Temporis* in the European Court of Human Rights" (2013) 84 *British Yearbook of International Law* 115.

41 Ibid, *Šilih v. Slovenia*, §161.

42 Ibid, §§162–163 (interior reference omitted).

43 For example, *Janowiec and Others v. Russia* [GC], nos. 55508/07 and 29520/09, Concurring Opinion of Judge Gyulumyan, 21 October 2013; *Janowiec and Others v. Russia* [GC], nos. 55508/07 and 29520/09, Joint Partly Dissenting Opinion of Judges Ziemele, De Gaetano, Laffranque and Keller, §§7 and 31, 21 October 2013.

In *Janowiec and Others v. Russia*, the Grand Chamber held that it could not consider the "underlying values" exception if the loss of life had taken place prior to 4 November 1950, the date when the European Convention on Human Rights was signed at the Barberini Palace in Rome. It said that "a Contracting Party cannot be held responsible under the Convention for not investigating even the most serious crimes under international law if they predated the Convention."[44] The Grand Chamber explained that "the events that might have triggered the obligation to investigate under Article 2 took place in early 1940, that is, more than ten years before the Convention came into existence." It said that "there were no elements capable of providing a bridge from the distant past into the recent post-entry into force period."[45]

The very substantial dissenting opinion of Judges Ziemele, De Gaetano, Laffranque and Keller harshly criticizes the majority for turning a "long history of justice delayed into a permanent case of justice denied."[46] With respect to the "underlying values" exception in *Šilih*, the dissenters noted that the majority simply did not apply it. The majority's decision "closes the Court's door to victims of any gross human rights violation that occurred prior to the existence of the Convention," they wrote.[47] By failing to implement the "humanitarian clause," the dissenters said that the Court has failed "to fulfil the role for which it was intended: to provide a Court that would act as a "conscience" for Europe."[48] It is indeed hard to be a "conscience" if one refuses to even consider the past. Indeed, where else does "conscience" come from if not the past?

In *Janowiec and Others*, it was argued that one factor justifying the extension of the temporal jurisdiction of the Court, on an exceptional basis, was the importance of truth seeking in order to enable nations to learn from their history and take measures to prevent future atrocities.[49] Reliance was placed upon the Updated Set of Principles drafted by Professor Orentlicher, as well as on the International Committee of the Red Cross rules of customary international law[50] and the case law of the Inter-American Court of Human Rights.[51] However, the Grand Chamber distinguished the procedural obligation of individual victims comprised in Article 2 from "other types of inquiries that may be carried out

44 *Janowiec and Others v. Russia* [GC], nos. 55508/07 and 29520/09, §151, 21 October 2013.
45 Ibid, §160.
46 Ibid, Joint Partly Dissenting Opinion of Judges Ziemele, De Gaetano, Laffranque and Keller, §36.
47 Ibid, §33.
48 Ibid.
49 Ibid, §§124 and 126, 21 October 2013.
50 J.-M. Henckaerts and L. Doswald-Beck, (eds.), *Customary International Humanitarian Law*, Vol. I, Cambridge: Cambridge University Press, 2005, Rule 117.
51 I/A Court H.R., *Case of Heliodoro-Portugal v. Panama*. Preliminary Objections, Merits, Reparations, and Costs. Judgment of 12, August 2008. Series C No. 186; I/A Court H.R., *Case of Gomes Lund et al. ("Guerrilha do Araguaia') v. Brazil*. Preliminary Objections, Merits, Reparations, and Costs. Judgment of 24, November 2010. Series C No. 219.

for other purposes, such as establishing a historical truth."[52] The four dissenting judges said that in addition to the rights of the individual victims, "it is equally clear that the obligation to investigate and prosecute those responsible for grave human rights and serious humanitarian law violations serves fundamental public interests by allowing a nation to learn from its history and by combating impunity."[53]

4. TEMPORAL LIMITS ON THE GENOCIDE CONVENTION

There is another recent example of judicial reluctance to look too far into the past, this time in a judgment of the International Court of Justice. The debate concerned the retroactive application of the Convention on the Prevention and Punishment of the Crime of Genocide. The Convention was adopted by the UN General Assembly on 9 December 1948, a date that has henceforth been marked as the International Day of Commemoration and Dignity of the Victims of Genocide.[54] The Convention's preamble states that "at all periods of history genocide has inflicted great losses on humanity," adding that its purpose is "to liberate mankind from such an odious scourge."[55] The preamble also makes reference to General Assembly Resolution 96(I), adopted two years earlier, that affirmed that "[m]any instances of such crimes of genocide have occurred when racial, religious, political and other groups have been destroyed, entirely or in part."

In a 2008 ruling, the International Court of Justice clearly left the door open on the question of temporal scope of the Convention, noting "that there is no express provision in the Genocide Convention limiting its jurisdiction *ratione temporis*."[56] But in February 2015, in its final judgment in the case of *Croatia v. Serbia*, the Court stated definitively that "the substantive provisions of the Convention do not impose upon a State obligations in relation to acts said to

52 *Janowiec and Others v. Russia* [GC], nos. 55508/07 and 29520/09, §143, 21 October 2013. However, see: ibid, Joint Partly Dissenting Opinion of Judges Ziemele, De Gaetano, Laffranque and Keller, §§8 and 9, 21 October 2013.

53 Ibid, Joint Partly Dissenting Opinion of Judges Ziemele, De Gaetano, Laffranque and Keller, §24, 21 October 2013.

54 Prevention of genocide, UN Doc. A/HRC/28/34, PP 22.

55 Convention on the Prevention and Punishment of the Crime of Genocide, (1951) 78 *UNTS* 277, preamble.

56 *Application of the Convention on the Prevention and Punishment of the Crime of Genocide (Croatia v. Serbia), Preliminary Objections, Judgment, I.C.J. Reports 2008*, p. 412, para. 123. See also: *Application of the Convention on the Prevention and Punishment of the Crime of Genocide, Preliminary Objections, Judgment, I.C.J. Reports 1996 (II)*, p. 617, para. 34.

have occurred before that State became bound by the Convention."[57] Like the European Court of Human Rights, the International Court of Justice pointed to the presumption against retroactivity in Article 28 of the Vienna Convention on the Law of Treaties. It acknowledged that the presumption was rebuttable, providing examples of international criminal law treaties with retroactive or retrospective effect, such as the Convention on the Non-Applicability of Statutory Limitations to War Crimes and Crimes against Humanity. On the other hand, the International Court of Justice cited references in the *travaux préparatoires* of the Genocide Convention where a few states suggested it was "intended to apply to acts taking place in the future and not to be applicable to those which had occurred during the Second World War or at other times in the past."[58]

5. THE PASSAGE OF TIME

Neither the European Court of Human Rights nor the International Court of Justice can be faulted for reaching a conclusion that is not patently unreasonable. Their findings are in line with much of the academic commentary, as well as with precedent. Perhaps the only implausible element is the fixing of the European Court on 4 November 1950 as the starting date for the right to truth. To the extent that it was deemed necessary to set a "critical date," it might have been more logical to pick that of the entry into force of the European Convention, in line with the approach of the International Court of Justice, or the date of adoption of the Universal Declaration of Human Rights on 10 December 1948, given that the European Convention, according to the final recital of its preamble, was intended "to take the first steps for the collective enforcement of certain of the Rights stated in the Universal Declaration." But this is a detail. At a time when there is a growing movement within human rights law to affirm a right to truth and to insist upon the importance of historical memory, these two courts seem to have drawn a curtain on the past in or around the year 1950.

Some will say in defence of these judgments that the courtroom is not the place to adjudicate such matters. This message also emerges from a December 2014 decision of the European Court of Human Rights in an application filed by Yevgeniy Yakovlevich Dzhugashvili, a grandson of Joseph Stalin. The applicant had unsuccessfully sued a Russian journalist for defamation concerning an article about the Katyń massacre that described his grandfather as "a bloodthirsty cannibal."[59] Declaring the application inadmissible, the Chamber said "it is an integral part of freedom of expression, guaranteed under Article 10

---

57 *Application of the Convention on the Prevention and Punishment of the Crime of Genocide (Croatia v. Serbia), Judgment*, 3 February 2015, para. 100.

58 Ibid, para. 97.

59 *Dzhugashvili v. Russia*, no. 41123/10, 9 December 2014, para 5.

of the Convention, to seek historical truth. It is not the Court's role to arbitrate the underlying historical issues, which are part of a continuing debate between historians." It added that "[a] contrary finding would open the way to a judicial intervention in historical debate and inevitably shift the respective historical discussions from public forums to courtrooms."[60]

It may well be that other institutions, such as truth commissions, are better suited to the complex task of detailed examination of the past. But the suspicion lingers that far from rising to the challenge of dealing with historical truth, the European Court of Human Rights and the International Court of Justice are turning their backs on the "bloody, black chapters" to which Judge Kovler referred in his dissent in *Janowiec*. Truth is often linked with reconciliation, as the names of many recent commissions bear out. But human experience suggests that sometimes reconciliation is better achieved without clarifying the truth or acknowledging it. Perhaps this is a *leitmotif* in the two judgments.

That there is a right to truth applicable to recent decades seems today to be beyond dispute. The ruling of the Grand Chamber of the European Court shuts out pre-1950 atrocities, but at the same time it seems to clear the way for inquiries into events of the second half of the twentieth century, even with respect to states that did not ratify the European Convention until the 1990s. Nor does there appear to be much dispute about the distant past when there is little suggestion that states intentionally conceal documents and lock their archives, even if legitimate debates about historical events persist. With respect to these very old atrocities of distant centuries and millennia, states are content to mutter apologies, with varying degrees of sincerity. But there is a problematic grey area, starting at about 1950 and going back several decades, perhaps a century, when the right to truth still seems to be important, yet its recognition encounters resistance, as it did recently in Strasbourg and The Hague.

In recent rulings on the incompatibility of genocide denial legislation with freedom of expression, the European Court has referred to "the time factor." A seven-judge Chamber said that where debates on historical issues are concerned, "the passing of time makes it inappropriate to deal with certain remarks about historical events, many years on, with the same severity as just a few years before. That forms part of the efforts that every country must make to debate its own history openly and dispassionately."[61] The Grand Chamber in the same case, after citing an earlier precedent where the impugned speech concerned events 40 years earlier, said that with respect to the Armenian genocide of 1915, "the lapse of time between the applicant's statements and the tragic events to which he was referring was considerably longer, about

[60] Ibid, para 33. See also *Perincek v. Switzerland*, no. 27510/08, §99, 17 December 2013; *Irodalom Kft v. Hungary*, no. 64520/10, §63, 3 December 2013; *Putistin v. Ukraine*, no. 16882/03, Concurring Opinion of Judge Lemmens, 21 November 2013.

[61] *Perinçek v. Switzerland*, no. 27510/08, §103, 17 December 2013.

ninety years, and at the time when he made the statements there were surely very few, if any, survivors of these events." The Grand Chamber noted that some of the interveners in the case had emphasized "that this was still a live issue for many Armenians, especially those in the diaspora." It said that "the time element cannot be disregarded. Whereas events of relatively recent vintage may be so traumatic as to warrant, for a period of time, an enhanced degree of regulation of statements relating to them, the need for such regulation is bound to recede with the passage of time."[62] The European Court has made similar pronouncements in cases dealing with Nazi sympathizers in wartime Switzerland,[63] supporters of communism in modern-day Hungary,[64] torturers in Algeria,[65] the defence of French collaborators during the Second World War,[66] as well as in cases dealing with individual reputation and image.[67]

The European Court's "passage of time" approach seems rather close to a familiar concept in law, that of statutory limitation or prescription. We accept the rationale for such notions when personal rights such as protection of reputation are concerned. At the same time, the whole concept is rejected when the core international crimes, including genocide, are concerned.[68] In the Armenian genocide case, however, the Court seemed to be saying to the descendants of victims of the "crime of crimes" that as a century had passed since the atrocities were committed, perhaps they were insisting too much. It is hard to reconcile this with the prohibition of statutory limitation on atrocity crimes.

6. CONCLUSION

The right to truth is closely related to the rights to justice and to reparations. In some cases, at the heart of campaigns for historical truth may lie the hope of some compensation, of restored property, of financial gain. But it is also associated with a sense that knowledge of historical truth is intrinsically important. It contributes in a general way to justice, the rule of law, democratic governance and social wellbeing. For reasons that mere law cannot explain, many of us still feel emotionally connected to the not-so-distant past, to the grey area. Some formulate this as an individual right, based on lineage to increasingly distant generations. The treatment of their immediate ancestors is important, although

62 *Perinçek v. Switzerland* [GC], no. 27510/08, §250, 15 October 2015.

63 *Monnat v. Switzerland*, no. 73604/01, §64, ECHR 2006-X.

64 *Vajnai v. Hungary*, no. 33629/06, §49, ECHR 2008.

65 *Orban and Others v. France*, no. 20985/05, §52, 15 January 2009.

66 *Lehideux and Isorni v. France*, 23 September 1998, §55, *Reports of Judgments and Decisions* 1998-VII.

67 *Editions Plon v. France*, no. 58148/00, §53, ECHR 2004-IV; *Smolorz v. Poland*, no. 17446/07, §38, 16 October 2012; *Hachette Filipacchi Associés v. France*, no. 71111/01, §47, 14 June 2007.

68 Rome Statute of the International Criminal Court, (2002) 2187 UNTS 90, art. 29.

the concern generally grows cold as the timeframe becomes more remote. More generally, the "people," to use the expression of the Joinet and Orentlicher Principles, insist upon knowing the truth about this grey area, much of it well before our birth, yet somehow close enough to engage us directly. In his report on the Spanish Civil War, Special Rapporteur de Greiff has made an intriguing foray into this fog of history. The consequences of his initiative are difficult to assess. He will doubtless receive many entreaties to look at other situations, cases, massacres and atrocities. Only time will tell just how far back human rights law will succeed in establishing a right to truth and whether, like the two prestigious courts, it will also decide to bolt the door to the past.

CORRUPTION, INEQUALITY AND BOKO HARAM IN NIGERIA

Tity AGBAHEY and Gilles Olakounlé YABI

The State social order is founded on ideals of Freedom, Equality and Justice.

In furtherance of the social order–

(a) every citizen shall have equality of rights, obligations and opportunities before the law;

(b) the sanctity of the human person shall be recognised and human dignity shall be maintained and enhanced;

(c) governmental actions shall be humane;

(d) exploitation of human or natural resources in any form whatsoever for reasons, other than the good of the community, shall be prevented; and

(e) the independence, impartiality and integrity of courts of law, and easy accessibility thereto shall be secured and maintained.[1]

Most constitutions in the world have such idealistic words in their preambles and first chapters, but not all of them put such emphasis on social justice and social order. Nigeria is certainly one of the places where the contrast between the sanctity of the principles of equality and justice on the one hand, and the daily reality of extreme inequality and unlimited injustice on the other hand is

1 Constitution of the Federal Republic of Nigeria (1999), Chapter II, Article 17, <http://www.nigeria-law.org/ConstitutionOfTheFederalRepublicOfNigeria.htm>, accessed 5 July 2015.

the most shocking. In the words of Muhammadu Buhari, the former military ruler who was elected as the new President of Nigeria in March 2015: "Together, we co-operated to surprise the world that had come to expect only the worst from Nigeria."[2] The surprise came from the exceptionally credible and peaceful presidential election, which led to the first-ever democratic alternation of power in the history of Nigeria.

Nigerians, West Africa and the African continent needed good news as bloody conflicts and an upsurge in the number of terrorist acts were casting serious doubts on the recent positive perceptions of economic prospects for the continent. Buhari's election generated an unprecedented wave of hopes throughout Nigeria. But the new president knew that turning around Nigeria might be the most difficult undertaking a leader on the planet could think of. Nigerians unequivocally voted for Buhari and his opposition party because they believed that a new administration could put an end to deadly violence in the country, especially in the north confronted with Boko Haram's campaign of terror, and at the same time aggressively fight a battle against corruption and outrageous economic and social inequalities.

1. FROM A SECTARIAN MOVEMENT TO MONSTROUS VIOLENCE: BOKO HARAM AS A REFLECTION OF NIGERIA'S CONTRADICTIONS

Nigeria is the most populous country in Africa, being home to around 174 million people scattered across 36 states and the federal capital Abuja, and more than 200 ethnic groups. Its peoples are also one of the most vibrant and innovative. For instance, its \$3 billion "Nollywood" is the world's second-largest movie industry, surpassing Hollywood and right behind India's Bollywood.[3] But for most of its history as an independent sovereign country, Nigeria has been making headlines for unsavoury performances: military coups, corruption scandals, urban violence and deadly conflicts in several parts of the federation, with insurgent groups challenging the state's monopoly of violence or identity-based communities fighting against each other.

While insecurity and rebellions have not completely ceased in recent years in the southern oil-producing regions of the Niger Delta and in the Middle Belt, where ethno-religious violence driven by political and economic rights have killed thousands of people over the years, the most popular two words which have come to define Nigeria since 2010 are Boko Haram. It has been roughly translated

2 "Read President Buhari's inaugural speech", 29 May 2015, *The Vanguard Nigeria*, <http://www.vanguardngr.com/2015/05/read-president-buhari-inaugural-speech>, accessed 6 July 2015.

3 J. Bright, "Meet 'Nollywood': The second largest movie industry in the world", *Fortune*, 24 June 2015, <http://fortune.com/2015/06/24/nollywood-movie-industry>, accessed 6 July 2015.

as "western education is forbidden." Some experts disagree on the accuracy of that translation, especially as Boko Haram is the name given to the group by others, not its official name. Set up by Mohamed Yusuf, the organization's real name is "Jama'atu Ahlis Sunna Lidda'Awati Wal-Jihad", which means "Group of the People of Sunnah for Preaching and Jihad." They did not gain serious attention nationally and internationally until 2009, when the occasional clashes between the group and security forces became recurrent and more and more deadly in the Borno and Yobe states in North-East Nigeria.[4]

Settled in a large mosque in Maiduguri, Yusuf and hundreds of his followers became the enemies of the state and federal authorities after having been tolerated for more than five years. The attack against their headquarters led to the death of an estimated 300 members of the sect, while the police arrested Yusuf himself. Police officers then executed him before he could face any prosecution, and before he could talk and possibly explain how his initially small group got the financial resources and political space to reach such numbers and strength. Several sources consistently identified well-known political elites of the region as early supporters and financiers of Yusuf's Islamist sect.[5] In electoral democracy, numbers are important, and numbers of motivated ideologically driven and physically fit young adults and adolescents count even more. Politics in Nigeria, from the local to the federal levels, has had a tradition of accommodating targeted and calculated violence using those youths called "area boys" to intimidate adversaries and sometimes kill them or their followers. Yusuf's boys were a different kind of "area boys", quite disciplined ones, which would make them extremely reliable.

Yusuf was described as a charismatic preacher. Trained in Islamic theology in Saudi Arabia, he developed a consistent ideological discourse presenting an extremely radical version of Sunni Islam as the only acceptable alternative to a failed and corrupt Nigerian federal state. For a number of years, some political entrepreneurs thought they could use and control Boko Haram, while others, including the authorities, thought that the sect was just another extremist group carrying little danger outside isolated pockets in the states of Borno and Yobe. What happens everywhere when dangerous groups are supported for opportunistic short-sight reasons, then happened. Yusuf's followers were more serious than everyone expected about their ideology and their ultimate objective of destroying the current political and social order and replacing it with a brand new Islamic caliphate. By killing Yusuf while in custody and pushing

---

4 In March 2015, Boko Haram officially pledged allegiance to the "Islamic State" (IS, also known as Daesh) and claimed to be the "Islamic State in West Africa." It is unclear to what extent this allegiance has changed the nature, objectives and strategy of a group, which appears more and more internally divided and weakened.

5 International Crisis Group, "Curbing violence in Nigeria (II): The Boko Haram insurgency", Africa Report No. 216, 3 April 2014.

a large number of his indoctrinated followers into the remote rural areas of the North-East and into the neighbouring countries of Cameroon, Chad and Niger, Nigerian political and military leaders set the stage for the comeback of a much more devastating version of Boko Haram.

When the group reappeared in 2010 under a new leader, Abubakar Shekau, it turned extremely violent and started diversifying its targets, attacking not only symbols of the state but also Muslim religious leaders who spoke out against it, churches, school institutions, ordinary civilians in markets, villages and even mosques. The group also diversified its operating techniques, getting much more sophisticated and organized in its attacks, and relying more and more on the extremely powerful weapon of terrorist groups: suicide bombers. For some time, Nigerians and many other Africans claimed that it was not in the genes of sub-Saharan Africans to blow themselves up as they embraced life very much, even when their daily life was a permanent battle for economic survival. Dozens of suicide attacks in northern Nigeria have since proved this deterministic view to be wrong.

2. TURBULENT POLITICS, AN UNLIKELY NATION AND THE OIL CURSE: HISTORY MATTERS

So what happened in northern Nigeria when Yusuf, his comrades and younger followers were growing up? What was happening politically, economically, socially and culturally in the states of Yobe, Borno and generally in the North-East during the 1980s and 1990s, when the future thousands of troops of Boko Haram were growing up and shaping their personalities? What kind of education was offered to the little boys born in those regions of the federation and what models of successful personal trajectories and prospects for life transformation were available to them? Few people in Nigeria asked these questions when discussing the outrageous violence being inflicted to the peoples of the North-East by Boko Haram insurgents and by those who have been fighting them unsuccessfully, the Nigerian military. Boko Haram's violence became monstrous, but the group itself was less a monster antithetical to Nigerian society than a product and a reflection of Nigeria as it is: a rich, dynamic and innovative country, as well as an exceptionally corrupt and ruthless one for the poor and the weak.

Mohamed Yusuf was born in 1970 and was 39 when he was killed in 2009. The year in which Yusuf was born was also the year of the end of the bloody civil war of Biafra in Nigeria. The war was fought between 1967 and 1970 by the federal army general and head of state Yakubu Gowon on the one hand, and the troops of Lieutenant Colonel Chukwuemeka Ojukwu, the military governor of the predominantly ethnic Igbo eastern region who declared the secession of the Republic of Biafra, on the other. One million deaths later, mostly as a result of hunger and disease, the secessionist rebellion was defeated and Nigeria retained its unity as one nation. The Biafra war exposed one of the key determinants of politics in Nigeria: the competition for power and resources between the elites representing the three most significant ethno-linguistic communities in the country, to wit, the Hausa/Fulani in the North, the Yoruba in the South-West and the Igbo in the South-East. While the federal system managed to create space for political representation and protection of the many smaller ethnic communities, the political order is still significantly dependent on the perceived balance of interests between the three biggest cultural blocks.

Nigeria has had a turbulent political history, oriented as in other African countries by the ways in which the European colonial powers have defined and decided to defend their own interests. In Nigeria, the colonial power was the British Empire, which created a unified country in 1914 by merging the Northern Nigeria Protectorate and the Southern Nigeria Protectorate. The country was roughly and unevenly divided between a predominantly Muslim North and a predominantly Animist South, which became progressively Christian as European missionaries settled and developed Christian education. The British rulers had decided to respect, to some extent, the political organization of the Islamized emirates of the North and restrict the extension of the British education system to the southern Animists, where missionaries had a free hand.[6] This differentiated treatment had long-lasting consequences, as Western-educated Nigerians at the time of independence in 1960 were mostly southerners. The North still had its influential intellectual elites whose prestige came from their Islamic erudition. Northern Nigeria was the host of the respected Sokoto Caliphate.[7]

The contradictions of the formation of a united Nigeria under British rule and conditions of independence set the stage for turbulent politics. The discovery of vast reserves of oil made the control of power even more ferocious and yet influenced by the former colonial rulers. In his memoirs,[8] the writer and poet Wole Soyinka, the 1986 Nobel Laureate for Literature, delivers a fascinating account of Nigerian political independence until the beginning of the second term of President Olusegun Obasanjo, whose election by universal suffrage in 1999 marked the long-delayed return to democracy. Soyinka described how warning signs of the greed of future political leaders were already visible on the eve of independence, the responsibility of British colonial masters who organized the transfer of power after creating an "unlikely nation", the inauguration of electoral rigging, the rise of political violence and identity-based electoral

6 International Crisis Group, "Nigeria: Want in the midst of plenty", Africa Report No. 113, 19 July 2006.

7 International Crisis Group, "Northern Nigeria: Background to conflict", Africa Report No. 168, 20 December 2010.

8 W. Soyinka, *You Must Set Forth at Dawn. A Memoir*, Random House, New York, 2006.

politics. Because he was a young adult during those first years of independent Nigeria and interacted directly with most of the leaders of the 1980s and 1990s, Soyinka offers rare insights on the personalities of the successive military rulers and their sustained contribution to the decline of the nation.

A bloody coup d'état in January 1966 was the first in a long series. The Federal Prime Minister, the Ministers of the Northern and the Western Regions and many army officers were murdered. The emergence on the political scene of a federal army itself split into rival groups marked by the ethnic and regional origin of its officers and non-commissioned officers ushered in an era of instability and authoritarian regimes. In July 1966, another coup was followed by assassinations, purges and mass violence against civilians who had the misfortune to belong to the same ethnic group as the perpetrators and beneficiaries of the first coup, in that case the Igbos.[9] The events paved the way for the Biafra civil war, which was also nurtured and aggravated by rivalries between foreign powers fighting for influence in the most important and oil-rich country in west Africa. From the mid-1970s to 1999, except for short periods of interim civilian governments, military dictators governed Nigeria.

3. ELITES WERE BUSY STEALING WHILE THE FRUSTRATED BOYS WERE GETTING READY

In the 1990s, a decade in which it is reasonable to assume that most current members of Boko Haram militants were born, two strongmen were in charge of the destiny of the nation: General Ibrahim Babangida (1985–1993) and, from November 1993, General Sani Abacha. Both generals were from the northern military elite. Abacha was an ethnic Kanuri from Borno State, the same group as many members of Boko Haram, but he was born and grew up in Kano, the metropolis of northern Nigeria. Abacha opened a new page in violent authoritarianism and staggering corruption. When he died – officially of a heart attack – in June 1998, there was a feeling of relief in the country. Under Abacha's rule, dozens of journalists, trade unionists, military officers and civil society activists were sent to prison. Nine militants of the Movement for Survival of Ogoni People who denounced the pollution of their environment and their marginalization by the federal government and the oil company Royal Dutch Shell were sentenced to death and hanged in November 1995. A renowned journalist and popular writer Ken Saro-Wiwa was one of them.[10]

---

9 Ibid.

10 "Nigeria's military leaders hang playwright and 8 other activists", *Associated Press*, 11 November 1995.

The Abacha regime marked history even more for its blatant level of corruption than for its brutality. In July 1998, after the death of the president, his wife was arrested with 38 suitcases filled with dollars and pounds.[11] Estimates of the money embezzled by the Abacha clan vary between US$5.5 billion and US$13.6 billion. A total of US$4 billion was channelled into accounts in Switzerland.[12] The staggering sums diverted directly from the coffers of the Central Bank during just four years in power gives an idea of the magnitude of systemic corruption in Nigeria under all regimes that have succeeded since the early 1970s.[13] If the majority of the 140 million Nigerians – at that time – were living in abject poverty, the first explanation was undoubtedly the abyssal level of corruption. Nigerian billionaires were not only former military heads of state and their close collaborators, but also included a few hundred former state governors, government officials, parliamentarians, business men and women enjoying close relations with oil and financial networks in the country and internationally.

When future Boko Haram recruits were growing up and learning about life, those who had responsibility for taking care of Nigeria's security, economic and social development at the federal and state levels were busy stealing the country's resources. Abacha's family and associates were clearly more interested in embezzling money for themselves and their future than in focusing on economic development, education, health and the cultural advancement of the Kanuri and other inhabitants of Borno and other northern states. They were concerned with siphoning funds out of Nigeria to banks in Europe and America. This example shows how corruption and bad governance in Nigeria has little to do with ethnic, regional origins or the religious affiliation of leaders. It has to do with the dramatic gap between the powerful rich elites and the several dozens of millions of extremely poor, uneducated, neglected and isolated men, women and children.

When the haves were celebrating their wealth and to some extent stimulating economic growth and modernity in Lagos and other southern states, the pool of the idle, uneducated and frustrated have-nots was quietly growing in several parts of the federation. In most of the North-East, someone had something to offer, an orderly vision of the world and life governed by an uncompromising

---

11 One of Abacha's sons was found with $100 million in cash. The London accounts of the Abacha family alone held as much as $60 million at one time. Several other accounts were opened in the United States and Switzerland. See K. Srinivasan, "Money laundering and capital flight", May 2006, <http://networkideas.org/feathm/may2006/Kannan_Srinivasan.pdf>, accessed 7 July 2015.

12 "Late Nigerian dictator looted nearly $500 million, Swiss say", *The New York Times*, 19 August 2004.

13 M. Mark, "Nigerian police recover part of Sani Abacha's $4.3bn hoard from robbers", *The Guardian*, 5 October 2012, <http://www.theguardian.com/world/2012/oct/05/nigeria-sani-abacha-jewellery-police>, accessed 7 July 2015.

reading of Islamic law, as he was taught in Saudi Arabia. Yusuf, and later Shekau, met their followers, and as soon as they reached sufficiently large numbers and strength, they began recruiting by force. When corruption exceeds a certain threshold, when it ceases to be a deviation from the norm and becomes consubstantial with the political, economic and social fabric of the country, it also becomes synonymous with total indifference to "others", those who are different because they are poor and because they cannot even understand the basics of the language of modernity and globalization. In Nigeria, that threshold seems to have been reached a long time ago.

The nomination of former Nigeria Central Bank governor Lamido Sanusi as the new Emir of the northern State of Kano in June 2014 came as a relief to many people involved in the political landscape. This new position meant that he would be officially outside of political matters and would show the self-restraint that comes with the position of Emir, the highest Muslim authority in Kano. The former governor had made the news in September 2013 when he sent a letter to then President Goodluck Jonathan to bring to his attention the missing US$50 billion in oil revenues not paid to the Central Bank by the Nigerian National Petroleum Corporation (NNPC), the powerful national oil company. Transparency International had in 2011 ranked that company as the least transparent of 44 state-run oil companies.[14] The NNPC evoked miscalculations and the missing amount was reduced to US$20 billion, still a huge amount of money. In February 2014, the governor was sacked.[15] The core issue of the missing money was left unaddressed.

The 2014 Transparency International Corruption Perception Index ranked Nigeria 136th out of 174 countries,[16] keeping it in the stable group of the most corrupt countries in the world. Surveyed by Transparency International in 2013, 94% of Nigerians thought that political parties were corrupt and 92% thought that the police was.[17] Corruption in Nigeria is more than an ethical issue; it has a direct impact on the economy and people's quality of life. In 2012, it was estimated that corruption has cost Nigeria US$35 billion over the past ten years.[18] Politics in Nigeria is a game played by either the military or very

---

14 Transparency International and Revenue Watch Institute, "Promoting revenue transparency: 2011 report on oil and gas companies", <https://www.transparency.org/news/feature/promoting_revenue_transparency_2011_report_on_oil_and_gas_companies>, accessed 1 August 2017.

15 "Nigeria Central Bank head Lamido Sanusi ousted", *BBC News*, 20 February 2014, <http://www.bbc.com/news/world-africa-26270561>, accessed 7 July 2015.

16 Transparency International, "Corruption Perception Index 2014", <http://www.transparency.org/cpi2014/results>, accessed 6 July 2015.

17 Transparency International, <http://www.transparency.org/gcb2013/country/?country=nigeria>, accessed 7 July 2015.

18 S. Allison, "Nigeria: How to lose $35bn", *The Guardian*, 13 November 2012, <http://www.theguardian.com/world/2012/nov/13/nigeria-oil-corruption-ridabu>, accessed 7 July 2015.

wealthy people, or both. Although the 2015 elections have been praised for being fair and remarkable in leading to an unprecedented alternation of power, they still brought back to power a former military ruler supported by a group of people who are rich, powerful and have all been actively present in Nigerian politics for decades. Doing politics in Nigeria costs a lot and pays very well. Nigerian lawmakers are amongst the best paid in the world. Their annual official earnings represent 116 times the country's gross domestic product (GDP) per person.[19] This happens in a country where 46% of the population is poor.[20] In the words of former governor Lamido Sanusi, "since [Nigeria] found oil, [the state] has existed not to serve the people but as a site for rent extraction by a very small minority that controls political power."[21]

4. DID CORRUPTION AND EXTREME INEQUALITY ACTUALLY LEAD TO BOKO HARAM?

Nigeria's GDP has made it Africa's biggest economy since 2014, surpassing South Africa. But the distribution of wealth, incomes and opportunities is extremely unequal between and within cultural groups and regions. Researchers have studied and exposed the extent of "horizontal inequalities" in Nigeria.[22] Prospects for access to some public education, health and economic opportunities are significantly determined by the place of the country where one is born. As mentioned in an article published in 2007, only 25% of pregnant women had access to medical facilities in the North-West of Nigeria compared to 85% in the South-East. The maternal mortality rate was 939% higher in the North-West than in the South-West (1,549 compared to 165 per 100,000 live births).[23] The concentration of poverty in the northern regions, especially in the North-East and North-West, has been confirmed by the latest available figures released in 2014. The North-West and North-East together accounted for 52% of the

19 "Paying lawmakers, rewarding work, more than they deserve?", *The Economist*, 20 July 2013, <http://www.economist.com/news/international/21582040-more-they-deserve-rewarding-work>, accessed 7 July 2015.

20 World Bank, "Nigeria Economic Report", 2 July 2014.

21 L. Sanusi, "TEDx youth", August 2013, <http://tedxtalks.ted.com/video/Overcoming-the-fear-of-vested-i>, accessed 7 July 2015.

22 F. Stewart "Horizontal inequalities as a cause of conflict", Bradford Development Lecture: November 2009, <http://www.brad.ac.uk/ssis/media/ssis/BDLStewart.pdf>, accessed 7 July 2015: "Horizontal inequalities are inequalities among groups of people that share a common identity. Such inequalities have economic, social, political and cultural status dimensions. Horizontal inequality differs from 'vertical' inequality in that the latter is a measure of inequality among individuals or households, not groups."

23 A. Langer, A. Mustapha and F. Stewart, "Horizontal inequalities in Nigeria, Ghana and Côte d'Ivoire: Issues and policies", *CRISE Working Paper* No. 45, March 2007.

poor in Nigeria. This figure reaches 66% when the North-Central region is added.[24] Besides, while the southern states have reduced their poverty rate in the last few years of national economic growth, it has remained unchanged in the North-West and has even increased in the North-East.[25] That is where Boko Haram has been pursuing its insurgency.

Among the different sub-categories most affected by inequalities and poverty in Nigeria are women and children, especially girls. A total of 49% of the Nigerian population is female and inequalities hit women the hardest. For instance, women constitute 60–79% of the rural workforce, but men are five times more likely to own land.[26] Being a woman in the northern part of the country worsens the situation: 70.8% of young women aged 20–29 in the North-West are unable to read or write compared to 9.7% in the South-East.[27] Nigeria's 10.5 million children who are out-of-school represent the largest number in the world. In the North, child marriage is the main reason that pushes girls out of schools. While the national rate of child marriage is 43%, it is as high as 76% in the North-West.[28]

Nigeria has made considerable efforts to try to ensure equal regional representation in politics and thus reduce horizontal inequalities in this field. The dislocation of this enormous and diverse country is always at stake, but the very choice of federalism and the power conferred on state governors and assemblies have reduced the risk of this happening. But what Nigeria has really succeeded in doing is not giving relatively equal opportunities to citizens from any region and any cultural group to benefit from key public services of education and health and ultimately economic opportunities. The political system instead succeeded in ensuring that the elites, regardless of their regional or ethnic background, could have reasonable access to portions of the national cake. Indeed, despite the political domination of the northern military elites for three decades and the official channelling of federal funds to all states, the extreme poverty of the northern regions and divergence with the other regions have been consistent.

So did inequalities, injustice and absence of the rule of law create Boko Haram? Did this lead to that? The relationship and causality are not so simple. Boko Haram emerged in a region where ideological divisions within Islam have led to recurrent tensions and episodes of deadly violence in the past. The "Muslim majority" in the North covers a complex reality as northern Nigerians are made of various Islamist trends and also large Christian minorities.[29]

24 World Bank, "Nigeria Economic Report", 2 July 2014.

25 Ibid.

26 British Council and DFID, Gender in Nigeria Report 2012, <https://www.britishcouncil.org/sites/default/files/british-council-gender-nigeria2012.pdf>, accessed 7 July 2015.

27 Ibid.

28 The percentage of women aged 20–24 who were married or in union before they were 18 years old. See <http://www.girlsnotbrides.org/child-marriage/nigeria>, accessed 7 July 2015.

29 Northern Nigeria here refers to the 12 states where Sharia law is in place: Bauchi, Borno, Gombe, Jigawa, Kaduna, Kano, Katsina, Kebbi, Niger, Sokoto, Yobe and Zamfara.

Although the practised Islam remains dominantly Sufi, reformist movements arose in the 1970s, one of the best known being the "Muslim Students Society of Nigeria (MSS)." A more radical offshoot of the MSS, the Islamic Movement of Nigeria, emerged as the Nigerian version of the "Muslim Brotherhood."[30] Back in the 1970s, the region experienced the religious campaign of Mohammed Marwa, nicknamed "Maitatsine" (meaning "the one who curses" in Hausa), a young man originally from northern Cameroon who claimed to be a prophet and had thousands of followers. Nigerian forces crushed the movement in a bloody battle in December 1980. Marwa was killed, but deadly violence erupted again in several northern states until 1985. Hence, it is in a region accustomed to extremist social uprisings that the Nigerians Taleban and later Boko Haram emerged.[31]

Inequalities, injustice and corruption may have not created Boko Haram, but these defining features of Nigerian governance have for decades made it possible for such a group to control, a perfect ground for recruitment, indoctrination and organization, and to become a formidable threat to the security of several million people. The responsibility of the elites for the destruction of the social fabric and local economies of large areas of Nigeria is overwhelming. When Yusuf, Shekau and their several thousands of future recruits were forging their personalities and deciding on what their lives would look like, the political and military leaders of their country were distracted by the competition for oil money and privileges. They could not find the time and energy to focus on public investments in education and health systems in the most disadvantaged states, or on encouraging agriculture, basic industries and enhanced formal trade between those states and neighbouring Cameroon, Chad and Niger. They could not see what was happening in the families, in the Islamic schools and in the minds of the growing youths in vast parts of the national territory.

Corruption and obsession with personal enrichment did not spare the very people who were supposed to be watching and detecting early signs of radicalization and violence: the police, the army, and the intelligence and other security sector senior officers. It is only from 2012–2013, when confronted by motivated Boko Haram fighters, that political authorities, Nigerians themselves and people from worried neighbouring countries, discovered what the once powerful Nigerian army had become: an undisciplined, ill-trained and badly equipped force. Beyond material conditions, soldiers consistently complained of the corruption and ineffectiveness of their senior commanders, and had no intention of risking their lives on the battleground.[32]

---

30 International Crisis Group, "Curbing violence in Nigeria (II): The Boko Haram insurgency", Africa Report No. 216, 3 April 2014.

31 Ibid.

32 Following the election of Muhammadu Buhari, the fight against Boko Haram took another turn. He adopted key measures, including the relocation of the nation's military headquarters

5. BACK TO GOOD OLD IDEALS: FREEDOM, EQUALITY AND JUSTICE DO MATTER

Let me assure you that if I am elected president, the world will have no cause to worry about Nigeria as it has had to recently; that Nigeria will return to its stabilizing role in West Africa; and that no inch of Nigerian territory will ever be lost to the enemy because we will pay special attention to the welfare of our soldiers in and out of service, we will give them adequate and modern arms and ammunitions to work with, we will improve intelligence gathering and border controls to choke Boko Haram's financial and equipment channels, we will be tough on terrorism and tough on its root causes by initiating a comprehensive economic development plan promoting infrastructural development, job creation, agriculture and industry in the affected areas. We will always act on time and not allow problems to irresponsibly fester, and I, Muhammadu Buhari, will always lead from the front and return Nigeria to its leadership role in regional and international efforts to combat terrorism.[33]

Speeches during electoral campaigns generally look like the preambles and first chapters of national constitutions. They are filled with nice words and promises of a better future for all. The new president of the most populous country of Africa did raise lots of expectations. Fighting Boko Haram on the one hand and systemic corruption on the other will keep the Nigerian administration busy for many years. Beyond governance, institutional and economic reforms, the key to safeguarding the confidence of Nigerians in democracy and in themselves will reside in their capacity to collectively take more seriously than they ever did the ideals enshrined in their country's constitution. "The State social order is founded on ideals of Freedom, Equality and Justice." Whether in Nigeria, the United States or Canada, the fight for the respect of those principles in the functioning of human societies is never definitively won.

---

from the federal capital Abuja to Maiduguri and the replacement of army chiefs. The army consequently won back many localities that were entirely controlled by the armed group. The other armies of the region, namely those of Cameroon, Niger and Chad, also gained ground. In December 2015, a very optimistic Buhari proudly claimed that Nigeria has "technically won the war" against Boko Haram. The group has been indisputably weakened, but isolated suicide attacks on easy civilian targets have continued and the humanitarian cost of the years of violence is exceptionally high and long-lasting.

33 "Prospects for democratic consolidation in Africa: Nigeria's transition", Africa Programme Meeting Transcript, General Muhammadu Buhari, Chatham House, Royal Institute for International Affairs, 26 February 2015, <http://www.chathamhouse.org/sites/files/chathamhouse/field/field_document/20150226BuhariSpeechQA.pdf>, accessed 7 July 2015.

SOCIAL AND ECONOMIC RIGHTS AND THE LEGAL IMAGINATION

Alana KLEIN

1. INTRODUCTION

The turn of the last millennium launched a period of renewed dynamism around social and economic rights (SERs) or human rights to food, housing, health care, education, and the like. Although these rights have formed part of the contemporary human rights canon, at least since the Universal Declaration of Human Rights, and are included in the majority of contemporary constitutions, there has been little dispute that SERs have been neglected relative to civil and political rights.[1] The reasons are historical, methodological, and deeply political.[2] By the year 2000, however, new constitutions were increasingly including such rights.[3] Courts were beginning to develop ways to adjudicate them across the

---

1 United Nations High Commissioner for Human Rights, "Fact Sheet No. 16 (Rev. 1), The Committee on Economic, Social and Cultural Rights" (July 1991), <http://www.ohchr.org/Documents/Publications/FactSheet16rev.1en.pdf>.

2 See J. STEINER, P. ALSTON and R. GOODMAN, *International Human Rights in Context: Law: Politics, Morals*, Oxford University Press, Oxford 2008, p. 269.

3 D.S. LAW and M. VERSTEEG, "The Evolution and Ideology of Global Constitutionalism" (2011) 99 *California Law Review* 1196 (Figure 2).

world,[4] most famously in South Africa[5] and India.[6] Prominent US scholars observing these developments were reversing long-held positions and were now opining that such rights could indeed be enforceable in courts.[7] International institutions and organizations were finally beginning to prioritize them.[8]

Canada's judiciary was not immune from this millennial energy. In the fall of 2002, soon after I became a law clerk for Supreme Court of Canada Justice Louise Arbour, the Court handed down its decision in *Gosselin v. Quebec*, its first response to an explicit constitutional, social and economic rights-based social welfare claim. The province of Quebec had introduced a law decreasing social assistance payments to persons under 30 who, for any reason, failed to participate in a workfare program. Canada's Charter of Rights and Freedoms[9] makes no specific mention of rights to welfare or to an adequate or minimum standard of living, and so Ms. Gosselin argued that the constitutional guarantees of life, liberty and security of the person in s. 7 of the Charter ought to be broadly interpreted so as to invalidate the law. The majority of the Court denied the claim on the basis that Ms. Gosselin had not demonstrated "actual hardship," though it left open the possibility that positive SERs might be read into s. 7 in a future case.[10] Justice Arbour, in a famous dissent, would have allowed the claim. "A minimum level of welfare is so closely connected to issues relating to one's basic health (or security of the person) and potentially even to one's survival (or life interest) that ... a positive right to life, liberty and security of the person must provide for it," she wrote.[11]

Later in the same term, a group of Francophone parents in Nova Scotia argued that the provincial government's failure to build French-language schools violated the Canadian Charter of Rights and Freedoms' only explicitly enumerated socio-economic right – the right to minority-language education.[12] The government conceded that it was under a positive constitutional obligation

---

4 See e.g. V. Gauri and D.M. Brinks (eds), *Courting Social Justice: Judicial Enforcement of Social and Economic Rights in the Developing World*, Cambridge University Press, Cambridge 2008; M. Langford (ed.), *Social Rights Jurisprudence: Emerging Trends in International and Comparative Law*, Cambridge University Press, Cambridge 2008.

5 *Government of the Republic of South Africa and Others v. Grootboom and Others* (CCT11/00) [2000] ZACC 19; 2001 (1) SA 46; 2000 (11) BCLR 1169 (4 October 2000).

6 *People's Union for Civil Liberties v. Union of India & Others*, Writ Petition (Civil) No. 196 of 2001 (8 May 2002).

7 See D.M. Beatty, *The Ultimate Rule of Law*, Oxford University Press, Oxford 2005, pp. 126–127 (discussing how Cass Sunstein and Dennis Davis underwent "profound conversions" to come to support constitutional SERs).

8 See M. Robinson, "Advancing Economic, Social and Cultural Rights: The Way Forward" (2004) 26 *Human Rights Quarterly* 866.

9 Canadian Charter of Rights and Freedoms, Part I of the Constitution Act, 1982, being Schedule B to the Canada Act 1982 (UK), c 11.

10 *Gosselin v. Quebec (Attorney General)* [2002] 4 SCR 429, para 83.

11 Ibid, para 358.

12 *Doucet-Boudreau v. Nova Scotia (Minister of Education)* [2003] 3 SCR 3, 2003 SCC 62.

to build the schools; the issue this time was about the remedy. The precise question was whether a court could retain jurisdiction to hear reports on the province's compliance with an order that it make its "best efforts" to provide school facilities and programs by particular dates. In a 5-4 decision, Justice Arbour, writing together with Justice Iacobucci for the majority, upheld the retention of jurisdiction. The decision stressed the importance of remedial flexibility so that judges could fulfil their constitutional mandate of ensuring effective, responsive, and meaningful protection of rights, including positive rights like the ones at stake in the case.[13]

I vividly recall discussing the latter decision with Justice Arbour at a lunch with the clerks. "I wanted to write a judgment that would keep judges' *creative juices flowing*," she declared over a glass of Chardonnay. The sentiment was classic Arbour – intellectually generous and emboldening, cultivating dynamism, the pithy expression of an idea whose complexity would continue to reveal itself with closer contemplation and inquiry. Arbour's commitment to invigorating socio-economic rights persisted after she left the bench to take up her position as UN High Commissioner for Human Rights.[14]

Since that millennial moment, Canada's constitutional jurisprudence on poverty-related claims, including social and economic rights claims, has undeniably stagnated,[15] a point to which I shall return. In other realms, however – in social rights advocacy, in scholarship, and in state and international institutions that have embraced the language of SERs – the question is famously no longer about *whether* such rights can be protected, but rather *how*.[16] Although there is continued disagreement about models and methodologies for the realization of socio-economic rights, most optimistic accounts have reflected common themes of flexibility, of engagement, and of opening up institutional, collective, and individual imaginations to novel and better ways of understanding and responding to economic and social abuses. The more pessimistic accounts, conversely, focus on how rights practice may constrain, limit, and effectively stem the flow of creativity and imagination among actors seeking social justice.

This chapter explores the themes of creativity and imagination in SER realization in a number of areas: constitutional jurisprudence, grassroots

---

13 Ibid, para 87.

14 See e.g. L. Arbour, "Economic and Social Justice for Societies in Transition" (2007) 40 *New York University Journal of International Law and Politics* 1; L. Arbour "LaFontaine-Baldwin Lecture 2005: Freedom from Want: From Charity to Entitlement – Libérer du besoin: de la charité à la justice," <http://www.ohchr.org/EN/NewsEvents/Pages/DisplayNews.aspx?NewsID=3004&LangID=E>.

15 See C. Sheppard, "'Bread and Roses': Economic Justice and Constitutional Rights" (2015) 5 *Oñati Socio-legal Series* 225.

16 See e.g. C. Sunstein, *Designing Democracy: What Constitutions Do*, Oxford University Press, New York 2001, p. 221; D. Landau, "The Reality of Social Rights Enforcement" (2012) 53 *Harvard International Law Journal* 402.

advocacy, and international institutions. It draws out commonalities among these areas of creativity, including the capacity to target multiple actors, the production of information, and fostering political inclusion. Drawing on the literature on social movements and access to justice, it concludes that dynamism in rights methodologies is inevitably necessary in rights frameworks that seek to root out exercises of power and domination that drive poverty and exclusion. It is those struggling with the enforcement of SERs who have needed to address this reality most squarely.

2. WHAT CREATIVITY AND WHY?

Much of the debate around the legal enforcement of SERs[17] has been framed in reaction or response to the enforcement of civil and political rights (CPRs), which have dominated the human rights landscape since the second half of the twentieth century.[18] Early opponents to SERs argued that compared to CPRs, SERs are vague, because they are subject to limits like "progressive realization" "within available resources,"[19] and because they are framed in terms of *adequate* food, housing, education, and adequacy is subjective.[20] They have argued they are more costly to enforce than other rights and therefore implicate difficult trade-offs that judges, rights advocacy organizations, and monitoring bodies lack capacity and legitimacy to pronounce upon.[21]

Social and economic rights proponents have been quick to point out that these ostensible infirmities may also be alleged against civil and political rights.[22] When, for example, does a detention qualify as arbitrary? And don't rights to a fair trial cost money?[23] In practice, however, even those friendly to SERs appear to have conceded that cost and complexity are an issue: yes, all

17 This is distinct from discussions about whether SERs ought to be ranked as fundamental rights as a moral matter. On this point, see J. King, *Judging Social Rights*, Cambridge University Press, Cambridge 2012, pp. 20–35.

18 See e.g. K. Roth, "Defending Economic, Social and Cultural Rights: Practical Issues Faced by an International Human Rights Organization" (2004) 26 *Human Rights Quarterly* 63–73; P. Farmer, *Pathologies of Power: Health, Human Rights, and the New War on the Poor*, University of California Press, Berkeley and Los Angeles 2004, pp. 220–221.

19 International Covenant on Economic, Social and Cultural Rights, adopted 16 December 1966, 993 UNTS 3 (entered into force 3 January 1976), Article 2(1).

20 M.J. Dennis and D.P. Stewart, "Justiciability of Economic, Social, and Cultural Rights: Should There Be an International Complaints Mechanism to Adjudicate the Rights to Food, Water, Housing, and Health?" (2004) 98 *American Journal of International Law* 462, 464.

21 Roth, *supra* note 18, p. 65.

22 See e.g. F.I. Michelman, "The Constitution, Social Rights and Liberal Political Justification" (2003) 1 *International Journal of Constitutional Law* 13–34; S. Fredman, *Human Rights Transformed: Positive Rights and Positive Duties*, Oxford University Press, Oxford 2008, p. 2.

23 S. Holmes and C.R. Sunstein, *The Cost of Rights: Why Liberty Depends on Taxes*, W.W. Norton & Company, New York, 2000.

rights cost, but SERs threaten to take up more of a government's budget and therefore to re-align the legislature's priorities.[24] Yes, all rights are vague, but the very concepts of "progressive realization" and "within available resources" suggest infinite contextual variability. Such concerns have led SER advocates to concede – or perhaps, rather, to argue – that traditional tools of human rights such as naming and shaming and litigation focusing on identifiable, immediately remediable human rights violations may be insufficient or ill-suited to the task of SER enforcement in many circumstances.[25]

2.1. TRADITIONAL APPROACHES

One early and initially dominant response among SER proponents has been to whittle down the content of SERs into something that better fits the traditional paradigm. The "violations approach"[26] and the "minimum core content"[27] are variations on this theme. In this vein, the Committee on Economic, Social and Cultural Rights' General Comment 14 on the Right to the Highest Attainable Standard of Health lists both illustrations of violations of the right to health as well as minimum core obligations[28] (though it has also developed further methods for assessing progressive realization beyond the minimum core).[29] However, approaches that seek to render SERs enforceable by delimiting their content have been criticized for being arbitrary in what they prioritize substantively; for preferring a bare minimum survival level far short of what would be required for a dignified life; and for nonetheless failing to specify with sufficient clarity which health goods, facilities, and services fall within the minimum core.[30] On the other hand, they have been defended for underscoring and

---

24 M. Tushnet, "Reflections on Judicial Enforcement of Social and Economic Rights in the Twenty-First Century" (2011) 4 *National University of Juridical Sciences Law Review* 177, 179; King, *supra* note 17, pp. 7–8.

25 G. MacNaughton and P. Hunt, "Health Impact Assessment: The Contribution of the Right to the Highest Attainable Standard of Health" (2009) 123 *Public Health* 302.

26 A.R. Chapman, "A 'Violations Approach' for Monitoring the International Covenant on Economic, Social and Cultural Rights" (1996) 18 *Human Rights Quarterly* 23.

27 See K.G. Young, "The Minimum Core of Economic and Social Rights: A Concept in Search of Content" (2008) 33 *Yale Journal of International Law* 113.

28 UN Economic and Social Council (ECOSOC), Committee on Economic, Social and Cultural Rights, General Comment No. 14: The Right to the Highest Attainable Standard of Health (art. 12), UN Doc. E/C.12/2000/4, paras 30, 43–44, 46–52.

29 *Ibid*, paras 53–62.

30 Young, *supra* note 27; J. Cohen, "Minimalism about Human Rights: The Most We Can Hope for?" (2004) 12 *Journal of Political Philosophy* 190; L. Forman, G. Ooms, A. Chapman, E. Friedman, A. Waris, E. Lamprea and M. Mulumba, "What Could a Strengthened Right to Health Bring to the Post-2014 Health Development Agenda?: Interrogating the Role of the Minimum Core Concept in Advancing Global Health Needs" (2013) 13 *BMC International Health and Human Rights* 48.

signalling to states and to judges that states must be spending on the poorest members of society: "International law is useful here as general guidance to constitutional courts for use in constitutional interpretation; it need not and should not resolve all the details."[31]

A response that similarly relies on traditional judicial methods has been simply to treat social and economic rights like any legal claim and enforce them absolutely and individually. This has effectively been the case in Brazil and Colombia, where litigants may, via a simplified action called the *tutela*, make a constitutional claim against the government or heavily regulated private insurers for the failure to fund or provide essential health goods or services.[32] In Colombia, judges initially limited the action to those with the greatest need, arguably reflecting a conception similar to the minimum core. Over time, however, the action came to be open to all.[33] The typical result is that the court orders provision of the medicine any time a litigant successfully demonstrates medical need.[34] Although this approach has been praised for raising the profile of SERs and changing perceptions among public administrators,[35] the dominant assessment among observers is that individualized enforcement has done little to distribute health care more equitably; rather, it has overburdened the courts and favoured the interests of members of the middle and upper classes, as these are the ones who appear more likely to litigate, to litigate successfully, and to have judgments enforced.[36]

2.2. CREATIVE APPROACHES

A set of approaches increasingly favoured in the scholarly literature and human rights practice stress flexibility in relation to the content of rights, modes of realization, or both.[37] These approaches, which are fiercely debated even as they are favoured, tend to de-emphasize the connection between a bounded, consistent, pre-defined judicially enforced content for SERs and their meaningful realization. For some, the content of SERs has been made

---

31 Landau, *supra* note 16, p. 453.

32 Landau, *supra* note 16; O.L.M. Ferraz. "Harming the Poor through Social Rights Litigation: Lessons from Brazil" (2010–2011) 89 *Texas Law Review* 1643.

33 Landau, *supra* note 16, pp. 420, 426.

34 *Ibid*, p. 424; Ferraz, *supra* note 32, p. 1660.

35 See F.F. Hoffmann and F.R.N.M. Bents, "Accountability for Social and Economic Rights in Brazil" in Gauri and Brinks (eds), *supra* note 4, pp. 100, 141; O.L.M. Ferraz, "Brazil: Health Inequalities, Rights, and Courts: The Social Impact of Judicialization of Health" in A.E. Yamin and S. Gloppen (eds), *Litigation Health Rights: Can Courts Bring More Justice to Health?*, Harvard University Press, Cambridge, MA 2011.

36 Hoffman and Bents, *supra* note 35, pp. 141–142; Landau, *supra* note 16, pp. 421–427; Ferraz, "Harming the Poor," *supra* note 32, pp. 1661–1662.

37 King, *supra* note 17; Landau, *supra* note 16, pp. 275–285.

sufficiently clear through treaties, bills of rights, scholarly literature and the like; the problem lies is rendering these rights "useful as a means of leverage for spreading human survival, dignity and hope" for those living in poverty.[38] Others maintain that SERs must always be fluid and flexible,[39] and that creative approaches are necessary to ensure that their content and enforcement do not become unduly ossified[40] or co-opted.

Necessarily varied, these approaches include evaluation of the reasonableness or proportionality of government action, and prompt or even require accountability, participation, and consultation of marginalized groups. They also demand that the effectiveness of rights-based action be understood more holistically, for example, based on the extent to which they in practice act as catalysts for social change or empowerment of the marginalized around the rights in question.[41] Together, they offer a more open-textured idea of what it means to operationalize SERs as legal rights. These approaches, often described as creative, have expanded the imaginations of rights adjudicators, advocates, and scholars to new ways to identify and root out abuses of power in the context of SERs. It would be impossible in this short chapter to fully canvas these approaches, but the following gives a sense of the field.

2.2.1. In Adjudication

In terms of judicial enforcement, the experience of the South African Constitutional Court is the most discussed and is perhaps most emblematic of the creative reimagining standards of judicial review and enforcement.[42] In its 2000 decision in *Grootboom*, the Court pioneered the "reasonableness approach" to adjudicating SERs. It found a state of affairs in which a group of plaintiffs were forcibly evicted from informal settlements and forced to live in appalling conditions on a sports field to be unconstitutional.[43] Rather than create an individual right and remedy for the plaintiff to housing "immediately upon demand," set out a clear pre-defined minimum core content to the housing

---

38 J.D. Sachs and L.E. Sachs, "Foreword" in L.E. White and J. Perelman (eds), *Stones of Hope: How African Activists Reclaim Human Rights to Challenge Global Poverty*, Stanford University Press, Stanford 2011, p. xii.

39 X. Contiades and A. Fotiadou, "Social Rights in the Age of Proportionality: Global Economic Crisis and Constitutional Litigation" (2012) 10 *International Journal of Constitutional Law* 660.

40 See H. Hershkoff, "Transforming Legal Theory in Light of Practice: The Judicial Application of Social and Economic Rights to Private Orderings" in Gauri and Brinks (eds), *supra* note 4, p. 299.

41 K.G. Young, "A Typology of Economic and Social Rights Adjudication: Exploring the Catalytic Function of Judicial Review" (2011) 8 *International Journal of Constitutional Law* 385.

42 Landau, *supra* note 16, p. 408.

43 *Grootboom*, *supra* note 4, para 3.

right in question,[44] or detail a housing plan that the government was required to implement, the Court simply declared the status quo unreasonable and demanded that the political branches devise a housing plan that took sufficient account of those in desperate need.[45] Although the approach was initially praised for its creativity in rendering such rights justiciable without overly straining the judicial role,[46] it soon came under criticism for not going far enough. Irene Grootboom herself died at the age of 44, still without housing, and some argued that little changed in housing policy in South Africa as a result of the decision.[47]

The Court has since added new factors to be included in the reasonableness evaluation, including, for example, that state policies must be transparent.[48] It has also since experimented with more flexible and dynamic remedial approaches. For example, in a series of housing rights cases, it developed what has been called an "engagement" model.[49] In these cases, the Court, upon finding or apprehending a constitutional rights violation in the course of an eviction, has ordered evicting municipalities to meaningfully engage with claimants, via negotiation or mediation, to manage even lawful evictions in ways that respect the constitutional right to housing, as broadly set out by the courts. It has even gone so far as to set agendas for such negotiation, bearing in mind the reasons why the parties are not progressing. Brian Ray argues that the approach is infinitely flexible: courts may appoint a mediator, order that certain groups be included or even removed from the negotiation, impose sanctions for failing to engage, or even make substantive policy decisions where engagement fails.[50] In this sense, he approaches the more complex structural remedies that some have argued strain judicial capacity and legitimacy too far. The focus, however, remains on leveraging the power of the claimants through forcing information and securing a spot for them at the table, with the threat of more aggressive intervention in the background.[51] Further, Ray observes, the South African Constitutional Court has built a constitutional requirement for governments to engage with affected actors in policy development affecting SERS, stating

---

44 *Ibid*, paras 31–32.

45 *Ibid*, paras 44, 95.

46 See e.g. M. Tushnet, *Weak Courts, Strong Rights: Judicial Review and Social Welfare Rights in Comparative Constitutional Law*, Princeton University Press, Princeton 2008.

47 P. Joubert, "Grootboom Dies Homeless and Penniless" *Mail & Guardian Online*, <http://mg.co.za/article/2008-08-08-grootboom-dies-homeless-and-penniless>.

48 *Minister of Health and Others v. Treatment Action Campaign and Others (No. 2)* (CCT8/02) [2002] ZACC 15; 2002 (5) SA 721; 2002 (10) BCLR 1033 (5 July 2002), para 123.

49 B. Ray, "Engagement's Possibilities and Limits as a Socioeconomic Rights Remedy" (2010) 9 *Washington University Global Studies Law Review* 399. S. Liebenberg, "Engaging the Paradoxes of the Universal and Particular in Human Rights Adjudication: The Possibilities and Pitfalls of 'Meaningful Engagement'" (2012) 12 *African Human Rights Law Journal* 1.

50 Ray, *supra* note 49, p. 414.

51 B. Ray, "Polycentrism, Political Mobilization and the Promise of Socioeconomic Rights" (2009) 45 *Stanford Journal of International Law* 151, 187–188. Liebenberg, *supra* note 49, p. 29.

in one case that "the process of engagement should take place before litigation commences unless it is not possible or reasonable to do so because of urgency or some other compelling reason."[52] He calls this a constitutional requirement of political engagement for the implementation of SERs.[53]

More skeptical scholars like David Landau have pointed out that the engagement model remains rare even in South Africa, that it has not always succeeded where it has been used, and that judges in other countries, such as Colombia, have been reluctant to take up the example or to develop their own innovative models of structural remedy.[54] Liebenberg is concerned that courts are abandoning their role in setting the normative content of rights by focusing simply on settling disputes without creating a sufficient framework for evaluating the outcomes of the engagement exercise.[55] Yet these scholars, like most who focus on the judicial role in SER enforcement, remain generally supportive of the idea that judges ought to use remedial creativity through structural engagement to get to the root of the political reasons behind institutional intransigence when gentler nudges don't work.[56] South African legal scholar Theunis Roux describes how he, like many fellow South African scholars, was initially concerned that by rejecting the minimum core content approach and stronger enforcement, the Constitutional Court of South Africa was abdicating its responsibility. However, he argues that: "As soon as one accepts … that the [Court's] strategy may have been to devise a review standard that allowed it greater flexibility to manage its relationship with political branches, much of this criticism falls away."[57] Katharine G. Young has likewise described the judicial function in this model as "representation reinforcing."[58]

Another feature of judicial innovation has been in the application of constitutional law in private law disputes. Here again, courts have not specifically delineated a complete set of rights and duties that apply to private actors. Rather, as Helen Hershkoff notes, there are more subtle "radiating effects of [constitutional SER guarantees] in private law cases involving common law rules that reconfigure social relations and destabilise entrenched hierarchy."[59]

52 *Occupiers of 51 Olivia Road, Berea Township and 197 Main Street Johannesburg v. City of Johannesburg and Others* (24/07) [2008] ZACC 1; 2008 (3) SA 208 (CC); 2008 (5) BCLR 475 (CC) (19 February 2008), para 30.

53 Ray, *supra* note 49, p. 418.

54 Landau, *supra* note 16, p. 455.

55 Liebenberg, *supra* note 49, p. 27.

56 Landau, *supra* note 16; Liebenberg, *supra* note 49, p. 29. See also M. Tushnet, "A Response to David Landau" (2012) 53 *Harvard International Law Journal* 156.

57 T. Roux, "Principle and Pragmatism in the Constitutional Court of South Africa" (2008) 7 *International Journal of Constitutional Law* 106.

58 K.G. Young, *Constituting Economic and Social Rights*, Oxford University Press, Oxford 2012, p. 191. See similarly Liebenberg, *supra* note 49, p. 29.

59 Hershkoff, *supra* note 40, p. 273.

In India, for example, courts have evaluated the fairness of the terms of a contract between private insurers and their beneficiaries in light of SER guarantees.[60]

In South Africa, constitutional SERs have come to be interpreted to impose obligations on private parties, though not of the same nature as the obligations such rights impose on states. Thus, for example, evictions from private property may only be carried out when it is reasonable in all the circumstances,[61] including "the constitutional vision of a caring society based on good neighbourliness and shared concern."[62] Reasonableness will depend in part on whether "proper discussions, and mediation where appropriate, have been attempted."[63] This obligation has resulted in innovative judicial orders that creatively blur the traditional distinction between public and private law. Thus, the South African Constitutional Court, balancing highly contextual factors, did not grant an order for landowner Mr. Modderklip to evict informal settlers on his land, but rather ordered the state to compensate Modderklip for the indigent occupiers' use of the land until alternative accommodation could be found. This represents a shift from the default private law assumption that landowners have an absolute right to exclude others from their land, acknowledges explicitly how private rights are intertwined with public law, and extends the obligation of inclusion, if embryonically, to relationships among private parties.

2.2.2. *In the "Law from Below"*

A trend in SER scholarship has been a move away from the focus on abstract questions like appropriate models of judicial review and toward an examination of the role rights and rights-language play in particular on-the-ground struggles for social and economic justice.[64] In this tradition, for example, Lucie White and Jeremy Perelman's edited collection canvasses four case studies of SER advocacy in sub-Saharan Africa. They examine how "creative" or "inventive"[65] advocacy practices and campaigns may "disrupt unfair patterns of distribution" and "strengthen citizens" capacities to claim their own SERs,"[66] independent of losses

---

60 *LIC of India v. Consumer Education & Research Centre and Others*, Manu/SC/0772/1995.

61 *Juma Musjid Primary School v. Essay N.O.* 2011 8 BCLR 761 (CC) at paras 54–60.

62 *President of the Republic of South Africa and Another v. Modderklip Boerdery (Pty) Ltd.* (Constitutional Court) CCT 20/04 (13 May 2005); *Port Elizabeth Municipality v. Various Occupiers* (CCT 53/03) [2004] ZACC 7; 2005 (1) SA 217 (CC); 2004 (12) BCLR 1268 (CC) (1 October 2004).

63 *Port Elizabeth*, *supra* note 62, para 43.

64 See e.g. White and Perelman, *supra* note 38; K. Young, "Social Movements and Economic and Social Rights" in *Constituting Economic and Social Rights*, pp. 223–255; H. Lessard, "Participatory Inclusion and Women's Rights to Social Security" in B. Goldblatt and L. Lamarche (eds), *Women's Rights to Social Security and Social Protection*, Hart, Oxford 2014, pp. 41–64; M. Langford, B. Cousins, J. Dugard and T. Modlingozi, (eds), *Socio-economic Rights in South Africa: Symbols or Substance?*, Cambridge University Press, Cambridge 2013.

65 Perelman and White, "Introduction" in White and Perelman, *supra* note 38, p. 12.

66 *Ibid*, 7.

or victories before formal rights-adjudicating or monitoring bodies. Langford and colleagues similarly consider, through case studies in South Africa, the material, symbolic, and political impacts of a range of rights-based strategies including protest, litigation, policy research, and awareness-raising.[67]

Within this analysis, a number of themes emerge. First, authors view grassroots SER advocacy as a ripe vehicle for "jurisgenesis," Robert Cover's famous term for how different "cultural worlds" create legal meaning, reinterpreting legal frameworks to better reflect their conceptions of justice.[68] For example, Perelman and Young in a series of writings describe a multi-pronged advocacy campaign to realize the right to health in Ghana.[69] The campaign concerned Mohammed Zakari, an elderly and impecunious farmer who was detained in a hospital for failing to pay the health-care user fees, despite the fact that those who could not afford to pay were exempted by law. The authors describe how the members of a community, in a groundswell of support for Zakari, used litigation, petitions, and protests, all infused with the language of the right to health. These actions not only changed official practices in relation to user fees and Zakari's case in particular; they also enlivened, legitimized, and integrated into state practices the community's own understanding about their rights.[70] Of course, opportunities for norm-generation from below will not always emerge from grassroots involvement in SER practice. As Hester Lessard notes, the extent to which women's groups taking up human rights discourse in relation to social security "participate in giving meaning to, and transforming, the content of human rights"[71] depends crucially on how spaces for participation in advocacy are designed. However, the very indeterminacy of SERs, perceived as an obstacle in traditional human rights practice, enhances their capacity to reflect community conceptions of justice in human rights advocacy.

Studies of grassroots SER activism "from below" also reveal how it creates space for creative negotiation of relationships among plural legal and normative orders.[72] Discussing the Zakari case again, White and Perelman note that activists were divided about whether to stage an unlicensed protest demanding Zakari's release. Some viewed the march as a "moral imperative," while others felt that

---

67 Langford et al., *supra* note 64.

68 See Young, *Constituting Social and Economic Rights*, *supra* note 58, p. 235; Lessard, *supra* note 64, pp. 53–55; and White and Perelman, *supra* note 38, p. 164, all citing R. Cover, "The Supreme Court, 1982 Term – Forward: Nomos and Narrative" (1982) 97 *Harvard Law Review* 4.

69 J. Perelman and K.G. Young, "Rights as Footprints" in White and Perelman, *supra* note 38, p. 122; Young, "Social Movements," *supra* note 64.

70 Young, *Constituting Social and Economic Rights*, *supra* note 68, p. 235.

71 Lessard, *supra* note 64, p. 51.

72 See e.g. B. De Sousa Santos and C.A. Rodriguez-Garavito, "Law, Politics and the Subaltern in Counter-Hegemonic Globalization" in B. De Sousa Santos and C.A. Rodriguez-Garavito (eds), *Law and Globalization from Below: Towards a Cosmopolitan Legality*, Cambridge University Press, Cambridge 2005, pp. 1–26.

respect for the rule of law precluded it. White and Perelman note that advocates were able to have a substantive moral discussion about the values these different normative/legal orders protected rather than simply defaulting to equating morality with legality.[73] In the context of land use rights, legal anthropologist Laurel Rose recounts case studies of two women in different ethnic groups in Swaziland and Malawi as they strategically negotiate plural legal orders in order to obtain land when neither formal state nor customary law obviously granted it to them.[74] This careful study of grassroots-level work reveals how women were able to leverage what power they did have by engaging a range of powerful actors, including but not limited to state and traditional authorities, using norms that included but transcended the formal customary and state law.

Finally, grassroots efforts, arguably with less strain than judicial approaches, are sufficiently flexible to target both public and private actors and to draw links between them. The global campaign for access to affordable generic medicines in the context of HIV/AIDS, for example, is often described in terms of its capacity to target drug companies, government actors, and international organizations such as the World Trade Organization.[75]

The point of these studies is not to generate a sanguine view of grassroots advocacy as superior to litigation. On the contrary, authors call for a "sceptical approach to any received wisdom on claims of success or failure."[76] The argument is that by attending to grassroots efforts, by recognizing them as law-creating, we see how rights may be useful in leveraging political power to render SERs meaningful and relevant to the lived experience of rights claimants. Further, creative advocates may use the human rights lens in order to target the many forces, beyond official state action, that produce and frustrate SER realization in practice.

2.2.3. *In International Institutional Practice*

In the international sphere, SERs have been a fertile area for the development of human rights methods beyond traditional tools like naming and shaming and individual complaints. UN institutions charged with developing the content of and monitoring state compliance with the International Covenant on Economic, Social and Cultural Rights were early developers and adopters of methodologies

---

73 White and Perelman, *supra* note 38, pp. 159–160.

74 L.L. Rose, "Women's Strategies for Customary Land Access in Swaziland and Malawi: A Comparative Study" (2002) 49 *Africa Today* 123.

75 See e.g. P. Nelson and E. Dorsey, "New Rights Advocacy in a Global Public Domain" (2007) 13 *European Journal of International Relations* 187.

76 M. Langford, "Introduction: Civil Society and Socio-Economic Rights" in M. Langford et al., *supra* note 64, pp. 1, 3.

like indicators, benchmarks, and human rights impact assessments,[77] as well as of methods aimed at facilitating the inclusion of marginalized groups and individuals in policy-making relevant to SERs.[78]

Human rights indicators,[79] along with benchmarks for progress, were initially developed as a "creative way to overcome the difficulties in assessing state compliance"[80] with the moving target that is the obligation of progressive realization. In relation to the right to the highest attainable standard of physical and mental health, for example, indicators might include gender disaggregated assessments of life expectancies, proportions of deaths from suicide, the proportion of people covered by health insurance, whether the state has a policy on sexual and reproductive health, or even whether the state has ratified the relevant international treaties.[81] The idea is that states develop and report in relation to these indicators as part of their international obligations with regard to the right to health, so that laggards may be identified.

Increasingly, however, indicators are being refined and developed to serve as a novel means of *driving* SER realization itself.[82] The importance of the governance and participation-enhancing features of indicators is evident in the discussion over how such indicators should be defined in the first place. Initially, UN institutions sought to develop a definitive list of universal indicators for SERs, through the assistance of experts.[83] In the end, however, they landed on the side of asking states to develop their *own* indicators through "participatory and transparent processes,"[84] so that these might be informed by local realities and respond to those whose voices may not resonate in ordinary political processes.[85] In other words, the process of developing indicators was viewed as

---

77 See e.g. P. Hunt, *Report of the Special Rapporteur on the right of everyone to the enjoyment of the highest attainable standard of physical and mental health*, UNGAOR, 2007, 4th sess, UN Doc. A/HRC/4/28 para. 25; A. Rosga and M.L. Satterthwaite, "The Trust in Indicators: Measuring Human Rights" (2008) 27 *Berkeley Journal of International Law* 270–279.

78 Lessard, *supra* note 64, pp. 55–60.

79 An indicator, in this context, is a "piece of information used to measure whether a right is being fulfilled or enjoyed in a given situation." See M. Green, "What We Talk about When We Talk about Indicators: Current Approaches to Human Rights Measurement" (2001) 23 *Human Rights Quarterly* 1062, p. 1065.

80 M. Sepúlveda Carmona, *The Nature of the Obligations under the International Covenant on Economic, Social and Cultural Rights*, Intersentia, Utrecht 2003, p. 319. See also P. Hunt, *Report of the Special Rapporteur on the right of everyone to the enjoyment of the highest attainable standard of physical and mental health*, UNGAOR, 2007, 4th sess, UN Doc. A/HRC/4/28, paras 26, 29, 87.

81 Office of the UN High Commissioner for Human Rights (OHCHR), *Human Rights Indictors: A Guide to Measurement and Implementation* HR/PUB/12/5. United Nations, New York and Geneva 2012, p. 90.

82 Ibid, pp. 109–124.

83 Rosga and Satterthwaite, *supra* note 77, pp. 288, 294.

84 General Comment 14, *supra* note 28, para. 43(f).

85 OHCHR, *Report on Indicators for Promoting and Monitoring the Implementation of Human Rights*, 15 n.17, UN Doc. HRI/MC/2008/3 (6 June 2008).

a way of refocusing policy debate and providing space for those most affected to set the terms of discussion. Further, the indicators themselves, once developed, are viewed as tools that might empower civil society to hold governments to account.[86]

Human rights impact assessments make use of indicators in similar ways. Impact assessments are tools for prospectively evaluating the impact of a policy program or intervention, public or private, for its effects on human rights and the distribution of those effects within a population.[87] A kind of human rights "mainstreaming," these are being developed as a means of broadening policy space for discussion of health impacts in areas where policymakers might otherwise ignore them,[88] prior to the post-hoc monitoring work of the human rights bodies.

Some argue that these methods have had the perverse effect of shutting down, rather than opening up, the imaginations of human rights actors.[89] Pointing to their origins in the corporate world, critics contend that in practice, these approaches are technocratic, distort human rights discourse, and exclude marginalized groups from human rights processes. They obscure abuses that are less susceptible to being quantified. They turn political processes of judging and evaluating, which civil society actors have always done, into technical exercises best done by experts. They encourage those who are evaluated to "game" systems to meet the demands of indicator-based evaluation. They create an unrealistic demand for short-term and verifiable results. Further, civil society organizations must now justify their own accomplishments in terms that are cognizable by quantitative indicators as they may obtain funding only for projects that are sufficiently "evidence-based."

The problem these critics expose is the complex way in which the relationship between knowledge and power plays out in the process of developing and using indicators. An illustration: Alicia Ely Yamin and Vanessa Boulanger describe how the choice of indicators related to the Millennium Development Goal of improving maternal health was fraught with ideological difficulties.[90] The goal initially entailed only one target: the reduction of the maternal mortality ratio.

---

86 OHCHR, *Guide to Measurement*, *supra* note 81, p. 109.

87 See, e.g. MacNaughton and Hunt, *supra* note 25.

88 See e.g. L. Forman and G. MacNaughton, "Moving Theory into Practice: Human Rights Impact Assessment of Intellectual Property Rights in Trade Agreements" (2015) 7(1) *Journal of Human Rights Practice* 109.

89 See e.g. S.E. Merry, "Measuring the World: Indicators, Human Rights and Global Governance" (2001) 52 *Current Anthropology* 583; P. Gready, "Reasons to Be Cautious About Evidence and Evaluation: Rights-Based Approaches to Development and the Emerging Culture of Evaluation" (2009) 1 *Journal of Human Rights Practice* 380.

90 A. Ely Yamin and V.M. Boulanger, "Why Global Goals and Indicators Matter: The Experience of Sexual and Reproductive Health and Rights in the Millennium Development Goals" (2014) 15 *Journal of Human Development and Capabilities* 218.

Several years into the process, women's rights advocates managed, despite opposition from conservative political forces, to add a target related to access to reproductive health. However, due to political opposition, access to safe abortions was not included among the indicators for this target, despite the fact that 13% of maternal deaths result from unsafe abortions. ("Family planning to delay or avoid pregnancy" was, after some struggle, included.) The exclusion of access to abortion from indicators related to maternal health has permitted pro-life advocates in Nicaragua, for example, to point to declining maternal mortality rates in the country in order to argue that a 2008 ban on abortion does impinge on women's health,[91] though clearly mortality rates would be further reduced with access to safe abortion.

If the value of indicators and the like lies in their capacity to reveal rather than obscure hidden agendas and preferences, and open up institutions to the participation of the most vulnerable, very careful attention must be paid to their design and to the new terrain of struggle that they create in order to ensure that knowledge puts power in the hands of those who need it rather than those who will abuse it. Further, it should be noted that this approach is not necessarily incompatible with traditional approaches like the minimum core.[92]

3. COMMON THEMES IN CONTEXT

This chapter has canvassed a number of creative approaches toward SER realization developed in human rights scholarship and practice since the turn of the millennium. Although each has been justified as a way of overcoming the capacity and legitimacy concerns typically alleged in relation to adjudication of SERs relative to CPRs, they also respond to a deeper skepticism about the relationship between legal and human rights practice more broadly and progressive social change.

First, each area of SER innovation reflects a broadened role for human rights law enforcement beyond delineating the boundary between what states are responsible for on the one hand and private activity on the other. In the case of SERs, it has always been recognized that private actors (such as teachers, private schools, or textbook publishers in the case of education, or physicians, nurses, and insurers in the case of health) are involved in the production and distribution of goods and services necessary for rights realization.[93] This is only

91 Yamin and Boulanger, *supra* note 90, p. 225, citing Amnesty International, *The Total Abortion Ban in Nicaragua*, Amnesty International, London 2009.

92 See A. Pillay, "In Defense of Reasonableness: Giving Effect to Socio-economic Rights" (2007) 8(4) *ESR Review* 3; S. Yeshanew, "Combining the 'Minimum Core' and 'Reasonableness' Models of Reviewing Socio-economic Rights" (2008) 9(3) *ESR Review* 8.

93 Gauri and Brinks, "Introduction" in Gauri and Brinks (eds), *supra* note 4, pp. 1–37.

more the case since the massive welfare state retrenchment in many countries over the last 50 years or so. In fact, the argument that human rights are matters between the state and the individual has never been fully convincing.[94] Rights are increasingly understood as the product of multiple actors, including non-state actors, with the state contributing to the legal framework within which rights may be realized or not. Yet this need to transcend the state/private binary is especially important in relation to poverty-related claims, which have tended to attract arguments that blame the poor for their condition and to de-emphasize complex systemic causes.[95]

Second, the above frameworks, and their critiques, place and maintain attention on law's vulnerability to co-optation by powerful elite interests.[96] This is a subject that has received a great deal of attention in the broader literature on law and social movements and access to justice. This literature has long noted how legal institutions, and particularly courts, are expensive to access, and may divert resources from other forms of political mobilization. Claimants must want to – and know how to – frame their claims in legal terms that are cognizable by the convening authority. These fora, in turn, are by necessary implication composed of the least marginalized and least hospitable to the most marginalized.[97] As a consequence, critical scholars have contended, position within social hierarchies will determine whether people will "perceive an experience as an injury, blame someone else, claim redress, or get their claims accepted."[98] Claims are made in a way that fits the general value system of the convening authority, and this value system comes to be seen as the exclusive or only legitimate normativity, crowding out other potential sources, including the more radical demands.[99]

Methods like reasonableness review combined with engagement remedies, the attention to pluralistic grassroots advocacy, and participatory approaches

94 See e.g. G. Teubner, "The 'State' of Private Networks: The Emerging Legal Regime of Polycorporatism in Germany" (1993) 1993 *Brigham Young University Law Review* 553, pp. 553–554.

95 See e.g. J. Hendry, "Developments in Equality Rights in the Economic and Social Sphere under the Charter" (2007) 21 *National Journal of Constitutional Law*, Suppl Constitutional Update 77, pp. 96–97.

96 See e.g. G.N. Rosenberg, *The Hollow Hope: Can Courts Bring about Social Change?*, University of Chicago Press, Chicago 1991; N. Stammers, "Social Movements and the Social Construction of Human Rights" (1999) 21 *Human Rights Quarterly* 980, 997. O. Lobel, "The Paradox of Extralegal Activism: Critical Legal Consciousness and Transformative Politics" (2012) *Harvard Law Review* 937, pp. 948–959.

97 S.C. McGuire and R.A. MacDonald, "Small Claims Court Cant" (1996) 34 *Osgoode Hall Law Journal* 509; L.E. White, "Mobilization in the Margins of the Lawsuit: Making Space for Clients to Speak" (1987–1988) 16 *New York University Review of Law and Social Change* 535, p. 542.

98 W.L.F. Felstiner, R.L. Abel and A. Sarat, "The Emergence and Transformation of Disputes: Naming, Blaming, Claiming ..." (1980)15 *Law and Society Review* 631, 636.

99 See R.A. MacDonald, "Access to Justice and Law Reform" (1990) 10 *Windsor Yearbook of Access to Justice* 287–337.

to human rights monitoring do not purport to solve these problems completely. They continue to make use of traditional human rights institutions, which remain costly to access and are primarily composed of powerful actors. And these mechanisms carry the risk, as illustrated by the problems associated with "evaluation culture," of domination by the more powerful. These methods do, however, address concerns about co-optation more directly. Engagement remedies and participatory methodologies for the development of indicators, for example, aim to make space for the needs and experiences of rights claimants to inform the content of rights and the means by which rights realization are measured and enforced, rather than leaving such norm-creation to courts alone. They are designed to be information-forcing, to reveal the factors that drive rights realization that may be hidden or obscured, which might make it easy to blame the poor for their predicament. And where they fail to leverage the political power of marginalized groups to shape that content, they leave space for further development of the models.

4. JUDICIAL STAGNATION IN CANADA

Canadian jurisprudence appears to have taken few cues from global innovation. While there have been two prominent housing rights victories in recent years, for example, both have relied on relatively traditional conceptions of SERs as negative rights of freedom from government interference; in these cases, claimants successfully challenged municipal bylaws that penalized the erection of temporary shelters in parks.[100]

A far bolder effort to challenge systemic government failures is reflected in *Tanudjaja v. Attorney General (Canada)*. In that case, four people with precarious access to housing in Ontario claimed that the federal and provincial governments' failure to adopt housing strategies, in the context of their systematic erosion of social programs related to housing through the 1990s, violated their constitutional rights.[101] Homelessness, they contended, was the result of both action and inaction on the part of the provincial and federal governments.[102] The claimants in *Tanudjaja* sought recognition of the violation of a positive right to housing under s. 7 of the *Charter*, an order that both levels of government develop and implement housing strategies, and a retention of jurisdiction to monitor the implementation of those orders.[103]

100 *Victoria (City) v. Adams*, 2009 BCCA 563; *BC/Yukon Association of Drug Survivors v. Abbotsford (City)*, 2014 BCSC 1817.

101 For a rich description of the context, nature and legal underpinnings of the claim from the co-counsel in the case, see T. Heffernan, F. Faraday and P. Rosenthal, "Fighting for the Right to Housing in Canada" (2015) 24 *Journal of Law and Social Policy* 10.

102 *Tanudjaja v. Canada (Attorney General)*, 2014 ONCA 852, para 16.

103 *Ibid*, para 15.

The claimants' approach in *Tanudjaja* was clearly informed by the creative approaches to SER enforcement described above. First, they explicitly engaged the systemic nature of government action contributing to homelessness, denying rigid state/private binaries that have stymied poverty-based claims in the past. Instead of challenging an individual law, for example, the claimants challenged the "*cumulative effect* of an *interconnected system* of government action" sustaining and supporting homelessness.[104] In their arguments before the courts, they sought to build on then-Justice Arbour's contributions in *Gosselin* (which would have recognized the state's positive obligation to fulfil SERs) and *Doucet-Boudreau* (which acknowledged the need for flexibility and innovation in SER remedies, approving judicial supervision of party engagement).[105] Interveners evoked South African models of judicial engagement in support of the claimants' request that the court declare a rights violation and supervise the governments' development and implementation of a housing policy to remedy the violation.[106] The claimants also drew on recommendations from UN bodies, including the Committee on Economic, Social and Cultural Rights' call on Canada to "implement a national strategy for reduction of homelessness that includes measurable goals and timetables, consultation and collaboration with affected communities, complaints procedures, and transparent accountability mechanisms."[107] They emphasized the importance of grassroots community organizing, mobilization, and alliance-building, including through legal education, observing that "litigation and its outcome are neither the only nor the dominant outcome."[108]

The claim was rejected prior to trial for disclosing no reasonable cause of action,[109] a decision upheld on appeal, and finally (without reasons) by the Supreme Court of Canada.[110] The judgments at first instance and on appeal rehearsed the usual concerns about the justiciability of SERs. The motion judge expressed sympathy for the applicants, but felt that the application was "misconceived" and that the courtroom was not the "proper place to resolve the issues involved."[111] The majority in the Court of Appeal concluded that

---

104 *Ibid*, Factum of the Appellants, <http://socialrightscura.ca/documents/legal/motion%20to%20strike/CA%20R2H%20Appellant%20Factum.pdf>, para 5.

105 *Ibid.*

106 *Ibid*, Factum of the Intervener, David Asper Centre for Constitutional Rights, <http://socialrightscura.ca/documents/R2HOCA/Asper-OCA.pdf>, paras 28–29.

107 See Heffernan, Faraday and Rosenthal, *supra* note 101, p. 23, citing M. Khotari, Report of the Special Rapporteur on adequate housing as a component of the right to an adequate standard of living, and on the right of non-discrimination in this context, Mission to Canada (9 to 22 October 2007), UN Human Rights Council, 10th Session, UN Doc. A/HRC/10/7 Add. 3 (7 February 2009), para 59, which in turn cites CESCR, Concluding observations, 22 May 2006, E/C.12/CAN/CO/4–E/C.12/CAN/CO/5, para 62.

108 Heffernan, Faraday and Rosenthal, *supra* note 101, p. 15.

109 *Tanudjaja v. Attorney General (Canada)* (Application), 2013 ONSC 5410.

110 *Tanudjaja v. Canada (Attorney General)*, 2015 CanLII 36780 (SCC).

111 *Tanudjaja v. Canada (Attorney General)*, 2014 ONCA 852, para 4.

this was a "political issue" and was therefore not a "legal issue";[112] that it didn't concern sufficiently specific state actions and laws to "engage the decision-making capacity of the courts";[113] that the claim was of too broad and diffuse a nature to lend itself to analysis under available legal tools;[114] and that courts lacked a "judicially discoverable and manageable standard for assessing in general whether housing policy is adequate."[115] Justice Feldman, dissenting at the Court of Appeal, held that the novel claim should at least be heard. In her view, the claim, however novel, raised significant issues of public importance and basic to the life and wellbeing of the claimants, it was "brought by counsel on behalf of a large, marginalized, vulnerable and disadvantaged group who face profound barriers to access to justice," and it was supported with an ample record that deserved to be heard.[116]

Canadian scholars like Margot Young have criticized the majority judgment of the Court of Appeal in *Tanudjaja* for its "resort to stale platitudes" around justiciability, political questions, and the like, and for its failure to take seriously innovations in other jurisdictions that may legitimately leverage constitutional litigation to support political struggle around housing.[117] Tracy Heffernan, Fay Faraday and Peter Rosenthal, who argued the case, bemoaned the courts' refusal to even engage with the 10,000 pages of evidence adduced to demonstrate the complex ways in which state action creates, supports, and sustains the discrimination and marginalization that leads to homelessness.[118]

Despite – or perhaps in response to – judges' restiveness, political actors are now driving the recognition of the inextricable relationship between law and politics to a matter like housing. Canada's First ever National Housing Strategy, introduced in 2017, explicitly recognizes housing as a human right to be recognized in law, and whose progressive realization is to be driven by accountability, transparency, and the participation of those most marginalized from policy making processes.[119] The judiciary may find itself forced to engage more creatively to interpret and apply this novel kind of law once the promised legislation is finally in place.

---

112 Ibid, para 23.

113 Ibid, para 26.

114 Ibid, para 32.

115 Ibid, para 34.

116 Ibid, paras 43, 88.

117 M. Young, "Charter Eviction: Litigating out of House and Home" (2015) 24 *Journal of Law and Social Policy* 46, pp. 62, 66. See also D. Des Baillets, "The International Human Right to Housing & the Canadian Charter: A Case Comment on *Tanudjaja v Canada (Attorney General)*" (2015) 32 *Windsor Yearbook of Access to Justice* 121.

118 Heffernan, Faraday and Rosenthal, *supra* note 101, p. 45.

119 Government of Canada, 2017. Canada's National Housing Strategy: A Place to Call Home. Ottawa: Canadian Mortgage and Housing Corporation, available at: <https://www.placetocallhome.ca/pdfs/Canada-National-Housing-Strategy.pdf>.

5. CONCLUSION

Social and economic rights claims, including housing claims, are challenging precisely because there are multiple factors that generate and contribute to phenomena like homelessness. The very difficulty of identifying these systemic factors may lead some to determine that poverty is the fault of the individual. This latter view may be convenient for bodies seeking to assign responsibility, but this does not make it the truth. The last 15 years have shown that legal actors can and do respond to calls to uncover and respond to systemic injustices and political exclusion that undermine SERs. Though creative approaches to SER enforcement do not offer any panacea for the problem of uneven distributions of power that drive SER abuses, they at least engage directly with political processes, broadly understood, by seeking to make them more inclusive and accountable. They acknowledge, as Louise Arbour did in 2005, that the realization of social and economic rights is an "inherently political undertaking."[120]

[120] Arbour, "Freedom from Want," *supra* note 14.

BUILDING A CULTURE OF INCLUSIVITY IN A DIVERSE SOCIETY[1]

Hina JILANI

1. INTRODUCTION

The world is currently experiencing a regression in the protection of human rights (including international humanitarian law). Non-state actors and states, including those who once led the charge in developing an international legal order based, in part, on the protection of human rights, frequently violate or

[1] This chapter is based on a speech delivered at the 6th Annual Desmond Tutu International Peace Lecture, Cape Town, South Africa, October 2016 (online: <http://theelders.org/article/building-culture-inclusivity-diverse-society>). The author thanks Moussa Bienvenu Haba, PhD student at Université Laval, for his valuable contribution to this chapter.

condone their violation. The trivialization of these violations in the name of security imperatives, sectarian religious ideologies and unbridled economic development must motivate us to redouble our efforts in the defence of fundamental rights. More than ever, it is important to remember that peace and security, respect for human rights, democratic governance and economic development are all inextricably linked. Consequently, national policies must be based on respect for human rights and be inclusive so that all segments of society feel equally protected by the state. In this contribution, I will first delve into how human rights, democracy, international peace and security are intertwined in all respects. I will then turn to the need for national efforts aimed at fostering a greater respect of human rights, emphasizing in this regard the role civil society has played in my country, Pakistan, for several decades.

2. HUMAN RIGHTS, DEMOCRACY, PEACE AND SECURITY IN A TROUBLED WORLD

Human rights are not an exclusively municipal or national concern; quite the contrary. Human rights are universal, indivisible and have a direct impact on international peace and security.

2.1. HUMAN RIGHTS VIOLATIONS AS THREATS TO PEACE AND SECURITY

Contemporary threats to peace and security extend far beyond wars between states. Peace can no longer be equated with the absence of war – so-called negative peace. The peace we should strive for – positive peace – must be based on the cooperation between groups or nations and the elimination of the root causes of conflicts.[2] This approach is embodied in the now well-established mechanisms of peace-building, which aim to prevent the resumption of hostilities by defining and supporting structures to strengthen peace.[3] The internal governance of states is therefore an essential element of peace.

Unfortunately, these days, many communities are besieged by violence in the name of religion, ethnicity and the rejection of diverse identities. Communal tensions bred by intolerance, hatred and extremism destroy the values of

2 For a more detailed analysis of negative and positive peace, see Johan Galtung, *War and Defense: Essays in Peace Research*, Volume 1 (Copenhagen: Christian Ejlers, 1975) at 76–108.

3 Report of the United Nations Secretary-General, *An Agenda for Peace: Preventive Diplomacy, Peacemaking and Peace-Keeping*, UNGAOR, 47th Sess, UN Doc. A/47/277 (1992), paras 21 and 57.

humanity and can lead to massive and systemic human rights violations, such as those resulting from apartheid, colonialism or foreign domination and occupation.

People's inability to recognize the merits of diversity has not only produced oppressive societies and divided nations, but has also diminished the possibilities of finding a common interest in promoting peace to achieve the welfare of all. Internal armed conflicts, terrorist campaigns, insurgencies, food crises and long-term political or economic instability have placed the human security of vast populations in peril. Large-scale movements of people fleeing for their lives or escaping various forms of persecution is a continuing crisis that has a direct link to social and political repression. The cumulative impact of these conditions is affecting global peace. Thus, the persistence of internal strifes in many parts of the world is no longer only a matter of internal national concern. This is why, after almost three decades, a new paradigm has developed at the international level according to which serious violations of human rights and international humanitarian law (IHL) occurring in a country may be characterized as threats to international peace and security.

This paradigm has materialized in the rise of international criminal justice. Indeed, the Security Council resolutions establishing the International Criminal Tribunal for the Former Yugoslavia[4] and the International Criminal Tribunal for Rwanda[5] are based on the recognition that serious human rights violations and IHL in these two countries constitute threats to international peace and security. In this way, they express the conviction that the establishment of international criminal tribunals to prosecute the perpetrators is an appropriate measure to maintain or to restore international peace and security.[6] The International Criminal Court (ICC) has legitimized this practice of the Security Council. Indeed, Article 13(b) of the Rome Statute[7] states that the Security Council acting under Chapter VII of the United Nations (UN) Charter may refer a situation to the ICC when it considers that this situation constitutes a threat to international peace and security.

However, the consequences of long drawn-out conflicts are now encompassing a wider sphere of political and economic interests than ever, making it more challenging than was the case in the past to find acceptable solutions.

---

4 Security Council, "Tribunal (former Yugoslavia)" (ICTY), SC Res 827, UNSCOR, 1993, UN Doc. S/RES/827 (1993) [ICTY, SC Res 827].

5 Security Council, Rwanda: "Establishment of an International Tribunal and adoption of the Statute of the Tribunal" (ICTR), SC Res 955, UNSCOR, 1994, UN Doc. S/RES/955 (1994) [ICTR, SC Res 955].

6 ICTY, SC Res 827, *supra* note 4, paras 4 and 6 of the Preamble; ICTR, SC Res 955, *supra* note 5, paras 5 and 7 of the Preamble.

7 Rome Statute of the International Criminal Court, 17 July 1998, 2187 UNTS 3 (entered into force 1 July 2002).

2.2. ANTI-DEMOCRATIC GOVERNANCE AS A CAUSE AND AGGRAVATING FACTOR OF CRISES AND CONFLICTS

I support the premise that a democratic society is one in which all human rights are fully respected and created for "equality of condition, not simply of opportunity."[8] It is through this approach that we can develop links between democracy and human rights, stressing the inter-dependency and indivisibility of political and civil rights on the one hand, and economic, social and cultural rights on the other. Thus, it highlights the importance of establishing or strengthening a genuine rule of law within states with the aim of maintaining peace and security at both the national and international levels. According to Louise Arbour, the rule of law "reflects the idea of equality in a substantive way: not just that no one is above the law, but that everyone is equal before and under the law, and is entitled to its equal protection and equal benefit. It requires that laws be just, and justly enforced."[9] Two essential pillars of the rule of law seem to emerge. First, the existence of the law: rule of law is characterized by the power of law and not by the power of men. But the mere existence of law is not sufficient, even where it is in accordance with fundamental rights (the right to life and physical integrity, freedom of expression and assembly, the right to privacy, etc.) and the principles of democracy (the people's power, separation of powers, free and fair elections, etc.).[10] The law must also be applied in a fair, just and equal way. The erosion or the absence of the rule of law, characterized by repressive national policies and impunity, is one of the structural causes of contemporary crises and conflicts.[11]

Unfortunately, we are experiencing a decline in the quality of world leadership. This lack of political vision is likely to lower capacities of states to address the causes of conflicts. This collective failure to restore hope for peace and people's security has given more critical dimensions to the present crisis. Indeed, responses to conflict and crisis, whether political or economic, instead of restoring security, have themselves become part of the problem. This is apparent from situations that prevail in several parts of the world.

---

8 Vitit Muntarbhorn and Charles Taylor, *Roads to Democracy: Human Rights and Democratic Development in Thailand*, (Bangkok/Montreal: International Centre for Human Rights and Democratic Development, 1994).

9 Louise Arbour, *Statement on the occasion of the high-level meeting of the General Assembly on the Rule of Law at the National and international levels*, UNGAOR, 67th Sess (2012).

10 Olivier Corten, "Rapport général, l'état de droit en droit international: Quelle valeur ajoutée?" in Colloque de Bruxelles, *L'État de droit en droit international* (Paris: Pedone, 2009) 11 at 11–12.

11 See generally Augustine Kposowa, "Erosion of the rule of law as a contributing factor in civil conflict: The case of Sierra Leone" (2006) 7(1) *Police Practice and Research* 35–48; Laurie Nathan, "The four horsemen of the apocalypse: The structural causes of crisis in Africa" (2000) 25:2 *Peace & Change* 188 at 189; *Report of Secretary-General, The Rule of Law and transitional justice in conflict and post-conflict societies*, UNSCOR, 2011, UN Doc. S/2011/634 (2004), para 6.

In Asia and in Africa, for instance, several countries have emerged or are in the process of transitioning from authoritarian rule, armed conflicts or struggles for the right to self-determination. Many countries in both continents have adopted national constitutions with strong guarantees for the protection of human rights. With few exceptions, most of these countries in these regions have enjoyed periods of political stability during which credible elections were held. Despite these significant advancements, political and economic conditions in many of these countries remain volatile. Some of these countries show visible signs of reversal of these initial advancements and are trapped in a perpetual state of transition. This is largely due to inadequate attention given to the establishment or the restoration of the rule of law and to inculcating a culture of respect for human rights in state institutions, as well as in governance practices.

Transition to democracy has remained merely procedural. Little has been done by governments to build the state's capacity to protect people. These trends are creating conditions in which the re-emergence of social, economic and political crises have impeded prospects for sustainable democracy, respect for human rights and the potential for development. Above all, these trends have considerably diminished the prospects for international peace and security. Governments are disregarding human rights norms and principles to the detriment of the interests of the most marginalized communities. The denial of economic, social and cultural rights is increasingly becoming a motive for public protest.

In many countries, stability rather than development has become an imperative to be achieved through the use of state force to repress popular movements and protests against economic and social disempowerment. This mode of governance has resulted in the narrowing of the space for dialogue and an increased public resentment against authorities.

Flaws in the agenda for economic development pursued by many states reflect the growing poverty and social exclusion of large parts of the population. Serious violations of economic, social and cultural rights have become carved into the actions of the state. The affected populations find that in the current environment of globalization, their own governments are either unable or unwilling to adjust to the difficulties they face. Exploitation of labour and depletion of the environment are some of the forms of serious violations resulting from the new economic arrangements. Indigenous populations are often particularly affected by such violations.

In my region, multinational corporations and other non-state agencies have acquired an enormous degree of control over the lives and liberties of the people. There are several examples where the coercive power of the state has been used against communities and human rights defenders, at times at the behest of powerful economic interests.

Leaders of indigenous and other minority communities, leaders of the movements of the poor, environmental and anti-globalization activists, trade union leaders and defenders of the rights of displaced persons, migrants and refugees are increasingly being targeted. These trends could lead to a further increase in violations and a future human rights crisis in that region. It is thus imperative to find approaches to economic development that secure people's social and cultural progress through means that do not create conflicts of interests between communities and become the basis of further tension or civil strife.

The political conditions and the practices of governance adopted by states determine the degree of risk and insecurity to which people in general, and some communities in particular, become exposed. An appreciable weakness in the rule of law has been observed in different countries where insufficiently representative democracies prevail, with little or no scope for citizen participation and with no accountability or transparency.

At the same time, public institutions are increasingly being used to perpetuate and strengthen the interests of certain sectors. Institutions for policing and prosecution suffer from inefficiency and corruption, and the independence of the judiciaries is becoming severely strained. Internal monitoring systems are either non-existent or have failed to enforce compliance with human rights norms in the practices or policies that are adopted by state institutions. Severe restrictions in many countries on freedom of information, expression and assembly, particularly in the name of religious ideology or the security or integrity of the state, have limited the access to evidence or to sites of violations, thereby frustrating attempts to monitor situations and to report violations.

2.3. HUMAN RIGHTS VERSUS HUMAN SECURITY: IS THERE A DILEMMA?

National security laws have been imposed in the severest forms in many countries of the world. In some countries, such laws are permanent parts of the domestic legal framework; this has effectively weakened fundamental human rights and has diminished the efficiency of their enforcement mechanisms.

In areas where armed conflict or political tensions are current, emergency or special laws are imposed to suspend fundamental freedoms and to restrict access to civilian courts. The introduction of rules of exceptions, for example through special legislation for security in general or against terrorism in particular, has affected the ability of national judicial systems to protect people from arbitrary actions.

The social climate created in the name of countering terrorism has led to instability without ensuring security. Anti-terrorism measures have been adopted in regions destabilized by political conflict and, in many cases, economic depression. Some governments have used the current climate to abuse the enhanced powers they gained in the campaign against terrorism to target political opposition, movements for self-determination and those defending human rights.

It is true that terrorism is a major threat to peace and security in contemporary times. Those involved in the defence and promotion minority rights, women's rights, religious tolerance and accommodation of ethnic or racial diversity have been some of the first victims of terrorism and extremism. These people are the frontline of counter-terrorism, working to preserve peace and democracy.

This struggle of the human rights community against terrorism and extremism pre-date the terrorist attacks of the 11 September 2001 in New York. It has long been a visible human rights activity in parts of the world where the roots of terrorism are the strongest, and there are several examples from Pakistan and Afghanistan. Human rights defenders increasingly argue that many counter-terrorism measures effectively erode human rights norms. They also defend the idea that lasting peace and security can only be achieved through compliance with these standards.

In the post-9/11 era, many states have failed to acknowledge that existing conflicts are rooted in the varying political or social claims of different sections of their population and the failure of the state to offer equitable solutions. They have characterized their response to all kinds of opposition as counter-terrorism. This trend of deliberately miscasting the context of the conflict, the emergency of a state of exception created for countering acts of terrorism, poses a threat to the rule of law and the respect for human rights.

A perception that security imperatives justify departures from established human rights standards has been deliberately nourished to condone these deviations. This has encouraged xenophobia, intolerance and hatred in many societies. Other significant sources of conflict or tension include the politics of identity, the difficulties of managing pluralism and diversity, increasing poverty and the diminishing role of the state in providing social security.

When societies fail to challenge the misconceived idea of the trade-off between security and human rights, most often they get neither, and minorities and other vulnerable groups typically pay the greater price. Such assaults on the rule of law and human rights are likely to become more and more entrenched if the current trends are not reversed.

3. LITIGATION AND POPULAR MOBILIZATION AS MEANS TO SOCIAL CHANGE[12]

For the promotion of human rights, a bottom-up approach, driven by national civil society, should prevail. In the face of the decline of human rights protection

[12] This section is based in part on the contribution the author made in a panel on 6 April 2000 (in Philip Alston et al., "What is access to justice? Identifying the unmet legal needs of the poor" (2000) 24 *Fordham international Law Journal* 187 at 205–213).

around the world, it is useful and revealing to discuss the human rights situation in Pakistan through the continuing struggle of civil society movements. In the present section, I will first underline the importance of civil society for the vitality of democratic governance, which, despite its limitations, appears to be the best way to promote respect for human rights. I will then illustrate this point in underlining strategies used by civil society in Pakistan, notably litigation and popular demonstrations, against certain systemic and endemic violations of fundamental rights.

3.1. CIVIL SOCIETY IN DEMOCRATIC GOVERNANCE AS A MOTOR FOR SOCIAL CHANGE

The measure of a society's level of democratic development is reflected in the vitality of its civil society. The institutionalization of norms and practices in democratic governance allows for the creation of effective mechanisms for facilitating interactive relationships between the state and its civil society. Under these conditions, the citizen not only has access to the state but is also equipped with the means to systematically monitoring state policy decisions and their implementation. Another element indicating the level of democracy is the power of the majority to secure their rights and legitimate interests against the vested interests of powerful elites. A necessary condition for a fully functioning democracy is the respect for the entire body of human rights not only in their formal recognition and promotion by the state but also in the effective exercise of these rights by civil society and citizens, both collectively and individually. The vitality of civil society enhances its capacity to manage the tensions of pluralism. Citizenship does not abolish class conflict or diversity. Nevertheless, it does imply some consensus on what constitutes the "common good" and how to reconcile it with pluralism. Such reconciliation is only possible where there is "agreement that 'public interest' does exist and that the parties have the right to participate in its elaboration and in the obligation of submission to society's laws."[13] It is the responsibility of the state to cultivate the notion of citizenship and its implications for citizen behaviour amongst the population.

The prospects for equal justice are largely determined by the social, economic and political environment in which institutions function. In most parts of the world, as was mentioned above, economic disparities, unequal social relationships and the political marginalization of groups and communities

---

13 Nancy Thede et al., *The Democratic Development Exercise: A Discussion Paper. Terms of Reference and Analytical Framework* (Montreal: International Centre for Human Rights and Democratic Development, Occasional Paper, July 1996).

persist to various degrees. It is true that the growth of inequality is proportional to the deficiency of democratic conduct in structures of governance. However, democracy as a political system, or the existence of democratic institutions alone, is no guarantee for the empowerment of all sections of the society. In order to address the issues of equity, the system has to be sufficiently imbued with values of human rights, not only in law but at all levels of social belief. In the absence of these values, democracy is merely procedural and fails to eliminate disparity and exploitation, or to create institutions that can dispense justice or satisfy the needs of the common citizen in the face of the vested interests of the powerful elite. Mobilization for change, or movements for change, face even greater challenges when the political environment restricts the freedom of movement, of association and of expression to an extent that mobilization becomes a very difficult process to achieve. It is in these conditions that the use of litigation becomes a partner or is used as a support for the movement for change.

Nevertheless, this strategy is not without its problems, especially when it is used in an environment where neither the law nor the institutions which are administering the law have the sensitivity that is necessary in order to not only give equal access to justice, but also to dispense justice, keeping in mind that there are conditions of equality in the society. The use of law becomes very contentious and the promotion or the respect of the rule of law becomes extremely difficult in conditions where the law itself becomes an instrument of oppression. The concept of the respect for the rule of law, as already stated, presumes the law to be just and equitable, and that the institutions for the administration of justice are fully sensitive to the inequality of conditions in which law is being applied. When the word "law" is taken to apply to any state command or mere whim exerted as an act of power, the rule of law becomes meaningless and "law" moves away from "justice."

Institutions that have become the victims of hampered political growth and that are amenable to manipulation are incapable of enforcing justice or influencing social attitudes. More importantly, they retain no power to ensure that the conduct of the state complies with human rights standards. It is in this context that I will discuss my experience as a human rights lawyer and member of organizations that have used litigation as a strategy for change. It has been a mixed experience, and we have learned many lessons in the process of using the law and the courts to gain and improve access to justice for the more marginalized communities and the more vulnerable and disadvantaged sections of society. One of the major realities that we have come to understand is that improving access to justice is ultimately a political process and no strategy will succeed if it ignores this fact. Litigation cannot be an alternative to the political process for change; it can only be a support for it and can only build the support for it. To better illustrate the role of litigation in social change, I will now discuss some of the experiences of Pakistan.

3.2. PAKISTAN: CIVIL SOCIETY ACTIONS FOR SOCIAL CHANGE

The role of civil society in promoting human rights in Pakistan, and therefore social change, can be illustrated in the fight against bonded labour and violence against women.

3.2.1. Bonded Labour in Pakistan: The Fight against a Modern Form of Slavery

The Constitution of Pakistan states that all persons are equal before the law and are entitled to the equal protection of the law. It also states – or rather presumes – that slavery is non-existent in Pakistan and that all practices which are slave-like are prohibited. Nevertheless, the truth is that slave-like practices – indeed, slavery itself – are very much in existence in Pakistan in the form of bonded labour, in the form of apprenticeship practices and also in the nature of certain social practices which relate to women, such as forced marriages. So this constitutional guarantee does not really mean very much when the realities are neither confronted nor addressed. Bonded labour, not only in the agricultural sector but also in the industrial sector, has been a reality for a long time in Pakistan. For years, at least one particular industry, that of brick kilns, was using bonded labour and had built its prosperity on the exploitation of the labour which they forced into bondage.

In fact, because of economic disparities and growing inequality in the ownership of land, numerous landless peasants have moved to urban areas. These landless peasants became most vulnerable to the exploitative practice of bonded labour. In the early 1980s, when we were called upon to address this issue, there were hundreds of thousands of people living on the peripheries of the urban areas who were working in brick kiln industries and were actually bonded slaves of the owners. They were given a sum of money as an advance payment because when they had come from the villages, they had absolutely nothing on which to survive. They were given this advance in order to buy some necessities of life. This advance was taken as a debt and it multiplied so quickly that by the time these people realized that they were under debt, the debt was too big for them to ever pay off. The result was that not only a particular family but also their children and children's children were bonded into labour.

This practice was discovered through legal action. When *habeas corpus* petitions were filed for release and liberation of these bonded labourers, it was then that the issue of bonded labour became visible. The court cases regarding the liberation or release of bonded labour acted as catalysts for a change of an exploitative practice. Now, institutions can either give you the strength to take an issue forward and achieve success or they can become an obstacle to the change that is sought. It took us years and nearly 1,000 *habeas corpus* petitions to convince the courts in Pakistan that there was no law that authorized the detention and forced confinement of people by employers, even if the debt was a legitimate debt. It was even more difficult for us to convince the courts that the kind of practice to which these people were subjected and the kind of debt which bound them can never be a legitimate debt; it is exploitative and clearly violates established norms of social justice and human rights. Ultimately, the courts did understand that, but the understanding was very reluctantly translated into judicial pronouncements. The reason for this, as mentioned above, is that all social institutions that are dominated by a power elite become subject to the interests of that elite. While the courts came to understand that there was no law and that the Constitution does not allow the loss of liberty for anyone except in accordance with law, they were not willing to concede the arguments made against the practice of bonded labour.

Even today, in spite of hard-fought legislative reforms, bonded labour laws have yet to be implemented and this pernicious slavery is far from being eradicated. According to the Human Rights Commission of Pakistan (HRCP) 2015 report, debt bondage continues to be inflicted on an estimated 2.6 million workers in the brick kiln and agriculture sectors.[14] In light of this continuing situation, the mobilization of civil society is necessary more than ever. In 2016, as many as 3,604 bonded labourers were released in the province of Sindh by order of the district courts and thanks to the work and legal aid of HRCP.[15]

3.2.2. *Violence against Women in Pakistan: A Long Journey for Women's Human Rights*

For women's human rights, access to justice is rendered more complicated because the law itself discriminates against women, promotes and reinforces attitudes that have led to increased violence against them, and in some ways condones and justifies unequal treatment. It is troubling that certain institutions, including the judiciary, have in fact promoted the attitudes which have made women more vulnerable to abuse and have justified discrimination against them in the name of either religion, culture or tradition. In this situation, it became very difficult to use the law and expect that women would be empowered or that any significant change would take place with regard to their social, economic, or political rights. So, how did human rights organizations shine a spotlight on issues regarding women through the courts?

As far as individual cases are concerned, most of the women who need to litigate do so with respect to laws that concern domestic or personal issues.

14 Human Rights Commission of Pakistan, *State of Human Rights in 2015: Labour*, at 4. Online: <http://hrcp-web.org/hrcpweb/wp-content/uploads/2016/04/Labour-2016.pdf>.

15 Human Rights Commission of Pakistan, *State of Human Rights in 2016*, at 187–188. Online: <http://hrcp-web.org/hrcpweb/wp-content/uploads/2017/05/State-of-Human-Rights-in-2016.pdf> [HRCP, Report 2016].

Where these laws are unequal, it becomes difficult for women to expect justice from the courts. It therefore becomes important for legal aid lawyers to bring these cases to court in order to show the inadequacy of the law and to document the resulting inequities. We also found that in order to bring about a change with regard to women, to encourage them to use laws which could be beneficial and to encourage them to join our efforts to bring to light the inadequacies of the law, they needed much more support.

By ratifying the Convention on the Elimination of All Forms of Discrimination against Women (CEDAW)[16] in 1996, Pakistan committed to ensuring the equality of men and women and to abolishing all forms of discrimination against women. However, the country failed in this regard: the World Economic Forum's (WEF) Global Gender Gap Report 2016 declared Pakistan second last in the world regarding gender equality (143/144) and made it the lowest-scoring country in South Asia.[17] Pakistan ranked 112th in the first edition of the report in 2006 and since then its position has been worsening every year. It was ranked 135th in 2013, 141st in 2014 and 143rd in 2015.

Women in Pakistan are not only marginalized, they are a category of the population that is actually at risk. The scope of violence that is perpetuated against women has to be understood in the context, again, of the law and the Constitution. This illustrates how even accepted norms of social justice or accepted standards of human rights when applied to women are conditioned by other considerations. The Constitution of Pakistan guarantees life, liberty and the security of the person. Nevertheless, if we look at the plight of women, their rights to life and liberty are not guaranteed, because they are conditioned to their conforming to certain social norms. We are speaking about practices like honour killings (which are the extreme form of domestic violence that takes women's lives), acid attacks, sexual violence and other domestic violence. It was only through court action that these practices were shown by legal aid lawyers to contravene the Constitution and violate women's fundamental rights. It was an uphill task to sensitize institutions that were not independent of the executive and free from social pressures – institutions that had not played a role in changing social reality, and had usually mirrored social biases and prejudices.

Honour killing and rape are forms of violence that are characteristic of a social and moral order of Pakistan that perpetuates inequalities between men and women. The basis of men's supposed "superiority" over women within this

---

16 Convention on the Elimination of All Forms of Discrimination against Women (CEDAW), 18 December 1979, 1249 UNTS 13 (entered into force 3 September 1981).

17 World Economic Forum, *The Global Gender Gap Report 2016*, Geneva, 26 October 2016, at 284–285. Online: <http://www3.weforum.org/docs/GGGR16/WEF_Global_Gender_Gap_Report_2016.pdf>.

order is founded on two concepts: the "commodification" of women and the honour of men.[18] First, based on this patriarchal system, every relationship between men and women is based on men's ownership of women. Second, a man will only be considered "respectable" and "honourable" if he is able to control the sexual behaviour of his wife, daughters, sisters and even mother, and his value as a man depends on the "virtue" of the women around him.[19] Thus, when one examines violence against women and the response of the justice system in Pakistan, it clearly appears that the divisions between law, justice, culture and religion are often blurred. Let us analyze further the practices of honour killing and rape in Pakistan and the relative power of litigation in this regard.

3.2.2.1. Honour Killing

When the murder of a woman is termed an "honour killing" in a court of law, it perpetuates the harmful attitudes that have bred the practice. There is no honour in killing anyone. Hundreds of thousands of women and girls were murdered by family members on the pretext of defending the family honour. In 2016, the HRCP related some cases of this cruel practice that were reported to them in these terms:

> On April 28, a 15-member Jirga in Abbottabad ordered the killing of a 16-year-old girl by burning her to death for helping her friend escape the village to marry of her free will. The girl was taken from her home to an uninhabited house where she was drugged, killed, and placed in the backseat of a parked van, which was set on fire. Two similar cases were also reported in June where the victims were burnt to death in the name of honour. First, a 19-year-old schoolteacher was killed after being tortured and set alight by the school principal as a punishment for refusing a marriage proposal from his son. She had been forced to leave her job because of constant harassment by her boss for refusing to marry his son who was twice her age. She had named the school principal and four others to be responsible for death in a statement she gave two days before succumbing to her injuries. A week later, a 17-year-old girl from Lahore was set ablaze by her mother for bringing shame to the family by eloping and contracting a love-marriage with a man whose ethnicity was not acceptable to the girl's mother. The mother confessed to the murder and was taken into police custody. Another case that gained prominence in 2016 was the murder of Qandeel Baloch, a 26-year-old social media activist. On July 17, Qandeel was strangled by her own brother who claimed that she had brought shame to him and his family, and who later also confessed to the murder.[20]

18 Maliha Zia Lari and Sarah Zaman, *Sexual Violence and the Law in Pakistan* (Karachi: War against Rape Publications, 2011), at 4.

19 Ibid at 5.

20 HRCP, Report 2016, *supra* note 15 at 159.

The perpetuation of this practice, which resisted decades of efforts by women's movements, is made possible by a certain clemency of the laws and the courts toward the perpetrators of these killings. In fact, as per the longstanding *Qisas* and *Diyat* laws in Pakistan, there was a legal loophole that allowed perpetrators to escape liability after being pardoned by the victim's families. The action of civil society, for several decades, by way of trials and protests has shown to the general population the problem related to honour crimes and the incongruity of Pakistani laws that permit the impunity of perpetrators in violation of fundamental guarantees enshrined in the country's constitution. It is true that more recent reforms in laws have made an effort to mitigate the negative effect of certain provisions of the criminal law on *Qisas* and *Diyat*. However, it is also true that statistics confirm that there is no reduction in the incidence of this crime or in impunity for the perpetrators.

Several incidents of the killing of women in the name of honour were followed by strong protests by civil society. This issue became central to the quest for full respect for women's fundamental rights to life and to dignity. The focus of the human rights and women's rights movements on eliminating the practice of "honour" has resulted in amendments to the criminal law in October 2016. The amended provisions stipulate that an individual found guilty of murder on the pretext of honour is punishable by life imprisonment, even if the victim's family pardons the offender.[21] Thus, although it is deplorable to observe that the practice of honour killing has not diminished, the awareness within Pakistani society is much greater. Many people who said publicly that this was part of our culture do not dare to affirm it openly today. To be clear, this victory belongs to the women's rights movement in Pakistan; it is not a state victory.

3.2.2.2. Rape

While it is not possible to give reliable statistical information on the incidence of rape in Pakistan, there is sufficient evidence to affirm that it remains one of the major crimes against women. Several hundred cases of rape are reported every year from different parts of the country. Yet these are estimated to be only a fraction of the actual number of cases. Social stigma associated with rape and a corrupt, inefficient and a gender-biased law enforcement system prevent women from reporting the crime. There are many deterrents to the reporting of rape and the pursuit of justice. A case of rape or gang rape can take as long as three to four years before a verdict is reached in the courts. Another deterrent is that the process is so traumatic for the rape survivor that families take a decision to avoid it altogether. The conviction rate is also extremely low (only 2–4%), with death as the maximum sentence for gang rape.

21 Ibid at 155.

There is a dark period in Pakistan's legal and political history that has left its mark on the legal framework and the justice system. In 1979, under a campaign of "Islamization" led by the military regime of General Zia, new legislation, known as the Hudood Ordinances, was introduced, which dealt with offences such as adultery, rape, murder, theft and the drinking of alcohol. The most glaring injustice of this law was that no person could be awarded the maximum punishment for these offences unless they were proved by the testimony of four male adult Muslim witnesses in the case of rape and adultery, and two male Muslims in other cases. Women were thereby declared incompetent and unreliable as witnesses, even when they themselves were the victims of the crime, as in the case of rape. Also, this law created a very dangerous situation for women. If a woman complained of rape, and the prosecution was unable to prove the offence against the accused man, the woman's complaint could be taken as a confession of *Zina* (adultery or extramarital sex), the maximum punishment for which was stoning to death. Further, she could also become liable to punishment for the offence of *Qazaf* (false accusation of rape or adultery against any person). The maximum punishment for this offence was flogging with 80 lashes. There are numerous instances in which women actually suffered the injustices of this law. Despite the actions of women's rights movements such as the Women's Action Forum, created precisely to resist oppressive state laws in the early 1980s, the *Zina* Law became a deterrent to the denunciation of rape.

In 2006, however, civil society's longstanding action led to the adoption of the Protection of Women Act, which removed the crime of rape (*Zina-bil-Jabr*) from the Hudood Ordinances and added it to Pakistan's Penal Code. By this amendment, rape became an offence under the Penal Code, and therefore under the jurisdiction of criminal courts, with convictions based on forensic and circumstantial evidence regulated by the Law of Evidence Order of 1984.[22] Additionally, the practice of converting rape cases to *Zina* cases was abolished under the reform.[23]

In addition, the adoption in October 2016 of the Anti-Rape Law strengthens the legal architecture of repression of rape in Pakistan. Indeed, the Anti-Rape Law gives legal cover to the collection and use of DNA evidence to prove that rape has been committed.[24] The amendment on this point ruled against the will of the Council of Islamic Ideology, which keeps insisting that DNA cannot be taken as primary evidence in rape cases and can only be taken as corroborating evidence, advocating that the four witnesses requirement is to be considered

---

22 Hanibal Goitom, "Islamic law in Pakistan – Global legal collection highlights" Law Library of Congress (24 December 2013). Online: <http://blogs.loc.gov/law/2013/12/islamic-law-in-pakistan-global-legal-collection-highlights>.

23 Ibid.

24 HRCP, Report 2016, *supra* note 15 at 155–156.

the primary evidence in considering rape.[25] This demonstrates the retreat of the hold of the Islamist lobbies over the state apparatus and society in general. However, while being less numerous and influential than in the past, they are no less clever and virulent, in particular because of their increasingly professional capacity to intimidate individuals and the state in order to extract concessions in their favour to the detriment of human rights. This is unfortunately symptomatic of contemporary Pakistani society, which is plagued by a culture of violence, religious radicalism and drugs inherited from the war in Afghanistan. The Anti-Rape Law prescribes strict investigation procedures and any officer who does not inquire diligently is punishable by a three-year jail term, a fine or both. The new law also provides that anyone who rapes a minor or a mentally or physically disabled person or a public servant such as a police officer, jailer or medical officer will be liable to the death penalty or life imprisonment. Victims and witnesses are not required to be present for the trials in person and may appear through audio-visual means, and the media are strictly prohibited from publishing the name or any information related to the victim.[26]

These are some of the conditions in which movements for social change find themselves. In isolation, a strictly legal strategy does not work. Human rights activists and lawyers are constantly required to make judgment calls on the choice of forum to project or resolve issues. In my experience, there have been issues that were more successfully pursued in courts and there were others that needed more public projection to dislodge deliberately created biases. For instance, we chose not to challenge the law of evidence that reduced the legal capacity of women to be witnesses in a court of law. Instead, we took the issue to the streets through public demonstrations and protests, and it is there that we were able to highlight not only the injustices of the law, but also the weaknesses of the institutions in their ability to dispense justice in the presence of biased and discriminatory laws. When groups and organizations join hands to bring about a change in the social and political lives of people, they become more and more conscious of what they need to change. It is not just for legal reform that social movements have to work; they have to work to reform the institutional culture. The culture of institutions, in fact, determines whether they will condone, accept and justify discrimination and inequality or whether they will, despite inadequacies and deficiencies of the law, uphold the standards of justice and equality. Many of the organizations that work for social change, either through political movement or through more legal strategies, do not base their work on the availability of resources. We know that resources are always

---

25 Umer Nagiana, "Rape cases: DNA tests not admissible as main evidence says CII" *The Express Tribune* (30 May 2013). Online: <https://tribune.com.pk/story/556392/rape-cases-dna-tests-not-admissible-as-main-evidence-cii-front-page/>.

26 HRCP, Report 2016, *supra* note 15 at 156.

scarce. However, the only resource on which we depend is the resource of commitment: the commitment to change, the commitment to the creating an environment in which the scope for access to justice is wider, and toward this end we concentrate on eliminating intolerance, discrimination, violence and on upholding international standards of social justice and equality.

4. CONCLUSION

Human rights laws are not drafted with peace and political stability in mind. Rather, their basic purpose is to provide states with the framework that allows them to respond effectively to even the most serious of crises. Human rights are never a luxury to be set aside in times of difficulties.

International law is the foundation that helps states to respond effectively to the difficulties that arise, including civil strife, armed insurgency and terrorism. Preservation of peace and security is a core objective of the UN Charter. Respect of human rights is another, as initially reflected in the Charter and then laid down more precisely in the Universal Declaration of Human Rights and subsequent treaties. History has eloquently illustrated how closely linked these two objectives are. Human rights violations are almost always the underlying cause or consequence of deterioration in peace and security.

Bringing an end to armed conflict and restoring peace and security typically require progress in addressing ongoing human rights violations and ending impunity for past violations. However, it is far less challenging to identify human rights concerns and to set an agenda for change than it is to bring about conditions – political, economic and social – that would allow the realization of these rights.

Repeated and prolonged periods of political crisis and economic instability in many parts of the world have restrained progress towards a stable environment in which respect for human rights can flourish. The role of the state in protection of individuals has diminished. These trends continue to impede progress for democracy, respect for human rights and the rule of law.

Effective judicial systems must be supported by complete judicial independence if people are to draw real benefits from protections that are normally available under a constitutional framework. Initiatives aimed at the legal empowerment of the poor, to relieve social exclusion and discrimination, labour exploitation, eviction from land and at displacement and for conferring the right to control over natural resources would contribute toward bringing peace to communities.

Such a move forward requires a creative relationship between states and civil society, so that people's dignity and security are placed at the centre of any approach toward governance. A significant development in the recent years is the growing strength and capacity of civil society in many parts of the world. Civil society actors have played a significant role in inducing the recognition by states of the concepts of participatory democracy, transparency and accountability.

Human rights defenders and other civil society actors have taken important initiatives to transform societies that still carry biases which drive discrimination, hatred and violence. International cooperation and a sense of collective responsibility to end violence remain critical elements in removing the threats to peace and security.

There are many challenges that are testing the resolve of the international community to promote accommodation and tolerance in order to prevent the erosion of peace and harmony. I end with the fervent hope that such a result at the international level leads the world out of the crises we are confronting today and that people learn the value of peaceful coexistence and shared progress.

MADE IN CANADA

A Failed War on Drugs

J. Michael SPRATT

On 21 February 2010, while Michael Swan was watching Canada's gold medal hockey team play the United States, three young men from Toronto were driving down a dark highway toward Ottawa. The "Toronto three," as they would come to be known, had a plan to make some easy money. They were going to steal Michael Swan's marijuana.

Swan was murdered later that night – killed by a single bullet that pierced his lung and tore apart his heart.

There was nothing particularly unique about Michael Swan. He was a typical teenager, he came from a good family, he had a tight circle of friends and, like almost half of all Canadians have done, he smoked marijuana.[1] He also sold marijuana, mostly to his friends, but rumours that he had a large supply of marijuana had travelled to Toronto.

In the early hours of 22 February 2010, the Toronto three, their faces masked, burst into Swan's house. They ordered Swan to tell them where he kept his supply of pot. Swan did not answer quickly enough and was shot. He died on the floor of his bedroom. Killed over a few pounds of pot.

1 Health Canada, "The Canadian Alcohol and Drug Use Monitoring Survey (CADUMS)," 2012, <http://www.hc-sc.gc.ca/hc-ps/drugs-drogues/stat/_2012/summary-sommaire-eng.php> accessed 10 July 2015.

I represented one of the Toronto three. Like Swan, he was 19 years old. He had no prior criminal record. He did not shoot Swan, but he was there when it happened. He was convicted of second-degree murder and received a life sentence. All of the Toronto three were convicted and all are serving life sentences.

Some cases stick with you; this is an occupational hazard for a criminal defence lawyer. Often we remember cases because of the result, the unexpected victory or the wrongful conviction. I remember the Swan case because of the heart-breaking victim impact statements given by his parents. Michael Swan's mother told the court that she hated her life: "I wish I could go to sleep and never wake up." Michael's father told the court about the guilt he lives with: "Ultimately, it was my job to protect my child, to identify the dangers and do whatever was required to deal with them. I thought I was doing this, but it proved not to be enough. I must live with this guilt for the rest of my life."[2]

Swan was killed, three young men were sentenced to life and a family was destroyed. This is one of the many grim faces of the criminalization of drugs.

Swan is not the only casualty of the war on drugs.[3] Murder is not the only harm created and perpetuated by the drug war: overdoses, addiction, petty crime, increasing prison populations, homelessness and the spread of disease can all be tied to the failed war.

Despite this tragic collateral damage, the war not only persists, but has also intensified, at least in Canada. It seems old habits die hard, and Canada is left behind as politics trump health and safety.

1. A FAILED WAR

In September 2014, the Global Commission on Drug Policy (GCDP) released a report entitled "Taking Control: Pathways to Drug Policies that Work." This Report provided a critical and substantive analysis of current global drug policy.[4] The GCDP was composed of international experts, former presidents and prime ministers, and Louise Arbour.[5]

---

2 G. Dimmock, "Slain Barrhaven teen Michael Swan memorialized in graffiti," *Ottawa Citizen*, 11 March 2015, <http://ottawacitizen.com/news/local-news/0312-barrhaven> accessed 10 July 2015.

3 In the Canadian context, the "war on drugs" is defined by criminalization and other anti-drug legislation, as opposed to an explicit policy as seen in some other jurisdictions.

4 Global Commission on Drug Policy, "Taking Control: Pathways to Drug Policies that Work," 2014.

5 It is worth recalling that during her time on the Supreme Court of Canada, Louise Arbour authored the most powerful minority opinion on harm-based drug policy in Canadian history in *R. v. Malmo-Levine; R. v. Caine* [2003] 3 SCR 571, finding that the harm associated with marijuana use does not justify the state's decision to use imprisonment as a sanction against the prohibition of its possession.

At its core, the Commission's report emphasized that a fundamental shift in policy – health, social and criminal – was required in order to alleviate the harms associated with drug use. The report was unequivocal: past approaches to drug policy premised on a punitive law enforcement paradigm have failed.

In other words, the world's so-called war on drugs has been a complete and abject failure. As a criminal defence lawyer, this comes as no surprise. Every day I see the ravages that illegal drugs inflict on our communities. Canada has a drug problem, but it is a problem of policy. Canadian politicians are still waging an outdated war.

There is no need to engage in an exhaustive review of the history of Canadian drug policy. One need not trace the lineage of the 1908 Opium Act[6] through to modern-day mandatory minimum drug sentences to conclude that the criminalization of narcotics has failed to eliminate drugs. The spoils of the tough-on-crime drug war are laid bare on our streets and in our jails. In Canada, we incarcerate more people than ever, despite the fact that since 1998, the proportional crime rate, excluding drug offences, in Canada has decreased by 43.5%. However, the proportional crime rate for drug offences has only decreased by 15.9% during that same time period.[7]

Sadly, it has also done nothing to eliminate the disastrous harms associated with narcotics. In 2011, the Supreme Court of Canada considered a subset of these harms, those associated with injectable drug use, in Vancouver's downtown eastside.[8] A survey of approximately 1,000 intravenous drug users demonstrated the ills associated with drug use. On average, the surveyed users had been addicted to injectable drugs for 15 years. A total of 87% were infected with the hepatitis C virus (HCV) and 17% with the human immunodeficiency virus (HIV). A total of 20% were homeless, 80% had been incarcerated, 38% were involved in the sex trade and 59% reported a non-fatal overdose in their lifetime. Of course, those who had died due to an overdose were not captured by the survey's conclusions.

The war on drugs has not eliminated narcotics. It has not reduced the amount of drug crime. It has not reduced the harm that drugs inflict on our society. Punitive law enforcement paradigms have indeed failed. But the GCDP's report was hopeful that a global paradigm shift had already begun. Change, it said, was in the air, as the international community had begun to embrace pragmatic reforms.

In Canada, the report fell on deaf ears, drowned out by sustained, outdated and harmful political rhetoric. Turning its back on the wave of international reform, Canada's Conservative government legislated punitive mandatory

6 Opium Act, SC 1908, c 50.

7 Statistics Canada, "Table 252-0051 – Incident-based crime statistics, by detailed violations, annual," CANSIM (database), accessed 15 May 2017.

8 *Canada (Attorney General) v. PHS Community Services Society*, 2011 SCC 44, para. 9.

minimum sentences for many drug offences, rejected a therapeutic evidence-based drug policy and sought to demonize those who disagreed as being soft on crime.

For over a decade, Canada's escalation of the war on drugs was not only out of step with the Commission's GCDP's recommendations, but also risked the health and safety of both drug users and communities. However, change may be in the air. In November 2015 the Conservative government was defeated by Justin Trudeau's Liberal party and its harsh rhetoric was replaced by sunny ways and the promise of evidence-based policy.

However, after almost three years in power, the new Liberal government's criminal justice and legislative track record has not matched its lofty promises. Simply reversing the Conservative government's poor policy is not enough.

2. THROWING AWAY THE KEY

In 2011, the Conservative government introduced the Safe Streets and Communities Act (SSCA), an omnibus piece of legislation designed to get tough on crime.[9] For the last decade in the Canadian political climate, being "tough on crime" has often meant simplistic policies and punitive criminal sanctions that stress punishment over rehabilitation.[10] The SSCA was no exception; it continued the Conservative tradition of increasing or imposing mandatory minimum penalties for a number of drug offences. In other words, the SSCA stands in direct contradiction to the recommendations of the GCDP's report.

The Conservative government defended minimum sentences as a historically accepted criminal justice tool. Minimum sentences have indeed formed part of Canadian criminal law since the first iteration of the Criminal Code in 1892. At that time, there were only six offences that mandated a minimum term of imprisonment. As noted by Nichole Crutcher, "the bulk of these early mandatory minimum penalties were directed at enforcing the legitimacy of public institutions" and focused on institutional fraud.[11] This was not a surprising state of affairs, given the relative infancy of the Canadian federal system. By 2005, the number of minimum penalties in the Criminal Code had increased to 29. The Conservative government came

---

9 Safe Streets and Communities Act, SC 2012, c 1.

10 On 19 October 2015, Stephen Harper's Conservative government was defeated in the 42nd general election by the Liberal Party, led by Justin Trudeau. The new Liberal government swept into power with a promise to govern based on evidence, not ideology. As part of this promise, the new government has vowed to reform Canadian drug laws. Time will tell if Trudeau's election platform manifests in substantive policy change.

11 N. Crutcher, "The Legislative History of Mandatory Minimum Penalties of Imprisonment in Canada" (2001) 39(2–3) *Osgoode Hall Law Journal* 273, <http://digitalcommons.osgoode.yorku.ca/ohlj/vol39/iss2/2> accessed 10 July 2015.

to power in 2006 and over the following ten years, the number of minimum sentences had doubled.[12] They now apply to more than 60 offences.[13]

So, it should have come as no surprise that the SSCA relied heavily on mandatory sentencing to accomplish its goals of increasing community safety. Among the new mandatory minimum sentences for certain drug offences, the SSCA included up to a mandatory two-year prison sentence for trafficking or possession for the purpose of trafficking any illegal drug, including marijuana, if the offence was committed near a school or place frequented by minors,[14] if the offender had a prior related conviction or if the offender was in possession of a weapon during the offence.

The SSCA also imposed mandatory minimum sentences for the production of prohibited drugs, including a mandatory minimum sentence of six months in jail for growing six marijuana plants. This punitive custodial narcotic sentencing is precisely the opposite of what the GCDP report recommends.

The GCDP was right to recommend restraint in sentencing for drug crimes. Most of the evidence and expert opinion suggests that minimum sentences are poor public policy. The purported justification for minimum drug sentences is to deter crime and keep communities safe (the legislation was, after all, called the Safe Streets and Communities Act). But minimum sentences don't deter crime, nor do they assist in the rehabilitation and reintegration of offenders.[15]

Most importantly, minimum punishments have been found, time and time again,[16] to violate the Canadian Charter of Rights and Freedoms.[17] As an example, in February 2015, the British Columbia Supreme Court found

---

12 Although minimum sentences have been introduced by every government in recent history, the new Liberal government has announced that it intends to review the use of minimum sentences. However, the current government's stated intention to review minimum sentences has not yet resulted in a repeal.

13 S. Dhillon, "B.C. rights group says mandatory minimum sentences don't deter crime," *Globe and Mail*, 8 September 2014, <http://www.theglobeandmail.com/news/british-columbia/bc-rights-group-says-mandatory-minimum-sentences-dont-deter-crime/article20487562> accessed 10 July 2015.

14 *R. v. Dickey*, 2015 BCSC 191, upheld by the British Columbia Court of Appeal (*R. v. Dickey*, 2016 BCCA 177). The government argued that a disused, boarded-up school building triggered the imposition of a two-year minimum prison sentence. The Court rejected the government's submissions and struck down the minimum sentences imposed by section 5(3)(a)(ii)(A) and (C) of the Controlled Drugs and Substances Act as cruel and unusual punishment.

15 For example, see J.V. Roberts, *Mandatory Sentences of Imprisonment in Common law Jurisdictions: Some Representative Model* (Ottawa: Department of Justice, 2005), <http://www.justice.gc.ca/eng/rp-pr/csj-sjc/ccs-ajc/rr05_10/rr05_10.pdf> accessed 29 February 2016. The Roberts report found that: "Minimum sentences are not an effective sentencing tool: that is, they constrain judicial discretion without offering any increased crime prevention benefits. Nevertheless, mandatory sentences remain popular with some Canadian politicians."

16 See *R. v. Nur*, 2015 SCC 15; *R v Vu*, 2015 ONSC 7965; and *R. v. Smickle*, 2013 ONCA 678.

17 Constitution Act, 1982, being Schedule B to the Canada Act 1982 (UK), c 11.

the SCCA's minimum sentences to be unconstitutional.[18] The facts before the court were simple: Mr Dickey, a 27-year-old with no prior record for drug-related offences and no prior drug history with police, sold $100 of cocaine to an undercover police officer. He faced a minimum sentence of two years in prison.

Mr Dickey was addicted to cocaine. He started using drugs after a workplace accident that left him in constant pain. Immediately following his arrest, he took steps to beat his addiction and found productive employment. The court found that Mr Dickey was a small-scale, unsophisticated dealer, who committed the offence to support his own addiction.

In light of Mr Dickey's personal circumstances, the court found that the one-size-fits-all approach to sentencing advanced by minimum sentences amounted to cruel and unusual punishment; a punishment so beyond what would be proper or proportionate as to be grossly disproportionate. This was a damning finding given that in 1977, the Supreme Court of Canada described a cruel and unusual sentence as one that is "so excessive as to outrage standards of decency."[19]

The government was undoubtedly aware that punitive legislation that relies upon minimum sentences stood on shaky constitutional ground. One indication of the potential problem was communicated to the government in 2007 by the Parliamentary Information and Research Service Department, which prepared a detailed legislative summary with respect to mandatory minimum sentences for firearms offences. The legislative summary concluded that "mandatory minimum terms of imprisonment are generally inconsistent with the fundamental principle that a sentence must be proportionate to the gravity of the offence and the degree of responsibility of the offender, as they do not allow a judge to make any exception in an appropriate case." The summary went on to predict that "mandatory minimum sentences may constitute cruel and unusual punishment, in violation of the Canadian Charter of Rights and Freedoms."[20]

As it turns out, the Parliamentary Information and Research Service department was correct. Despite the Conservative government's best efforts (it spent almost $7 million defending unconstitutional laws),[21] minimum sentences for both drugs and firearms[22] have been found to violate the Charter.

---

18 *R. v. Dickey*, 2015 BCSC 191; 2015 BCSC 625 (s. 1 decision).

19 *R. v. Miller* [1977] 2 SCR 680 at 688.

20 Law and Government Division, Bill C-2: An Act to amend the Criminal Code and to Make Consequential Amendments to Other Acts (Legislative summary), 29 October 2007, <http://www.parl.gc.ca/About/Parliament/LegislativeSummaries/bills_ls.asp?source=library_prb&ls=C2&Parl=39&Ses=2&Language=E&Mode=1#part1> accessed 10 July 2015.

21 A. Minsky, "Conservatives spend almost $7M defending unconstitutional legislation," Global News, 17 June 2015, <http://globalnews.ca/news/2055556/conservatives-spend-almost-7m-defending-unconstitutional-legislation/> accessed 10 July 2015.

22 *R. v. Nur*, 2015 SCC 15.

The real fraud is that minimum sentences don't even deliver the benefits the government promises. Minimum sentences don't reduce crime and don't make for safer communities. This is contention has been supported by the Supreme Court of Canada, which, after a review of the criminological evidence, recognized that "empirical evidence suggests that mandatory minimum sentences do not, in fact, deter crimes."[23]

But again, the Conservative government should have known this. A study published in 2002 and referenced in government documents concluded that the existing research generally did not support the use of mandatory minimum sentences for the purpose of deterrence or for the purpose of reducing sentencing disparity.[24] The government was also made aware that one Canadian meta-analysis found little difference in general recidivism rates, regardless of length of incarceration or whether the offender was given a prison or community sanction. In fact, the study concluded that mandatory prison sentences actually produced slight increases in recidivism.[25]

Evidence may matter in court, but it apparently held little sway over former Prime Minister Stephen Harper government's policy choices. Under Conservative management, the Canadian government devoted ever-increasing resources to the prosecution and incarceration of individuals charged with drug offences. While crime rates have been falling, federal spending on punishment has risen to $2.7 billion – an increase of about a billion dollars since 2006.[26] The average cost of warehousing a federal inmate has increased from $88,000 in 2006 to more than $117,788 today.[27]

Obviously money spent on punishment is money not available for harm reduction, rehabilitation and crime prevention. However, the dangers of minimum sentences are much more pernicious than simple economics. Minimum sentences are a simplistic solution that end up disproportionately impacting already vulnerable and marginalized populations – including those who are struggling with substance abuse. A study conducted by British Columbia's Pivot Legal Society, which included extensive interviews with street drug users, concluded that the "path to recovery from drug dependence does

---

23 Ibid, para. 114.

24 T. Gabor and N. Crutcher, "Mandatory minimum penalties: Their effects on crime, sentencing disparities, and justice system expenditures," 2002, prepared for the Research and Statistics Division (Department of Justice Canada).

25 Public Works and Government Services Canada, "The Effects of Prison Sentences on Recidivism", 1999, Cat. No. J42-87/1999E, <http://www.publicsafety.gc.ca/cnt/rsrcs/pblctns/ffcts-prsn-sntncs-rcdvsm/index-eng.aspx> accessed 10 July 2015.

26 K. Mackrael, "Justice spending rising sharply as crime rates fall, budget watchdog warns," *Globe and Mail*, 20 March 2013, <http://www.theglobeandmail.com/news/politics/justice-spending-rising-sharply-as-crime-rates-fall-budget-watchdog-warns/article9983443/> accessed 14 May 2017.

27 M. Spratt, "Life behind bars: The politics of despair," *iPolitics*, 28 January 2015, <http://ipolitics.ca/2015/01/28/life-death-prison-and-the-politics-of-despair/> accessed 10 July 2015.

not involve a lengthy jail sentence. Instead, jail terms are disruptive life events that serve to further marginalize individuals and compound the very harms they ostensibly seek to eradicate."[28]

Like all of the former Conservative government's drug policies, minimum sentences are about politics, embodied by a simplistic tough-on-crime rhetoric. Any attempt to reform or modernize Canadian drug laws is met with partisan attacks and fundraising emails.[29] During the 2015 federal election, both the Liberal Party and the New Democratic Party of Canada indicated a willingness to consider the legalization or decriminalization of some drugs. Indeed, one of the Liberal Party's central campaign promises was to legalize, regulate and restrict access to marijuana.[30]

On 13 April 2017, the Liberal government introduced legislation to sort of legalize marijuana.[31] The legislation became law in October 2018, but not without criticism. Marijuana is still illegal in many circumstances. For example, youth are criminalized more than adults, the new legislation comes significant immigration consequences, and some worry that the reliance on police discretion will only further systemic discrimination.

But this is not why the Conservatives opposed the legislation. They could not resist falling back into their tough on crime rhetoric. In 2015, the former Conservative government responded to the Liberal's intention to legalize marijuana with partisan attacks delivered by the Parliamentary Secretary to the Minister of Public Safety and Emergency Preparedness, Roxanne James:

> Mr. Speaker, unlike the Liberal Party, we have been very clear. We have no intention of legalizing or decriminalizing marijuana. The chiefs of police have also been very clear that they do not support legalizing marijuana.
>
> Now that he has joined the Liberal Party, Bill Blair has flip-flopped and now wants to legalize marijuana, which would make it easier for children to smoke pot. Already he puts it on equal footing with alcohol and is already planning to, as he says "tax the thing" and "control the price."

---

28 S. Bernstein, "Throwing away the keys: The human and social cost of mandatory minimum sentences," *Pivot Legal Society*, 30 May 2013, <http://www.pivotlegal.org/throwing_away_the_keys_the_human_and> accessed 10 July 2015.

29 A 2013 Conservative fundraising email concluded with "support strong leadership – and stand up against Justin Trudeau's plan to bring more illegal drugs into our communities. Chip in $5 or more today and tell us you're with us." See A. Radia, "Harper Conservatives are still the best at raising money," *Yahoo*, 31 July 2013, <https://ca.news.yahoo.com/blogs/canada-politics/harper-conservatives-still-best-raising-money-175050301.html> accessed 10 July 2015.

30 Liberal Part of Canada Election Platform, 42nd General Election, 2015, <https://www.liberal.ca/realchange/marijuana/> accessed 29 February 2016.

31 Bill C-45, An Act Respecting Cannabis and to Amend the Controlled Drugs and Substances Act, the Criminal Code and Other Acts, 1nd Sess, 42st Parl, 2017, <http://www.parl.ca/DocumentViewer/en/42-1/bill/C-45/first-reading> accessed 20 July 2017.

> Unlike Mr. Blair and the Liberal Party, we do not intend to compromise on the safety of our youth. These drugs are illegal because of the harmful effects they have on users and on our society. One can only wonder how Mr. Blair can feel comfortable now that he belongs in the same basket as Liberal supporters such as drug-pushing Marc and Jodie Emery.[32]

The GCDP's report urged countries to rely on alternatives to incarceration for non-violent, low-level participants in illicit drug markets: "Governments devote ever-increasing resources to detecting, arresting and incarcerating people involved in illicit drug markets – with little or no evidence that such efforts reduce drug-related problems or deter others from engaging in similar activities."[33] Canada has taken a different approach in recent years, legislating punitive and mandatory sentencing regimes, misleading the public about the utility of minimum sentences and politicizing the debate by demonizing the opposition – all the while ignoring the disproportionate impact of the new laws on the poor and disadvantaged.

But the war on drugs and its associated harms do not end in a prison cell. The previous government widened the battlefield to include an attack on harm reduction sites and the health-care system – a foolish consistency is the hobgoblin of little minds.

3. INSITE: THE POLITICS OF HARM REDUCTION

There is no better microcosm of the harms associated with traditional drug policies than Vancouver's downtown eastside (DTES). The DTES is a small geographic area, only a few city blocks, yet it is home to more than 4,500 intravenous drug users. The personal histories of these users are tragic and yet sadly predictable: childhood physical and sexual abuse, mental illness, homelessness, disease and crime all colour their life histories.[34] There is no better descriptor of the lives of the DTES drug users than that offered by the Supreme Court: "Existence is bleak."[35]

These are the people most affected by punitive sentencing, but it is a safe bet that minimum sentences are the furthest things from their minds. Let's recall the disheartening survey of 1,000 DTES drug users cited by the court:

- an average of 15 years injecting drugs;
- the majority (51%) inject heroin and 32% inject cocaine;

---

32 *Edited Hansard*, 41st Parl, 2nd Sess, No 204 (30 April 2015).

33 Global Commission on Drug Policy, "Taking Control: Pathways to Drug Policies that Work," 2014, at 8.

34 *Canada (Attorney General) v. PHS Community Services Society*, 2011 SCC 44, paras. 7–8.

35 Ibid, para. 8.

- 87% are infected with the hepatitis C virus (HCV) and 17% with the human immunodeficiency virus (HIV);
- 20% are homeless and many more live in single-resident rooms;
- 80% have been incarcerated;
- 38% are involved in the sex trade;
- 21% are using methadone; and
- 59% have reported a non-fatal overdose in their lifetime.[36]

Fatal communicable diseases were at epidemic levels, fuelled by sharing dirty needles. Hundreds of overdose deaths were reported every year. A public health emergency was declared in 1997. This is the true face of the war on drugs.

So, in 2003, after years of planning and consultation, the Insite safe injection facility opened its doors. At Insite, intravenous drug users are provided with clean equipment, and trained nurses monitor their health and safety before and after injections. There is no spread of HIV or other diseases through dirty needles. There are also no deaths – despite 336 overdoses since 2006, there have been no fatalities.[37] Insite enjoyed the support of the community, perhaps since the surrounding area saw a decrease in crime.

Insite was a success story. The GCDP urged the adoption of measures that "focus on reducing both drug-related harms such as fatal overdoses, HIV/AIDS, hepatitis and other diseases as well as prohibition-related harms such as crime, violence, corruption, human rights violations, environmental degradation, displacement of communities, and the power of criminal organizations."[38] Insite was held as a positive example of the benefits of rethinking past drug policy.

And then the Conservative government shut Insite down. There was no special legislation or evidence-based decision-making; all it took was the stroke of a pen – or more accurately the lack of the Minister of Health's signature. Operating Insite required an exemption from the prohibitions of possession and trafficking of controlled substances under the Controlled Drugs and Substances Act.[39] In 2008, the Minister of Health refused to grant an exemption.

After three years of litigation (the federal government lost at every level of court at a cost of almost half a million dollars),[40] the Supreme Court of Canada found the Minister of Health's decision to be unreasonable. The Court not only found that Insite should have been granted an exemption, but also validated the positive benefits of harm reduction sites.

36 Ibid, para. 9.
37 Ibid, para. 141.
38 Global Commission on Drug Policy, "Taking Control: Pathways to Drug Policies that Work," 2014, at 7.
39 Controlled Drugs and Substances Act, SC 1996, c 19 s. 56.
40 M. Spratt, "The cost of unconstitutionality," 28 May 2015, <http://www.michaelspratt.com/law-blog/the-cost-of-unconstitutionality> accessed 10 July 2015.

The Supreme Court's decision was, however, not the end of the government's harm-reduction battle. The government's response was swift and typically partisan. The Conservative government first introduced Bill C-2, the Respect for Communities Act.[41] The legislation did little to address the problem identified by the Supreme Court (the government's unreasonable exercise of discretion to deny exemptions). Instead, the bill introduced 27 criteria that must be met before the government could even begin to consider a request for an exemption to operate an injection site. Even if all 27 criteria were met, the government could still say no. There was no mechanism in the legislation to ensure reasonableness.

The Canadian Medical Association characterized the 27 criteria as onerous[42] and Emmett Macfarlane, Associate Professor of Political Science at the University of Waterloo, concluded that "it's pretty obvious the federal government is intentionally making it as difficult as possible to get approval for new supervised-injection sites."[43] Bill C-2 is a pathway to "No," designed to frustrate injection site applications from ever even reaching the minister responsible for issuing exemptions.

Leaving aside the 27 criteria, the government's true intent was shown even more explicitly. The Supreme Court held that "where the evidence indicates that the site will decrease the risk of death and disease, and there is little or no evidence that it will have a negative impact on public safety, the Minister should generally grant an exemption."[44] But the preamble of Bill C-2 states that exemptions will only be granted in exceptional circumstances. There is a chasm of daylight between "generally grant" and "only in exceptional cases."

In the days that followed the introduction of Bill C-2, the government further clarified its thoughts on harm reduction in an email to party loyalists:

> Friend,
>
> Do you want a supervised drug consumption site in your community? These are facilities where drug addicts get to shoot up heroin and other illicit drugs.
>
> I don't want one anywhere near my home.

---

41 Bill C-2, An Act to Amend the Controlled Drugs and Substances Act, 2nd Sess, 41st Parl, 2013 (assented to 18 June 2015) SC 2015, c 22.

42 Senate, Standing Committee on Legal and Constitutional Affairs, Issue 31 (14 May 2015) (comments of Jeff Blackmer, Vice-President, Medical Professionalism, Canadian Medical Association), <http://www.parl.gc.ca/Content/SEN/Committee/412/lcjc/31ev-52140-e.htm?Language=E&Parl=41&Ses=2&comm_id=11> accessed 10 July 2015.

43 E. MacFarlane, "Denis Coderre vs. Ottawa on supervised-injection sites," Maclean's, 8 June 2015, <http://www.macleans.ca/politics/ottawa/coderre-vs-ottawa-on-supervised-injection-sites> accessed 10 July 2015.

44 *Canada (Attorney General) v. PHS Community Services Society*, 2011 SCC 44, para. 152.

> Yet, as I write this, special interests are trying to open up these supervised drug consumption sites in cities and towns across Canada – over the objections of local residents and law enforcement.
>
> We've had enough – that's why I am pleased the Harper government is acting to put the safety of our communities first.
>
> Today, the Harper government introduced tough new rules that will give local law enforcement, municipal leaders, and local residents a voice before a permit is granted for a supervised drug consumption site.
>
> The Trudeau Liberals and Mulcair NDP are against us. They want to repeat the experiment of Vancouver's Insite facility across the country – maybe even in your community.
>
> Because of the tough rules the Harper government introduced today, your voice will now matter.
>
> Add your name if you demand a say before a supervised drug consumption site is opened close to your family: http://www.conservative.ca/?page_id=3190
>
> Sincerely,
>
> Jenni Byrne
>
> National Campaign Manager, 2011[45]

The Conservative attacks continued in Parliament. Conservative MP Kellie Leitch called critics of the bill "pro-heroin."[46] Conservative MP Steven Fletcher explained the Conservatives' black-and-white approach to drug policy: "At the end of the day if people are breaking the law, they should face the consequences."[47] The Minister of Veteran Affairs, Julian Fantino, linked the issue of safe injection sites to international terrorism, saying that "the whole network of illicit drugs connects back to international organized crime and even some terrorist groups."[48]

Conservative Public Safety Minister Steven Blaney explained to the parliamentary committee considering Bill C-2 that he rejected the "radical pro-narcotic ideology" because safe injection sites "destabilize and disrupt an environment" and lead to an "increase in criminal activity and deterioration in quality of life."[49] Blaney's assertions stand in direct contrast to the

---

45 J. Byrne, Conservative Party of Canada email, 06 June 2013, <http://d3n8a8pro7vhmx.cloudfront.net/pivotlegal/pages/413/attachments/original/1370538270/CPC_email.pdf?1370538270> accessed 10 July 2015.

46 *Edited Hansard*, 41st Parl, 2nd Sess, No 003 (18 October 2013), at 1050 (Kellie Leitch).

47 *Edited Hansard*, 41st Parl, 2nd Sess, No 018 (18 November 2013), at 1225 (Steven Fletcher).

48 Ibid, at 1715 (Julian Fantino).

49 House of Commons, Standing Committee on Public Safety and National Security (2014 October 27) (Chair: Daryl Kramp).

evidence that was before the Supreme Court. Safe injection sites do not lead to increased crime, nor do they destabilize or lead to a poor environment. On the contrary, injection sites reduce crime, increase health and save lives.

The bills may change, but the Conservative song remained the same: legislation indicative of a punitive "war on drugs" mentality, partisan attacks and demonizing dissenting opinions. Evidence may matter in court, but not when it came to the government's outdated and harmful drug policies. In fighting to close Insite, just as in legislating punitive mandatory drug sentencing, the Conservative government exposed its adherence to an old and blind ideology and turned its back on the progress cited as a reason for optimism in the GCDP's report.

Clearly, at least for some in Canada, addicts belong either in jail or overdosing in a back alley. But again there is positive change in the air.

The new Liberal government, spurred into action by scores of Fentanyl deaths, introduced and passed legislation to reverse much of Bill C-2 resulting in new safe consumption sites.[50] There can be no question that the reversal of the Conservative legislation is a positive step toward rational drug policy. There is also no question that the death of many vulnerable Canadians can be laid at the feet of the previous government.

4. MEDICAL HEROIN AND POISONED POLITICS

In its report, the GCDP highlighted the Canadian medical trial of heroin-assisted therapy as a positive step toward more humane and effective drug strategies. Canada's experience with therapeutic heroin treatments was actually referenced in the GCDP's recommendations.[51] As with safe injections sites, perhaps this was a kiss of death.

In a 2014 speech to the Canadian Medical Association, Health Minister Rona Ambrose said, without a hint of irony, that Prime Minister Stephen Harper and his government are firm believers in evidence-based policy.[52] Ambrose claimed that "at the end of the day, for policymakers like me, it's the medical science and data-based evidence that must guide our decisions on health sector regulation and allocation of resources."[53]

---

50 S. Lunn, "Government agrees to make changes bill on supervised drug-injection site," *CBC*, 12 May 2017, <http://www.cbc.ca/news/politics/safe-injections-safe-injections-bill-amendments-1.4112252> accessed 14 May 2017.

51 Global Commission on Drug Policy, "Taking Control: Pathways to Drug Policies that Work," 2014, at 14.

52 W. Kondro, "Conservatives on health: Evidence-based and activist, Ambrose says," *iPolitics*, 8 August 2014, <http://ipolitics.ca/2014/08/18/conservatives-on-health-evidence-based-and-activist-ambrose-says> accessed 10 July 2015.

53 Ibid.

And that is precisely the type of decision-making process that is encouraged by the GCDP's report. Unfortunately, it stands in sharp contrast to the previous federal government's policy decisions. Actions speak louder than words.

In October 2013, a month after the publication of the GCDP's report, Ambrose announced that the Canadian government would no longer allow doctors to prescribe medicinal heroin, LSD, ecstasy or other illegal narcotics under Health Canada's Special Access Program.[54] Speaking with the Canadian Broadcasting Corporation, she claimed that there was no proof that therapeutic heroin treatment was effective:

> There is no evidence at this point that heroin … giving heroin to heroin addicts … is any way an effective treatment … As I said, there is no evidence that this is an effective, safe treatment … no clinical evidence … There is no clear evidence to suggest that this a safe treatment and it's not a good idea for Health Canada to be supporting giving heroin to heroin addicts when there's no scientific evidence that this is a safe treatment.[55]

Ambrose's position was adopted by the government and incorporated into the 2013 speech from the throne: "Canadian families expect safe and healthy communities in which to raise their children … Our Government will … close loopholes that allow for the feeding of addiction under the guise of treatment."[56]

In reality, there is copious evidence supporting the use of medical-grade opiates to treat addiction. In 2012, the European Monitoring Centre for Drug and Drug Addiction (EMCDDA) released a 176-page study on the use of doctor-supervised medicinal heroin:

> Over the past 15 years, six RCTs have been conducted involving more than 1,500 patients, and they provide strong evidence, both individually and collectively, in support of the efficacy of treatment with fully supervised self-administered injectable heroin, when compared with oral MMT, for long-term refractory heroin-dependent individuals. These have been conducted in six countries: Switzerland (Perneger et al., 1998); the Netherlands (van den Brink et al., 2003); Spain (March et al., 2006); Germany (Haasen et al., 2007), Canada (Oviedo-Joekes et al., 2009) and England (Strang et al., 2010).

---

54 Health Canada, "Heroin and other dangerous drugs are banned from Health Canada's Special Access Programme – Government of Canada puts safety and security of Canadians first and focuses on treatment and recovery, " Government of Canada, press release, 3 October 2013, <http://news.gc.ca/web/article-en.do?nid=778019> accessed 10 July 2015.

55 "Research for heroin addiction," *CBC Power and Politics*, 4 October 2013, <http://www.cbc.ca/player/News/Politics/ID/2410478140> accessed 10 July 2015.

56 Government of Canada, "Speech from the throne," 41st Parl, 2nd Sess, 16 October 2013, <http://speech.gc.ca/eng/full-speech> accessed 10 July 2015.

> Patients receiving SIH treatment achieved gains in physical and mental health, as well as social functioning, although improvements in those receiving SIH were not consistently or significantly superior to the control group across all trials, particularly in relation to psychosocial functioning.
>
> Reductions in the criminal activity of SIH patients were evident and were substantially greater when compared with patients under control conditions. Retention in treatment varied substantially across the trials. The available evidence suggests added value of SIH alongside supplementary doses of methadone for long-term treatment-refractory opioid users.
>
> Furthermore, efficacy of heroin provision as a treatment modality on several outcomes (retention, mortality) was corroborated by a systematic review conducted by the Cochrane Group. Although the inclusion criteria of studies in the latter review were stricter from a methodological point of view, converging conclusions on the efficacy of SIH further strengthens the current evidence of this. However, it is important to note that more serious adverse events have been reported to occur in patients receiving SIH than oral methadone. This suggests that SIH may be less safe and therefore require more resources and clinical attention in order to manage greater safety issues.
>
> Finally, countries that have conducted longer term (up to six years) follow-up studies have seen a high retention in SIH (55% at two years and 40% at six years), with patients sustaining gains in reduced "street" heroin use and marked improvements in social functioning (e.g. stable housing, drug-free social contacts and increased rate of employment).[57]

The results of the EMCDDA should have been predictable to Canada. In 2008, the North American Opiate Medication Initiative (NAOMI) evaluated the effectiveness of heroin-assisted treatment (HAT) in the Canadian context. NAOMI concluded that, when compared to patients engaged with traditional methadone treatment, HAT patients were 62% more likely to remain in treatment. Importantly, the study found that collateral harms associated with drug use – for example, external criminality – decreased by 40%.[58] That's the evidence, albeit inconvenient evidence from the government's point of view. Ignoring that evidence causes harm.

In May 2014, the Supreme Court of British Columbia granted an injunction against the government policy and restored patients' access to the treatment.[59] As part of that hearing, Dr. Evan Wood, a specialist in internal medicine,

---

57 European Monitoring Centre for Drugs and Drug Addiction, "New heroin-assisted treatment," 2012, <http://www.emcdda.europa.eu/publications/insights/heroin-assisted-treatment> accessed 10 July 2015.

58 E. Oviedo-Joekes et al., "The North American Opiate Medication Initiative (NAOMI): Profile of participants in North America's first trial of heroin-assisted treatment" (2008) 85(6) *Journal of Urban Health* 812.

59 *Providence Health Care Society v. Canada (Attorney General)*, 2014 BCSC 936.

epidemiology and addiction medicine, detailed the harms associated with Severe Opioid Disorder (a term used in the latest edition of the *Diagnostic and Statistical Manual of Mental Disorders*). According to Dr. Wood, opioid use disorder is associated with "a range of health and community concerns, including compulsive drug-seeking behaviour, infectious diseases and related risk behaviors (e.g., used syringe sharing, sex-trade involvement), fatal overdose and drug acquisition crime." Although not an expert in criminology, Dr. Wood also stated the obvious: illegal drug use contributes to the often violent illegal drug market and fuels organized crime syndicates.

Dr. Wood indicated that research suggests that when heroin treatment is abruptly discontinued, the majority of patients (in excess of 80%) will experience a severe health deterioration that places them at immediate risk of serious harm or death.

The court accepted Dr. Wood's evidence and, in granting an injunction, found that the government's decision to eliminate Health Canada's Special Access Program would result in harms that would be "clearly irreparable in nature."[60]

Again, the Conservatives responded with partisan attacks. On the Conservative Party of Canada website, under the title of "stop giving heroin to addicts," the Conservatives claimed that: "If the NDP or Liberals are elected in 2015, you can bet they would make this heroin-for-addicts program permanent. We can't let that happen. We'll keep fighting to keep our streets and communities safe, but we need your support."[61]

And just as there is no evidence that minimum sentences keep the streets safe or that safe injection sites increase crime, there is zero evidence that the Special Access Program endangered the safety of communities.

And then the new government overturned the Conservative ban on medical heroin.[62] Perhaps a bit of a trend can be noticed. The Liberal government took some political heat for its decision. Drug policy has always been used as a political wedge. In the end there was little lasting controversy, but undoubtedly there will be lasting positive results.

5. AN APPETITE FOR CHANGE

In Canada, suburban kids are killed over pot while life-long addicts overdose in back allies. Communicable diseases are spread through dirty needles and

---

60 Ibid, para 74.

61 Conservative Party of Canada, "Stop giving heroin to addicts," 22 September 2013, <http://www.conservative.ca/stop-giving-heroin-to-addicts/> accessed 10 July 2015.

62 A. Woo, "Health Canada overturns ban on medical heroin," Globe and Mail, 13 May 2016, <http://www.theglobeandmail.com/news/national/health-canada-proposes-to-allow-doctor-requests-to-prescribe-heroin/article30020597> accessed 14 May 2017.

the most serious addicts are denied treatments that have been proven to work. While an ever-increasing number of American states legalize marijuana, Canada has legislated increased minimum jail sentences. Over the last ten years, arrests for possession of marijuana have increased by 28%.[63]

The Conservative government fought for minimum sentences and lost. They tried to shut down Insite and lost. They tried to cancel the Special Access Program and lost. The common thread in all of these cases is the wilful ignorance of evidence that contradicted the previous government's ideology. The other commonality in all of these cases is the predictable partisan attacks.

The Conservative government turned its back on the international community and abandoned any pretence of evidence-based policy decisions. Indeed, there has been no more fictitious a statement than Rona Ambrose claiming that Conservative policy is guided by evidence. A seemingly unlimited amount of resources are expended fighting a losing war. But this gives the government too much credit. Canadian drug policy is not a war; it is a political wedge. While the government plays politics, lives are ruined and communities are put at risk.

The Toronto three may be serving a life sentence for killing Michael Swan, but the hands of the previous Conservative government are by no means clean of the harms associated with drug crime. But there is reason for optimism.

Canadian courts have resisted the government's unconstitutional measures at every step. Most recently, the Federal Court[64] declared that medical marijuana users have the constitutional right to consume the drug in ways other than smoking. Until recently, government policy required even young epileptic children to *smoke* their medicine, but no more.[65]

Predictably the Minister of Health (as she then was) Rona Ambrose's response was "outrage" at the Court's decisions, accusing them of steering young people toward marijuana use in the same fashion as Liberal Prime Minister Justin Trudeau.[66]

In early 2016, the Federal Court also struck down a Conservative law that would prohibit medical marijuana users from growing their own medicine

---

63 Statistics Canada, "Police-reported drug-related offences in Canada, 2013," 25 June 2015, <http://www.statcan.gc.ca/daily-quotidien/150625/dq150625b-eng.htm"> accessed 10 July 2015.

64 *Allard v. Canada*, 2016 FC 236.

65 "Thornhill parents treating epileptic daughter with marijuana oil," *CBC News*, 10 May 2015, <http://www.cbc.ca/news/canada/toronto/thornhill-parents-treating-epileptic-daughter-with-marijuana-oil-1.3068592> accessed 10 July 2015.

66 S. Fine, "Health Minister 'outraged' by Supreme Court ruling on medical marijuana," Globe and Mail, 11 June 2015, <http://www.theglobeandmail.com/news/national/medical-marijuana-users-can-bake-it-not-just-smoke-it-high-court-rules/article24912888> accessed 10 July 2015.

and would require them to purchase medicinal marijuana from authorized distributors at highly inflated costs.[67]

The current Liberal government's attitude toward drug policy certainly represents a marked departure from the rhetoric of the last ten years. It may be better to characterize the Liberal government's position as a systematic dismantling of the previous government's regressive drug policy: legal marijuana, more generous approvals of safe consumption sites and the reinstituting of medical heroin treatment. The previous government must be rolling over in its still-warm grave.

Perhaps the biggest danger to Canadian drug policy is the temptation to fall into the trap of complacency born of a comparative analysis of the Liberal and Conservative drug policy.

For example the Liberals have rejected calls to expunge the records of people criminalized for marijuana offences, preferring weaker pardon legislation. And even in this they have dragged their feet. A progressive policy on marijuana going forward does little for the almost half-million Canadians, a disproportionate number of whom are minorities, who have already been charged and convicted with possession of marijuana for personal use.[68] And then there is the decriminalization of other drugs. The Liberal government has constantly rejected calls to remove possession of hard drugs from the Criminal Code.

Just because the previous government set the bar so low, the current government should not be given a free pass. The Liberal government has done better than its predecessor, but there is still a wide margin for improvement.

We must always seek to do better if Canada is to see fewer lives destroyed, fewer Michael Swans and fewer young men like the Toronto three falling victim to the harms of drug use and drug crime.

---

67 *Allard v. Canada*, 2016 FC 236.

68 J.P. Tasker, "Tens of thousands of Canadians could soon be eligible for a pot pardon, but lawyers warn about limitations", 18 October 2018, <https://www.cbc.ca/news/politics/tasker-pot-pardons-limitations-1.4866610> accessed 12 November 2018.

UNACCOMPANIED CHILDREN OUT OF THEIR COUNTRY OF ORIGIN

Trapped in the Administrative Net

Pablo ESPINIELLA*

Ten years have passed since the Convention on the Rights of the Child, the almost universally ratified international human rights treaty, came of age.[1] The Convention constitutes the main and unchallenged normative standard on the rights of the child and their protection throughout the world. It applies to all children irrespective of their nationality or migration status. On that occasion, Louise Arbour, then United Nations High Commissioner for Human Rights, pointed out that the Convention had brought a global understanding that girls and boys are not the property of their parents or guardians, or objects of generosity or goodwill, but the subjects of rights, as are adults. Certainly, it has

* The views expressed in this chapter are those of the author and do not necessarily reflect the views of the United Nations.

1 Convention on the Rights of the Child, 20 November 1989, 1577 UNTS 3 (entered into force on 2 September 1990), in line with its Article 49. At the moment of finalization of this contribution, the Convention had been ratified by 196 states.

led to a major change in the way children should and must be treated, with rights and responsibilities appropriate to their age.[2]

Similarly, there has been a marked change in access to information on the effective protection of children worldwide, and on the progress and challenges in ensuring absolute respect for the provisions of the Convention at the national level. The establishment and work of the Committee on the Rights of the Child, created with the entry into force of the treaty and which monitors the observance of the Convention by states parties, has played a critical role during the last almost 30 years. The Committee has unpacked the rights enshrined in the Convention through its general comments and has identified the precise actions required by states parties[3] to guarantee those rights and to respond to the great challenges that are still faced in the effective protection of the human rights of children, in their capacity, as Arbour noted, as rights holders.

On the day the treaty turned 18, Arbour stated that it was essential to continue emphasizing the universality of human rights at the same time as the universal respect for the standards established in the Convention on the Rights of the Child. This premise resonates with particular emphasis and force today in the face of the events that we observe every day, with millions of migrants and refugees making their way to Europe crossing the Mediterranean, in the northern triangle of Central America and the seas of Asia – in short, around the entire planet in the context of large-scale movements that are mixed in character.[4]

The UN General Assembly has recognized the complexity of the reasons inherent in the current movement of persons. People are moving in search of new economic opportunities or escaping armed conflict, poverty, hunger, persecution and even in response to the adverse effects of climate change

---

2 Louise Arbour, UN High Commissioner for Human Rights, "Happy Birthday" in *18 Candles: The Convention on the Rights of the Child Reaches Majority, Happy Birthday* (Sion: Institut International des Droits des Enfants, 2009).

3 Office of the United Nations High Commissioner for Human Rights (OHCHR), Committee on the Rights of the Child, *General Comment No 5 on General Measures of Implementation of the Convention on the Rights of the Child*, 34th Sess, UN Doc. CRC/GC/2003/527, November 2003, at para 20: "welcomes the incorporation of the Convention into domestic law, which is the traditional approach to the implementation of international human rights instruments in some but not in all States. Incorporation should mean the provisions of the Convention can be directly invoked before the courts and applied by national authorities and that the Convention will prevail where there is a conflict with domestic legislation or common practice."

4 Zeid Ra'ad Al Hussein, UN High Commissioner for Human Rights, "Speech delivered at the High-level plenary meeting on addressing large movements of refugees and migrants," 3rd plenary meeting of the UN General Assembly, 71st Sess, 19 September 2016.

and natural disasters. These movements also occur in a context of great precariousness and insecurity due to the lack of appropriate mechanisms and procedures to ensure human rights protection throughout the process. As a result, the vulnerability faced by millions of people raises serious concerns.[5]

Despite the increasing recognition of the need to respect human rights during these mixed movements of people, public policies that should give effect to these norms often shy away from such a noble end. This occurs in the face of the pressure and challenges that these movements sometimes represent. These policies, which are often justified on questionable concerns of national sovereignty and security, are also influenced by migration regulations that result in a limitation of the rights guaranteed by international obligations.[6] Moreover, in states where rights for children are guaranteed even at the constitutional level, the protection is not always forthcoming for unaccompanied and separated children.

The challenges encountered by many states in the face of a major immigration crisis are undeniable. It is also undeniable that it is in such critical situations that the rule of law and its responses can demonstrate the strength of the pillars upon which it has been erected. I argue here that the advances achieved in the protection of children and childhood are often opposed to the gap in the protection of unaccompanied children or those separated from their relatives in the migration process.

Although there have been significant developments in numerous states enabling us to understand the magnitude of this phenomenon, particularly regarding data collection, it is still impossible to know the exact number of unaccompanied and separated children in transit or countries of destination with certainty. Significant progress has been made in particular over the past five years to record the presence of unaccompanied and separated children, either through asylum and refugee petition records or the records of foreign children subject to protection. However, when they exist, the information and data still continue to be fragmented and poorly disaggregated. What many states and institutions working on the issue have recognized is the exponential growth in recent years in the movement of unaccompanied and separated children across all regions.

The specific situation of children separated from their parents, but not necessarily from any member of their family in the broad sense, poses another major challenge. These minors are often registered as unaccompanied, but

5 New York Declaration for Refugees and Migrants, GA Res 71/1, UNGAOR, 71 Sess, UN Doc. A/RES/71/1, 3 October 2016.

6 UN Secretary General, *In Safety and Dignity: Addressing Large Movements of Refugees and Migrants*, UNGAOR, 70th Sess, UN Doc. A/70/59 (21 April 2016).

their situation also implies specific and additional protection issues. Generally, their situation is often not captured either by the "radars" of the general child protection mechanisms. The legal situation of children in both situations, unaccompanied or separated, does not really differ. What is different in both cases are the circumstances in which they reach the states of transit and destination. Therefore, special attention should also be given to the condition and circumstances of separated children. In the last few years, several regional and national human rights institutions have also made progress in understanding their particular situation and specific protection needs.

Moreover, significant legislative progress in providing strong guarantees for the protection of children and adolescents in general has been recorded, for example, by the Committee on the Rights of the Child through its concluding observations after consideration of the state party reports. However, in general practice, we find that when it comes to unaccompanied and separated children, the challenges and violation of their rights question the effectiveness of the general advances achieved for child protection. Despite the adoption of measures such as the presumption of the minority of age in order to avoid situations of vulnerability upon interception of the child or the immediate assignment of a tutor or guardian, the lack of effective implementation of these measures represents a great concern for the effective protection of these children.[7]

The role that the courts should and must play as the ultimate guarantor of rights in light of these challenges is critical. Ensuring the right to legal assistance from the moment of reception of these children and throughout the entire process of establishment of protection measures is of the utmost importance. It is also essential to ensure respect of the right of the child to have his or her voice heard, which is particularly relevant when the age determination process (a main focus of this contribution) is involved. The complexity of the issues that occur in connection with age determination processes today, particularly identifying who establishes and defines the best interests of these minors,[8] makes it particularly important to apply multidisciplinary approaches that allow the least possible margin of error because, in the end, the future and in many cases the life of the minor are at stake.[9]

Several questions are particularly pertinent at this time. Have the international standards of protection been applied uniformly and without discrimination to all children on the same territory? Are regulations applied selectively, rendering

---

7 Save the Children, *Children on the Move: A Crisis in the Northern Triangle, Mexico and USA* (Panama City: Save the Children, 2016).

8 Philip Alston and Bridget Gilmour-Walsh, *The Best Interests of the Child: Towards a Synthesis of Children's Rights and Cultural Voices* (Florence: UNICEF, International Child Development Centre, 1996).

9 European Council on Refugees and Exiles (ECRE), *Right to Justice; Quality Legal Assistance for Unaccompanied Children – Comparative Report* (ECRE, July 2014).

ineffective the fundamental principle of the treaty that ensures universal application to all children when it comes to unaccompanied and separated children? Have we departed from the achievements that Arbour pointed out and, in the case of unaccompanied minors, have we failed to observe, first, what their rights are as children and, second, what is needed for their effective protection regardless of their migration situation?

This chapter offers insights that may provide some answers to these questions. It sheds some light on a series of good practices that have proven efficient to continue offering guarantees and protection of the rights of these children in the face of large mixed movements of people. To this effect, it discusses the lack of legal protection faced by tens of thousands of unaccompanied children that have been separated from their families around the world, both in countries of transit and of destination, because their status as migrants usually prevails over that of their condition of minors.

Taking into account one of the issues that has emerged in recent years as a crucial first step toward the establishment of a gateway for protection services – "age determination" – this chapter also highlights the challenges that are faced for the effective protection of unaccompanied and separated children on equal terms with their peers in transit and host countries.

Although these reflections and the arguments put forward take account of situations present in all regions of the world, special attention is paid to the challenges and opportunities within the European Union. The situation of unaccompanied and separated children in the northern triangle of Central America[10] and the protection challenges they face is also spurring the attention of transit and destination countries.[11] Unaccompanied or separated children are undoubtedly at the centre of the greatest protection challenges today in the context of large mixed movements of people.[12]

10 "Migration crisis: The thorn in the side of Europe and North America," *The Prisma* (27 March 2017).

11 The Secretary General of the Organization of American States, Mr José Miguel Insulza, on the launching of the Declaration on Central American Unaccompanied Child Migrants in July 2014, explained that the General Secretariat has had two fundamental concerns on the issue of unaccompanied and separated children: "first the general way of addressing the crisis in some sectors, that have wanted to transform this into a national security issue" and, second, "the need to guarantee due process to the children in the framework of the procedures that are established by internal and international norms."

12 The United Nations Special Rapporteurs on the Human Rights of Migrants have been alerting others to the challenging situation of unaccompanied and separated children in all their reports to the UN Commission on Human Rights and the Human Rights Council. For references, see, for example, Jorge Bustamante (Special Rapporteur on the Human Rights of Migrants), *Promotion and Protection of All Human Rights, Civil, Political, Economic, Social and Cultural Rights, Including the Right to Development*, UNGAOR, 11th Sess, UN Doc. A/HRC/11/7 (14 May 2009); and François Crépeau (Special Rapporteur on the Human Rights of Migrants), *Report of the Special Rapporteur on the Human Rights of Migrants*, UNGAOR, 71st Sess, UN Doc. A/71/285 (4 August 2016).

1. CHILDREN OR MIGRANTS?

1.1. THE INTERNATIONAL LEGAL FRAMEWORK

The Universal Declaration of Human Rights provides in Article 1 that "all human beings are born free and equal in dignity and rights," establishing that the only condition is that of being human. This is a key element to find a definition of the legal status of unaccompanied and separated children outside of their country of origin that does not entail any discrimination aggravating their situation and further undermining their rights. Therefore, the first question is whether these children are considered as children as a primary consideration or if, on the contrary, their status as a migrant prevails.

The Committee on the Rights of the Child defines unaccompanied children outside of their country of origin as "children, who have been separated from both parents and other relatives and are not being cared for by an adult who, by law or custom, is responsible for doing so." The Committee also defines separated children as "children who have been separated from both parents, or from their previous legal or customary primary caregiver, but not necessarily from other relatives. These may, therefore, include children accompanied by other adult family members."[13] In both cases, the definition is in line with Article 1 of the Convention. This is also the definition applicable in the European Union.[14] It is also used by the Inter-American Court of Human Rights.[15] The condition of being outside of their country of origin or, in the case of stateless persons, the country of habitual residence is a key element to be taken into account within these definitions.

Four main principles govern the application and interpretation of all the rights in the treaty. These principles are non-discrimination;[16] the best interests of the child;[17] the right to life and development;[18] and the respect of the child's opinion and views in all aspects affecting them.[19] As Bruce Abramson notes in

---

13 OHCHR, Committee on the Rights of the Child, *General Comment No 6, Treatment of Unaccompanied and Separated Children*, 39th Sess, UN Doc. CRC/GC/2005/6, 1 September 2005, at paras 7–8.

14 EC, Council Directive 2001/55/EC of 20 July 2001 on minimum standards for giving temporary protection in the event of a mass influx of displaced persons and on measures promoting a balance of efforts between Member States in receiving such persons and bearing the consequences thereof [2001] OJ L212/12.

15 *Rights and Guarantees of Children in the Context of Migration and/or in Need of International Protection (The Argentine Republic, the Federative Republic of Brazil, the Republic of Paraguay and the Oriental Republic of Uruguay)* (2014), Advisory Opinion OC-21/14, Inter-Am Ct HR (Ser A) No 21.

16 Convention on the Rights of the Child, *supra* note 1, at Article 2.

17 Ibid, at Article 3.1.

18 Ibid, at Article 6.

19 Ibid, at Article 12.

his Commentary on Article 2 of the Convention, these four principles are like the front wheel of a child's bicycle.[20]

This internationally accepted definition moves away from appreciations that could be discriminatory or detrimental for the effective protection of these children, which would be the case when using terms such as "undocumented" or "irregular." Such connotations further increase the risks of social exclusion and discrimination. The situation of irregularity or regularity of a person outside of his or her country of origin is not an absolute and innate condition to that person, but an administrative circumstance that changes or can change.[21] Terminology that can be utilized to further deepen the vulnerabilities of the most unprotected, marginalized and excluded persons of our societies should be avoided.

Although in most cases unaccompanied and separated children in both Central America and the European Union are in the 14–17 age range, all persons under the age of 18 are children and, as such, are protected by the same rights and should be provided the same protection.[22] The European Parliament's resolution of 2013 on the situation of unaccompanied minors was pioneering on this matter by confirming that an unaccompanied and separated child outside of his or her country of origin is "above all a child who is potentially in danger and that child protection, rather than immigration policies, must be the leading principle for Member States and the European Union when dealing with them, thus respecting the core principle of the child's best interests."[23]

The need to reaffirm that these unaccompanied minors are first and foremost children might be seen as unnecessary when observing the number of ratifications of the Convention and the legislative developments that have occurred in these almost 30 years. However, one of the first challenges unaccompanied and separated children experience today is precisely that of their recognition as children in the first place. In its recently issued Joint General Comment on the general principles regarding the human rights of children in the context of international migration, the Committee firmly stresses that States should ensure that these children are treated as children.[24] In some

---

20 Bruce Abramson, *A Commentary on the United Nations Convention on the Rights of the Child, Article 2: The Right of Non-discrimination* (Leiden: Brill Online Books and Journals, 2008).

21 Raquel Fuentes Sanchez, "Menores Extranjeros no Acompañados" (2014) 3 *International Review of Social Work and Welfare*, at 105–106.

22 Convention on the Rights of the Child, *supra* note 1, at Article 2. The Convention applies to all children, whatever their race, religion or abilities; whatever they think or say, whatever type of family they come from. It doesn't matter where children live, what language they speak, what their parents do, whether they are boys or girls, what their culture is, whether they have a disability or whether they are rich or poor. No child should be treated unfairly on any basis.

23 EC, *European Parliament Resolution on the Situation of Unaccompanied Minors in the European Union 2012/2263 (INI)* [2013] P7_TA(2013)0387, 12 September 2013.

24 Committee on the Rights of the Child and Committee on the Protection of the Rights of all Migrant Workers and Members of their Families, Joint *General Comment No 3 (16 November 2017), General Principles Regarding the Human Rights of Children in the Context of International Migration.*

regions, age determination processes are increasingly becoming the cornerstone for the delivery or not of the effective protection services for children. In these processes, the four above-mentioned principles are often disregarded. Regrettably, migration policies therefore often take precedence.[25]

1.2. RECOGNITION OF THE PHENOMENON

The situation of unaccompanied and separated children and the challenges they face in the enjoyment and protection of their rights have certainly become increasingly visible over the last five years. This interest includes a need to better understand the magnitude of the phenomenon in order to offer durable solutions. Studies on the impact of this phenomenon and its ramifications within a rights-based approach have advanced, particularly in the European Union and the northern triangle region in Central America. The situation of separated children and the specific concerns and challenges in their effective protection has also received increased attention.[26]

These positive developments contrast with actions in practice when migratory and security measures take precedence over the existing frameworks for child protection. Although in theory they are identified as rights holders, in practice their immigration status is often the one determining their access or not to guaranteed rights for all the children in the territory of the country. Separated children are sometimes registered as accompanied by an adult without an in-depth analysis of the relationship between them, which could be abusive or inappropriate to the type of protection the child requires.

In recent years, the European Union has taken a number of legislative measures, including the above-mentioned directive and the adoption of a Plan of Action (2011–2014),[27] which together with other legislative developments on refuge and asylum have attempted to provide a general uniform framework for the protection of unaccompanied children in the territory of the European Union. The implementation of the Action Plan has been an important step forward in the efforts to harmonize, inter alia, the reception and protection systems in the member states.

---

25 Jorge Bustamante (Special Rapporteur on the Human Rights of Migrants), *Promotion and Protection of All Human Rights, Civil, Political, Economic, Social and Cultural Rights, including the Right to Development*, *supra* note 12.

26 European Union Agency for Fundamental Rights, *Current Migration Situation in the EU: Separated Children* (Vienna: European Union Agency for Fundamental Rights, December 2016).

27 EC, Commission, *Communication from Commission to the European Parliament and the Council – Action Plan on Unaccompanied Minors (20102–014) (SEC(2010)534)* (Brussels: EC, 6 May 2010). The Action Plan was launched to provide concrete responses to the arrival of unaccompanied minors in territory of the European Union and its Member States, while fully respecting the rights of the child and the principle of the best interests of the child.

This increased interest radically contrasts with the challenges that unaccompanied and separated children still face in practice. It is not always clear for states and relevant institutions how to deal with the complex legal frameworks that the particular situations of these children entail and to ensure that these minors are treated as children in the first place. This is an issue where national human rights institutions play an important role by drawing attention to the issue and proposing solutions for a rights-based approach that could guarantee the rights of these children.

The National Human Rights Commission of Mexico, for example, in its recent report on the challenges facing Central American unaccompanied children in the context of migration, reveals through diagnosis a first assessment of the vulnerabilities that these children face during their transit and stay in Mexico.[28] The report analyses the path that the management of the situation of unaccompanied children can take depending on the approach applied by child protection authorities or, on the contrary, by the authorities and institutions responsible for migration policy and management. It also refers to the specific protection challenges faced by separated children and, in particular, the importance of the early assignment of a guardian.[29]

Over the last five years, the European Parliament has also been drawing attention to the importance of monitoring this phenomenon. Acknowledging the difficulties faced by thousands of unaccompanied and separated children in the enjoyment of their rights, the European Parliament called in 2013 for the development of guidelines reflecting the legal basis and situation of unaccompanied and separated children in the territory of the European Union. The objective of these guidelines was to facilitate the implementation of a harmonized protection framework contributing to the reinforcement of the effective protection of the rights of these minors. Since then, numerous initiatives and projects have been launched supporting the legislative development, including data collection, as well as identifying good practices which could encourage states to undertake efforts to enhance protection at the national level. However, the recent decision by the European Union not to renew its Action Plan and the slow pace in the development of a pledged strategy accurately responding to the current challenges can be seen as a decline in the interest and attention paid to this issue. This is particularly challenging now, when this effort is most needed in the region.

Let's just take a moment to reflect on some figures and facts. The number of unaccompanied and separated children arriving in the territory of the

28 National Human Rights Commission of Mexico, *Report on the Situation of the Unaccompanied Children from Central America in the Context of International Migration and their Transit through Mexico, in Need of International Protection* (October 2016).

29 Committee on the Rights of the Child, *General Comment No 6, Treatment of Unaccompanied and Separated Children, supra* note 13, at para 21.

European Union, despite the difficulties in providing reliable data, has grown exponentially in the last three years. In 2015, according to Eurostat, 88,300 asylum seekers in the Member States of the European Union were considered unaccompanied children, compared to 23,000 in 2014. Clearly, these statistics do not include those who arrived but did not apply for asylum.[30]

In the current situation – called migratory crisis by European leaders – the High Commissioner for Refugees estimated that by the end of December 2015, almost one million refugees and migrants would have tried their luck in a desperate attempt to reach Europe, many of them children. In Sweden alone, by the end of November 2015, some 35,500 unaccompanied children had arrived in the country, more than twice as many as in 2014.[31] In Spain, for example, 3,341 unaccompanied children were registered in 2015,[32] while in Italy, 3,133 unaccompanied children had been registered in May 2016.[33] Countries such as Syria, Afghanistan, Eritrea, Somalia, Pakistan and regions such as sub-Saharan Africa are the majority of countries and regions of origin of these children.[34] According to the Office of the United Nations High Commissioner for Refugees, from September 2015 to February 2016, around 340 children drowned in the Mediterranean when trying to cross by sea either with their families or alone.[35]

The confirmation in the summer of 2014 of the presence of more than 59,000 unaccompanied and separated children in the United States, coming mostly from Central America, inevitably caused alarm in the region due to the protection challenges faced by these children. According to information from the High Commissioner for Refugees, in the Central American region 48% of the children who embarked on this journey did so as a result of violence and 29.2% for economic reasons linked to situations of poverty and exclusion. Many of the children heading north are indigenous from the poorest areas of the region; Honduras, Guatemala, El Salvador and Mexico being the main countries of origin of minors.[36]

---

30 Statistical office of the European Union (EUROSTAT), *Report on Unaccompanied Minors Claiming Asylum in EU Member States in 2015* (EUROSTAT, 19 May 2016).

31 Human Rights Watch, *Seeking Refuge, Unaccompanied Children in Sweden* (HRW, 9 June 2016).

32 *Memoria de la Fiscalia de España* (Madrid: Centro de Estudios Jurídicos, Ministerio de Justicia, 2015).

33 House of Lords, European Union Committee, *Children in Crisis: Unaccompanied Migrant Children in the EU* (Authority of the House of Lords, 26 July 2016).

34 UNHCR, *Global Trends Forced Displacement, 2015* (UNHCR, 20 June 2016).

35 See UNHCR, UNICEF, IOM (Joint Statement), "With growing numbers of child deaths at sea, UN agencies call for enhancing safety for refugees and migrants," Geneva, 16 February 2016.

36 United Nations High Commissioner for Refugees (UNHCR), *Children on the Run: Unaccompanied Children Leaving Central America and Mexico and the Need for International Protection* (Washington, D.C.: UNHCR, 13 March 2014).

Within the mixed movements of people, we find unaccompanied and separated children who, although they do not fit within the specific category or tight frameworks for asylum seekers or refuges in countries of destination, require special protection for the respect and enjoyment of their human rights. Many of them escape from situations of conflict, social and family violence, extreme poverty and in search of a space that allows them to develop as human beings and enjoy a life in full respect of their rights as children. The risks that these children face both on their long road to the final host country and upon arrival are undeniable.

Discrimination, exclusion and violence that lead these children to embark on a road that has proved fatal for a large number of them are the symptoms of structural problems in their countries of origin. In host countries and countries of transit, these children continue to face great challenges. According to the Convention, the state party has the obligation to provide them with protection, to act as their guardian and to guarantee their basic rights, such as health and education. However, many of these children are neither provided with a tutor nor given the necessary protection, remaining on the streets and exposed to multiple violations of their rights.[37] The early appointment of a guardian who can act with the required independence is also critically important in cases of unaccompanied victims of trafficking. It contributes to avoiding double victimization and ensuring effective early protection that could also facilitate an early recovery and rehabilitation.

1.3. MIGRATION POLICIES vs. CHILD PROTECTION FRAMEWORKS

The starting point of the above-described situation of vulnerability in many cases is when children are identified as migrants first rather than as children, or are identified as adults as a result of age determination processes that do not respect the minimum human rights standards. This situation is of particular concern for victims of trafficking and has a direct impact on the efforts to break ties with traffickers who may continue to harass and abuse these children.[38]

Migration policies can have a decisive influence on the interpretation of the norm. For example, in Spain, despite relevant developments in recognizing the rights and specific challenges faced by unaccompanied children, there is

[37] Platform for International Cooperation on Undocumented Migrants (PICUM), paper prepared for UNICEF Brussels Office, *Rights of Accompanied Children in an Irregular Situation* (PICUM, November 2011).

[38] Council of Europe, Group of Experts on Action against Trafficking in Human Beings (GRETA), *6th General Report 2016 Covering the Period from 1 January to 31 December 2016* (Council of Europe, March 2017).

a practical contradiction between two existing legal frameworks and logics: the first should protect the child without discrimination of any kind under its current child protection legal framework; and the second looks at ways of returning them to their countries of origin as a general principle, in the name of their best interests, through the current migration law (*ley de extranjeria*), referring to border control and channelling of the migration flows.[39] The systematic practice of the use of medical tests for age determination purposes, which often does not take into account the documentation of the child or other multidisciplinary methodologies, has been noted in various Supreme Court judgments and reflects this dichotomy between the two logics, an issue to which I return to below.[40] Furthermore, the financial crisis and the cuts in the budgets of social services over the last few years in many countries is also an important factor contributing to this interpretation and to the consideration of these children as migrants rather than children in need of immediate and effective protection.[41] However, it should be noted that in some countries the benefit of the doubt and the presumption of minority for these children is systematically applied, for example, in Mexico or in Italy. These actions are seen as a good practice, avoiding the protection gap and discrimination between the treatment of these unaccompanied and separated children and the protection to be provided to all the children in the host or transit country. This practice recognizes them first as children before considering their migration situation.

The benefit of the doubt and the presumption of minority from the first moment of identification, as well as the practice of ensuring that decisions on age determination are not the responsibility of a single institution with vested interests in migration policy and management, can be identified as good practices in ensuring the treatment of unaccompanied and separated minors first and foremost as children. However, the lack of effective guardianship for unaccompanied and separated children is another challenge and results from actions driven by the consideration of these children as migrants first. This issue affects the minor from the very first moment of his or her arrival in the host or transit country. The alleged minor from the point of his or her interception should benefit from the assignment of a guardian or tutor who can ensure that his or her rights are fully protected from the outset.

Due to the lack of uniformity in practice, children face different levels of protection depending on the country in which they arrive. There are even differences within the same country depending on the region or state in which

---

39 Lucia Aparicio Chofré, "Advances and challenges in the Spanish Regulation for Unaccompanied Minors" (2015) 20 *Iuris Tantum Revista Boliviana de Derecho* 120.

40 Defensor del Pueblo de España, *Informe anual 2016 y debates en las Cortes Generales* (Madrid: Defensor del Pueblo, 2017).

41 Kirsty McNeilk, Save the Children, "Problem of lone refugee children in EU 'is getting worse,'" *Politics Home* (26 April 2016).

the unaccompanied or separated children is found. In a situation like that in the European Union, this calls for a harmonization of the legislation and reception measures to ensure that all children are treated equally and equally protected regardless of the Member State in which they arrive, without discrimination of any kind.

Unfortunately, one of the major challenges faced by these children in their first contact with the competent authorities is the lack of credibility and suspicion regarding the reasons for their journey. Despite progress made on the impact of double victimization, such children are routinely subjected in Europe to continuous interviews about their family relationships and more specifically about their age, often directed from the beginning to determine their majority in order to keep them away from well-established and consolidated protection systems in fear of a collapse or destabilization of such systems.

In Central America, even if the presumption of minority is applied in most countries, unaccompanied and separated children face situations of great vulnerability and the protection systems at the national level remains underdeveloped.[42] These include summary expulsions, lack of access to effective and early guardianship or obstacles to enjoyment of basic services such as health or education. Although properly identified as children, they are often placed in facilities which, without being called detention centres, have great similarities and respond to the same characteristics.

Paradoxically, although the regions mentioned are thousands of miles away from each other, the protection challenges faced by unaccompanied and separated children, as well as by states for the effective protection of these children's rights, also show important similarities.

2. CONCRETE CHALLENGES: THE RESPECT OF THEIR BEST INTERESTS, INCLUDING IN AGE DETERMINATION PROCESSES

2.1. AGE DETERMINATION AND THE BEST INTERESTS OF THE CHILD

A large number of unaccompanied and separated children who arrive in the countries of transit and destination do so with documentation that proves that they are minors; however, many others lack such documentation. Hence, despite their conspicuous appearance as minors, some states have adopted a number of measures to determine the age of these minors as a first step in identifying

---

42 Save the Children, *Every Last Child: The Children the World Chooses to Forget* (London: Save the Children, 2016).

the type of protection to be provided, in Europe in particular. These measures, which could be seen as logical, have instead often become an obstacle to effective protection as a result of the lack of guarantees for the protection of rights in the process. These processes often place unaccompanied and separated children in a never-ending net of administrative procedures in which they remain highly unprotected.

The Convention, which does not contain any provision concerning age determination, refers to the need for birth registration.[43] This still presents great challenges in many countries, including the countries of origin of unaccompanied and separated children taking the route to Europe or in the northern triangle of Central America. In many cases, public administration, especially those in charge of applying migration policy, do not appear to take these challenges into account, questioning the veracity of the factual reasons for the lack of documentation. This approach has also led here to the confronting of two logics: on one side, the growth of control of immigration flows and, on the other, the protection of the child as a rights holder on an equal footing with children in the state of transit and destination.[44]

In the European Union, the determination of age and its effects on the effective protection of unaccompanied and separated children has taken on significant importance in recent years, also coinciding with the increased number of arrivals. In this regard, guidelines and guides have been developed to ensure the protection of rights and, in particular, the best interests of the child, both by European institutions and national human rights institutions. Something similar has happened in the United States under the former administration, particularly given the alarming situation of a large number of unaccompanied and separated children from Central America who are found to be unprotected. While it is important to recognize the practical challenges and the complexities for the operationalization of the best interests of the child, over the last ten years, numerous efforts and progress have been made to describe the formal process and safeguards to be observed in the determination of those best interests. These include adequate child participation in decisions affecting them without discrimination in the process, the critical importance of relevant decision-making with the required expertise at all levels, as well as the balancing of elements that can result in the best interests of the child.[45]

Migration trends are shifting rapidly. Countries such as Spain and Mexico have seen how in recent years they have gone from pure transit countries to

---

43 Convention on the Rights of the Child, *supra* note 1, at Article 7.

44 Elena Arce, *Minor and Migrant: Two Confronting Logics* (Malaga: University of Malaga, 2016) (to be published).

45 See, for example, the guidelines by the UNHCR, *UNHCR Guidelines on Determining the Best Interests of the Child* (UNHCR, May 2008); and Save the Children, *Best Interest Determination for Children on the Move: A Toolkit for Decision-Making* (Save the Children, September 2010).

increasingly becoming countries of destination.[46] The speed of change does not necessarily translate into adjustments at the same pace in mandatory protection frameworks. Clearly the challenges in identifying and certifying the child as a child will lead to a myriad of administrative situations that often leave these children in a situation of legal limbo, lack of protection and too often of violation of their rights.

The implications of a decision as important as age at such a crucial time has – as is clear from my interviews with these minors – short-term and long-term impacts that are very difficult to rectify at a later stage. Understanding the nature of these obstacles, as well as analyzing whether the cross-cutting systems of child protection effectively protect the child when the minor in question is foreign and unaccompanied, is a crucial imperative in this historical moment of cross-border mixed movements of people. This could serve to effectively assess the actions and policies that are needed to mitigate the challenges faced by these children in line with the standards internationally accepted by the states concerned.

The first measure that the Committee on the Rights of the Child[47] indicates in determining the protection needs is in fact the determination of whether the child is an unaccompanied and separated minor. In a visionary fashion, the Committee puts forward the guarantees that must be respected in order to ensure that these processes are carried out under the most scrupulous respect for the rights of the child and in his or her best interests. These measures should not only be based on the physical aspect, but must take into account multidisciplinary parameters, including psychological maturity, and must comply with criteria that respect human dignity, always granting in cases of discrepancy the benefit of the doubt and therefore the presumption of minority of age. The practices followed in some states proceeding with evidence of age determination, even in cases where there is documentation demonstrating the minority of age of the person concerned, are practices that may be found to be discriminatory and inefficient, often only leading to extending situations of lack of protection.

In view of this concern, the Office of the High Commissioner for Human Rights for Europe, located in Brussels, organized a judicial colloquium in June 2012 entitled "Implementation of Article 3 of the Convention on the Rights of the Child in Europe: the case of migrant children including unaccompanied and separated children." The judges participating in this colloquium, who represented various courts in several European Union Member States, as well as from the European Court of Human Rights in Strasbourg, raised concerns about the impacts that age determination processes have on the effective protection

46 United Nations Human Rights Council, Advisory Committee, *Global Issue of Unaccompanied Migrant Children and Adolescents and Human Rights – Progress Report*, UNHRCOR, 33rd Sess, UN Doc. A/HRC/33/53 (2016).

47 Committee on the Rights of the Child, *General Comment No 6, Treatment of Unaccompanied and Separated Children*, *supra* note 13.

of the children's rights. They warned of the need to apply a multidisciplinary approach to processes and procedures for age determination in order to guarantee the least possible margin of error and to respect the best interests of the child. This approach is largely limited by the great weight that some systems give to medical tests alone. It was also noted that age determination processes are often carried out even when there is documentation confirming the age of the person.

If it is decided not to grant the presumption of minority of age and to carry out determination procedures, it is necessary to make sure that the medical and social tests of age determination are complementary, since none on its own provides absolute certainty.[48] Particularly relevant in this regard is the study carried out by the Office of the Ombudsman of Spain under the title *Minors or Adults: Procedures for the Determination of Age*,[49] which underlines the scientific challenges relating to relying exclusively on the results of medical tests. In this seminar and in the study, the widespread use of medical tests for the determination of the age based on the so-called Greulich and Pyle (GP) Atlas[50] was presented as a matter of concern. This Atlas was developed in 1959 using data on children of Caucasian origin in the United States from socio-economically privileged sectors, so it is evident that its validity is highly questionable to the realities of today.

This method, as found by an analysis I did in 2015 and which included interviews with forensic experts, was never thought of as a forensic investigation method and its large margin of error of about 18 months entails a number of ethical questions about its use in decisions that will mark the future of a person for his or her whole life.[51] Even the French Academy of Medicine and the Public Health Council of France have established that the results obtained through measurement with this Atlas, in particular the results of chest X-rays, are not representative for children over 15 years of age, and concluded that this instrument is too imprecise due to its large margin of error.[52] In spite of these concerns, the method continues to be applied as the sole rule in many countries, disregarding that age should be determined, if absolutely necessary, with methods that reliably reflect reality.

In Italy, Spain, Sweden and the United Kingdom, the question of the margins of error of medical tests for age determination has been debated in recent years

48 Regional Office for Europe and UNICEF, *Judicial Implementation of Article 3 of the Convention on the Rights of the Child: The Case of Migrant Children* (UN Children's Fund (UNICEF), June 2012).

49 Maria Luisa Cava de Llano y Carrio (Spain Acting Ombudsman), *Minors or Adults: Procedures for the Determination of Age – Minors First, Foreigners Second* (2010).

50 Ibid, at 26.

51 See also Terry Smith and Laura Bownless, *Age Assessment Practices: A Literature Review and Annotated Bibliography* (New York: UNICEF, 2011).

52 Haut Conseil de la santé publique (France), *Avis relatif à l'évaluation de la minorité d'un jeune étranger isolé* (23 January 2014).

and been the subject of numerous court judgments and decisions. All these countries except Spain have implemented a series of mechanisms that protect the minor from the margins of error that such medical tests present through a series of additional controls that rely on other disciplines, such as psychology, or assessment by trained social workers who can make a holistic assessment of the situation of the child, including maturity. In most of these countries, however, it is recognized that age-setting systems are far from perfect, despite the inclusion of such guarantees. In many of them, because the decision on age can lead to a change in the civil status of the individual, the decision is left to the courts to ultimately establish the age of the subject of the law in question. In this context, judicial guarantees for rights protection are critically important. In Spain, for example, where the child prosecutor retains the decision-making powers in age determination processes, despite the concerns expressed by the Spanish courts, the question remains unresolved. The Committee on the Rights of the Child recently, in March 2018 following consideration of the reports of Spain on the status of implementation of the Convention on the Rights of the Child, expressed serious concern at this situation and urged Spain to review the protocol for unaccompanied foreign minors in line with the provisions in the Convention.[53]

These concerns have prompted some national parliaments, such as that in the United Kingdom, to request a number of studies and this has led to a number of efforts to establish some criteria that can safeguard the rights of boys and girls in these proceedings (the Merton Criteria).[54] Similar efforts have been carried out in Italy.[55] The Merton Criteria aim to reinforce the fundamental procedural rights that ensure the protection of children, so that they are treated as such until proven otherwise. These criteria include the obligation to explain to the child the process of determining the child's age and its implications; that physical appearance is not by itself a determinant of age; that in the process of determining age, the family and social background of the subject of law are taken into account; and, above all, that the necessary measures will be taken so that each case is considered on an individual basis and that no group actions are taken.

The Office of the Ombudsman of Spain pointed out, referring to the Committee on the Rights of the Child, that the age determination process must be carried out in the best interests of the child, with scientific criteria, safety and impartiality, avoiding at all times the risks that endanger their dignity and

---

53 Committee on the Rights of the Child, *Concluding Observations on the combined fifth and sixth periodic reports of Spain*, 5 March 2018, CRC/C/ESP/CO/5_6.

54 House of Lords, European Union Committee, *Children in Crisis: Unaccompanied Migrant Children in the EU*, *supra* note 32.

55 *Legge 7 Aprile 2017 n° 47 (Italy), Disposizioni in materia di misure di protezione dei minori stranieri non accompagnati*, G.U. Serie Generale n.93 del 21 Aprile 2017.

physical integrity. Pointing to the consensus that exists among the scientific community on the wide margins of error connected to the techniques for measurement of bone maturity and dental consistency, the Spanish Ombudsman's study also advocates for the benefit of doubt, the presumption of minority and the need to ensure the existence of an effective remedy regarding the decisions on their age taken by public administrations.[56]

The appropriate procedures for child protection may be affected by regulations that attribute a higher rank to migration pressure or the perception of growth of migration pressure. The condition of the minor or alleged minor is pushed aside by criteria that give primary consideration to the rights holders as migrants rather than as children, thereby placing greater emphasis on their documentation status. As a result, age determination processes are often tainted by actions or omissions that avoid guaranteeing the rights established in the Convention, as developed by the Committee, for the effective protection of the best interests of the minor.

Therefore, the need to verify and determine the age of a child for the purpose of determining his or her minority of age when documentation is not available is of increasing legal relevance for unaccompanied and separated children. Age determination processes, including uniformity of the regulations and of their interpretation, should ensure the best levels of protection for unaccompanied and separated children and should serve to mitigate the negative impacts that inconsistencies produce, for instance, as regards access to basic social services in equal terms with all children.[57] The best interests of the child should be the primary consideration not only in the general process but also in practice for each of the steps and measures for age determination. The best interests of the child should not automatically be his or her return to the country of origin, at least not without a thorough assessment of the realities and situations that led these children to flee to another country.

2.2. HUMAN RIGHTS CHALLENGES IN AGE DETERMINATION PROCESSES

Age determination is the axis that acts as an entry point to a future that provides children with the protection that is guaranteed by law or, unfortunately as often happens, as an exit point that denies this protection.[58] A child's status as a minor,

---

56 Ibid, at 23.

57 Vivien Feltz, *Age Assessment for Unaccompanied Minors: When European Countries Deny Children their Childhood* (Médecins du Monde International Network, 28 August 2015).

58 House of Lords, European Union Committee, *Children in Crisis: Unaccompanied Migrant Children in the EU*, *supra* note 32, at 18; UNHCR written evidence UK proceeding: "The outcomes of age assessment have great importance in determining how an individual will

in the absence of a person responsible for his or her protection and welfare, will determine in transit and countries of destination the measures concerning declaration of the situation of deprivation of parental care and therefore the need for the assignment of a guardianship or tutorship by the relevant administrations.

Particularly worrisome from a rights perspective are, for example, the efforts of some administrations to demonstrate, even when unaccompanied children are in possession of documentation determining their age as children, that they are adults and therefore do not fall within the parameters of protection that should be granted to a minor. In some instances the determination of majority also serves to justify detention procedures or swift expulsions. In spite of the opinions and judicial judgments[59] confirming that a minor in possession of documents that certify his or her minority of age cannot be considered an undocumented foreign minor, the validity of these documents is questioned in many situations in a systematic and indiscriminate way. The determination of the age of unaccompanied children who are in possession of any documentation proving their status as a minor should be based on such documentation.

The situations of abuse and violence from which these children escape are not taken into account systematically because the priority is to attend to their migration situation and status. Thus, their needs as children are systematically neglected in these cases. For example, Save the Children in Italy has found that 50% of the children they assist have acquired some type of sexually transmitted disease due to the forms of sexual exploitation they suffered in transit, as well as traumatic experiences which will mark their lives.[60] Many of them suffer depression, stress and post-traumatic stress disorders due to experiences in their countries of origin and transit that often, regrettably, may continue in countries of destination if they are not provided with the necessary protection and support. The lack of credibility and the assumption that these children are lying in their testimonies are unfortunately common attitudes among immigration

---

be treated both in the immigration and asylum process and also in relation to the care and support they receive. If a child is wrongly considered to be an adult, they may miss being supported by children's services; miss access to education or college; they may be dispersed to a different part of the country and might be accommodated or detained with adults."

59 The judgments from the Supreme Court in Spain on the protection of the rights of unaccompanied children and age determination processes are particularly relevant. Since 2014, the Supreme Court issued more than 11 judgments reiterating its jurisprudence of 24 September 2014, in which the Court judged in favour of a child who had been obliged to undergo medical testing to determine his age, even though the child was holding documentation stating his age as a minor. The Court stated that a child migrant with documentation stating his or her age cannot be considered as an undocumented migrant requiring to undergo through age determination testing to determine his or her age. See the Judgments by the Supreme Court of Spain N°452/2014; N°453/2014; N°11/2015; N°13/2015; N°318/2015; N°320/2015; N°452/2015; and N°453/2015.

60 Save the Children Italia, *Piccoli schiavi invisibili i volti della tratta e dello sfruttamento* (Save the Children Italia, 22 August 2014).

and border agents who do not necessarily have the training to deal with these situations.

The validity of documents proving minority of age is routinely questioned. In several countries, during a particular period of time, coinciding with the arrival of large numbers of individuals from specific countries, documentation relating to children was questioned systematically by migration authorities. This situation considerably increased the number of disputes over the age of the children arriving from these countries. This occurs even when the child is in possession of documents issued by the authorities of his or her country of origin declaring minority of age and in disregard of the benefit of the doubt that should be applied to effectively consider the child as a minor in order to provide him or her with the necessary protection.

Evidence from interviews with these minors shows that when unaccompanied or separated children are intercepted in countries of destination, they face new challenges that begin with the first contacts with the authorities due to attitudes of suspicion, a lack of clarity in the institutional responsibility for their protection and the lack of appropriate conditions to meet their needs upon arrival. It should not be forgotten that many of these children arrive without documentation that proves their age because it has been lost or because, as mentioned above, it is not common practice in their countries of origin to issue such documents. The weight of the testimony of the presumed minor is generally called into question when it is not given the necessary value as material evidence. The results of these processes will undoubtedly have a crucial impact on the child. When the presence of quality legal assistance is not guaranteed during the entire process of reception and age determination, fundamental rights are violated, including those related to due process.[61]

The prompt action of the authorities in the country of destination, as of the very first moment of reception, in compliance with the existing international human rights standards, may change the life of an unaccompanied boy or girl for better or worse. The story of Hakim,[62] one of the Afghan children I interviewed in Italy, is particularly interesting in this context. Hakim left his native village in northern Afghanistan and he turned 13 en route to Kabul. On the way, he was harassed several times, even though he was accompanied by two family friends who were adults. Their eyes were set on the United Kingdom, where a close uncle lived. On his trip to Greece, he passed through Pakistan, Iran and Turkey, where he had to face situations of violence, witnessed the violent death of one of his fellow travellers and feared for his physical integrity, with only

61 Fundacion Raices, *Solo por estar solo – Informe sobre la determinación de la edad en menores migrantes no acompañados* (Madrid: Fundacion Raices, 2014).

62 The author of this chapter interviewed Hakim in Pavia, Italy, on 12 December 2015. He then provided written authorization to present his story and he has reconfirmed it for the purposes of this chapter.

one bottle of water for more than 20 days, or after having spent days in the company of drug dealers and guards who beat them. Finally, he arrived in Greece and spent six months working on whatever he could or was able to in order to eat. He finally climbed aboard a freighter that he thought would take him to Italy and hid in the cargo hold of a truck. Upon arrival at a port, he climbed to the bottom of a truck that left the ship, but unfortunately it continued without stopping in port and took the highway. Finally, after having feared for his life, the truck stopped at a gas station. Hakim thought he was in Italy, but he was in France. He managed to get to Paris and from there to Calais to try to go to the United Kingdom and meet his uncle. After several months waiting to pass in Calais, one night, there was a raid and although tired due to severe sleep deprivation caused by fear and stress, he jumped onto a train that he thought would take him back to Paris. He fell asleep and does not know how, but the next thing he saw was the train stopped at a station.

Hakim was awakened by the Italian police because he was in Milan. He was asked about his age and he responded that he was 14 years old and that he came from Afghanistan. Without further questioning, he was transferred to the corresponding social protection services. His story and accounts were not questioned. Today, he is about to finish his university studies in Italy, where he has a made a new life. Although it is difficult to predict what would have happened to him if his age had been questioned because of his physical appearance, the reality is that many children in similar situations face very different realities. The divide between law and practice on the application of the principle of the best interests of the child and its implementation is still abysmal in the case of unaccompanied and separated minors, despite the progress made in translating the international standards into national legislative frameworks. Often in the age determination processes, little or no attention is paid to the word and testimony of the minor, contrary to what happened in Hakim's case. However, Hakim now faces other challenges since he turned 18. He has been trapped in lengthy administrative procedures, this time not due to his age determination as many other unaccompanied and separated children are obliged to face, but to remain and continue advancing in life in the country that has become his home country. He has taken the original opportunity offered and demonstrated his capacities to complete his studies and be able to rebuild his life. He speaks Italian better than any other language; he is fully integrated and his results at university are remarkable. However, his capacity to remain in Italy still largely remains attached to his capacity to provide sufficient financial means for himself.

If a child is erroneously declared of legal age, as could have been the case for Hakim and which is regrettably the case for many unaccompanied children, his or her opportunities to access protection services vanish at a stroke, as well as opportunities for education and access to basic social services appropriate for his or her age, and can even lead to detention and retention in facilities dedicated for adults. Detention of migrants in irregular situations should be a last resort, only permissible for the shortest period of time and if no other less coercive measure can be applied. It should never be applicable to children.[63] The declaration of legal age following processes of age determination, the credibility of which is dubious, as illustrated above, additionally vacates the effective guardianship protection that should accompany the child at all times of the process from the time of his or her reception to his or her coming of legal age.

3. CONCLUSIONS

The world continues to stare stunningly at the great precariousness of the current human mixed movements, which are currently one of the largest in history since World War II, involving thousands of children. Every day, more people leave their countries of origin to embark on a route with the hopes of a better and safer life and better opportunities in dignity. Thousands of children take this route with their parents, separated or simply alone and unaccompanied. The reception conditions in transit and countries of destination for unaccompanied and separated children must ensure their effective protection so as not to perpetuate the precariousness which they fled.

As is observed year after year, the tightening of border controls, as well as the limitation of access for these people to the minimum standards of protection of human rights in both regions, will not lead to a decrease in the arrival of minors. Despite the numerous rescues at sea and returns, the situations of violence in the countries of origin of these unaccompanied and separated children prevail and continue to push thousands of children to seek a better life in other places, away from the daily violence they experience.[64] The economic and demographic differences between countries, inequalities within countries and the effects of climate change will continue to be contributory factors to migration, including that of unaccompanied and separated children, in the coming decades.[65] The violence these children face in their countries of origin due to conflict, on the streets, in the family and as a result of the lack of food, education and opportunities is undeniable. The manner in which states parties

---

63 In March 2017, the European Union was to adopt a new recommendation on return procedures, which was observed by UN experts as "encouraging Member States to increase the use and length of detention of migrants, including of children." In a press statement launched on 9 March 2017, the UN experts, including the Special Rapporteur on the Rights of Migrants and the Committee on the Rights of the Child, urged the European Union to explore alternatives to increased detention and swift returns to uphold the human rights of migrants.

64 EC, Commission, *Mid-term Report on the Implementation of the Action Plan on Unaccompanied Minors* (Brussels: EC, COM(2012) 554, 28 September 2012).

65 International Organization for Migration (IOM), *World Migration Report 2010* (Geneva: IOM, 2010).

to the Convention have reacted to implement their obligations under this treaty and to respond to these trends has been varied, leading to uneven levels of protection for unaccompanied and separated children.[66]

The consideration of the child as a migrant and not as an unaccompanied and separated minor in need of protection in the first place has very serious consequences for the life and the future of the child. This consideration places the child in a lengthy and entangled administrative process. The administrative tangle in which thousands of children are trapped leaves many of them unprotected in the streets of even very wealthy cities with well-established social protection systems for minors in general. Determining the age of the unaccompanied and separated children, when this is absolutely necessary and is in their best interests, should be the way to provide them with effective protection and not to leave them out.

The Committee on the Rights of the Child could enhance its mechanisms to carefully review the situation of states undertaking age determination processes for unaccompanied and separated children based only on the results of medical tests, in particular when documentation exists confirming the minority of the person in question. It may be timely for the Committee to update its general comment on unaccompanied and separated children in light of the recently adopted joint General Comment and the new challenges that these children face in the context of the current mixed movements, as well as the recent developments and the good practices developed in the last five years, particularly in respect of the best interest of the child.

Reaffirming the importance of treating children as rights holders, which Arbour stated as being one of the key achievements since the adoption of the Convention, is now more relevant than ever. A strong commitment to ensure that the best interests of the child govern each of the actions taken in their regard is necessary. The opportunity for unaccompanied and separate children to recover a life in dignity as established by international human rights law depends on it. In the framework of the current commitments by the international community to proceed with the implementation of the 2030 Sustainable Development Agenda and the plans being drawn to achieve the Sustainable Development Goals, the situation of unaccompanied and separated children in the context of large movements of people should find a particular place so that they are not – once again – left behind.

---

66 Committee on the Rights of the Child, *General Comment No 5 on General Measures of Implementation of the Convention on the Rights of the Child*, *supra* note 3.

PART II

OF PEACE AND JUSTICE

THE DETERRENCE RATIONALE IN A CRIMINAL JUSTICE ACCOUNTABILITY REGIME

James K. STEWART*

1. INTRODUCTION

The deterrence rationale finds expression in the criminal justice accountability regime established by the Rome Statute of the International Criminal Court (ICC). The Preamble to the Statute links ending impunity, by the effective prosecution of the most serious crimes of concern to the international community, to the goal of contributing to the prevention of such crimes.[1] Although it is still early in the life of the ICC, some scholars have discerned a deterrent impact from

* The views expressed in this chapter are those of the author, who does not here purport to speak for the Prosecutor or her Office, or for the International Criminal Court. The author expresses his gratitude to Moussa Bienvenu Haba, doctoral student at Université Laval, Quebec, Canada, for his invaluable research assistance in the preparation of this chapter. Note that the original drafting of this text was finished before the Appeal in the *Bemba* case and the text has only been slightly modified accordingly.

1 It appears that general deterrence was one of the principal reasons for creating the ICC; see Cronin-Furman, Kate. 2013. Managing Expectations: International Criminal Trials and the Prospects for Deterrence of Mass Atrocity. *International Journal of Transitional Justice* 7: 434–454, p. 437.

the Court's activities.[2] While it is difficult to measure such an impact with any accuracy,[3] the ICC operates on the assumption that effective prosecution of the perpetrators of war crimes, crimes against humanity and genocide will serve to deter their commission.[4] Prevention may be a goal of uneven achievement, but many people believe that the ICC's involvement in situations does indeed have a preventive effect.

Whatever the long-term impact of the Court's work will be, the immediate purpose of the investigations and prosecutions brought so far under the Rome Statute has been to determine the individual criminal responsibility of persons accused of crimes committed in specific situations and to seek a just sentence for those found guilty. Without effective investigations and prosecutions, there can be no hope of deterrence and ultimately prevention. The Court, however, faces challenges in this endeavour. Certain warrants of arrest issued by the ICC are still unexecuted and fugitives continue to evade justice, while the Court is powerless to bring them to account without decisive cooperation and support from states. Nevertheless, where accused persons have been brought before the Court, a past somewhat uneven record has given way to a more impressive pattern of achievement. The rate of confirmation by Pre-Trial Chambers of charges against accused persons has increased, an indication of the improved quality of work being done by the Office of the Prosecutor (OTP).[5] The trials of these accused are in an advanced stage, but the ultimate results remain to be seen.

The basic premise of the Rome Statute is that states parties have primary responsibility for the investigation and prosecution of genocide, crimes against humanity and war crimes. The ICC is "a court of last resort," only able to intervene where states have been shown to be unable or unwilling to act themselves.[6] The OTP has used the cornerstone principle of complementarity of jurisdictions in a positive way to encourage appropriate national responses to Rome Statute crimes. Thus, an early preventive effect may be found in this practical approach

---

2 See Jo, Hyeran and Beth A. Simmons. 2014. Can the International Criminal Court Deter Atrocity? 1–53 (electronic copy available at: http://ssrn.com/abstract=2552820); and Dancy, Geoff, Bridget Marchesi, Florencia Montal and Kathryn Sikkink. 2015. The ICC's Deterrent Impact: What the Evidence Shows, *openGlobalRights*, reproduced in *openDemocracy*.

3 Jo and Simmons, p. 20: "Studying deterrence empirically is a difficult endeavor." See also Cronin-Furman, p. 435.

4 As Cronin-Furman puts it, p. 438: "[D]eterrence optimists seem to take for granted that more trials will mean more deterrence." Such optimism certainly underlies the objectives of the strategic planning of the Office of the Prosecutor (OTP).

5 The rate of confirmation of charges has recently increased to almost 86%, an improvement in performance of 23.3%, and the rate of confirmation of accused for trial to 100%, an improvement in performance of 28.6%: see Office of the Prosecutor Strategic Plan 2016–2018 (hereinafter "Strategic Plan 2016–2018").

6 Rome Statute of the International Criminal Court (hereinafter "RS"), Preamble and Articles 1 and 17–19.

to complementarity, even short of a criminal investigation or prosecution, as will be seen below.[7]

The Rome Statute system of international criminal justice is based on the premise that the effective investigation and prosecution of genocide, crimes against humanity and war crimes will serve to deter the future commission of such crimes. Realizing this objective will depend upon how effectively the criminal accountability regime that permeates the whole Statute is applied in specific situations.[8] The architecture of that regime resides in the provisions the Statute makes for the penalties that may be imposed upon convicted persons.

Furthermore, according to Jo and Simmons: "The ICC also deters because it mobilizes the international community as well as domestic civil society to demand justice."[9] ICC interventions, they suggest, are powerful because they are part of broader efforts to end impunity.[10] Reinforcing the global effort to end impunity for the most serious crimes of concern to the international community is one of the major goals of the ICC OTP.

2. THE DETERRENCE RATIONALE IN THE ROME STATUTE OF THE ICC

Evoking the horrors of the twentieth century, the framers of the Rome Statute of the ICC declared that "the most serious crimes of concern to the international community as a whole must not go unpunished" and "their effective prosecution must be ensured." Effective prosecution was required "to put an end to impunity" and "thus to contribute to the prevention" of genocide, crimes against humanity and war crimes.[11] Deterrence is therefore an express objective of the Rome Statute system of international criminal justice.

It may be true that the "idea that international criminal trials should have a general deterrent effect has become widespread only recently," since modern international criminal justice, dating back to the Nuremberg trials, "began with a focus on retribution."[12] However, it would be wise to recall the words of Robert H. Jackson, the lead American prosecutor before the International

---

7 See Olasolo, Hector. 2012. The Role of the International Criminal Court in Preventing Atrocity Crimes through Timely Intervention, in *Essays on International Criminal Justice*. Oxford: Hart Publishing, pp. 11–19.

8 As Cronin-Furman rightly observes, p. 453: "[T]he extent to which potential perpetrators can actually be deterred will require that the Court demonstrate that it can successfully prosecute and punish."

9 Jo and Simmons, p. 37.

10 Jo and Simmons, p. 38.

11 RS, Preamble and Articles 1, 5, 6, 7 and 8.

12 See Cronin-Furman, p. 436.

Military Tribunal at Nuremberg. He said in his opening statement: "The wrongs which we seek to condemn and punish have been so calculated, so malignant, and so devastating, that civilization cannot tolerate their being ignored, *because it cannot survive their being repeated* [emphasis added]."[13] These words would suggest that, at least in the eyes of that prosecutor, the trials of the Nazi regime leaders had as an objective the future prevention of such wrongs. Indeed, as a permanent institution, today the ICC is, according to Cronin-Furman, "the only institution in the existing international criminal justice system capable of producing any deterrent effect."[14] This is due principally to the ICC's potentially unlimited geographic jurisdiction and prospective temporal jurisdiction, despite procedural limitations upon how a case may come before the Court.[15]

The deterrence rationale underlines the criminal accountability regime that the Rome Statute creates. The sentencing regime of the Statute focuses upon factors such as the gravity of the crime committed and the individual circumstances of the convicted person. It provides for penalties of imprisonment and fines, orders of forfeiture of proceeds, and reparations to victims.[16] Such a regime places the emphasis upon doing justice in the individual case and derives from traditional criminal law concepts.[17] These concepts encompass individual and general deterrence, although they are not confined to these objectives exclusively.

The criminal accountability regime of the Rome Statute system of international criminal justice thus derives more from traditional concepts that have shaped criminal law than from any empirical proof of their effectiveness in deterring crimes. Social science research seeks to answer the question whether there is in fact any validity to the assumptions underlying the rationale.[18] In other

---

13 See "Second Day, Wednesday, 11/21/1945, Part 04", in Trial of the Major War Criminals before the International Military Tribunal. Volume II. Proceedings: 11/14/1945-11/30/1945 (official text in the English language) Nuremberg: IMT, 1947. pp. 98–102; for this, the writer thanks the Robert H. Jackson Center.

14 Cronin-Furman, p. 435. However, the sentence cited continues with the observation that the ICC "is likely [to have a deterrent effect] only under a narrow set of conditions." She explains what that narrow set of conditions is, a matter picked up again further on in this chapter. It should also be recognized that ad hoc judicial institutions, such as the International Criminal Tribunal for the former Yugoslavia (ICTY), the International Criminal Tribunal for Rwanda (ICTR), the Special Court for Sierra Leone (SCSL) and others, as well as investigations and prosecutions that have been conducted by the national authorities in Canada, Belgium, The Netherlands, Germany, Switzerland, Finland, Rwanda and elsewhere, have also contributed to the deterrent impact of international criminal justice.

15 Cronin-Furman, p. 441.

16 RS, Articles 76, 77, 78 and 79.

17 This proposition, which is obvious to any practitioner with experience in both domestic and international criminal law, is supported by the scholarly literature: see Cronin-Furman, p. 439.

18 No attempt will be made here to canvass the scholarly literature on the subject of how effective deterrence can be in the administration of international criminal law, but a selective reference to a few representative articles, it is hoped, will give some sense of the general trends in thinking on the subject.

words, does the deterrence rationale work in real life? Is the prevention of mass atrocities a realizable goal of international criminal justice? The investigation of mass atrocities and the prosecution, conviction and punishment of perpetrators of such crimes, with the measure of justice to victims and communities affected that this endeavour may bring, endure as important and valid objectives in themselves. But will they deter future crimes? Similar questions have preoccupied the administration of criminal justice – and not just international criminal justice – from the beginning.[19]

In domestic jurisdictions, deterrence of crime, especially serious crimes, such as homicide, sexual aggression, armed robbery, major fraud, drug trafficking and so on, remains a principal objective of the administration of criminal justice. No deterrence regime works perfectly. The prevalence, or not, of crime depends upon so many social, cultural, economic and demographic factors, in addition to the efficacy of law enforcement and the criminal justice system. However, on the level of international crimes, the challenge to the deterrence rationale may be of a different order entirely, since a judicial institution, such as the ICC, seeks to deter powerful actors, such as warlords and high-ranking state agents, and even heads of state, from committing the worst crimes, crimes of cruelty and terror on a mass scale. Such actors may feel themselves immune from investigation or prosecution. "Persons who intentionally terrorize civilians for their personal or political purposes are difficult to deter under any circumstances."[20] Disrupting this feeling of security, and breaking the cycle of impunity, must be a goal of the ICC's criminal justice accountability regime. Thus, its application may contribute to prevention, if powerful actors are compelled to pause and think before they act – and even be dissuaded from acting at all.

Some social science research, which will be mentioned further below, suggests that the creation, via the ICC, of a criminal justice accountability regime in itself may serve to deter violence by shaping policy and attitudes. Social scientists are exploring the impact of international criminal justice institutions, including the ICC, in an attempt to measure their efficacy in reducing violence and enhancing protection for human rights. Nevertheless, as already noted, the underlying assumption of international criminal justice, as framed in the ICC Statute, is that effective prosecution will contribute to the prevention of war crimes, crimes against humanity and genocide. So, in the meantime, the deterrence rationale of the ICC criminal accountability regime continues to be applied in the belief that effective prosecution, among other achievements, will contribute to prevention.

---

19 There is, it seems, a growing consensus in the deterrence literature that suggests that the swiftness, and especially the likelihood, of punishment may more effectively deter crime than the severity of punishment: see Jo and Simmons, pp. 8–9.

20 Jo and Simmons, p. 3; and see also Cronin-Furman, pp. 442 and 445, where she argues that: "Where potential offenders have 'overriding interests' in offending, deterrence is unlikely to operate."

Social scientists will continue to examine the impact of the ICC in both the short term and the long term, while the ICC continues to pursue its immediate mandate of seeing to justice in individual cases arising out of particular situations that qualify for intervention under the Rome Statute.

Achieving prevention of the crimes proscribed by the Rome Statute may be a far more complex and multifaceted process in the end, with prosecution being only one component. Future reduction in mass atrocities may ultimately be due to factors other than the punishment of perpetrators alone, such as the development of inclusive political institutions, strengthening of the rule of law, enhancement of a culture of respect for basic human rights and so on.[21] The process of prevention will be a complex one, with many factors coming into play. The ICC's interventions are intended to make an important contribution to this endeavour.

One focus of interest has been the so-called tension between peace and justice. Jo and Simmons argue that "as a general matter there is little evidence to suggest the peace versus justice trade-off is anything other than a false dichotomy."[22] From the standpoint of the OTP, this tension has been resolved, insofar as the Rome Statute and its application are concerned.[23] Peace without justice is not sustainable in the long run. The Rome Statute seems to imply as much, since its framers declared themselves to be "[r]esolved to guarantee lasting respect for and the enforcement of international justice," in the context of a determination to end impunity for the perpetrators of "grave crimes [that] threaten the peace, security and well-being of the world."[24] Thus, to achieve peace – that is, to deter or prevent war crimes, crimes against humanity and genocide – there must also be a measure of accountability for such crimes. Otherwise, embers of resentment over injustice may re-ignite conflicts, on either a short or a long fuse, if victims receive no redress.

3. ESTABLISHING THE TRUTH

While deterrence may be the ultimate objective of ICC prosecutions, these serve a multiplicity of purposes. Cronin-Furman observes that scholars and international lawyers, in arguing for the deterrent effect of international criminal trials, have drawn an analogy to domestic criminal law. Criminal punishment in domestic

---

21 See Jo and Simmons, p. 25.

22 Jo and Simmons, p. 5.

23 In its 2007 *Policy Paper on the Interests of Justice*, relating to how it interprets the concept of "the interests of justice" appearing in Article 53(1)(c) and (2)(c) RS, the OTP observed that "there is a difference between the concepts of the interests of justice and the interests of peace and … the latter falls within the mandate of institutions other than the Office of the Prosecutor." See also pp. 3 (especially footnote 5) and 8–9 of the policy paper.

24 RS, Preamble.

systems, she writes, is justified under three distinct philosophical rationales, namely, "expressivism, retributivism and consequentialism." Expressivism underscores the symbolic value of demonstrating society's commitment to the law and condemnation of its breaches. Retributivism mandates punishment as necessary to provide moral redress for crime. Consequentialism focuses on the practical ramifications of punishment, such as incapacitation, rehabilitation and deterrence.[25] All three rationales are relevant to the work of the ICC. Justice must be done in the individual case. This involves, in any given case, the need to reinforce the value of the rule of law, to recognize the suffering of victims and to end impunity for the perpetrators of international crimes. In achieving these goals of accountability, the trials undertaken by the ICC also incidentally serve another purpose: to establish the truth.

The ICC Statute thus obliges the Prosecutor to exercise her powers of investigation "to establish the truth."[26] Moreover, in the exercise of its functions and powers, a Trial Chamber has as a goal to establish the truth.[27] The Trial Chamber performs a fact-finding function essential to a criminal trial that seeks to determine, in a fair and impartial process, the truth of the allegations against the accused. Guilt or innocence must be decided before the Trial Chamber may hold any accused to account. It may also be argued that establishing the truth about particular crimes, apart from being essential for accountability, has intrinsic value – for the victims, for the communities affected by the crimes and for the historical record to make any narrative of denial simply untenable.[28]

If, after a trial, the allegations against the accused are proven to be true beyond reasonable doubt, then the sentencing provisions of the ICC Statute are applied to hold perpetrators accountable for their actions. The effective prosecution of the perpetrators of mass crimes, while establishing the truth and serving other valid purposes, may therefore contribute to the evolution of a broader culture of deterrence of atrocities and respect for human rights.

4. THE ICC CRIMINAL ACCOUNTABILITY REGIME

While the concept of a criminal accountability regime may be far broader, encompassing the constituent elements of the crimes charged and the process by which individual criminal responsibility is determined, the focus of the

25 Cronin-Furman, p. 439.

26 RS, Article 54.

27 This is apparent in the provisions relating to the functions and powers of the Trial Chamber, notably Articles 64, 66, 67, 68, 69, 70 and 71 RS, and expressed in provisions, such as those contained in Article 69(1) and (3), and Rule 66 of the Rules of Procedure and Evidence (RPE).

28 See how the importance of the truth for victims and their families is underscored in ICC-01/04-01/07: *Décision relative à la peine (article 76 du Statut)*, 23 May 2014 (hereinafter "*Katanga* Sentencing Judgment"), para. 38.

following discussion will be upon the penalties in the Rome Statute. While fear of investigation and prosecution itself may cause some potential perpetrators to hesitate – a possibility that is addressed further below – one must examine the sanctions regime that will be applied if investigations and prosecutions do result in convictions.

Generally speaking, under the Statute, persons convicted of war crimes, crimes against humanity or genocide are liable to a fixed term of imprisonment of up to 30 years or, when justified by the extreme gravity of the crime and their individual circumstances, a term of life imprisonment.[29] In addition to imprisonment, the Trial Chamber may order a fine and may also order the forfeiture of proceeds, property and assets derived directly or indirectly from the crime (without prejudice to the rights of good faith third parties).[30] A person convicted of multiple crimes is liable to receive a sentence for each crime, with the joint total sentence not to exceed the permitted maximum of either 30 years of imprisonment or life imprisonment, depending on the case.[31] The Rules of Procedure and Evidence (RPE) make detailed provision for the imposition of a sentence of imprisonment or a fine. The RPE develop the concepts of the gravity of the crime and the individual circumstances of the convicted person, requiring, among other considerations, the Trial Chamber to balance all relevant factors, including those that are mitigating and aggravating.[32]

Respecting the gravity of the crime and the circumstances of the convicted person, the RPE thus oblige Chambers to consider, among other factors: the extent of the damage caused, in particular the harm caused to victims and their families; the nature of the unlawful behaviour and the means used to commit the crime; the convicted person's degree of participation; the degree of intent; circumstances relating to the manner, time and location of the commission of the crimes; and the age, education, and social and economic condition of the person to be sentenced.[33]

The RPE list mitigating circumstances (for example, duress or cooperation with the Court) and aggravating circumstances (for example, abuse of power, the defencelessness of the victims, particular cruelty, discriminatory motives or other similar circumstances) in a way that is not exhaustive of the factors relevant to the determination of sentence.[34] The RPE also provide guidance regarding the imposition of fines and the making of forfeiture orders.[35]

---

29 RS, Article 77.
30 RS, Articles 77 and 79.
31 RS, Articles 77 and 78(3).
32 RPE, Rules 145–148.
33 RPE, Rule 145(1).
34 RPE, Rule 145(2).
35 RPE, Rules 146 and 147.

In sum, the Rome Statute confers a broad discretion upon a sentencing Chamber to determine just sanctions, while articulating many of the considerations that a Chamber should take into account in determining the penalty to impose: "[T]he Trial Chamber's determination involves an exercise of discretion with the aim to impose a proportionate sentence that reflects the culpability of the convicted person."[36] The provisions of the Rome Statute and the RPE thus provide "a comprehensive scheme for the determination and imposition of sentence."[37] They appear to be designed to meet the sentencing objectives that apply generally in international criminal law. These objectives have emerged from, among other sources, the experience of the ad hoc United Nations (UN) international criminal tribunals.

The sentencing practices of the UN international criminal tribunals, while adapted to the unique circumstances of the crimes they were established to address, themselves derive from traditional criminal law precepts about the purposes of sentencing. These purposes include the need to impose a sentence that fits the crime, and thus the gravity of the criminal conduct tends to be the most important sentencing factor: the sentence should be proportionate to the gravity of the crime and the degree of responsibility of the offender.[38] The sentence must reflect the condemnation of the criminal conduct by the international community; this requirement is often expressed by the concept of retribution. The sentence must also serve the objectives of deterrence and prevention. Rehabilitation has relevance as a sentencing factor, but, given the nature of the crimes of concern here, this factor receives little weight, save in connection with young offenders or possibly in the case of a guilty plea.[39] Thus, international criminal law sentencing regimes, like domestic criminal justice accountability systems, have always contained a deterrence component. The objective of prevention embraced by the Rome Statute in its Preamble simply continues this tradition.

So far, the ICC has applied the Rome Statute criminal justice accountability regime in five cases, namely, *Lubanga*, *Katanga*, *Bemba*, *Bemba et al.* and

36 ICC-01/04-01/06 A 4 A 6: Judgment on the appeals of the Prosecutor and Mr Thomas Lubanga Dyilo against the "Decision on Sentence pursuant to article 76 of the Statute", 1 December 2014 (hereinafter "*Lubanga* appeal judgment on sentence"), paras 1–4, 34 and 40–46.

37 *Lubanga* appeal judgment on sentence, para. 32.

38 This prominent feature of sentencing in international criminal justice accountability systems could fit within both expressive and retributive rationales for punishment, as well as serving the goal of deterrence.

39 For this succinct, but compendious, overview of the sentencing principles developed, in particular, at the ICTY and the ICTR, the writer is indebted to Helen Brady, Senior Appeals Counsel in the OTP at the ICC, and formerly Senior Appeals Counsel at the ICTY OTP, who shared memoranda on sentencing principles applicable at the ad hoc tribunals. A detailed exploration of the underlying sentencing decisions is beyond the scope of this chapter.

Al Mahdi, this last case being the first time the Court has engaged in proceedings on an admission of guilt.

In the case of Thomas Lubanga Dyilo, the Appeals Chamber, by a majority, dismissed the sentence appeals of both the defence and the prosecution and maintained the sentencing decision of the Trial Chamber.[40] The Trial Chamber found Thomas Lubanga guilty of the crimes of conscripting and enlisting children under 15 years of age and using them to participate actively in hostilities being conducted in Ituri, in the eastern Democratic Republic of the Congo (DRC); it sentenced him to a joint term of 14 years of imprisonment.[41] In doing so, the Trial Chamber recognized the importance of deterrence in sentencing for such crimes.[42] It considered in detail the sentencing factors in the Rome Statute and RPE outlined above, paying particular attention to the gravity of the crimes, as was reflected, notably, in the harm done to vulnerable victims and their families, the widespread nature of the crimes, and the degree of participation and intent of the convicted person.[43] The Trial Chamber also took into account mitigating factors, some of which were perhaps uniquely peculiar to these particular proceedings.[44] The *Lubanga* Chamber thus situated its sentencing task within the deterrence rationale of the Rome Statute's accountability regime.

Germain Katanga was convicted of crimes against humanity and war crimes that were committed at a village in Ituri, DRC.[45] Specifically, he was found guilty, as an accessory, of murder as both a crime against humanity and a war crime, attack against a civilian population as a war crime, destruction of enemy property as a war crime and pillaging as a war crime, but was acquitted of other charges.[46] He was sentenced to 12 years' imprisonment.[47] However, the defence and the prosecution withdrew their respective appeals in this case, so the sentence of 12 years imposed by the Trial Chamber stood without challenge.[48]

Adopting an approach to the interpretation of the sentencing provisions of the Rome Statute in line with the *Lubanga* sentence appeal judgment, the *Katanga* Trial Chamber once again underscored the importance of passing a sentence that would have a deterrent effect.[49] For the Chamber, however, the

---

40 *Lubanga* appeal judgment on sentence, para. 119.

41 ICC-01/04-01/06: Decision on Sentence pursuant to article 76 of the Statute, 10 July 2012 ("*Lubanga* trial decision on sentence"), paras 1, 98–99 and 107.

42 *Lubanga* trial decision on sentence, para. 16.

43 *Lubanga* trial decision on sentence, paras 36–53.

44 *Lubanga* trial decision on sentence, para. 91.

45 ICC-01/04-01/07-3436-tENG ("*Katanga* Trial Judgment"), pp. 658–659.

46 *Katanga* Trial Judgment, pp. 658–659.

47 *Katanga* Sentencing Judgment, paras 146–148 and 170.

48 ICC-01/04-01/07-3497 ("Defence's Notice of Discontinuance of Appeal"); ICC-01/04-01/07-3497-AnxA ("Defence's Submissions on Discontinuance of Appeal"); ICC-01/04-01/07-3498 ("Prosecution's Notice of Discontinuance of Appeal"), para. 2.

49 *Katanga* Sentencing Judgment, para. 37.

deterrent impact of a sentence resided less in its severity than in the certainty of its infliction.[50] In determining the sentence, the Chamber, having considered all of the relevant factors prescribed by the Statute and the RPE, imposed a sentence that took into account the cruel and discriminatory nature of the crimes, but recognized that Germain Katanga was not present at the scene of the attack and his criminal responsibility was as an accessory to the crimes committed by a group acting with a common purpose. The Chamber gave little weight to mitigating factors, such as Katanga's relative youth, but it did take into account his efforts to contribute to disarmament.[51] Thus, within its broad margin of discretion, the Trial Chamber attempted to balance the various sentencing factors that were particular to the case, while recognizing the overarching sentencing goal of deterrence.

The ICC Trial Chamber III found Jean-Pierre Bemba guilty as a military commander for the crimes against humanity of murder and rape, and the war crimes of murder, rape and pillaging, committed by his forces in the course of their operations in Central African Republic during 2002–2003, a finding that was reversed on appeal.[52] The judgment had served as a warning to military commanders, who, it was to be hoped, would be less sanguine about setting loose the dogs of war to terrorize and brutalize innocent civilian populations, given the risk that they may be held accountable under international criminal law for the depredations of the forces under their effective command and control. The *Bemba* case remains important for its emphasis on the repression of sexual and gender-based crimes. I shall mention the Chamber's conclusions on sentence, regardless of the acquittal on appeal, as it remains relevant for the arguments made here.

In approaching the matter of sentence, the *Bemba* Chamber had considered that the Preamble to the Rome Statute "establishes retribution and deterrence as the primary objectives of punishment at the ICC."[53] Retribution was not a matter of revenge, but rather "an expression of the international community's condemnation of the crimes." Deterrence encompassed both specific and general deterrence. While rehabilitation was relevant, it should not be given undue weight, in light of the nature of the crimes. The Chamber, applying the decision of the Appeals Chamber in *Lubanga*, held that the sentence must be

50 *Katanga* Sentencing Judgment, para. 38. In this, the Trial Chamber's observation finds support in the scholarly literature on deterrence: see Jo and Simmons, pp. 8–9; and Cronin-Furman, p. 441.

51 *Katanga* Sentencing Judgment, paras 141–147.

52 ICC-01/05-01/08, Judgment pursuant to Article 74 of the Statute, 21 March 2016, para. 742. ICC-01/05-01/08-3636-Red Judgment on the appeal of Mr Jean-Pierre Bemba Gombo against Trial Chamber III's "Judgment pursuant to Article 74 of the Statute", 8 June 2018.

53 ICC-01/05-01/08, Decision on Sentence pursuant to Article 76 of the Statute, 21 June 2016 ("*Bemba* Sentencing Judgment"), para. 10.

proportionate to the crime and the culpability of the convicted person: "[A] proportionate sentence also acknowledges the harm to the victims and promotes the restauration of peace and reconciliation."[54]

The Chamber had sentenced Bemba to 18 years in prison on the basis that "the highest sentence imposed, namely, 18 years for the crimes of rape, reflects the totality of Mr Bemba's culpability."[55] The war crime of rape and the crime against humanity of rape, for which Bemba was held criminally responsible as a commander, were committed, the Chamber found, with particular cruelty against particularly defenceless victims.[56] Further, the Chamber's finding that Bemba *knew* that the soldiers, over whom he had effective authority and control, were committing or about to commit the crimes against humanity of murder and rape and the war crimes of murder, rape and pillaging was also an important factor in the sentencing.[57]

In a separate trial before a different Trial Chamber, Bemba and four other individuals were convicted of offences against the administration of justice, contrary to Article 70 of the Rome Statute, in connection with actions they took in an attempt to affect the outcome of the *Bemba* trial. Their convictions and sentences were appealed. The Appeals Chamber confirmed the convictions in respect of most of the charges and granted the Prosecutor's appeal on sentences, finding that the Trial Chamber committed several errors with respect to the assessment of the gravity of the offences. The Appeals Chamber reversed the sentences of Mr Bemba and two others and remanded the matter to the Trial Chamber for a new determination. Considering Bemba's acquittal in the main case, on 15 June 2018, he was provisionally released pending the new determination of his sentence in *Bemba et al.* by the Trial Chamber.[58]

The *Al Mahdi* judgment and sentence provided the first opportunity for the Court to discuss sentencing in the context of a guilty plea. In respect of deterrence, the Chamber considered that "a sentence should be adequate to discourage a convicted person from recidivism (specific deterrence), as well as to ensure that those who would consider committing similar crimes will be

54 *Bemba* Sentencing Judgment, para. 11.

55 *Bemba* Sentencing Judgment, paras 90–96. The crimes of murder and pillaging attracted concurrent sentences of 16 years' imprisonment, while those of rape merited concurrent sentences of 18 years.

56 *Bemba* Sentencing Judgment, para. 93.

57 *Bemba* Sentencing Judgment, paras 59–67.

58 *The Prosecutor v. Jean-Pierre Bemba Gombo, Aimé Kilolo Musamba, Jean-Jacques Mangenda Kabongo, Fidèle Babala Wandu and Narcisse Arido*: ICC-01/05-01/13 (19 October 2016), Judgment pursuant to Article 74 of the Statute; ICC-01/05-01/13-2123-Corr (22 March 2017); Sentence pursuant to Article 76 of the Statute; and ICC-01/05-01/13 (24 April 2017); Appeals: see details and summary here: https://www.icc-cpi.int/Pages/item.aspx?name=pr1362; interim release: ICC-01/05-01/13 (12 June 2018), Decision on Mr Bemba's Application for Release.

dissuaded from doing so (general deterrence)".[59] The Chamber considered that the admission of guilt was a mitigating circumstance and "may have a deterrent effect on others tempted to commit similar acts in Mali and elsewhere".[60]

Considering the *Bemba* acquittal, the *Lubanga* case has provided the only lasting occasion for the ICC Appeals Chamber to address a post-trial judgment appeal on sentence, with the exception of the decision in the *Bemba et al.* case.[61] The ICC's jurisprudence on sentencing is therefore still in its infancy. In calibrating sentences that are proportionate to the gravity of the crime and the degree of participation of the convicted person, ICC judges must operate within the range of sanctions that the Rome Statute makes available to them. Only an extreme case will attract the heaviest penalty of life imprisonment. Many perpetrators will thus face sentences within a range having 30 years as the maximum term of imprisonment.

Thus, while some sentences, such as those imposed in the *Lubanga* and *Katanga* cases, given their relative leniency (depending upon one's point of view), may raise a question about the efficacy of the deterrence rationale in ICC sentencing, it may be right to say that effective deterrence lies more in the certainty of punishment than in the severity of the sanction. Moreover, Thomas Lubanga's conviction and sentence appear to have had a deterrent effect, as will be seen below. Furthermore, in the case of Jean-Pierre Bemba, the sentence of 18 years in prison was obviously meant to have a preventive impact upon the conduct of military commanders and, by extension, superiors generally who come within the provisions of the Rome Statute relating to command responsibility, especially in relation to sexual and gender-based crimes.[62]

It should be noted in passing that the Rome Statute and the RPE allow for the Court's review of a sentence to determine whether early release is justified.[63] Early release may only be considered once the convicted person has served two-thirds of his or her sentence, or 25 years in the case of life imprisonment.[64] The decision to grant early release is discretionary and is based upon a number of considerations enumerated in the Statute and the RPE.[65] The clear emphasis

---

59 ICC-01/12-01/15, *The Prosecutor v. Ahmad Al Faqi Al Madi*, Judgment and Sentence, 27 September 2016, para. 67.

60 *Ibid.*, para. 100.

61 See *supra* note 58 for the appeals of the other *Bemba* sentencing judgment concerning offences against the administration of justice. As mentioned above, the sentence appeals in *Bemba* were rendered moot, because, in a 3–2 decision, dated 8 June 2018, the Appeals Chamber, essentially upon its review of certain factual conclusions of the Trial Chamber, reversed his convictions and acquitted him: see, ICC-01/05-01/08 A.

62 See RS, Article 28. Note that the crimes of rape had attracted the highest penalty imposed in the *Bemba* case.

63 RS, Article 110; RPE, Rules 223 and 224. The provisions for reconsideration are not relevant to this discussion, but see Article 84 and Rules 159–161.

64 RS, Article 110(3).

65 See, generally, RS, Article 110 and RPE, Rule 223.

of these various provisions, although not their exclusive emphasis, is upon progress in rehabilitation and potential for resocialization. Rehabilitation and resocialization are well-known sentencing objectives in domestic criminal justice systems and so at the ICC, they also have their part to play in the administration of international criminal justice. The three judges of the ICC Appeals Chamber designated to consider the application of Thomas Lubanga for early release denied his application.[66] However, Germain Katanga's application for early release was granted by the Court.[67] He returned to the DRC, but only to face domestic prosecution for other crimes he allegedly committed.[68]

5. TO DETER WHOM?

From the perspective of the deterrence rationale in the Rome Statute, the following question arises: just whom should the ICC seek to deter? One would hope that the widest possible spectrum of perpetrators would become the target of investigation and prosecution where the evidence supported such action. Given the Rome Statute's principle of complementarity, this would primarily be the responsibility of states, with the ICC intervening only where national authorities lacked either the capacity or the willingness to do so. Combatting impunity is a shared responsibility.

Confronted with the immensity of its task, the ICC has had to decide just how to use its available resources to best effect, just as the ad hoc tribunals and courts have had to do. This has meant, generally speaking, that the OTP's investigative strategy has focused upon those individuals that the evidence suggests bear the greatest responsibility for the most serious crimes committed in a situation country.[69] Many lower-level, and even mid-level, perpetrators may thus escape ICC scrutiny and, if they are not caught by the national criminal law system, may elude justice altogether.

However, practical limitations on investigative possibilities or a lack of cooperation will result in an OTP strategy of building upward from

66 ICC-01/04-01/06-3173, Decision on the review concerning reduction of sentence of Mr Thomas Lubanga Dyilo, 22 September 2015. Lubanga has made another application for early release, but this too was denied: *The Prosecutor v. Thomas Lubanga Dyilo*: ICC-01/04-01/06-3375 – Second Decision on the review concerning reduction of sentence of Mr Thomas Lubanga Dyilo.

67 ICC-01/04/01/07, Decision on the review concerning reduction of sentence of Mr Germain Katanga, 13 November 2015.

68 See ICC-01/04-01/07, Decision pursuant to Article 108(1) of the Rome Statute, 7 April 2016; and ICC-01/04-01/07 OA 15, Decision on the admissibility of Mr Katanga's appeal against the "Decision pursuant to Article 108(1) of the Rome Statute," 9 June 2016.

69 See Strategic Plan 2016–2018, paras 35–36; this strategic plan builds on the previous strategic planning cycle of 2012–2015.

investigation and prosecution of certain mid-level and high-level perpetrators in order to ultimately achieve a reasonable prospect of conviction of those most responsible for the crimes. The OTP will also consider prosecuting lower-level perpetrators exceptionally, where their conduct has been particularly grave and has acquired notoriety.[70]

The upshot, of course, is that an "impunity gap" remains to be filled, which requires capacity at the national level or the development of such capacity, an objective to which the ICC can only contribute in a limited way, since it is outside of the scope of its mandate and beyond the reach of its resources. In its Strategic Plan 2016–2018, the OTP confronts this problem, which it has always recognized, and sets itself as an objective "to develop with partners a coordinated investigative and prosecutorial strategy to close the impunity gap."[71] In setting this goal, the OTP, while necessarily accepting the limitations upon its statutory mandate and available resources, will seek to be a catalyst to make the Rome Statute system of international criminal justice work as it was designed to do, with states shouldering the primary burden of bringing the perpetrators of Rome Statute crimes to justice, no matter what level in the hierarchy of perpetrators they are situated. The strategic goal also recognizes the often interconnected nature of criminality, with perpetrators of Rome Statute crimes often also being engaged in organized transnational or domestic criminal activity.

Certainly, the OTP must do its own work well if would-be perpetrators are to be worried enough about being tried in The Hague to desist before committing crimes. While observers of the Court have noted the many practical challenges the Court faces in gathering evidence and conducting quality fact-finding, "its willingness to prosecute has contributed to perceptions that impunity for egregious crimes is a diminishing option."[72] Improving the quality of its work in all domains has been one of the principal objectives of the OTP, as expressed in its strategic planning.[73]

6. PREVENTION STRATEGIES OF THE ICC PROSECUTOR

The massacres that ensued from the fall of Srebrenica in July 1995 occurred after the UN International Criminal Tribunal for the Former Yugoslavia (ICTY) was established and functioning. The existence of the ICTY, and thus the possibility of prosecution, did not prevent that tragedy from happening. Yet, after the

70 Strategic Plan 2016–2018, para. 36.
71 Strategic Plan 2016–2018, strategic goal 9 and paras 100–106.
72 Jo and Simmons, p. 39.
73 See, generally, the objectives established in the Strategic Plan 2016–2018.

convictions of key actors in the Srebrenica genocide, even highly placed political actors, such as Radovan Karadžić, the prosecution of others, both civilian and military, including Slobodan Milošević and Ratko Mladić, and the work of other courts respecting other conflicts, such as the International Criminal Tribunal for Rwanda (ICTR) and the Special Court for Sierra Leone (SCSL), it must now be clear: those responsible for mass atrocities face a far greater risk that they will eventually be called to account for their actions.

Investigation, prosecution and conviction of perpetrators will serve to break the cycle of impunity and help deter the commission of future crimes – such is the objective. It is in this spirit that the work of the ICC progresses, with the goal of bringing a measure of justice to victims and affected communities, and strengthening respect for human rights and the rule of law.

The OTP pursues the goal of prevention through its own operations and by encouraging national responses to international crimes. The latter approach is in line with the Rome Statute, which places primary responsibility for the investigation and prosecution of war crimes, crimes against humanity and genocide upon states. The ICC is a court of last resort and is only justified in intervening where states themselves either cannot or will not discharge their responsibilities under the Statute.[74] Whether the Court will intervene in a given situation is determined via the preliminary examination process. Along with investigations and prosecutions, the conduct of preliminary examinations is a core function of the OTP under the ICC Statute.[75]

The successful investigation and prosecution of Rome Statute crimes will be the most obvious and public vindication of the values that the Court exists to protect. Investigation and prosecution are important, but they do not embrace the whole prevention effort. Where justified, investigations and prosecutions follow from the preliminary examination of the given situations. Preliminary examination is an information-gathering process to determine issues of jurisdiction and admissibility. Since the ICC is a court of last resort, one necessary focus of a preliminary examination is to determine whether there are genuine national proceedings in existence that relate to substantially the same cases as the ICC Prosecutor would bring.[76] If there are, then these cases would be inadmissible before the ICC and the OTP will not intervene to investigate.

The concept of complementarity of jurisdictions that is a fundamental premise of the Rome Statute has led the OTP to adopt a positive approach to complementarity. Thus, since the OTP's jurisdiction is complementary to national jurisdictions, at the preliminary examination stage, the OTP often finds

---

74 See RS, Preamble and Articles 1 and 17–19.

75 See RS, Articles 15 and 53.

76 See ICC-01/09-3 (26 November 2009), paras 51 and 107; ICC-01/09-19-Corr (31 March 2010), paras 50, 182 and 188; ICC-02/11-14 (3 October 2011), paras 190–191.

itself encouraging national authorities to exercise their jurisdiction. There are many advantages to an effective local response to mass atrocity crimes: justice is delivered closer to the community where the crimes occurred, the rule of law and respect for human rights are strengthened at the national level, and the overall objectives of the Rome Statute system of international criminal justice – namely, ending impunity for the most serious crimes and contributing to their prevention – are advanced.

Ultimately, the ability of the ICC to deter crimes will depend upon the success with which it does its work, and the focus here must be initially, and especially, upon the OTP. The OTP must accomplish those actions over which it has control with the greatest possible skill and address, and manage, as well as it is able, those many factors that are beyond its control, but that impinge upon its ability to operate effectively. Such factors include the willingness of states parties to the Rome Statute and others to cooperate with the OTP, behaviour the OTP can attempt to influence through a variety of strategies, but which ultimately turns on the political decisions states themselves make, the security situations on the ground, which present risks that the OTP can manage, but which it may not be able to control and so on. The OTP can only strive to mitigate disadvantages and manage risks in any given situation, and to capitalize on opportunities it is able to generate.

There is a belief in many quarters – on the part of civil society in situation countries, human rights non-governmental organizations (NGOs) and even governments – that the mere presence of the ICC in a situation country through the preliminary examination process will have a preventive effect upon potential violence.[77] The OTP's *Policy Paper on Preliminary Examinations* recognizes this aspect of the preliminary examination process. One of the stated objectives of preliminary examinations is therefore to end impunity through a positive approach to complementarity, by encouraging national proceedings.[78]

Jo and Simmons believe that the complementarity principle bolsters the ICC's prosecutorial deterrence – a concept they posit alongside the concept of social deterrence in examining the total deterrent effect of the ICC's work – to the extent that it creates incentives for states to strengthen their own legal capacities. In their view, "the Rome Statute's 'complementarity regime' creates a channel for the ICC to support prosecutorial deterrence at the *national* level as well."[79] This view certainly accords with the OTP's strategic planning. For Sikkink and Kim, the ICC, as the back-up institution when the primary institutions for

77 The author bases this rather broad assertion upon his engagement since October 2012, well before he assumed office as Deputy Prosecutor at the ICC in March 2013, and in the years since with various actors in the domains cited; it is also implied in some of the social science research that will be discussed later on.

78 *Policy Paper on Preliminary Examinations*, paras 100–103. See also Olasolo, pp. 15–16.

79 Jo and Simmons, pp. 10–12.

enforcement at the national level fail, is "necessary to create a fully functioning international model."[80]

An example of such positive complementarity at work is Guinea: the authorities there are dealing with a politically motivated massacre and other crimes that occurred in September 2009. The OTP has not intervened to investigate, but continues to keep open a preliminary examination of the situation. The progress that Guinean judicial authorities have made in their investigation of the alleged crimes is "partly ascribable to the positive and constructive dynamic created between the OTP, the UN, civil society and the Guinean authorities."[81]

Colombia presents another, quite different, example. Colombia has a sophisticated legal and judicial system. It has also suffered decades of civil war, a conflict which the government in Bogotá has endeavored to end through a peace process engaging the guerrillas it has been fighting. The situation in Colombia thus raises the question of how, for a state party to the Rome Statute, transitional justice measures that are responsive to the requirements of the Rome Statute can be implemented as an integral feature of the peace process. The preliminary examination opened by the OTP remains open for now in order to allow the OTP to monitor developments in consultation with a variety of stakeholders, including the Colombian government. The issue of transitional justice for guerrillas is not the only justice issue the Colombian authorities must confront within the scope of the ICC Statute, since, for example, the investigation and prosecution of crimes alleged to have been committed by members of the Colombian military – the infamous "false positives" cases – continue to be a matter of concern for the OTP and for the authorities.[82]

These two examples are but illustrations of the variety of complex situations in which the OTP is involved, short of launching a full criminal investigation or prosecution, to encourage and support action by national authorities to address Rome Statute crimes effectively.

To enhance the preventive impact of the ICC, and thus deter violence and obviate the need for the Court to intervene, the OTP also attempts to perform an early warning function. The Office reacts promptly to information it collects

80 Sikkink, Kathryn and Hun Joon Kim. 2013. The Justice Cascade: The Origins and Effectiveness of Prosecutions of Human Rights Violations. *Annual Review of Law and Social Science* 9: 269–285, p. 272.

81 OTP, *Report on Preliminary Examination Activities 2015*, Guinea, p. 43, para. 185; see also pp. 42–43, paras 179–184. The writer also gained the impression from public remarks made in December 2014 at the Assembly of States Parties session in New York City by the Guinean Minister of Justice that the presence of the ICC in the background had strengthened the hand of the Minister to push forward with the cases he wished to see prosecuted.

82 The complex involvement of the OTP in the situation in Colombia is well beyond the scope of this chapter and is cited as but one example of positive complementarity in practice; for a fuller background to the OTP's current activities in relation to the situation in Colombia, see OTP, *Report on Preliminary Examination Activities 2015*, Colombia, pp. 32–39.

on upsurges in violence and engages with states, international organizations and NGOs to verify information about alleged crimes. It encourages intervention by national authorities or restraint on the part of political actors in sometimes highly fraught situations on the national scene.[83] The Prosecutor will occasionally issue public statements in connection with situation countries to caution against violence in the hope that the reminder about possible investigation and prosecution will serve to deter crimes.[84] However, the Prosecutor makes judicious use of such statements, reserving them for situations where she believes they can have a genuine impact.

There is a belief, supported by anecdotal evidence, that such cautionary statements do have an effect. Crisis situations in states parties to the Rome Statute often result in calls for the Prosecutor to issue statements that will serve to deter excesses. Opening a preliminary examination into a situation of possible Rome Statute crimes constitutes an even sturdier intervention on the Prosecutor's part, which may serve to deter violence, even in the absence of an investigation or prosecution. However, in some situations, ICC involvement, even where it has led to investigations and the initiation of prosecutions, has had little impact on levels of violence and human rights abuses; Sudan (Darfur) and Libya serve as dismaying examples.

During the UN Security Council Open Debate in September 2012, Rhadika Coomaraswamy, then Special Representative of the Secretary-General for Children and Armed Conflict, remarked, in relation to violations against children in conflict, that the possibility of appearing before the ICC had proven "an effective deterrent for military commanders, as well as a useful leverage in action plan dialogue."[85] Appearing as an expert witness before the *Lubanga* Trial Chamber at the ICC, she also testified as follows:

> Finally, your Honour, let me state how important the work of the ICC is to every one of us who works in the field. The willingness on the part of the Court to prosecute these cases has sent many armed groups to us – the United Nations – willing to negotiate action plans for the release of children; most recently yesterday in Nepal where the release of

83 *Policy Paper on Preliminary Examinations*, paras 104–105.

84 *Policy Paper on Preliminary Examinations*, para. 106. For example, the Prosecutor issued statements calling for restraint and warning those alleged to be committing crimes in the context of pre-election violence and the worsening security situation in Burundi, on 8 May and 6 November 2015, respectively. On 25 April 2016, she opened a preliminary examination of the situation in that country, then a state party to the Rome Statute. Note that the state withdrew from the Rome Statute effective on 27 October 2017, but the Pre-Trial Chamber authorised the Prosecutor to open *proprio motu* investigation on 25 October 2017 (public redacted version available on 9 November): ICC-01/17-9-Red, Public Redacted Version of "Decision Pursuant to Article 15 of the Rome Statute on the Authorization of an Investigation into the Situation in the Republic of Burundi", ICC-01/17-X-9-US-Exp, 25 October 2017.

85 19 September 2012 – UN Security Council Open Debate Statement.

> 3,000 children is about to begin today. We found your work to be so important and that is why we have sought to reflect the experiences of the child protection partners of the United Nations in the field and the child victims we attend to across the globe in our intervention here.[86]

This is eloquent testimony to the deterrent capacity of the Court.

On a panel at a conference held in Switzerland in 2014, a Deputy of the National Assembly of the DRC related that the ICC decision in *Lubanga* had heightened awareness about the problem of the use of child soldiers in his country. He was adamant that it had had a deterrent effect on the ground.[87]

There is also the wonderful story reported in the *New Yorker* about Christian militiamen in the Central African Republic releasing Muslim refugees they were abducting from a church compound when a nun told the militiamen that the Muslims were under the protection of the ICC and, if any harm came to them, the militiamen would be arrested and taken to The Hague.[88]

Such anecdotal evidence offers encouragement regarding the ability of the ICC to have a preventive impact. However, the challenge that international criminal justice faces is far greater than one such incident, even if the outcome there was a happy one. Certainly, the reception the ICC has received in situation countries, such as the Central African Republic, suggests that a strong belief does exist in the preventive potential of action by the ICC in conducting preliminary examinations of situations, even short of investigation and prosecution. The situation in the Central African Republic, of course, led to a far stronger intervention by the OTP, when the Prosecutor opened investigations respecting the actions of both sides to the conflict there.[89]

7. WILL EFFECTIVE PROSECUTION DETER THE FUTURE COMMISSION OF CRIMES?

Social scientists have been examining the deterrent impact of the ICC and international criminal justice endeavours generally. Referring to their own work and to other recent empirical studies, which focus upon either the effect of the ICC in ongoing conflicts or the Court's impact on law and violence in the

86 ICC-01/04-01/06-T-223-ENG ET WT 07-01-2010 16/77 NB T, lines 11–18.

87 As related to the writer by the Senior Special Assistant to the Prosecutor, Sam Shoamanesh, with reference to remarks made by Juvénal Munubo Mubi, Deputy, National Assembly of the DRC, on a panel on "Youth and Human Security: Perspectives," held on 14 October 2014 in Bern, as part of the Annual Conference of the Human Security Division of the Swiss Federal Department of Foreign Affairs.

88 Anderson, Jon Lee, "The Mission: A Last Defense against Genocide," *The New Yorker*, 20 October 2014.

89 See press release ICC-OTP-30130116-PR869.

longer term, Dancy, Marchesi, Montal and Sikkink have offered this guarded, but positive, appraisal:

> The results of recent empirical studies lead us to support this cautious consensus about the positive benefits of international criminal justice. Research is beginning to show that human rights prosecutions are associated with improvement in core human rights over the intermediate term, and, at a minimum, do not exacerbate conflict or undermine democracy. From the point of view of a short-term policy option, these are quite positive findings – stronger, for example, than the findings on the impact of other tactics like economic sanctions, trade linkage or foreign military intervention on human rights performance. When future panic about an ICC "crisis" arises, this evidence is worth keeping in mind.[90]

The commitment of states to conduct investigations and prosecutions may signal a stronger resolve to protect human rights and prevent mass atrocities. Simmons and Danner suggest that adherence to the Rome Statute, in and of itself, may be a signal by a state that it is voluntarily abandoning the option of engaging in unlimited violence so as to create incentives for other actors to alter their behaviour as well.[91]

The initial findings of Simmons and Danner do not show that the ICC will deter all or even most atrocities in future. However, they found that there was:

> convincing evidence that governments least able credibly to prosecute war-related atrocities were among those most likely to embrace the new international criminal law regime, as well as behavioural evidence that this commitment meant something to domestic adversaries. This finding is consistent with a new stream of legal research that explores the significance of international law and institutions to bind governments' hands in ways that allow them to achieve results that would not be possible in the absence of international legal institutions.[92]

The results they speak of relate to the ratcheting down of violence and the enhancement of peace-making.

There is skepticism too about the ability of the ICC to accomplish deterrence or prevention. Jo and Simmons provide a convenient – and critical – overview of the criticisms of the Court, noting that "the ICC almost by definition raises hopes and expectations beyond anything we have seen since the Nuremberg

---

90 Dancy, Geoff, Bridget Marchesi, Florencia Montal and Kathryn Sikkink. 2015. The ICC's deterrent impact: What the evidence shows, *openGlobalRights*, reproduced in *openDemocracy*. (The "crisis" referred to was the reaction to the Prosecutor's withdrawal of the charges against Uhuru Kenyatta.)

91 See Simmons, Beth Ann and Allison Danner. 2010. Credible Commitments and the International Criminal Court. *International Organization* 64(2): 225–256, p. 234.

92 Simmons and Danner, p. 254.

and Tokyo trials."[93] Cronin-Furman, as a thoughtful critic of the ICC, has concluded that "individuals who bear the 'greatest responsibility' for the 'most serious crimes' are likely to be those who are hardest to deter." On the other hand, she continues, "commanders who fail to prevent and punish the violation of their subordinates do not face overwhelming incentives to allow mass atrocity and therefore are more likely to be deterred by prosecutions of similarly situated individuals."[94] Based on her conclusions, Cronin-Furman questions the wisdom of the OTP's strategy of investigating those persons bearing the greatest responsibility for the most serious crimes, since she maintains that charges against such persons are those least likely to have a true deterrent effect.[95] For her, "the Court's [the OTP's] choices of charges to pursue do not maximize the chances of a general deterrent effect on the commission of mass atrocity."[96]

Nevertheless, it would seem from the OTP's perspective that whatever success the ICC may have in achieving deterrence respecting one set of potential offenders as opposed to another, the imperatives of the Rome Statute itself leave the Prosecutor with little choice but to pursue both – and there is certainly room for expressive and retributive justice, as well as deterrence, in the ICC criminal justice accountability regime.

On their part, Kim and Sikkink have found that "prosecution processes and convictions of high-level state officials appear to have a stronger deterrent effect when compared to prosecutions and convictions of low-level officials."[97] Moreover, it would appear that the whole process of prosecution is likely to improve human rights, even where dismissals of charges or acquittals result, although "a sustained failure to convict could diminish belief in the likelihood of punishment."[98] Such findings only serve to underscore the importance of the OTP's effort to improve the quality and effectiveness of its preliminary examinations, investigations and prosecutions.

Jo and Simmons, in their research, specify two broad channels of general deterrence, namely, prosecutorial deterrence and social deterrence. Prosecutorial deterrence operates through the legal process resulting in court-imposed sanctions, while social deterrence derives from extra-legal social costs of violations of the law.[99] Regarding prosecutorial deterrence, Jo and Simmons note that individuals are deterred from violating the law when the chances of detection and legal sanction increase. This facet of deterrence encompasses both

---

93 See Jo and Simmons, pp. 4–6.
94 Cronin-Furman, p. 453.
95 See Strategic Plan 2012–2015; Cronin-Furman, pp. 453–454.
96 Cronin-Furman, p. 436.
97 Kim, Hun Joon and Kathryn Sikkink. 2012–2013. How Do Human Rights Prosecutions Improve Human Rights after Transition? *Interdisciplinary Journal of Human Rights Law* 7: 69–90, pp. 71 and 87.
98 Kim and Sikkink, p. 87.
99 Jo and Simmons, p. 7.

the investigation and prosecution of crimes by the ICC and the application of the complementarity regime: "In sum, prosecutorial deterrence is expected to be enhanced by any condition that makes prosecution more likely in a given jurisdiction."[100]

Regarding social deterrence, Jo and Simmons observe: "The ICC is the institutional manifestation of a movement, years in the making, to punish international crimes and put them firmly beyond the pale."[101] Potential offenders are often deterred from violating the law more as the result of the anticipated social response, they write, than the likelihood of prosecution and punishment by formal legal processes. The social, psychic, material and reputational costs of transgressing community values may serve as an effective deterrent. "Importantly, this range of informal social pressure is both elicited and legitimated by the normative focal power of a criminal tribunal." The authors conclude: "As the ICC takes action, it not only raises expectations of prosecutions, it shapes social expectations about what constitutes justice more broadly."[102]

In the view of Jo and Simmons, "there are grounds for cautious optimism that the ICC is contributing in important ways to violence reduction in some of the most brutal places in the world."[103] They observe that: "The absolute risk of punishment by the ICC remains small, but it is not negligible and is much higher than was the case when impunity was the default."[104]

In a recent article on the research they have been doing, Jo and Simmons repeat their cautious optimism. They report that the ICC can indeed deter civilian killings, but only under the right conditions. Having examined all of the situations subject to investigation or prosecution by the ICC, as well as many other situations, they found that the ICC had some deterrent impact upon national governments and their forces. Where ratification of the Rome Statute has conferred jurisdiction upon the ICC, there have been domestic legal reforms, and the Court has indicated a clear intention to prosecute by initiating investigations. They report that "intentional killings drop most in places under the Court's jurisdiction and where human rights groups are on the rise. Local social context matters." They found, however, only limited evidence of a deterrent effect upon rebel groups, but noted that "rebel groups seem to be strongly deterred when investigations begin." In conclusion, they suggest: "There is now some reason to think the ICC saves some lives – but the ICC is also deeply embedded in the world of politics and faces challenges in securing state support and capturing criminals."[105]

---

100 See Jo and Simmons, pp. 7–12.
101 Jo and Simmons, p. 12.
102 See Jo and Simmons, pp. 12–16.
103 Jo and Simmons, p. 4.
104 Jo and Simmons, p. 16.
105 Jo, Hyeron and Beth A. Simmons. 2016. Running the Numbers on ICC Deterrence: When Does it Actually Work? *openGlobalRights*, reproduced in *openDemocracy*.

The social science research canvassed above may be a modest vindication of the work of the Court, but it is enough to inspire a continued effort to end impunity with the aim of contributing to prevention. Thus, while opinion may be divided on whether the ICC has, or will have, a positively preventive impact on the commission of international crimes, social science research does offer hope that it will.

For its part, the OTP, while being aware of the research on the deterrent effect of ICC actions, so far avoids drawing upon it to measure its performance, precisely because of the difficulty of evaluating that effect with accuracy and confidence in any given circumstances. For now, the endeavour to measure the preventive effect of the Court is best left to scholars and other observers of the Court. The performance indicators being developed by the OTP, and the Court generally, focus for the moment upon matters that are within the Court's control, more or less, and that are more easily susceptible of measurement.

8. CONCLUSION

In recent cases, the OTP has enjoyed success before the Pre-Trial Chambers in securing the confirmation of charges. The coming years will tell whether similar successes will result from the trials before the Trial Chambers. What success will mean for prevention only time will tell. However, if the ICC can hold perpetrators of the most serious crimes to account, following sound investigations and as a positive outcome of fair and efficient trials, then it can indeed hope to achieve a deterrent impact.

The ability of the OTP to inspire state action in response to international crimes, through the operation of the concept of positive complementarity, also enhances the protection of human rights. This too is a part of the Court's prevention strategy, which has had a positive impact.

Moreover, the influence the Court enjoys in shaping attitudes and policies, with respect to the protection of human rights, strengthens the cause of prevention. The ICC provides a moral compass to guide both state and individual actors away from violent actions and toward the more benign resolution of conflicts.

In an often volatile, violent and dangerous world, the ICC offers the promise of an independent, impartial and fair administration of international criminal justice. This guarantee enhances the Court's credibility and improves its ability to deter mass atrocities. The capacity of international criminal justice to prevent the occurrence of mass atrocities may prove to be uneven and imperfect. This is, however, no reason to despair of the fight to end impunity.

PEACE AND JUSTICE

Human Rights Fact-Finding in Raging Conflicts

Mona RISHMAWI[1]

1 Louise Arbour, one of the greatest international investigators of our time, hugely influenced the author's thinking about United Nations human rights and criminal investigations. Nevertheless, the views expressed are those of the author, who writes in her personal capacity. They also do not necessarily reflect the views of the United Nations or of any other institution. The author wishes to thank Professor Andrew Clapham for his comments and insights, which enriched the piece. The author is also deeply grateful to her colleagues and friends Takhmina Karimov, Ruth Marshall and Zaved Mahmood for their expert review of the text.

1. INTRODUCTION

Louise Arbour began her term as High Commissioner on 1 July 2004 at a difficult time for human rights in general and for the Office of the United Nations High Commissioner for Human Rights (OHCHR) in particular. The tense international atmosphere following the terrorist attacks on the United States on 11 September 2001 was still at its peak. Armed conflicts in Afghanistan and Iraq were ongoing. Guantanamo was being filled by detainees and the relevance of international law was being questioned. Darfur was undergoing a slow but steady deadly conflict that started to gain international attention. The United Nations (UN) system was affected by the debate on the legality of the Iraq war and the Oil for Food corruption allegations.[2] Moreover, there were public campaigns against the UN human rights system accusing it of bias and partiality.[3]

Only ten months before Arbour took the helm, the OHCHR had been devastated by the killing of the UN High Commissioner for Human Rights Sérgio Vieira de Mello and 21 others in a terrorist attack on the Canal Hotel in Baghdad, which also left many injured, including OHCHR staff. Shocked and shaken, the OHCHR in particular and the UN human rights system in general needed a strong intellectual and strategic leader to steer the ship into safe waters. And that was Louise Arbour.

With her background as a distinguished jurist, judge and international prosecutor, Arbour focused her efforts on bringing back faith in human rights as a legal regime and the absolute need for its implementation. Fact-finding was central to her approach, believing that ascertaining facts is an indispensable prerequisite to bringing respect for the rule of law. She invested in developing accountability processes that could be carried out according to a fair, credible and predictable methodology.

This chapter will narrate the story of fact-finding, largely within the UN human rights context. After discussing the approaches and types of fact-finding, it will examine some challenges that face fact-finding in the human rights field. The specific role of Louise Arbour will be situated in this story,

---

2 United Nations, "The United Nations is Extremely Concerned about the Serious Allegations of Corruption Surrounding the Oil-for-Food Program" (21 April 2004), online: <http://www.un.org/News/dh/iraq/oip/facts-oilforfood.htm>; Ewen MacAskill and Julian Borger, "Iraq War was Illegal and Breached UN Charter, Says Annan," *The Guardian* (16 September 2004), online: <https://www.theguardian.com/world/2004/sep/16/iraq.iraq>.

3 Barbara Crossette, "For First Time, U.S. is Excluded From U.N. Human Rights Panel," *The New York Times* (4 May 2001), online: <http://www.nytimes.com/2001/05/04/world/for-first-time-us-is-excluded-from-un-human-rights-panel.html>; Anne Applebaum, "The U.N.'s Human Rights Rituals," *The Washington Post* (16 April 2003), online: <http://www.anneapplebaum.com/2003/04/16/the-uns-human-rights-rituals/>.

particularly the strategies she developed to address some of the dilemmas that were faced. Issues pertaining to legal regimes and the differences between human rights investigations and criminal investigations, such as standards of proof, witness protection and follow up, will be highlighted.

2. APPROACHES TO FACT-FINDING

The science and art of fact-finding is essential for many disciplines. For instance, it is a key component of diagnosing medical problems, health risks, environmental degradation and natural disasters. It also occupies a central place in the legal field, playing a major role in the implementation of law, whether it relates to dispute resolution, adjudication or assessment of damages. The premise is that professional and credible examination of facts, and impartial assessments against established legal principles, leads to justice.

Fact-finding can also serve as political early warning and as a confidence-building tool. It may contribute to building a better understanding of applicable rules amongst communities and to lowering the level of tension. Timely and accurate knowledge of the facts may lead to violations being prevented. Understanding the economic and social roots of conflicts, as well as economic and social trends and political developments, are essential for avoiding dangerous escalation.[4] Such examination is an important peace-making and peace-building tool that enhances understanding and therefore respect for the international rule of law.[5]

While it often follows precise rules, there are moral and philosophical aspects that are generally relevant to fact-finding beyond a specific social or scientific field. In 1947, Immanuel Lewy, writing in the aftermath of the Second World War, explored the moral issues surrounding the assertion of facts.[6] He explained that when we speak of facts, "we pick out some bundles of happenings and separate them from their context, giving them shape and color."[7] His basic conclusion is that facts often depend on the lens of the valuation system from which they are

4 United Nations Secretary-General (UNSG), *An Agenda for Peace: Preventive Diplomacy, Peacemaking and Peacekeeping*, UNGAOR, 47th sess, UN Doc. A/47/277, 12 June 1992 at para 25.

5 UNSG, *Strengthening and Coordinating United Nations Rule of Law Activities*, UNGAOR, 67th sess, UN Doc. A/67/290, 10 August 2012 at para 19.

6 Immanuel Lewy, "Valuation in Fact-Finding" (1947) 44(21) *Journal of Philosophy* 575–578 at 576.

7 Ibid. Immanuel Lewy wrote: "When we describe the prosperity of a country, the behaviour of an ethnic group, the working conditions of a factory, or a state, we select some important or characteristic phenomena and neglect some others which seem to us irrelevant. Time and space make such reduction inevitable. Since we select and discern between important and irrelevant happenings, we have introduced a subjective factor, our valuation."

viewed. The timing of the exercise plays a role in shaping its accuracy, as well as the quality and expertise of those who carry out these functions.[8]

Writing before the era of extensive international regulation, Lewy explains that in the pre-Nazi period, a group of scholars attempted to create a political science approach based on the gathering of experiences and observations, without ideological valuations.[9] He was intrigued, as he put it, by the thought of freeing politics, religion and social science from emotional prejudices, from class, national or other vested interests. He saw this as the greatest step forward in unifying humanity.[10]

In 1948, the Universal Declaration of Human Rights provided an instrument for an international valuation against which policies and conduct could be measured. After all, it was adopted by the UN General Assembly "as a common standard of achievement for all peoples and all nations."[11] What ensued was a persistent effort to develop a system that enables objective assessments of human rights obligations that a state has voluntarily accepted. This has resulted in the elaboration of numerous treaties, declarations and norms.

With the development of this legal framework, methods to assess implementation immediately began. Leading non-governmental human rights organizations like Amnesty International, the International Commission of Jurists and later Human Rights Watch started to develop techniques to monitor the application of human rights in specific situations. This movement at the international level was echoed by a movement at the national level, with strong domestic human rights groups in almost every country in the world developing their own approaches of assessing their state's compliance with its own human rights obligations.

Attempts to standardize the fact-finding methods followed. Already in 1980, a special sub-committee of the International Law Association developed the Belgrade Minimal Rules of Procedure for International Human Rights.[12] In 1991, the UN General Assembly adopted the Declaration on Fact-Finding by the United Nations in the Field of the Maintenance of International Peace and Security.[13] This Declaration provides for a definition of fact-finding, as will be detailed below. While this Declaration continues to guide the UN fact-finding work in general, more tailored standards were developed to guide the UN human

8 Ibid at 578.

9 Ibid.

10 Ibid.

11 Universal Declaration of Human Rights, GA Res 217 (111), UNGAOR, 3d sess, Supp No 13, UN Doc. A/810 (1948) 71; see preamble.

12 Thomas M. Franck, "The Belgrade Minimal Rules of Procedure for International Fact-Finding Missions" (1981) 75(1) *Human Rights American Journal of International Law* 163–165.

13 *Declaration on Fact-Finding by the United Nations in the Field of the Maintenance of International Peace and Security*, GA Res 46/59, UNGAOR, 46th sess, UN Doc. A/C.6/46/L.9, 9 December 1991.

rights work in this area. Particularly relevant are the Updated Set of Principles for the Protection and Promotion of Human Rights through Action to Combat Impunity, which were elaborated by Professor Diane Orentlicher in 2005, upon the request of the then UN Commission on Human Rights.[14]

There has also been growing academic interest in this area of work. Several research projects have been carried out to study these inquires and to develop guidance for practitioners focusing in particular on independent International Commissions of Inquiry.[15] The OHCHR, which carries out most international investigations, continues to provide professional guidance to these bodies and reflect on lessons learnt.[16] The UN human rights special procedures system has also looked at the impact of these bodies at the international and national levels and has offered specific advice in this area.[17]

It should be noted that the international methods for fact-finding were mostly borrowed from national legal systems, particularly from the Commonwealth countries, which have been deploying such mechanisms for centuries.[18] Many states have an elaborate national regime for inquiries. In her capacity as a national judge, Louise Arbour herself led the Commission of Inquiry into certain events beginning on 22 April 1994 at the Prison for Women in Kingston, Ontario.[19] As states appear to be resorting to national commissions of inquiry, human rights experts have been studying the conditions that render such commissions effective.[20]

---

14 *Updated Set of Principles for the Protection and Promotion of Human Rights through Action to Combat Impunity*, UNESCOR, 61th sess, UN Docs. E/CN.4/2005/102 and E/CN.4/2005/102/Add.1, 8 February 2005. Those principles update a 1997 version developed by Mr Louis Joinet, who was the Special Rapporteur on the question of impunity of perpetrators of violations of human rights of the then Sub-Commission on Prevention of Discrimination and Protection of Minorities. *Revised Final Report Prepared by Mr. Joinet Pursuant to Sub-Commission Decision 1996/119*, UNESCOR, 49th sess, UN Doc. E/CN.4/Sub.2/1997/20/Rev.1, annex II, 2 October 1997.

15 See e.g. Harvard Humanitarian Initiative, *HPCR Advanced Practitioner's Handbook on Commissions of Inquiry: Monitoring, Reporting, and Fact-Finding*, 2015, online: <https://hhi.harvard.edu/publications/hpcr-advanced-practitioners-handbook-commissions-inquiry>; Cherif Bassiouni and Christina Abraham (eds), *Siracusa Guidelines for International, Regional and National Fact-Finding Bodies*, Cambridge, Interstentia, 2013.

16 See e.g. Commissions of Inquiry and Fact-Finding Missions on International Human Rights and Humanitarian Law, *Guidance and Practice*, OHRC, New York and Geneva, 2015.

17 Phillip Alston, *Report of the Special Rapporteur on Extrajudicial, Summary or Arbitrary Executions*, UNHRCOR, 8th sess, UN Doc. A/HRC/8/3, 2 May 2008; Juan E. Méndez, *Report of the Special Rapporteur on Torture and Other Cruel, Inhuman or Degrading Treatment or Punishment*, UNHRCOR, 19th sess, UN Doc. A/HRC/19/61, 1 March 2012.

18 On an early survey of national commissions of inquiry, see e.g. Harold F. Gosnell, "British Royal Commissions of Inquiry" (1934) 49(1) *Political Science Quarterly* 84–118.

19 Commission of Inquiry into Certain Events at the Prison for Women in Kingston, 1996, online: <http://www.justicebehindthewalls.net/resources/arbour_report/arbour_rpt.htm>.

20 See e.g. *supra* note 17.

3. TYPES OF FACT-FINDING

The General Assembly's Declaration on Fact-Finding by the United Nations in the Field of the Maintenance of International Peace and Security defines fact-finding as "any activity designed to obtain detailed knowledge of the relevant facts of any dispute or situation which the competent United Nations organs need in order to exercise effectively their functions in relation to the maintenance of international peace and security."[21] In more general terms, as already stated, fact-finding is about reconstructing what actually happened through individual experiences, narratives, details and specificity. It explores the various elements of conduct and assesses them against predetermined rules.

Antonio Cassese in his last work, *Realizing Utopia*,[22] proposes cooperation with the parties in the investigation as the variable to distinguish between two types of investigations that he terms "monitoring" and "fact-finding." For him, monitoring is a process that is focused on verifying compliance with and inducing respect for international legal standards. He considers fact-finding to be "a method of establishing facts resort to which is not contingent on the will of the States concerned."[23]

Irrespective of what the actual investigative activity is called, placing the emphasis on the cooperation of the parties with the inquiry has some historical roots. There is also the issue of the consent of the parties, which differs from their cooperation.[24] Given the fact that, unlike domestic systems, very few institutions at the international level have subpoena and summons powers, the manner in which the inquiry is decided is also of relevance. Taking into account the three variables of cooperation, consent and who carries out the inquiry, one can in fact distinguish between four types of international inquiries.

3.1. TYPE 1: INVESTIGATIONS BY INDEPENDENT EXPERTS RELYING ON THE CONSENT OF THE PARTIES

The first generation of inquiries was fully anchored on the need for the consent and cooperation of the parties. As Antonio Cassese explains, the

---

21 *Supra* note 13 at para 2.

22 Antonio Cassese (ed), *Realizing Utopia: the Future of International Law*, Oxford, Oxford University Press, 2012 at 295.

23 Ibid.

24 While the concepts of consent and cooperation are related as expressions of agency, sovereignty and autonomy, they are not the same. Consent generally refers to the voluntary acceptance of the act and an agreement of minds. Cooperation may not entail an acceptance of the measure, but some tolerance that enables the parties to go along with it.

institution of Commissions of Inquiry at the international level dates back to the 1899 and 1907 Hague Peace Conferences.[25] The treaties resulting from these meetings, namely the 1899 and 1907 Conventions for the Pacific Settlement of International Disputes, included some elaborate rules on international Commissions of Inquiry.[26] At that time, this method was reserved for disputes of an international nature arising from a difference of opinion on points of facts "involving neither honour nor vital interests." The two Conventions specifically stipulate that international Commissions of Inquiry can be constituted only by special agreement between the parties in conflict. Part III of each of the Convention contains detailed rules regarding the structure and functioning of these Commissions.[27]

The issue of the consent of the parties remained an important feature of the 1949 Geneva Conventions, which provide that "an enquiry shall be instituted in a manner to be decided between the interested Parties concerning any alleged violation of the Convention."[28] The investigations are then carried out by "qualified persons" agreed upon by the parties.[29]

When devising the inquiry rules in 1977 in the context of Article 90 of Additional Protocol I to the Geneva Conventions of 12 August 1949, relating to the Protection of Victims of International Armed Conflicts (Protocol I), the agreement of the parties remained paramount. Protocol I creates a permanent International Fact-Finding Commission that was established in 1991 and has been placed at the disposal of the parties to Protocol I, and to be utilized by

25 *Supra* note 22 at 295.

26 See Title III of the Hague Convention (I) For the Pacific Settlement of International Disputes, 29 July 1899, and Title III of the Hague Convention (I) For the Pacific Settlement of International Disputes, 18 October 1907.

27 The predecessor to the Geneva Conventions, the 1929 Geneva Convention for the Amelioration of the Condition of the Wounded and Sick in Armies in the Field also contained a provision under Article 30 providing for inquiry mechanism.

28 Article 52 of Geneva Convention (I) on Wounded and Sick in Armed Forces in the Field, 12 August 1949, 75 UNTS 970; Article 53 of Geneva Convention (II) on Wounded, Sick and Shipwrecked of Armed Forces at Sea, 12 August 1949, 75 UNTS 971; Article 132 of Geneva Convention (III) on Prisoners of War, 12 August 1949, 75 UNTS 972; and Article 149 of Geneva Convention (IV) on Civilian Persons in Time of War, 12 August 1949, 75 UNTS 973 (all entered into force 21 October 1950). The wording of the inquiry identical in all four instruments reads as follows: "At the request of a Party to the conflict, an enquiry shall be instituted, in a manner to be decided between the interested Parties, concerning any alleged violation of the Convention."

29 For further elaboration on this point see Théo Boutrouche, "Commentary on Article 149 of the Geneva Convention (IV) Relative to the Protection of Civilian Persons in Time of War. Geneva, 12 August 1949; Good Offices, Conciliation, and Enquiry" in Andrew Clapham, Paula Gaeta and Marco Sassòli (eds), *The 1949 Geneva Conventions: A Commentary*, Oxford, Oxford University Press, 2015 at 561–574.

others on a voluntary basis.[30] At the time of writing, 76 states have recognized its competence, yet it has not been called upon because there have been no agreements between parties to any conflict to avail themselves of its services.[31]

The role of fact-finding with the agreement of the parties has also long been recognized by the UN. The UN has since 1946 relied on fact-finding processes to investigate a range of issues, including border disputes, inter-state disputes, international crimes and, in limited cases, national crimes, such as the investigation into the assassination of Rafik Hariri in Lebanon[32] or of Benazir Bhutto in Pakistan.[33] At one stage, the UN General Assembly even toyed with the idea of establishing a permanent fact-finding body, highlighting the usefulness of impartial fact-finding as a means toward the settlement of disputes.[34]

The consent and the cooperation of the states concerned were essential in carrying out these mandates. There are also examples of the UN being requested by the state concerned to carry out human rights investigations, such as the case of the investigation set up by the Secretary-General regarding Timor-Leste in 2006 and conducted by the OHCHR.[35]

3.2. TYPE 2: INVESTIGATIONS BY INDEPENDENT EXPERTS IN THE ABSENCE OF CONSENT

This type of inquiry came with the development of the UN human rights system. Following the 1973 coup against President Salvador Allende by General

---

30 The International (Humanitarian) Fact-Finding Commission was established in 1991 and it has added an addendum "humanitarian" in order to distinguish itself from other international fact-finding missions and commissions.

31 On the Commission, see its official website: <http://www.ihffc.org>; see also Frits Kalshoven, "The International Humanitarian Fact-Finding Commission: A Sleeping Beauty?" (2002) 4 *Humanitäres Völkerrecht – Informationsschriften* 213–216.

32 United Nations, "Security Council Unanimously Endorses Findings of Investigation of Murder of Rafik Hariri, Call for Syria's Full, Unconditional Cooperation," press release, SC/8543 (31 October 2005), online: <https://www.un.org/press/en/2005/sc8543.doc.htm>.

33 Heraldo Munoz Valenzuela, Marzuki Darusman and Peter FitzGerald, *Report of the United Nations Commission of Inquiry into the Facts and Circumstances of the Assassination of Former Pakistani Prime Minister Mohtarma Benazir Bhutto*, New York, 15 April 2010, online: <https://www.un.org/News/dh/infocus/Pakistan/UN_Bhutto_Report_15April2010.pdf>.

34 See *Repertory of Practice of United Nations Organs* (<http://legal.un.org/repertory/dtSearch/Search_Forms/dtSearch.html>), *sub verbo* "Article 34," online: <http://legal.un.org/repertory/art34/english/rep_supp3_vol2_art34.pdf> and *sub verbo* "Article 33," online: <http://legal.un.org/repertory/art33/english/rep_supp4_vol1_art33.pdf>.

35 The Independent Special Commission of Inquiry for Timor-Leste set up in 2006 by the UN-Secretary-General. See *Report of the United Nations Independent Special Commission of Inquiry for Timor-Leste*, Geneva, 2 October 2006, online: <http://www.ohchr.org/Documents/Countries/COITimorLeste.pdf>.

Augusto Pinochet, the UN Commission on Human Rights established in 1975 an ad hoc Working Group to inquire into the situation of human rights in Chile. In 1979, this working group was replaced by a Special Rapporteur and two experts to study the fate of the disappeared in Chile. In 1980, the Commission established the Working Group on Enforced or Involuntary Disappearances to deal with the question of enforced disappearances throughout the world. The UN Human Rights Council continues to develop these monitoring bodies within the UN human rights system, which are known as Special Procedures. As of 30 September 2016, there are 43 *thematic*[36] and 14 *country* mandates.[37]

The mandate holders report to the UN Human Rights Council and often to the UN General Assembly on the situation in various countries. When visiting the concerned countries, they require freedom of inquiry, which can be achieved through unhindered access to places such as prisons and detention centres, contact with civil society groups, access to documentation, and confidential and unsupervised contact with witnesses and other persons.[38] If such access is not guaranteed, the mandate holders often carry out their examination on the basis of interviews with victims, witnesses and experts outside the concerned country.

In this category we also find the commissions of inquiry and fact-finding missions established by the UN inter-governmental system, which are supported by the OHCHR. While such institutions have been utilized by the

---

36 The covered thematic issues are: the plight of people of African-Descent, Albinism, arbitrary detention, business and human rights, cultural rights, disabilities, disappearances, discrimination against women in law and practice, right to education, environment and human rights, equitable international order, extreme poverty, right to food, foreign debt and human rights, freedom of assembly, freedom of expression, hazardous substance and human rights, right to health, right to housing, human rights defenders, independence of judges and lawyers, indigenous peoples, internally displaced persons, international solidarity, mercenaries, migrants, minorities, older persons, the right to privacy, racism and xenophobia, religion and belief, sale of children, sexual orientation and gender identity, slavery, summary or arbitrary executions, counter-terrorism and human rights, torture, trafficking in persons, transitional justice, unilateral coercive measures, violence against women, and the right to water and sanitation.
See United Nations Human Rights Office of the High Commissioner, "Thematic Mandates," online: <http://spinternet.ohchr.org/_Layouts/SpecialProceduresInternet/ViewAllCountryMandates.aspx?Type=™>.

37 The country mandates relate to Belarus, Cambodia, the Central African Republic, Cote d'Ivoire, Eritrea, Haiti, Iran, Mali, Myanmar, the Occupied Palestinian Territories, the People's Republic of Korea, Somalia, Sudan and the Syrian Arab Republic.
See United Nations Human Rights Office of the High Commissioner, "Country Mandates," online: <http://spinternet.ohchr.org/_Layouts/SpecialProceduresInternet/ViewAllCountryMandates.aspx>.

38 *Terms of Reference for Fact-Finding Missions by Special Rapporteurs/Representatives of the Commission on Human Rights*, ESCOR, 54th sess, UN Doc. E/CN.4/1998/45, Appendix V, 1998.

UN for decades, the establishment of the UN Human Rights Council in 2005 has led to the elaboration of various investigative models, as will be discussed below in relation to type 3.

Historically, most Commissions of Inquiry have been established by the Security Council (SC), the General Assembly (GA) and the former UN Commission on Human Rights. The body establishing the Commission normally specifies its mandate. Commissions established by the Security Council have been created under Chapter VII of the UN Charter, such as those on Darfur in 2004[39] and on the Central African Republic in 2013.[40] When established under Chapter VII, even if the state concerned does not consent to them, it usually cooperates with them.

3.3. TYPE 3: MANDATES TO THE OHCHR TO INVESTIGATE IRRESPECTIVE OF CONSENT

Since 1992, the OHCHR has provided support to and deployed close to 60 commissions of inquiry and fact-finding missions.[41] With the UN Human Rights Council growing stronger and more confident in its role to address violations, it has developed various models of investigative bodies, also requesting the OHCHR to carry out human rights investigations irrespective of the consent of the state concerned. These investigations have been directed at both states and non-state actors and have been taking place in the context of armed conflict and beyond, sometimes covering several countries.

The first request by the UN Human Rights Council for such investigation emerged in the context of the situation in Syria. The UN Human Rights Council, meeting in a Special Session on 29 April 2011, requested the OHCHR "to dispatch urgently a mission to the Syrian Arab Republic to investigate all alleged violations of international human rights law and to establish the facts and circumstances of such violations and of the crimes perpetrated, with a view to avoiding impunity and ensuring full accountability."[42] It also called upon the Government of Syria to cooperate fully with the Office and to grant access

39 UN Security Council Resolution 1564 (2004), SC Res 1564, 2004, UNSCOR, UN Doc. S/RES/1564(2004), 18 September 2004.

40 UN Security Council Resolution 2127 (2013), SC Res 2127, 2013, UNSCOR, UN Doc. S/RES/2127(2013), 5 December 2013.

41 International Commissions of Inquiry, Commissions on Human Rights, Fact-Finding Missions and other Investigations, "Introduction," online: <http://www.ohchr.org/EN/HRBodies/HRC/Pages/COIs.aspx>.

42 *Resolution adopted by the Human Rights Council – The Current Human Rights Situation in the Syrian Arab Republic in the Context of Recent Events*, UNHRCOR, 16th sess, UN Doc. A/HRC/RES/S-16/1, 29 April 2009.

to the OHCHR. Syria did not cooperate with the OHCHR.[43] Nevertheless, High Commissioner Navi Pillay published the results of her investigations, noting the failure of the Government of Syria to cooperate with the OHCHR with regard to access to the country. In her report, she pointed to serious violations of human rights that may amount to crimes against humanity.[44]

An almost identical request was made on 1 September 2014 following a UN Human Rights Council Special Session on the human rights situation in Iraq in light of abuses committed by so-called Islamic State in Iraq and the Levant (ISIL) and associated groups.[45] In his report dated 31 October 2014, High Commissioner Zeid Ra'ad Al Hussein stressed the violations committed by ISIL, including a suggestion of genocide against the Yezidi community, as well as war crimes and crimes against humanity. He also reported on violations perpetrated by other parties to the conflict amounting to war crimes.[46] Regarding the situation in Libya, the UN Human Rights Council requested the High Commissioner to "dispatch a mission to investigate violations and abuses of international human rights law that have been committed in Libya since the beginning of 2014, and to establish the facts and circumstances of such abuses and violations, with a view to avoiding impunity and ensuring full accountability."[47] In June 2015, the Human Rights Council also requested a comprehensive assessment of allegations of violations and abuses of human rights with regard to South Sudan also with a view to ensuring accountability.[48]

---

43 Ibid.

44 *Report of the United Nations High Commissioner for Human Rights on the Situation of Human Rights in the Syrian Arab Republic*, UNHCROR, 18th sess, UN Doc. A/HRC/18/53, 15 September 2011.

45 *HRC Resolution S-22/1, the Human Rights Situation in Iraq in the Light of Abuses Committed by the So-Called Islamic State in Iraq and the Levant and Associated Groups*, UNHCROR, 22nd sess, UN Doc. A/HCR/RES/S-22/1, 3 September 2014. Paragraph 10 "*Requests* the Office of the High Commissioner urgently to dispatch a mission to Iraq to investigate alleged violations and abuses of international human rights law committed by the so-called Islamic State in Iraq and the Levant and associated terrorist groups, and to establish the facts and circumstances of such abuses and violations, with a view to avoiding impunity and ensuring full accountability …".

46 *Report of the Office of the United Nations High Commissioner for Human Rights on the Human Rights Situation in Iraq in the Light of Abuses Committed by the So-Called Islamic State in Iraq and the Levant and Associated Groups*, UNHRCOR, 18th sess, UN Doc. A/HRC/28/18, 27 February 2015.

47 *HRC Resolution 28/30 – Technical Assistance and Capacity-Building to Improve Human Rights in Libya*, HCR Res 28/30, UNHCROR, 28th sess, UN Doc. A/HCR/28/L.7/Rev.1, 27 March 2015.

48 See *HRC Resolution 29/13 – Mission by the Office of the United Nations High Commissioner for Human Rights to Improve Human Rights, Accountability and Reconciliation in South Sudan*, HCR Res 29/13, UNHCROR, 29th sess, UN Doc. A/HCR/29/L.8, 2 July 2015 at para 14(a) requests the OHCHR "urgently to undertake a mission to engage with the Government of

The engagement on the situation of Sri Lanka stands out as perhaps the most significant in helping a country to move forward in advancing its respect for human rights. The international community has agonized about this situation for a long time, particularly as the conflict between the Government of Sri Lanka and the Liberation Tigers of Tamil Eelam (LTTE) intensified in 2002 and reached an end in 2009. Several measures were taken, including the establishment of a Panel of Experts by the Secretary-General in 2011 to address alleged violations of international humanitarian law and human rights law committed during the operations against the LTTE.[49] The report on Sri Lanka was made public and led to other UN actions, particularly by the UN Human Rights Council, and paved the way for further action.

Several resolutions by the UN Human Rights Council followed. The most significant was Resolution 25/1, adopted in March 2014. It requested the High Commissioner to undertake a comprehensive investigation into alleged serious violations and abuses of human rights and related crimes by both parties in Sri Lanka during the conflict period and its immediate aftermath and to establish the facts and circumstances of such alleged violations and of the crimes perpetrated with a view to avoiding impunity and ensuring accountability.[50]

The investigation lasted for about a year and a half.[51] It started under the leadership of High Commissioner Navi Pillay and was concluded in September 2015 during the tenure of High Commissioner Zeid Ra'ad Al Hussein. It was conducted without the cooperation of Sri Lanka on the basis of extensive documentation already available on the period under investigation, as well as a desk review of existing material, including government publications, civil society reports, audio-visual material and satellite images, reports of the UN Special Procedures and treaty bodies.[52]

South Sudan, to monitor and report on the situation of human rights, and to undertake a comprehensive assessment of allegations of violations and abuses of human rights with a view to ensuring accountability and complementarity with the African Union Commission of Inquiry."

49 Marzuki Darusman, Steven R. Ratner and Yasmin Sooka, *Report of the Secretary-General's Panel of Experts on Accountability in Sri Lanka*, New York, 31 March 2011.

50 *HRC Resolution 25/1 – Promoting Reconciliation, Accountability and Human Rights in Sri Lanka*, HCR Res 25/1, UNHCROR, 25th sess, UN Doc. A/HCR/25/L.1/Rev.1, 9 April 2014. In its Resolution 25/1, the Human Rights Council requested the OHCHR to undertake a comprehensive investigation into alleged serious violations of human rights during the period covered by the Lessons Learnt and Reconciliation Commission. This period starts from 2012 and arguably could last until today.

51 See *Promoting Reconciliation, Accountability and Human Rights in Sri Lanka – Note by the Secretariat*, UNHRCOR, 28th sess, UN Doc. A/HRC/28/23, 27 February 2015.

52 *Report of the OHCHR Investigation on Sri Lanka (OISL)*, UNHCROR, 30th sess, UN Doc. A/HRC/30/CRP.2, 16 September 2015 at para 20.

The report and its 261-page annex tell the story of a brutal war that claimed the lives of thousands of people, with vast numbers of disappearances, torture, rape and sexual violence, child recruitment and destruction of property.[53] As the report indicates, the findings of the investigation were born out of the past failure of the Government of Sri Lanka to address accountability for the most serious human rights violations and crimes. It makes specific recommendations regarding truth, justice and accountability to address past violations, including the establishment of a hybrid court.

The report was released in an opportune time when Sri Lanka itself was undergoing some crucial change. The presidential election held on 8 January 2015 resulted in the common opposition candidate, Mathiripala Sirisena, defeating the incumbent President Mahinda Rajapaksa with the support of a broad coalition derived from all ethnic communities and spread over the ideological spectrum. A new Cabinet was formed with the former opposition leader, Ranil Wickremesinghe, as Prime Minister. The new government saw in the report opportunities to reshape the country around human rights principles. Championed by Foreign Minister Mangala Samaraweera, the government positively approached the UN Human Rights Council, making specific commitments. This resulted in the Council adopting by consensus a landmark resolution with the co-sponsorship of Sri Lanka,[54] noting with appreciation the High Commissioner's report, including the findings and conclusions of the comprehensive OHCHR investigation, and encouraging the Government of Sri Lanka to implement the recommendations contained therein. The Council also requested the OHCHR to continue to assess progress on the implementation of its recommendations and other relevant processes related to reconciliation, accountability and human rights, and to update it on such progress. This landmark process demonstrates how human rights investigations can play a critical role in transforming a situation.

Another particularly complex investigation concerned the actions by Boko Haram. The request stemmed from a Special Session of the UN Human Rights Council.[55] To carry out this investigation, the OHCHR deployed human rights officers to countries affected by Boko Haram to collect information on human rights abuses and violations and violations of international humanitarian law (IHL). The report of this investigation was primarily based on over 350 confidential interviews which the OHCHR conducted with individuals from

---

53 *Comprehensive Report of the Office of the United Nations High Commissioner for Human Rights on Sri Lanka*, UNHCROR, 30th sess, UN Doc. A/HRC/30/61, 28 September 2015 and *supra* note 52.

54 *HRC Resolution 30/1 on Promoting Reconciliation, Accountability and Human Rights in Sri Lanka*, HCR Res 30/1, UNHCROR, 30th sess, UN Doc. A/HCR/30/L.29, 1 October 2015.

55 *HRC Resolution S-23/1 – Atrocities Committed by the Terrorist Group Boko Haram and its Effects on Human Rights in the Affected States*, HCR Res S-23/1, UNHCROR, 23rd sess, UN Doc. A/HCR/RES/S-23/1, 1 April 2015.

diverse ethnic and religious groups, including 210 women and girls, as well as refugees and internally displaced persons (IDPs).[56] The report focused on regions where Boko Haram has been active, namely the far north region of Cameroon, the southwest region of Chad, the southeast region of Niger and the northeast region of Nigeria. While the investigation was carried out with the consent of the concerned countries, similar to the report on ISIL in Iraq, it pointed out the failure of the concerned countries to adequately protect people from Boko Haram and referred to allegations of serious violations of human rights and IHL committed by some Government forces during counter-insurgency operations.[57]

3.4. TYPE 4: THE UN ACTING ON ITS OWN INITIATIVE

This type of inquiry is the most contentious one as it is carried out by the UN on its own initiative. In 1992, in his report to the General Assembly and the Security Council known as *Agenda for Peace*, Secretary-General Boutros Boutros-Ghali already flagged that fact-finding can be a confidence-building measure. He said that preventive steps must be based upon timely and accurate knowledge of the facts. He recommended the increased resort to fact-finding, in accordance with the Charter. He also said that this fact-finding could be initiated either by the Secretary-General, to enable him to meet his responsibilities under the Charter, including Article 99, or by the Security Council or the General Assembly.[58]

Article 99 of the UN Charter indicates that the Secretary-General has the authority to bring to the attention of the Security Council any matter which in his opinion may threaten the maintenance of international peace and security. Without specifically citing this provision of the Charter, the Secretary-General has used his discretionary power to establish a number of inquiries, with various scopes. Sometimes he did so at the request of the concerned state; other times, he did so on his own initiative. For instance, in 2009, Secretary-General Ban Ki-Moon established a Commission of Inquiry to determine the facts and circumstances of the events of 28 September 2009 in Guinea, where the forceful military response to thousands protesting against military rule in a stadium resulted in dozens of people being killed or wounded.[59] Looting and sexual violence were also alleged. The government of Guinea later

56 *Report of the United Nations High Commissioner for Human Rights on Violations and Abuses Committed by Boko Haram and the Impact on Human Rights in the Affected Countries*, UNHCROR, 30th sess, UN Doc. A/HRC/30/67, 29 September 2015 at para 3.

57 Ibid at para 79.

58 *Supra* note 4 at para 25.

59 United Nations, "Secretary-General Announces Members of Guinea Commission of Inquiry to Investigate Events of 28 September," press release, SG/SM/12581-AFR/1902 (30 October 2009), online: <https://www.un.org/press/en/2009/sgsm12581.doc.htm>.

welcomed the UN action and the inquiry report was eventually submitted to the Security Council.[60]

The Secretary-General also established a Panel of Experts to consider the situation in Sri Lanka that was mentioned above.[61] The Sri Lanka and Guinea assessments were supported by the OHCHR, with other UN entities participating.

The High Commissioner for Human Rights also has the legislative authority to exercise investigative power *proprio motu*. General Assembly Resolution 48/141 bestowed on the High Commissioner a wide mandate to promote and protect the enjoyment and full realization, by all people, of all rights. The ability of the High Commissioner to send fact-finding missions was specifically deliberated during the drafting of the resolution. While the reference to fact-finding was eventually removed in the final text, the High Commissioner's right of initiative was maintained, especially with the call on the High Commissioner to play an active role in preventing the continuation of human rights violations around the world.[62]

During her term as High Commissioner, Arbour convinced the UN system of the utility of issuing periodic public reports on situations, particularly when there is a UN peace mission with a human rights component. Some of these reports, such as on civilian casualties in Afghanistan, received wide media attention and have become flagship reports for the UN as a whole.[63]

Arbour also embarked on complex investigations. Under the authority of her mandate, investigations were launched into the human rights situation in several countries. It is particularly worth noting the investigation into the violence in Kenya,[64] and the mapping exercises of the situations in Afghanistan[65] and the Democratic Republic of Congo (DRC),[66] which will be discussed later.

---

60 *Report of the International Commission of Inquiry Mandated to Establish the Facts and Circumstances of the Events of 28 September 2009 in Guinea*, SCOR, 2009, UN Doc. S/2009/693, 18 December 2009.

61 *Supra* note 49.

62 Andrew Clapham, "Creating the High Commissioner for Human Rights: The Outside Story" (1994) 5 *European Journal of International Law* 556–568, online: <http://ejil.org/pdfs/5/1/1267.pdf>.

63 See, for instance, Mujib Mashal, "Civilian Casualties in Afghan War are Unabated in 2016," *The New York Times* (17 April 2016), online: <http://www.nytimes.com/2016/04/18/world/middleeast/civilian-casualties-in-afghan-war-are-unabated-in-2016.html?_r=0>.

64 OHCHR Fact-Finding Mission to Kenya, 6–28 February 2008. For more information, see *Report from OHCHR Fact-Finding Mission to Kenya*, Geneva, 6–28 February 2008, online: <http://www.ohchr.org/documents/press/ohchrkenyareport.pdf>.

65 OHCHR Mandated Mission on Accountability in Afghanistan, 2001.

66 A mapping exercise documenting gross human rights violations committed between 1993 and 2003. For more information, see OHCHR, "DRC: Mapping human rights violations 1993–2003," online: <http://www.ohchr.org/EN/Countries/AfricaRegion/Pages/RDCProjetMapping.aspx>.

4. LOUISE ARBOUR AND UN HUMAN RIGHTS FACT-FINDING: TELLING THE STORY

Less than three months after Louise Arbour became the UN High Commissioner for Human Rights, the Security Council, on 18 September 2004, adopted Resolution 1564 regarding the situation in Darfur. The resolution requested the Secretary-General, *inter alia* to "rapidly establish an international commission of inquiry in order immediately to investigate reports of violations of international humanitarian law and human rights law in Darfur by all parties, to determine also whether or not acts of genocide have occurred, and to identify the perpetrators of such violations with a view to ensuring that those responsible are held accountable."[67]

Secretary-General Kofi Annan appointed a five-member body chaired by former International Criminal Tribunal for the former Yugoslavia (ICTY) President Judge Antonio Cassese.[68] Given Arbour's background as the Chief Prosecutor for the ICTY and the International Criminal Tribunal for Rwanda (ICTR), Secretary-General Annan also decided that the Commission's Secretariat should be the Office of the High Commissioner for Human Rights.[69]

The situation in Darfur was dire, with reports of killings, destruction and rape on a daily basis. The international community, particularly the Security Council, was looking for an appropriate response to the crisis. This was clear in the request to qualify violations in terms of international crimes, including to determine whether genocide was committed, as well as to identify perpetrators. Both Arbour and Cassese saw in this mandate an opportunity to shape UN human rights fact-finding work, particularly during conflict.

4.1. DESIGNING A MODEL

Establishing the Secretariat was Arbour's task and she was keen to build a structure that would be adequate to address the complexity of the task, while acting as a model for fact-finding work in the future. Building on her experience as an international prosecutor, she immediately saw a nexus between a human rights investigation and a criminal investigation, particularly since the Darfur

---

67 UN Security Council Resolution 1564 (2004), SC Res 1564(2004), UNSCOR, 2004, UN Doc. S/RES/1564(2004), 1 October 2004 at para 12.

68 The other members were Mr Mohammed Fayek (Egypt), Ms Hina Jilani (Pakistan), Mr Dumisa Ntsebeza (South Africa) and Ms Theresa Striggner-Scott (Ghana). See International Commission of Inquiry on Darfur, *Report of the International Commission of Inquiry on Darfur to the United Nations Secretary-General*, Geneva, 25 January 2005, online: <http://www.un.org/news/dh/sudan/com_inq_darfur.pdf>.

69 Ibid. The author was the head of the Secretariat to the Commission.

Commission had been given a mandate to determine whether genocide was committed and to identify perpetrators. She wanted this job done professionally and fairly, so she called on some of the investigators she had relied on as Chief Prosecutor and designed the Commission to include a criminal investigative team.[70] The investigators were guided by a research team proficient in human rights law and methodology.

The 176-page report of the International Commission of Inquiry on Darfur was submitted within three months, as the Security Council requested, and provided the international community with a strong direction regarding accountability. After intense deliberations, on 31 March 2005, the UN Security Council referred the situation in Darfur to the International Criminal Court (ICC).[71]

The human rights community was thrilled by the success of the referral and confidence was boosted in the ability of the OHCHR to organize and conduct such thorough investigations under Louise Arbour's leadership. She began looking for opportunities to consolidate these gains.

4.2. BUILDING ON THE FIRST SUCCESS: THE OHCHR ACTION PLAN

The chance to strengthen the work of Arbour's Office in this area immediately arrived when Secretary-General Kofi Annan presented a five-year progress

70 The Secretariat of the Commission was composed of more than 30 people, including lawyers, criminal investigators, forensic experts, military analysts and experts in sexual violence. Overall, the Commission received more than 20,000 pages of material from different sources. It reviewed and analysed published, public reports on Darfur, other reports that were brought to the attention of the Commission in response to its requests for information, as well as other types of information. A database was developed where bibliographic and evidentiary details were recorded. The incidents analysis carried out by the research team was also recorded in the database as a way to facilitate swift access by the Commissioners and staff to resource material and source information.

71 UN Security Council Resolution 1593 (2005), SC Res 1593(2005), UNSCOR, 2005, UN Doc. S/RES/1593(2005), 31 March 2005. This was an unprecedented step that many thought a few months earlier would be impossible due to the fierce opposition of President George W. Bush to the ICC. Four states abstained in the vote: Algeria, Brazil, China and the United States. United Nations, "Security Council Refers Situation in Darfur, Sudan, to Prosecutor of International Criminal Court," press release, SC/8351 (31 March 2005), online: <http://www.un.org/press/en/2005/sc8351.doc.htm>. However, Resolution 1593 included a clear exemption for nationals of states not parties to the Rome Statute from ICC jurisdiction and placed them under the "exclusive jurisdiction" of their respective states. See Operative Paragraph 6 of Security Council Resolution 1593 (2005). The resolution also instructed that none of the expenses incurred in connection with the referral, including expenses related to investigations or prosecutions, were to be borne by the UN, but by the ICC itself. See Operative Paragraph 7 of Security Council Resolution 1593 (2005). These conditions were replicated five years later, in the case of the referral of the situation in Libya to the (ICC). UN Security Council Resolution 1970 (2011), SC res 1970(2011), UNSCOR, 2011, S/RES/1970 (2011), 26 February 2011.

report in 2005 on the implementation of the 2000 Millennium Declaration, as had been requested of him by the UN General Assembly.[72] Arbour convinced Annan to include amongst the priority areas identified in the report the strengthening of the OHCHR, with additional resources and staff to play a more active role in the deliberations of the Security Council and of the Peacebuilding Commission. Annan asked Arbour for an action plan, which she promptly submitted.[73]

The Action Plan highlighted that the OHCHR is increasingly required to provide more sustainable support and legal expertise for commissions of inquiry or fact-finding missions investigating human rights violations. In her report, Arbour stressed that these tasks must be carried out diligently and thoroughly.[74] She also indicated that the OHCHR should be ready to swiftly deploy human rights officers to carry out fact-finding missions.[75] Through the Action Plan, not only did she double the resources provided to her Office from the UN regular budget, but she also created structures to enable the OHCHR to conduct investigations.

When the election violence took place during the Kenya elections in December 2007, Arbour was ready. A team of OHCHR staff was deployed in February 2008 and conducted an investigation over 22 days from 6 to 28 February 2008.[76] The investigation looked into violations during a specific period that followed the December 2007 presidential elections.[77] The report of the mission was drafted, taking into account the political negotiations underway and which were being mediated by then former Secretary-General Annan.[78]

---

72 *Report of the Secretary-General, In Larger Freedom: Towards Development, Security and Human Rights for All*, UNGAOR, 59th sess, UN Doc. A/59/2005, 21 March 2005.

73 The United Nations High Commissioner for Human Rights, *The OHCHR Plan of Action: Protection and Empowerment*, Geneva, May 2005, online: <http://www2.ohchr.org/english/planaction.pdf>.

74 Ibid at para 62.

75 Ibid at para 63.

76 The mission also formulated recommendations on possible accountability mechanisms. It concluded that the state failed to take all appropriate measures to meet its obligations "to protect the rights of its citizens to life and physical integrity, property, democratic rights, freedom of expression, assembly and movement." It also found that while the violations of democratic rights provided the trigger for the bulk of the street violence and human rights violations, a number of underlying causes also contributed to fuelling the outburst: "Violations of economic and social rights pre-existed the recent violence as evidenced in the lack of access to water, food, health, decent housing together with the rate of youth unemployment and the gross inequality reported by civil society organisations." *Report from OHCHR Fact-Finding Mission to Kenya, supra* note 64.

77 Ibid.

78 Ibid. The mission welcomed that the 4 March 2008 agreement included general parameters and principles for the establishment of a Truth Justice and Reconciliation Commission. It provided specific recommendations as to the elements that should be included in the legislation so as to render it effective. The report also recommended specific measures for witness protection and that the independent investigations conducted by the civil society and

Arbour also engaged her Office in complex long-term investigations. She is credited for initiating an extensive "mapping"[79] of human rights violations carried out in the DRC between 1993 and 2003.[80] The story of this mapping runs as follows: in late 2005, three mass graves were discovered in the eastern part of the DRC. Given the long history of massacres in the DRC and the presence of a UN peace-keeping operation in that country, Arbour convinced the UN that it needed to look at these mass graves in a holistic manner.[81] The objective of the mapping was threefold: to map out the most serious violations of human rights and international humanitarian law committed in the territory of the DRC during the specified period; to assess the national capacities to address these violations; and to formulate options aimed at assisting the Government of the DRC in identifying appropriate transitional justice mechanisms to deal with the legacy of these violations in terms of truth, justice, reparation and reform.[82] The report was submitted to Arbour toward the end of her mandate as High Commissioner and was released by her successor Navi Pillay in August 2010.

5. HUMAN RIGHTS AND JUSTICE: SOME DILEMMAS WHEN INVESTIGATING

While human rights and criminal investigations are different in nature, these two types of investigations can be mutually reinforcing. To start with, human

national human rights commission should be supported. The mission and its report served as a template for the various actors in Kenya, as well as the international community, to address the situation in Kenya after the violence.

79 The term "mapping" is used in this context to refer to the exercise of diagnosing human rights violations. It is a method of inquiry that is done to document violations that occur over a lengthy period of time to provide a general overview of the situation. It can be a mix of broad-brush assumptions as well as inquiries into specific emblematic events. It also involves gathering hypotheses about key historical events as well as the collection of segregated data. It follows basic human rights information collection methods.

80 *Report of the Mapping Exercise Documenting the Most Serious Violations of Human Rights and International Humanitarian Law Committed within the Territory of the Democratic Republic of the Congo between March 1993 and June 2003*, August 2010, online: <http://www.ohchr.org/Documents/Countries/CD/DRC_MAPPING_REPORT_FINAL_EN.pdf>.

81 In June 2006, the UN announced its intention to send a human rights team to conduct a mapping exercise in the DRC and report to the Security Council. This led to intense discussions between the UN and the DRC Government. In May 2007, the UN Secretary-General approved the terms of reference of this exercise and asked the OHCHR to lead it. The actual work began in July 2008. Between October 2008 and May 2009, a total of 33 staff worked on the project in the DRC, including Congolese and international human rights experts. Of these, some 20 human rights officers were deployed across the country, operating out of five field offices, to gather documents and information from witnesses. The 550-page report contained descriptions of 617 alleged violent incidents occurring in the DRC between March 1993 and June 2003.

82 *Supra* note 80.

rights investigations can focus on state responsibility, the responsibility of non-state actors under certain circumstances and individual responsibility. Criminal investigations, however, focus only on individual responsibility. IHL also enters into this mix, with inquiries under IHL focusing on the obligations of the parties to the conflict, and on individual responsibility when violations amount to war crimes.

Three issues illustrate this point: the applicable legal regime, standards and methods, and witness protection. Each of these will be briefly discussed below.

5.1. THE APPLICABLE LEGAL REGIME

Many of the situations under a human rights investigation are subject to multiple rules of international law. The most common overlap is between international human rights law, humanitarian law and international criminal law. As a result, much of the literature about human rights fact-finding concentrates on this nexus.

The multiplicity of regimes applicable to a particular situation is not unique to our context. As the International Law Commission (ILC) explains, international law is not a random collection of norms, but is composed of rules and principles that have a meaningful relationship between them.[83] It is a dynamic legal system which benefits from systemic integration and rejects fragmentation.[84] When several norms have bearings on a single issue, the ILC suggests that, to the extent possible, the rules should be interpreted "to give rise to a single set of compatible obligations."[85] It calls this approach the principle of harmonization.[86]

In several of its rulings, the International Court of Justice has reiterated the concept of the complementarity of human rights law and IHL.[87] In its Advisory Opinion on the *Legality of the Threat or Use of Nuclear Weapons*, the Court thought that this relationship was that of *lex specialis* or special law.[88] The ILC helps us to understand what this means by clarifying that the special law

83 International Law Commission, *Conclusions of the Work of the Study Group on the Fragmentation of International Law: Difficulties Arising from the Diversification and Expansion of International Law*, United Nations, 2006, online: <http://legal.un.org/ilc/texts/instruments/english/draft_articles/1_9_2006.pdf> at Conclusion 1.

84 Ibid.

85 Ibid at Conclusion 4.

86 Ibid at Conclusion 2.

87 *Legality of the Threat or Use of Nuclear Weapons Case*, Advisory Opinion [1996] ICJ Rep 226; *Legal Consequences of the Construction of a Wall in the Occupied Palestinian Territory*, Advisory Opinion [2004] ICJ Rep 136; and *Armed Activities on the Territory of the Congo (Democratic Republic of the Congo v. Uganda)*, Judgment [2005] ICJ Rep 168.

88 *Legality of the Threat or Use of Nuclear Weapons*, *supra* note 87 at para 25.

concept may be used "to apply, clarify, update, or modify as well as set aside the general law."[89] In its Advisory Opinion on the *Wall*, the Court explains, there are three possible scenarios: "some rights may be exclusively matters of international humanitarian law; others may be exclusively matters of human rights law; yet others may be matters of both these branches of international law."[90] This concurrent application creates a need to resolve the primacy of norms between the general and special law.

It is now fully recognized that human rights law applies at all times, while IHL applies when the existence of armed conflict is established. So, in all situations, human rights law remains the general law and, in specific situations, IHL may be considered as *lex specialis*. Being the general law, human rights law will "continue to give direction for the interpretation and application of the relevant special law and will become fully applicable in situations not provided for by the latter."[91]

Moreover, as the ILC explains, when determining the applicable legal regime, it cannot be presumed that a special law applies when, for instance, it might frustrate the purpose of the general law, or negatively affect the balance of rights and obligations established in the general law.[92] In particular, certain types of general law rules may not be derogated from by the special law. These, according to the ILC, include in particular *jus cogens* norms, which it clarifies to mean the prohibition of aggression, slavery and the slave trade, genocide, racial discrimination and apartheid, torture and self-determination, as well as basic rules of IHL applicable in armed conflict.[93]

---

89 *Supra* note 83 at Conclusion 8.

90 *Legal Consequences of the Construction of a Wall in the Occupied Palestinian Territory*, Advisory Opinion [2004] ICJ Rep 106, online: <http://www.icj-cij.org/docket/files/131/1671.pdf>.

91 *Supra* note 83 at Conclusion 9.

92 Ibid at Conclusion 10.

93 Ibid at Conclusions 10 and 33. The UN Human Rights Committee expanded the list of *jus cogens* for the purposes of discouraging certain reservations to the International Covenant on Civil and Political Rights, stating that reservations that offend peremptory norms would not be compatible with the object and purpose of the Covenant. It therefore considered that "a State may not reserve the right to engage in slavery, to torture, to subject persons to cruel, inhuman or degrading treatment or punishment, to arbitrarily deprive persons of their lives, to arbitrarily arrest and detain persons, to deny freedom of thought, conscience and religion, to presume a person guilty unless he proves his innocence, to execute pregnant women or children, to permit the advocacy of national, racial or religious hatred, to deny to persons of marriageable age the right to marry, or to deny to minorities the right to enjoy their own culture, profess their own religion, or use their own language. And while reservations to particular clauses of article 14 may be acceptable, a general reservation to the right to a fair trial would not be." Human Rights Committee, *General Comment No. 24: Issues Relating to Reservations Made upon Ratification or Accession to the Covenant or the Optional Protocols Thereto, or in Relation to Declarations under article 41 of the Covenant*, HRCOR, 52th sess, UN Doc. CCPR/C/21/Rev.1/Add.6, 11 April 1994 at para 8, online: <http://tbinternet.ohchr.org/_layouts/treatybodyexternal/Download.aspx?symbolno=CCPR%2fC%2f21%2fRev.1%2fAdd.6&Lang=en>.

5.2. STANDARDS AND METHODS

In his excellent article on the challenges facing credible fact-finding in IHL, Theo Boutruche considers factors that can be relevant to both human rights and humanitarian law investigations.[94] He explores complex scenarios from the point of view of IHL, particularly with regard to gathering information about the perception of the attacker and the defender in the context of conflict at the time of the attacks. He cites several examples from fact-finding missions regarding the difficulty of looking at questions such as the determination of civilian and military targets, the efficacy of precautions, and the role of institutions such as the police and military peace-keepers to illustrate the complexity of assessing the lawfulness of the conduct of military operations.

There is no doubt that there are complexities in assessing the competing claims under different legal rules. Irrespective of the obligations of the parties to a conflict, individuals enduring the conflict also have human rights. A human rights assessment looks at the situation from the perspective of the impact of the conduct on the inherent rights of these individuals, while an IHL inquiry assesses whether the parties respected their IHL obligations. An international criminal law investigation assesses whether the material and mental elements of a recognized crime exist. These perspectives are all complementary and each serves a purpose.

The ICC Trial Chamber summarized the differences between criminal investigations and human rights fact-finding. It noted that "conducting an investigation into human rights violations is not subject to the same rules as those for a criminal investigation. Reports are prepared in a non-adversarial manner; they are essentially based on oral testimony, sometimes derived from hearsay, and the identity of sources is always redacted."[95]

With an early warning purpose, human rights investigations necessarily rely on a lower threshold than criminal investigations. Their main objective is to alert the concerned government and the international community about conduct, patterns or policies that have a harmful impact on life and liberty. Their aim is to stop the violence and encourage decisive action.

While investigations cannot be too cautious, they must not be reckless. They must be careful in assessing the quality and credibility of information

94 Théo Boutruche, "Credible Fact-Finding and Allegations of International Humanitarian Law Violations: Challenges in Theory and Practice" (2011) 16(1) *Journal of Conflict and Security Law* 105–140.

95 *Situation in the Democratic Republic of the Congo in the Case of The Prosecutor v. Mathieu Ngudjolo*, ICC-01/04–02/12-3, Judgment pursuant to Article 74 of the Statute (18 December 2012) at para 294 (International Criminal Court).

that is required to make factual and legal assessments, using only corroborated material. This is particularly important as the reports receive intense scrutiny by States, civil society, the media and the victims of the violations. The scrutiny often focuses on the political context of the investigations,[96] or on the legal analysis and methodology, the impartiality of the investigations or the conclusions and recommendations.[97] All of these must be accurate and beyond reproach.

Still, human rights investigations are not judicial investigations. Even when they apply a criminal law framework, they need not prove their point beyond reasonable doubt. They make tentative assessments, often only finding that there are reasonable grounds to consider that certain violations may amount to crimes having been or currently being committed. An academic study in the standards used by Commissions of Inquiry found that in effect, similar standards are used, though sometimes are differently expressed.[98]

Since 2004, a number of former judges and prosecutors have served as members of UN Commissions of Inquiry; their presence has reinforced the seriousness with which the reports are taken by stakeholders and various bodies.[99] In the case concerning *Armed Activities on the Territory of the Congo (Democratic Republic of the Congo v. Uganda)*, the International Court of Justice said that "evidence obtained by examination of persons directly involved, and who were subsequently cross-examined by judges skilled in examination and

---

96 See e.g. Steven R. Ratner, "The Political Dimension of International Human Rights Fact-Finding" (2013) 107 *Proceedings of the Annual Meeting (American Society of International Law)* 70–72.

97 See e.g. Patryk I. Labuda, "What Lies beneath the 'G' Word? Genocide-Labelling and Fact-Finding at the UN" (28 May 2015), online: <http://www.ejiltalk.org/what-lies-beneath-the-g-word-genocide-labelling-and-fact-finding-at-the-un/>.

98 Stephen Wilkinson, "Standards of Proof in International Humanitarian and Human Rights Fact-Finding and Inquiry Missions," Geneva Academy of International Humanitarian Law and Human Rights Research Project, 2014, online: <https://www.geneva-academy.ch/our-projects/our-projects/armed-conflict/detail/26-standards-of-proof-in-fact-finding>.

99 In addition to Judge Nino Cassese, who presided over the Darfur Commission in 2004–2005, the former ICTY Prosecutor Judge Goldstone presided over the Commission that considered the situation in the Occupied Palestinian Territory and Southern Israel in 2009; Mr Mohammed Bedjaoui, former ICJ President, was the Chairman of the International Commission of Inquiry on Guinea; former ICC President Philippe Kirsch presided over the Commission of Inquiry on Libya; Ms Christine Chanet, Judge of the Court of Cassation of France and member of the UN Human Rights Committee, chaired the International Fact-Finding Mission on Israeli Settlements; and we have Madame Carla Del Ponte as a member of the Syria Commission of Inquiry, Judge Michael Kirby of the High Court of Australia and former UN Special Representative of the Secretary-General on Cambodia chairing the North Korea COI, and Mr Bernard Muna, a former magistrate who was Deputy Chief Prosecutor for the ICTR, who now chairs the Commission of Inquiry on the Central African Republic.

experienced in assessing large amounts of factual information, some of it of a technical nature, merits special attention."[100]

The example of the human rights investigation that took place in August 2010, by Philip Alston, the then Special Rapporteur on extrajudicial, summary or arbitrary executions, provides an indication of how a diligent human rights investigation in a complex conflict setting is done. He received some video footage alleging extrajudicial executions by Sri Lankan soldiers.[101] Alston commissioned three outside experts in forensic pathology, forensic video analysis and firearm evidence to examine the video, after concluding that the investigations carried out by the government had not been thorough or impartial. The three experts strongly suggested that "the video is authentic."[102] Alston hence called for the establishment of an independent inquiry to carry out an impartial investigation into war crimes and other grave violations of international humanitarian and human rights law allegedly committed in Sri Lanka.[103] This has paved the way for a mandate to OHCHR in 2014 to conduct a comprehensive investigation.[104]

Human rights investigations also help in supporting criminal investigations. If a preliminary human rights examination of facts leads to the conclusion that war crimes, crimes against humanity, genocide or gross violations of human rights and IHL may have been committed, then there will be calls that there should not be an amnesty for the violations.[105] This will impact the work of the mediators in a specific conflict, particularly if they are acting on behalf of the UN and would open the door for criminal investigations.

5.3. WITNESS PROTECTION

In her magnificent work, *Paperwork and the Will of Capital: An Account of Flora as Witness*, exposed during the 2015 Venice Biennale, the US artist Taryn

---

100 *Armed Activities on the Territory of the Congo (DRC v. Uganda)*, [2005] ICJ Rep 35 at para 61, referring to Report of the Porter Commission.

101 UN News Center, "Deeming Sri Lanka execution video authentic, UN expert calls for war crimes probe" (7 January 2010), online: <http://www.un.org/apps/news/story.asp?NewsID=33423#.WQdKG_ThC3A>.

102 In a news release, Alston added that there are a small number of characteristics of the video which the experts were unable to explain, including the movement of certain victims in the video, 17 frames at the end of the video, and the date of 17 July 2009 encoded in the video (the conflict was officially declared over in May 2009). "Each of these characteristics can, however, be explained in a manner entirely consistent with the conclusion that the videotape appears to be authentic."

103 *Supra* note 101.

104 *Supra* note 50.

105 Office of the United Nations High Commissioner for Human Rights, "Rule-of-Law Tools for Post-Conflict States – Amnesties" (2009), online: <http://www.ohchr.org/Documents/Publications/Amnesties_en.pdf>.

Simon presents images of the floral arrangements used during the actual official signing ceremony of various international treaties and agreements as silent witnesses to these events. As the flowers decay, they illustrate the gradual collapse of the agreements they have observed. The inspired installation is a reminder of those who stand by as events pass by them, often becoming the victims of what they have witnessed.

There are many silent witnesses to human rights violations. They are often the victims. Credible human rights investigations depend on documenting their experiences. The process of documentation must take into account two considerations. The first is *do no harm* and the second is confidentiality.

Do no harm is a cardinal principle that underlies the methodology of human rights monitoring and investigation. When gathering information during an investigation, there is a necessity to exercise judgment to balance the need for the information and the potential risk of harm to the information providers.

This issue was extensively explained by Arbour in her capacity as UN High Commissioner for Human Rights in an *amicus curiae* brief submitted before the ICC on 10 October 2006 in the case regarding the situation in Darfur.[106] The Pre-Trial Chamber requested the brief, asking Arbour to focus on "issues concerning the protection of victims and the preservation of evidence in Darfur, Sudan."[107] In her intervention, Arbour described the OHCHR's experience in engaging in on-the-ground monitoring and investigation of serious human rights violations in the context of armed conflict. She offered some observations on the issue of protection of victims, arguing that the risks to victims must be assessed in the light of a variety of factors. These include the advantage to the overall protection of a population that can be derived from an international presence, including criminal investigations. She said that while risks to victims and witnesses may not be completely eliminated, they can be mitigated by specific well-tested measures. In this context, the deterrent effect of an international presence, including a criminal investigation, may advance the overall protection of witnesses, and this must be taken into account.

In her capacity as UN High Commissioner for Human Rights, Arbour also examined the need to respect the confidentiality of witnesses in another brief before the Special Court for Sierra Leone. On 16 December 2005, in a case known as *Prosecutor v. Brima*, Arbour as *amicus* addressed the question of whether a former UN human rights advisor could be compelled to answer questions related to the names of his informants or sources of information on

106 *Situation in Darfur*, ICC-02/05-19, Observations of the United Nations High Commissioner for Human Rights Invited in Application of Rule 103 of the Rules of Procedure and Evidence (10 October 2006) (International Criminal Court).

107 *Situation in Darfur*, ICC-02/05-10, Decision Inviting Observations in Application of Rule 103 of the Rules of Procedure and Evidence (24 July 2006) (International Criminal Court).

the ground that he obtained the information from these sources on conditions of confidentiality.[108] She asserted a privilege for protecting the identities of confidential sources of UN human rights officers, indicating that the trust and confidence relationship built with the community with whom they work is vital to fulfilling their functions. "Irreparable damage" would be caused if this confidentiality could not be maintained. She explained that protecting the identities of confidential sources cannot be the subject of any balancing of competing interests, but is rather the subject of a specific exception.

The Sierra Leone Court agreed that the witness must not be compelled to reveal the sources and clarified that the information provider, who in this case was a UN human rights officer, "must be empowered to guarantee anonymity to a confidential source."[109] This guarantee of non-disclosure of identity cannot depend on the chance that a future court might compel the office to break this promise.[110] While by now the need for protection of witnesses and victims is recognized by law, there is much more work that must be done to give effect to this promise. Often without the testimonies of courageous individuals, it is hard to break the cycle of impunity. Considering the elements needed for effective witness and victim protection is an issue that Arbour nudged the OHCHR to invest in.[111]

6. CONCLUSION

Louise Arbour approached her mandate as the UN High Commissioner for Human Rights with a vision. A distinguished jurist who has faith in humanity, she embraced on the law and searched for facts as the best way to address the plight of victims. She has made an enormous contribution to human rights

108 *Prosecutor v. Alex Tamba Brima, Brima Bazzy Kamara, Santigi Borbor Kanu (Brima Case)*, No. SCSL-04-16-AR73(B), Decision on Prosecution Appeal against Decision on Oral Application for Witness TF1-150 to Testify without Being Compelled to Answer Questions on Grounds of Confidentiality – Amicus Curiae Brief of the United Nations High Commissioner for Human Rights (16 December 2005) (Special Court for Sierra Leone), online: <http://www.rscsl.org/Documents/Decisions/AFRC/Appeal/435/SCSL-04-16-AR73-451.pdf>. See also *Annual Report of the United Nations High Commissioner for Human Rights and Reports of the Office of the High Commissioner and the Secretary-General*, HCROR, 12th sess, UN Doc. A/HRC/12/19, 21 August 2009; *Report of the United Nations High Commissioner for Human Rights on the Right to the Truth*, HCROR, 15th sess, UN Doc. A/HRC/ 15/33, 28 July 2010.

109 *Prosecutor v. Alex Tamba Brima, Brima Bazzy Kamara, Santigi Borbor Kanu (Brima Case)*, No. SCSL-04-16-AR73(B), Decision on Prosecution Appeal against Decision on Oral Application for Witness TF1-150 to Testify without Being Compelled to Answer Questions on Grounds of Confidentiality (26 May 2006) at para 33 (Special Court for Sierra Leone).

110 Ibid.

111 See also reports to the Human Rights Council on the right to truth, *supra* note 108.

by applying it as a legal regime that must be respected and implemented. Her intellectual rigour and practical mind enabled her to resolve dilemmas and address problems, she set an example of how human rights work should be carried out at the highest level. She has been a role model for many human rights investigators throughout the world, demonstrating how integrity, impartiality and independence, armed with knowledge, expertise and skill can work for the benefit of humanity. Thank you Louise Arbour.

"EXCEPTIONAL MEASURES" IN TIMES OF CRISIS

Terrorism, National Security and the Rule of Law

Lisa N. Oldring*

A decade ago, in a pivotal address at Chatham House in February 2006, Louise Arbour, the then United Nations (UN) High Commissioner for Human Rights, reflected on an environment referred to by some at that time as the "new normal."[1] She questioned whether the response of governments to the unprecedented threat posed by international terrorism following 9/11 meant that the world had entered a different legal landscape that presented a fundamental challenge to the protection of human rights. And with good cause. The "new normal" had raised a wide range of human rights issues. Among the hallmarks of the post-9/11 era identified by Arbour were challenges to the important safeguards regulating arrests and interrogations by law enforcement, and the role of national courts in supervising counter-terrorism measures, including fair trial rights and the

* Senior advisor on human rights and security policies with the Office of the United Nations High Commissioner for Human Rights. The views expressed herein are those of the author and do not necessarily reflect the views of the United Nations.

1 L. Arbour, UN High Commissioner for Human Rights, "In our name and on our behalf," delivered at Chatham House, 15 February 2006. Available at: <www.chathamhouse.org/sites/files/chathamhouse/public/Research/International%20Law/ilparbour.pdf>.

use of special and military courts. There were problems with the way some governments sought to define terrorism and related offences in their national legislation, and in their determination of states of emergency and the existence of armed conflict. Challenges to the principle of non-discrimination, including the techniques used to screen terrorist suspects, and the protection of vulnerable groups, including human rights defenders, non-citizens and journalists, also raised concerns. The rights to privacy and to property were also challenged by new methods of investigation, information collection and sharing, and through the compilation of sanctions lists and the freezing assets of persons suspected of terrorism.

Particularly egregious and widespread, at that time, were questionable practices related to judicial and administrative detention, incommunicado detention and the secret detention of individuals suspected of terrorist activity. Arbour focused her remarks at Chatham House on two such issues: the alleged use of secret detention centres and irregular transfers of persons suspected of engagement in terrorist activities, and the use of diplomatic assurances to justify the return and transfer of suspects to countries where they would face a risk of torture. These practices, she suggested, characterized the "new normal." They reflected the fact that terrorist suspects were being arrested, detained and interrogated with no apparent intention of bringing them to trial. Although this system of abductions, extra-legal transfers and secret detentions represented a repudiation of the law and of the justice system, the "unprecedented level of secrecy" surrounding what democratic governments were doing in our name and on our behalf had severely curtailed examination and debate of these issues. For Arbour, this raised fundamental questions: as the pursuit of terrorist suspects seemed to have little to do with criminal or international law as we then knew it, what was it about? Under what legal framework, if any, did it purport to operate and who was accountable to whom?

Later that same year, as though in response to these critical questions, Member States gathered at the UN General Assembly to unanimously adopt a Global Counter-Terrorism Strategy, with "measures to ensure respect for human rights for all and the rule of law" as the explicit and fundamental basis. The adoption of the Global Strategy was a watershed. Through it, all governments agreed to embrace a holistic, integrated approach to addressing terrorism, effectively and through a rule of law framework, and with full respect for their obligations under the UN Charter as well as international human rights, humanitarian, refugee and criminal law. The Strategy was elaborated through a four-pillar Plan of Action, which included a commitment by states to make every effort to "develop and maintain an effective and rule of law-based national criminal justice system that can ensure, in accordance with … obligations under international law, that any person who participates in the financing, planning, preparation or perpetration of terrorist acts or in support of terrorist acts is brought to justice, on the basis of the principle to extradite or prosecute, with due respect for human rights and fundamental freedoms."[2]

Since its adoption in 2006, the Global Counter-Terrorism Strategy has been reaffirmed by all UN Member States, most recently at the sixth biennial review in June 2018. The UN Security Council has also repeatedly asserted that counter-terrorism measures taken by states must comply with their obligations under international law, recognizing that "effective counter-terrorism measures and respect for human rights, fundamental freedoms and the rule of law are complementary and mutually reinforcing, and are an essential part of a successful counter-terrorism effort."[3]

However, the practice of states in the decade since the adoption of the Global Strategy raises a number of critical rule of law issues. In response to real or perceived security threats, governments have rushed to adopt emergency or other exceptional legislation, at times bypassing ordinary democratic legislative processes.[4] Criminal justice rules, practices and policies have been modified, ostensibly in response to security imperatives, while limitations have been imposed on individuals' privacy, freedom of expression, peaceful assembly and movement. Far-reaching surveillance practices have been introduced and maintained, without adequate procedural safeguards or effective oversight. While illegal practices including abductions, extra-legal transfers, secret detention and torture have been exposed and repudiated, at least by some governments, their exposure and condemnation has not resulted in systematic investigation, accountability or justice for victims. In some cases, efforts to ensure accountability for serious human rights violations have been thwarted by broad assertions of executive privilege, including state secrecy.

The decade since the adoption of the Global Strategy has been marked, in many respects, by the "normalization" of exceptional measures. Policies and practices that once would have been considered extraordinary in liberal democratic societies, such as the extended and in some cases indefinite detention of individuals without charge, the use of secretive judicial processes to authorize measures that may violate the law and mass surveillance of individuals' communications without warrant, are no longer exceptional. Some of these practices have become entrenched and either justified as consistent with or even

---

2 UN Global Counter-Terrorism Strategy, GA Resolution 60/288, 8 September 2006, Pillar IV, para 4.

3 S/PRST/2013/1, 15 January 2013.

4 See, for example, Report of the Special Rapporteur on the promotion and protection of human rights and fundamental freedoms while countering terrorism, 27 February 2018, A/HRC/37/62, as well as reports of the UN High Commissioner for Human Rights to the Human Rights Council on the protection of human rights and fundamental freedoms while countering terrorism, UN Docs A/HRC/16/50; A/HRC/22/26; A/HRC/28/28.

established in law. One author has referred to this progressive entrenchment of exceptional measures into law as a "normative shift from a liberal to an authoritarian form of legality."[5] Others have expressed concerns over mistakes of "institutionalized illegality" in the name of security.[6] The UN Special Rapporteur has highlighted her concerns at the "absorption of normally exceptional national security powers and counter-terrorism measures in the ordinary law of many states", noting that the dividing line between the exercise of such powers and the ordinary criminal and civil processes of some states becomes hard to distinguish, with consequences for the protection of rights which becomes "increasingly fraught and difficult to deliver in practice".[7]

This chapter reflects upon the normalization of exceptional measures in the context of national security. Part 1 provides a brief overview of the importance of the rule of law in a national security context and emphasizes the extent to which legitimate security concerns can be accommodated within a rule of law framework. Part 2 examines the shift toward the normalization of exceptional measures that has occurred, notably through the adoption of overly broad security legislation at the global and national levels, and the expansion of executive powers, including through a broadening of intelligence powers and of state secrecy privilege.

1. THE RULE OF LAW IN A NATIONAL SECURITY CONTEXT

The rule of law is a fundamental principle that asserts equality before and under the law, and the entitlement of all to equal protection and equal benefit of the law. According to the UN, it is a governance principle:

> in which all persons, institutions and entities, public and private, including the State itself, are accountable to laws that are publicly promulgated, equally enforced and independently adjudicated, and which are consistent with international human rights norms and standards. It requires, as well, measures to ensure adherence to the principles of supremacy of law, equality before the law, accountability to the law, fairness in the application of the law, separation of powers, participation in decision-making, legal certainty, avoidance of arbitrariness and procedural and legal transparency.[8]

---

5 R. Diab, *The Harbinger Theory: How the Post-9/11 Emergency Became Permanent and the Case for Reform*, Oxford University Press, Oxford, 2015, p 12.

6 C. Forcese and K. Roach, *False Security: The Radicalization of Canadian Anti-Terrorism*, Irwin Law Inc, Toronto, 2015, p 8.

7 Report of the Special Rapporteur on the promotion and protection of human rights and fundamental freedoms while countering terrorism, 27 September 2017, A/72/43280, para 12.

8 Report of the UN Secretary-General, *The Rule of Law and Transitional Justice in Conflict and Post-conflict Societies*, 23 August 2004, S/2004/616, para 6.

Integral to this is the notion that applicable laws must ensure predictability and certainty, such that they have a power-restraining effect to prevent excesses and abuses by executives and agents of the state, and ensure accountability through a system of checks and balances.

The rule of law is also described in terms of four key requirements, each of which is of central relevance in the national security context: a government and its officials and agents that are accountable under the law; laws that are clear, publicized, stable and fair, and protect fundamental rights; the process by which the laws are enacted, administered and enforced is accessible, fair and efficient; and access to justice is provided by competent, independent and ethical adjudicators or representatives and judicial officers who are of sufficient number, have adequate resources and are representative of the makeup of the communities they serve.[9] As distinct from a "rule *by* law," which amounts to a formalistic "law and order" approach, the rule of law includes certain human rights requirements, thus reflecting the ideals of equality and accountability. As Louise Arbour has reasoned, this is so because "rules serve a higher purpose than the mere orderly regulation of human conduct; laws must also enhance liberty, security and equality and strive to attain a perfect balance between law and justice."[10]

As others have highlighted in detail, not only can legitimate security imperatives be accommodated within the rule of law and with full respect for international law, they are most effective when anchored in these legal principles, norms and standards.[11] Human rights law, for example, contains within its provisions a deliberate balance between respect for the inherent dignity and freedom of each individual, and the legitimate needs of others. As such, most security measures can be adopted and implemented without restricting or interfering with human rights. In the limited situations where there may be a need to limit the enjoyment of specific rights in order to protect national security, this can be done within the flexibilities built into the international human rights law framework. Indeed, the international legal framework was developed to weather crises through an integrated set of mechanisms for exceptionality, with clear boundaries around those rights that are absolute and non-derogable. In spite of these in-built flexibilities, the way in which many states continue to respond to real or perceived threats to national security has challenged fundamental rule of law principles and has resulted in the violation of fundamental human rights.

---

9 J. Botero and A. Ponce, "Measuring the rule of law," World Justice Project Working Paper Series (Washington, November 2011).

10 L. Arbour, "The Rule of Law," *International Herald Tribune*, 26 September 2012.

11 Multi-national Counter-Terrorism Expert Network, "UN reform, the rule of law and counter-terrorism: How can past lessons inform future responses?", University of Nottingham, UK (Nottingham, March 2012); A.M. Salinas de Frias, K.L.H. Samuel and N.D. White, *Counter-Terrorism: International Law and Practice*, Oxford University Press, Oxford, 2012.

2. EXCEPTIONAL MEASURES IN TIMES OF CRISIS

2.1. NORMALIZING EXCEPTIONAL MEASURES THROUGH LAW

In accordance with the rule of law, clarity and precision in the legal definition of an activity as criminal is a baseline for ensuring both the effectiveness of the law and the accountability of agents of the state that are responsible for enforcing it. A law that is vague or overly broad provides neither fair notice to individuals of what conduct is prohibited or potential consequences for violation of that law, nor clear standards for those entrusted with law enforcement, thus leaving open the possibility of abuses. Then-Justice Louise Arbour elaborated on this notion in her dissenting opinion in *Canadian Foundation for Children, Youth and the Law v. Canada (Attorney General)*, where she emphasized that a "vague law violates the principles of fundamental justice because it does not provide 'fair warning' to individuals as to the legality of their actions and because it increases the amount of discretion given to law enforcement officials in their application of the law, which may lead to arbitrary enforcement."[12] In brief, legal certainty serves to ensure that those subject to the law are protected against the arbitrary use of state power, whilst allowing for the effective function of criminal justice processes.

The years since 9/11 have seen a proliferation of national security and counter-terrorism legislation. More than 140 governments have adopted new security legislation, in many cases without precise definitions of the types of acts and/or organizations the laws are meant to target.[13] Legislative reforms have been implemented in some cases without meaningful democratic reflection and debate, without in-built checks and balances such as sunset clauses and provision for periodic parliamentary review.[14] In many cases the legislation has been based upon broad, ambiguous or vaguely defined concepts such as "public order," "public safety," "national security" or "anti-terrorism," leaving open the potential for abuse while also limiting the effectiveness of such legislation to achieve its stated purpose.[15] Criminal legislation in many countries includes offences related

---

12 *Canadian Foundation for Children, Youth and the Law v. Canada (Attorney General)* [2004] 1 SCR 76, 2004 SCC 4, Arbour J (dissent).

13 "In the name of Security: Counterterrorism laws worldwide since September 11", Human Rights Watch, 29 June 2012, available at: <https://www.hrw.org/report/2012/06/29/name-security/counterterrorism-laws-worldwide-september-11>.

14 See, for example, Study of Bill C-51 (Antiterrorism Act 2015), Submissions to the Senate Standing Committee, 2 April 2015, available at: <www.antiterrorlaw.ca; https://ccla.org/cclanewsite/wp-content/uploads/2015/07/Notice-of-Application-Re-Bill-C-51-C1382903xA0E3A.pdf>.

15 For recent examples, see: "Two UN rights experts urge France to bring its draft counter-terrorism law in compliance with its international human rights obligations", 27 September 2017, available at: <http://www.ohchr.org/EN/NewsEvents/Pages/DisplayNews.aspx?NewsID=22165&

to speech that is seen to directly or indirectly encourage terrorism, through the expansion of prohibitions on incitement to broader and less-defined areas such as "apology," "praising," "glorification or indirect encouragement" or "public justification" of terrorism. Such provisions reflect a weakening of the causal link that would normally be required in law between the speech (or other form of expression) and the risk that a criminal act may be committed.[16]

2.1.1. *Supranational Legislation*

The impetus for states to adopt security legislation in recent years is rooted in the international legal obligations of states to prevent and suppress terrorism. These obligations are enshrined in declarations, resolutions, and multilateral and regional treaties that proscribe acts related, for example, to the financing of terrorism, hostage-taking, maritime navigation and attacks against internationally protected persons.[17] A number of universal treaties aim to ensure that specific acts are criminalized and investigated, and that suspects are prosecuted or extradited, with various measures of international cooperation.[18]

While many of these instruments include a component definition of terrorist activity, none provides a comprehensive definition of terrorism.[19] Multilateral

---

LangID=E>; "UK independent reviewer of terrorism legislation criticises too-broad definition of terrorism," 22 July 2014, available at: <https://terrorismlegislationreviewer.independent.gov.uk/wp-content/uploads/2014/07/22-July-2014-PRESS-RELEASE.pdf>; "UN experts urge Ethiopia to stop using anti-terrorism legislation to curb human rights," UN OHCHR press release, 18 September 2014; "Statement by the United Nations Special Rapporteur on the rights to freedom of peaceful assembly and of association at the conclusion of his visit to the Republic of Rwanda," UN OHCHR press release, 27 January 2014. See also Report of the UN High Commissioner for Human Rights on the protection of human rights and fundamental freedoms while countering terrorism, 19 December 2014, A/HRC/28/28, paras 21–30; Report on Counter-Terrorism Measures and Human Rights adopted by the Venice Commission at its 83rd Plenary Session (Venice, 4 June 2010), para 33; and Report of the Secretary-General on Protecting Human Rights and Fundamental Freedoms while Countering Terrorism, A/72/316, 11 August 2017, paras 26–33.

16 See General Comment 34 of the UN Human Rights Committee, which suggests that offences such as the "encouragement of terrorism" and "extremist activity" or "praising," "glorifying" or "justifying" terrorism should be clearly defined to ensure that they do not lead to unnecessary or disproportionate interference with freedom of expression. CCPR/C/GC/34.

17 International Convention for the Suppression of the Financing of Terrorism, adopted by the General Assembly of the United Nations on 9 December 1999; International Convention against the Taking of Hostages, adopted by the General Assembly of the United Nations on 17 December 1979; Convention for the Suppression of Unlawful Acts against the Safety of Maritime Navigation, done at Rome on 10 March 1988; Convention on the Prevention and Punishment of Crimes against Internationally Protected Persons, including Diplomatic Agents, adopted by the General Assembly of the United Nations on 14 December 1973.

18 A complete list of the universal counter-terrorism treaties is available at: <http://www.un.org/en/terrorism/instruments.shtml>.

19 See also the decision of the Special Tribunal for Lebanon, Appeals Chamber, "Interlocutory decision on the applicable law: terrorism, conspiracy, homicide, perpetration, cumulative

efforts to enshrine a definition of terrorism in a binding, comprehensive, international counter-terrorism instrument have continued for over a decade, stalling primarily over a lack of agreement on the distinction between acts of terrorism and the "legitimate struggle of peoples in the exercise of their right to self-determination or under foreign occupation"; whether "state terrorism" should fall within its scope; and whether the activities of armed forces of a state in peacetime should be considered within the scope of the Convention.[20] Similarly, although "national security" often provides the legal rationale for criminal and other legislation at the national level, the concept is not defined in international law. A recent study of national legal regimes and practices related to national security and related legislation in EU Member States highlighted the "fuzziness and legal uncertainties inherent to the very term 'national security'" and noted that "the few definitional features that appear in [EU Member States'] legal regimes and doctrinal practices fail to meet legal certainty and rule of law standards."[21]

At the international level, the Security Council has played a predominant role in shaping Member States' security legislation, insofar as it has imposed binding obligations on them to take legislative and other measures to counter terrorism. Resolution 1267, adopted by the Security Council in 1999, had already established a sanctions mechanism that, together with subsequent resolutions, includes an arms embargo, a travel ban and asset-freezing against any individual or entity affiliated with al-Qaida.[22] The subsequent adoption of Security Council Resolution 1373 in the critical days following the horrific 9/11 terrorist attacks signalled a turning point.[23] First, it reflected the notion that *any* act of terrorism was a threat to international peace and security (thus triggering the Chapter VII authority of the Council). Second, it imposed a number of permanent, general legislative obligations on all states. Acting under Chapter VII of the UN Charter, through Resolution 1373 the Council mandated governments to enact legislation to prevent and suppress the financing of terrorist acts, criminalize direct and indirect terrorist funding, freeze the assets

charging," Case No. STL-11-01/I, 16 February 2011, as well as a critique of the decision (insofar as it address the definition of terrorism) in B. Saul, "Legislating from a radical Hague: The United Nations Special Tribunal for Lebanon invents an international crime of transnational terrorism" (2011) 24 *Leiden Journal of International Law* 655.

20 Draft Comprehensive Convention against International Terrorism, A/59/894, and reports of the Ad Hoc Committee established by General Assembly Resolution 51/210 of 17 December 1996, 13th and 15th sessions, A/64/37 and A/66/37. See also B. Saul, *Defining Terrorism in International Law*, Oxford University Press, Oxford, 2008.

21 European Parliament Directorate-General for Internal Policies, *National Security and Secret Evidence in Legislation and before the Courts: Exploring the Challenges, Study for the LIBE Committee*, European Parliament, Brussels, 2014, p 9.

22 UNSC Res 1267 (15 October 1999) UN Doc. S/RES/1267.

23 UNSC Res 1373 (28 September 2001) UN Doc. S/RES/1373.

of terrorists and any participants or accomplices, and prohibit individuals from providing financial or any other support to terrorists. It further required all states to ensure that "such terrorist acts are established as serious criminal offences in domestic laws and regulations" with punishment commensurate with the seriousness of the act, to implement immigration reforms, to bring terrorists to justice, and to strengthen international cooperation in criminal matters, among other measures. The resolution also established the Counter-Terrorism Committee with a mandate to monitor states' implementation of Resolution 1373, including national legislative measures.

Significantly, while it imposed mandatory obligations on states to enact counter-terrorism legislation, Resolution 1373 did not define the word "terrorism," nor did it provide guidance on what constitutes a "terrorist act," or who counts as a "terrorist" or a "participant." Moreover, as the resolution did not include specific provision for ensuring that all of the measures it required states to adopt were compliant with international human rights law, the interpretive discretion was left to individual states, raising the prospect that it could (and would) be used by some states as grounds for abuse.[24] The lack of definition of those key terms also created challenges for effective international cooperation and mutual legal assistance, as well as the establishment of a uniform measure for compliance.

Other resolutions have added to the Security Council legislative regime, covering issues ranging from the proliferation of nuclear, chemical and biological weapons,[25] to international cooperation in the fight against terrorism,[26] to the prevention and prohibition of incitement to commit terrorist acts,[27] gradually incorporating certain human rights and rule of law protections. Resolution 1566 constructively offered an operational definition of terrorism in line with the principle of legality, with specific characteristics of conduct to be suppressed in the fight against international terrorism, although by the time of its adoption in 2004, many governments had already adopted broad new anti-terrorism legislation

24 The problems created by the lack of definition immediately became apparent, as highlighted in the 2002 report of the Special Representative of the Secretary-General on human rights defenders, Hina Jilani, who noted the danger that, in the aftermath of 9/11, "some governments may be using the global war on terrorism as a pretext to infringe human rights and to clamp down on human rights defenders." E/CN.4/2002/106, 27 February 2002, para 96. The Special Representative provided examples of the negative effects of vague legislative definitions of terrorism in her 2003 report: "such legislation has been used in the arrest and detention of, among others, trade unionists, student leaders, political activists, members of religious groups, academics, lawyers, journalists and non-governmental organization workers in response to their human rights activities." A/58/380, 18 September 2003, para 31.

25 UNSC Res 1540 (28 April 2004) UN Doc. S/RES/1540.

26 UNSC Res 1566 (8 October 2004) UN Doc. S/RES/1566.

27 UNSC Res 1624 (14 September 2005) UN Doc. S/RES/1624.

in accordance with the mandate and reporting requirements established under Resolution 1373.[28]

However, more recent efforts by some governments to deter and punish individuals who have or seek to become "foreign terrorist fighters" also raise serious human rights challenges. In its Resolution 2170, the Security Council called upon Member States to take national measures to suppress the flow of fighters to join terrorist groups, reiterating the obligations deriving from previous counter-terrorism resolutions to prevent the movement of terrorists and their supply with arms or financial support. In September 2014, the Council adopted Resolution 2178, which imposed further broad new legal obligations on all states, without any geographic or temporal limitation, to prevent the "recruiting, organizing, transporting or equipping of individuals who travel to a State other than their States of residence or nationality for the purpose of the perpetration, planning of, or participation in terrorist acts."[29] The Resolution required states to establish criminal offences which would allow for the prosecution of such individuals for their intention to travel in order to participate in terrorist acts. This requirement raised alarm bells for commentators including the UN Special Rapporteur on human rights and counter-terrorism, who noted that "a Security Council requirement for nations to adopt legislation regulating people's intent to participate in a particular action (the exact contours of which may be hazy at best in individual cases), ought to concern all of us with even a passing knowledge of the difference between a choate and inchoate criminal offence".[30]

Resolution 2178 contained an important reaffirmation of the obligation of all Member States to comply with international human rights law when fighting terrorism, noting that a failure to comply with human rights and other international obligations has contributed to increased radicalization and fostered a sense of impunity. However, set against the backdrop of the human rights record of many states, including those that had already used the term "extremism" "not as part of a strategy to counter violent extremism but as an offence in itself,"[31] it could fuel the adoption by governments of repressive measures against otherwise lawful,

---

28 S/RES/1566 (2004), para 3: "criminal acts, including against civilians, committed with the intent to cause death or serious bodily injury, or taking of hostages, with the purpose to provoke a state of terror in the general public or in a group of persons or particular persons, intimidate a population or compel a government or an international organization to do or to abstain from doing any act, which constitute offences within the scope of and as defined in the international conventions and protocols relating to terrorism."

29 UNSC Res 2178 (24 September 2014) UN Doc. S/RES/2178.

30 F.N. Aolain, "The UN Security Council, Global Watch Lists, Biometrics, and the Threat to the Rule of Law", *Just Security*, 17 January 2018, available at: <https://www.justsecurity.org/51075/security-council-global-watch-lists-biometrics/>.

31 Report of the Special Rapporteur on the promotion and protection of human rights and fundamental freedoms while countering terrorism, A/HRC/31/65, 22 February 2016, para 21.

non-violent activities of groups or individuals,[32] with further implications for the accountability of state agents.[33] The impact of Security Council resolutions 2354(2017) on "countering terrorist narratives" and 2396(2017) on returning and relocating "foreign terrorist fighters" have similarly raised well-founded concerns from the perspective of human rights and the rule of law.[34]

Challenges have arisen in the context of other efforts by states seeking to address the challenge of countering violent extremism as and when conducive to terrorism.[35] The Plan of Action to Prevent Violent Extremism, which was issued in January 2016 by the UN Secretary-General and with a strong human rights focus, explicitly addressed some of the conceptual and definitional challenges, noting that violent extremism "is a diverse phenomenon, without clear definition." The Plan of Action also provided that "definitions of 'terrorism' and 'violent extremism' are the prerogative of Member States and must be consistent with their obligations under international law, in particular international human rights law."[36] In his report to the Human Rights Council in March 2016, the UN Special Rapporteur highlighted the "inherent risks of relying on poorly defined concepts," noting further that the lack of semantic and conceptual clarity around the notion of violent extremism inhibits "any in-depth examination of strategies and policies to counter violent extremism on human rights, as well as on their effectiveness in reducing the threat of terrorism."[37] The Special

32 Report of the United Nations High Commissioner for Human Rights on the protection of human rights and fundamental freedoms while countering terrorism, A/HRC/28/28, 19 December 2014, para 46; Report of the Special Rapporteur on the promotion and protection of human rights and fundamental freedoms while countering terrorism, A/HRC/31/65, 22 February 2016.

33 Report of the United Nations High Commissioner for Human Rights on the protection of human rights and fundamental freedoms while countering terrorism, A/HRC/28/28, 19 December 2014, para 47; see also M. Scheinin, "Back to post-9/11 panic? Security Council Resolution on Foreign Terrorist Fighters," *Just Security*, 23 September 2014, available at: <https://www.justsecurity.org/15407/post-911-panic-security-council-resolution-foreign-terrorist-fighters-scheinin>.

34 See FIDH, "Countering terrorist narratives at the expense of human rights? The UN Security Council sets the alarming tone", 24 May 2017, available at: <https://www.fidh.org/en/international-advocacy/united-nations/security-council/countering-terrorist-narratives-at-the-expense-of-human-rights-the-un>; and F.N. Aolain, 'The UN Security Council, Global Watch Lists, Biometrics, and the Threat to the Rule of Law", *Just Security*, 17 January 2018, available at: <https://www.justsecurity.org/51075/security-council-global-watch-lists-biometrics/>.

35 For example, Security Council resolution See also Plan of Action to Prevent Violent Extremism Report of the Secretary-General, A/70/674, 24 December 2015. For a summary of recent international, regional and national initiatives, see the Report of the Special Rapporteur on the promotion and protection of human rights and fundamental freedoms while countering terrorism, A/HRC/31/65, 22 February 2016, para 9.

36 Plan of Action to Prevent Violent Extremism Report of the Secretary-General, A/70/674, 24 December 2015, paras 5, 15, 20, 40, 43, 49 and 50.

37 Report of the Special Rapporteur on the promotion and protection of human rights and fundamental freedoms while countering terrorism, A/HRC/31/65, 22 February 2016, paras 21 and 55.

Rapporteur reiterated the recommendation made by the Secretary-General in the Plan of Action for states to focus their efforts on the implementation of the first and fourth pillars of the Global Counter-Terrorism Strategy as the only holistic, effective and sustainable approach and, further, that they should ensure that all strategies and policies adopted by states to counter violent extremism are firmly grounded in and comply with international human rights law.[38]

2.1.2. National Legislation

While not defined explicitly in a comprehensive way under international law, concepts of national security and counter-terrorism are indeed pervasive in national legislation, providing the basis in many countries for expansive executive, intelligence-gathering and law enforcement powers. National laws criminalize various acts associated with terrorism, including preparatory offences, endow police with enhanced powers of investigation and arrest in relation to such offences, establish regimes for mass communications surveillance as well as the targeted surveillance of individuals, and provide for asset-freezing and the imposition of travel bans on "terrorists" and "terrorist organisations" as well as trade sanctions against countries that reportedly harbour or support terrorists. Acting on Security Council mandates, states have implemented measures including blocking the validity of travel documents, revoking citizenship, freezing financial assets and the prosecution and punishment of individuals for acts ranging from recruitment and incitement to the planning of terrorist acts.[39]

According to international law, states have an obligation to criminalize terrorist activity. Of the universal counter-terrorism instruments, 16 define a specific offence and require states parties to establish the offence as criminal under national legislation.[40] In view of its serious potential consequences, the precise definition in national criminal law of "terrorist-related crimes" is critical to ensure the effectiveness of such legislation to prevent and address activity which is truly "terrorist" in nature.[41] It is equally important to prevent human rights violations by agents of the state, as well as to ensure that perpetrators of any

---

38 Report of the Special Rapporteur on the promotion and protection of human rights and fundamental freedoms while countering terrorism, A/HRC/31/65, 22 February 2016, para 56. See also Report of the High Commissioner for Human Rights on best practices and lessons learned on how protecting and promoting human rights contribute to preventing and countering violent extremism, A/HRC/33/29, 21 July 2016.

39 See, for example, Report of the United Nations High Commissioner for Human Rights on the protection of human rights and fundamental freedoms while countering terrorism, A/HRC/28/28, 19 December 2014, para 33.

40 On the criminalization of terrorist activities, see United Nations Office on Drugs and Crime, *Human Rights and Criminal Justice Responses to Terrorism*, Counter-Terrorism Legal Training Curriculum Module 4, United Nations, New York, 2014, Chapter 2.

41 Ibid, p 33.

violations are held to account through a rule of law framework. An imprecise, vague or overly broad definition can lead to the criminalization of innocent conduct or a broadening of proscribed conduct through judicial interpretation.[42] States therefore must define the material and mental elements of terrorist offences in accordance with their general criminal law, while ensuring that any new provisions also comply with their other obligations under international law, including human rights law. In the definition of terrorism-related crimes, this includes adhering to the principle of legality, which prohibits not only the application of *ex post facto* laws, but also requires that the criminalized conduct be described in clear and unambiguous language that gives "fair notice" of what conduct is prohibited, narrowly defines the punishable offence and distinguishes it from conduct that is either not punishable or is punishable by other penalties.[43]

The impact of overly broad or vague counter-terrorism legislation enacted by many states in the years immediately following the adoption of Security Council Resolution 1373 in 2001 has been documented in detail.[44] Set against the lessons learned through these experiences, the implementation of new or newly-revised counter-terrorism legislation containing similarly broad or vague terminology has raised serious concerns over the potential for abuse. Such potential is explicit in some legislation, for example, where terrorism is defined to include such acts as "insulting the reputation of the State or its position," a provision that effectively criminalizes any discourse critical of the government or its policies.[45] National security legislation has also left open the door to abuse where it defines national security broadly, for example, as "the condition in which the country's government, sovereignty, unification, territorial integrity, well-being of its people, sustainable development of its economy and society and other major interests are relatively safe and not subject to internal and external threats," with punitive measures for individual violations.[46] The extraordinarily

42 For these reasons, common law jurisdictions incorporate a "void for vagueness" doctrine, which dictates that a law is void if its prohibitions are not defined with clarity and precision.

43 International Covenant on Civil and Political Rights, Article 15. See also UN General Assembly Resolution 63/185, which underscores these principles and urges Member States to "ensure that their laws criminalizing acts of terrorism are accessible, formulated with sufficient precision, non-discriminatory, non-retroactive and in accordance with international law, including human rights law."

44 See, for example, International Commission of Jurists, *Assessing Damage, Urging Action: Report of the Eminent Jurists Panel on Terrorism, Counter-Terrorism and Human Rights*, Geneva, 2009; K. Roach, *The 9/11 Effect: Comparative Counter-Terrorism*, Cambridge University Press, New York, 2011; B. Saul, *Defining Terrorism in International Law*, Oxford University Press, Oxford, 2008.

45 Report of the United Nations High Commissioner for Human Rights on the protection of human rights and fundamental freedoms while countering terrorism, A/HRC/28/28, 19 December 2014, para 22.

46 T. Mitchell, "China passes sweeping national security law," *Financial Times*, 1 July 2015, available at: <www.ft.com/intl/cms/s/0/5dfa8360-1fdb-11e5-aa5a-398b2169cf79.html#axzz3nR05LDx.r>.

broad scope of such legislation, together with the vagueness of its terminology and definitions, has prompted concerns that it leaves the door open to further restrictions of rights and freedoms, as well as tighter controls on civil society. One expert has noted that overly broad counter-terror laws are "undesirable even if they are not misused," with legislative restraint needed to avoid "creep" and ensure that counter-terrorism mandates are legitimate and confined to their proper purpose.[47]

Concerns over the potential for abuse of overly broad or vague national security legislation must be considered in the light of recent experiences in states that have clamped down on the legitimate activity of journalists, human rights defenders, minority groups, members of the political opposition or others, with authorities charging individuals or groups with "inciting" or "encouraging" terrorism. As highlighted in one recent comprehensive study, counter-terrorism legislation, policy and guidelines such as those developed by the Financial Action Task Force (FATF), in particular the FATF recommendation concerning "the adequacy of laws and regulations that relate to entities that can be abused for the financing of terrorism," have had a negative impact on the operational space for civil society. The study cites counter-terrorism measures officially intended to prohibit material support to terrorist organizations, which have "restricted NGOs' access to foreign funding, often due to ambiguous or overtly broad definitions of 'terrorism' and 'material support' or a lack of due process requirements."[48] The activities of civil society organizations have been restricted significantly, with more than 60 countries reportedly adopting laws curtailing the activity of non-governmental organizations and civil society groups, while 96 countries have taken steps to inhibit them from operating at full capacity through a global pushback that appears part of the "new normal."[49]

2.2. NORMALIZING EXCEPTIONAL MEASURES THROUGH ENHANCED EXECUTIVE POWERS

Preventing and countering terrorism poses a unique and serious challenge for governments, and for traditional law enforcement in particular, and one

47 D. Anderson, QC, "UK independent reviewer of terrorism legislation in the United Kingdom criticises too-broad definition of terrorism," 22 July 2014, available at: <https://terrorismlegislationreviewer.independent.gov.uk/wp-content/uploads/2014/07/22-July-2014-PRESS-RELEASE.pdf>.

48 T. Carothers and S. Brechenmacher, *Closing Space: Democracy and Human Rights Support under Fire*, Carnegie Endowment for International Peace, Washington, D.C., 2014, p 30. See also the report of the UN Special Rapporteur on the promotion and protection of human rights and fundamental freedoms while countering terrorism A/69/365, which highlights concerns that such restrictions have been used by some states as a "cover for imposing politically motivated restrictions on civil society funding."

49 Ibid, p 29.

that has required intelligence agencies to play an increasingly prominent role. While intelligence alone may not prevent a terrorist attack, the combination of intelligence and law enforcement is the primary means to identify and possibly thwart such criminal activity, and can be critical in ensuring that perpetrators are brought to justice.

However, the expansion of intelligence authority in many countries and the increase in intelligence-led law enforcement characteristic of the post-9/11 era raise a number of rule of law issues and have contributed to the normalization of otherwise exceptional measures. With increasingly blurred lines between criminal justice and national security, this expansion has often occurred without adequate consideration of the procedural safeguards and oversight necessary to protect against abuses and ensure accountability, where abuses occur. With the increased focus on the prevention of terrorism, the powers of intelligence agencies have been broadened beyond their traditional core functions related to the collection, analysis and dissemination of information relevant to the protection of national security, in some instances even taking on law enforcement powers such as arrest, detention, search and seizure, and the use of force.[50]

While such powers are not prohibited under international law per se, the agency endowed with such powers must comply with human rights standards, along with domestic laws that would normally govern law enforcement. Yet intelligence services in some jurisdictions have been mandated with powers to make arrests without a warrant and to detain without explicit safeguards, including guarantees of due process rights such as the right to counsel.[51] National laws on surveillance of electronic communications have expanded the power of the executive over the collection, analysis and storage of communications content or metadata, without the requirement of prior authorization or judicial review.[52] Intelligence agencies have been endowed with the power to detain terror suspects for prolonged periods of time and for the sole purpose of intelligence gathering in situations that arguably amount to an arbitrary deprivation of liberty.[53] In Canada, national security legislation which had effectively authorized intelligence services to breach constitutional rights, with

---

50 For example, covert lethal drone operations continue to be conducted by the CIA, in spite of repeated calls for such operations to be subsumed under military command to ensure greater transparency, oversight and accountability. See also Report of the United Nations High Commissioner for Human Rights on the protection of human rights and fundamental freedoms while countering terrorism, A/HRC/28/28, paras 24 and 25.

51 "South Sudan fires Interior Minister as Security Law implemented," 14 April 2015, available at: <www.bloomberg.com/news/articles/2015-04-14/south-sudan-fires-interior-minister-as-security-law-implemented>.

52 "UN rights experts urge France to protect fundamental freedoms while countering terrorism," UN press release, 19 January 2016.

53 "South Sudan: Government must end arbitrary detentions by the intelligence agency," Amnesty International, 15 April 2016; "Sudanese National Intelligence Service empowered to violate human rights," Amnesty International, 19 March 2015.

a warrant issued by a judge in a secretive process,[54] was criticized as amounting to a perversion of the rule of law, the role of the judiciary and the separation of powers.[55] While new wide-reaching national security legislation was introduced before Parliament in 2017 in the form of Bill C-59, ostensibly with a view to addressing these and other issues, civil society organizations and individual experts have voiced concerns over a number of provisions reflected in the Bill.[56]

The fundamental tenets of the rule of law require that the powers and competences of intelligence services are outlined clearly and precisely in law, and that intelligence services are constituted through, and operate under, publicly available laws that comply with international and domestic law. As organs of the state, like other executive bodies, intelligence agencies are bound by the relevant provisions of national and international law, including human rights law. As a consequence, states cannot rely upon either domestic law or security objectives to justify violations of international human rights law or indeed any other international legal obligations.[57] National legislation governing the functioning of intelligence services should also explicitly provide for adequate control and oversight, as well as ensuring that oversight institutions are empowered through an adequate mandate, expertise and resources.[58] Reviews of oversight structures and experiences across a number of jurisdictions suggest that accountability is most effective where intelligence agencies are overseen by a combination of internal, executive, parliamentary, judicial and expert institutions, including at least one civilian institution that is independent of the executive and the intelligence agency, adequately empowered and sufficiently resourced to carry out its functions.[59] Policies and mechanisms should also be in place to enable an

---

54 Canada Anti-Terrorism Act 2015, S.C. 2015, c. 20 (also referred to as Bill C-51), s 12.1(3): "The Service shall not take measures to reduce a threat to the security of Canada if those measures will contravene a right or freedom guaranteed by the Canadian Charter of Rights and Freedoms or will be contrary to other Canadian law, unless the Service is authorized to take them by a warrant issued under section 21.1."

55 Amnesty International, *Insecurity and Human Rights: Concerns and Recommendations with Respect to Bill C-51, the Anti-Terrorism Act, 2015*, submitted to the House of Commons Standing Committee on Public Safety and National Security, 9 March 2015.

56 See, for example, "Civil Society Statement Regarding Bill C-59, *An Act respecting national security matters*" (5 April 2018), available at: <http://iclmg.ca/civil-society-statement-c59/>.

57 Report of the Special Rapporteur on the promotion and protection of human rights and fundamental freedoms while countering terrorism: Compilation of good practices on legal and institutional frameworks and measures that ensure respect for human rights by intelligence agencies while countering terrorism, including on their oversight, A/HRC/14/46, 17 May 2010, para 12.

58 Ibid, para 12. See also, for example, "Open letter to Parliament: Amend C-51 or kill it," *National Post* (27 February 2015), available at: <http://news.nationalpost.com/full-comment/open-letter-to-parliament-amend-c-51-or-kill-it>.

59 Report of the Special Rapporteur on the promotion and protection of human rights and fundamental freedoms while countering terrorism: Compilation of good practices on legal and institutional frameworks and measures that ensure respect for human rights by intelligence agencies while countering terrorism, including on their oversight, A/HRC/14/46, 17 May 2010, para 12.

independent investigation into alleged human rights violations by intelligence agencies, such that they are able to establish facts and ensure accountability.

The increase in intelligence-led law enforcement has also had an impact on criminal justice, as national security considerations have permeated criminal processes related to counter-terrorism.[60] As intelligence and justice ultimately have different, though overlapping objectives, their increased interaction has raised issues that present challenges to the principles and aims of both. The reliance on intelligence for criminal justice purposes, for example, has created issues related to differences in evidentiary standards, as intelligence-gathering procedures are generally subject to lower legal thresholds than those governing the collection of evidence for use in a criminal proceeding. The inherently secretive nature of intelligence also means that it may not be subject to testing in the context of criminal legal proceedings, raising further questions of reliability; at the same time, the accused may be denied the right to review and challenge evidence when disclosure of intelligence submitted as evidence is suppressed.[61] The expansion of intelligence cooperation has included more extensive sharing of raw data on individuals collected through the internet or via mobile devices, prompting questions with regard to judicial accountability, including difficulties in assessing the quality, lawfulness and accuracy of information.[62] A study of European Union Member States revealed an increasingly blurred distinction between "information" and "intelligence," which, in turn, has contributed to "ambiguity in the nature and validity of secret materials when presented as 'evidence' in court."[63] The increase in the sharing of information between law enforcement and intelligence agencies in different jurisdictions has also raised risks that such information may have been obtained by illegal means, creating additional problems of accountability.

The enhancement of executive powers in the post-9/11 environment has also impacted upon accountability in other ways. A core indicator of respect for the rule of law, accountability is an obligation that entails the adoption of policies, laws and practices that are accessible, open to meaningful public scrutiny

---

60 European Parliament Directorate-General for Internal Policies, *National Security and Secret Evidence in Legislation and before the Courts: Exploring the Challenges, Study for the LIBE Committee*, European Parliament, Brussels, 2014.

61 Report of the United Nations High Commissioner for Human Rights on the protection of human rights and fundamental freedoms while countering terrorism, A/HRC/16/50, 15 December 2010.

62 See European Parliament Directorate-General for Internal Policies, *National Security and Secret Evidence in Legislation and before the Courts: Exploring the Challenges, Study for the LIBE Committee*, European Parliament, Brussels, 2014, Section 2 and Annex I. See also Report of the UN High Commissioner for Human Rights on the Right to Privacy in the Digital Age, A/HRC/27/37.

63 European Parliament Directorate-General for Internal Policies, *National Security and Secret Evidence in Legislation and before the Courts: Exploring the Challenges, Study for the LIBE Committee*, European Parliament, Brussels, 2014.

and subject to effective oversight, in order to ensure a system of balanced and effective checks and balances. Respect for the rule of law also requires putting in place and implementing effective accountability mechanisms for violations of human rights, including where these occur in the national security realm.[64] This includes individual criminal responsibility, where violations amount to crimes, as well as responsive civil and administrative policies and procedures to address grievances.

The investigation of an alleged violation of human rights law by a state in its counter-terror operations is fundamental to ensure accountability and prevent future violations. Wherever there is credible evidence to suggest that there has been a serious violation of human rights, the state must conduct a prompt, independent, impartial and thorough investigation.[65] Victims of gross human rights violations have a legal right to an effective remedy and to know the truth – that is, to seek and obtain information on the causes and conditions pertaining to gross violations of human rights law and to learn the truth in regard to these violations.[66] This right entails a duty on the state to ensure the cessation of any ongoing violation, as well as to have this right "determined by competent judicial, administrative or legislative authorities, or by any other competent authority provided for by the legal system of the State, and to develop the possibilities of judicial remedy."[67] Some have argued that where a strong case is made, but the party accused of a serious violation (such as an alleged unlawful killing, in violation of human rights law) fails to make available the information needed for an informed determination to be made as to whether a violation has taken place, there should be a presumption that a violation has occurred. Otherwise the state may have "an irresistible incentive … to maintain as much secrecy as possible and then shield behind the justification that national security prevents any disclosure."[68]

---

64 The obligation to seek accountability is explicitly referred to in instruments of international human rights law and has been reinforced by interpretations of the law. The International Covenant on Civil and Political Rights, the Convention against Torture and Other Cruel, Inhuman or Degrading Treatment or Punishment, the International Convention for the Protection of All Persons from Enforced Disappearance, and the Optional Protocols to the Convention on the Rights of the Child on the involvement of children in armed conflict and on the sale of children, child prostitution and child pornography impose an obligation on all States Parties to provide an effective remedy for violations of the rights and freedoms contained in these treaties, including a duty to investigate and punish those responsible.

65 Human Rights Committee General Comment 31[80], The Nature of the General Legal Obligation Imposed on States Parties to the Covenant, CCPR/C/21/Rev.1/Add.13, 26 May 2004, para 18.

66 UN Basic Principles and Guidelines on the Right to a Remedy and Reparation for Gross Violations of International Human Rights Law and Serious Violations of International Humanitarian Law, GA Resolution 60/147, 16 December 2005, Annex, para 24.

67 Article 2, paragraph 3(b) ICCPR.

68 P. Alston, "IHL, transparency and the Heyns' UN Drones Report," *Just Security*, 23 October 2013, available at: <https://www.justsecurity.org/2420/ihl-transparency-heyns-report>.

The invocation of a state secrets privilege has, in many cases, prevented accountability for serious human rights violations. Although the concept of a "state secrets" privilege was originally conceived to address cases where it may be necessary to exclude specific evidence, the exposure of which would necessarily harm national security, its use in some states has expanded from an evidentiary privilege to a "justiciability doctrine" in order to effectively exclude entire lawsuits.[69] Investigations and prosecutions in relation to the alleged involvement of states in renditions have been obstructed by the non-disclosure of information and evidence deemed prejudicial to security interests. The state secrets doctrine been invoked in a number of cases as grounds for dismissal of legal proceedings in cases related to the extraordinary rendition and torture of detainees.[70] Legal action brought on behalf of individuals killed by armed drones has also been thwarted by "the position taken by States that judicial inquiry into decisions regarding the use of drones was inappropriate," while requests for judicial review are routinely met with "assertions of exclusive executive decision-making authority in matters of national security, immunity for officials, and the need for secrecy with regard to relevant government information."[71]

Recent developments suggest that there is recognition of a need for reform to contain the excessive use of state secrecy and ensure accountability, in line with the rule of law. Courts at the national level have ruled against the state where state secrecy was invoked as grounds for refusal by the government, for example, to provide testimony and access to information to a parliamentary inquiry into alleged cooperation of its intelligence services in renditions.[72] In another case brought against the government by an individual who had been erroneously included on an official yet secretive no-fly list, the judge asserted that

---

69 Report of the UN High Commissioner for Human Rights on the promotion and protection of human rights while countering terrorism, A/HRC/16/50, 15 December 2010. The Special Rapporteur on the promotion and protection of human rights and fundamental freedoms while countering terrorism has also raised concerns over the increasing use of state secrecy provisions and public interest immunities by Germany, Italy, Poland, Romania, the former Yugoslav Republic of Macedonia, the United Kingdom or the United States "to conceal illegal acts from oversight bodies or judicial authorities, or to protect itself from criticism, embarrassment and – most importantly – liability." A/HRC/10/3, 4 February 2009, para. 59.

70 *Binyam Mohamed et al v. Jeppesen DataPlan, Inc*, United States Court of Appeals for the Ninth Circuit No. 08-15693, 8 September 2010; *Arar v Ashcroft*, 585 F.3d 559 (2d Cir. 2009) (*en banc*).

71 Summary of the Human Rights Council interactive panel discussion of experts on the use of remotely piloted aircraft or armed drones in compliance with international law, A/HRC/28/38, 15 December 2014, para 20. The UN Special Rapporteur on the promotion and protection of human rights and fundamental freedoms while countering terrorism has suggested that the lack of transparency by states regarding their use of drones as the single greatest obstacle to an evaluation of the impact of armed drones on civilians, as it made it extremely difficult to assess the legality of their use and ensure accountability.

72 Available at: <www.bundesverfassungsgericht.de/entscheidungen/es20090617_2bve000307.html>.

the government had overreached in its invocation of the state secrets privilege and ruled in favour of the plaintiff.[73]

At the regional level, already in 2002 the Inter-American Court of Human Rights had asserted that "public bodies cannot shield themselves behind the protective cloak of official secrets to avoid or obstruct the investigation of illegal acts ascribed to members of its own bodies."[74] More recently, in Europe, guidelines on eradicating impunity for serious human rights violations were adopted by the Committee of Ministers on 30 March 2011, following a request by the Parliamentary Assembly of the Council of Europe for guidelines which would stress that "state secrecy and immunities do not prevent effective, independent and impartial investigations into serious human rights violations" and "that those responsible should be held to account."[75] Following the publication of the US Senate report on the use of torture by the CIA in February 2015, the European Parliament condemned the "obstacles encountered by national parliamentary and judicial investigations into some Member States' involvement in the CIA programme, the abuse of state secrecy, and the undue classification of documents resulting in the termination of criminal proceedings and leading to de facto impunity of perpetrators of human rights violations."[76] In looking forward, the European Parliament has underscored the critical importance of accountability in order to "protect and promote human rights effectively in the internal and external policies of the EU," as well as to ensure "legitimate and effective security policies based on the rule of law."[77]

3. CONCLUSIONS

While the policies and practices of governments in the post-9/11 global environment reveal the increasing entrenchment of exceptional measures, states have nonetheless continued to assert their commitment to uphold the rule of law and respect international law in the adoption and implementation of counter-terrorism measures. Learning from the collective experiences of the recent past will be critical if this apparent disconnect is to be redressed.

---

73 *Ibrahim v Department of Homeland Security et al*, Case 3:06-cv-00545-WHA, 14 January 2014. See also S. Stellin, "Who is watching the watch lists?", *The New York Times*, 30 November 2013, available at: <http://www.nytimes.com/2013/12/01/sunday-review/who-is-watching-the-watch-lists.html?_r=0&pagewanted=all>.

74 IACtHR, *Myrna Mack Chang v. Guatemala*, Judgment of 22 February 2002 (Reparations and Costs), (Ser. C) no. 91 (2002).

75 Council of Europe Parliamentary Assembly, Recommendation 1876, "State of human rights in Europe: The need to eradicate impunity," adopted 24 June 2009.

76 European Parliament resolution of 11 February 2015 on the US Senate report on the use of torture by the CIA, 2014/2997(RSP), para 7.

77 Ibid, para D.

In looking forward, some have highlighted the importance of an objective and evidence-based approach to counter-terrorism through policies which address threats or acts of terrorism as essentially criminal in nature. Others have suggested that terrorism should be incorporated into an "all-risks" approach to national security, alongside other threats such as cybercrime and climate-related disasters.[78] Each of these approaches would potentially serve to normalize government responses to terrorism, within a rule of law framework and through a more faithful adherence to human rights, rather than perpetuate the rationale for extraordinary or exceptional measures.

In closing, it bears repeating that the rule of law is both underpinned by and the backbone of the protection of fundamental human rights, including the rights to life, liberty and security of the person. National security policies that are grounded in the rule of law and incorporate the protection of human rights among their chief objectives are most likely to deliver on the promise inherent in these rights. After all, the purpose of law in a free and democratic society, as Louise Arbour has reminded us, is "to liberate, not to restrain. It is to create a safe and just environment in which human conduct is regulated and power is constrained so that maximum freedom and safety is attained by all."[79]

---

78 K. Roach, *The 9/11 Effect: Comparative Counter-Terrorism*, Cambridge University Press, New York, 2011, p 460.

79 Statement by the Honourable Louise Arbour, President and CEO of the International Crisis Group, on the occasion of the High-level Meeting of the 67th Session of the General Assembly, 24 September 2012.

WHEN THE END LACKS THE MEANS

National Prosecutions of International Crimes and Canada's Paper Tiger Approach

Fannie LAFONTAINE*

1. INTRODUCTION

"I postulate, essentially, that as we now stand, we should expect a continued growth in the reach of national courts for international crimes committed outside

* The reflections in this chapter are expansions of previous research and parts of it were originally published in French by the Centre for International Governance Innovation (CIGI) in the series "Canada et droit international: 150 ans d'histoire et perspectives d'avenir", document no 12, and in the CIGI book *Reflections on Canada's Past, Present and Future in International Law/Réflexions sur le passé, le présent et l'avenir du Canada en matière de droit international* in 2018 and translated here with CIGI's permission, with thanks: Fannie Lafontaine, "Criminels de guerre au Canada? La valse-hésitation historique entre poursuites et expulsions", available at: <https://www.cigionline.org/sites/default/files/documents/Reflections%20Series%20Paper%20no.12%20LafontaineWEB_0.pdf>.

their territory, above and beyond any activities that the ICC may undertake in its own right in the foreseeable future."[1] Louise Arbour's 2003 prediction, or "speculation" as she put it, at the moment that the International Criminal Court (ICC) was just coming into existence, has proven to be quite accurate.

Numbers are difficult to ascertain, but scholars and organizations count that a few dozen countries have been involved in the prosecution of genocide, war crimes and crimes against humanity in the last decades, resulting in hundreds of convictions.[2] Courts of states where crimes occurred are very busy: for instance, the *ad hoc* international tribunals – the International Criminal Tribunal for the former Yugoslavia (ICTY) and the International Criminal Tribunal for Rwanda (ICTR) – have transferred some accused persons to Serbia, Bosnia and Herzegovina and Rwanda,[3] and national courts there have already tried thousands of perpetrators.[4] Latin American countries have now prosecuted hundreds of suspects of international crimes associated with the brutal dictatorships of the 1970s.[5] Numerous suspects have also been prosecuted on the basis of universal jurisdiction in a growing number of states and more than ever on different continents: Argentina, Austria, Belgium, Canada, Denmark, Finland, France, Germany, the Netherlands, Norway, Senegal, South Africa, Spain, Sweden, Switzerland, the United Kingdom and others.

Universal jurisdiction can be defined as: "The assertion by one state of its jurisdiction over crimes allegedly committed in the territory of another state by nationals of another state against nationals of another state where the crime alleged poses no direct threat to the vital interests of the state asserting jurisdiction."[6] The number of cases based on universal jurisdiction has increased

1 Louise Arbour, "Will the ICC Have an Impact on Universal Jurisdiction?" (2003) 1 *Journal of International Criminal Justice* 585, at 585.

2 Joseph Rikhof, "Prosecution of International Crimes – A Historical and Empirical Overview" (2014) 2(2) *Bergen Journal of Criminal Law and Criminal Justice* 108–140; Maximo Langer, "Universal Jurisdiction is Not Disappearing: The Shift from 'Global Enforcer' to 'No Safe Haven' Universal Jurisdiction" (2015) 13 *Journal of International Criminal Justice* 245.

3 Transfers are made pursuant to art. 11*bis* of the Tribunals' respective Rules of Procedure and Evidence and can also be made by the International Residual Mechanism for Criminal Tribunals (art. 6 of its Statute, S/RES/1966 (2010)).

4 Rwanda has prosecuted over 10,000 perpetrators in its criminal courts, and more than one million others have been processed through the *gacaca*; see e.g. William Schabas, "Genocide Trials and *Gacaca* Courts" (2005) 3 *Journal of International Criminal Justice* 879.

5 A March 2015 report of the special section of the Attorney General's office in Argentina highlights that 456 cases are active, with over 500 previous convictions: Procuraduría de Crímenes contra la Humanidad, *Actualización de datos sobre el proceso de justicia por crímenes de lesa humanidad. Datos al 18 de marzo de 2015*. See also Naomi Roht-Arriaza, "After Amnesties are Gone: Latin American National Courts and the New Contours of the Fight against Impunity" (2015) 37(2) *Human Rights Quarterly* 341–382.

6 AU-EU Technical Ad Hoc Expert Group on the Principle of Universal Jurisdiction: EC, Council, *The AU-EU Expert Report on the Principle of Universal Jurisdiction*, EC, Brussels 2009, at para. 8.

steadily: close followers have documented that in 2017, specialized war crimes units within states have publicly investigated, prosecuted or brought to justice 126 suspects of international crimes, with 13 convictions. Hundreds of other cases are being investigated confidentially.[7] Universal jurisdiction – despite innumerable writings that had announced its fall[8] – also features quite highly on international and regional political and judicial agendas.[9]

Despite undeniable advances, the international normative system providing for states' obligations to investigate, prosecute or extradite international crimes is outdated and insufficient, and does not foster effective "horizontal" cooperation between states. Also, the capacity and will of states to contribute to the global fight against impunity remains very uneven across the globe. This unevenness manifests itself in various ways, but one stands out as particularly worrying: while some states simply do not have the capacity to ensure domestic war crimes trials, others do have the capacity, but simply lack the will.

Canada has historically been a leading voice for international accountability. Armed with an internationally renowned legislation criminalizing international offences and providing for broad bases of jurisdiction, and an inter-departmental war crimes program, Canada also prides itself as being an example and a leader as to how to deal with roaming suspected war criminals who cross its borders. But beyond the rhetoric, the record is grim. Canada symbolizes both the promise and the limits of the decentralized international response to the need to ensure accountability for international crimes.

This chapter critically assesses the Canadian approach to war criminals present on its territory in the light of the international law framework related to the responsibility of states in the fight against impunity. Canada's policy

---

7 TRIAL International, REDRESS, FIDH, ECCHR and FIBGAR, *Make Way for Justice #4: Universal Jurisdiction Annual Review 2018*, available at: <https://trialinternational.org/wp-content/uploads/2018/03/UJAR-Make-way-for-Justice-2018.pdf>.

8 The mid-1990s enthusiasm for universal jurisdiction was followed by inevitable setbacks. States like Belgium and Spain that had adopted an expansive view of universal jurisdiction amended their laws, the African Union has decried an "abusive" recourse to universal jurisdiction, and diplomatic tensions exerted a lot of pressure on certain states; see e.g. Antonio Cassese, "Is the Bell Tolling for Universality? A Plea for a Sensitive Notion of Universal Jurisdiction" (2003) 1 *Journal of International Criminal Justice* 589; Fannie Lafontaine, "La compétence universelle et l'Afrique : ingérence ou complémentarité?" (2014) XLV (1) *Études internationales* 129.

9 As examples, the topic of universal jurisdiction is discussed at the Sixth Committee of the United Nations General Assembly; the closely related concept of the *aut dedere aut judicare* obligation was on the agenda of the International Law Commission; the International Court of Justice in 2012 delivered a judgment on the issue of *aut dedere aut judicare* and universal jurisdiction pursuant to the Convention against Torture; the Council of the European Union established a "European Network of contact points in respect of persons responsible for genocide, crimes against humanity and war crimes" to strengthen Member States' capacities in the investigation and prosecution of the core crimes, including on the basis of universal jurisdiction (EU Genocide Network); and Interpol launched projects to help international courts, but also states, in locating fugitives suspected of atrocity crimes.

explicitly combines criminal and administrative remedies. Between the duty to punish the perpetrators of international crimes and the responsibility to exclude them from the protection of international refugee law,[10] international law penetrates Canadian law through two distinct legal branches with objectives that are sometimes contradictory and sometimes complementary.

The study first delves into the historical context of the Canadian approach, a history which, as will become obvious, is repeating itself (section 2). It then tackles challenges that Canada currently faces in the implementation of its international duties and highlights the gross imbalance in the use of criminal and administrative remedies. It looks into a potential dilemma in this regard – namely, it is impossible to prosecute all alleged war criminals present on the territory, and other existing measures (for example, the expulsion to the country of origin) may not be entirely respectful of international law and not satisfactory from the victims' point of view (section 3). Finally, this chapter proposes a reflection on what could be called "alternative universal justice." It aims to help spark ideas on innovative ways out of the dilemma, which would recognize the impossibility of prosecuting all potential suspects of international crimes present on the territory of a third state, while taking into account the fundamental principles of accountability, satisfaction and reparation. It discusses some measures that Canada could adopt or improve at home in order to become a true actor on the international justice stage (section 4).

2. WHERE FROM: THE HISTORICAL CONTEXT OF THE CANADIAN APPROACH

Following a long tradition as an international leader on humanitarian issues and human rights, Canada is often considered a champion in relation to the fight against impunity for genocide, crimes against humanity and war crimes. It has been a strong supporter of the ICC, being one of the main actors behind its creation,[11] one of the first states to ratify the Rome Statute[12] and the first to adopt an implementation act, the Crimes Against Humanity and War Crimes Act.[13] The Canadian government adopted a "no safe haven" policy, pledging

10 Convention Relating to the Status of Refugees, 28 July 1951, 189 UNTS 150, art 1F(a).

11 See Valerie Oosterveld, "Canada and the Development of International Criminal Law: What Role for the Future?", CIGI series – Canada in International Law at 150 and Beyond | Paper No. 16 – March 2018, available at: <https://www.cigionline.org/sites/default/files/documents/Reflections%20Series%20Paper%20no.16web.pdf>.

12 Rome Statute of the International Criminal Court, 17 July 1998, (2002) 2187 UNTS 159. Canada signed the Statute on 18 December 1998 and ratified it on 7 July 2000.

13 Crimes against Humanity and War Crimes Act, SC 2000, c 24 (enacted on 29 June 2000) (hereinafter "War Crimes Act").

to fight against impunity and to not provide refuge to international criminals. But this noble reputation is put to the test in practice. Canada's haunted past toward suspected war criminals crossing its borders seems to explain today's unsatisfactory reality. What the future holds may depend on the capacity and the will to question and rethink the current paradigm.

2.1. FROM INACTION TO A SLOW HARD AWAKENING

Canada has a long and twisted history with respect to the prosecution of war criminals.[14] With the exception of the trials held immediately after World War II under the War Crimes Act that was applicable at the time,[15] the issue of accountability for World War II war crimes slowly disappeared from the agenda. Cold War considerations certainly played an important role in the policy of inaction of Canada and other victorious nations concerning the repression of international crimes. The new East–West tensions had accelerated the need to secure the cooperation of former members of the secret services of the Axis countries. Also, the arresting of Nazi war criminals and their collaborators was seen as a less crucial issue than the economic reconstruction of the country, and the anti-communist ideology of these possible new immigrants provided quite a good fit with the dominant ideology of the 1950s. The policy of inaction persisted until the end of the 1970s, despite unrelenting pressures from the Canadian Jewish Congress and repeated demands from the Simon Wiesenthal Center and others. The government even refused to comply with extradition requests from certain countries, arguing that no prescriptions of customary or conventional international law obliged it to extradite persons suspected of war crimes or crimes against humanity. The Royal Canadian Mounted Police (RCMP) justified its policy of inaction by pointing to the fact that Canadian

---

14 For a more thorough historical background, see Fannie LAFONTAINE, *Prosecuting Genocide, Crimes against Humanity and War Crimes in Canadian Courts*, Carswell, Toronto 2012 and the references given therein.

15 War Crimes Act, SC 1946, c 73, which was adopted mainly to give jurisdiction to Canadian military tribunals based in Europe so that they could judge enemy combatants for "offences against laws and customs of war" against members of the Canadian or allied armed forces. Many of these trials took place in Aurich, Germany, and the most well-known is the case of Kurt Meyer, who was judged for having ordered the execution of Canadian prisoners of war and received the death sentence (which was later commuted). The summary of this judgment can be found in: United Nations War Crimes Commission, *Law Reports of Trials of War Criminals* (London, His Majesty's Stationery Office, 1947–1949) vol. 4 at p. 97. For a presentation on these trials, see e.g. Jules DESCHÊNES, "Toward International Criminal Justice" (1994) 5 *Crim LF* 249, at 254. Some trials were also held in Canada: e.g. *R v. Krebs* [1943] 4 DLR 553, 80 CCC 279 (Mag Ct Ont); *R v. Schindler* [1944] 3 WWR 125, 82 CCC 206 (Police Ct Alb); *R v. Brosig* [1945] 2 DLR 232, 83 CCC 199 (CA Ont); *R v. Kaehler* [1945] 3 DLR 272, 83 CCC 353 (CS A Alb); *R v. Perzenowski* [1946] 3 WWR 678 (CS A Alb).

courts did not have jurisdiction over these offences according to the Criminal Code or any other law.[16]

This Canadian inaction in the Cold War era was not an isolated stance. There were numerous exercises worldwide of domestic jurisdiction related to crimes committed during World War II in its aftermath, with the various military trials held by the victorious powers pursuant to Control Council No. 10 and other legislative bases, and by Germany itself.[17] The international treaties adopted at that time – in particular, the Genocide Convention and the Geneva Conventions – logically provide, to different degrees, for the duties of states to investigate and prosecute, or extradite, *génocidaires* and war criminals, and the 1951 Refugee Convention declares, as noted above, that those suspected of involvement in the commission of international crimes are undeserving of refugee protection. But the "dark ages" of the idea of individual criminal responsibility for violations of international law that followed Nuremberg and Tokyo, caused by the Cold War, also affected the development of the idea of justice at the national level. After the thousands of convictions in the aftermath of World War II, there was a considerable loss of appetite for justice for war crimes. There were national efforts here and there, with uneven success. However, some well-known trials that occurred during this period for Nazi war crimes had tremendous resonance, such as those of Adolf Eichmann in Israel in 1961, and Paul Touvier and Klaus Barbie in France, who were initially convicted in absentia then retried in 1994 and 1987 respectively for crimes against humanity. The idea of accountability for atrocity crimes never died.

During the 1980s, the government modified its official policy regarding the presence in Canada of Nazi war criminals and this question became one of the priorities of the Justice Department. The *Rauca* case[18] constituted the first occasion for the Canadian government to show its willingness to implement its new and supposedly less tolerant policy regarding Nazi war criminals present in the country. The government accepted to extradite to the Federal Republic of Germany this Canadian citizen against whom grave accusations were made of having participated as an officer in the killing of thousands of Jews in Lithuania. Rauca was extradited to Germany and died in prison while awaiting trial.

This policy change in the 1980s was notably driven by the public outcry following the publication of important books, such as *None is Too Many* by authors Abella and Troper, that had demonstrated a deliberate policy

---

16 See Alain Joffe, "Les crimes contre l'humanité dans le *Code criminel* : Une contribution canadienne au droit international" (1995) 9 *Revue québécoise de droit international* 52, at 55.

17 See Michael Wahid Hanna, "An Historical Overview of National Prosecutions for International Crimes" in Cherif Bassiouni (ed.), *International Criminal Law*, vol. III, Martinus Nijhoff Publishers, Leiden 2008, p. 297 at pp. 304–309.

18 *Re Federal Republic of Germany and Rauca* (1983), 41 OR (2d) 225, 145 DLR (3d) 638 (CA Ont).

implemented by high-level public servants during the war to limit Jewish immigration in Canada as much as possible.[19] The title of the book makes reference to the answer of a high-level immigration public servant to a question concerning Canada's intentions to raise the quotas of Jewish immigration in light of the Nazi persecution of the Jews in Europe. The answer would have been: "none is too many." This was easily contrasted with what appeared to be the few efforts deployed to bar the entry of Nazi war criminals after the war[20] – or, worse, to prosecute them – and prompted a renewed interest in Parliament on the issue of war criminals in Canada.

The progressive emergence in Parliament of a consciousness of the importance of the war criminals issue coincided with the constitutional reform process which culminated in the patriation of the Canadian Constitution and the enactment of the Canadian Charter of Rights and Freedoms, inspired by international documents such as the Universal Declaration of Human Rights and the International Covenant on Civil and Political Rights. Included in the Charter was Article 11(g), inspired from the same international instruments, which reads:

> Any person charged with an offence has the right:
>
> (...)
>
> g) not to be found guilty on account of any act or omission unless, at the time of the act or omission, it constituted an offence under Canadian or international law or was criminal according to the general principles of law recognized by the community of nations

The aim of this provision is to ensure that those responsible for war crimes and crimes against humanity are not able to escape criminal punishment in the name of the *nulla peona sine lege* principle. It confirms the retrospective (rather than retroactive)[21] effect of Canadian laws that impose criminal sanctions

---

19 Irving ABELLA and Harold TROPER, *None is Too Many*, Lester & Orpen Dennys Ltd, Toronto 1982.

20 Howard MARGOLIAN, *Unauthorized Entry: The Truth about Nazi War Criminals in Canada, 1946–1956*, University of Toronto Press, Toronto 2000, who evaluates at around 2,000 the number of Nazi war criminals and collaborators who gained admission to Canada and who endeavours to explain how this became possible in the confusing post-war and subsequent Cold War eras.

21 Elmer A. DRIEDGER, "Statutes: Retroactive Retrospective Reflections" (1978), 56 *Can Bar Rev* 264, at 268–269: "A retroactive statute is one that operates as of a time prior to its enactment. A retrospective statute is one that operates for the future only. It is prospective, but it imposes new results in respect of a past event. A retroactive statute *operates backwards*. A retrospective statute *operates forwards*, but it looks backwards in that it attaches new consequences *for the future* to an event that took place before the statute was enacted. A retroactive statute changes the law from what it was; a retrospective statute changes the law from what it otherwise would be with respect to a prior event" (emphasis in original).

ex post facto for actions which, at the time when they were committed, constituted crimes according to Canadian law or, at least, according to international law.

Then, after about 40 years of inaction following World War II, the government modified the Criminal Code in 1987 in order to allow Canada to exercise jurisdiction over crimes against humanity and war crimes committed outside Canada by creating a legal fiction permitting these crimes to be prosecuted as if they had taken place in Canada.[22] These legislative modifications were essential in the absence of appropriate legal foundations to prosecute crimes committed abroad, as well as to do so retrospectively. They answered the recommendations made in the report of the Commission of Inquiry on War Criminals, presided by the late Honorable Jules Deschênes,[23] which had been set up in 1985 in the midst of a developing interest for Nazi war crimes in the public sphere, but also because of the public outcry that followed a rumour to the effect that Dr. Josef Mengele, an infamous Nazi criminal, had applied for a Canadian visa under a pseudonym.

The Commission concluded that in accordance with s. 11(g) of the Charter, Parliament could promulgate laws with a retrospective effect to allow for the prosecution and punishment of war criminals. It recommended that the Criminal Code be used as the preferred legal instrument to repress not only the war crimes and crimes against humanity committed during World War II, but also those that were committed or would be committed at a later stage. The Commission also recommended that amendments be made to immigration and citizenship laws to allow for the revocation of citizenship and expulsion of anyone who would have lied to the immigration authorities about their war criminal past. The Commission recommended that the government envisage criminal prosecutions against the 29 individuals in respect of whom the Commission had conducted detailed inquiries and to proceed at a later stage to further inquiries in respect of 220 other files. The Canadian government accepted most of the Commission's recommendations.

At that time, the Canadian government chose to mostly pursue the criminal prosecutions option. This strategy was to be tested in the following years, without much success in terms of convictions. Four prosecutions were initiated between 1987 and 1994, with none leading to a conviction. The first war crimes charges were laid against Mr. Imre Finta, who was charged with involvement in kidnapping and manslaughter while an officer in the Hungarian *Gendarmerie* during World War II. His trial before a jury of the Ontario Supreme Court ended in acquittal, and the Crown's appeal was dismissed by the Ontario Court

---

22 Criminal Code, RSC 1985, c C-46, s. 3.71, modified by the Crimes against Humanity and War Crimes Act in 2000.

23 Commission of Inquiry on War Criminals, *Report, Part I: Public*, Minister of Supply and Services Canada, 1986, Privy Council Office, available at: <http://publications.gc.ca/collections/collection_2014/bcp-pco/CP32-52-1986-1-eng.pdf>.

of Appeal in late April 1992 (Arbour JA, as she then was, participating to the majority judgment) and by the Supreme Court of Canada in March 1994.[24] This case became a seminal case with respect to international crimes in Canada, and to some extent a reference for other jurisdictions, but paradoxically it also signed the death warrant of any such future prosecutions under the Criminal Code. Not only had the authorities suffered a chilling effect by their lack of success before criminal courts, but the Supreme Court also interpreted the provisions of the Criminal Code in a manner that imposed a very high threshold for proving crimes against humanity and war crimes.[25] As of then, criminal prosecutions stopped being an option and immigration measures were preferred. The slow awakening had been difficult.

2.2. ENTERING THE MODERN INTERNATIONAL CRIMINAL JUSTICE ERA

2.2.1. The New "System"

At about the same time, though, an international momentum was rebuilding for individual accountability for international crimes. The establishment of the ICTY in 1993 and of the ICTR in 1994 created renewed enthusiasm for criminal prosecutions of serious violations of human rights and enthused states to exercise jurisdiction over these crimes, including based on universal jurisdiction. With suspects of crimes committed during these conflicts roaming around the world among refugee populations and the reviving of the legal principles of Nuremberg through the statutes of the *ad hoc* tribunals, states began to adopt laws or enforce existing ones (for instance, the implementing legislations of the Geneva Conventions), giving life to the principle of universal jurisdiction. The *ad hoc* tribunals produced a substantial body of jurisprudence – which was lacking in the past – on which domestic courts could rely for an authoritative interpretation of international law. Belgium and Spain famously adopted an expansive version of universal jurisdiction, General Pinochet was arrested in London in 1998 on an extradition request from Spain, which wished to exercise jurisdiction for crimes committed in Chile, and the ICC Statute was adopted in

---

24 *R v. Finta* [1994] 1 SCR 701.

25 See especially at 814–818 of the judgment, where the Court explains elements of the *actus reus* and *mens rea* of crimes against humanity that are almost impossible for the Crown to prove and which were subsequently rejected by Canadian and international jurisprudence (notably: "for example, robbery, without the *additional component of barbarous cruelty* is not a crime against humanity" or "[t]o convict someone of an offence when it has not been established beyond a reasonable doubt that he or she was aware of conditions that would bring to his or her actions the requisite *added dimension of cruelty and barbarism* violates the principles of fundamental justice") (emphasis added).

Rome, inciting states into action at the domestic level. Canada, chilled as it was by its unsatisfactory attempts at domestic war crimes trials, was carried along by this renewed wave of excitement for international criminal law. As we will see, it brought to life at the national level – in a sophisticated manner – the rules and norms of the new international justice order. Interestingly, though, if the evolution of the legal regime at the international level in the late 1990s certainly created a momentum for domestic efforts, it did not create formal obligations for states.

The ICC has not followed the model of the *ad hoc* tribunals, which was based on the primacy of the international jurisdictions over national jurisdictions.[26] The ICC drops the logic of vertical hierarchy and is "complementary to national jurisdictions."[27] Its statute affirms in the preamble that it is "the duty of every State to exercise its criminal jurisdiction over those responsible for international crimes" and that "the most serious crimes of concern to the international community as a whole must not go unpunished and that their effective prosecution must be ensured by taking measures at the national level and by enhancing international cooperation." Complementarity has replaced primacy as the *leitmotif* of international criminal justice.[28]

The ICC is thus based on the hope that post-conflict dynamics may not always prevent domestic war crimes trials. It is also based on the idea that it forms part of a system of accountability for core international crimes, composed of a network of national jurisdictions willing and able to investigate and prosecute such crimes wherever they are committed. The ICC has raised expectations that the principle of complementarity would have a "catalyzing effect" at the domestic level, not only by inciting investigations and prosecutions of international crimes in national courts, but also by spurring reforms of domestic legal norms and justice systems. The idea that the ICC would be subsidiary to national jurisdictions is also a continuation of the growing understanding "that international justice is an instrument to strengthen domestic justice efforts."[29]

However, despite an increasing reliance on states to enforce the prohibitions of international criminal law, the international normative system presents many gaps that can hinder inter-state cooperation, such as extradition and mutual legal assistance. There is no explicit obligation in the ICC Statute to criminalize

26 UN Security Council, Statute of the International Criminal Tribunal for the Former Yugoslavia (as amended on 17 May 2002), 25 May 1993, art. 9; UN Security Council; Statute of the International Criminal Tribunal for Rwanda (as last amended on 13 October 2006), 8 November 1994, art. 8.

27 Preamble, Recital 10 and art. 1 of the Rome Statute.

28 Payam Akhavan, "Complementarity Conundrums: The ICC Clock in Transitional Times" (2016) 14 *Journal of International Criminal Justice* 1043, at 1045.

29 Carsten Stahn, "Introduction: Bridge over Troubled Waters?" in Carsten Stahn and Mohammed M. El Zeidy (eds), *The International Criminal Court and Complementarity: From Theory to Practice*, Cambridge University Press, Cambridge 2011, at p. 2.

the crimes of genocide, crimes against humanity and war crimes as such or to establish jurisdiction over the crimes, and certainly no obligation to assert jurisdiction on the basis of universality. Nor does the Statute provide for an *aut dedere aut judicare* obligation, namely an obligation to extradite or prosecute, which implies that the state where a suspect is found must ensure that its courts can exercise all possible forms of jurisdiction, including universal jurisdiction. The consequence for a "failure" to do so would be that a particular case, for example, could be declared admissible by the Court. But it does not imply a breach of international law as such.

The obligation to extradite or prosecute is mandated in other international treaties, but numerous international crimes – most crimes against humanity, war crimes other than grave breaches, war crimes in non-international armed conflict and genocide – are not covered by a treaty obligation to extradite or prosecute.[30] A rule of customary international law to that effect may be emerging, but a safer view at the moment is that the existing rule is permissive rather than mandatory.[31] The *aut dedere aut judicare* obligation creates a powerful tool to achieve justice. Interpreting the regime of the Convention against Torture, the International Court of Justice has confirmed that: "Extradition is an option offered to the State by the Convention, whereas prosecution is an international obligation under the Convention, the violation of which is a wrongful act engaging the responsibility of the State."[32]

At the present time, there appears to be a gap in international law concerning the obligation to prosecute or extradite over certain categories of atrocity crimes. The ICC has created a momentum toward a relatively broad embrace of universal jurisdiction and criminalization of international crimes in national law. Various states, including Canada, have made no distinction in their laws based on a formal legal obligation and have criminalized and provided for universal jurisdiction for all of the core crimes. However, the unevenness of international obligations hinders the effective "horizontal" cooperation between states in the investigation and prosecution of international crimes, and can provide a useful justification for political unwillingness, as will be seen below.

2.2.2. Canada's Way Back In

The War Crimes Act adopted in 2000 aims to implement the Rome Statute, but one of its main objectives is also to reinforce Canada's capacity to prosecute and

30 Report of the Working Group on the Obligation to Extradite or Prosecute (*aut dedere aut judicare*), UN Doc. A/CN.4/L.829, para. 20.

31 Final Report of the Working Group on the Obligation to Extradite or Prosecute (*aut dedere aut judicare*), UN Doc. A/CN.4/L.844, paras 8–20.

32 *Questions relating to the Obligation to Prosecute or Extradite (Belgium v. Senegal)*, Judgment [2012] ICJ Rep 422 [95].

sanction people accused of international crimes, wherever they were committed. Thanks to the evolution of international law leading to the adoption of the Rome Statute, to the codification therein of numerous principles of customary international law and to the vibrant body of scholarship that has accompanied the process, the interpretations of international crimes *à la Finta* could perhaps be avoided, strengthening Canada's ability to prosecute such crimes.

It is essential to understand that the actions (but mostly the inaction) of the post-World War II era, as well as the unsuccessful attempts at criminal prosecutions and the following changes in government policy, represent the hesitations, the false starts and the failures that characterize the advent of the War Crimes Act. They are also useful to explain the Canadian authorities' caution before introducing the first prosecution under the new law in the *Munyaneza* case, discussed below, and their general reluctance – still to this day – to use criminal law for violations of international law committed outside Canada.

The War Crimes Act indeed represents only one of the measures that the Canadian government can use to tackle the question of alleged war criminals present on its territory. The combination of criminal and administrative remedies in the Canadian approach can be illustrated by sampling the very different outcomes that have faced individuals present in the country who were suspected of international crimes, such as Léon Mugesera, Désiré Munyaneza, Jorge Vinicio Sosa Orante, Branko Rogan and Jacques Mungwarere. They have faced very different consequences for their alleged actions. Two have been prosecuted (Munyaneza and Mungwarere), one was removed from Canada (Mugesera, although note that procedures have been launched to that effect against Mungwarere after he was acquitted in his criminal trial), one has faced extradition proceedings (Sosa Orantes) and one faced the revocation of his Canadian citizenship and his removal from Canada (Rogan; Sosa Orantes now faces a similar fate). The first two individuals who were subject to prosecution stand as the only ones who have faced this repressive consequence in the past 20 years. The others are some of the most well-known cases of hundreds of similar cases, where expulsion from the country is the ultimate (desired) outcome.

Canada's "no safe haven" policy therefore encompasses many remedies, both criminal and administrative, which could be grouped into three categories. The first category aims at preventing the admission to Canada of people who are or have been involved in war crimes, crimes against humanity or genocide, which includes the denial of visas. This effective measure has prevented more than 2,500 persons suspected of involvement in international crimes from gaining access to Canada.[33] The other two categories apply once a suspect has

[33] Canadian Department of Justice, Evaluation Division, Office of Strategic Planning and Performance Management, *Crimes against Humanity and War Crimes Program Summative Evaluation – Final Report*, Ottawa, October 2008, at 44 (hereinafter *2008 Evaluation*

entered or lives in Canada. The second category comprises the most repressive measures, which are prosecution in Canada under the War Crimes Act, extradition to a foreign government, and surrender to an international tribunal. The third category contains the other remedies, which are more focused on national interests than in ensuring that justice is done for the suspected crimes: revocation of citizenship under the Citizenship Act[34] and deportation under the Immigration and Refugee Protection Act;[35] exclusion from the protection of the 1951 United Nations Convention relating to the Status of Refugees; and inquiry for inadmissibility and removal from Canada under the Immigration and Refugee Protection Act.

The availability of these various remedies is, in principle, a promising strategy. An approach that strives to implement obligations emanating from two distinct branches of international law in a complementary way is theoretically beyond reproach. Obviously, no state can prosecute hundreds of cases related to crimes committed abroad, due to a lack of evidence, lack of cooperation of the territorial state and numerous other reasons. The problem is when exclusion under refugee law and state-centric immigration rules are used as the main tool to ensure accountability for international crimes, defeating both the purpose of the exclusion clause and undermining the inter-connected system to fight against impunity.

3. WHERE AT: PROSECUTE LITTLE AND EXPEL A LOT

According to the twelfth report of Canada's Crimes against Humanity and War Crimes Program, as of March 2011, 527 persons had been removed and two had been prosecuted since the program's inception in 1998.[36] Statistics from the thirteenth and last published report are less clear, but since 2011, at least 99 people have been removed and many others are subject to a pending expulsion.

Report), available at: <http://www.justice.gc.ca/eng/rp-pr/cp-pm/eval/rep-rap/08/war-guerre/war.pdf>. The second evaluation report, published in August 2016, mentions 2,810 people for the years 2003 to 2015; Ministry of Justice, Evaluation Division, *Crimes against Humanity and War Crimes Program Evaluation*, 2016, at p. 44 (hereinafter *2016 Evaluation Report*) available at: <http://www.justice.gc.ca/eng/rp-pr/cp-pm/eval/rep-rap/2016/cahwc-cchcg/cahwc-cchcg.pdf>. Note that the fairness of the determination procedure is sometimes contested. Stories are sometimes picked up by the media and will eventually call for clarification by the authorities. See e.g. Louise LEDUC, "Un Haïtien accusé de crime de guerre par le Canada", *LaPresse*, 10 May 2011, available at: <https://www.lapresse.ca/actualites/justice-et-faits-divers/201105/09/01-4397748-un-haitien-accuse-de-crime-de-guerre-par-le-canada.php>.

34 Citizenship Act, LRC 1985, c C-29, s. 10.1.

35 Immigration and Refugee Protection Act, SC 2001, c 27, s. 35.

36 *Canada's Program on Crimes against Humanity and War Crimes, 12th Report*, 2008–2011, p. 18, available at: <http://cbsa.gc.ca/security-securite/wc-cg/wc-cg2011-eng.html>.

No new prosecution has been instigated since then.[37] There have been "one and a half" extraditions since the inception of the program, the only ones since the *Rauca* case in the early 1980s. These will be discussed below.

On the prosecution front, the *Munyaneza* case was the first opportunity to apply the new War Crimes Act. On 22 May 2009, Munyaneza was found guilty at trial by Justice Denis of the Superior Court of Quebec of seven counts of genocide, crimes against humanity and war crimes for acts of murder, sexual violence and looting committed in Rwanda in 1994.[38] On 29 October 2009, in its sentencing judgment,[39] Justice Denis imposed life imprisonment and fixed parole eligibility after 25 years spent in prison, which is automatically imposed for first-degree – premeditated – murder.

The verdict and sentence were confirmed by the Quebec Court of Appeal on 7 May 2014.[40] The Court of Appeal delivered a legally and factually strong judgment which confirms that Canada can rely on a solid legislation that fulfils the main objective behind its adoption, namely to preserve and improve its ability to prosecute and sentence people accused of international crimes.[41] Its importance cannot be understated, considering that all cases in Canada that relate to the application of international criminal law had emanated from the immigration and refugee law fields, from various quasi-judicial bodies or from the Federal Court, the Federal Court of Appeal and the Supreme Court, on two occasions in *Mugesera*[42] and *Ezokola*,[43] sitting in judicial review of such proceedings. The decision in a criminal context by an appeals court thus represents a unique precedent. However, the success of the War Crimes Act depends maybe not so much on the strength of its provisions and on credible judicial interpretation,

---

37 *Canada's Program on Crimes against Humanity and War Crimes, 13th Report*, 2011–2015, p. 11, available at: <http://www.justice.gc.ca/eng/rp-pr/cj-jp/wc-cdg/wc20112015-cdg20112015/wc20112015-cdg20112015.pdf>. A total of 138 removals between 2010 and 2015 are also mentioned in the *2016 Evaluation Report*, *supra* note 33 at 49.

38 *R v. Munyaneza*, 2009 QCCS 2201. For an analysis, see Fannie Lafontaine, "Canada's Crimes against Humanity and War Crimes Act on Trial: An Analysis of the *Munyaneza* Case" (2010) 8 *Journal of International Criminal Justice* 269; Robert J. Currie and Ion Stancu, "*R v. Munyaneza*: Pondering Canada's First Core Crimes Conviction" (2010) 10 *Int'l Crim L Rev* 829.

39 *R v. Munyaneza*, 2009 QCCS 4865.

40 *Munyaneza v. R*, 2014 QCCA 906. Leave to appeal to the Supreme Court of Canada was denied: *Munyaneza v. R*, 2014 CSC (Qc) (Criminal) (Authorization) (35993).

41 See Fannie Lafontaine, "La compétence universelle au Canada : le droit chemin tracé par la Cour d'appel du Québec dans *Munyaneza*", (2014) 27(1) *RQDI* 161–180.

42 *Mugesera v. Canada (Minister of Citizenship and Immigration)* 2005 SCC 40. This key decision provided guidance on the definition of international crimes, the standard of proof and other issues, and has influenced profoundly the domestic approach to international crimes.

43 *Ezokola v. Canada (Citizenship and Immigration)* 2013 SCC 40. This important decision concerned the proper test to be applied to "complicity" in the determination process of whether a person should be excluded from refugee status for having "committed" genocide, crimes against humanity or war crimes.

but on the political will to use its full potential against international criminals present on Canadian territory.

Munyaneza might have been the sign of a new, more aggressive approach toward alleged war criminals present on Canadian soil. However, what we are noticing now is not that different from what was happening 20 years ago after the prosecution debacle in the *Finta* case: Canada prefers to use immigration measures and prosecutions are not an option that is seriously considered. The second trial after *Munyaneza* ended with the accused, Jacques Mungwarere, being acquitted at trial.[44] The Crown did not file an appeal, thus perhaps putting the nail in the coffin of the Canadian prosecutorial authorities' renewed confidence in their ability to bring about criminal prosecutions based on universal jurisdiction. In fact, ten days before the judgment was issued in the criminal trial, the Minister – obviously not very confident about the prosecution's outcome – submitted an application to the Refugee Protection Division to revoke Mungwarere's refugee status. It was revoked on 10 September 2014 on the basis that he had made misrepresentations in his refugee claim, with respect to, among other things, what he was doing during the genocide.

The authorities then moved on to obtain Mungwarere's removal from Canada, based on the fact that he was inadmissible for his involvement in violations of international human rights. On 2 June 2016, the Immigration and Refugee Board of Canada's Immigration Division issued a deportation order against him. He applied for judicial review before the Federal Court of Canada. The Court concluded that moving to obtain the removal under immigration rules after an acquittal in a criminal trial did not amount to an abuse of process. It decided that there was no identity of object between the criminal trial and the immigration hearing. The respective burdens of evidence were very different and could not satisfy the criteria for issue estoppel.[45] The Court nonetheless quashed the decision for being unreasonable as a whole, for not addressing the new evidence submitted and for merely considering the findings of fact from the trial judgment. It has to be said that the judge at the criminal trial, Justice Charbonneau, found that witnesses for the Crown had fabricated evidence and that the bulk of the remaining credible evidence did not suffice for the Crown to prove beyond reasonable doubt the essential elements of the alleged crimes. However, strangely, he concluded his decision by saying that "at the most, the evidence establishes a probability of culpability", a sweet candy offered deliberately or not to the authorities for their immigration procedures.

In any case, the deportation order is no longer valid and the fate of Mr. Mungwarere is under the jurisdiction of the Minister, who could start the process anew, stay still or provide him with a status to remain in Canada

---

[44] *R v. Jacques Mungwarere*, 2013 ONCS 4594, 5 July 2013.

[45] *Mungwarere v. Canada (Public Safety and Emergency Preparedness)* 2017 CF 708.

for "humanitarian reasons." In the meantime, Mungwarere is in a legal limbo, a frequently arising dilemma in which individuals are "undesirable but unreturnable" due to risks of torture, ill-treatment, unfair trial or other reasons.[46] If anything, the *Mungwarere* case unequivocally confirms the virtual paralysis of the prosecution option. Immigration measures are essentially what Canada has to offer in the global effort to hold perpetrators of international crimes to account.

The preferred option is sometimes more openly acknowledged. In July 2011, in a bold move to prove that Canada is not a safe haven for alleged perpetrators of international crimes, the Canadian authorities publicly released a list of 30 rejected refugee claimants or immigrants, soliciting the public's assistance in hunting down the fugitives.[47] Despite having "reasonable grounds to believe" that the 30 suspects had committed or had been complicit in the commission of genocide, war crimes or crimes against humanity, the Canadian authorities did not intend to prosecute the accused once they were arrested. Indeed, all 30 individuals were subjected to removal orders from Canada. The "most wanted" list became very controversial for numerous reasons: the Canadian approach to suspected war criminals present in Canada was questioned,[48] while the public exposure of individuals as "war criminals" without sufficient justification raised issues of privacy[49] and exposed the border agency's limited capacity, will or competence to track down individuals who are the subject of deportation orders.[50]

---

46 Jennifer Bond, "Unwanted But Unremovable: Canada's Treatment of 'Criminal' Migrants Who Cannot be Removed" (2017) 36(1) *Refugee Survey Quarterly* 168; Joke Reijven and Joris Van Wijk. "Caught in Limbo: How Alleged Perpetrators of International Crimes Who Applied for Asylum in the Netherlands are Affected by a Fundamental System Error in International Law" (2014) 26(2) *Int J Refugee Law* 248.

47 Canada Border Services Agency, "Government of Canada Enlists Help of Canadians to Enforce Canada's Immigrations Laws – Government Will Not Tolerate War Criminals in Our Communities", 21 July 2011, available at: <http://news.gc.ca/web/article-en.do?nid=612409>.

48 See e.g. the public debate between Amnesty International and the Public Safety Minister Jason Kenney with respect to the July 2011 hunt for fugitive alleged war criminals undertaken by the Canadian government: Alex Neve and Béatrice Vaugrante, "Amnesty International Canada Open Letter to Ministers Toews and Kenney about 'Wanted by the CBSA,'" 2 August 2011, available at: <http://www.amnesty.ca/news/news-item/amnesty-international-canada-open-letter-to-ministers-toews-and-kenney>, and Jason Kenney, cited in Tonda MacCharles, "Kenney Gets into Letter-Writing Scrap with Amnesty International", *Toronto Star*, 10 August 2011, available at: <http://www.thestar.com/news/canada/2011/08/10/kenney_gets_into_letterwriting_scrap_with_amnesty_international.html>.

49 The public tagging of the individuals as "war criminals" was condemned by the Privacy Commissioner: Canadian Press, "Border Agency's War Crimes Tag 'Potentially Misleading,'" 5 December 2013, available at: <http://www.cbc.ca/news/politics/border-agency-s-war-crimes-tag-potentially-misleading-1.2451893>.

50 Michael Friscolanti, "Maclean's Tracked Down an Accused War Criminal Ottawa Couldn't Find: Just How Hard are They Looking?", *Maclean's*, 9 January 2014, available at: <http://www.macleans.ca/news/world/macleans-tracked-down-an-accused-war-criminal-ottawa-couldnt-find>.

It also made clear the political opinion of the moment concerning Canada's international obligations: "Canada is not the UN. It's not our responsibility to make sure each one of these [alleged war criminals present in Canada] faces justice."[51]

As for extradition, it could be called the ghost of the Canadian War Crimes Program. Mr. Rauca was the last person to be extradited from Canada for war crimes until 2007, when Michael Seifert, a former German SS member, was extradited to Italy.[52] Jorge Vinicio Sosa Orantes was also extradited from Canada to the United States, but to answer immigration fraud charges with regard to his citizenship application there.[53] Notably, Guatemala had already requested Sosa Orantes' extradition from Canada for serious human rights violations. Sosa Orantes was involved in the Dos Erres massacre, during which hundreds of civilians were killed.[54] On 10 February 2014, he was found guilty in California of having omitted to mention his role in the Guatemalan army when he applied for his American citizenship. He was convicted to ten years' imprisonment, the maximum sentence for immigration-related crimes, and his American citizenship was revoked.[55] He could be deported after the end of his jail sentence, even more so because Guatemala requested his extradition. That said, for Canada's purposes, this is an extradition procedure that is not directly linked to charges for international crimes as such.[56] It is the half-extradition generously counted in above when summarizing the war crimes program's achievements.

---

51 Laura Payton, "War Crimes Prosecution Not up to Canada, Toews Says: 6th War Crimes Suspect in Canadian custody", *CBC News*, 3 August 2011, citing the then Public Safety Minister, available at: <http://www.cbc.ca/news/canada/story/2011/08/03/war-crimes-suspect-toronto-arrest.html>.

52 *Italy v. Seifert*, 2007 BCCA 407, 246 BCAC 46; leave to appeal to the Supreme Court of Canada was denied: [2007] SCCA 503 (QL), available at: <https://scc-csc.lexum.com/scc-csc/scc-l-csc-a/fr/5809/1/document.do>.

53 *United States of America v. Sosa*, 2011 ABQB 534; *United States of America v. Sosa*, 2012 ABCA 242; leave to appeal to the SCC was refused: 2013 CanLII 2390, 24 January 2013.

54 See especially the second letter from the CCIJ and LWBC, available at: <https://www.ccij.ca/content/uploads/2015/07/Sosa-CCI-ASF-Letter-to-Minister-of-Justice-Sept-22-2011-FINAL-VERSION-CLEAN.pdf>.

55 Department of Justice, Office of Public Affairs, "Former Guatemalan Special Forces Officer Sentenced for Covering up Involvement in 1982 Massacre", press release, Washington DC, 10 February 2014, available at: <https://www.justice.gov/opa/pr/former-guatemalan-special-forces-officer-sentenced-covering-involvement-1982-massacre>. This was mostly confirmed on appeal by the US Court of Appeals, Ninth Circuit, *United States v. Sosa*, 608 Fed Appx 464, 2015 US App LEXIS 7057, 2015 WL 1908879 (9th Cir Cal, 28 April 2015), available at: <https://law.justia.com/cases/federal/appellate-courts/ca9/14-50072/14-50072-2015-04-28.html>.

56 As noted above, following Sosa Orantes' conviction in the United States for crimes linked to immigration, Canada initiated proceedings to revoke his citizenship: Canadian Press, "Jorge Vinicio Sosa Orantes, Accused Guatemalan War Criminal, May Lose Canadian Citizenship", *Huffington Post*, 16 April 2017, available at: <http://www.huffingtonpost.ca/2017/04/16/jorge-vinicio-sosa-orante_n_16052344.html>.

The numbers are telling, and in that regard the obvious should perhaps be recalled: deportation or removal of war criminals from Canada certainly cannot replace criminal prosecutions, nor can it be a substitute for extradition.[57] The reliance on administrative remedies, such as deportation and removal from the country, may serve the limited purpose of not allowing Canada to become a safe haven for war criminals, but it does very little to serve the broader objective of ensuring accountability for the core crimes on Canadian territory or abroad.

While the annual budget of the Canadian war crimes program is CAD15.6 million, an amount that remained unchanged since 1998, the cost of a single prosecution is evaluated at more than CAD5 million.[58] According to the Program Evaluation Report released in 2008: "There is a strong cost effectiveness argument for using the criminal prosecution remedy sparingly."[59] The report, while confirming that "[t]he 2007 decision of the War Crimes Steering Committee to place greater emphasis on immigration remedies (in terms of allocating resources) can be seen as appropriate from a cost effectiveness point of view given the apparent costs of prosecution cases and the budgetary limitations of the Program", affirms at the same time that: "The limited resources available for criminal investigation, in relation to the inventory of serious cases, place an important limitation on the Program's contribution to the objective of denying safe haven through non-civil remedies."[60] The report thus concludes that: "There is considerable evidence that the Program will require increased financial resources if it is to be effective in addressing the no safe haven policy in the future."[61] The 2016 Evaluation Report reached similar conclusions and noted that a program with such a limited budget "clearly could not conduct many prosecutions of suspected war criminals" and that: "The Program's resource constraints have affected its ability to pursue criminal investigations and prosecutions."[62] Clearly, financial considerations can severely restrict the capacity of states to fulfil their international obligations. In reality, in Canada, money is the main guiding principle in the prosecutor's decision on whether or not to prosecute.

---

[57] Anne Warner Laforest, *Extradition to and from Canada*, 3rd ed, Canada Law Book, Ontario 1991 at p. 42: "The aims of extradition and deportation are clearly distinct. The object of extradition is to return a fugitive offender to the country which has requested him for trial or punishment for an offence committed within its jurisdiction. Deportation, on the other hand, is governed by the public policy of the state that wishes to dispose an undesirable alien."

[58] *2008 Evaluation Report*, *supra* note33 at pp. 2, 47; see also *2016 Evaluation Report*, which mentions costs of up to 6 million Canadian dollars (*supra* note 33 at p. 73).

[59] Ibid, p. 48.

[60] Ibid, pp. 48, 61.

[61] *2008 Evaluation Report, supra* note 33 at p. 60.

[62] *2016 Evaluation Report, supra* note 33 at p. 73.

It is obvious that states have a legitimate interest in maintaining a manageable caseload, which inevitably draws on public resources. States are also justified in taking into account the "potential political fallout of universal jurisdiction proceedings."[63] Though political and financial concerns should not be prioritized over the risk that alleged offenders go unpunished or over the extent of Canada's international obligations in this regard, it has to be acknowledged that: "Concerns about the potentially real consequences of universal jurisdiction proceedings on interstate relations are not trivial."[64]

From a practical standpoint, prosecutions based on universal jurisdiction are very complex. Prosecutorial authorities (and defence teams)[65] may face important obstacles in trying to gather evidence and witnesses' testimonies abroad, which require a third state's cooperation and which may not always be forthcoming. In addition, not all cases can meet the criteria of a "reasonable prospect of conviction" necessary to warrant, for the Attorney General, the launch of a criminal procedure, notably whether there is sufficient evidence that could prove, for each accused, every element of the crime.[66]

There is an apparently insoluble dilemma surrounding the available recourses to deal with war criminals present in third states like Canada. On the one hand, prosecution and extradition – the remedies most respectful of states' international responsibilities, if not obligations – are expensive, complicated and/or cumbersome. On the other hand, deportations and removals are quite unsatisfactory as they offer a very mild version of justice: there is no proper accountability of the alleged perpetrator, no satisfaction or reparation to the victims and very little truth telling associated with the processes. A debate ensues between those who call for more justice – the "idealists" – and those who insist on third states' inherently limited role in the global endeavour of putting an end to impunity for international crimes – the "pragmatists."

It is suggested that more thought should be invested in finding alternatives to these two apparently irreconcilable positions. The following section offers some thoughts that might be seen as a launchpad for a reflection on possible ways to become pragmatic idealists.

---

63 Bruce BROOMHALL, *International Justice and the International Criminal Court*, Oxford University Press, Oxford 2003, at p. 418.

64 Ibid.

65 Fannie LAFONTAINE and Fabrice BOUSQUET, "Les douze travaux de Me X : La défense d'un accusé avant procès sous la *Loi sur les crimes contre l'humanité et les crimes de guerre*", (2015) 19 *Can Crim L Rev* 295; Fannie LAFONTAINE and Fabrice BOUSQUET, "Défendre un accusé pendant un procès pour génocide, crimes contre l'humanité et crimes de guerre au Canada : mission impossible?" (2017) 2 *Can Crim L Rev* 22.

66 Ministry of Justice, Public Prosecution Service of Canada, *The Federal Prosecution Service Deskbook*, Part II, Section 2.3, Point 3.1, available at: <http://www.ppsc-sppc.gc.ca/eng/pub/fpsd-sfpg/fps-sfp/fpd/toc.html>.

4. WHERE TO: RETHINKING THE APPROACH

4.1. MORE RESOURCES FOR PROSECUTION

It is first important to insist on the obvious and the inevitable. The extent of Canada's international responsibilities, as well as the genuineness of its commitment to international criminal justice, must be adequately reflected in the budget allocated to its War Crimes Program. The budget must be important enough for the program to be credible. As it is, Canada is effectively paralysed on the criminal prosecution option, as was concluded in the program's Evaluation Report published in 2016. True leadership in the fight against impunity must be directed at the proper functioning of the international institutions that have collectively been established for that purpose, such as the ICC, but Canada must equally commit to putting to use its national institutions toward the realization of the same fundamental accountability objective. The current stalled budget is ludicrous and "pays" lip service to the international criminal justice global enterprise.

That more money should be made available to pursue the criminal investigation and prosecution option is a given. Canada is not the only country being criticized for not investing enough in its domestic war crimes effort, the last in line being Switzerland, which is also conducting some politically sensitive cases.[67] But at a more systemic level, there is a fundamental problem with the decision to confine the budget for criminal prosecutions within a wide-ranging program that must stretch the resources between widely differently-purposed activities, such as measures abroad aimed at preventing entry into Canada and refugee law and immigration proceedings ultimately aimed at removal. This is inadequate and damaging for various reasons.

The severe budget limitations effectively subject prosecutorial discretion on whether to prosecute genocide, crimes against humanity and war crimes to abnormal and unjustified criteria. In Canada, the decision to prosecute in general cases takes into account two criteria: the existence of a reasonable prospect of conviction and the public interest. Generally, the graver the offence, the more likely it is that a prosecution will take place. Provided there is sufficient evidence, it is certain, for instance, that a prosecutor will launch a prosecution for the crime of murder. I have discussed elsewhere at length the considerations

---

67 Nicolas Borsinger, "Se donner enfin les moyens de poursuivre les criminels de guerre", *Le temps*, 19 March 2018, available at: <https://www.letemps.ch/opinions/se-donner-enfin-moyens-poursuivre-criminels-guerre?utm_content=Suisse&utm_source=facebook&utm_campaign=social&utm_medium=TRIAL+International>; Fati Mansour, "Ces crimes de guerre qui embarrassent le parquet fédéral", *Le temps*, 19 November 2017, available at: <https://www.letemps.ch/suisse/crimes-guerre-embarrassent-parquet-federal>.

that could be relevant in the specific context of prosecutions for international crimes committed abroad, such as lack of evidence, lack of cooperation from a third state, risk to security, the possibility of trial in another jurisdiction (this idea of "subsidiarity" is addressed below) and, arguably, serious diplomatic counter-measures.[68]

Interestingly, on the issue of whether to prosecute, treaties with an obligation *aut dedere aut judicare* provide that upon examination of the information available, "authorities shall take their decision in the same manner as in the case of any ordinary offence of a serious nature under the law of that State" (see, e.g. Article 7(1) and (2) of the Convention against Torture). This apparently innocuous prescription can actually carry great weight. In Canada, financial considerations will not prevent the prosecution of crimes which otherwise meet the applicable criteria for prosecution. But in the current context, these criteria are effectively irrelevant for genocide, crimes against humanity and war crimes. Clearly, the decision on whether to prosecute is not taken "in the same manner" and the main guiding principle is very different from that for ordinary offences, and it is not glamorous; essentially, it is money.

The inconsistency is even more bothersome with respect to other international crimes that are provided for elsewhere in the Criminal Code, such as torture or incitement to genocide. The decision to prosecute these crimes will be based on the criteria usually applicable to the exercise of prosecutorial discretion – a reasonable prospect of conviction and the public interest. The costs of prosecution for these crimes are not constrained within a particular program and are part of the general criminal justice budget. It is true that prosecutions for these crimes are also generally only possible with the consent of the Attorney General,[69] a requirement aimed at preventing negative diplomatic effects. But financial considerations should normally not come into play. If the general criteria for prosecution are met, prosecution should happen. It is illogical and counter-productive to effectively confine prosecutorial discretion for crimes pursuant to the War Crimes Act to considerations that are totally unrelated to the basic and legitimate reasons that base the decision as to whether to prosecute other international crimes of similar gravity. Numerous countries, like France, the Netherlands and Germany, despite the creation of specialized war crimes units, do not confine the money necessary for prosecution to a separate budgetary envelope. This might serve to explain at least in part why according to the organization TRIAL, France had 12 pending universal jurisdiction cases in 2017, Germany had 15 and the Netherlands had three.[70]

---

68 Lafontaine, *Prosecuting Genocide*, *supra* note 14 at pp. 60–92.

69 Crimes against Humanity and War Crimes Act, s. 9(3); s. 318(3) of the Criminal Code (advocating genocide) and s. 7(7) (for torture if the accused is not a Canadian citizen).

70 TRIAL International, *supra* note 7 at pp. 102–104.

However, it must be acknowledged that even if resources were significantly increased, numerous suspects of international crimes could not be prosecuted. Recourse to other remedies is essential in order to fulfil the War Crimes Program's objectives of ensuring both that Canada does not offer a safe haven to war criminals and that the principle of accountability is upheld.

4.2. PROACTIVE STANCE ON EXTRADITION AND "CONCERNED EXPULSIONS"

Considering the need for considerable resources for prosecution, their inherent complexity and the appropriateness on certain occasions to favour prosecution where the crimes have occurred, it seems that Canada should endeavour to promote more frequent recourse to extradition, a comparatively lower cost remedy and a central if neglected component of the *aut dedere aut judicare* principle.

In Canada, the procedures for transfers to international tribunals, including the ICC, and for extradition to third countries, are well provided for by the Extradition Act (1999). Extradition is generally restricted to those states with which Canada has entered into an extradition treaty or which are designated as extradition partners by legislation.[71] Extradition from Canada is usually done upon request from a third state. Lack of requests or the lack of an extradition treaty with a given third state could be invoked as justification for the very rare recourse to extradition in war crimes cases. However, the lack of an extradition treaty is not an obstacle, as s. 10 of the Extradition Act allows the Minister of Foreign Affairs, with the agreement of the Minister of Justice, to "enter into a specific agreement with a state or entity for the purpose of giving effect to a request for extradition in a particular case." Nothing prevents the Canadian authorities from actively engaging with foreign governments with a view to encouraging extradition where the circumstances so warrant (including fair trial and security concerns). Simply sharing the information about the presence of an alleged war criminal on Canadian soil can trigger an interest in seeking extradition. This proactive stance is clearly consistent with the *aut dedere aut judicare* principle, which offers an alternative to the custodial state: prosecute or extradite. This shift would need more explicit cooperation between the actors of the War Crimes Program and the authorities responsible for extradition issues, including Global Affairs Canada (Foreign Affairs), which strangely (or tellingly) is not an official partner of the War Crimes Program.[72]

---

71 Extradition Act, SC 1999, c. 18, ss. 2–3.

72 *2016 Evaluation Report*, *supra* note 33 at section 2.5.

Extradition is the poor alternative of the *aut dedere aut judicare* obligation; indeed, there are relatively few extradition requests around the world for war crimes.[73] The current passive attitude of custodial states as regards extradition is at odds with the idea that inter-state cooperation is key to the fight against the impunity of perpetrators of international crimes, as demonstrated by the widespread use of *aut dedere aut judicare* clauses in treaties related to international crimes. Extradition of course has its own rules and there are a number of reasons why extradition to the territorial state will be impossible. There are issues of dual nationality and dual criminality, but, most importantly, non-refoulement obligations and the ability of the custodial state to refuse extradition where the suspect would risk a flagrant denial of justice. These considerations, for instance, have blocked extraditions to Rwanda for years, but they are the strict minimum, the basic reasons that will, in certain cases put the custodial state in a well-justified position to not favour subsidiarity. The perfect system would then take heed of the International Court of Justice's decision in *Belgium v. Senegal*, according to which, as noted above, prosecution is an obligation and extradition an option.

However, in a pragmatic understanding of the capacities of third states as regards war crimes prosecutions, where neither extradition nor prosecution is possible, states such as Canada should endeavour to adopt a collaborative approach with states where expulsion or deportation of an alleged war criminal is considered. Rather than proceed with the removal without any consideration for the fate of the person suspected of having participated in an international crime, the sending state should try to ensure that investigations and prosecutions will be undertaken by the receiving state, with all due fair trial guarantees. This would alleviate the legitimate concern that the vast majority of alleged war criminals found on Canadian territory are expelled without measures aimed at ensuring that their criminal liability is established, whether in Canada or elsewhere. These "concerned expulsions" could contribute to reshape the "no safe haven" policy from a purely state-centric standpoint into a more cooperative stance toward the fight against impunity. In appropriate circumstances, they could also cover some distance to better reconcile the complementary objectives of refugee law's exclusion clause and the duties to ensure accountability for international crimes.

Canada's continued interest and support after the removal of a suspect should concern the capacity and will of the receiving state to prosecute genuinely and fairly. There are at least two distinct but related aspects to consider. The first concerns the fate of the person transferred. Mechanisms can be designed by states to maximize the chances that receiving states conduct genuine

---

73 Fannie Lafontaine, "National Jurisdictions" in William A. Schabas (ed.), *Cambridge Companion to International Criminal Law*, Cambridge University Press, Cambridge 2016, at p. 171.

proceedings in accordance with international standards. Two such mechanisms are monitoring and diplomatic assurances, which ideally should be combined. Monitoring, carried out by non-governmental organizations, other independent observers or even state representatives, is not a waterproof guarantee, but it certainly adds a level of bilateral and international scrutiny that serves well the idea of subsidiarity and the ultimate objective of ensuring genuine justice for the worst crimes. A state that prosecutes a high-level transferred suspect may in many cases be in the international spotlight for a little while, but monitoring can ensure that the trial does not fall into oblivion once the headlines have passed on to the next story. Diplomatic assurances, on their part, are quite controversial. They have a shadowy history in the context of torture and counter-terrorism and they have been harshly criticized, including by Louise Arbour.[74] Where they concern fair trial guarantees (not torture or mistreatment) and if they are truly followed up on, diplomatic assurances, as imperfect as they might be, can contribute to ensuring that sending states do not completely avoid their international responsibilities in cases where they decide to expel (or extradite) instead of prosecute, just as they add a certain level of diplomatic and political pressure on the receiving state.[75] Canada partly (and controversially) relied on Rwanda's diplomatic assurances to decide on the expulsion of Léon Mugesera following a "risk assessment" of an unusually long period of almost eight years after his expulsion was ordered by the Supreme Court of Canada in 2005.[76] Although the process was one of expulsion and not of extradition, it was clear that Mugesera was going to be arrested upon arrival and tried in Rwanda, and similar principles were applied.[77] Canada never followed up on the diplomatic guarantees and Mugesera's human rights were jeopardized, with respect to his conditions of detentions, health issues and numerous fair trial guarantees, etc.[78] Canada's complete lack of interest and follow-up despite a certain level of public outcry and pre-occupying judicial decisions concerning Rwanda's treatment of Mugesera is, needless to say, a counter-example.

The second element to ponder in the evolution of the thinking concerning expulsions is Canada's enormous potential to contribute to capacity-building in receiving states. It has some expertise in judicial cooperation, which could usefully be offered to the country to which the alleged offender is deported.

---

74 Address by Louise Arbour, UN High Commissioner for Human Rights at Chatham House and the British Institute of International and Comparative Law, 15 February 2006.

75 See the broader discussion in Fannie Lafontaine, "Universal Jurisdiction: The Realistic Utopia" (2012) 10 *Journal of International Criminal Justice* 1277, at 1299.

76 *Mugesera, supra* note 42.

77 For the Minister's decision, see *Motifs d'une décision en application de l'alinéa 115(2)b) de la Loi sur l'immigration et la protection des réfugiés (LIPR)*, numéro de dossier HQ7-65767, on file with author, at p. 53, and the discussion on fair trial guarantees generally at pp. 57–63.

78 African Court for Human Rights, *Leon Mugesera v. Republic of Rwanda*, Application No. 012/2017, Order for Provisional Measures, 28 September 2017.

Canadian authorities could thus contribute to the promotion of guarantees of non-repetition by training judges and prosecutors in relation to the conduct of international crimes investigations and trials, and by offering to share evidence gathered in Canada on a specific case with the receiving state. Generally speaking, some programs of international cooperation in Canada could be specifically targeted at "deportation countries", and could be implemented with the help of Canadian NGOs whose expertise touches upon judicial training and international criminal justice, such as Lawyers without Borders Canada. Such measures could help to ensure that the destination countries of deported alleged war criminals are equipped for investigations and eventual criminal prosecutions. State cooperation in training and technical assistance has been recognized by many as essential to reinforcing national judicial systems and for "bridging the gap between international and national justice."[79]

4.3. A TRANSPARENT DECISION-MAKING PROCESS

Transparency to victims must be enhanced in the current Canadian War Crimes Program, as there is an opaque veil surrounding the process of deciding whether to prosecute. The criteria upon which Canada bases a decision whether to investigate or whether to prosecute are provided only in internal guidelines – the *Federal Prosecution Service Deskbook* – and in scarce information provided on the War Crimes Program's website. No enforceable legal criteria exist to circumscribe the exercise of discretion. Other countries have asserted specific criteria in their legislation.[80] The importance of discretion in relation to the prosecution of international crimes is beyond doubt. The fact that certain states such as Germany and Belgium, where there is normally an obligation to prosecute, have adopted a special regime with respect to the prosecution of international crimes is quite telling in this regard.[81]

---

79 See European Commission, "Joint Staff Working Document on Advancing the Principle of Complementarity: Toolkit for Bridging the Gap between International & National Justice", Brussels, 31 January 2013, available at: <http://www.europarl.europa.eu/meetdocs/2009_2014/documents/droi/dv/702_1854_/702_1854_en.pdf>; ICC, Assembly of State Parties, "Report of the Bureau on Stocktaking: Complementarity – Taking Stock of the Principle of Complementarity: Bridging the Impunity Gap", ICC-ASP/8/51, 18 March 2010, at paras 17, 20–21, 28, 30, 34, 39, available at: <https://www.icc-cpi.int/iccdocs/asp_docs/ASP8R/ICC-ASP-8-51-ENG.pdf>; ICC, Assembly of State Parties, "Report of the Bureau on Complementarity,", ICC-ASP/9/26, 17 November 2010, at para. 13, available at: <https://www.icc-cpi.int/iccdocs/asp_docs/ASP9/ICC-ASP-9-26-ENG.pdf>.

80 See in Germany, Code of Criminal Procedure, s. 153f; South Africa, Rome Statute of the International Criminal Court Act, 2002 (South African ICC Act), s. 5(1)(3); Belgium, Preliminary Title of the Code of Criminal Procedure, ss. 10 and 12; Spain, Ley orgánica del poder judicial, s. 23(4).

81 In Germany, Ntanda Nsereko mentions that this discretion was designed "to save the German state from the financial burden and the heavy workload that the obligation to prosecute in

That being said, the need for broad prosecutorial discretion does not do away with the importance of transparency and accountability in the decision-making process. This is of particular concern for the victims, who are sometimes faced with the presence of an alleged perpetrator in their neighbourhood and who may question the subsequent inaction from the prosecutorial authorities. Inaction that is not followed by explanation may significantly lessen victims' and the public's confidence in the administration of justice. It is thus crucial to ensure that the reasons for a decision not to prosecute are made available, as is frequently done by the German federal prosecutor,[82] or as is statutorily provided in the South African legislation.[83]

The Canadian *Federal Prosecution Service Deskbook* recommends that where a decision is made not to institute proceedings, a record of the reasons for that decision be kept. It also indicates that in certain circumstances, such reasons may have to be explained to investigative agencies or to victims, and may sometimes be publicly communicated in order to maintain confidence in the administration of justice.[84] The recent Canadian Victims Bill of Rights,[85] which applies to prosecutions undertaken under the War Crimes Act (s. 2), goes even further in that regard.[86] This obligation is particularly important in the context of core crimes prosecutions, which will remain few in number in comparison to the number of potential suspects of war crimes present in Canada and to the much broader recourse to other remedies. We are not aware that such communications initiatives have ever been taken with respect to alleged war criminals in Canada.

Also, the War Crimes Program, initially quite proactive and visible, has obviously been hampered by budget restrictions, despite the energetic and competent presence of renowned lawyers and investigators among its staff. Its website is now quite parsimonious of the information it shares, and it is spread out between the Justice Department and other departments, such as the Royal Canadian Mounted Police and the Canadian Border Service Agency, so that a concerned citizen's search for information is made to be quite complicated. Furthermore, the annual reports are published late – they are now only called "reports" because they have not been published annually – and are not easy to

all cases would engender." See Daniel D. Ntanda Nsereko, "Prosecutorial Discretion before National Courts and International Tribunals" (2005) 3(1) *Journal of International Criminal Justice* 124, at 127.

82 Katherine Gallagher, "Universal Jurisdiction in Practice: Efforts to Hold Donald Rumsfeld and Other High-Level United States Officials Accountable for Torture", (2009) 7(5) *Journal of International Criminal Justice* 1087, at 1103.

83 South African ICC Act, s. 5(5).

84 *The Federal Prosecution Service Deskbook*, *supra* note 66, section 15.3.2.

85 SC 2015, c 13, s. 2.

86 However, s. 5 seems to limit the application of the Act to crimes committed in Canada. This further demonstrates the vulnerability faced by victims of international crimes committed abroad once they are in Canada.

find. In addition, the administrative processes leading to deportation or expulsion are often confidential, except where they reach the judicial review stage, and it is almost impossible for victims to know what was taken into consideration in an assessment of exclusion or non-admissibility to refugee status. Information provided to victims may be key to their perceptions of "justice" and to their confidence in the judicial system in general, be it international or domestic.[87] Such transparency is an almost costless measure that is particularly important in countries such as Canada, where victims have almost no possibility of seeking judicial review of a decision not to prosecute, which would obviously be the ultimate remedy to ensuring transparency and accountability of the exercise of prosecutorial discretion.[88]

4.4. ALTERNATIVE MEASURES FOCUSED ON TRUTH, RECONCILIATION AND REPARATION

In some cases, neither prosecution nor expulsion is an option for a suspected war criminal. In general, there are also situations where expulsion is likely not the most favourable option in a holistic understanding of justice.

For one thing, due to the long processing times of refugee or immigration claims in Canada, people suspected of being perpetrators of international crimes have very often forged strong family or professional ties with Canada by the time of the issuance of their removal order. Expulsions very often result in broken families and vulnerable economic situations if the offender happens to have children born on Canadian soil and is the main provider of the family. Expulsion to a state that the perpetrator left a long time ago is often not ideal for rehabilitation.

For another thing, deportation may provide a sense of satisfaction for victims who are in Canada, because they know that the alleged perpetrator will not then enjoy the economic opportunities offered by Canada and because expulsion of a person for their alleged past involvement in the commission of international crimes is a de facto official acknowledgement and denunciation of the actions of the individual. However, because most immigration and refugee inadmissibility hearings are held *in camera*, the victims of these alleged offenders do not have a say in the expulsion process and cannot voice their objections to the removal of their tormentors to countries where they would seldom be brought to justice for their actions. Expulsion is not accompanied by proper accountability of the alleged perpetrator, whether in Canada or abroad; there is no reparation to the victims and very little truth telling associated with the processes.

---

87 Jo-Anne Wemmers and Emilie Raymond, "La justice et les victimes : L'importance de l'information pour les victimes" (2011) 44(2) *Criminologie* 157, at 164–167.

88 Lafontaine, *Prosecuting Genocide*, *supra* note 14 at 86.

Finally, numerous individuals who are subject to a removal order cannot be sent back, as noted above, for various reasons, including the risk of mistreatment and torture. These "undesirable but unreturnable" persons are often caught in a legal limbo that imposes significant hardship on them, but Canada does not seem to have a coherent or even deliberate policy regarding their treatment.[89]

It is perhaps time to craft innovative measures inspired by transitional justice, where human rights and victims' interests in truth, reconciliation and reparation are paramount. The idea of alternative justice is not foreign to Canadian criminal law. Section 717 of the Criminal Code, for instance, provides that alternative measures to prosecution can be envisaged, provided these are not inconsistent with the protection of society and that certain conditions are met, including the existence of a program authorized by the Attorney General, the free participation and consent of the person alleged to have committed an offence and, most importantly, the acceptation of responsibility for the act or omission that forms the basis of the offence by that person.

This could serve as inspiration for similar programs specific to suspects of international crimes. More often than not, individuals who have participated in core crimes no longer represent a danger to society, particularly to the society into which they integrated after the commission of their crimes. Nothing prevents the crafting of a program in Canada or other states which could include public apologies to victims, public recognition of involvement in crimes, compensation to victims or to communities, community service with the victims' communities, etc. Measures could involve giving a number of hours per week to an NGO of the victims' community, or rendering a percentage of the suspect's salary to an NGO, in Canada or abroad, or to a Trust Fund for Victims – that of the ICC or that contemplated in the War Crimes Act, etc. Such programs could include measures in Canada and/or the country where the crimes were committed, according to the circumstances; notably, the presence of communities of victims in Canada and the level of collaboration Canada enjoys with the territorial state. Such a program could be accompanied – where appropriate – by a status that allows the repentant suspect to stay in Canada if their compensation is considerable and the remorse is genuine. The costs of such programs could be kept at a reasonable level, even if investigations would still be required to identify suspects. Such investigations and information gathering are already being carried out in relation to existing remedies as regards numerous potential suspects found on Canadian territory. Obviously, monitoring the program would imply that non-respect of the completion deadline, lack of genuine remorse or of full commitment, or any partial execution of an agreed measure could lead to the launch of a criminal prosecution, extradition or deportation, according to the circumstances. Research into victims' needs in third states such

89 Bond, "Unwanted But Unremovable", *supra* note 46.

as Canada[90] and public consultation with victims could contribute to the design of a sensitive program that could be truly ground-breaking in its approach to "universal justice."

4.5. THE CRIMES AGAINST HUMANITY FUND

Finally, an interesting consequence of the ICC Statute is the creation of reparation mechanisms in domestic legal systems, including in countries like Canada where victims normally have minimal involvement in criminal proceedings. Canada has created the Crimes against Humanity Fund as part of its national implementing legislation (s. 30 of the War Crimes Act). If such initiatives do not involuntarily act "at cross-purposes to the ICC Trust Fund for Victims",[91] they can be crucial tools for victims in national proceedings for ICC crimes and a positive indirect consequence of the complementarity principle.

The Canadian Trust Fund is not yet operational and has therefore played no role in the two prosecutions undertaken thus far under the War Crimes Act. It currently plays no part in the general Canadian approach to justice for international crimes. However, its potential – despite likely difficulties in terms of funding and implementation – is tremendous. Considering the different categories of victims that international crimes create and their various needs, particularly where victims are in third states, the fund could channel innovative initiatives of reparation – think of scholarships or tax credits – including but not limited to psychological support of victims acting as witnesses in criminal trials in Canada. Reparation could be collective and could be done in synergy with the ICC Trust Fund if the situation calls for collaboration, or with the territorial state in certain circumstances.

5. CONCLUSION

"It took a very long time for the legacy of Nuremberg to start taking hold. The momentum, however, is irreversible."[92]

---

90 See Amissi Manirabona and Jo-Anne Wemmers, "It Doesn't Go away with Time: Victims' Need for Reparation Following Crimes against Humanity" in Jo-Anne Wemmers (ed.), *Reparation for Victims of Crimes against Humanity: The Healing Role of Reparation*, Routledge, New York 2014, at pp. 71–91.

91 Carla Ferstman, "The Reparation Regime of the International Criminal Court: Practical Considerations", (2002) 15(3) *Leiden J of Int'l L* 667, at 686.

92 Lecture by Louise Arbour, President and CEO, International Crisis Group to the Dutch Auschwitz Committee, Royal Tropical Institute, Amsterdam, 27 January 2010, at p. 7, on file with the author.

The promise of the new system of international justice largely depends on the capacity and will of states to put their legal systems to use for the global fight against impunity. Universal jurisdiction has a role to play in closing the impunity gap. Beyond the evidence and the rhetoric, many challenges remain: international obligations are inconsistent, practical and political obstacles lead to scarce prosecutions, extradition is underused, and victims' needs and rights are neglected. The next few decades will require a move from an unduly state-centric "no safe haven" idea to a conscience of the necessity of being proactive members of a global system directed at a single and common goal. Canada can and must gain its leadership back on this matter.

Currently, despite the impressive developments in international law and the implementation of its vast War Crimes Program, Canada is walking along the path it forged for itself in its inglorious past. Despite a robust implementation legislation adopted in the aftermath of the ratification of the Rome Statute, criminal prosecutions based on universal jurisdiction are a stillborn remedy within the program, sacrificed for budgetary considerations wholly inconsistent with Canada's international obligations. Extradition, for its part, is the ghost remedy, being almost never used despite its clear advantages in terms of cost and its central role in the *aut dedere aut judicare* equation at the heart of the international fight against impunity. Canada rests passively on the absence of extradition requests coming from foreign states, without exploring the avenues that a proactive stance might open up. The massive and quasi-exclusive reliance on immigration remedies to deal with the presence of suspected war criminals on its territory emphasizes the "no safe heaven" policy while neglecting the requirements of international law with regards to criminal accountability for the gravest crimes.

Eighteen years after the adoption of the War Crimes Act, two criminal prosecutions with different outcomes and independent assessments that underscore the shortcomings in the War Crimes Program's conception and the serious consequences of its infinitely limited budget, it is time to creatively question the traditional remedies available in Canada to face the presence of alleged war criminals within its borders. Beyond the "prosecute little and expel a lot" dilemma, how can the requirements of international law be reconciled with the inherent limitations of third states with respect to the prosecution of crimes committed abroad, as well as the rights and expectations of the victims? This chapter has explored avenues to consider for the important work that has to be undertaken to make Canada a true stakeholder in the fight against impunity at the national level: a serious increase in resources, proportional to the needs of complex legal proceedings for international crimes; better cohesion between stakeholders and a proactive attitude regarding extradition; concerned removals that follow up on the fate of the transferred suspect and that are accompanied by technical and legal cooperation to the receiving country; and greater transparency with respect to victims and an activation of the Crimes against Humanity Fund. Other possibilities need to be explored, by government, academics and activists alike, such as the prosecution of individuals under ss. 127 and 128 of the Immigration and Refugee Protection Act for concealing the commission of war crimes. This avenue is the favourite one in the US – as we saw above in the case of Jorge Sosa Orantes – although it came about by default because of the absence strong substantive war crimes legislation. In appropriate cases, perhaps this avenue of accountability for immigration crimes linked to the commission of international crimes, implying different evidence requirements, could be a half-way house between a trial for genocide, crimes against humanity or war crimes as such and mere deportation. In all these cases, a true political commitment, paired with resources allowing Canada to gain back its leadership role in the fight against impunity, is the cornerstone on which other initiatives that could compensate for the current gaps depend.

There will be no turning back to the old normal of impunity. It is time to look ahead and for Canada to really embrace the momentum. The theoretical tango between prosecutions and expulsions is history repeating itself. It is stale and unsatisfactory. Canada must be creative and committed; it can free itself from its old demons and strive to ensure the delivery of novel forms of justice here for international crimes committed elsewhere, wherever that may be.

THE INDEPENDENCE OF INTERNATIONAL PROSECUTORS

Where Law Meets Realpolitik

Luc Côté

On 24 March 1999, 19 European and North American countries have said with their deeds what some of them were reluctant to say with words. They have voluntarily submitted themselves to the jurisdiction of a pre-existing International Tribunal, whose mandate applies to the theatre of their chosen military operations, whose reach is unqualified by nationality, whose investigations are triggered at the sole discretion of the Prosecutor and who has primacy over national courts.[1]

Louise Arbour, ICTY Prosecutor

---

1 International Criminal Tribunal for the former Yugoslavia, press release, JL/PIU/401-E, "Introductory Statement by Justice Louise Arbour, Prosecutor ICTY and ICTR at the Launch of the ICC Coalition's Global Ratification Campaign" (The Hague, 13 May 1999), online: <http://www.icty.org/fr/press/introductory-statement-justice-louise-arbour-prosecutor-icty-and-ictr-launch-icc-coalitions> (accessed 6 September 2016).

This statement from Louise Arbour, pronounced a few weeks after NATO countries began a bombing campaign of Serbia claiming a duty of humanitarian intervention, constituted a spectacular affirmation of the independence of the international prosecutor. Not devoid of certain defiance, it was considered unacceptable by the leaders of NATO. The Prosecutor had picked the wrong target. "Don't bite the hand that feeds you" was, in essence, what NATO's spokesman Jamie Shea told her.[2] A few weeks before, when Arbour cautioned Madeleine Albright that the ICTY had jurisdiction over the military actions of NATO in the Federal Republic of Yugoslavia, the former US Secretary of State was also skeptical: "You'd better check with your legal advisors," Arbour told her. For most political figures at the time, the ICTY and its Prosecutor were still seen as diplomatic tools, a "sword of Damocles" never intended to come down on anyone's head, certainly not theirs!

Both independence and impartiality were personal qualities and attitudes that Louise Arbour had experienced and cherished during her previous careers as university professor, judge – at the Ontario Superior Court and Court of Appeal – and head of a Commission of Inquiry on events that occurred at the Kingston Prison for Women. However, being a fully independent prosecutor was something new, not only for her, but also as an institution. While it is common wisdom that prosecutors should act independently and impartially, domestic prosecutors as an institution generally do not benefit from the same basic legal guarantees of independence that are provided to the judiciary in all legal systems. Furthermore, in many countries, domestic prosecutors are not considered independent; they remain subordinates and have to answer to the executive branch of the government.[3]

Operating in a totally different setting – the international community – which "lacks any central government with the attendant separation of powers and checks and balances,"[4] international tribunals have paved the way to the

2 Quoted in Pierre Hazan, *Justice in the Time of War: The True Story behind the International Criminal Tribunal for the Former Yugoslavia* (College Station: Texas A&M University Press, 2004) at 132: "I am certain that when Justice Arbour goes to Kosovo and looks at the facts she will be indicting people of Yugoslav nationality and I don't anticipate any others at this stage … NATO countries are those that have provided the finance to set up the Tribunal, we are amongst the majority financiers … I think we have to distinguish between the theoretical and the practical. I believe that when Justice Arbour starts her investigation, she will because we will allow her to. It's not Milosević that has allowed Justice Arbour her visa to go to Kosovo to carry out her investigations. If her court, as we want, is to be allowed access, it will be because of NATO so NATO is the friend of the Tribunal" (17 May 1999 Transcript of NATO press conference by Jamie Shea and Major General W. Jertz in Brussels Transcribed by M2 PRESSWIRE © 1999).

3 See, for example, *Medvedyev and Others v. France*, No 3394/03 (10 July 2008) ECtHR at para 61: "the French public prosecutor … lacks the independence in respect of the executive"; see also *Schiesser v. Switzerland*, No 7710/76 (4 December 1979) ECtHR at paras 29–30.

4 *Prosecuror v. Tihomir Blaskic*, IT-95-14, Judgment on the Request of the Republic of Croatia for Review of the Decision of Trial Chamber II of 18 July 1997 (29 October 1997) at para 40

institution of an "officially declared" independent prosecutor in their respective statutes. In international tribunals established after those in Nuremberg and Tokyo,[5] the Office of the Prosecutor is often considered as "a separate organ of the court."[6] The Prosecutor, as required by statute, shall "act independently,"[7] notably by not seeking or receiving instruction from any government or from any external source. More importantly, in order to assert the functional independence of their prosecutors, the statutes of international criminal jurisdictions have provided them with discretionary powers in key sectors: selection of the investigation to conduct, of the individuals to prosecute and of the crimes to charge in the indictment.

As such, independent international prosecutors were often described as "a new species in the international landscape: they are 'homini novi'."[8] They hold the most political office in international criminal justice. By selecting who will be prosecuted, when proceedings will be set in motion and what crimes will be charged, prosecutors cannot ignore the political dimension of their decisions, which lie at the heart of international relations and, in some cases, of the peaceful settlement of conflicts. Furthermore, international prosecutors were given the lead of the whole investigation process within each new court, putting on their shoulders uncharacteristic new responsibilities which make it necessary to establish relations and secure cooperation from state actors. David J. Scheffer, the former US Ambassador at Large for War Crimes Issues,

---

(International Criminal Tribunal for the former Yugoslavia, Appeals Chamber). See also *Prosecuror v. Dusko Tadic*, IT-94-1, Decision on the Defence Motion for Interlocutory Appeal on Jurisdiction (2 October 1995) at para 43 (International Criminal Tribunal for the former Yugoslavia, Appeals Chamber): "It is clear that the legislative, executive and judicial division of powers which is largely followed in most municipal systems does not apply to the international setting nor, more specifically, to the setting of an international organization such as the United Nations."

5 The Charters of the Nuremberg and Tokyo Tribunals did not provide for the independence of their prosecutors from their governments. On the contrary, the prosecutors of both these "military" tribunals were under the direct authorities of their respective states. See William Schabas, "Prosecutorial Discretion v. Judicial Activism" (2008) 6 *Journal of International Criminal Justice* 732: "To be entirely accurate, these [Nuremberg prosecutors] were not "independent" prosecutors but rather the representatives of their own governments, and their role, at least in part, was surely to ensure that the interests of their respective states were protected."

6 Article 44, International Criminal Court Statute, 17 July 1998, 2187 UNTS 3, 37 ILM 1002 [ICC Statute]; Article 11, Updated Statute of the International Criminal Tribunal for the Former Yugoslavia, SC Res 1877 (2009), UNSCOR, 2009, UN Doc. S/RES/1877; Article 10, International Criminal Tribunal for Rwanda Statute, CS Res 955 (1994), UNSCOR, 1994, UN Doc. S/RES/955.

7 Article 41(1) ICC Statute; Article 17(2) ICTY Statute; Article 16(2) ICTR Statute.

8 Cesare P. Romano, "Judges and Prosecutors of Internationalized Criminal Courts" in Cesare P. Romano, André Nollkaemper and Jann K. Kleffner, *Internationalized Criminal Courts and Tribunals* (New York: Oxford University Press, 2004) at 269.

captures very well this political dimension of the international prosecutor's job, who "has to be as much of a diplomat as a criminal prosecutor ... The only way the court efficiency operates is if the prosecutor in particular successfully negotiates their way to cooperation state by state."[9]

During her entire tenure as Prosecutor of the International Criminal Tribunal for the former Yugoslavia (ICTY) and the International Criminal Tribunal for Rwanda (ICTR), Louise Arbour's diplomatic skills were put to the test. This was the case in her relationship with NATO – a crucial partner of the ICTY – as illustrated in her statement quoted above; it was also the case in relation to her capacity to indict the former President of the Federal Republic of Yugoslavia, Slobodan Milosević.

This chapter intends to look at how prosecutors are truly independent in the context of international relations, where states occupy the high ground. While the independence of international prosecutors finds its main source in law, which lays down the basic safeguards that ensure the independent exercise of their functions, in practice it remains constantly undermined by political actors, mainly by states. This chapter proposes to explore both these avenues, looking at the establishment of the "de jure" independence of prosecutors and how it is impaired by the powerful role played by states, whose interests do not always coincide with the interests of justice.

1. THE INDEPENDENCE OF THE INTERNATIONAL PROSECUTOR IN THE STATUTES

An effective international court requires not only a Prosecutor who is independent and able to access necessary information, but an institutional framework which ensures that he or she is able to make vital decisions without undue pressure or restraint. In many ways the credibility of the Court depends on whether the Prosecutor is able to act independently and in an atmosphere which does not create perceptions of bias or partiality.[10]

Being independent is often understood as acting on one's own volition, free from direct or indirect interference. It connotes not only a state of mind, but also a status or relationship to others, thus requiring some objective safeguards to rely upon. Institutional independence goes beyond any individual prosecutor and refers to the "Office of the Prosecution" as such, which is viewed as a distinct

---

9 Interview by Victor Peskin in September 2004, quoted in Victor Peskin, *International Justice in Rwanda and the Balkans* (New York: Cambridge University Press, 2008) at 239–240.

10 Medard R. Rwelamira, "Composition and Administration of the Court" in Roy S.K. Lee (ed), *The International Criminal Court: The Making of the Rome Statute – Issues, Negotiations, Results* (The Hague: Kluwer Law International, 1999) at 167. Medard Rwelamira was the first Director of the Permanent Secretariat of the Assembly of States Parties to the Rome Statute.

institution in itself. In Canada, it was referred to as "collective" independence[11] by the Supreme Court. It is concerned both with the status of the prosecutorial institution as guaranteed in the statute, as well as with the formal independence from other actors – states, international organizations, non-governmental organizations (NGOs) – including other organs of the court.

1.1. INSTITUTIONAL INDEPENDENCE

Most of the international criminal jurisdictions created after Nuremberg and Tokyo have recognized in their statutes the institutional independence of their prosecutors using two main features: first, provisions that characterize the Office of the Prosecutor as a "separate organ of the Court"[12] affirm its independence both as part of and with regard to the judicial institution as such; and second, provisions that stipulate that the Prosecutor "shall act independently" and "shall not seek or receive instructions from any external source"[13] confirm his or her independence towards third parties such as states and other governmental organizations and NGOs. Even if it is articulated in very few words in the statutes, one cannot underestimate the importance of institutional independence. It is at the core of the notion of independence of the international prosecutor and constitutes the best safeguard and the main tool in their political, legal and administrative relationships with all other actors involved in international criminal justice.

1.1.1. "An Organ of the Court"

The status of "an organ of the court" entails different consequences with respect to the independence of the Office of the Prosecutor. It reinforces the Prosecutor's independence: as an "organ of the court," the Office of the Prosecutor becomes an integral part of the whole judicial institution, that is, of "a competent, independent and impartial tribunal established by law."[14] The Prosecutor is not only independent as an individual or as an institution of its own; it is an organ of an independent tribunal and thus is an essential attribute of the right to a fair trial.

Paradoxically, being "an organ of the court" comes at a high price: prosecutorial independence will inevitably be gauged and judged in the light

---

11 See the decision of the Supreme Court of Canada, *Valente v. The Queen* [1985] 2 SCR 673 at 685.

12 Article 44 International Criminal Court (ICC) Statute; Article 11 ICTY Statute; Article 10 ICTR Statute.

13 Article 42 ICC Statute; Article 17(2) ICTY Statute; Article 16(2) ICTR Statute.

14 Article 14(1) ICCPR.

of the independence – real and perceived – of the international criminal jurisdiction to which it belongs. Therefore, the broader perception of the independence of the Prosecutor will be tainted by the reputation of the whole tribunal, the political intricacies of its creation by victorious or powerful states, its "imposed justice"[15] on unwilling states, etc. The Prosecutor cannot escape the political reality that the international criminal jurisdictions created by the United Nations Security Council (UNSC) are seen by many as instruments of a type of selective justice. A prosecutor may be statutorily independent, but he or she nevertheless belongs to an institution that was set up with a clear and limited mandate dictated by political interests and reasons.

1.1.2. "Acting Independently ... Without Seeking or Receiving Instructions from Any Government or from Any Other Source"

Prosecutorial independence is stipulated in non-ambiguous terms in both the ICTY and ICTR Statutes: "The Prosecutor shall act independently ... [and] shall not seek or receive instructions from any Government or from any other source."[16] Similar wording was included in the International Criminal Court (ICC) Statute.[17] These provisions reflect what is nowadays accepted as the norm governing the exercise of prosecutorial authority in international criminal jurisdictions, namely "autonomy and independence."[18] They impose a clear duty on prosecutors to guard the institutional independence of their office by acting independently, by not seeking or receiving instructions from any sources. Acting otherwise would jeopardize the independence of the whole judicial institution and trigger the Prosecutor's accountability.

If the Prosecutor cannot seek, act or receive *instructions* from any sources, it does not prevent him or her from seeking collaboration and receiving information from anyone. As a matter of fact, the whole system of international

15 Frédéric Mégret, "The Internationalization of the Judgment of Terrorism: The Special Tribunal for Lebanon Precedent (Une justice pénale internationalisée pour juger le terrorisme: Réflexions à propos du Tribunal spécial pour le Liban)" (2009) SSRN Electronic Journal. Online: <http://ssrn.com/abstract=1501190> (accessed 6 September 2016): "International criminal justice was more often 'imposed' than 'invited.' It was certainly the case of Nuremberg and Tokyo where allied powers as victors forced international tribunals on the defeated. It was also the case with the *ad hoc* for former Yugoslavia and Rwanda, both imposed by the Security Council."

16 Article 17(2) ICTY Statute; Article 16(2) ICTR Statute.

17 Article 42(1) ICC Statute: "The Office of the Prosecutor shall act independently as a separate organ of the Court ... A member of the Office shall not seek or act on instructions from any external source."

18 *Prosecutor v. Sesay, Gbao and Kallon (Prosecutor v. Sesay)*, SCSL-04-15-T, Decision on Motion Seeking Disclosure of the Relationship Between the United States of America's Government and/or Administration and/or Intelligence and/or Security Services and the Investigation Department of the Office of the Prosecutor (2 May 2005) at para 22 (Special Court for Sierra Leone, Trial Chamber I).

criminal justice is reliant upon some measure of state cooperation. As recognized by the ICTY Chamber of Appeals in *Blaskić*:

> [I]t is self-evident that the International Tribunal, in order to bring to trial persons living under the jurisdiction of Sovereign States not being endowed with enforcement agents of its own, must rely upon the cooperation of the States. The International Tribunal must turn to States if it is effectively to investigate crimes, collect evidence, summon witnesses and have indictees arrested and surrendered to the International Tribunal.[19]

As such, if the Prosecutor has the "power to question suspects, victims and witnesses, to collect evidence and to conduct on-site investigations," the ICTY and ICTR Statutes also acknowledge that "in carrying out these tasks, the Prosecutor may, as appropriate, seek the assistance of the State authorities concerned."[20] The ICC Statute also provides that with respect to investigations, the Prosecutor may "seek the cooperation of any State or intergovernmental organization" and even "enter into such arrangements or agreements ... as may be necessary to facilitate the cooperation."[21] Therefore, a prosecutor's simple request or demand for "assistance or cooperation" cannot be construed as seeking or receiving "instructions" from any sources that would jeopardize prosecutorial independence.[22]

1.2. FUNCTIONAL INDEPENDENCE: PROSECUTORIAL DISCRETION

In addition to relying on their statutory provisions to anchor their independence, international prosecutors also need the means and powers to fulfil their goals independently and impartially. Functional independence is in many respects the operational manifestation of institutional independence. In other words, it focuses more on the operation of the Prosecutor's office, the way it is functioning rather than the structure and the guarantees attached to it.

The core of functional independence consists of what is commonly described as the "freedom in decision making."[23] In criminal law, it is encompassed in what

19 *Prosecuror v. Tihomir Blaskic*, IT-95-14, Judgment on the Request of the Republic of Croatia for Review of the Decision of Trial Chamber II of 18 July 1997, *supra* note 4 at para 26.

20 Article 17(2) ICTR Statute; Article 18(2) ICTY Statute.

21 Article 54 (3) ICC Statute.

22 *Prosecutor v. Sesay, supra* note 18 at para 43: "It would do violence to the plain meaning and context of the Statute and the Rules if conceptually the words '*instructions*' and '*assistance*' were construed as being synonymous and interchangeable."

23 *Nahimana, Barayagwiza and Ngeze v. Prosecutor*, ICTR-99-52-A, Judgement (28 November 2007) at para 19 (International Criminal Tribunal for Rwanda, Appeals Chamber): "Independence is a functional attribute which implies that ... the individual possessing it ... has complete freedom in decision making."

is commonly referred to as *prosecutorial discretion*, which implies the ability to choose between two or more solutions or courses of action. It constitutes the main element of the Prosecutor's functional independence. Applied to international prosecutors, it involves their capacity to independently and impartially select cases to investigate, suspects to indict and crimes to include in the indictments.[24] As Louise Arbour rightly pointed out, "domestic prosecution is never really seriously called upon to be selective in the prosecution of serious crimes," while the international prosecutor "has to be highly selective before committing resources to investigate and prosecute."[25] International prosecutors are confronted with "the most important criminal investigations ever conducted in History ... [where] the number of potential suspects is considerable, witnesses number into tens of thousands and victims into millions."[26] In reality, "contemporary armed conflicts may generate several hundred thousand violations of international criminal law."[27] As a practical matter, difficult choices have to be made. Selectivity is inevitable and desirable given the large numbers of crimes committed and suspects implicated, and the scarcity of judicial resources.

While domestic prosecutors rely mainly on the strength of the evidence that a serious crime was committed to decide to prosecute, reliance on that criterion alone is of little help to international prosecutors, leaving them with too many cases to cope with. In international criminal law, the exercise of prosecutorial discretion requires taking into account a wide range of other criteria, "including the gravity of the crimes in question, the leadership role and the level of responsibility of the suspect, the effective allocation of resources within the Office of the Prosecutor, the relationship of the case to the overall prosecution strategy, and other similar considerations."[28]

---

24 "Among the implications of functional prosecutorial independence are that the Office of the Prosecutor operates in its own right ... to select or prioritize specific cases, to proceed or not proceed with a full investigation or formal charges, or to conduct its investigations and prosecutions in any particular manner": Morten Bergsmo and Frederik Harhoff, "Article 42" in Otto Triffterer (ed), *Commentary on the Rome Statute of the International Criminal Court: Observers' Notes, Article by Article*, 2nd ed (Oxford: Hart, 2008) at 973; see Article 18 ICTY Statute; Article 17 ICTR Statute.

25 Louise Arbour, "Progress and Challenges in International Criminal Justice" (1997) 21(2) *Fordham International Law Journal* 531.

26 See Florence Hartmann, "Entretien avec Richard GOLDSTONE, Le Tribunal des tragédies" (1995) 67 *Politique internationale* 291, translated by the author.

27 Morten Bergsmo, "The Theme of Selection and Prioritization Criteria and Why it is Relevant" in Morten Bergsmo (ed), *Criteria for Prioritizing and Selecting Core International Crimes Cases* (Oslo: Torkel Opsahl Academic EPublisher, Forum for International Criminal and International Law Publication Series, 2009).

28 *Prosecutor v. Delalic, Mucic, Delic and Landzo ("Celebici Case")*, Prosecution Response, Respondent's Brief of the Prosecution (17 September 1999) at para 15.5. See also *Prosecutor v. Delalic, Mucic, Delic and Landzo* (hereinafter "*Celebici Case*"), IT-96-21-A, Judgment (20 February 2001) at para 602 (International Criminal Tribunal for the former Yugoslavia, Appeals Chamber): "In the present context, indeed in many criminal justice

The most important exercise of prosecutorial discretion resides clearly in the decisions to initiate an investigation and to prosecute specific individuals *proprio motu*. These decisions are also the most controversial and "political" ones: *what* events/crimes will be examined and investigated, and ultimately *who* will be suspected and eventually indicted are the two main issues that everyone is concerned with in the political arena. It also explains the fierce debates over the Prosecutor's *proprio motu* powers to initiate investigations during the Rome negotiations of the ICC Statute.[29]

According to some observers, the best way to "ensure that the prosecutor will be independent is to provide that the prosecutor has the power on his or her own initiative to initiate investigations and seek the approval of the appropriate judicial chamber of the court to begin a prosecution, without interference by any political body."[30] And in order to exercise his or her discretionary powers efficiently and in total fairness, a prosecutor needs to be independent, to act independently and to be shielded from political interference. Here, prosecutorial discretion and prosecutorial independence can be seen as the opposite sides of the same coin, prosecutorial discretion being the foundation of prosecutorial independence, and the latter reinforcing the exercise of the former. These two concepts are clearly linked; for example, the standards of the International Association of Prosecutors address the issue of prosecutorial discretion under the title "Independence": "The use of prosecutorial discretion, when permitted in a particular jurisdiction, should be exercised independently and be free from political interference."[31]

The symbiotic relationship between prosecutorial independence and prosecutorial discretion – particularly the *proprio motu* power to initiate

---

systems, the entity responsible for prosecutions has finite financial and human resources and cannot realistically be expected to prosecute every offender which may fall within the strict terms of its jurisdiction. It must of necessity make decisions as to the nature of the crimes and the offenders to be prosecuted. It is beyond question that the Prosecutor has a broad discretion in relation to the initiation of investigations and in the preparation of indictments."

29 Morten Bergsmo and Jelena Pejic, "Article 15: Prosecutor" in Otto Triffterer (ed), *Commentary on the Rome Statute of the International Criminal Court* (Baden-Baden: Nomos Verlagsgesellschaft, 1999) at 360: "The ability of the ICC Prosecutor to initiate investigations proprio motu was the most controversial aspect of the Court's trigger mechanism and was one of the main political/legal issues that had to be resolved before the Statute could be assured of adoption. Both opponents and proponents of the Prosecutor's proprio motu powers – and the chasm was very wide – agreed that their inclusion or absence of would fundamentally affect the Court's structure and functioning."

30 Amnesty International, *The International Criminal Court: Making the Right Choices – Part II Organizing the Court and Ensuring a Fair Trial* (Amnesty International, IOR 40/01/97, 30 June 1997) at 9.

31 International Association of Prosecutors, "Standards of Professional Responsibility and Statement of the Essential Duties and Rights of Prosecutors" (23 April 1999) at Article 2, online: <http://www.iap-association.org/getattachment/34e49dfe-d5db-4598-91da-16183bb12418/Standards_English.aspx>.

an investigation – became an explosive issue that nearly derailed the negotiations of the ICC Statute.[32] On the one hand, numerous states, as well as many international NGOs, saw in an independent prosecutor with discretionary powers to initiate investigations and prosecute individuals "the only one truly effective method to ensure that all cases which should be brought before the court are brought."[33] On the other hand, some states feared that a powerful and uncontrollable prosecutor vested with that *proprio motu* "overreaching power" to trigger the court's jurisdiction could threaten their sovereignty, a fear unequivocally rejected by Louise Arbour in front of the Preparatory Committee on the Establishment of the ICC in December 1997, where she stated:

> [T]here is more to fear from an impotent than from an overreaching Prosecutor. It is trite to recognize that an institution should not be constructed on the assumption that it will be run by incompetent people, acting in bad faith for improper purposes.[34]

These two perceptions, albeit reflecting opposing schools of political theory,[35] confirm that the real power of an international prosecutor, the reason to fear and/or to trust him or her, rests in the independent exercise of his or her discretionary powers.

2. THE INDEPENDENCE OF THE INTERNATIONAL PROSECUTOR BEYOND THE STATUTES: THE ROLE OF STATES

> *The ICTY has escaped its creator, but not its environment. I am convinced of the independence of the judges with regard to the Security Council. The more complex question remains on the relationship between the prosecutor and the states. States can*

32 "The ability of the ICC Prosecutor to initiate investigations *proprio motu* was the most controversial aspect of the Court's trigger mechanism and was one of the main political/legal issues that had to be resolved before the Statute could be assured of adoption. Both opponents and proponents of the Prosecutor's *proprio motu* powers – and the chasm was very wide – agreed that their inclusion or absence of would fundamentally affect the Court's structure and functioning." Morten Bergsmo and Jelena Pejic, "Article 15: Prosecutor," *supra* note 29 at 360.

33 Amnesty International, *The International Criminal Court: 16 Fundamental Principles for a Just, Fair and Effective International Criminal Court* (Amnesty International, IOR 40/012/1998, 1 May 1998).

34 "Statement by Justice Louise Arbour to the Preparatory Committee on the Establishment of an International Criminal Court" *ICTY Yearbook 1997* (8 December 1997) at 229.

35 Matthew R. Brubacher, "Prosecutorial Discretion within the International Criminal Court" (2004) 2(1) *Journal of International Criminal Justice* 71 at 72: "Although participants in the Preparatory Committees came from diverse legal backgrounds and with an even greater variety of specific interests, their approaches generally fell into one of two main categories: liberalists and realists."

> *measure out the oxygen that they feed to the tribunal in order to speed it up or slow it down, even if it is not simply a puppet in their hands.*[36]

These comments offered by a judge of the ICTY dramatically highlight the power of states over the independence of international prosecutors. Although prosecutors are "independent" of states, as stipulated by statute, they remain subject – like the whole tribunal – to the willingness of states to see them succeed. Early on the President of the ICTY acknowledged that "if States are willing to cooperate, Tribunals will be able to fulfill their mandate. If not … Tribunals become completely powerless."[37] The reality is that "without decisive international community intervention on behalf of war crimes tribunals – whether in the form of persuasion, incentives, or coercion – cooperation from targeted states will rarely be forthcoming."[38]

Beyond the statutes, prosecutorial independence is particularly vulnerable to states' goodwill. International prosecutors need the collaboration of states to carry out their investigative functions, to gather the evidence necessary to arrest suspects of international crimes and to prosecute them. While international prosecutors have their own means of inquiry allowing them to conduct an investigation independently, their access to the crime scene undoubtedly requires the authorization of sovereign states. Furthermore, the complexity of crimes and, even more so, the difficulty in establishing the responsibility of senior officers can hinder the prosecution's efforts if some forms of state collaboration is not forthcoming. Critical elements of evidence may remain irretrievable, particularly in relation to the personal responsibility of the senior officers.[39]

As ICTY Prosecutor, Louise Arbour acknowledged these difficulties:

> Refugee accounts are critical, but they are not enough on their own. The victims didn't see the command structures or the people giving the orders at the highest levels. We therefore need the sophisticated kind of assistance that only states can provide.[40]

---

36 Comment from an ICTY judge as quoted by Pierre Hazan, *Justice in the Time of War: The True Story behind the International Criminal Tribunal for the Former Yugoslavia*, *supra* note 2 at 129.

37 Antonio Cassese, "La répression des infractions internationales – Présentation" in Hervé Ascensio, Emmanuel Decaux and Alain Pellet (eds), *Droit international pénal* (Paris: Pédone, 2000) at 621 (translated by the author).

38 See Victor Peskin, *International Justice in Rwanda and the Balkans*, *supra* note 9 at 236.

39 *Prosecutor v. Blaskic*, ICTY-95-94, Decision on the Objection of the Republic of Croatia to the Issuance of a Subpoena Duces Tecum (18 July 1997) at para 34 (International Criminal Tribunal for the former Yugoslavia, Trial Chamber II): "The tangible evidence required for proof of the guilt or innocence of those persons appearing before it will often be in the possession of States. Many of the crimes listed in Articles 2, 3 and 5 of the Statute relate to the conduct of military operations and therefore the records of those operations may constitute vital evidence. The fact that these are government documents should not automatically bar their production."

40 Institute for War and Peace Reporting (IWPR), "ICTY's Kosovo Investigation: Suspicions of Manipulation," Institute for War and Peace Reporting Tribunal Update no. 122 (19 April 1999).

As she noted, this kind of state assistance and collaboration would not be given eagerly:

> There is no doubt that there might be extremely valuable information contained in the intelligence archives of many countries. But it would be extremely surprising if that information surfaced in international trial, when so little ever surfaces in domestic trials in any country. The difficulty of access to this kind of information, first of all is obtaining an acknowledgement that it exists.[41]

However, if states do not want the Prosecutor "to discover critical evidence, recruit significant witnesses or arrest individuals in their jurisdictions, they can simply choose not to cooperate: evidence can be concealed, witnesses hounded and fugitives hidden."[42] While states do have a legal obligation to cooperate with certain tribunals – the ICTY, the ICTR and the ICC[43] – the sanction for non-compliance rests exclusively in the hands of political bodies, namely the UNSC or the Assembly of the States Parties. The history of the ICTR and the ICTY, and more recently of the UNSC in relation to Sudan has shown the great leniency of the UNSC towards uncooperative states.[44]

Realpolitik dictates that states evaluate their need to cooperate in light of their own geopolitical interests rather than according to their desire to see justice done. In other words, as stated by Louise Arbour, "generally speaking, everyone cooperates with the Tribunal in direct proportion to their self-interests. Croatia, for example, collaborates fully on certain investigations that serve its interests, less so on the ones that bother it."[45]

Online: <https://iwpr.net/global-voices/ictys-kosovo-investigation-suspicions> (hereinafter "IWPR Tribunal Update 122").

41 Ibid.

42 Carla Del Ponte, *Madame Prosecutor* (New York: Other Press, 2008) at 41.

43 See Article 29 ICTY Statute; Article 28 ICTR Statute. For the ICC, the obligation to cooperate is limited to States Parties: Articles 86 and 93 ICC Statute.

44 Gary J. Bass, *Stay the Hand of Vengeance: The Politics of War Crimes Tribunals* (Princeton: Princeton University Press, 2000) at 244: "Cassese formally protested five times, and each time got roughly the same reply from the Security Council. 'We deplore their attitude [to Serbia]; we condemn their attitude. Either deplore or condemn,' Cassese said. 'Maybe next time they'll find a third word.'" Theodore Meron, "Comments in the International Law Association Panel on the Yugoslav Tribunal: November 13, 1998" (1999) 5(2) *ILSA Journal of International & Comparative Law* 347: "the Security Council has not been consistently helpful. Verbal admonitions, even made under Chapter VII, not accompanied by credible sanctions or threats of use of force have not proved adequate to force compliance. The need to back up international criminal tribunals with power, power of enforcement, has been demonstrated once again."

45 Author's translation of a statement from Louise Arbour in "Le Tribunal pénal international est devenu un processus irréversible," *Le Monde* (15 September 1999), interview conducted by Rémy Ourdan and Claire Tréan: "D'une façon générale, tout le monde coopère avec le Tribunal en proportion directe de son intérêt propre. La Croatie, par exemple, coopère très bien sur certaines enquêtes qui peuvent servir ses intérêts, pas sur d''autres, qui la dérangent."

As a result, one can say that international prosecutors are not completely shielded from some degree of manipulation by states, which control an important part of the information that they need to perform their duties.[46] That being said, political control over international prosecutors and tribunals rarely takes a brutal or explicit form; rather, it expresses itself in a more indirect but just as efficient manner, "for instance, by withdrawing funds or withdrawing State cooperation."[47] The Prosecutor may be independent under the statute; he or she nevertheless remains dependent on states to carry out important components of his or her mandate.

This explains the importance of the international prosecutor's diplomatic skills, turning him or her into an active political actor. For David J. Scheffer, an international prosecutor "has to be as much of a diplomat as a criminal prosecutor ... The only way the court efficiency operates is if the prosecutor successfully negotiates their way to cooperation state by state."[48] However, working closely with states is a double-edged sword for international prosecutors, who must always be cautious not to create the appearance of trading off their independence for better collaboration. To generate state cooperation, international prosecutors do not have many tools. Often unable to count on the strong support of the UNSC, their main tool consists of "the use of adversarial and conciliatory strategies – from shaming to negotiation."[49] In doing so, their best ally – if not their only one – remains undoubtedly their independence guaranteed by international statutes. Unfortunately, in many cases, this will prove to be insufficient.

2.1. INDEPENDENCE IN PRACTICE: THE CASE OF THE ICTY

Surprisingly, a brief look at the early years of the ICTY reveals that most of the initial threats to prosecutorial independence came from its allies, both within and outside the institution. Right from the outset, the judges themselves stepped out of their judicial reserve to openly criticize the prosecutorial

46 Aleksa Djilas, "The Politicised Tribunal" IWPR Tribunal Update No, 230 – Part 1 (16–21 July 2001): "Paranoia aside, political control does exist – though not in the blunt and direct way presumed. In fact, since the tribunal does not have its own police force, its indictments rely in part on evidence gathered by the US and other NATO intelligence services. Intelligence services give evidence only when their governments tell them to, and they provide only so much information as is considered politically useful. Needless to say, the CIA would never send evidence that in any way incriminated US politicians, diplomats, generals or the CIA itself."

47 Louise Arbour, Albin Eser, Kai Ambos and Andrew Sander (eds), *The Prosecutor of a Permanent International Criminal Court* (Freiburg im Breisgau: Iuscrim, 2000) at 636.

48 See Victor Peskin, *International Justice in Rwanda and the Balkans*, *supra* note 9 at 239–240.

49 Ibid at 237.

investigative strategy[50] – the bottom-up approach of targeting low-level suspects before getting to the senior leaders – a move denounced by the then Prosecutor as an intrusion in his exclusive competence over the investigation and an encroachment on his independence.[51] Other parts of the UN were not overly supportive, providing insufficient resources and administrative backing, which ultimately undermined the functioning of the prosecution office.[52] The UN itself showed some difficulties in understanding the specific nature of a "judicial" organ and its inherent and necessary independence, including that of its Prosecutor. For instance, the first ICTY Prosecutor, Richard Goldstone, was called out by Secretary-General Boutros Boutros-Ghali, who was surprised that "the tribunal had indicted Karadžić without consulting him and without seeking his views on the matter."[53]

As to the "friendly states," the ones that originally supported the setting up of the tribunal by the UNSC, they remained ambivalent in relation to the exact role of the new judicial institution, seeing it more as a means of pressure or "sword of Damocles" to serve the purpose of diplomacy,[54] which ultimately cast doubt on its independence.[55] In the beginning, the ICTY was seen by many as

---

50 Claudia Angermaier, "Case Selection and Prioritization Criteria in the Work of the International Criminal Tribunal for the ex-Yugoslavia" in Morten Bergsmo (ed), *Criteria for Prioritizing and Selecting Core International Crimes Cases, supra* note 27 at 29: "Antonio Cassese views was that there was no interference with specific cases, but only a review of the general case selection policy in order to ensure that the Prosecutor acted in conformity with the general goals laid down in the ICTY Statute." See also Antonio Cassese, "The ICTY: A Living and Vital Reality" (2004) 2 *Journal of International Criminal Justice* 586.

51 See Richard Goldstone, "A View from the Prosecution" (2004) 2 *Journal of International Criminal Justice* at 380–381.

52 Richard Goldstone, *For Humanity: Reflections of a War Crime Investigator* (New Haven: Yale University Press, 2000) at 77: "I had assumed that a United Nations tribunal, which was a sub-organ of the Security Council itself and established by the unanimous vote of its members, would adequately be funded and well supported by the international body. That, unfortunately, turned out to be a naïve assumption."

53 Ibid at 102–103: "He [the Secretary-General] made it clear that had I consulted him, he would have advised me not to indict Karadic before peace had been brokered in Bosnia. "See also a Letter from the Secretary-General to the ICTY Prosecutor complaining about methods used to obtain Milosevič's transfer, quoted in Carla Del Ponte, *Madame Prosecutor, supra* note 42 at 105: "While naturally wishing to respect your independence as Prosecutor, I would accordingly encourage you in the future to confine your interventions to matters that are more directly within the sphere of your lawful concern."

54 "The tribunal was evidently intended by many countries to be just another kind of reprimand, not an actual court with defendants in the dock. Even Albright did not seem confident that anyone would ever be arrested: 'The Tribunal will issue indictments whether or not suspects can be taken in custody. They will become international pariahs.'" Gary J. Bass, *Stay the Hand of Vengeance: The Politics of War Crimes Tribunals, supra* note 44 at 215; see also Pierre Hazan, *Justice in the Time of War: The True Story behind the International Criminal Tribunal for the Former Yugoslavia, supra* note 2 at 192.

55 "The politicians used it as a sword of Damocles ... they want to instrumentalize international justice, to use it as a means of pressure, in the same way they use threats of sanctions or air strikes. This strategy politicized the Tribunal and inevitably damaged its image."

"the 'fig leaf' of the international community, established to hide its shame for inaction in the former Yugoslavia, particularly in Bosnia."[56]

During the following years of the ICTY, prosecutors resisted thick and thin to external pressures and managed to establish and preserve their independence, though it undoubtedly remains vulnerable in the inauspicious field of international relations. The following two episodes from the time of Louise Arbour's tenure as Prosecutor of the ICTY illustrate the challenges and limits of exercising independent prosecutorial functions in the realm of realpolitik: the NATO bombing campaign case reveals the dilemmas of investigating an ally as best evidence of your independence; and the indictment of President Milosević offers a clear example of the critical importance of state support to ensure the Prosecutor's success in highly political environments, in what has been labelled by Arbour as "coinciding interests."[57]

2.2. THE NATO AFFAIR

The NATO affair can be best described as a shilly-shallying episode – *une valse-hésitation* – where prosecutorial independence had its ups and downs. It started on a high note with Louise Arbour's bold affirmation of prosecutorial independence quoted at the beginning of this chapter: the NATO bombing campaign against the Federal Republic of Yugoslavia came under ICTY jurisdiction and would be carefully scrutinized. It ended on a low note with the publication of a baffling report where Prosecutor Carla Del Ponte recommended not investigating NATO since "the investigations are unlikely to result in the acquisition of sufficient evidence to substantiate charges against high level accused,"[58] due notably to the fact that NATO's answers to the Prosecutor's specific questions were "couched in general terms and failed to address the specific incidents"!

Obviously, the whole "affair" was delicate. On the one hand, NATO was a close and vital partner of the ICTY Prosecutor in her investigations and arrest operations in Bosnia; and at least three influential members of NATO were

---

Pierre Hazan, *Justice in the Time of War: The True Story behind the International Criminal Tribunal for the Former Yugoslavia*, *supra* note 2 at 192.

56 Richard Goldstone, "A View from the Prosecution," *supra* note 51 at 77.

57 Words of ICTY Prosecutor Louise Arbour in IWPR, "ICTY's Kosovo Investigation: Suspicions of Manipulation," Institute for War and Peace Reporting Tribunal Update no. 122, *supra* note 40: "'There are circumstances in which justice and politics interests coincide,' she said last week. Arbour further denied the suggestions that she was given the green light by the Western governments to indict Yugoslav President Slobodan Milosević. The question is not whether we are free [to indict Milosević] but whether we will now be better equipped by those who may hold information in moving forward in this investigation."

58 *Final Report to the Prosecutor by the Committee Established to Review the NATO Bombing Campaign against the Federal Republic of Yugoslavia* (ICTY, 13 June 2000) at para 90 *in fine*.

instrumental in bringing the resolution that created the ICTY. On the other hand, the ICTY Prosecutor was in possession of information from different sources[59] accusing NATO forces of violations of international humanitarian law. In terms of independence, or the appearance of it, it was important for the Prosecutor to act. After all, as Louise Arbour pointed out, the "greatest threat to the legitimacy of the [International Criminal] Court would be the credible suggestion of political manipulation of the Office of the Prosecutor, or of the Court itself, for political expediency."[60]

In order to defuse any accusations of bias or lack of independence, confronted with the significant political impact of the decisions to investigate or not and to prosecute or not, a call for more transparency is essential. Most disagreements surface on how such a decision is taken or, to be more precise, on which criteria it is based. Therefore, these decisions need to be "explained in a manner which avoids giving rise to such a credible suggestion."[61] In the NATO affair, Louise Arbour took an innovative step – with a view of avoiding any suspicion of bias on her part – and appointed a committee within her office "to assess the allegations and material accompanying them, and advise the Prosecutor and Deputy Prosecutor whether or not there is a sufficient basis to proceed with an investigation into some or all the allegations or into other incidents related to the NATO bombing."[62] The decision was made public on 2 June 2000, when the new ICTY Prosecutor, Carla Del Ponte, stated in front of the UNSC that "there was 'no basis' for opening an investigation into allegations that war crimes had been committed by NATO personnel and leaders during the alliance's air campaign against the Federal Republic of Yugoslavia last year."[63]

This decision raised suspicions about the prosecution's independence and impartiality; the Prosecutor was accused of using double standards in the exercise of her discretion when applied to "friendly" powers.[64] In order to counter

59 See Amnesty International, *NATO/Federal Republic of Yugoslavia: "Collateral Damage" or Unlawful Killings? Violations of the Laws of War by NATO during Operation Allied Forces* (Amnesty International, EUR 70/18/00, June 2000); Human Rights Watch, *Civilian Deaths in the NATO Air Campaign* (Human Rights Watch, February 2000).

60 Louise Arbour, "The Need for an Independent and Effective Prosecutor in the Permanent International Criminal Court" (1999) 17 *Windsor Yearbook of Access to Justice* 213.

61 See James A. Goldston, "More Candour about Criteria: The Exercise of Discretion by the Prosecutor of the International Criminal Court" (2010) 8 *Journal of International Criminal Justice* 390.

62 *Final Report*, *supra* note 58 at para 3.

63 United Nations, press release, SC/6870, "Prosecutor for International Tribunals Briefs Security Council" (2 June 2000).

64 See, for example, Claudio Gidron and Avner Cordone, "Faut-t-il juger l'OTAN," *Le Monde Diplomatique* (July 2000) at 1: "La demande, souvent martelée par l'OTAN, d'être jugée à la lumière de la cause humanitaire qu'elle poursuivait peut être lue comme un plaidoyer pour être jugée selon des normes plus tolérantes que celles appliquées à la RFY. Aucune organisation impartiale ne peut admettre de tels doubles standards et de jauger avec deux poids deux mesures." See also Natalino Ronzitti, "Is the *Non Liquet* of the Final Report by the

mounting criticisms and defuse accusations that prosecutorial independence and impartiality had been left aside in the decision not to open an investigation against NATO, the Prosecutor published the report of the committee set up to analyze and assess the allegations. This was an unprecedented move in the field of prosecutorial discretion,[65] something that should be acknowledged as an important step toward greater transparency. Unfortunately, if the publication of the report was intended to establish the independence and impartiality of Del Ponte's office, it failed miserably, due in large part to the weak nature of its content.[66] Globally, the report fell short of reinforcing the appearance of prosecutorial independence. For example, the report stated that apart from issues of evidence and law, it also took into account a number of other factors concerning the prospects of obtaining sufficient evidence to prove that the crime had been committed "by an individual who merits prosecution in the international forum,"[67] but regrettably it stopped short of revealing what makes someone a meritorious candidate for prosecution!

The two main reasons supporting the recommendation not to investigate are highly questionable: the first is that "the law is not sufficiently clear" and the second is that "the investigations are unlikely to result in the acquisition of sufficient evidence to substantiate charges against high level accused or against lower accused for particularly heinous offences."[68] As a critic rightfully said, "difficulties in interpretation are not a good excuse for not starting an investigation."[69] The second reason touches on something familiar, the anticipated non-collaboration of NATO in getting all of the evidence needed, while the Prosecutor had not yet deployed any investigative activities.[70] It seems like

---

Committee Established to Review the NATO Bombing Campaign against the Federal Republic of Yugoslavia Acceptable?" (2000) 82(840) *International Review of the Red Cross* 1018.

65 The OTP has never before made public the internal process leading to a decision on whether to investigate a case. The deputy prosecutor said that the OTP would do so on this occasion to ensure the process was as transparent as possible and to demonstrate that the Tribunal is not a "political tool of NATO." IWPR, "NATO Case" IWPR Tribunal Update no. 179 (5–10 June 2000).

66 It is not the objective of this chapter to analyse this report in depth; others have done so extensively. See, for example, "Symposium: The International Legal Fallout from Kosovo" (2001) 12 *European Journal of International Law* 331–356; Louis Henkin, "Editorial Comments: NATO's Kosovo Intervention" (1999) 93 *American Journal of International Law* 824–863.

67 *Final Report*, *supra* note 58 at para 5.

68 Ibid at para 90 *in fine*.

69 Natalino Ronzitti, "Is the *Non Liquet* of the Final Report by the Committee Established to Review the NATO Bombing Campaign against the Federal Republic of Yugoslavia Acceptable?", *supra* note 64.

70 *Final Report*, *supra* note 58 at para 90: "*The committee has conducted its review* relying essentially upon public documents, *including statements made by NATO and NATO countries at press conferences and public documents produced by the FRY.* It has tended to assume that the NATO and NATO countries' press statements are generally reliable and that explanations have been honestly given. The committee must note, however, that when the OTP requested NATO to answer specific questions about specific incidents, the NATO reply was couched

the Prosecutor gave up before the fight – not quite what is expected from an impartial and independent prosecutor.[71]

During this period, the ICTY Prosecutor Carla Del Ponte kept on sending contradictory signals about her willingness to act: "If I am not willing to do that [press charges if there is conclusive evidence against NATO], I am not in the right place: I must give up the mission!"[72] Then, following the diplomatic storm caused by her declaration, she issued a statement saying that "there is no formal inquiry into the actions of NATO."[73] She admitted months after the report was released that not all aspects of the NATO bombing campaign had been fully examined.[74] In her memoir, looking back at the whole NATO affair, she wrote straightforwardly: "I understood that I had collided with the edge of the political universe in which the tribunal was allowed to function."[75]

If a proper investigation had been opened, it is very likely that the Prosecutor would have taken the same decision – not to prosecute NATO military forces – but based on more convincing arguments, reducing much of the perceived partiality and lack of independence that the NATO case as engendered.

2.3. THE INDICTMENT OF PRESIDENT MILOSEVIĆ

The historical importance of President Slobodan Milosević's indictment before the ICTY on 24 May 1999 is undeniable.[76] There is no doubt that Milosević was

in general terms and failed to address the specific incidents. *The committee has not spoken to those involved in directing or carrying out the bombing campaign.*"

71 An internal and confidential document of the ICRC is highly critical of the report: "We may reasonably ask the question if this is *a priori* favoritism to one of the parties of the conflict is compatible with the Prosecutor's avowed impartiality," quoted by Pierre Hazan, *Justice in the Time of War: The True Story behind the International Criminal Tribunal for the Former Yugoslavia*, *supra* note 2 at 136; see also Paolo Benvenuti, "The ICTY Prosecutor and the Review of the NATO Bombing Campaign against the Federal Republic of Yugoslavia" (2001) 12 *European Journal of International Law* 503 at 507: "In short the report displayed a one-sided attitude hardly consistent with the prosecutor's duty of independence and impartiality as envisaged in the ICTY Statute."

72 "Dossier of Nato 'Crimes' Lands in Prosecutor's Lap," *London Sunday Observer* (26 December 1999).

73 IWPR, "Nato Not under OTP Investigation," IWPR Tribunal Update no. 158 (27–31 December 1999): "The statement triggered quite a storm between The Hague, NATO HQ in Brussels and the US administration in Washington. In order to put an end to such speculations and calm the resultant storm caused in the midst of the Millennium holidays, Del Ponte issued the following statement: "NATO is not under investigation by the Office of the Prosecutor of the International Criminal Tribunal for the former Yugoslavia. There is no formal inquiry into the actions of NATO during the conflict in Kosovo."

74 Carla Del Ponte in comments recorded by Alain Franco, "Balkans-Rwanda: la fin de l'impunité" (2001) 90 *Politique Internationale* at 316–317.

75 Carla Del Ponte, *Madame Prosecutor*, *supra* note 42 at 60.

76 IWPR, "ICTY's Kosovo Investigation: Suspicions of Manipulation," *supra* note 40: "As pointed out by Justice Arbour in her application to Judge Hunt, "this indictment is the first in

a prime target of the prosecution since the setting up of the ICTY and the bloody conflict in Bosnia, but there was not enough evidence to indict him.[77] The war in Kosovo dramatically changed the rules of the game and opened up new opportunities for the Prosecutor. Milosević had lost what little credibility he still had in the eyes of some Western diplomats for his failure to attend the last round of peace negotiations in Rambouillet: he was no longer a credible interlocutor. The tone of the US State Department shifted dramatically at the time: "He is not simply part of the problem; Milosević is the problem."[78] The beginning of the civil war in Kosovo followed by the NATO bombing campaign in Serbia would not only cause numerous sufferings, but would also paradoxically favour "unprecedented levels of cooperation":[79] the Americans, the British, the French and the Germans suddenly converged at The Hague and offered their "new" collaboration to the Prosecutor, providing crucial information "to ensure that those who commit these crimes will be held responsible."[80] Louise Arbour's euphemistic expression of "coinciding interests" is useful to explain that new era of collaboration: "there are circumstances in which justice and politics interests coincide."[81]

Here the Prosecutor was confronted with realpolitik, on the thin line between legitimate cooperation with states in the interests of justice and serving

---

the history of this Tribunal to charge a Head of State during an on-going armed conflict with the commission of serious violations of international humanitarian law."

77 Louise Arbour in Rémy Ourdan and Claire Tréan, "Le Tribunal pénal international est devenu un processus irréversible," *supra* note 45: "In Bosnia, the chain of command is much more difficult to prove, while in Kosovo crimes are limited in time and space, and the chain of command is much more direct" (translated by the author).

78 Quoted by Pierre Hazan, *Justice in the Time of War: The True Story behind the International Criminal Tribunal for the Former Yugoslavia, supra* note 2 at 130.

79 IWPR, "ICTY's Kosovo Investigation: Suspicions of Manipulation," *supra* note 40: "The 'coinciding interests' have, therefore, brought us to the point of what Tribunal Deputy Prosecutor Graham Blewitt last week described as 'unprecedented levels of cooperation.'"

80 Pierre Hazan, *Justice in the Time of War: The True Story behind the International Criminal Tribunal for the Former Yugoslavia, supra* note 2 at 130–131: "The American government supports this unprecedented collaboration to document these cases to help ensure that all potential sources of information will be tapped ... says Koh, the American Under-Secretary of State ... The next day, Foreign Minister Robin Cook of Great Britain declares: we have authorized the handover of British intelligence material to the War Crimes Tribunal ... one of the largest releases of intelligence material ever authorized by the British." IWPR, "ICTY's Kosovo Investigation: Suspicions of Manipulation," *supra* note 40: "the German Defence Minister Rudolf Scharping in Bonn on April 19, handed Arbour a series of aerial photographs taken by drone reconnaissance aircraft, which show both the destruction of villages in Kosovo and refugees being stripped of identity papers and belongings by Yugoslav troops ... the French government promised its full co-operation. This included the gathering of eyewitnesses, providing security for investigators, protecting refugees, transmitting information of military nature, including that gathered on the chains of command."

81 IWPR, "ICTY's Kosovo Investigation: Suspicions of Manipulation," *supra* note 40: "The Chief Prosecutor, Louise Arbour, however, sees no reason to worry about this, and does not believe the Tribunal's work has been compromised by accepting offers of co-operation. 'There are circumstances in which justice and politics interests coincide,' she said last week.'"

the political agendas of powerful actors. It is true that states control access to important elements of evidence; without it, the Prosecutor's investigation will be more difficult, in some case even impossible to achieve. It is also true that state "collaboration" is often, if not always, dictated by self-interest; by "leaking" some important information in the hands of the prosecutor, states do influence – some would say manipulate – the justice process.[82] However, states cannot dictate the conduct of an independent prosecutor; the ultimate decision to indict Milosević, and the moment and the extent of the indictment, rested solely with the Prosecutor.[83] As Louise Arbour stated very clearly at the time, "the question is not whether we are free [to indict Milosević] but whether we will now be better equipped by those who may hold information in moving forward in this investigation."[84] Paraphrasing the ICTY judge already quoted above, states can measure out the oxygen that they feed to the Prosecutor in order to speed him or her up or slow him or her down, but the Prosecutor remains independent and "is not simply a puppet in their hands."[85]

3. CONCLUSION

International criminal law is at the crossroads of public international law and criminal law. It is, as described by Louise Arbour, an "unlikely union" which presented "the extraordinary difficulty of trying to marry together principles of international law (a profoundly consensual body of law that is essentially concerned with regulating conduct between *states*) with the criminal law (a body of law that is profoundly coercive), which is primarily concerned with *personal* liability."[86] International criminal tribunals are thus the offspring

---

82 Pierre Hazan, *Justice in the Time of War: The True Story behind the International Criminal Tribunal for the Former Yugoslavia*, *supra* note 2 at 129: "Is she being manipulated? Is she the legal arm of the Atlantic Alliance? … Arbour energetically refutes these accusations, 'There are circumstances in which justice and political interests coincide,' she says. From her mouth, it is an implicit criticism of the West, which demonstrate[s] no such devotion to the tribunal when Bosnia was burning and bloody."

83 Louise Arbour in IWPR, "Arbour, Milosević and 'Yesterday's Men,'" IWPR Tribunal Update no. 128 (31 May–5 June 1999): "We were not told by the Security Council to investigate and then go and consult with various governments to see if it suits their political agenda for us to move forward."

84 The critical matter for the Office of the Prosecutor (OTP), concluded Arbour, "is not to be given a political mandate [which already exists in the form of Security Council Resolution 827 and Statute of the Tribunal] but to be provided with the information that would allow us to move." Quoted in IWPR, "ICTY's Kosovo Investigation: Suspicions of Manipulation," *supra* note 40.

85 See comment from an ICTY judge as quoted by Pierre Hazan, *Justice in the Time of War: The True Story behind the International Criminal Tribunal for the Former Yugoslavia*, *supra* note 36.

86 Louise Arbour, "Progress and Challenges in International Criminal Justice" (1997) 21(2) *Fordham International Law Journal* 531.

of international law and criminal law, the former being known for its lack of means of implementation and sanction and the latter for exactly the opposite. International criminal law can be seen as a hybrid between both legal branches that has led to a law that can be enforced like criminal law, but that is left largely to the discretion of states to implement, much like public international law.

In this context, international prosecutors cannot fully escape the political context of the international criminal tribunals' creation and of their place and role within it. As we have seen, a prosecutor may be statutorily independent, but he or she is nevertheless part of a political context where state actors still have the upper hand. Furthermore, international prosecutors are organs of tribunals that were created by political bodies acting with political purposes often concealed beneath the cloak of good intentions served in diplomatic language. For state actors – and unfortunately that includes the UN – justice becomes a means to achieve their political goals, not the opposite. This is the message sent year after year with the recourse to selective international justice by the most powerful political actors of our world: from direct instruments of the victors (Nuremberg and Tokyo), to tools masking their impotence (former Yugoslavia)[87] or their indifference (Rwanda),[88] to instruments of political sanctions (Special Tribunal for Lebanon), and to vehicles for some states in helping to silence the opposition (Special Court for Sierra Leone) or to control the narrative (Extraordinary Chambers in the Courts of Cambodia). Despite its more universal jurisdiction, the ICC does not completely escape being used for political purposes by the UNSC or states' self-referrals. This reality of being seen as instruments of 'selective justice" constitutes undoubtedly the first challenge for the independence and impartiality of international prosecutors; it was justly depicted by an author as "being tainted by the original sin."[89]

87 "The governments wanted to hide their political impotence behind the existence of a tribunal" (Judge Cassese); "The ICTY had been created as a catharsis, a moral executor of the Security Council, which at its core refused to intervene politically and militarily in Yugoslavia" (another ICTY judge). Quoted by Pierre Hazan, *Justice in the Time of War: The True Story behind the International Criminal Tribunal for the Former Yugoslavia*, *supra* note 2 at 49.

88 Alison Des Forges, *Leave None to Tell the Story: Genocide in Rwanda* (New York and Paris: Human Rights Watch & International Federation of Human Rights, 1999) at 2: "Policymakers in France, Belgium, and the United States and the United Nations all knew of the preparations for massive slaughter and failed to take the necessary steps to prevent it. Aware from the start that Tutsi were being targeted for elimination, the leading foreign actors refused to acknowledge the genocide … and declined for weeks to use their political and moral authority to challenge the legitimacy of the genocidal government." Richard Falk, *Human Rights Horizons: The Pursuit of Justice in a Globalizing World* (New York: Routledge, 2000) at 180: "The events in Rwanda and Burundi also confirm this pattern of indifference: only minimal efforts were made by the international community to protect the target of genocide or to punish the main perpetrators. No strategic interests were at stake."

89 See Antonio Cassese, "La répression des infractions internationales – Présentation," *supra* note 37; Pierre Hazan, *Justice in the Time of War: The True Story behind the International Criminal Tribunal for the Former Yugoslavia, supra* note 2 at 36.

The central question is thus whether an international prosecutor "can operate in a highly politicized context and fulfill an explicit political purpose," without compromising his or her independence and impartiality and becoming itself politicized, taking down with him or her the fundamental right to "a fair and public hearing by a competent, independent and impartial tribunal."[90] In her very insightful book on the law, politics and diplomacy of the ICTY, Rachel Kerr summarizes the difficult relationship between the "political and judicial" nature of these new institutions in these words:

> The tribunal was a tool of politics, but it was a judicial, not a political tool. The distinction is crucial. It means that the Tribunal itself, once created, was independent. The independent status of the Tribunal meant that it developed a momentum of its own, so that, in time, it mattered less what the precise motives for its establishment were.[91]

Once created, international criminal tribunals – and their prosecutors – do develop a "momentum of their own"; they do escape from their creators, although not completely. Without the collaboration of sovereign states, the tribunals and their prosecutors are doomed to fail. And through their specific investigative function, international prosecutors are condemned to deal with states more than any other organ of the court; in such a role, independence becomes their most prized attribute and their only line of defence toward powerful states.

From Nuremberg to The Hague, prosecutorial independence went from the Dark Ages to the "siècle des lumières," from non-existent to fully recognized and guaranteed by statutes. More generally, the statutory history of the modern international criminal tribunals demonstrates a strong desire to protect the independence of the prosecution, which culminated in the Rome Statute of the ICC. Better guarantees and greater transparency are both essential ingredients to ensure institutional, individual and functional independence of a new generation of international prosecutors. Paradoxically, while the independence of international prosecutors provides a formal or legal shield from political interference, it nevertheless turns them into political actors in the field of international relations. If international prosecutors cannot escape this reality (they unmistakably need state collaboration to succeed), the exercise of their core functions – their decisions to investigate and prosecute – should be devoid of political considerations. The fundamental aspect of independence is "that the prosecutor should not be required to account to a political body for his or her professional decisions or to take instructions from politicians on the exercise of prosecutorial discretion."[92]

---

90 Rachel Kerr, *The International Criminal Tribunal for the Former Yugoslavia: An Exercise in Law, Politics, and Diplomacy* (New York: Oxford University Press, 2004) at 40.

91 Ibid at 39–40.

92 Richard Goldstone, *For Humanity: Reflections of a War Crimes Investigator* (New Haven: Yale University Press, 2000) at 132.

If politics play a role upstream (in the creation of most international criminal tribunals and the appointment of their prosecutors) and downstream (in the decision to defer or shut down the institution), it leaves enough space in between for a prosecutor to assert his or her independence beyond the political interests of the founders. Still, any attempt to immunize prosecutors from their political surroundings and to protect them from perceptions of politicization is almost an impossible task: every utterance is immediately interpreted and exploited for political ends by one side or the other, as are the silences. The reality is that *no* international prosecutors were able to exercise their functions without being accused by one side or another of partiality or not being independent – all the more reason to avoid giving grounds to such accusations and leave the political issues with the political bodies, such as questions of peace, security and reconciliation.

International prosecutors were born in turmoil, in the aftermath of violent conflicts, often where the international community turned a blind eye. Heirs of the powerful, burdened by an unachievable mandate, they nevertheless succeeded over the years in emancipating themselves from their creators and fulfilling their mission with independence and impartiality. Safeguarding this independence presents their main challenge in today's difficult political context. To be independent, an international prosecutor needs proper institutional, individual and functional guarantees provided by statute. To appear independent, he or she needs to act as such, showing impartiality and measure in his or her conduct, something that unfortunately no law can provide.

TORTURE, JURISDICTION AND IMMUNITY

Theories and Practices in Search of One Another

François LAROCQUE*

1. INTRODUCTION

That the prohibition of torture has attained the status of a peremptory norm of international law has been beyond question for some time.[1] The torture victim's right to civil redress is also generally uncontroversial and widely recognized in international law,[2] as well as in the domestic law of certain

* This chapter is reprinted with permission. It originally appeared in Alexander Orekhaleshvili (ed.), *Research Handbook on Jurisdiction and Immunities in International Law* (Cheltenham: Edward Elgar, 2015).

1 *Filártiga v. Peña-Irala*, 630 F2d 876 (2d Cir 1980); *Questions Relating to the Obligation to Prosecute or Extradite (Belgium v. Senegal)*, Judgment, ICJ Reports 2012, p 422 at para 99.

2 *Convention Against Torture and Other Cruel, Inhuman or Degrading Treatment or Punishment*, 1465 UNTS 85, Article 14 (CAT); Committee against Torture, *General Comment No 3 – Implementation of Article 14 by State Parties*, CAT/C/GC/3, 13 December 2012 (*General Comment No 3*); *Basic Principles and Guidelines on the Right to a Remedy and Reparation for Victims of Gross Violations of International Human Rights Law and Serious*

states, either through specific legislative schemes,[3] the general law of torts or obligations[4] and, in many civil law countries, through the normal operation of the criminal law.[5] More controversial, however, is the scope of the adjudicative jurisdiction of national courts with respect to civil claims for torture. It has been contended, at least since the 1990s, that national courts have the jurisdiction to adjudicate civil claims for torture, even in circumstances when the alleged torture has occurred in another country, that is, outside the territorial jurisdiction of the forum.[6] More specifically, it has been argued that the universal *criminal* jurisdiction to prosecute individual torturers entails the recognition of a corresponding principle of universal *civil* jurisdiction to hold states and their functionaries liable for torture.[7] A related question is whether this putative universal civil jurisdiction with respect to torture, like its criminal counterpart, is inimical to the application of immunities.[8]

The idea that the peremptory prohibition of torture has given rise to a type of universal civil jurisdiction has found some acceptance in the literature, but does not yet form part of the mainstream.[9] It might be that the impetus

---

Violations of International Humanitarian Law, GA Res/60/147, UN Doc. A/Res/60/147, December 16, 2005.

3 Alien Tort Statute (ATS) and Torture Victim Protection Act, 28 USC §1350 (TVPA); Torture Prohibition Act, RSY 2002, c 220.

4 Beth Stevens et al., *International Human Rights Litigation in US Courts*, 2nd edn (Leiden: Martinus Nijhoff, 2008) at pp 120–127; François Larocque, "The Tort of Torture" (2009) 17 *Tort Law Review* 158.

5 *Sosa v. Alvarez-Machain*, 542 US 692 at 762 (Breyer J); *Kiobel v. Royal Dutch Petroleum*, 133 S Ct 1659 at 1676 (2013); *Prosecutor v. Max Joseph Milde* (2008), 92 RDI 618 (Ct Cass It); *Ely Ould Dah v. France* (2009) 48 ILM 884 (ECtHR).

6 Harold Hongju Koh, "Transnational Public Law Litigation" (1991) 100 *Yale LJ* 2347; Benedetto Conforti and Francesco Francioni (eds), *Enforcing International Human Rights in Domestic Courts* (The Hague: Kluwer International, 1997); Craig Scott (ed), *Torture as Tort: Comparative Perspectives on the Development of Transnational Human Rights Litigation* (Oxford: Hart Publishing, 2001); François Larocque, *Civil Actions for Uncivilized Acts: The Adjudicative Jurisdiction of Common Law Courts in Transnational Human Rights Proceedings* (Toronto: Irwin Law, 2010).

7 Kathryn Lee Boyd, "Universal Jurisdiction and Structural Reasonableness" (2004) 40 *Texas Int'l LJ* 1; Jane Wright, "Retribution But No Recompense: A Critique of the Torturer's Immunity from Civil Suit" (2010) 30 *Oxford J Leg St* 143 at 151–162.

8 Lorna MacGregor, "State Immunity and Human Rights" (2013) 11 *JICJ* 125; Roger O'Keefe, "State Immunity and Human Rights: Heads and Walls, Hearts and Minds" (2011) 44 *Vanderbilt J Transnt'l L* 999; Christopher Keith Hall, "The Duty of States Parties to the Convention against Torture to Provide Procedures Permitting Victims to Recover Reparations for Torture Committed Abroad" (2008) 18:5 *EJIL* 921; Craig Forcese, "De-immunizing Torture: Reconciling Human Rights and State Immunity" (2007) 52 *McGill LJ* 127; François Larocque, "La Loi sur l'immunité des états canadienne et la torture" (2010) 55 *McGill LJ* 81.

9 Jeffrey Blum and Ralph Steinhardt, "Federal Jurisdiction over International Human Rights Claims: The Alien Tort Claims Act after *Filártiga v. Peña-Irala*" (1981) 22 *Harv Int'l L J* 53; *Restatement (Third) of the Foreign Relations Law of the United States* (St Paul, MN: ALI Publishers, 1987) at §404; Brief of the *Amicus Curiae* European Commission in *Sosa v. Alvarez-Machain*, 2004 WL 177036 (hereinafter "EC Brief in *Sosa*"); Beth van Schaack, "Justice without Borders: Universal Civil Jurisdiction" (2005) 99 *ASIL Proceedings* 120;

to fully theorize a putative principle of universal civil jurisdiction has been stifled by a consistent stream of national court rulings, since the 1990s, holding that the law of state immunity constitutes an absolute bar to civil claims for extraterritorial torture.[10] The implicit conceit of these decisions appears to be that since acts of torture attract immunity, it is of little import whether national courts possess the adjudicative jurisdiction to entertain civil claims with respect to extraterritorial torture. It is noteworthy that almost[11] none of these national court decisions even attempted to address the logically prior question of jurisdiction before dismissing the plaintiffs' case on the basis of immunity. This line of jurisprudence was essentially confirmed by the International Court of Justice (ICJ) in the case on *Jurisdictional Immunities of the State*, which held that states enjoy immunity at international law in civil claims for violations of international humanitarian law committed by occupying military forces during wartime.[12]

There are lingering inconsistencies between the theories and practices surrounding torture, jurisdiction and immunity, which are perhaps symptomatic of a deeper problem. The community of nations is united in its unequivocal condemnation of torture, yet torture is regularly employed with impunity in prison cells, interrogation rooms and so-called "blacksites" throughout the world. Torture survivors and victims' families are explicitly entitled to a range of civil remedies for pain, suffering and death, yet in the vast majority of cases, they are denied justice and access to a court of law for the determination of their rights. The prohibition of torture in international law forms part of the

---

Donald Francis Donovan and Anthea Roberts, "The Emerging Recognition of Universal Civil Jurisdiction" (2006) 100 *AJIL* 142; Lorna MacGregor, "The Need to Resolve the Paradoxes of the Civil Dimension of Universal Jurisdiction" (2005) 99 *ASIL Proceedings* 125; Kate Parlett, "Universal Civil Jurisdiction for Torture" (2007) 4 *EHRLR* 385. See *contra* Menno T Kamminga, "Universal Civil Jurisdiction: Is it Legal? Is it Desirable?" (2005) 99 *ASIL Proceedings* 123; Curtis A Bradley, "Universal Jurisdiction and US Law" (2001) *U Chi Legal Forum* 323; Eugene Kontorovich, "The Piracy Analogy: Modern Universal Jurisdiction's Hollow Foundation" (2004) 45 *Harv Int'l LJ* 183.

10 *Al-Adsani v. Kuwait* (1995), 103 ILR 420 (QB), aff'd (1996), 107 ILR 536 (CA); *Al-Adsani v. United Kingdom* (2001) 34 EHRR 273; *Arar v. Syrian Republic*, [2005] OJ No 752 (SCJ); *Bouzari v. Islamic Republic of Iran* [2002] OJ No 1624 (SCJ), aff'd (2004), 71 OR (3d) 675 (CA); *Mitchell v. Al-Dali*, Case No A2 2004/0489 (QB), aff'd *sub nom Jones v. Saudi-Arabia*, [2004] EWCA Civ 1394, varied [2006] UKHL 26; *Jones and Others v. United Kingdom*, App nos. 34356/06 and 40528/06 (ECtHR, 14 January 2014); *Fang and Others v. Jiang Zemin and Others* [2007] NZAR 420 (HC); *Steen v. Islamic Republic of Iran*, 2011 ONSC 6464 aff'd 2013 ONCA 30; *Kazemi (Estate of) v. Islamic Republic of Iran*, 2011 QCCS 196, varied *sub nom Islamic Republic of Iran v. Hashemi*, 2012 QCCA 1449, aff'd *sub nom Kazemi Estate v. Islamic Republic of Iran*, 2014 SCC 62.

11 *Bouzari* (2002); see also *Saleh v. United Arab Emirates* (2003) 15 CCLT (3d) 231 (SCJO) (*Saleh*) (claim for extraterritorial torture dismissed for lack of real and substantial connection to Ontario without raising state immunity)

12 *Jurisdictional Immunities of the State (Germany v. Italy: Greece Intervening)*, Judgment, ICJ Reports 99.

theoretically inviolable and hierarchically superior *jus cogens*, yet its civil enforcement is routinely eschewed on the basis of ordinary and hierarchically inferior *jus dispositivum*, such as state immunity. The unhappy disconnect between the legal prohibition of torture (what *ought* to be done) and the real-world impunity surrounding torture (what is *actually* done) is a particularly troubling type of performative contradiction, because it not only risks invalidating the prescription itself, but also threatens the integrity of the international legal system as a whole. The enduring malaise of international law is its propensity to repudiate its own effectiveness.

If the consequences of international law's self-denying tendencies were purely theoretical, they would matter a great deal more to academic lawyers than to anyone else. But the reality is quite different. By failing to walk the walk in the area of human rights, the international law of human rights is failing the individuals it purports to protect: the tormented and battered men, women and children who have suffered or died from state-sanctioned abuse. Instead of finding relief or vindication in the law, torture victims and survivors' families have been systemically turned away by an international legal system that prioritizes the impersonal dignity of sovereign states over the inherent dignity of the human person. Where torture, jurisdiction and immunity are concerned, international law is quite tragically a "travesty."[13] Indeed, as Philip Allot once lamented:

> Law constrains or it is a travesty to call it law. Law enters decisively into the willing of its subjects or it is a travesty to call it law. Law transcends the power of the powerful and transforms the situation of the weak or it is a travesty to call it law. A legal system which does its best to make sense of murder, theft, exploitation, oppression, abuse of power and injustice, perpetrated by public authorities in the public interest is a perversion of a legal system.[14]

This chapter will describe this sad state of affairs and propose possible paths through the gloom, with a view to resolving some inconsistencies between theories and practices surrounding torture, jurisdiction and immunity.

2. TORTURE

2.1. IN THEORY

It is hardly necessary to devote much time and space in this chapter to the demonstration of torture prohibition's special status at international law.

---

13 *Al-Adsani v. United Kingdom* (2001) 34 EHRR 273, dissenting opinion of Judge Loucaides, para 1.

14 Philip Allott, *Eunomia: New Order for a New World* (Oxford, Oxford University Press, 2001).

It will suffice, for the present purposes, to recall that the ban on torture has been incorporated in every important human rights declaration and treaty since the creation of the United Nations (UN).[15] In 1986, Peter Kooijmans, the Special Rapporteur on Torture (as he then was), observed: "If ever a phenomenon was outlawed unreservedly and unequivocally it is torture."[16] If any doubts lingered as to the strength of its international legal prohibition, these were surely jettisoned in 2012 when the ICJ finally felt able to recognize the prohibition of torture as *jus cogens*.[17]

The decisions of national courts also consistently express the enhanced status of the legal norms prohibiting torture, and do so with the literary gravitas that characterizes much of Western international legal writing.[18] Indeed, one of the striking features of the national jurisprudence in civil proceedings with respect to torture is the lyrical tone of the prose used to describe its unlawfulness. Consider, for example, Judge Kaufman's famous dictum that "the torturer has become, like the pirate and the slave trader before him, *hostis humani generis*, an enemy of all mankind."[19] In that sentence, one of many poetic crescendos in a self-consciously historic decision, Judge Kaufman equated torture to other forms of egregious abuses – piracy and slavery – in order to convey the normative weight and scope he understood the torture prohibition to possess.

Even in those cases where the immunity of the torturing state or state official is ultimately upheld and the plaintiff denied a remedy, judges couch their decisions in the lexicon of moral aversion, perhaps to express genuine

---

15 Universal Declaration of Human Rights (adopted 10 December 1948 UNGA Res 217 A(III), Article 5; Geneva Conventions (I–IV) (adopted 12 August 1949, entered into force 21 October 1950) (I) 75 UNTS 31 (II) 75 UNTS 85 (III) 75 UNTS 135 (IV) 75 UNTS 287, Article 3; European Convention for the Protection of Human Rights and Fundamental Freedoms (adopted 4 November 1950, entered into force 3 September 1953), ETS 5, 213 UNTS 221, Article 3 (ECHR); International Covenant on Civil and Political Rights (adopted 16 December 1966, entered into force 23 March 1976) 999 UNTS 171, Article 7; American Convention on Human Rights (adopted 21 November 1969, entered into force 18 July 1978) OAS Treaty Series No 36, 1144 UNTS 123, Article 5; Declaration on the Protection of All Persons from Being Subjected to Torture and Other Cruel, Inhuman or Degrading Treatment or Punishment, 30 UN GAOR Supp (No. 34) at 91, UN Doc. A/10034 (1975); African Charter on Human and Peoples' Rights (adopted 27 June 1981, entered into force 21 October 1986) CAB/LEG/67/3 rev 5, 21 ILM 58, Article 5; Convention against Torture and Other Cruel, Inhuman or Degrading Treatment or Punishment (adopted 10 December 1984, entered into force 26 June 1987), 1465 UNTS 85, Article 14 (CAT); Arab Charter on Human Rights (adopted 22 May 22 2004, entered into force 15 March 2008) (2005)12 IHHR 893, Article 8; ASEAN Human Rights Declaration (adopted 18 November 2012), Article 14 (available at: http://www.refworld.org/docid/50c9fea82.html).

16 Peter Kooijmans, *Report of the Special Rapporteur on Torture and other Cruel, Inhumane or Degrading Treatment or Punishment*, E/CN.4/1986/15 (19 February 1986) at p 3.

17 *Obligation to Prosecute or Extradite*, *supra* note 1 at para 99.

18 Philip Allott, "Language, Method and the Nature of International Law" (1971) 45 *BYIL* 70.

19 *Filártiga*, *supra* note 1 at 890.

sympathy with the claimants, but also to convey the symbolic importance of the international proscription of torture. For example, the decision of the Quebec Court of Appeal in *Kazemi* opens with a lapidary assertion: "Torture of a human being is evil and abhorrent."[20] The Supreme Court of Canada also referred to acts of torture suffered by Zahra Kazemi as "a tragedy," "horrific," "atrocious" and "shock[ing] the conscience."[21]

These statements, however, pale in comparison with the House of Lords' positively epic characterizations of the torture prohibition at common law. In *A(FC) and Others v Secretary of State for the Home Department (No 2)*, a case on the admissibility in English courts of evidence obtained through torture, the Lords each expressed in their own words (though Lord Carswell found some inspiration in Tennyson) the nature of the common law's absolute revulsion of torture and of its poisoned fruits.[22] In a rare display of Blackstonian hubris, Lord Hoffmann described the special nature of the torture prohibition in English law as follows:

> Just as the writ of *habeas corpus* is not only a special (and nowadays infrequent) remedy for challenging unlawful detention but also carries a symbolic significance as a touchstone of English liberty which influences the rest of our law, so the rejection of torture by the common law has a special iconic importance as the touchstone of a humane and civilised legal system. Not only that: the abolition of torture, which was used by the state in Elizabethan and Jacobean times to obtain evidence admitted in trials before the court of Star Chamber, was achieved as part of the great constitutional struggle and civil war which made the government subject to the law. Its rejection has a constitutional resonance for the English people which cannot be overestimated.[23]

So it is that the torture prohibition at international and domestic law enjoys an "iconic" and "constitutional resonance."[24] It is, *in theory*, one the hallmarks of modernity and the basic expression of humanity's highest aspirations to live free from fear and violence.

Jeremy Waldron proposes that the prohibition of torture can be conceptualized as a "legal archetype," not in the Lockean or Jungian sense, but in a manner more akin to a Dworkininan principle.[25] As a legal archetype,

---

20 *Kazemi* (2012), *supra* note 10 at para 7.

21 *Kazemi* (2014), *supra* note 10 at paras 1, 3 and 95.

22 *A(FC) and Others v. Secretary of State for the Home Department (No 2)*, (2005) UKHL 71 at paras 11–12 (Lord Bingham), paras 64–65 (Lord Nicholls), para 100 (Lord Hope), para 129 (Lord Rodger), paras 146–152 (Lord Carswell).

23 Ibid at para 83 (Lord Hoffmann).

24 Ibid. Indeed, many countries have included the torture prohibition in their constitutional bill of rights. See e.g. Canadian Charter of Rights and Freedoms, section 12; Constitution of the United States of America, Eighth Amendment; Constitution of the Islamic Republic of Iran, Article 38, South African Bill of Rights, Article 12.

25 Jeremy Waldron, "Torture and Positive Law: Jurisprudence for the White House" (2005) 105 *Columbia Law Review* 1681 at 1718–1728.

the prohibition of torture operates in the background and foreground of a given legal system, alongside other positive legal rules, epitomizing a fundamental policy that is emblematic of the entire *corpus juris*. Viewed in this light, the universal stance against torture can be understood as the normative distillation of a common understanding about the very nature of the rule of law, a deeply felt intuition that law, not violence, is the surest way forward for humanity. Waldron puts it this way:

> Law is not brutal in its operation. Law is not savage. Law does not rule through abject fear and terror, or by breaking the will of those whom it confronts. If law is forceful or coercive, it gets its way by nonbrutal methods which respect rather than mutilate the dignity and agency of those who are its subjects. The idea is that even where law has to operate forcefully, there will not be the connection that has existed in other times or places between law and brutality. People may fear and be deterred by legal sanctions; they may dread lawsuits; they may even on occasion be forced by legal means or legally empowered officials to do things or go places against their will. But even when this happens, they will not be herded like cattle or broken like horses; they will not be beaten like dumb animals or treated as bodies to be manipulated. Instead, there will be an enduring connection between the spirit of law and respect for human dignity, respect for human dignity even in extremis, where law is at its most forceful and its subjects at their most vulnerable. I think the rule against torture functions as an archetype of this very general policy.

Like Lord Hoffmann, Waldron compares the iconic significance of the ban on torture to the writ of habeas corpus,[26] and also (perhaps less convincingly) to the US Constitution's Second Amendment and to groundbreaking precedents like *Brown v Board of Education* and *Donoghue v Stephenson*.[27] One might add *Marbury v Madison* and *Edwards v Canada*[28] to the list of Anglo-North American jurisprudential archetypes. As dominant features of the legal system, the effect of legal archetypes is to exert a gravitational force on every other rule, pulling them into their orbit and controlling their development. Or, to borrow Lord Hoffmann's phrasing, the torture prohibition "carries a symbolic significance … which influences the rest of our law."[29]

---

26 Ibid at pp 1724–1726.

27 *Brown v. Board of Education*, 347 US 483 (1954) (desegregating US schools and discrediting all legally sanctioned forms of racial discrimination); *Donoghue v. Stephenson* [1932] AC 562 (HL) (establishing a general principle of duty of care in the private law of negligence).

28 *Marbury v. Madison*, 5 US (Crach) 137 (1803) (establishing the judiciary's power to declare the law and interpret the constitution); *Edwards v.* Canada, (1930) AC 124 (PC) (establishing the "living tree" doctrine of constitutional interpretation for Canada and recognizing women as "persons").

29 *A(FC)*, supra note 22.

2.2. TORTURE IN PRACTICE

Noting the universal abhorrence with which torture is viewed, Judge Kaufman commented in *Filártiga* that the "prohibition of torture is often honoured in the breach."[30] Shakespearean distortion aside,[31] His Honour's point is that, despite its international condemnation, torture is routinely resorted to in every corner of the world, either to elicit statements and confessions or to punish and intimidate. Sometimes torture occurs on the zealous initiative of sadistic lower-level officials, while at other times as a result of a direct order from high-ranking superiors. As Amnesty International acknowledges, "a comprehensive and categorical statistical assessment of the global scale of torture is impossible."[32] However, between January 2009 and May 2013, the organization received "reports of torture and other ill-treatment committed by state officials in 141 countries, and from every world region," with most cases originating from countries that are party to the Convention against Torture (CAT).[33]

This paradox is exacerbated by the fact that the practice of torture is by no means limited to the dark, damp dungeons of failed states and rogue regimes. Sadly, the use of torture has become a dishonourable stain on the constitutions of democratic states that, since 11 September 2001, regularly sacrifice fundamental human rights on the altar of national security. Waldron forcefully decried the "dishonour" the United States brought upon itself in Abu Ghraib and Guantanamo, and further noted that "the use of torture has in recent decades disfigured the security polices of France (in Algeria), Britain (in Northern Ireland), Israel (in the Occupied Territories), and now the United States (in Iraq, Afghanistan, and Cuba)."[34]

---

30 *Filártiga, supra* note 1 at 884, note 15.

31 Judge Kaufman's phrase was almost certainly inspired from a passage in *Hamlet* (Act 1, Scene IV), in which the titular character laments his uncle's excessive drinking habits: "But to my mind, though I am native here, and to the manner born, it is a custom more honor'd in the breach than the observance." Hamlet means, with respect to a vile or bad custom, that it is more honourable to disregard the practice. Judge Kaufman used the sentence to mean the exact opposite, namely, that the torture prohibition is an honourable custom that is unfortunately often ignored.

32 Amnesty International, *Torture in 2014: 30 Years of Broken Promises* at p 10. Available at: https://www.amnesty.org/en/documents/ACT40/004/2014/en/.

33 Ibid.

34 Waldron, "Torture and Positive Law," *supra* note 25 at 1681, 1684. In light of the actions of its peace-keeping force in Somalia, Canada can also claim its own place in this league. For an overview of the misconduct of Canadian soldiers in Somalia and of the subsequent enquiry and proceedings, see: http://www.cbc.ca/archives/categories/war-conflict/peacekeeping/the-somalia-affair/topic-the-somalia-affair.html. Canada is also alleged to have facilitated the torture of prisoners in Afghanistan. See: http://www.theglobeandmail.com/news/politics/canada-complicit-in-torture-of-innocent-afghans-diplomat-says/article1347481.

It is a distinctively twenty-first-century phenomenon that those states that use torture also adamantly deny it[35] or, more often, attempt to legally characterize their methods as amounting to something less than torture. This phenomenon is perhaps, as Koskenniemi warned, a consequence of international human rights law's post-war descent into the mainstream of positivism.[36] By codifying the prohibition of torture in treaties and statutes, and by providing definitions of what torture *is*, we have unwittingly opened the possibility of delineating what it is *not*. Human rights treaties and statutes, including those relating to torture, are inherently vulnerable to "analytic distinctions whose one social function is the legitimation of oppressive practices through the strategy of the exception: once you define a right, you delimit it. And once you delimit it, you offer a formally valid argument for someone to deny that right."[37]

The US government's War on Terror has provided the perfect rhetorical ecosystem in which arguments defending the use of torture can emerge and flourish.[38] Notable jurists such as Professor John Yoo, then the Deputy Attorney General of the United States, advised the Bush administration that the Geneva Conventions' common Article 3 did not apply to the US military campaign against al-Qaida and the Taliban, and by extension to the treatment of its prisoners and detainees.[39] Similarly, federal Judge Jay Bybee, who served in the Office of Legal Counsel of the Department of Justice between 2001 and 2003, advised the Bush administration on the standards of conduct required under US federal laws and the CAT.[40] He concluded that only acts of an extreme nature specifically intended to inflict severe pain or suffering rise to the level of "torture" within the meaning of the CAT, and that certain acts might be cruel, inhumane and degrading, but still "not produce pain and suffering of the requisite intensity to fall within [the legal] proscription of torture."[41] Official legal opinions such as these received academic support from Harvard law professor Alan Dershowitz, who published entire books arguing that the use of non-lethal torture methods could be morally and legally justifiable to

35 "That states engage in official torture cannot be doubted ... all that engage in torture deny it": *Siderman de Blake v. Republic of Argentina*, 965 F2d 699 at 717 (9th Cir 1992).

36 Martti Kosekenniemi, "'The Pull of the Mainstream': Book Review of *Human Rights and Humanitarian Law as Customary Norms* by Theodore Meron" (1990) 88(6) *Mich L Rev* 1946.

37 Ibid at 1962.

38 Karen Greenberg and Joshua Datel (eds), *The Torture Papers: The Road to Abu Ghraib* (Cambridge: Cambridge University Press, 2005); Karen Greenberg, *The Torture Debate in America* (Cambridge: Cambridge University Press, 2006).

39 Memorandum from John Yoo, Deputy Assistant Attorney General, and Robert J Delahunty, Special Counsel, to William J. Haynes II, General Counsel, Department of Defense 1 (9 January 2002).

40 Memorandum from Jay S Bybee, Assistant Attorney General, Office of Legal Counsel, to Alberto R. Gonzales, Counsel to the President, Regarding Standards of Conduct for Interrogation under 18 USC §§2340–2340A (1 August 2002) (on file with author).

41 Ibid at p 1.

extract information from so-called "ticking bomb terrorists" in order to save lives.[42] Dershowitz further advised that the use of torture in such circumstances should be authorized by emergency court order,[43] a proposal that essentially revives the torture warrants that were historically obtained under the Crown prerogative in proceedings of the Star Chamber.[44] The last torture warrant in English legal history was issued in 1640.[45]

With respect to torture, ours is a time of great hypocrisy. Our theory of torture is not reflected in our practices. Our deeds do not match our declarations. We affect a false appearance of virtue, denouncing and banning torture in absolute terms, while dissimulating an authentic propensity to use it when it is convenient or believed to be necessary. It is a monumental failing, one that can perhaps be fatalistically forgiven on account that we are (all too) human. To paraphrase Romans, we know the law to be good, but we are unable to carry it out. We do not do the good we want, but the evil we do not want is what we keep doing.[46] In our darkest hour, we try to convince ourselves, like Yoo, Bybee and Dershowitz, that torture is the virtuous thing to do, espousing for duration of the argument, a near-sighted and exclusionary view of the collective good. One or dozens must suffer, we rationalize, so that thousands may live. Perhaps a more generous assessment is that humanity is hypocritical with respect to torture in the etymological sense of the word.[47] Perhaps, according to this more generous view, it is not that we are incapable of not resorting to torture, even in times of perceived urgency, but simply that we have not yet decided to live up to our own ideals. This possibility will be discussed further in the final section of this chapter.

3. JURISDICTION AND EXTRATERRITORIAL TORTURE

This section will examine an important inconsistency that persists with respect to jurisdiction and extraterritorial torture. It will be argued that in this area,

42 See Alan M Dershowitz, *Why Terrorism Works: Understanding the Threat, Responding to the Challenge* (New Haven: Yale University Press, 2002) at pp 132–164; Alan M Dershowitz, *Shouting Fire: Civil Liberties in a Turbulent Age* (Boston: Little, Brown & Co, 2002) at p 470. See *contra* François Larocque, "The Choice of Torture", *The Lawyer's Weekly* (2 May 2003) at p 4.

43 Dershowitz, *Why Terrorism Works*, *ibid.*

44 Sir William Holdsworth, *A History of English Law*, vol 5, 3rd edn (London, Sweet & Maxwell, 1945) at pp 194–195. See also David Hope, "Torture" (2004) 53 *ICLQ* 807 at 810–811; John H Langbein, *Torture and the Law of Proof* (Chicago, University of Chicago Press, 1977) at pp 3–69; AL Lowell, "The Judicial Use of Torture" (1897) 11 *Harv L Rev* 220 at 233, 290–300.

45 *A(FC), supra* note 22 at para 12 (Lord Bingham). See also para 64 (Lord Nicholls), para 83 (Lord Hoffmann), para 147 (Lord Carswell) and para 160 (Lord Brown).

46 Romans 7:14–19.

47 The literal meaning of the Greek ὑπόκρισις is to *under* (hypo) + *decide, determine, judge* (crisis). See "hypocrisy," *OED Online*. Oxford University Press, March 2014.

too, international legal theories and practices needlessly diverge, leading to unsatisfactory results.

3.1. IN THEORY

Jurisdiction generally refers to the authority of the state to make and apply law within its own territory.[48] However, when torture survivors and victims' families initiate proceedings in the civil courts of one country with respect to acts of torture that occurred in another country, they are in effect asking the forum court to extend their jurisdiction to matters and persons situated outside their *prima facie* sphere of power. The appropriateness of such extraterritorial jurisdiction therefore arises.

In criminal matters, it is well established since *The Lotus* case that international law imposes very few restrictions on the exercise of extraterritorial jurisdiction.[49] Save for the clear interdiction on the exercise of state power within the boundaries of another state without the latter's consent,[50] each state may, as a function of its sovereignty, extend its criminal laws to extraterritorial matters or persons and based on a variety of rationales. Most international law textbooks identify five permissive principles under which states assert extraterritorial jurisdiction in criminal law matters.[51]

> These five general principles are: first, the *territorial principle*, determining jurisdiction by reference to the place where the offence is committed; second, the *nationality principle*, determining jurisdiction by reference to the nationality or national character of the person committing the offence; third, the *protective principle*, determining jurisdiction by the national interest injured by the offence; fourth, the *universality principle*, determining jurisdiction by the custody of the person committing the offence; and fifth, the *passive personality principle*, determining

48 Michael Akehurst, "Jurisdiction in International Law" (1972) 46 *BYIL* 146; Derek W Bowett, "Jurisdiction: Changing Patterns of Authority over Activities and Resources" (1983) 53 *BYIL* 26; Ian Brownlie, *Principles of Public International Law*, 6th edn(Oxford: Oxford University Press, 2003) at p 297; Michael Byers, *Custom, Power and the Powers of Rules: International Relations and Customary International Law* (Cambridge: Cambridge University Press, 1999) at p 53; Patrick Capps, Malcolm Evans and Stratos Konstadinidis (eds), *Asserting Jurisdiction: International and European Legal Perspectives* (Oxford: Hart, 2003) at p xix; *Harvard Research on Jurisdiction with Respect to Crime*, Edwin Dickinson (Rapp) (1935) 29 *AJIL Supp* 429 at pp 467–632; Vaughan Lowe, "Jurisdiction" in Malcolm Evans (ed), *International Law* (Oxford: Oxford University Press, 2003) at p 336; Robert Jennings and Andrew Wattas (eds), *Oppenheim's International Law*, 9th edn (London: Longman, 1992) at p 456.

49 *The SS Lotus* (1927) PCIJ, Series A, No 10 at p 18.

50 Ibid at p 19; *R v. Hape*, (2007) 2 SCR 292 at para 60.

51 Akehurst, *supra* note 48 at pp 152–169; Brownlie, *supra* note 48 at Chapter 15; Lowe, *supra* note 48 at pp 336–343; Antonio Cassese, *International Criminal Law* (Oxford: Oxford University Press, 2003) at Chapter 15; Malcolm Shaw, *International Law* (Cambridge: Cambridge University Press, 2003) at Chapter 12.

jurisdiction by reference to the nationality or national character of the person injured by the offence.[52]

The various principles of extraterritorial criminal jurisdiction form part of international law as "general principles of law recognized by civilized nations."[53] They are both normative and descriptive principles. They are normative in the sense that they permit the use of extraterritorial jurisdiction in appropriate circumstances.[54] They are descriptive in the sense that each principle represents an acceptable justification for the assertion of jurisdiction over foreign nationals in criminal matters, such that they can be taken as "evidence of the reasonableness of the exercise of jurisdiction."[55]

Since the coming into force of the CAT,[56] criminal jurisdiction over acts of extraterritorial torture is generally underwritten by the universality principle, though some have argued that international law permitted universal jurisdiction with respect to torture well before 1988.[57] Other jurisdictional grounds – such as nationality or passive personality – might also come into play depending on the particular facts of a given case. The great innovation of the CAT is that it *obligates* States Parties to exercise universal jurisdiction over any alleged torturer that is present on their territory.[58] The CAT also requires States Parties to investigate and punish acts of torture occurring on their territory (the territoriality principle) and at the hands of their own nationals (the nationality principle).[59] By contrast, the CAT merely *allows* a State Party ("if that State considers it appropriate") to assert jurisdiction in matters where the torture victim is a national (passive personality).[60]

Extraterritorial civil jurisdiction in international law is not nearly as well theorized as in the criminal sphere. This discrepancy is puzzling because, in general, international law views civil and criminal exercises of extraterritorial jurisdiction in the same light, since both types of adjudication amount in substance to the exercise of state power. As Brownlie put it, "there is in principle no great difference between the problems created by the assertion of civil and criminal jurisdiction over aliens."[61] Similarly, according to Jessup: "From the

---

52 *Harvard Research*, *supra* note 48 at pp 444–445.

53 United Nations, Statute of the International Court of Justice, 18 April 1946, Article 38(1)c); *Harvard Research*, *supra* note 48.

54 *Harvard Research*, *supra* note 48 at pp 444–445; *The Lotus*, *supra* note 49 at p 20.

55 Brownlie, *supra* note 48 at p 305.

56 CAT, *supra* note 15.

57 Most notably Lord Millett in *R v. Bow Street Metropolitan Stipendiary Magistrate and Others, Ex parte Pinochet Ugarte (No 3)* (2000) 1 AC 147 at p 276 (HL) (hereinafter *Pinochet No 3*).

58 CAT, *supra* note 15, Article 5§2.

59 Ibid, Article 5§1(a) and (b).

60 Ibid, Article 5§1(c).

61 Brownlie, above note 48 at 298; Francis A Mann, "The Doctrine of Jurisdiction in International Law" (1964-I) 111 *RC* 1 at pp 43–51; Luc Reydams, *Universal Jurisdiction: International and*

standpoint of considering transnational law there seems to be little reason for attempting to distinguish between civil and criminal cases in determining jurisdiction."[62]

International law is certainly not indifferent to the exercise of extraterritorial jurisdiction in civil proceedings. For instance, there is widespread consensus that extraterritorial civil jurisdiction should only be asserted where the defendant attorns to the forum or where there is a meaningful nexus between the forum and the claim.[63] The relevant connecting factors are fundamentally territorial in nature, and include the convenience of the parties having regard to their place of domicile, the location of the evidence and of witnesses, and, crucially, the place where the wrongful acts took place. Clearly, in the context of civil proceedings for extraterritorial acts of torture, the assessment of such factors, in the vast majority of cases, will lead to the conclusion that the foreign country where the torture occurred is the most natural forum. As the Human Rights Committee of the International Law Association British Branch observed, in such cases, "the forum with which the action has its closest and most real connection is the forum in which the acts complained of ... took place. The relevant witnesses will (usually) be there; relevant documents (if any) will be there; and the governing law will almost certainly (applying English choice of law rules) be the law of the foreign forum."[64] Accordingly, a flexible approach is needed in civil proceedings for extraterritorial torture, an approach that takes into account and gives appropriate weight to the particular subject matter of the proceedings and that does not insist on direct territorial connections in cases where none could ever exist.

Two related principles are emerging as viable alternatives to the traditional real and substantial connection requirement and could supply an appropriate jurisdictional basis in civil proceedings with respect to extraterritorial torture: the principles of necessity and universality.

3.1.1. *Forum of Necessity Jurisdiction*

Under the doctrine of forum of necessity, civil courts enjoy a residual discretion to assert personal jurisdiction over a defendant in exceptional circumstances,

---

Municipal Legal Perspectives (Oxford: Oxford University Press, 2003) at pp 2–3. But see Akehurst, *supra* note 48 at p 170.

62 Philip Jessup, *Transnational Law* (New Haven: Yale University Press, 1956) at p 64.

63 Council Regulation (EC) No 44/2001 of 22 December 2000 on jurisdiction and the recognition and enforcement of judgments in civil and commercial matters (OJ L 12 of 16 January 2001); *Spiliada Maritime Corp v. Cansulex Ltd* (1987) AC 460 (HL); *Club Resorts Ltd v. Van Breda*, 2012 SCC 17; Lowe, *supra* note 48 at p 336; Brownlie, *supra* note 48 at p 297.

64 International Law Association, Committee on International Human Rights Law and Practice, "Report on Civil Actions in the English Courts for Serious Human Rights Violations Abroad" (2001) 2 *EHRLR* 129 at p 146.

even in the absence of meaningful territorial connections between the claim and the forum. The objective of forum of necessity jurisdiction is to provide plaintiffs with access to a court in circumstances where it is impossible or unreasonable to expect them to commence proceedings elsewhere. It ensures access to justice in cases where it would otherwise be denied.

The idea of forum of necessity apparently first appeared in Switzerland with the adoption of the *Loi fédérale du 18 décembre 1987 sur le droit international privé* ("Swiss Act")[65] and it has since been adopted by other countries, such as Canada.[66] During the drafting of the Swiss Act, Professor Frank Vischer, one of the statute's principal authors, described the underlying policy objective of the doctrine as follows:

> A general forum of necessity in Switzerland is offered to foreigners when the absence of this forum has a totally inappropriate effect for the claimant, in the sense of an international denial of justice. The grant of this forum of necessity must be applied in a restrictive way, but its availability stems from the fact that there may always be situations not foreseen by the legislator making it absolutely imperative to provide access to our courts.[67]

In a subsequent commentary, Professor Vischer further emphasized that the doctrine's main international legal function was to prevent denials of justice by providing plaintiffs with access to national courts:

> The negative conflict can lead to a "déni de justice" for the claimant, if he cannot obtain jurisdiction on the grounds that no State considers its courts competent. It is generally recognized that public international law demands that States should take the necessary precautions to provide respective jurisdiction or order to avoid denial of justice. The European Convention on Human Rights even confers on the prohibition of denial of justice the quality of being a human right (Art. 6§1).[68]

However, as will be discussed below, the right to access a court of law for the determination of one's rights – even fundamental rights such as the right to

---

65 *Loi fédérale du 18 décembre 1987 sur le droit international privé*, RS 291, s 3 ("3. *Lorsque la présente loi ne prévoit aucun for en Suisse et qu'une procédure à l'étranger se révèle impossible ou qu'on ne peut raisonnablement exiger qu'elle y soit introduite, les autorités judiciaires ou administratives suisses du lieu avec lequel la cause présente un lien suffisant sont compétentes.*") (hereinafter "Swiss Act").

66 Quebec Civil Code, SQ 1991, c 64, Article 3136; Court Jurisdiction and Proceedings Transfer Act, SBC 2003, c 28, s 6; Court Jurisdiction and Proceedings Transfer Act, SNS 2003, c 2, s 7; *Van Breda v. Village Resorts Ltd* (2010), 98 OR (3rd) 721, 2010 ONCA 84 at para 100 (recognizing forum of necessity jurisdiction at common law).

67 Frank Vischer, "Drafting National Legislation on Conflict of Laws: The Swiss Experience" (1977) 41 *L & Contemp Prob* 131 at p 136.

68 Frank Vischer, "General Course on Private International Law" (1992) 232 *RC* 9 at p 204.

remedy in cases of torture – is ultimately weighed against other concerns and considerations, such as international relations and immunities.[69]

While the outer limits of forum of necessity jurisdiction remain to be established, it is nevertheless possible to identify a range of cases in which its use is clearly appropriate. These include tort claims relating to egregious human rights violations instituted by plaintiffs who cannot return to the forum where the harm occurred without risking their lives or further injury. The Court of Appeal for Ontario pointed to the doctrine of forum of necessity "as a possible basis for jurisdiction" in cases relating to extraterritorial torture, such as *Bouzari v Islamic Republic of Iran*.[70] Torture victims and their families are often unable to seek civil redress in the countries where the abuse occurred because they would be at risk of violence or death, or because the judicial systems in those countries are unable or unwilling to process their claims. In these exceptional situations, commencing proceedings in the place where the violations took place is either a practical impossibility or an unreasonable expectation to place upon the plaintiff, or both.

In *Lamborghini*, the Quebec Court of Appeal held that the forum of necessity provision of the Quebec Civil Code applies to situations where proceedings cannot be commenced in the natural forum due to perilous circumstances for the plaintiffs:

> [L'article 3136] veut régler certains problèmes d'accès à la justice, pour un plaideur qui se trouve dans le territoire québécois, lorsque le forum étranger normalement compétent lui est inaccessible pour des raisons exceptionnelles, comme une impossibilité en droit ou une impossibilité pratique, presqu'absolue. Ainsi, on peut penser à celles résultant de la rupture des relations diplomatiques ou commerciales avec un État étranger ou de la nécessité de la protection d'un réfugié politique, ou à l'existence d'un danger physique sérieux, si l'on entame un débat devant le tribunal étranger.[71]

While less-than-perilous circumstances may also justify the assertion of jurisdiction on the basis of necessity, the doctrine clearly applies in cases where survivors of human rights violations cannot sue in the place where the harm occurred without risk to life or limb. Indeed, the entire body of international human rights law, and particularly those conventional and customary norms that have attained the status of *jus cogens*, such as the prohibition against torture, would be made illusory if there were no court available to apply that law.

---

69 See below notes 110–119 and accompanying text.

70 *Van Breda, supra* note 66 at para 54.

71 *Lamborghini (Canada) Inc v. Automobili Lamborghini SPA* [1996] QJ No 4175 at para 44 (CA). See also *Josephson (Litigation Guardian of) v. Balfour Recreation Commission*, 2010 BCSC 603 at para 89 for an unofficial English translation of the salient passages of *Lamborghini*.

3.1.2. *Universal Civil Jurisdiction and Extraterritorial Torture*

The other emerging principle that is relevant to the present discussion is universal civil jurisdiction. While such a principle does not yet form part of the mainstream, it has generated an increasing amount of commentary from courts[72] and scholars.[73]

From the outset, it is important to define what is meant by "universal jurisdiction" in order to avoid any misconceptions as to the scope of its underlying principle. For the purposes of the present discussion, universal jurisdiction is understood as the presence-based adjudicative authority of a state over persons who are alleged to have committed international crimes.[74] As Judges Higgins, Kooijmans and Buergenthal noted in the *Arrest Warrant* case, what by "the loose use of language … has come to be referred to as 'universal jurisdiction' … is really an obligatory territorial jurisdiction over persons, albeit in relation to acts committed elsewhere."[75] To be sure, universal jurisdiction does not refer to unlimited judicial power over extraterritorial events and persons on the basis, for instance, that the wrongful conduct at issue is prohibited by a peremptory norm of international law. Aside from the discredited Belgian statute that purported to authorize *in absentia* jurisdiction over extraterritorial persons and grave violations of international humanitarian law,[76] there is little practice in support of so-called "pure"[77] universal adjudicative jurisdiction. In cases where it applies, for example on the basis of a treaty such as the CAT, the exercise of universal jurisdiction by national courts requires some link to the forum, usually in the form of the offender/defendant's presence in the territory.[78]

72 *Arrest Warrant of 11 April 2000 (Congo v. Belgium)*, ICJ Reports 2002 at p 79, Separate Concurring Opinion of Judges Higgins, Kooijmans and Buergenthal at para 48 (hereinafter "*Arrest Warrant* case"); *Sosa, supra* note 5 at p 772; *Xuncax v. Gramajo*, 886 F Supp 162 at p 182 (D Mass 1995).

73 See *supra* note 9.

74 Antonio Cassese, "Is the Bell Tolling for Universality? A Plea for a Sensible Notion of Universal Jurisdiction" (2003) 1 *JICJ* 589; Roger O'Keefe, "Universal Jurisdiction: Clarifying the Basic Concept" (2004) 2 *JICJ* 735.

75 *Arrest Warrant* case, *supra* note 72, Separate Concurring Opinion of Judges Higgins, Kooijmans and Buergenthal at para 41.

76 See *Loi du 16 juin 1993 relative à la répression des infractions graves aux Conventions internationales de Genève du 12 août 1949 et aux Protocoles I et 11 du 8 juin 1977, additionnels à ces Conventions*, replaced by *Loi du 10 février 1999 relative à la répression des violations graves du droit international humanitaire*, 38 ILM 918 (1999), amended by *Loi modifiant la loi du 16 juin 1993 relative 6 la répression des violations graves du droit international humanitaire et l'article 144e du Code judiciaire* (23 April 2003), 42 ILM 749 (2003) replaced by *Loi relative à la répression des violations graves du droit international humanitaire* (5 August 2003), 42 ILM 1258 (2003).

77 *Arrest Warrant* case, *supra* note 72, Separate Concurring Opinion of Judges Higgins, Kooijmans and Buergenthal at para 45.

78 Institut de droit international, *Universal Criminal Jurisdiction with Regard to the Crime of Genocide, Crimes against Humanity and War Crimes*, Rapp: Christian Tomuschat,

As Lowe observed, there appears to be two "strands" of conduct that give rise to universal jurisdiction. The first consists of "heinous crimes, such as genocide, crimes against humanity and serious war crimes."[79] It is the particularly egregious nature of the acts that justifies the exercise of universal jurisdiction. The second strand includes serious wrongs for which no redress or legal sanction is likely to be available, owing to the particular circumstances surrounding their perpetration.[80] Piracy and aircraft hijacking are said to fall in this category because they are committed outside the territorial jurisdiction of all states and can potentially involve the nationals of any state.[81] Systemic or social circumstances, such as wartime, civil unrest and governmental corruption, may also conspire to make redress or justice impossible and validate the exercise of universal jurisdiction.[82] Aside from piracy, international law recognizes the use of universal jurisdiction in criminal proceedings for torture,[83] genocide, war crimes and crimes against humanity.[84] Generally, universal jurisdiction appears to attach to crimes that have achieved the status of peremptory norms of international law (*jus cogens*). This comports with an understanding of peremptory norms as coextensive with and protective of world public order and of international security interests, the underlying rationale of universal jurisdiction.[85]

The various rationales that form the basis for universal criminal jurisdiction arguably produce equally credible and persuasive arguments in support of universal jurisdiction in civil proceedings. The justifications put forth in support of universal civil jurisdiction tend to follow two distinct yet interrelated lines of arguments. The first line addresses the international legal plausibility of universal civil jurisdiction. For instance, the American Law Institute adopts the view, predicated on *The Lotus* case, that universal civil jurisdiction is permissible in international law insofar as it is not prohibited: "In general,

17th Commission, Warsaw Session, 2005, Article 3b. For a useful summary of national practice, see UN Secretary-General, *The Scope and Application of the Principle of Universal Jurisdiction*, Report of the Secretary-General prepared on the basis of comments and observations of governments, UN GAOR, 65th Sess, UN Doc. A/65/181 (29 July 2010). See also *Ould Dah, supra* note 5 at p 894.

79 Lowe, *supra* note 48 at p 343; EC Brief in *Sosa*, *supra* note 9 at p 15.

80 Lowe, *supra* note 48.

81 But see *Kiobel*, *supra* note 5 at p 1672–1675, where Breyer J observes that piracy unavoidably involves the boarding of a ship at sea which "falls within the [territorial] jurisdiction of the nation whose flag it flies."

82 *United States v. Yousef*, 327 F3d 56 at p 105 (2d Cir 2003); Willard B Cowles, "Universality of Jurisdiction over War Crimes" (1945) 33 *Cal L Rev* 177 at p 194.

83 *Supra* notes 56–57 and accompanying text.

84 Rome Statute of the International Criminal Court, 17 July 1998, UN Doc. A/CONF183/9, 2187 UNTS 90.

85 Alexander Orakhelashvili, "State Immunity and International Public Order" (2002) 45 *GYIL* 227 at p 255; see also generally, Alexander Orakhelashvili, *Peremptory Norms in International Law* (Oxford: Oxford University Press, 2006).

jurisdiction on the basis of universal interests has been exercised in the form of criminal law, but international law does not preclude the application of non-criminal law on this basis, for example, by providing a remedy in tort or restitutions for victims of piracy."[86] The second line of argument addresses the broad structural differences and commonalties between criminal punishment and civil redress. One such argument was put forth by Reydams, for whom universal civil jurisdiction logically follows from its relevance in criminal matters. Because civil jurisdiction is considered less intrusive, he argued, it ought to apply *mutatis mutandis* in the same manner as criminal jurisdiction: "The presumption is that if universal criminal jurisdiction is permissible under international law, universal civil jurisdiction is also permissible (*qui peut le plus peut le moins*, the greater includes the lesser)."[87]

The distinguished editors of the 9th edition of *Oppenheim's International Law* cite *Filártiga*[88] and point to the Alien Tort Statute (ATS)[89] in support of the proposition that serious violations of human rights, such as torture, are subject to universal civil jurisdiction.[90] While the jurisdiction exercised under the ATS has been unquestionably far-reaching,[91] there is reason to question whether the ATS is in fact predicated solely on the principle of universality. In their concurring opinion in the *Arrest Warrant* case, Judges Higgins, Kooijmans and Buergenthal described the ATS as "the beginnings of a very broad form of extraterritorial jurisdiction."[92] The judges stopped short of characterizing the ATS as granting universal jurisdiction and noted moreover that the US model had "not attracted the approbation of States generally."[93] Indeed, the international response to ATS jurisdiction has been variegated.[94]

86 *Restatement of the Law (3d) of Foreign Relations Law of the United States* (St. Paul, Minn., ALI Publishers, 1988) at §404 cmt. b.

87 Reydams, *supra* note 61 at pp 2–3. See, *contra*, Sir Franklin Berman, "Jurisdiction: The State" in Capps et al, *Asserting Jurisdiction, supra* note 48 at p 13.

88 See *supra* note 1.

89 *Supra* note 3.

90 Sir Robert Jennings and Arthur Watts (eds), *Oppenheim's International Law*, 9th edn (London: Longman, 1992) at pp 469–470.

91 Larocque, *Civil Actions for Uncivilized Acts, supra* note 6, c 2.

92 *Arrest Warrant of 11 April 2000 (Congo v. Belgium)*, ICJ Reports 2002, 79, Separate Concurring Opinion of Judges Higgins, Kooijmans and Buergenthal at §48.

93 Ibid.

94 For example, Ecuador initially approved of the ATS proceedings in *Aguinda v. Texaco Inc*, 1994 US Dist LEXIS 4718 (SDNY 1994), then later protested in *Jota v. Texaco*, 157 F3d 153 (2d Cir 1998). Similarly, South Africa protested against US civil jurisdiction in *In Re South African Apartheid Litigation*, 238 F Supp 2d 1379 (SDNY 2002), but supported broad-based, justice-oriented civil jurisdiction in *Connelly v. RTZ Corporation plc* (1998) AC 854 (HL) and *Lubbe v. Cape plc* (2000) 1 WLR 1545 (HL). See also *Doe v. Exxon Mobile Corp*, 654 F3d 11 at p 64, note 56 (CADC) for a list of foreign states that approved and later objected to ATS jurisdiction.

Moreover, in *Kiobel*, the US Supreme Court held that claims brought under the ATS were subject to the presumption against extraterritoriality.[95] Under US law, it is presumed that "legislation of Congress, unless a contrary intent appears, is meant to apply only within the territorial jurisdiction of the United States."[96] Accordingly, plaintiffs who wish to sue in the US under the ATS must, since *Kiobel*, show that their "claims touch and concern the territory of the United States, [and] do so with sufficient force to displace the presumption against extraterritorial application."[97] While the Court was unanimous as to the disposition in *Kiobel* – i.e. that no jurisdiction lied under the ATS in that specific case where the corporate defendant had weak ties to the United States – the judges diverged (5–4) on the usefulness of the presumption against extraterritoriality. Rather than invoking the presumption, Justice Breyer would have limited ATS jurisdiction to cases where "(1) the alleged tort occurs on American soil, (2) the defendant is an American national, or (3) the defendant's conduct substantially and adversely affects an important American national interest, and that includes a distinct interest in preventing the United States from becoming a safe harbor (free of civil as well as criminal liability) for a torturer or other common enemy of mankind."[98] Arguably, there is no great difference between the majority's "touch and concern" standard and the minority's reliance on established principles of so-called "foreign relations law," as both approaches ultimately hinge on showing some kind of nexus between ATS claims and the forum. In short, after *Kiobel*, ATS jurisdiction can no longer be touted as being universal (if it ever was). Rather more reasonably, ATS jurisdiction over extraterritorial violations of international law depends on the existence of meaningful connections between the claim and the territory of the United States. In this sense, the post-*Kiobel* ATS is more aligned with the generally accepted practice and principles that govern the exercise of extraterritorial civil jurisdiction.[99]

In *Sosa*, the European Commission argued that the ATS could defensibly be interpreted as providing for a type of universal civil jurisdiction over a limited set of offences, which included torture, but only if it is exercised consistently

95 For analysis of *Kiobel* and its significance, see Austen Parrish, "Kiobel, Unilateralism and Retreat from Extraterritoriality" (2013) 28 *Maryland J Int'l L* 208; Jordan J Paust, "Human Rights through the ATS after *Kiobel*: Partial Extraterritoriality, Misconceptions and Elusive and Problematic Judicially-Created Criteria" (2014) 6 *Duke Forum for Law and Social Change* 31; Anthony Colangelo, "*Kiobel*: Muddling the Distinction between Prescriptive and Adjudicative Jurisdiction" (2013) 28 *Maryland J Int'l L* 62.

96 *Morrison v. National Australian Bank Ltd* (2010), 130 S Ct 2869 at p 2877; *EEOC v. Arabian American Oil Co*, 499 US 244 at p 248 (1991). See also William S Dodge, "Understanding the Presumption against Extraterritoriality" (1998) 16 *Berkley J Int'l L* 85.

97 *Kiobel, supra* note 5 at p 1669 (Roberts CJ).

98 Ibid at p 1671 (Breyer J).

99 Eugene Kontorovich, "*Kiobel* Surprise: Unexpected by Scholars But Consistent with International Trends" (2014) 89 *Notre Dame L Rev* 1671.

with international law and only when the ends of justice so require. The European Commission argued that "to the extent recognized, [universal civil jurisdiction] should apply only to a narrow category of conduct and should be exercised only when the claimant would otherwise be subject to a denial of justice."[100] Under this view, universal civil jurisdiction could serve a similar function to the doctrine of forum of necessity: while the former is predicated on the importance of enforcing a specific category of international norms, the latter is focused preventing denials of justice in analogous cases. European support for a cautious, justice-oriented version of universal civil jurisdiction is not surprising given Europe's leading role in the work of the Hague Conference on Private International Law, where a version of universal civil jurisdiction was once on the agenda. In its *Preliminary Draft Convention on Jurisdiction and Foreign Judgments in Civil and Commercial Matters*, the Conference had proposed the right of states to assert broad extraterritorial civil jurisdiction over a core category of violations of international law, subject to the ability of forum to properly assert personal jurisdiction over the defendant.[101] This proposal ultimately proved too contentious and was eventually set aside,[102] but the favoured approach was in line with the European Commission's submissions in *Sosa*, namely, that universal jurisdiction should be exercised in respect of violations of peremptory norms of international law, in circumstances where the claimant faces the prospect of being denied justice and the claim presented a sufficient nexus to the forum.

The availability of monetary damages in certain countries in the context of criminal prosecutions further supports the recognition of universal civil jurisdiction. Indeed, in many civil law countries, victims of crime are permitted to join criminal proceedings as a "partie civile" and obtain damages as part of the court's sentence.[103] In his concurrent opinion in *Sosa*, Justice Breyer explained the significance of such remedies in relation to universal civil jurisdiction:

> The fact this procedural consensus exists [viz. a consensus that "universal jurisdiction exists to prosecute a subset" of certain universally condemned behaviour which

---

100 EC brief in *Sosa, supra* note 9 at pp 26–27.

101 Hague Conference on Private International Law, *Preliminary Draft Convention on Jurisdiction and Foreign Judgments in Civil and Commercial Matters* (30 October 1999) Preliminary Document No 11. For analysis of the drafting history of the preliminary draft convention, see Beth Van Schaack, "In Defense of Civil Redress: The Domestic Enforcement of Human Rights Norms in the Context of Proposed Hague Judgments Convention" (2001) 42 *Harv J Int'l L*.141.

102 Donovan and Roberts, *supra* note 73 at p 151–152.

103 Such civil actions are possible in Austria, Belgium, Denmark, Finland, France, Germany, Greece, Italy, Luxembourg, the Netherlands, Portugal, Spain and Sweden. EC Brief in *Sosa*, above note 9 at n.48; Van Schaack, *supra* note 101 at p 143. Canadian courts can also award damages upon sentencing in certain circumstances: Canadian Criminal Code, RSC 1985, c C-48, s 738.

> includes torture] suggests that recognition of universal jurisdiction in respect of a limited set of norms is consistent with principles of international comity. That is, allowing every nation's courts to adjudicate foreign conduct involving foreign parties in such cases will not significantly threaten the practical harmony that comity principles seek to protect. That consensus concerns criminal jurisdiction, but consensus as to universal criminal jurisdiction itself suggests that universal tort jurisdiction would be no more threatening. Cf. Restatement para. 404, Comment b. That is because the criminal courts of many nations combine civil and criminal proceedings, allowing those injured by criminal conduct to be represented and to recover damages in the criminal proceedings itself.[104]

The fact that certain states allow the award of damages under their laws in relation to crimes, including crimes of universal competence, lends credence to the proposition that civil jurisdiction over the same wrongful conduct does not require a huge leap of faith. While the criminal sentence that orders the offender to pay compensation or make restitution is not the same as an award for damages at the outcome of a civil trial, this overlap of remedies reflects the broader point, made by the European Commission in *Sosa*, that "criminal punishment and civil liability operate with different intensity to vindicate important standards of conduct and deter future wrongdoing."[105]

3.2. IN PRACTICE

The assertion of adjudicative jurisdiction by national courts over foreign nationals with respect to extraterritorial violations of peremptory norms of international law is a relatively new phenomenon. Starting in the second half of the twentieth century, a handful of *causes célèbres* stand out.[106] The coming into force of the Rome Statute and the establishment of the International Criminal Court (ICC) – which operates on the basis of complementarity[107] – have

104 *Sosa, supra* note 5 at p 762 (Breyer J). See also *Kiobel, supra* note 5 at p 1676, where Breyer J echoes this point. See also *Prosecutor v. Furundzija* ICTY IT-95–17/1-T (10 December 1998) at para 155, raising the possibility of initiating civil proceedings for crimes of universal competence.

105 EC Brief in *Sosa, supra* note 9 at 22.

106 *Israel (AG) v. Adolf Eichmann* (1961), 36 ILR 5 (Israel Dst Ct), confirmed by (1962) 36 ILR 277 (Israel Sup Ct); *R v. Finta*, (1994) 1 SCR 701; *Pinochet No 3, supra* note 57.

107 Rome Statute of the International Criminal Court (17 July 1998) UN Doc. A/CONF.183/9, 2187 UNTS 90 (*Rome Statute*). Under the Rome Statute, national courts have primary jurisdiction over international crimes (Preamble, Article 1). The ICC has complementary jurisdiction and may only exercise it if national courts are unwilling or unable to carry out criminal investigations and prosecutions. The subsidiary nature of the ICC's jurisdiction rests on two rationales. First, to avoid inundating the ICC with cases from all over the world, it was decided that states should have the first opportunity to prosecute international criminals, given that it is in fact their duty to do so. Second, the ICC's complementary jurisdiction

given rise to a further handful of national prosecutions for core crimes.[108]

The idea of civil jurisdiction over non-nationals with respect to extraterritorial violations of international law is still in its early phase of development and, for the moment, is mostly limited to the United States.[109] Even though the First US Congress enacted the ATS in 1789,[110] lawsuits for extraterritorial human rights violations did not begin until after the groundbreaking decision in *Filártiga* in 1980. Outside of the United States, tort claims for extraterritorial human rights violations remain few and far between.[111]

Despite there being, according to Brownlie, "no great difference between the problems created by the assertion of civil and criminal jurisdiction over aliens,"[112] the guarded treatment that civil claims for extraterritorial human rights violations continue to receive suggests that – at least in the minds of

---

is respectful of each state's sovereignty. If a state is willing and able to conduct a fair trial under one of the usual jurisdictional grounds (e.g. territoriality, nationality or universality), the ICC should not usurp that state's jurisdiction in a given case. In short, complementarity is about deference to a given state's power and duty to put its national laws and judicial system to the service of the international community by prosecuting and punishing acts that threaten world public order. See also Antonio Cassese et al, *The Rome Statute of the International Criminal Court: A Commentary* (Oxford: Oxford University Press, 2002), Chapter 18.1; Jann K. Kleffner, *Complementarity in the Rome Statute and National Criminal Jurisdictions* (Oxford: Oxford University Press, 2008) at c. 6.

108 See, for example, *R v. Munyaneza*, 2009 QCSC 2201 confirmed by 2014 QCCA 96 (accused found guilty in Canada of genocide, crimes against humanity and war crimes committed in Rwanda); *General Prosecutor v. François Bazaramba*, Eastern Uusimaa District Court, 11 June 2010, confirmed by Helsinki Court of Appeal, 30 March 2012 (accused found guilty in Finland of genocide committed in Rwanda); *Public Prosecutor v. Sadi Budingo*, Oslo District Court, 14 February 2013, confirmed by Norwegian Borgarting Court of Appeal, 16 January 2015 (accused found guilty in Norway for genocide committed in Rwanda); *Prosecutor v. Onesphore Rwabukombe, Oberlandesgericht*, Frankfurt am Main, 18 February 2014 (accused found guilty in Germany for genocide committed in Rwandan); *Affaire Pascal Simbikangwa*, Cour d'Assise de Paris, 14 March 2014 (accused found guilty in France of crimes against humanity and genocide in Rwanda). See also *Affaire Ely Ould Dah*, Cour d'Assise du Gard, 1 July 2005 (on the basis of the CAT and national universal jurisdiction legislation, the accused was found guilty *in absentia* in France of torture committed in Mauritania). For a survey of slightly less recent European activity in this area, see Wolfgang Kaleck, "From Pinochet to Rumsfeld: Universal Jurisdiction in Europe 1998–2008" (2009) 30 *Mich J Int'l L* 937.

109 See generally Stevens, *supra* note 4.

110 William Casto, "The Federal Court's Protective Jurisdiction over Torts Committed in Violation of the Law of Nations" (1986) 18 *Conn L Rev* 467; Anne-Marie Burley, "The Alien Tort Statute and the Judiciary Act of 1789: A Badge of Honor" (1989) 83 *AJIL* 461; William Dodge, "The Historical Origins of the Alien Tort Statute: A Response to the Originalists" (1996) 19 *Hastings Int'l & Comp L Rev* 221.

111 See *supra* notes 10 and 11. See also *Bouzari v. Bahremani*, 2013 ONSC 6337 (in a fresh claim for the same acts at issue in *Bouzari*, *supra* note 10, the defendant moved to have Ontario proceedings dismissed on the basis that England was the most appropriate forum).

112 Brownlie, *supra* note 48 at p 298.

certain judges and commentators – there is indeed a difference between civil and criminal jurisdiction. Common objections are raised to the assertion of civil jurisdiction over extraterritorial human rights abuses.[113] For example, the broad jurisdiction exercised by US federal courts since *Filártiga* has been likened to a type of legal "hegemony or imperialism"[114] where courts appoint themselves as "the *custos morum* of the whole world."[115] It is also sometimes argued that such litigation might cause embarrassment to the executive branch and have a chilling effect on international relations.[116] Finally, some commentators argue that even if jurisdiction were asserted, a successful judgment would prove too difficult to enforce.[117] Of course, such arguments can and have been made with respect to universal criminal jurisdiction,[118] but they do not necessarily lead to the conclusion that national courts cannot enforce those international norms that entitle victims of egregious human rights abuses to civil redress, such as torture. Arguably, these considerations, important as they are, point to the need for heightened judicial forbearance, not categorical abstention.

The 2013 decision in *Kiobel* is illustrative. After more than three decades of litigation under the ATS, the Supreme Court has ruled that ATS claims (not the statute itself) are subject to the presumption against extraterritoriality.[119] This in turn has already and quite predictably had the effect of reducing the volume of ATS cases by causing the dismissal of matters deemed to be insufficiently connected to the United States.[120] This novel application of the presumption against extraterritoriality as a limit on adjudicative jurisdiction is perhaps difficult to explain in an increasingly connected world, where people, capital and information cross borders with increasing ease and frequency,

---

113 See generally Jan Klabbers, "Doing the Right Thing? Foreign Tort Law and Human Rights" in *Torture as Tort, supra* note 6 at p 562 (Doing the Right Thing); Curtis Bradley, "The Cost of International Human Rights Litigation" (2001) 2 *Chi J Int'l L* 457 (The Cost of IHRL); *Hearts and Minds, supra* note 8; Larocque, *Civil Actions for Uncivilized Acts, supra* note 6 at pp 306–313.

114 Hazel Fox, "Approaches of Domestic Courts to the Assertion of International Jurisdiction" in Capps et al, *Asserting Jurisdiction, supra* note 48 at p 187.

115 *Kiobel, supra* note 5 at p 1674.

116 Curtis A Bradley, "The Cost of International Human Rights Litigation" (2001) 2 *Chi J Int'l L* 457 at 461; *Sosa, supra* note 5 at pp 727–728; *Kiobel, supra* note 5 at p 1664.

117 Hazel Fox, "Private Law Damages as a Method of State Accountability: The Tort Exception to State Immunity" (1993) *Third World Legal Studies* 107 at p 118.

118 See, for example, Henry Kissinger, "The Pitfalls of Universal Jurisdiction" (2001) 80(4) *Foreign Affairs* 150.

119 *Kiobel, supra* note 5 at pp 1664–1665.

120 See for example, *Balintulo v. Daimler AG et al*, 727 F.3d 174 (2nd Cir, 2014); *Al Shimari v. CACI International Inc*, 727 F.3d 174 (EDVA, 2013) overturned by 758 F.3d 516 (4th Cir, 2014); *Giraldo v. Drummond Co*, 2013 US Dist LEXIS 103981 (EDAL, 2013) affirmed by 2015 US App LEXIS 4863 (11th Cir, 2015). See also Ralph Steinhardt, "The ATS after Kiobel," *ASIL Unbound* (31 January 2014), online: http://shar.es/1gsEnb.

but it is a defensible judicial policy that properly leaves the door open to the assertion of civil jurisdiction over allegations of serious violations of international human rights. In his terse concurring opinion in *Kiobel*, Justice Kennedy emphasized that "in those disputes, the proper implementation of the presumption against extraterritorial application may require some further elaboration and explanation."[121]

The exercise of civil jurisdiction over extraterritorial acts of torture is mandated at international law, at least for the 153 States Parties to the CAT. In 2012, the Committee against Torture issued its General Comment on Article 14 of the CAT.[122] This article codifies, *inter alia*, the obligation of each State Party to "ensure in its legal system that the victim of an act of torture obtains redress and has an enforceable right to fair and adequate compensation, including the means for as full rehabilitation as possible."[123] There lingered a debate in the case law[124] and literature[125] as to whether Article 14 obligated States Parties to provide civil redress to victims who were tortured in the forum (the territoriality principle) or whether it established an obligation to assert jurisdiction over acts of extraterritorial torture as well (the universality principle). It is now clear, in the authoritative view of the Committee, that:

> [T]he application of article 14 is not limited to victims who were harmed in the territory of the State party or by or against nationals of the State party. The Committee has commended the efforts of States parties for providing civil remedies for victims who were subjected to torture or ill-treatment outside their territory. This is particularly important when a victim is unable to exercise the rights guaranteed under article 14 in the territory where the violation took place. Indeed, article 14 requires States parties to ensure that all victims of torture and ill-treatment are able to access remedy and obtain redress.[126]

Despite the absence of any territorial language in Article 14, the Committee against Torture has taken the view that the CAT requires States Parties to provide "all" victims of torture with a remedy through their civil jurisdiction,

---

121 *Kiobel, supra* note 5 at p 1669.

122 Committee against Torture, *General Comment No 3: Implementation of Article 14 by State Parties* (13 December 2012) CAT/C/GC/3.

123 CAT, *supra* note 2, Article 14.

124 See, for example *Bouzari* (2002), *supra* note 10 at paras 44–55; *Bouzari* (2004), *supra* note 10 at paras 76–83; *Jones* (2006), *supra* note 10 at paras 25 (Lord Bingham) and 46 (Lord Hoffmann); *Kazemi* (2014), *supra* note 10 at paras 140–150 (LeBel J) and 214–226 (Abella J).

125 See, for example, Manfred Nowak and Elizabeth McArthur, *The United Nations Convention against Torture: A Commentary* (Oxford: Oxford University Press, 2008) at pp 492 and 502; Andrew Byrnes, "Civil Remedies for Torture Committed Abroad: An Obligation under the Convention against Torture?" in Scott (ed),*Torture as Tort, supra* note 6 at pp 546 and 548; Larocque, *Civil Actions for Uncivilized Acts, supra* note 6 at pp 260–266.

126 *General Comment No 3, supra* note 122 at para 22.

irrespective of where the torture occurred. It can now be argued that Article 14 mandates a broad civil extraterritorial jurisdiction equivalent to the criminal jurisdiction provided for under Article 5, though the Committee could have been more not explicit on that point. It is also worth pointing out that the Committee buttressed its interpretation of Article 14 with the underlying policy objective of the doctrine of forum of necessity,[127] stating that a broad approach to civil jurisdiction was "particularly important when a victim is unable to exercise the rights guaranteed under article 14 in the territory where the violation took place."[128]

Unfortunately, national courts routinely disregard the views of the Committee against Torture. In *Jones*, which was admittedly released before the publication of the Committee's General Comment on Article 14, the House of Lords was blatantly dismissive of the treaty body's interpretations of the CAT. Lord Bingham characterized the weight of the Committee's recommendations as being "slight," while Lord Hoffmann regarded "it has having no value."[129] This aspect of the House of Lords' decision has been justly criticized.[130] The Supreme Court of Canada took a more conciliatory view of the Committee's work in *Kazemi*, recognizing its commentaries and recommendations as "importan[t]," "useful" and forming "part of a dialogue within the international community."[131] Nevertheless, in the Court's view, the Committee's interpretations should not be given more weight than the "pronouncements of States parties and judicial authorities" and ultimately "do not overrule adjudicative interpretations of the articles in the CAT."[132] This last statement is unexceptionable as a matter of Canadian law, but it unhappily undermines the object and framework of the CAT. National courts should adopt the Committee's commentaries and recommendations not as evidence of some widespread international practice, but rather as persuasive authority regarding the evolving scope of the States Parties' obligations under the CAT, with a view of furthering that treaty's purpose "to make more effective the struggle against torture."[133] The gravitational pull of the torture prohibition in both international law and national law commands as much.

As long as national courts remain unwilling to take direction from the Committee on the proper interpretation of the CAT, the assertion of jurisdiction over acts of extraterritorial torture will be governed by a patchwork of

---

127 *Supra* notes 67–68 and accompanying text.

128 *General Comment No 3*, *supra* note 122 at para 22.

129 *Jones* (2006), *supra* note 10 at para 23 (Lord Bingham) and para 57 (Lord Hoffmann).

130 Nowak and McArthur, *The United Nations Convention*, *supra* note 125 at p 500; Larocque, *Civil Actions for Uncivilized Acts*, *supra* note 6 at pp 264–266; Alexander Orakhelashvili, "State Immunity and Hierarchy of Norms: Why the House of Lords Got it Wrong" (2008) 18(5) *EJIL* 955 at p 963.

131 *Kazemi 2014*, *supra* note 10 at paras 147–148 (LeBel J) and paras 224–226 (Abella J).

132 Ibid at paras 147–148.

133 CAT, *supra* note 2, preamble.

asymmetrical rules that will vary according to the nature of the proceedings and the legal tradition of the forum. For instance, if an alleged torturer travels to a civil law State Party, like France, he may be both criminally prosecuted and civilly sued under the CAT for his wrongdoing.[134] If, however, he opts to visit London or Toronto, he need only fear a criminal indictment since the courts of those countries will not take civil jurisdiction over him unless the plaintiffs can establish a territorial link between their civil claim and the forum[135] or show some form of legal or practical necessity.[136] With great respect to Lord Bingham, the untenable distinction between criminal proceedings (which are subject to universal jurisdiction) and civil proceedings (which are not) can be "wished away."[137] The interpretation of Article 14 advanced by the Committee profitably harmonizes the panoply of possible international responses to torture by applying the same jurisdictional principle to both civil and criminal proceedings, thereby reinforcing the CAT's overarching purpose and policy.

Wishful thinking aside, it may be that the development of a cogent principle of universal civil jurisdiction for torture has been stifled by the nearly unanimous chain of national court decisions, since the 1990s, holding that the law of state immunity constitutes an absolute bar to civil claims for extraterritorial torture.[138] The implicit conceit of these decisions appears to be that since acts of torture attract immunity, it is of little import whether national courts possess the adjudicative jurisdiction to entertain civil claims with respect to extraterritorial torture. This issue will be examined in the final section of this chapter.

4. STATE IMMUNITY AND TORTURE

This section highlights some problems that arise between the peremptory prohibition of torture at international law and the doctrine of state immunity.

4.1. IN THEORY

The law of state immunity can be stated easily enough and the underlying principles are relatively straightforward. Simply put, in its modern form, state immunity is a procedural rule that operates to prevent the national courts of one

134 See *Ould Dah*, *supra* note 5.
135 See *Saleh*, *supra* note 11.
136 See *Bahremani*, *supra* note 111.
137 *Jones* (2006), *supra* note 10 at para 32.
138 *Supra* note 5.

state from exercising their adjudicative jurisdiction over the sovereign conduct of another state. This broad definition warrants a number of qualifications.

First, it is essential to emphasize that state immunity is a doctrine of judicial restraint that operates as an exception to the primary rules of territorial jurisdiction of the forum. As the ICJ stated in the *Arrest Warrant* case, "it is only where a State has jurisdiction under international law in relation to a particular matter that there can be any question of immunities in regard of the exercise of that jurisdiction."[139] More recently, in the *Jurisdictional Immunities* case, the ICJ characterized state immunity as "a departure from the principle of territorial sovereignty and the jurisdiction which flows from it."[140] Higgins described the relationship between jurisdiction and immunity as follows:

> It is very easy to elevate sovereign immunity into a superior principle of international law and to lose sight of the essential reality that it is an exception to the normal doctrine of jurisdiction. It is a derogation from the normal rule of territorial sovereignty. It is sovereign immunity which is the exception to jurisdiction and not jurisdiction which is the exception to a basic rule of immunity. An exception to the normal rules of jurisdiction should only be granted when international law requires – that is to say, when it is consonant with justice and with the equitable protection of the parties. It is not to be granted "as of right."[141]

As with most questions, it matters where one begins when reasoning about state immunity. As Keitner has argued, by starting from a "baseline" of immunity rather than jurisdiction, national courts run the risk of overextending the doctrine beyond what is required at international law.[142] Unfortunately, as illustrated by Lord Bingham's comments in *Jones*, the normative and logical priority of jurisdiction over immunity is not always well understood by national courts.[143] *Ex falso sequitur quodlibet.*

Second, contrary to diplomatic or head-of-state immunity, which are immunities *ratione personae* that inure to certain individuals while they

139 *Arrest Warrant* case, *supra* note 72 at para 46.

140 *Jurisdictional Immunities* case, *supra* note 12 at para 57.

141 Rosalyn Higgins, "Certain Unresolved Aspects of the Law of State Immunity" (1982) 29 *Neth Int'l L Rev* 265 at p 271. See also Lee M Caplan, "State Immunity, Human Rights, and *Jus Cogens*: A Critique of the Normative Hierarchy Theory" (2003) 97 *AJIL* 741 at p 744. ("[A]s a fundamental matter, state immunity operates as an exception to the principle of adjudicatory jurisdiction"); Lorna MacGregor, "Torture and State Immunity: Deflecting Impunity, Distorting Sovereignty" (2007) 18 *EJIL* 903 at p 912.

142 Chimène Keitner, "Foreign Official Immunity and the 'Baseline' Problem" (2011) 80 *Fordham L Rev* 605 at p 621. See also *Jurisdictional Immunities* case, *supra* note 12 at para 55 ("States sometimes decide to accord an immunity more extensive than that required by international law").

143 See, for example, Lord Bingham's misstatement of the law in *Jones*, *supra* note 10 at para 14 ("the rule of international law is not that a state should not exercise over another state a jurisdiction which it has but that (save in cases recognised by international law) a state has no jurisdiction over another state. I do not understand how a state can be said to deny access to its court if it has no access to give").

exercise specific government functions, state immunity is a subject-matter immunity that applies *ratione materiae* to particular state acts or conduct.[144] The doctrine was once believed to be absolute, mostly by common law courts,[145] but this paradigm has been replaced by the modern restrictive doctrine under which only official or sovereign acts of state (acts *jure imperii*) attract immunity, that is, acts performed in a public capacity by or on behalf of the state. Under the restrictive doctrine, therefore, the characterization of state acts as being sovereign or non-sovereign becomes the decisive issue.[146] The proper methodology entails a case-by-case assessment of "whether the act, by its nature or purpose, has contributed to the exercise of the foreign State's sovereignty."[147] As will be seen below, the question of whether a state act that violates a peremptory norm of international law, such as the prohibition of torture, can be considered *jure imperii* has been recently settled, albeit on the basis of reasoning that strains both logic and credibility.

Third, the non-justiciability of official state acts derives from the principle of state equality in international law, traditionally expressed by the maxim *par in parem non habet imperium.*[148] Immunity was historically extended as a matter of courtesy and reciprocity among sovereigns and is still understood as "play[ing] a large role in international relations."[149] Despite state immunity's "messy" origins and character – to borrow Peter's evocative phrasing[150] – it is important to recall that the doctrine was first administered and developed by national courts[151] and was only later recognized as a rule of customary international law.[152] As Lord Denning MR summed up the situation in 1977:

> Each country delimits for itself the bounds of sovereign immunity. Each creates for itself the exceptions from it. It is, I think, for the courts of this country to define the rule

144 *Pinochet No 3, supra* note 57 at p 269; *Holland v. Lampen-Wolfe,* [2000] 1 WLR 1573 at p 1583 (HL); *Verlinden BV v. Central Bank of Nigeria*, 461 US 480 at 493 (1983).

145 *The Cristina* (1938) AC 485 at p 490 (HL); *Ex parte Republic of Peru* 318 US 578 (1943); *Dessaules v. Republic of Poland* (1944) SCR 275; Hazel Fox and Philippa Webb, *The Law of State Immunity*, 3rd ed (Oxford: Oxford University Press, 2013) at p 26. On the history of state immunity, see Sir Ian Sinclair, "The Law of Sovereign Immunity: Recent Developments" (1980-II) 167 *RC* 113 at p 198; Hersh Lauterpacht, "The Problem of Jurisdictional Immunities of Foreign States" (1951) 28 *BYIL* 220 at p 228; Sompong Sucharitkul, "Immunities of Foreign States before National Authorities" (1976-I) 149 *RC* 89; Peter D. Trooboff, "Foreign State Immunity: Emerging Consensus on Principles" (1986-V) 200 *RC* 245.

146 James Crawford, "International Law and Foreign Sovereigns: Distinguishing Immune Transactions" (1983) 54 *BYIL* 75; Lauterpacht, ibid at pp 222–226.

147 *Case of Sabeh El Leil v. France*, App No. 34869/05 (29 June 2011) at para 24 (ECHR).

148 *Jurisdictional Immunities* case, *supra* note 12 at para 57; *Kazemi* (2014), *supra* note 10 at para 35.

149 *Kazemi* (2014), *supra* note 10 at p 38; *Jurisdictional Immunities* case, *supra* note 12; *Jones* (2006), *supra* note 10 at para 18; *Al-Adsani* (2001), *supra* note 10 at para 54.

150 Anne Peters, "Immune against Constitutionalisation?" in Anne Peters et al (eds), *Immunities in the Age of Global Constitutionalisation* (Leiden: Brill Nijhoff, 2015) 1.

151 *Trendtex Trading Corp v. Central Bank of Nigeria,* (1977) 2 WLR 456 (CA); *The Philippine Admiral* [1976] 2 WLR 214 at pp 232–233 (PC); *Jaffe v. Miller* (1993), 13 OR (3d) 745 at p752 (CA).

152 *Jurisdictional Immunities* case, *supra* note 12 at paras 54, 58; *Kazemi* (2014), *supra* note 10.

> as best they can, seeking guidance from the decisions of the courts of other countries, from the jurists who have studied the problem, from treaties and conventions and, above all, defining the rule in terms which are consonant with justice rather than adverse to it.[153]

In the late twentieth century, many countries of the Anglo-American legal world adopted legislation codifying the doctrine of restrictive immunity,[154] while other countries continued to develop the rule as a matter of common law.[155] Interestingly, the courts in many civil law countries – which traditionally favour legislation over judge-made law – continue to administer the restrictive theory of immunity without the benefit of legislation, on the basis of customary international law and their respective constitutions.[156] The US, UK and Canadian codifications[157] were intended to uniformly implement the restrictive principle and to depoliticize the adjudication of civil claims.[158] Unfortunately, the US, UK and Canadian statutes appear to have caused the national courts of those countries to abdicate their traditional law-making function in the area of state immunity.[159] In these countries, being dualist legal systems with respect to the domestic reception of international norms, the law of state immunity has been statutorily frozen in its dishevelled 1970s form and, in the absence of legislative amendment, rendered impermeable to modern-day developments in international law. Accordingly, if any change to the customary international law of state immunity is to occur, it must necessarily emanate from the national legislatures or from the less fettered courts of civil law countries.[160]

---

153 *Trendtex, supra* note 151 at p 364.

154 E.g. Australia, Canada, Malaysia, Pakistan, the United Kingdom and the United States.

155 E.g. Kenya, Ireland, New Zealand, Nigeria and Zimbabwe.

156 For a dramatic recent example, see Sentenza nº 238/2014 della Corte Costituzionale, 23 October 2014, where the Italian Constitutional Court struck down legislation intended to implement the ICJ's judgment in the *Jurisdictional Immunities* case (*supra* note 12) and to ratify the UNCSI (*infra* note 164), on the basis that the statutes conflicted with the basic tenets of the Italian constitutional order, including the right to access justice to protect fundamental human rights. The English translation of the Corte Costituzionale's decision 238/2014 is available on the Court's website: http://www.cortecostituzionale.it/ActionPagina_1240.do.

157 Foreign Sovereign Immunities Act, 28 USC §1330 (1976); State Immunity Act, 1978, c 33 (UK); State Immunity Act, RSC 1985, c S-18.

158 Larocque, *Civil Actions for Uncivilized Acts, supra* note 6 at pp 243–244.

159 *Amerada Hess Shipping Corp v. Republic of Argentina*, 488 US 428 at 434 (1989); *Kazemi* (2014), *supra* note 10 at paras 54–56; *Jones 2006, supra* note 10. It has been argued, at least with respect to the Canadian statute, that Parliament never intended to occupy the field and extinguish the pre-existing common law of state immunity. See Larocque, "La Loi sur l'immunité des états canadienne et la torture," *supra* note 8; Larocque, *Civil Actions for Uncivilized Acts, supra* note 6 at pp 273–275.

160 The Italian Constitutional Court decision 238/2014, *supra* note 156, is evidence that the law of state immunity remains in flux.

Finally, while the restrictive doctrine of state immunity undoubtedly forms part of customary international law, it is not regarded as *jus cogens*, and its footing in the law of treaties remains precarious. Aside from an early convention relating to immunity of state-owned vessels[161] the first multilateral convention on the general topic of state immunity was the European Convention on State Immunity,[162] which remains unpopular, having been ratified by only eight European states since coming into force in 1976.[163] The newer United Nations Convention on the Jurisdictional Immunities of States and their Property (UNCSI), which opened for signature in 2004, is not faring much better.[164] Not only has the UNCSI not yet come into force, but at the time of writing, only 17 states have ratified it.[165] Moreover, several States Parties have filed declarations noting the UNCSI's silence on the right of victims to civil redress for extraterritorial human rights violations and holding the UNCSI as being without prejudice to any future international legal development concerning the protection of human rights.[166] Consequently, the binding sources of international law on state immunity remain largely unwritten.

4.2. IN PRACTICE

While the basic principle of state immunity can be rather easily summarized, the doctrine's practical application has proven much more difficult to manage, particularly in the context of civil claims for violations of fundamental human rights, such as torture. The practical challenges posed by immunity in such cases stem in part from conflicting views on the doctrine's scope and purpose, as well as from its relationship to other norms of international public order.

Initially an expression of political courtesy and reciprocity extended among sovereigns and governments, state immunity gradually became a question of law to be administered by the judiciary. However, as stated above, the adoption of state immunity legislation in the United States, the United Kingdom and Canada has caused the courts of these countries to divest themselves of

---

161 Brussels Convention for the Unification of Certain Rules Relating to the Immunity of State Owned Vessels, 10 April 1926, 176 LNTS 199 (1926).

162 European Convention on State Immunity ETS No 074 (1972).

163 At the time of writing, the European Convention on State Immunity has been ratified or acceded to by Austria, Belgium, Cyprus, Germany, Luxembourg, the Netherlands, Switzerland and the United Kingdom.

164 United Nations Convention on the Jurisdictional Immunities of States and their Property, 2 December 2004, A/RES/59/38 [UNCSI].

165 Pursuant to Article 30, the UNCSI will come into force on the 30th day following the deposit of the 30th instrument of ratification.

166 See the declarations of Finland, Italy, Norway and Sweden, Switzerland: http://tiny.cc/anz8wx.

their historical creative function in this area, thus leaving emerging problems and phenomena to be resolved on the basis of stultified statutes. The Anglo-Canadian torture cases are illustrative. The courts in *Bouzari*, *Jones* and *Kazemi* were all asked to interpret their respective state immunity statutes consistently with evolving international norms respecting torture and the rights of victims to civil redress.[167] While the wording of the statutes admittedly do not leave much room for judicial innovation,[168] it was arguably still open to the courts to a find an interpretive solution, either by reading-in a new exception for torture (which would have entailed a finding that such an exception existed in international law or was mandated by the domestic constitution) or, conversely, by excluding torture from the ambit of the immunity conferred by the statutes.[169] Under this second approach, which starts from a baseline of jurisdiction, the statutes are characterized as narrow codifications of the restrictive principle of state immunity, where the exceptional immunity granted by Parliament attaches only to true sovereign acts of foreign states. To succeed in a case like *Bouzari, Jones* and *Kazemi*, this argument requires the court to find that torture cannot be, for immunity purposes, an official or sovereign act of state. Of course, such a finding has become immeasurably more difficult to make after the *Jurisdictional Immunities* case.[170]

Ultimately, the courts in *Bouzari*, *Jones* and *Kazemi* all found that the denial of immunity with respect to torture was not required under constitutional or international law and, perhaps as significantly, that such a development was foreclosed in any event by the words of the state immunity statutes. Justice LeBel summed up the situation in *Kazemi*:

> With regard to exceptions to state immunity, Professor H. H. Koh famously asked, "if contracts, why not torture?" The answer is simple. Parliament has decided as much.
>
> State immunity is a complex doctrine that is shaped by constantly evolving international relations. Determining the exceptions to immunity requires a thorough knowledge of diplomacy and international politics and a careful weighing of national interests. Since the introduction of the *SIA*, such a task belongs to Parliament or the government, though decisions and laws pertaining to international affairs may be subject to constitutional scrutiny under the *Charter* ... It is not, however, this Court's task to intervene in delicate international policy making.

---

167 *Supra* note 10.

168 The UK's State Immunity Act, 1978, c 33, s 1(1) provides: "A State is immune from the jurisdiction of the courts of the United Kingdom except as provided in the following provisions of this Part of this Act." Similarly, the Canadian State Immunity Act, RSC 1985, c I–18, s 3(1) provides: "Except as provided by this Act, a foreign state is immune from the jurisdiction of any court in Canada."

169 Ibid.

170 *Jurisdictional Immunities* case, *supra* note 12 at para 60 (holding that state acts that breach the peremptory norms of international law can still be acts *jure imperii* for immunity purposes).

> Parliament has the power and the capacity to decide whether Canadian courts should exercise civil jurisdiction. Parliament has the ability to change the current state of the law on exceptions to state immunity … and allow those in situations like Mr. Hashemi and his mother's estate to seek redress in Canadian courts. Parliament has simply chosen not to do it yet.[171]

In deciding that Canada's State Immunity Act barred civil claims for torture, the Supreme Court of Canada emphasized the role of state immunity in "diplomacy and international politics" and shored up this characterization in strong Diceyan terms, noting that it was up to Parliament, and no longer the courts, to affect change in the law of state immunity.

It is an unfortunate turn of events that legislation explicitly enacted to introduce the principle of restrictive immunity in jurisdictions that had hitherto adhered to an absolutist paradigm has been decisively interpreted as barring any further judicial development of the law. It was not what Parliament intended.[172] While legislatures can and indeed must take the lead in defining the broad principles that govern immunities, national courts should be able to develop these principles, as Lord Denning suggested in *Trendtex*, in light of evolving international law and "in terms which are consonant with justice rather than adverse to it."[173] Unfortunately, state immunity's political origins and its continuing role in modern-day international relations have compromised its ontological and axiological status as *law*. Consider, for instance, the US and Canadian legislative amendments establishing a terrorism exception in their respective state immunity legislation. In the United States, the 1996 Antiterrorism and Effective Death Penalty Act,[174] codified as part of the Foreign Sovereign Immunities Act (FSIA) in 28 USC §1605(a)(7), allows US citizens to bring a claim for compensatory and punitive damages against certain designated foreign states[175] for death or personal injury

171 *Kazemi* (2014), *supra* note 10 at paras 168–170 (citations omitted).

172 When the bill that became the State Immunity Act was being studied in parliamentary committee, the principal drafter of the Act emphasized that courts were expected to interpret the statute in light of changing international law. See Senate of Canada, Minutes of the Permanent Committee on Justice and Legal Affairs, February 1982, at pp 59:17 and 60:17 ("Well, we did not intend to have this [Act] come back on a periodic review. Not that it would stand for perhaps a thousand years but we hope that the courts would be able to have that flexibility to interpret it in the light of new factual situations, new transactions … Therefore, it is imperative to have a reasonably flexible and supple bill, one that will allow Canadian courts to reflect changing international norms in this area"). See generally, Larocque, "La Loi sur l'immunité des états canadienne et la torture," *supra* note 8.

173 *Trendtex, supra* note 151 at p 364.

174 Antiterrorism and Effective Death Penalty Act, Pub L 104–132, §221, 221 Stat 1214 (24 April 1996).

175 The designation is made pursuant to §6(j) of the Export Administration Act of 1979, 50 USC App 2405(j) and §620A of the Foreign Assistance Act of 1961, 22 USC 2371. At the time of writing, Cuba, Iran, Sudan and Syria are designated state sponsors of terrorism for immunity

arising from an act of torture, extrajudicial killing, aircraft sabotage, hostage taking or for supporting such activities, provided the plaintiff gave the foreign state a reasonable opportunity to resolve the matter through arbitration. Similarly, Canada's 2012 Justice for Victims of Terrorism Act[176] permits Canadian citizens and permanent residents to sue certain designated foreign states[177] for loss or injuries arising from terrorism-related activities, provided the plaintiff afforded the foreign state with a reasonable opportunity to arbitrate the claim. The US terrorism exception has been widely criticized[178] and the Canadian model is potentially problematic as well since both statutes ultimately grant or deny immunity by executive fiat, and not through a principled assessment of the legal character of the impugned state act, as customarily required under the restrictive doctrine.

It is interesting to note, nevertheless, that both the US and Canadian statutes provide for the selective denial of immunity, in part at least, on the basis of terrorism's international unlawfulness. The preamble of the Justice for Victims of Terrorism Act (JVTA) recalls "that terrorism is a matter of national concern that affects the security of the nation" and that "United Nations Security Council Resolution 1373 (2001) reaffirms that acts of international terrorism constitute a threat to international peace and security, and reaffirms the need to combat by all means, in accordance with the Charter of the United Nations, threats to international peace and security caused by acts of terrorism."[179] One wonders if it might therefore be inferred that Canada and the United States, as a matter of *opinio juris*, both consider the denial of immunity for terrorism as being justified in light of that particular act's international criminality. If so, then the politically driven US and Canadian amendments might be partly redeemed as codifying the kind of qualitative assessment of state conduct that the restrictive principle of state immunity

purposes. In April 2015, in line with government efforts to normalize relations with Cuba, the US State Department recommend the rescission of that country's designation. See US State Department, State Sponsors of Terrorism: http://go.usa.gov/32VHW.

176 Justice for Victims of Terrorism Act, SC 2012, c 1, s 4 (JVTA).

177 The designation is made pursuant to s 6.1(2) of the State Immunity Act, RSC 1985, c I–18. At the time of writing, Iran and Syria are designated for immunity purposes. See Canada, "Canada Lists Both Iran and Syria as State Supporters of Terrorism," news release (7 September 2012): http://tiny.cc/ucz8wx.

178 Ronald Bettauer, "Germany Sues Italy at the International Court of Justice on Foreign Sovereign Immunity – Legal Underpinnings and Implications for U.S. Law" (2009) 13(22) *ASIL Insight* 1 at p 5: "Fox sees the U.S. legislation as 'partisan' and not a satisfactory precedent for other states to adopt. Gattini calls the U.S. approach 'of dubious value' because of its 'unilateral nature and political overtones.' Bankas called subsection (a)(7) and the pre-2008 amendments to it 'draconian in many respects and therefore may be vigorously contested by defendant states.' Professor van Alabeek says that 'the terrorist state exception to the FSIA causes the United States to violate its obligations under international law.'" (References omitted).

179 JVTA, *supra* note 176, preamble.

requires. Moreover, the US and Canadian enactments can arguably be taken to stand for the notion that state immunity is privilege that can be lost or removed in appropriate circumstances ("when it is consonant with justice and with the equitable protection of the parties")[180] rather than an automatic and absolute attribute of sovereignty.

Of course, such a conception of state immunity runs counter to the orthodox view, namely, that "States generally proceed on the basis that there is a right to immunity under international law,"[181] even when the impugned state conduct violates international law. The ICJ held in the *Jurisdictional Immunities* case that the international illegality of the impugned state act has no bearing on its characterization as *jure imperii* for the purposes of determining immunity.[182] This case, it will be recalled, concerned war crimes and crimes against humanity perpetrated by the Third Reich during World War II. It is an unusual feature of the case that both parties agreed that the acts at issue – the murder of civilian populations in occupied territories and the forced deportation of civilian inhabitants as well as prisoners of war to slave labour – were prohibited by peremptory norms of international law, yet nevertheless constituted acts *jure imperii*.[183] With this unfortunate concession, Italy's only remaining rhetorical avenue was to argue that Germany's unlawful actions did not attract immunity because at least some of them occurred on Italian territory or, conversely, because "those acts involved the most serious violations of rules of international law of a peremptory character for which no alternative means of redress was available."[184] This chapter will not address the Court's response to the first argument,[185] but will focus instead on the Court's endorsement of the view espoused by the various national courts in civil claims for torture,[186] to wit, state immunity applies to conduct that contravenes international *jus cogens*.

Flagging the US's Antiterrorism and Effective Death Penalty Act as an outlier,[187] the ICJ held "that, under customary international law as it presently stands, a State is not deprived of immunity by reason of the fact that it is accused of serious violations of international human rights law or the international law of armed conflict."[188] Then, turning to the *jus cogens* argument, the Court

---

180 Higgins, "Certain Unresolved Aspects of the Law of State Immunity," *supra* note 141 at p 271.

181 *Jurisdictional Immunities* case, *supra* note 12 at para 56.

182 Ibid at para 60.

183 Ibid. The Court noted "that Italy, in response to a question posed by a member of the Court, recognized that those acts had to be characterized as *acta jure imperii*, notwithstanding that they were unlawful." This was an unfortunate concession on the part of Italy.

184 Ibid at para 61.

185 Ibid at paras 62–79.

186 Ibid at para 85. See also *supra* note 10.

187 Ibid at para 88. The ICJ's decision was issued three weeks before the Canadian JVTA came into force. See *supra* notes 174–179 and accompanying text.

188 Ibid at para 91.

found that there existed no conflict between the substantive peremptory prohibition of war crimes and crimes against humanity and the hierarchically inferior procedural rule of state immunity. It held that:

> [T]he two sets of rules address different matters. The rules of State immunity are procedural in character and are confined to determining whether or not the courts of one State may exercise jurisdiction in respect of another State. They do not bear upon the question whether or not the conduct in respect of which the proceedings are brought was lawful or unlawful.[189]

In this holding, the ICJ adopted the line of reasoning famously advanced by Fox and endorsed by the House of Lords in *Jones* and the Supreme Court of Canada in *Kazemi*, namely, that: "State immunity is a procedural rule going to the jurisdiction of a national court. It does not go to substantive law; it does not contradict a prohibition contained in a *jus cogens* norm but merely diverts any breach of it to a different method of settlement. Arguably, then, there is no substantive content in the procedural plea of State immunity upon which a *jus cogens* mandate can bite."[190]

This reasoning warrants a few observations. First, Lord Bingham's easy acceptance of the proposition that a procedural rule (state immunity) remains unaffected by its interaction with peremptory substantive rule (the torture prohibition) should be contrasted with his Lordship's own indignation, a mere few months earlier, at the suggestion that a procedural rule (on the admissibility of evidence) could survive its interaction with a substantive peremptory norm of international and constitutional law (the torture prohibition). In *A(FC)*, Lord Bingham stated:

> But the English common law has regarded torture and its fruits with abhorrence for over 500 years, and that abhorrence is now shared by over 140 countries which have acceded to the Torture Convention. I am startled, even a little dismayed, at the suggestion (and the acceptance by the Court of Appeal majority) that this deeply-rooted tradition and an international obligation solemnly and explicitly undertaken can be overridden by a statute and a procedural rule which make no mention of torture at all.[191]

One wonders why or how the *jus cogens* character of the torture prohibition in international law and the constitutional resonance it carries in common law should imperatively be honoured in the law of evidence, but not in the law of state immunity.

---

189 *Jurisdictional Immunities* case, *supra* note 12 at para 93.

190 Fox and Webb, *The Law of State Immunity*, *supra* note 145 at p 21; *Jones* (2006), *supra* note 10 at para 24 (Lord Bingham) and para 44 (Lord Hoffmann); *Kazemi* (2014), *supra* note 10 at para 161.

191 *A(FC)*, *supra* note 22 at para 51.

Second, as Orakhelashvili correctly pointed out, "international law knows of no straightforward distinction between 'substantive' and 'procedural' norms. All international norms derive from the agreement of states or acceptance by the international community as a whole, and there are neither established criteria nor a recognized agency to split them into such categories."[192] A norm forms part of *jus cogens* or it does not. Once the international community recognizes the peremptory character of a given norm – such as torture – all other norms of international law must be interpreted and applied consistently with that characterization. Courts should strive to avoid inconsistencies by giving full effect to the peremptoriness of the international norms they apply, irrespective of the substantive or procedural nature of that effect, subject only to specific and contrary direction from the national legislature. As the Supreme Court of Canada stated in *R v Hape*: "Parliamentary sovereignty dictates that a legislature may violate international law, but that it must do so expressly. Absent an express derogation, the courts may look to prohibitive rules of customary international law to aid in the interpretation of Canadian law and the development of the common law."[193] In other words, it is the entire body of domestic law – be it substantive or procedural, statutory or common law – that must be interpreted and developed consistently with international law.

Another related question is the apparent inconsistency in the law of state immunity with respect to criminal and civil proceedings. The House of Lords held in *Jones* and *Pinochet No 3* that the universal criminal jurisdiction over torture "implies" the removal of immunity *ratione materiae* in criminal matters, but not in civil proceedings,[194] presumably because the concept of universal civil jurisdiction was not well established at international law. Accordingly, if such a notion were to become part of general international law, it too, "by necessary implication," would cause the removal of immunity *ratione materiae* in civil proceedings.[195] But in *Jones*, Lord Bingham went on to state that "the distinction between criminal proceedings (which were the subject of universal jurisdiction under the Torture Convention) and civil proceedings (which were not) was fundamental to [the *Pinochet No 3*] decision. This is not a distinction which can be wished away."[196] With respect, Lord Bingham's account of *Pinochet No 3* is incomplete. While the universal criminal jurisdiction mandated under the CAT was unquestionably central to the denial of immunity in that case, some of the Lords also shored up their conclusion on the basis of the overriding effect of peremptory norms with respect to conflicting

192 Orakhelashvili, "State Immunity and Hierarchy of Norms," *supra* note 130 at p 968.
193 *Hape, supra* note 50 at para 39.
194 *Jones* (2006), *supra* note 10 at para 89 (per Lord Hoffmann); *Pinochet No 3, supra* note 57 at p 205 (per Lord Browne-Wilkinson) and at p 264 (per Lord Hutton).
195 *Jones* (2006), *supra* note 10at para 71 (per Lord Hoffmann).
196 Ibid at para 32 (per Lord Bingham).

immunities.[197] It is thus unclear why peremptory norms could not have the same overriding effect in civil proceedings.

5. CONCLUSION: FINDING A WAY THROUGH TO TOMORROW

This chapter has sought to highlight some of the problems and inconsistencies that have marked the debates and decisions involving issues of torture, jurisdiction and state immunity. The latest decisions to grapple with these problems – the European Court of Human Rights in *Jones* and Supreme Court of Canada in *Kazemi* – will almost certainly not be the last. But, as Webb has remarked, those decisions leave us in a "strange situation"[198] in which state immunity is routinely lifted in banal commercial cases, maritime cases *in rem* and local torts, but not in matters involving the most fundamental norms of international law. This untenable situation is maintained by anachronistic thinking about sovereignty and the state. As Webb put it, the formalistic "distinctions being drawn in immunities cases – civil/criminal, procedural/ substantive, employment/human rights – are hard to reconcile with broader movements for accountability at the international level."[199]

Many of the cases discussed in this chapter contain the hopeful evocation of a future world where such untenable distinctions no longer exist, where the CAT is fully implemented and civil redress is finally made available to all victims of torture.[200] But that world, the courts have melancholically concluded, is not "yet"[201] ours. Accordingly, one may ask, with dissenting Judge Ferrari Bravo, "Quousque tandem?"[202] The unashamedly optimistic answer – which the author believes to be the correct one – is no longer than a "thought-instant."[203] It takes no more than a single "thought-instant to

197 See e.g. *Pinochet No 3*, *supra* note 57 at p 247 (per Lord Hutton), at p 278 (per Lord Millet) and at p 289 (per Lord Phillips).

198 Philippa Webb, "*Jones v. UK*: The Re-integration of State and Official Immunity?" *EJIL Talk!* (14 January 2014): http://tinyurl.com/pa6lggg.

199 Ibid.

200 See e.g. *Bouzari* (2004), *supra* note 10, at para 95 ("In the future, perhaps as the international human rights movement gathers greater force, this balance may change"); *Kazemi* (2012), *supra* note 10 at para 56 ("The Committee points to a 'possible or even hoped for future' of conventional international law").

201 *Jurisdictional Immunities* case, *supra* note 12 at para 91; *Al-Adsani* (2001), *supra* note 10 at para 66; *Jones* (2014), *supra* note 10 at para 198; *Kazemi* (2014), *supra* note 10 at para 148; *Kalogeropoulou and others v. Greece and Germany*, 12 December 2002, ECHR Reports 2002-X at p 417.

202 *Al-Adsani* (2001), *supra* note 10, Dissenting opinion of Judge Ferrari Bravo.

203 Philip Allott, *Eunomia: New Order for a New World* (Oxford: Oxford University Press, 2001), at p xxxii.

transform one's idea of international society from a state-centered to a human-centered mental universe. In the very next moment, one has a wholly new world-view, with wholly new values, wholly new possibilities, and wholly new purposes."[204] It takes no more than a thought-instant to decide that states that breach the peremptory norms of international law should not benefit from the protection of that law.

As Judges Higgins, Koojimans and Burgenthal stated in their Joint Separate Opinion in the *Arrest Warrant* case, the notion of *acta jure imperii* is continually evolving, "reflecting the changing priorities of society."[205] In this connection, given the growing salience of peremptory norms and human rights, it seems, despite the ICJ's view in the *Jurisdictional Immunities* case, that the peremptory illegality of torture should somehow be factored into its characterization as a sovereign or non-sovereign act and in the ultimate grant or denial of immunity. In proposing a path forward, it is helpful to refer to some theory of the state and of the power it wields, as well as to some theory of international law as a whole, and both will be normative, not merely descriptive. Under the view that states are the ultimate embodiment of social power, including the power to make and break laws, torture – that is, extraordinary state-directed violence against an individual – can be conceived as the sovereign act par excellence. Under this worldview, described by Marshall CJ in *The Schooner Exchange*,[206] the planet is inhabited by equal and independent sovereigns, owing nothing to each other but that which they politely concede. However, through constant and deliberate practice, in their mutual interest and for that of their citizens, states have outlawed torture, imbuing that prohibition with the full force of their combined sovereignties, elevating it amongst those rules that govern the formation of all others. Arguably, by so restricting their respective sovereignties, states have permanently excluded torture from the panoply of possible policies that they may pursue, *ipso facto* gaining in protection what they have lost in prerogative. In other words, the sovereign discretion to commit the violence of torture has been reallocated to the empowerment of its peremptory prohibition. Thus, every time and everywhere torture is ordered, it is never an exercise of social power, but simply the utterance of words, just words, not law, mere *flatus vocis*, not *acta jure imperii*. Following this conception of things, the *jus cogens* illegality of torture becomes a decisive component of the contextual characterization of state acts, resulting in its *ab initio* removal from the ambit of immunity.

---

204 *Ibid*, at pp xxxii–xxxiii.

205 *Arrest Warrant* case, *supra* note 72, Separate Opinion of Judges Higgins, Koojimans and Burgenthal, para 72.

206 *The Schooner Exchange v. McFaddon*, 11 US 116 (1812).

Put differently, we must conceive of a new world where state sovereignty and power serves humanity's highest aspirations of peace and freedom from fear and violence. State acts that breach these tenets of world public order are *ultra vires* and must not be countenanced by any court of law. This is hardly a new idea. One of its most eloquent articulations is owed to the learned judge of the Court of First Instance of Leivadia in *Prefecture of Voiotia v Federal Republic of Germany*, who stated that the "acts of a state that violate *jus cogens* norms do not have the character of sovereign acts. In such cases it is considered that the accused state did not act within the ambit of its capacity as a sovereign. Acts contrary to *jus cogens* norms are null and void, and cannot constitute a source of legal rights or privileges, such as the claim to immunity."[207] To hold up a qualified conception of state sovereignty and international society is not to simultaneously repudiate the principle of equality of states, but merely to recognize that while states are equal, they are not above the law that they themselves have created and that sustains their very existence.

[207] *Prefecture of Voiotia v. Federal Republic of Germany*, No. 137/1997, 30 October 1997, as cited in Jordan J Paust, "Genocide in Rwanda, State Responsibility to Prosecute or Extradite, and Nonimmunity for Heads of State and Other Public Officials" (2011) 34:1 *Houston J Int'l L* 57 at p 73, note 63.

REVISITING CHALLENGES TO INTERNATIONAL HUMANITARIAN LAW

Tim McCormack*

* The research for this chapter was supported under the Australian Research Council's *Discovery Projects* funding scheme (project no. DP130100432). The author thanks Fannie Lafontaine for the generous invitation to contribute to this *festchrift*.

1. A GLOBAL CONTRIBUTOR

It is a special pleasure for me to write in honor of Louise Arbour because she is a person I hold in the highest esteem and whom I am privileged to consider a friend. I first met Louise in 1998 in Canberra. Australia's Department of Foreign Affairs and Trade, the Pacific Delegation of the International Committee of the Red Cross and Australian Red Cross had joined forces to organize a roundtable of South East Asian and South Pacific States to discuss the Rome Statute, then recently opened for signature. Louise was the Prosecutor for the International Criminal Tribunals for the Former Yugoslavia and for Rwanda at the time, and she had travelled for a full day of her life from The Hague to speak to the gathered representatives. She spoke passionately about the importance of a collective commitment to global justice and of the historical significance of the creation of the world's first permanent international criminal court. And people listened to her as they always do. Few people are imbued with such commanding presence as to "fill" any room they enter. Louise Arbour is exceptional. I was enthralled all those years ago and have been ever since. Louise commands the attention of others and her relatively diminutive height is testament to the irrelevance of physical stature for meritorious contribution in the world. For me, Louise is the quintessential "pocket rocket."

My friendship with Louise was initiated following the Canberra roundtable when she and I joined a group of organizers for a post-roundtable social debrief. I have little if any recollection of the content of our discussions, but I do remember laughing long and loud as we thoroughly enjoyed the conviviality of the evening. It is one thing to share values and philosophical approach to one's profession; it is an additional blessing to experience deep satisfaction in eating, drinking and laughing together. In the 18 years since we first met, I have stayed in touch with Louise principally by catching up whenever we happen to have been in the same place – in The Hague, Ottawa, Geneva, Brussels, Melbourne and most recently in Vancouver. Louise has always made time for me in her hectic schedule and I have always come away from time spent with her both grateful and inspired.

Justice of the Court of Appeal for Ontario; Prosecutor of the International Criminal Tribunal for the former Yugoslavia (ICTY) and the International Criminal Tribunal for Rwanda (ICTR); Justice of the Supreme Court of Canada, UN High Commissioner for Human Rights; President and CEO of the International Crisis Group: only a small handful of people are ever appointed to such positions and those privileged few would rightly consider their appointment to one or other institution as the pinnacle of their careers. To have held all of these positions with indefatigable dynamism and with unswerving commitment to professionalism and integrity is truly extraordinary. Louise has lots to give; a great deal was asked of her, she gave freely of herself and the world is a better place because of her contributions. And this is no eulogy! Louise is, thankfully, still very much alive and why wait until a person is no longer with us to acknowledge some of the contributions they have made?

The selection of general subject matter for this piece was obvious for me. International humanitarian law is my area of expertise and it also happens to have been the mutual subject matter of professional interest when Louise and I first met. On 29 February 1996, the UN Security Council adopted Resolution 1047 and appointed Louise "Prosecutor of the International Tribunal for the Prosecution of Persons Responsible for Serious Violations of International Humanitarian Law Committed in the Territory of the Former Yugoslavia and the International Tribunal for Rwanda" to succeed the inaugural Prosecutor, Richard Goldstone. A few months later, on 1 August 1996, I was appointed the Foundation Australian Red Cross Professor of International Humanitarian Law at the University of Melbourne Law School. I do not mean to infer that I somehow equate these two appointments – by no means. My own appointment paled into insignificance compared to the responsibilities assigned to Louise. Instead, I am merely noting the coincidence of timing of our respective appointments which both explicitly mandated an international humanitarian law focus and which facilitated our friendship.

A few months after I was first appointed to the new Chair, I delivered my inaugural public professorial lecture in which I reflected upon contemporary challenges to international humanitarian law.[1] My intention here is to take both a retrospective and a prospective approach: to reflect upon the challenges to international humanitarian law which loomed large in 1996 and to discuss the extent to which those same challenges (or evolved manifestations of them) are still relevant or have been displaced by developments over the past two decades; and to identify key twenty-first-century challenges to international humanitarian law which have emerged or are likely to do so – many of them inconceivable 20 years ago. The title of my public professorial lecture was "From Solferino to Sarajevo: A Continuing Role for International Humanitarian Law?" and there are both temporal and material reasons for reflecting on the lecture as a basis for my contribution to this *festschrift*. Temporally, the lecture more or less coincided with the commencement of my friendship with Louise and now, twenty-three years on from our respective appointments – an opportune moment for reflection. Materially, I focused in 1996 on challenges to international humanitarian law from the then ongoing Balkans conflicts and, of course, those same conflicts were very much the focus of Louise's responsibilities at the time. In attempting to identify and articulate prospective challenges to international humanitarian law, my motivation is the confidence of knowing that Louise is

1 A revised version of the lecture was published as: Timothy L H McCormack, "From Solferino to Sarajevo: A Continuing Role for International Humanitarian Law?" (1997) 21 *Melbourne University Law Review* 621–649.

not content with how things were or continue to be. The Louise I admire is constantly thinking about incremental improvement in the state of the world and so I am confident she will also be interested in my prospective analysis.

2. INTERNATIONAL CRIMINAL INSTITUTION BUILDING AND MORE EFFECTIVE ENFORCEMENT OF INTERNATIONAL HUMANITARIAN LAW

2.1. 1996 CONCERNS: MOVING BEYOND AD HOC TRIBUNALS FOR SPECIFIC CONFLICTS

In 1996, when Louise was appointed Prosecutor of the ICTY and the ICTR, the contemporary international criminal justice project was still very much in its infancy. The ICTY was not three years old and the ICTR had not even existed for two years. In the case of the ICTY, the first judges had been appointed in November 1993, but there were then no rules of procedure, no chief prosecutor and, consequently, no indictments, no cases and no accused in custody. Louise's predecessor, Richard Goldstone, commenced in The Hague in August 1994 and it was only 18 months later that Louise took over from him. By March 1996, when she arrived in The Hague, delivery of judgment in the first trial – that of Duško Tadić – was still 14 months away.

However, it would be a complete misrepresentation to imply that newly appointed officials of the tribunals were idle. By the time Richard Goldstone had arrived in The Hague, the judges had already drafted the Rules of Evidence and Procedure and the Deputy Prosecutor, my compatriot Graham Blewitt, "had set up the structures of the Office of the Prosecutor (OTP), recruited the first investigators and begun mounting investigations."[2] Those early investigations were not straightforward because hostilities were ongoing throughout – particularly in Bosnia-Herzegovina – right up until the signing of the Dayton Accords in late 1995.[3] Most early ICTY witnesses were refugees who had fled the conflict and were temporarily provided asylum in foreign states. In retrospect, given start-up times at the International Criminal Court (ICC) and in other international criminal tribunals, it was a significant achievement to have issued

2 ICTY, Office of the Prosecutor, "History" at: http://www.icty.org/en/about/office-of-the-prosecutor/history.

3 See General Framework Agreement for Peace in Bosnia and Herzegovina, 21 November 1995 presented to the UN Security Council as UN SCOR Doc. S/1995/999 (30 November 1995) and to the General Assembly as UN GAOR Doc. A/50/79C (30 November 1995). Text of the Agreement, signed in Dayton, Ohio, is available at: http://peacemaker.un.org/sites/peacemaker.un.org/files/BA_951121_DaytonAgreement.pdf.

the indictment against Duško Tadić in February 1995 (within 14 months of the appointment of the judges of the ICTY), to have secured transfer of custody of Tadić from Germany and to have commenced trial proceedings against him before the end of April 1995.[4]

Skepticism about the likely efficacy of the ICTY was rife when Louise took up her appointment. A widely held view at the time was that the Tribunal would only ever deal with "small fish"[5] and never with the political and/or military elites most responsible for atrocities in the Balkans conflicts. The arrest of Tadić, and the inauguration of ICTY jurisdiction against someone of his relatively low-ranking status, only fuelled the skepticism. Fortunately, while armchair critics lamented the inefficacy of the institution, the Tribunal plowed on with its work. Although the *Tadić* Trial Judgment was not delivered until July 1997,[6] significant jurisprudence had already emerged from trial proceedings before Louise was appointed to her position. In particular, the decision of the Appeals Chamber on Tadić's challenge to the jurisdiction of the Tribunal[7] profoundly influenced the subsequent development of international humanitarian law in at least two respects. First, paragraph 70 of that decision is consistently and persistently cited in all subsequent international criminal jurisprudence as the seminal articulation of the threshold criteria for an armed conflict:

> an armed conflict exists whenever there is a resort to armed force between States or protracted armed violence between governmental authorities and organized armed groups or between such groups within a State. International humanitarian law applies from the initiation of such armed conflicts and extends beyond the cessation of hostilities until a general conclusion of peace is reached; or, in the case of internal conflicts, a peaceful settlement is achieved. Until that moment, international humanitarian law continues to apply in the whole territory of the warring States or, in the case of internal conflicts, the whole territory under the control of a party, whether or not actual combat takes place there.

Paragraph 70 is perhaps one of the most regularly cited of any early ICTY statement of international humanitarian law, in part because the relevant treaty law – the 1949 Geneva Conventions and the 1977 Additional Protocols – are silent on the definition of an armed conflict.

---

4 See, for example, the transcript of the opening of the trial on 26 April 1995 at: http://www.icty.org/x/cases/tadic/trans/en/950426ia.htm.

5 The choice of a pescatorial metaphor to describe relative levels of criminal responsibility has always intrigued me. Perhaps size relative to rank in the food chain is most dramatically obvious in fish.

6 See *Prosecutor v. Duško Tadić a.k.a. "Dule,"* "Opinion and Judgment," IT-94-1-T, 7 May 1997 at: http://www.icty.org/x/cases/tadic/tjug/en/tad-tsj70507JT2-e.pdf.

7 *Prosecutor v. Duško Tadić a.k.a. "Dule,"* "Decision on the Defence Motion for Interlocutory Appeal on Jurisdiction," IT-94-1-A, 2 October 1995 at: http://www.icty.org/x/cases/tadic/acdec/en/51002.htm.

Second, the Appeals Chamber clarified the scope of Article 3 of the ICTY Statute on violations of "the laws and customs of war" as extending individual criminal liability to serious violations of customary international humanitarian law, including that applicable to non-international armed conflicts.[8] This breakthrough clarification was cited repeatedly in the negotiations for the Rome Statute to establish the ICC, for example, and the extent of the ICC's jurisdiction over war crimes in non-international armed conflicts in Article 8(2)(c) and 8(2)(e) would have been inconceivable in the absence of the combined effect of the Appeals Chamber's authoritative finding in *Tadić* and the wording of Article 4 of the Statute of the ICTR.[9]

Louise presided over a period of intense activity in the ICTY Office of the Prosecutor, a period described by the ICTY itself as one in:

> which the Tribunal reached maturity and saw a huge increase in trial activity as tens of accused persons were brought to its custody. It was Prosecutor Arbour who introduced the use of so-called "sealed indictments" and persuaded the international agencies present in the former Yugoslavia to start arresting indictees.[10]

Louise never shied from issuing indictments against those her Office believed were the most responsible for ICTY Statute offences, including against the incumbent President of Serbia at the time, Slobodan Milošević. This decision was also derided: Milošević was entrenched in power and, according to some, there was no prospect that the leader himself would ever be brought into custody and transferred to The Hague. On reflection now, the decision was inspired. Politics can shift and security of incumbency is rarely guaranteed for life. The issuance of the Milošević indictment and his subsequent transfer to The Hague has resonance for contemporary proceedings against those apparently entrenched in high political office.

Writing in 1996 on the issue of more effective enforcement of international humanitarian law, I discussed some of the appalling violations of the law which had emerged from the Balkans conflicts at that time and the desperate need for effective enforcement mechanisms.[11] While applauding the establishment of the ICTY, I did discuss the limitations of the ad hoc tribunal model – selectively established for some conflicts but not for others – and whether or not a permanent international criminal court – a potential antidote to the ad hoc template – would eventuate. The International Law Commission had

---

8 Ibid, paras 96–136.

9 Article 4 of the Statute is entitled "Violations of Article 3 Common to the Geneva Conventions and of Additional Protocol II" and the provision extends the subject-matter jurisdiction of the ICTR over war crimes perpetrated in the non-international armed conflict in Rwanda.

10 See the "Biography" entry for Louise Arbour at: http://www.icty.org/en/about/office-of-the-prosecutor/former-prosecutors.

11 McCormack, *supra* note 1, at 638–642.

produced its Draft Code of Crimes against the Peace and Security of Mankind[12] and that initiative had provided a catalyst for the adoption of a Draft Statute for an International Criminal Court.[13] A Diplomatic Conference in Rome was scheduled for June 1998 by the UN General Assembly,[14] but it was unclear in 1996 whether the Conference would eventuate and, even if so, what its prospects for success really were.

2.2. TWO DECADES OF DEVELOPMENT: THE WORLD'S FIRST PERMANENT INTERNATIONAL CRIMINAL COURT

So much has happened to advance the international criminal justice project over the past two decades that the prevailing uncertainty in 1996 is now but a distant memory. The 1998 Diplomatic Conference resulted in the adoption of the Rome Statute and the requisite 60 states deposited their instruments of ratification in less than four years following its opening for signature. The most optimistic projection I heard during and following the Rome Conference was five years for entry into force, but more pessimistic voices predicted a minimum of 20 years – if ever. Most commentators underestimated the depth of resolve among states for the materialization of the ICC – a demonstrably palpable resolve in the rush to be included in the Original States Parties following the triggering of entry into force in April 2002.[15] Now, 14 years after the initial swearing-in of the founding

---

12 International Law Commission, "Draft Code of Crimes against the Peace and Security of Mankind with Commentaries" in Report of the Commission to the General Assembly on the Work of its Forty-Eighth Session, *Yearbook of the International Law Commission 1996, Volume II, Part 2* (2005) 15–54. The text of the Report including the Draft Code and Commentaries is available at: http://legal.un.org/ilc/publications/yearbooks/english/ilc_1996_v2_p2.pdf. For an analysis of the substantive crimes in the Draft Code, see: Timothy L H McCormack and Gerry Simpson, "The International Law Commission's Draft Code of Crimes against the Peace and Security of Mankind: An Appraisal of the Substantive Provisions" (1994) 5 *Criminal Law Forum* 1–55.

13 The UN describes the contribution of the International Law Commission's Draft Statute for an International Criminal Court to the subsequent calling of the Rome Diplomatic Conference as follows: "the International Law Commission successfully completed its work on the draft statute for an international criminal court and in 1994 submitted the draft statute to the General Assembly. To consider major substantive issues arising from that draft statute, the General Assembly established the Ad Hoc Committee on the Establishment of an International Criminal Court, which met twice in 1995. After the General Assembly had considered the Committee's report, it created the Preparatory Committee on the Establishment of an International Criminal Court to prepare a widely acceptable consolidated draft text for submission to a diplomatic conference. The Preparatory Committee, which met from 1996 to 1998, held its final session in March and April of 1998 and completed the drafting of the text." See: http://legal.un.org/icc/general/overview.htm.

14 See 51 UN GAOR (88th mtg), UN Doc. A/RES/51/207 (17 December 1996).

15 The deposit of Panama's instrument of ratification on 21 March 2002 brought the number of ratifications to 56. Then, on 11 April 2002, a cluster of ten more states deposited their instruments of ratification passing the critical number of 60 required to trigger ratification

judges and Prosecutor and the establishment of the Court in March 2003, the ICC has: opened formal investigations in nine separate country situations, including the first non-African situation;[16] issued a total of 40 demands for appearance (32 arrest warrants and eight summonses to appear) across eight of the country situations;[17] concluded seven trials and terminated proceedings in an additional six cases;[18] and moved into its permanent premises in The Hague.[19]

The contributions of the ICC to more effective enforcement of international humanitarian law are not limited to trial proceedings in The Hague. I have written elsewhere of the incentive created by the complementarity formula in the Rome Statute for both States Parties and non-States Parties to implement comprehensive domestic criminal legislation to cover all of the crimes within the subject-matter jurisdiction of the Court. Many states have wanted to ensure that they could never be characterized as "unable genuinely" to conduct trial proceedings – at least not on the basis of a lack of domestic criminal subject-matter jurisdiction over conduct allegedly constituting ICC crimes.[20] Consequently, there has been a revolutionary domestic legislative effort resulting in an unprecedented capacity

on 1 July 2002. Once it was known that the Statute was entering into force, another ten states deposited their instruments of ratification on or before 1 July 2002 to bring the total number of original States Parties to 76. My own state of Australia was a good example of the resolve I have referred to. Australia wanted to be among the original States Parties upon entry into force of the Statute and, following the attainment of the requisite 60 ratifications in April 2002, the Australian Government significantly increased the pace on domestic preparations for ratification and just managed to ratify on 1 July 2002. For more details on aspects of the Australian domestic process leading to ratification, see the Hon David Harper, "Australia's Road to Ratification of the International Criminal Court," (2014) 1 *Australian Red Cross International Humanitarian Law Magazine* 26–27. The issue is available online at: http://www.redcross.org.au/files/IHL_Magazine_Sept_2014.pdf.

16 In chronological order of the opening of formal investigations, those country situations are: the Democratic Republic of the Congo (DRC); Uganda; the Central African Republic (CAR); Sudan (Darfur); Kenya; Libya; Côte D'Ivoire; Mali; and Georgia.

17 No arrest warrants have yet been issued in relation to the Georgia situation, the Prosecutor only having received approval to commence a formal investigation of that situation on 27 January 2016.

18 The four concluded trials were against Lubanga, Katanga and Ngudjolo in relation to the DRC and against Bemba in relation to the CAR. The eight terminations have either resulted from deaths of the accused (Odhiambo in Uganda, Gaddafi in Libya and Jerbo in Darfur), from a refusal by the Pre-Trial Chamber to confirm charges against the accused (Mbarushimana in the DRC, Abu Garda in Darfur), because the Prosecutor has had to withdraw charges against the accused (Kenyatta in Kenya) or because the Trial Chamber has terminated proceedings against the accused (Ruto and Sang, both in Kenya).

19 The Court moved into its new permanent premises in December 2015 and the building was officially opened by the King of the Netherlands on 19 April 2016. See: https://www.icc-cpi.int/en_menus/icc/press%20and%20media/press%20releases/Pages/pr1208.aspx.

20 See, for example, Katherine L Doherty and Timothy L H McCormack, "Complementarity as a Catalyst for Comprehensive Domestic Penal Legislation" (1999) 5 *University of California, Davis Journal of International Law and Policy* 147–180; and Tim McCormack, "The Contribution of the International Criminal Court to Increasing Respect for International Humanitarian Law," (2009) 27 *University of Tasmania Law Review* 22–46.

to prosecute international crimes before national courts.[21] This development is welcome, although well-crafted and comprehensive domestic legislation does not automatically translate into increased prosecution of international crimes.

Fortunately, there is growing evidence of states taking domestic investigation of international crimes more seriously as a consequence of the existence of the ICC and the Court's potential jurisdictional reach. Two examples in different factual circumstances illustrate the point. The first involves the armed forces of a State Party, the United Kingdom, on the physical territory of a non-State Party, Iraq; and the second involves the armed forces of a non-State Party, Israel, on the physical territory of a "State Party",[22] Palestine.

Allegations of torture and mistreatment of detainees by UK military forces in the south of Iraq emerged in the course of UK domestic litigation – particularly pertaining to the death of Baha Mousa in UK military custody in Basra in 2003.[23] Court-martial proceedings were conducted against seven members of the Queen's Lancashire Regiment of the British Armed Forces,[24] civil proceedings were initiated by relatives of six Iraqi nationals killed by UK military forces in Iraq including members of Mousa's family,[25] and an official public inquiry into the death of Mousa was chaired by the retired Lord Justice of Appeal, Sir William Gage.[26]

The Prosecutor of the ICC at the time, Luis Moreno Ocampo, received over 240 communications alleging various ICC crimes in Iraq, including wilful

21 Again, my own country of Australia is a good example. Gillian Triggs described this as "a quiet revolution in Australian domestic criminal law" because Australia had never previously had comprehensive domestic criminal legislation to cover all international crimes. To facilitate Australian ratification of the Rome Statute, new legislation was enacted ensuring that all the substantive crimes in the Rome Statute can now be prosecuted by Australian courts. See Gillian Triggs, "Implementation of the Rome Statute for the International Criminal Court: A Quiet Revolution in Australian Law," (2003) 25 *Sydney Law Review* 507–534.

22 Palestine's legal status is contested. Following the Palestinian Authority's deposit of its instrument of accession to the Rome Statute and the announcement of the Prosecutor to open a Preliminary Examination into the situation in Palestine, Prime Minister Benjamin Netanyahu of Israel condemned the Prosecutor's decision, claiming that it was "absurd for the ICC to ignore international law and agreements, under which the Palestinians don't have a state and can only get one through direct negotiations with Israel." See "PM Netanyahu on the Decision of the ICC Prosecutor," press release, Israel Ministry of Foreign Affairs, 17 January 2015 at: http://mfa.gov.il/MFA/PressRoom/2015/Pages/PM-Netanyahu-on-decision-of-the-ICC-prosecutor-17-Jan-2015.aspx. My characterization of Palestine as a "State Party" to the Rome Statute here is without prejudice to the resolution of that issue.

23 See Gerry Simpson, "The Death of Baha Mousa" (2007) 8(2) *Melbourne Journal of International Law* 340–355.

24 See *R v. Payne* at: http://www.internationalcrimesdatabase.org/Case/811.

25 *R (Al-Skeini) v. Secretary of State for Defence* [2007] QB 140 at first instance. The case was appealed to Court of Appeal and to the House of Lords, and finally to the European Court of Human Rights. For a summary of the procedural history, see: http://www.internationalcrimesdatabase.org/Case/965/Al-Skeini-and-others.

26 The Report of the Public Inquiry is available at: https://www.gov.uk/government/uploads/system/uploads/attachment_data/file/279190/1452_i.pdf.

killing, torture and inhumane treatment. In response to those communications, the Prosecutor explained that Iraq was not a State Party to the Rome Statute and so, pursuant to Article 12, the Court only had jurisdiction over ICC crimes allegedly perpetrated by nationals of a State Party.[27] The United Kingdom was one such State Party whose nationals (military forces) had been deployed in Iraq. The Prosecutor had received multiple communications of abuse, mistreatment and torture of Iraqi detainees in the custody of UK military forces. The Prosecutor "concluded that there was a reasonable basis for believing that crimes within the jurisdiction of the Court had been committed, namely willful killing and inhuman treatment," but announced that, in the absence of more detailed information, he was unable to determine that the alleged crimes were of sufficient gravity to warrant seeking approval to open a formal investigation. In response to the Prosecutor's announcement, the European Centre for Constitutional and Human Rights in Berlin, in conjunction with Public Interest Lawyers (a law firm with offices in London and in Birmingham), prepared a 250-page dossier of evidence detailing large-scale mistreatment of detainees in the custody of UK military forces in Iraq.[28] Having received this new information, the ICC Prosecutor, Fatou Bensouda, announced that she was re-opening the preliminary examination of the situation in Iraq.[29]

In 2010, the UK Government established the Iraq Historic Allegations Team (IHAT) "to review and investigate allegations of abuse by Iraqi civilians by UK armed forces personnel in Iraq during the period of 2003 to July 2009."[30] Following Bensouda's announcement of the decision to re-open the Preliminary Examination, the UK authorities substantially increased the resources of the IHAT and, according to the official website, discovered more than 1,300 cases involving in excess of 1,500 separate incidents of alleged ill-treatment in detention or of death by shooting warranting investigation.[31] The UK authorities should

27 See "OPT Response to Communications Received Concerning Iraq," 9 February 2006, available at: https://www.icc-cpi.int/NR/rdonlyres/04D143C8-19FB-466C-AB77-4CDB2FDEBEF7/143682/OTP_letter_to_senders_re_Iraq_9_February_2006.pdf.

28 See ECCHR and PIL, "Communication to the Office of the Prosecutor of the International Criminal Court: The Responsibility of Officials of the United Kingdom for War Crimes Involving Systematic Detainee Abuse in Iraq from 2003–2008," 10 January 2014. The text of the dossier is available to download at: http://www.ecchr.eu/en/our_work/international-crimes-and-accountability/united-kingdom.html.

29 "Prosecutor of the International Criminal Court, Fatou Bensouda, Re-opens the Preliminary Examination of the Situation in Iraq," 13 May 2016. The text of the announcement is available at: https://www.icc-cpi.int/en_menus/icc/structure%20of%20the%20court/office%20of%20the%20prosecutor/reports%20and%20statements/statement/Pages/otp-statement-iraq-13-05-2014.aspx.

30 See: https://www.gov.uk/government/groups/iraq-historic-allegations-team-ihat.

31 For a detailed summary of incidents of alleged ill-treatment, see: https://www.gov.uk/government/uploads/system/uploads/attachment_data/file/509659/20160322-IHAT_Allocated_Cases_as_per_31_December_2015.pdf.

be applauded for taking the investigation of these allegations seriously, even if the motivation is to avoid ICC exercise of jurisdiction (on the possible basis of an apparent lack of willingness by the United Kingdom to exercise its primary jurisdiction as the state of nationality). There is an understandable tendency for military authorities to explain violations of international humanitarian law as the acts of a few "bad apples" rather than a systemic failure of command responsibility. If one consequence of the existence of the ICC is to act as a catalyst for states to take their national investigative responsibilities more seriously, this will be a significant contribution.

The second example of "positive complementarity" involves increased scrutiny of the conduct of Israeli Defense Forces (IDF) members on the physical territory of Palestine. Following the so-called "Mavi Marmara Incident" in 2010 – the interdiction by the IDF of the flotilla of vessels attempting to run the maritime blockade of Gaza – the Government of Israel created an independent public commission of inquiry headed by Jakob Turkel, a former Justice of Israel's Supreme Court (the Turkel Commission). The Commission produced its First Report on the Maritime Incident of 31 May 2010 in January 2011[32] and then initiated its Second Phase to consider Israel's Mechanisms for Examining and Investigating Complaints and Claims of Violations of the Laws of Armed Conflict According to International Law. In its Second Report produced in March 2013,[33] the Commission concluded that Israel's mechanisms for examining and investigating complaints and claims of violations of the Law of Armed Conflict generally complied with its obligations under international law. However, the Commission also made 18 recommendations for further improvement. Recommendation 5 is entitled "Fact-Finding Assessment" and is the critical recommendation for current purposes. Previously the Israeli Military Advocate-General's (MAG) principal source of documentation for considering whether or not to open a criminal investigation was the IDF "operational debrief." The Turkel Commission expressed some concern that the operational debrief is prepared by members of the very IDF unit whose conduct is in question. Consequently, the Commission recommended that the IDF establish an independent Fact-Finding Assessment mechanism to assist the MAG in his considerations.[34]

---

32 Turkel Commission: The Public Commission to Examine the Maritime Incident of 31 May 2010, *Report: Part I*, January 2011. Available at: http://www.turkel-committee.gov.il/files/wordocs//8707200211english.pdf.

33 Turkel Commission: The Public Commission to Examine the Maritime Incident of 31 May 2010, *Report: Part II – Israel's Mechanisms for Examining and Investigating Complaints and Claims of Violations of the Laws of Armed Conflict According to International Law*, March 2013. Available at: http://www.turkel-committee.gov.il/files/newDoc3/The%20Turkel%20Report%20for%20website.pdf. In the interests of transparency and disclosure, I served as one of two independent international observers for Phase II of the Turkel Commission of Enquiry.

34 Ibid, Recommendation 5, pp 378–382.

According to the IDF website:

> At the beginning of the 2014 Gaza Conflict, in accordance with one of the recommendations of the Turkel Commission, the IDF Chief of the General Staff ordered the establishment of a permanent new General Staff Mechanism for Fact-Finding Assessment ("FFA Mechanism") to examine exceptional incidents that allegedly occurred during the ongoing conflict. The examination conducted by the FFA Mechanism is intended to provide the MAG with as much information as possible so that the MAG may decide whether to open a criminal investigation. The FFA Mechanism relies on high-ranking IDF reserve and active-duty officers with military operational, legal, and investigative experience outside the chain of command of the operational activity under examination. These examinations may also help to inform the IDF's "lessons-learned" process, so that steps may be considered in an effort to minimise the risk of such incidents recurring in the future. In some cases, where credible allegations prima facie give rise to a reasonable suspicion of criminal wrongdoing, the MAG may open a criminal investigation without requiring an FFA examination.[35]

In the aftermath of the IDF's 2014 incursion into Gaza, the FFA Mechanism was established and commenced its work immediately. Several incidents in Gaza were referred to the MAG in addition to those the MAG had already determined warranted a criminal investigation.[36] The Israeli authorities are clearly conscious of international criticism of IDF conduct, and increased independent scrutiny of operational decisions is intended to demonstrate Israel's capacity to undertake independent and impartial proceedings in the face of alleged serious violations of international humanitarian law.[37] Following the announcement of the opening of a Preliminary Examination into the Palestine situation by Fatou Bensouda on 16 January 2015,[38] such increased scrutiny has only become more important if Israel wishes to exercise its primary right of national jurisdiction and to avoid the ICC exercising complementary jurisdiction on the basis of an apparent lack of willingness on the part of Israel as the state of nationality.

---

35 See: https://www.idfblog.com/blog/2015/06/22/israels-investigation-alleged-violations-law-armed-conflict.

36 See, for example, Mitch Ginsburg, "IDF Opens Criminal Probe into 5 Cases in Wake of Gaza Op," *The Times of Israel*, 10 September 2014, available at: http://www.timesofisrael.com/idf-to-open-criminal-probe-into-2-deadly-gaza-strikes; Isabel Kershner, "Israel, Facing Criticism, to Investigate Possible Military Misconduct in Gaza," *The New York Times*, 10 September 2014, available at: http://www.nytimes.com/2014/09/11/world/middleeast/gaza-strip-israel-criminal-investigation.html.

37 See, for example, Yoav Zitun and Itamar Eichner, "IDF Extends Criminal Investigations into Protective Edge," *Y-Net News*, 12 June 2015, available at: http://www.ynetnews.com/articles/0,7340,L-4667770,00.html.

38 ICC, "The Prosecutor of the International Criminal Court, Fatou Bensouda, Opens a Preliminary Examination of the Situation in Palestine," press release, 16 January 2015 at: https://www.icc-cpi.int/en_menus/icc/press%20and%20media/press%20releases/Pages/pr1083.aspx.

The ICC is, of course, not the only relevant development over the past two decades. The establishment of the ICTY and the ICTR created a momentum which not only facilitated the establishment of the ICC but also spawned a proliferation of ad hoc and hybrid international criminal tribunals, including the Serious Crimes Unit (SCU) for East Timor in Dili,[39] the Special Court for Sierra Leone (SCSL) in Freetown,[40] the Extraordinary Chambers in the Courts of Cambodia (ECCC) in Phnom Penh,[41] the Special Tribunal for Lebanon (STL) in The Hague[42] and the newly announced Kosovo Relocated Specialist Judicial Institution to also be established in The Hague.[43] This burgeoning of new institutions to try international crimes is symptomatic of an increasing global expectation that those responsible for atrocities be held accountable – an expectation that has also manifested itself in domestic criminal proceedings, including, for example, the extradition proceedings against Augusto Pinochet in London.[44]

By any measure, developments to increase enforcement of serious violations of international humanitarian law over the past two decades have been dramatic. In 2019, it is hard to believe there was ever any cause for doubt about the momentum for development back in 1996. Much of the credit for these developments can be traced back to the decision of the UN Security Council in 1993 to establish the ICTY and for the approach of Louise and others in the early years of the Tribunal to render it an effective institution.

2.3. FUTURE CHALLENGES: STILL NO COMPREHENSIVE AND SYSTEMATIC SYSTEM OF GLOBAL CRIMINAL JUSTICE

While developments in international criminal justice over the past 20 years offer cause for celebration, the project is far from complete. Every ad hoc tribunal has faced its own challenges. The ICTY in The Hague and the ICTR in Arusha were both physically removed from the location of the crimes and criticisms have been levelled at the relative lack of local "ownership" of the trial process.

39 See Caitlin Reiger and Marieke Weirda, *The Serious Crimes Process in Timor-Leste: In Retrospect*, International Center for Transitional Justice Prosecutions Case Studies Series, March 2006. Available at: https://www.ictj.org/sites/default/files/ICTJ-TimorLeste-Criminal-Process-2006-English.pdf.

40 See the website of the Residual Special Court for Sierra Leone: http://www.rscsl.org.

41 See the website of the Extraordinary Chambers in the Courts of Cambodia: http://www.eccc.gov.kh/en.

42 See the website of the Special Tribunal for Lebanon: http://www.stl-tsl.org/en.

43 See the announcement of the establishment of the Kosovo Tribunal: https://www.government.nl/latest/news/2016/01/15/kosovo-court-to-be-established-in-the-hague.

44 I have written elsewhere of what I characterize here as increasing global expectation. See, for example, McCormack (2009), *supra* note 20.

But those hybrid tribunals which have been established locally have been beset with their own challenges. The most senior individual tried by the SCSL, Charles Taylor of Liberia, was tried not in Freetown but in The Hague. The SCSL conducted three trials in Freetown – one each for the three parties to the conflict, but Sam Hinga Norman, the senior Sierra Leonean government official on trial, died in custody. The Special Court was intended to help train Sierra Leonean judges, prosecutors and defence counsel, but serious questions remain about the efficacy of any capacity building by a court dominated by foreign nationals.[45] The ECCC has been plagued by allegations of political interference by Prime Minister Hun Sen, who reluctantly allowed the trials against the most senior Khmer Rouge leaders, but has refused to allow any expansion of the list of potential accused.[46] Neither the STL in The Hague (physically distant from the site of the Beirut assassination of Rafik Hariri) nor the SCU for Timor Leste in Dili (precisely where many of the 1999 atrocities occurred) have enjoyed any success in gaining custody of those allegedly most responsible for respective atrocities. The STL is conducting its first trial *in absentia*,[47] but queries remain about the merits of proceedings in the absence of the accused.[48]

The permanent ICC – an alternative model to ad hoc tribunals for specific situations – also faces many of its own challenges. The Court has no police powers of arrest and is dependent upon states and international organizations to cooperate in the execution of arrest warrants. Some States Parties, with explicit Rome Statute treaty obligations to cooperate, have refused to do so. The South African Government's complicity in Omar Al-Bashir's hasty departure from South Africa while the Supreme Court was ordering Al-Bashir's arrest is the most glaring recent example.[49] Other States Parties have obstructed the Court's

---

45 For a detailed assessment of the efficacy of the Special Court, see, for example: Charles Chenor Jalloh, "Special Court for Sierra Leone: Achieving Justice?" (2011) 32 *Michigan Journal of International Law* 395–460; and Tom Perriello and Marieke Wierda, *The Special Court for Sierra Leone under Scrutiny*, International Center for Transitional Justice Prosecutions Case Studies Series, March 2006. Available at: https://www1.umn.edu/humanrts/instree/SCSL/Case-studies-ICTJ.pdf.

46 See, for example, Susan Lamb, *Reconciliation v. Accountability: The Extraordinary Chambers in the Courts of Cambodia*, Forum for International Criminal and Humanitarian Law Policy Brief Series, No. 34, 2015. Brief available at: https://www.fichl.org/fileadmin/fichl/documents/FICHL_Policy_Brief_Series/150521_PBS_No._34__2015___Lamb_.pdf; and Heather Ryan and Laura McGrew, *Performance and Perception: The Impact of the Extraordinary Chambers in the Courts of Cambodia*, Open Society Justice Initiative Report, 2016. Report available at: https://www.opensocietyfoundations.org/sites/default/files/performance-perception-eccc-20160211.pdf.

47 *Ayyash et al* Trial against the co-accused Salim Jamil Ayyash, Mustafa Amine Badreddine, Hussein Hassan Oneissi, Assad Hassan Sabra and Hassan Habib Merhi. For information on the trial, see: http://www.specialtribunalforlebanon.com/en/the-cases/about-the-trial.

48 See Chris Jenks, "Notice Otherwise Given: Will *in Absentia* Trials at the Special Tribunal for Lebanon Violate Human Rights?" (2009) 33 *Fordham International Law Journal* 57–100.

49 See Milton Nkosi, "South Africa Criticized over Sudan's Omar al-Bashir's Exit," *BBC World News*, 24 June 2015, available at: http://www.bbc.com/news/world-africa-33254003. For a

work and the Prosecutor's decision to withdraw the charges against Uhuru Kenyatta,[50] and the Pre-Trial Chamber's decision to dismiss the case against William Ruto and Joshua Sang[51] in the midst of swirling allegations of bribery of witnesses and political interference[52] have established disappointing precedents for undermining the Court's efficacy. Beyond situations involving States Parties to the Statute, the Court has only limited jurisdiction and is dependent upon the UN Security Council for referral of situations.[53] The Council's 2005 referral of the situation in Darfur, Sudan was a significant breakthrough in the Court's experience. Unfortunately, the Council's enthusiasm for facilitating the Court's engagement with Darfur has not been matched with subsequent resolve to bring those allegedly most responsible for atrocities to justice. Mr Ocampo's decision to seek approval for the issuance of an arrest warrant against Al-Bashir was roundly criticized – principally because it was thought to create unwanted complications for the separate process to conclude a peace agreement in the south of Sudan.[54] As it happened, Ocampo's initiative did not prove to be an impediment to conflict resolution elsewhere in the country, but many wondered whether Security Council members might be reluctant to refer other situations to the Prosecutor in the future. In February 2011, all such concerns evaporated when the Council referred the situation in Libya and extended a role to the Court in an international crisis in real time. Ocampo wasted no time in requesting the issuance of arrest warrants against Muammar Gaddafi, his son Saif Gaddafi and Abdullah Al-Senussi.[55] However, those who naively assumed

summary of the various judicial proceedings in the case, including links to filings in the proceedings and to the decisions of the North Gauteng High Court and of the Supreme Court of Appeal, see: http://www.southernafricalitigationcentre.org/cases/ongoing-cases/south-africasudan-seeking-implementation-of-icc-arrest-warrant-for-president-bashir.

50 *The Prosecutor v Uhuru Muigai Kenyatta*, "Notice of Withdrawal of the Charges against Uhuru Muigai Kenyatta," ICC-01/09-02/11, 5 December 2014 at: https://www.icc-cpi.int/iccdocs/doc/doc1879204.pdf.

51 *The Prosecutor v. William Samoei Ruto and Joshua Arap Sang*, "Decision on Defence Applications for Judgments of Acquittal," ICC-01/09-01/11, 5 April 2016 at: https://www.icc-cpi.int/iccdocs/doc/doc2228553.pdf.

52 Arrest warrants have been issued against three suspects in two cases for alleged offences against the administration of justice consisting in corruptly or attempting to corruptly influence ICC witnesses. See *The Prosecutor v Walter Osapiri Barasa* ICC-01/09-01/13 (https://www.icc-cpi.int/kenya/barasa) and *The Prosecutor v. Paul Gicheru and Philip Kipkoech Bett* ICC-01/09-01/15 (https://www.icc-cpi.int/kenya/gicheru-bett). All three accused are currently at large and no proceedings against them will occur *in absentia*.

53 Article 13(b) of the Rome Statute.

54 See, for example, Alex de Waal and Gregory Stanton, "Should President Omar al-Bashir of Sudan be Charged and Arrested by the International Criminal Court?: An Exchange of Views," (2009) 4(3) *Genocide Studies and Prevention* 329–353, at 329–335.

55 Mr Ocampo requested the issuance of all three warrants for arrest in May 2011 and the Pre-Trial Chamber agreed to the request and ordered the issuance of the arrest warrants in June 2011. See *The Prosecutor v. Saif Al-Islam Gaddafi*, Case Information Sheet, 26 March 2015, available at: https://www.icc-cpi.int/iccdocs/PIDS/publications/GaddafiEng.pdf.

that UN Security Council Resolution 1973 represented some new commitment of Council Member States to optimize the potential of the Court were soon to be disappointed, given the lack of political will to refer other situations, including the final months of the civil war in Sri Lanka or the obstruction of Russia and China to the attempted referral of the Syrian situation.

I will never forget a breakfast meeting I enjoyed with Louise in Melbourne in 2010 shortly after the International Crisis Group (ICG) had produced its report on war crimes perpetrated in the latter months of the conflict on the Jaffna Peninsula in the north of Sri Lanka.[56] The deliberate targeting of Tamil civilians, hospitals and humanitarian relief operations had been extensively documented, but Louise and I were most upset by the anecdotal suggestions that the "Sri Lankan Model" was in vogue in conversations around the world. The regime of Mahinda Rajapaksa had allegedly evicted all journalists from the war zone in order to use overwhelming force to finally crush the Liberation Tigers of Tamil Eelam (LTTE) once and for all. And, given the relative lack of criticism of the strategy in multilateral circles, the approach was being spruiked as a successful approach to dealing with protracted insurgencies. Louise and I were appalled at the prospect of impunity for those most responsible and the precedent that would set for other regimes in similar circumstances. We lamented the lack of appetite amongst Security Council members for referral of the Sri Lankan conflict to the ICC Prosecutor, knowing full well that the Rajapaksa regime would resist all efforts to establish any external accountability mechanism. I note that Louise has not relented in her calls for an independent international inquiry into the conduct of operations in those chilling final months of the Sri Lankan conflict.[57]

The then Israeli Foreign Minister, Avigdor Lieberman, was quoted as criticizing Fatou Bensouda for opening a Preliminary Examination into the situation in Palestine, but not one for Syria, alleging an anti-Israel bias given her apparent indifference to the then more than 200,000 dead from the Syrian conflict.[58] Such suggestions reflect a comprehensive misunderstanding of the limitations to the ICC's jurisdiction. In the absence of a UN Security Council referral of the Syrian situation to the Prosecutor, the ICC has no jurisdiction over alleged violations of the Rome Statute perpetrated on the physical territory of Syria unless the conduct in question is perpetrated by nationals of a State Party to the Rome Statute – government armed forces intervening in Syria or

56 International Crisis Group, *War Crimes in Sri Lanka*, Asia Report No. 191, 17 May 2010, available at: http://www.crisisgroup.org/en/regions/asia/south-asia/sri-lanka/191-war-crimes-in-sri-lanka.aspx.

57 See Louise Arbour, "Let the UN Unmask the Criminals of Sri Lanka's War," *The New York Times*, 28 February 2014, available at: http://www.crisisgroup.org/en/regions/asia/south-asia/sri-lanka/op-eds/arbour-let-the-un-unmask-the-criminals-of-sri-lankas-war.aspx.

58 See Jonathan Lis, "ICC Opens Initial Probe into Possible War Crimes in Palestinian Territories," *Haaretz*, 16 January 2015, available at: http://www.haaretz.com/israel-news/1.637518.

foreign fighters who are nationals of States Parties. France attempted to facilitate referral of the Syrian situation, but the draft resolution was vetoed by Russia and China.[59] The reality is that the ICC does not represent a comprehensive and systematic system of international criminal justice. For those, including Louise and I, who believe that the ICC represents an advance over all that precedes it, we must also acknowledge that it remains far from an ideal institution and that there is still much to do to improve the current version of international criminal justice.

I remain encouraged by a long-term view of incremental progress. Think of the situation 100 years ago at the end of World War I. The victorious Allies chose not to establish criminal tribunals for German and Ottoman defendants and allowed the Central Powers instead to conduct their own national trials.[60] It is impossible to argue that there has been no demonstrable progress over the past century toward the goal of individual criminal accountability and a more comprehensive system of international criminal justice. Even the last 20 years reveal significant advances – many of which are attributable to the Security Council's decision to establish the ICTY and to Louise and others like her who have worked so assiduously on multiple fronts. Another 20 years from now, let alone another century from now, any objective reflection on developments since 2019 will undoubtedly reveal some significant steps forward, as well as some setbacks and new challenges.

3. SPECTACULAR TECHNOLOGICAL ADVANCES AND THE ADAPTABILITY OF INTERNATIONAL HUMANITARIAN LAW

3.1. 1996 CONCERNS: THE CHEMICAL WEAPONS CONVENTION AS PRECEDENT FOR FUTURE DISARMAMENT REGIMES

In 1996, I focused more extensively on developments in arms control and disarmament than on any other issue. I started with the spectacular technological developments since the Battle of Solferino in 1859. In the period immediately following the battle, there were no weapons of mass destruction, no aircrafts,

---

59 See "Referral of Syria to International Criminal Court Fails as Negative Votes Prevent Security Council from Adopting Draft Resolution," UN press release, 22 May 2014, available at: http://www.un.org/press/en/2014/sc11407.doc.htm.

60 The post-World War I decision not to impose Allied Tribunals on the defeated Germans and Ottomans, despite the inclusion of *pro forma* provisions in the respective peace treaties, is now well known. One of the earliest analyses of the Allied decision was Gary Jonathan Bass, *Stay the Hand of Vengeance: The Politics of War Crimes Tribunals* (Princeton, Princeton University Press, 2000).

no machine-powered vessels, no missiles and no long-range or machine-driven artillery. I made the observation in 1996 that neither weapons of mass destruction nor automatic weapons were needed to cause prodigious carnage on the battlefield of Solferino (80,000 dead in one day of fighting) in 1859 and nor were such weapons needed to cause the almost one million deaths in the Rwandan Genocide in 1994.[61] But, of course, military applications of technology have developed spectacularly across more than 100 years and Henri Dunant could never have imagined fighter aircraft, helicopters, aircraft carries, submarines, inter-continental ballistic missiles and machine guns, let alone chemical, biological and nuclear weapons.

The period immediately following the Cold War was a watershed moment for multilateral arms control, facilitating, as it did, unprecedented international cooperation to finalize agreement on key treaty regimes – particularly the Chemical Weapons Convention (CWC)[62] in 1993. The conclusion of that treaty represented a major breakthrough both because of its comprehensive prohibition of an entire category of weapons and because of its unprecedented measures for verification of compliance amongst States Parties, which set a new benchmark for subsequent arms control and disarmament agreements.[63]

The proposed CWC had languished in the discussion/negotiation phase since the 1960s and even following almost 30 years, the "Rolling Text" of the draft convention was still riddled with square brackets and contested wording. The then Australian Foreign Minister, Gareth Evans, undertook a major initiative to conclude negotiations on the CWC by preparing a draft alternative text "clean" of all square brackets. The concept was to use the existing Rolling Text, but to remove all square brackets by selecting compromise language to potentially resolve key sticking points and to demonstrate what a final convention text could resemble.[64] The Australian initiative was a stunning success. Evans presented the text to the Conference on Disarmament at UN Headquarters in Geneva in March 1992,[65] and the Conference adopted the new Convention and opened it

61 McCormack, *supra* note 1, at 627.

62 Convention on the Prohibition of the Development, Production, Stockpiling and Use of Chemical Weapons and on their Destruction, 13 January 1993, 1974 *United Nations Treaty Series* 45.

63 See, for example, Robert J Mathews, "The First Review Conference of the Chemical Weapons Convention: A Drafter's Perspective" in Ramesh Thakur and Ere Haru (eds), *The Chemical Weapons Convention: Implementation, Challenges and Opportunities* (Tokyo, United Nations University Press 2006) 44–74.

64 For a more detailed analysis of the Australian initiative, see Martine Letts, Robert J Mathews, Timothy L H McCormack and Christos Moraitis, "The Conclusion of the Chemical Weapons Convention: An Australian Perspective" (1993) 14 *Arms Control* 311–332.

65 See the extract of Senator Gareth Evans' speech to the UN Conference on Disarmament in Geneva on 19 March 1992 in (1992) 14 *Australian Yearbook of International Law* 682–686.

for signature in 1993.[66] The Convention involved a comprehensive prohibition on the production, possession, transfer and use of an entire category of weapons.

One major challenge for the prohibition of chemical weapons had always been the so-called "dual use" dilemma: the same basic chemicals used in toxic chemical weapons have many beneficial peaceful purposes – in agriculture, pharmaceutical drugs, domestic paints and solvents, for example. The worldwide industry produced massive quantities of chemicals worth billions of dollars annually and any effective verification regime required industry cooperation. A key aspect of the Australian CWC initiative was to engage the global chemical industry,[67] which came on board in strong support for conclusion of convention negotiations and expressing a willingness to cooperate with verification measures. Consequently, the final CWC established an unprecedented verification regime to be managed by a new collective of expert chemical inspectors employed by the Convention's new Organisation for the Prohibition of Chemical Weapons (OPCW).[68]

In 1996 the CWC had not yet entered into force (this occurred in 1997) and nor had the headquarters of the OPCW been constructed in the host city, The Hague. My focus two decades ago was on initiatives to encourage states to join the treaty regime and on outreach activities occurring in various states around the world. There was never any suggestion that the new convention would not enter into force and, instead, I discussed the momentum from the breakthrough of the CWC for other arms control and disarmament initiatives.[69]

Following the opening for signature of the CWC in 1993, States Parties to the Certain Conventional Weapons Convention (CCW)[70] had adopted two new Protocols to the Convention. Protocol IV prohibiting laser weapons designed to cause human blindness[71] also constituted a refreshing change in disarmament negotiations because it was the first multilateral treaty to ban a category of weapons before they had been deployed in battle. Usually tortuous disarmament negotiations only follow in the wake of an egregious use of the weapons that

---

66 Convention on the Prohibition of the Development, Production, Stockpiling and Use of Chemical Weapons and on their Destruction, 13 January 1993, 1974 *United Nations Treaty Series* 45.

67 See Speech of the Australian Prime Minister, R J Hawke, to open the Government-Industry Conference against Chemical Weapons (GICCW), Canberra, 18 September 1989 at: http://pmtranscripts.dpmc.gov.au/release/transcript-7744.

68 See website of the OPCW at: https://www.opcw.org.

69 McCormack, *supra* note 1, at 631–632.

70 Convention on Prohibitions or Restrictions on the Use of Certain Conventional Weapons Which May Be Deemed to Be Excessively Injurious or to Have Indiscriminate Effects, 10 April 1981, 1342 *United Nations Treaty Series* 137.

71 Protocol on Blinding Laser Weapons, 13 October 1995, 1380 *United Nations Treaty Series* 370.

acts as a catalyst for subsequent multilateral action. In contrast, the other newly adopted protocol was a major disappointment. Amended Protocol II[72] revisited the legal regulation of anti-personnel landmines. Some states had wanted to adopt a comprehensive treaty prohibition on anti-personnel landmines and were disappointed with the CCW process only resulting in a treaty regime for the adoption of "smart mines": those containing a minimum amount of detectable metal and incorporating either self-deactivating or self-destructing capability. The CCW process is consensus-based and so any single state can veto a particular disarmament initiative. One consequence though is that the lowest common denominator reality often disappoints those with a more progressive agenda. In 1996, I lauded the achievement of Protocol IV and lamented the relative lack of progress inherent in Amended Protocol II.

A key humanitarian challenge in 1996 involved the deleterious impact of anti-personnel landmines. The International Committee of the Red Cross (ICRC) estimated at the time that as many as 24,000 people a year were killed or maimed by landmines and that there were as many as 120 million sown landmines in the ground then being cleared at a rate of approximately 100,000 per year, while an additional two million new landmines were being sown annually.[73] The overwhelming majority of the sown landmines were remnants from past conflicts lying in the ground and ready to explode in many cases decades after the cessation of hostilities. Tragically, the ubiquity of these weapons often precluded the working of arable land, exacerbating dire economic circumstances and causing death and maiming of civilians who had inadvertently stepped on and detonated them. Unusually for the ICRC, the deleterious impact of anti-personnel landmines on civilians had become so widespread and so damaging that the organization departed from its usual approach of neutrality in disarmament negotiations to publicly advocate for a comprehensive treaty prohibition.[74]

3.2. TWO DECADES OF DEVELOPMENT: NEW COMPREHENSIVE TREATY PROHIBITIONS

Since 1996, the CWC has not only entered into force but has attained close to universal participation with 192 States Parties.[75] The most high-profile recent accession to the Convention involved Syria following confirmation of extensive

---

72 Amended Protocol on Prohibitions or Restrictions on the Use of Mines, Booby-Traps and Other Devices, 3 May 1996, 2048 *United Nations Treaty Series* 93.

73 McCormack, *supra* note 1, 635, citing ICRC, *Landmines Must Be Stopped* (1996).

74 Ibid, 637.

75 For comprehensive details on CWC States Parties, see the OPCW website at: https://www.opcw.org/about-opcw/member-states.

use of chemical weapons (CWs), which sparked an unusually unanimous outpouring of multilateral condemnation.[76] OPCW inspectors played a significant role in verifying Syria's stockpile of CWs and in overseeing its destruction in what is arguably the one highpoint for the advancement of international law in the face of egregious disregard for it that has been so characteristic of the Syrian conflict. Tragically, however, Syria's accession to the CWC and the subsequent destruction of its declared national stockpile of toxic chemicals has not resulted in a cessation of CW attacks. In the third and final report of the UN-OPCW Joint Investigative Mission deployed to Syria to investigate alleged CW attacks, the Mission personnel have reported "sufficient information" to conclude that the Assad regime has used chlorine gas and that ISIL forces have used sulfur mustard.[77] Even these findings by the Joint Investigative Mission have not appeared to have deterred ongoing alleged uses of chlorine gas[78] and Syria now has the dubious record of becoming the first State Party to the CWC on whose physical territory CWs have allegedly been deployed.

As explained earlier, the CWC set important precedents both in terms of scope of prohibition (development, production, stockpiling, transfer, use and destruction of existing stockpiles) and of the intrusiveness of the verification regime. Some key subsequent disarmament initiatives followed the CWC model.

Following the conclusion of the First Review Conference to the Certain Conventional Weapons Convention,[79] a number of states were disappointed with the limited scope of Amended Protocol II and with the failure to reach an agreement on a process to work toward a comprehensive prohibition on

---

76 Allegations of Syrian use of CWs had circulated throughout 2013, but the deadliest attack occurred in the Damascus suburb of Ghouta on 21 August 2013. UN investigations confirmed use of the nerve agent sarin in that attack and the regime of Bashar al-Assad was roundly condemned. On 14 September 2013, just over three weeks after the Ghouta attack, Syria deposited its instrument of accession to the CWC on the same day that the United States and Russia agreed on a program for the elimination of Syria's CW stockpile. On 27 September 2013, the UN Security Council adopted Resolution 2118 and, *inter alia*, expressed deep outrage at the confirmed use of CWs in August 2013, condemned the killing of civilians in that attack and affirmed that the use of CWs is a serious violation of international law.

77 See "Third Report of the Organisation for the Prohibition of Chemical Weapons – United Nations Joint Investigative Mission," presented to the UN Security Council by the UN Secretary-General, 24 August 2016. Available at: http://www.securitycouncilreport.org/atf/cf/%7B65BFCF9B-6D27-4E9C-8CD3-CF6E4FF96FF9%7D/s_2016_738.pdf.

78 As recently as 6 September 2016, the Assad regime has been accused of dropping chlorine gas bombs on Aleppo in northern Syria. See: "Chlorine Gas Bombs Dropped on Syrian City of Aleppo Poison Dozens of Children," *The Telegraph*, 7 September 2016, available at: http://www.telegraph.co.uk/news/2016/09/07/chlorine-bombs-dropped-on-syrian-city-of-aleppo-leave-dozens-cho.

79 See the "Final Report" of the Review Conference of the State Parties to the Convention on Prohibitions or Restrictions on the Use of Certain Conventional Weapons Which May Be Deemed to Be Excessively Injurious or Have Indiscriminate Effects, 3 May 1996. Available at: http://www.un.org/Depts/ddar/ccw/ccw.htm.

anti-personnel landmines. Canada hosted an "international strategy conference" in Ottawa in October 1996 entitled "Towards a Global Ban on Anti-Personnel Mines" involving 50 participating states, an additional 24 observer states and several pro-ban non-governmental organizations (NGOs) and international organizations.[80] At the conclusion of that conference, the Canadian Foreign Minister invited states to return to Ottawa a year later to adopt the text of a comprehensive multilateral treaty prohibition on anti-personnel landmines. In September 1997, at a Diplomatic Conference in Oslo, the "Ottawa Convention" was adopted.[81] Following the model of the CWC, the Ottawa Convention includes a comprehensive prohibition on anti-personnel landmines[82] and measures for verification of compliance.[83]

My initial reaction on the celebrations of the opening for signature of the Ottawa Convention was skeptical. Signatory States did not include the biggest users or producers of landmines and, consequently, I was concerned that the treaty would achieve little for the victims of anti-personnel landmines around the world.[84] In retrospect, I underestimated the potential of a new multilateral disarmament treaty to influence attitudes to the continued use of the weapon – even by those states not party to the new treaty regime. As a direct consequence of the growing influence of the Ottawa Treaty prohibition, there is a de facto moratorium on the export of anti-personnel landmines and the United States, originally so implacably opposed to the Ottawa Treaty, is now openly discussing the possibility of joining the treaty regime.[85] There are salutary lessons here for the progressive development of international law – that the emergence of a new treaty prohibition can increase the stigma attached to the export and the use of the category of weapons in question, even for those states which have chosen not to participate in the new treaty.

---

80 See "Report on Activities" of "Towards a Global Ban on Anti-Personnel Mines: International Strategy Conference" at: https://idl-bnc.idrc.ca/dspace/bitstream/10625/27887/1/120310.pdf.

81 Convention on the Prohibition of the Use, Stockpiling, Production and Transfer of Anti-Personnel Mines and on Their Destruction, 17 September 1997, 2056 *United Nations Treaty Series* 211.

82 See Article 1 – General Obligations.

83 See Article 8 – Facilitation and Clarification of Compliance.

84 Some commentators are still concerned by the lack of participation in the Ottawa Convention of the world's largest manufacturers and users of anti-personnel landmines. For example, Bill Boothby states that: "It does matter that militarily significant States like India, Pakistan, the United States, China and the Russian Federation are not, and, in the case of some them, appear to have no intention of becoming, party to the Ottawa Convention. Without their participation, the global aspect of the treaty ban is impaired." William H Boothby, *Weapons and the Law of Armed Conflict* (Oxford: Oxford University Press, 2nd edn, 2016), 378.

85 See, for example, Felicia Schwartz, "U.S. Moves Closer to Compliance with Treaty Banning Land Mines: Obama Administration Pledges to Cease Use Everywhere Except Korean Peninsula," *The Wall Street Journal*, 23 September 2014 at: http://www.wsj.com/articles/u-s-moves-closer-to-compliance-with-treaty-banning-land-mines-1411509618.

In addition to the deleterious consequences of anti-personnel landmines, the ICRC also became concerned in the 1990s about the often devastating impact of other forms of unexploded ordnance, including "artillery shells, mortar shells, hand grenades, cluster munitions, bombs and similar weapons,"[86] following the end of armed conflict. In 2000, the ICRC proposed the negotiation of a new Protocol to the CCW on "explosive remnants of war" in order to reduce the threat posed by unexploded ordnance after the end of conflicts. The CCW established a Group of Governmental Experts to identify ways to tackle the problem and the new Protocol V on Explosive Remnants of War was adopted and opened for signature in 2003. Again, a number of states wanted to go further than a general treaty on mapping and clearing the explosive remnants of war. In particular, concerns were centred on the deleterious humanitarian impact on civilian populations of cluster munitions. Cluster weapons involve the dispersal of multiple sub-munitions, often over a wide physical area. The use of such munitions in civilian residential areas can involve widespread damage to civilian objects and extensive civilian deaths. In addition, it is inevitable that a proportion of sub-munitions will fail to detonate on impact and will instead explode when subsequently disturbed. Dud sub-munitions create a particular unexploded ordnance problem, causing human death or maiming and/or obstructing commercial or agricultural activities. Some states wanted to push for a comprehensive treaty ban on cluster munitions, but the consensual-based CCW was not amenable. Instead, Norway seized the initiative and led a negotiation process similar to the Ottawa Convention, which resulted in the opening for signature of the so-called "Oslo Convention" – the Convention on Cluster Munitions.

3.3. FUTURE CHALLENGES: EMERGING MILITARY TECHNOLOGIES

These past 20 years or so represent something of a halcyon period in arms control and disarmament – a relatively short period of time immediately following the Cold War in which an unprecedented level of multilateral cooperation resulted in some key breakthrough developments. However, the environment of cooperation and willingness to relinquish certain categories of weapons should not be overstated. Nuclear weapons are an excellent example. Despite the opening for signature of the new Treaty on the Prohibition of Nuclear Weapons in September 2017,[87] all the major nuclear weapons possessor states are

86 ICRC, Protocol on Explosive Remnants of War (Protocol V to the CCW Convention), 28 November 2003 at: https://www.icrc.org/ihl/INTRO/610.

87 Treaty on the Prohibition of Nuclear Weapons, 20 September 2017, U.N. Doc. A/CONF.229/2017/L.3/Rev.1.

opposed to joining the treaty. It is unclear whether any of those states could be encouraged to forego their possession of nuclear weapons and become States Parties to the treaty. Indeed, the prospect of horizontal nuclear proliferation – across a growing number of states – seems increasingly likely if not inevitable.

Given Russian expansionism in Crimea and Eastern Ukraine, and increasing murmurings of bellicose action beyond those situations, one wonders whether hypothetically it would even be possible now to conclude the CWC negotiations? The one glaring example of multilateral cooperation including between the United States and Russia – pressuring Bashar Al-Assad to join the CWC and to finally relinquish his stockpile of CWs – was arguably an aberration. On the same day that Assad announced his accession to the CWC, his forces undertook an attack on a hospital in rebel-held territory.[88] Indiscriminate attacks, by government forces, by rebel forces and by ISIS forces, have continued unabated in Syria, with no agreement even to refer the situation to the Prosecutor of the ICC – let alone on more substantive action. In the years since Syria acceded to the CWC, there have been ongoing allegations of the use of CWs by Assad regime forces and by ISIS raising questions about just how comprehensive the OPCW destruction of the Syrian CW stockpile really was.

In the midst of discouraging news about the ongoing use of CW, new technological developments will undoubtedly raise novel challenges to the existing regime of international humanitarian law. Henri Dunant's conclusion to *A Memory of Solferino* in 1862 was particularly prescient:

> If the new and frightful weapons of destruction which are now at the disposal of the nations, seem destined to abridge the duration of future wars, it appears likely, on the other hand, that future battles will only become more and more murderous. Moreover, in this age when surprise plays so important a part, is it not possible that wars may arise, from one quarter or another, in the most sudden and unexpected fashion? And do not these considerations alone constitute more than adequate reason for taking precautions against surprise?[89]

Dramatic technological developments over the past 150 years or so are likely to be eclipsed in future decades because of the increasing rapidity of technological advances. Military applications of information technologies and robotics raise the spectre of new modalities for the deployment of lethal military force and the adaptability of international humanitarian law will undoubtedly be tested.

---

88 See, for example, "Warplanes Bomb Hospital in Rebel-Held Territory," *ABC News*, 13 September 2013 at: http://www.abc.net.au/news/2013-09-13/syria-signs-up-to-global-poison-gas-ban-as-us-and-russia-hold-t/4955092.

89 Henri Dunant, *Un Souvenir de Solferino* (1862). I quote from the 1986 translation *A Memory of Solferino* published by the International Committee of the Red Cross (at 182). The original English translation of Dunant's reflections was published by the American Red Cross in 1939.

The information technology revolution is breathtaking in its pace of development and truly global in its reach. The Internet used only to be thought of as linking computers "plugged in" to a network, but the advent of wireless communication and spectacular advances in electronic connectivity have resulted in the notion of the "Internet of things."[90] So much of daily life is now controlled by electronic systems which operate more conveniently, and often more accurately, efficiently and effectively than manual systems ever could. But with increased connectivity comes increased vulnerability – to manipulation, exfiltration, loss of functionality, damage and loss of control. On average, almost one million computer network attacks occur every day around the world.[91] Exploitation of programming flaws in software and the release of targeted malware are not only commonplace but also increasingly innovative, sophisticated and audacious.[92] The international community is now used to cyber-espionage and to the exfiltration of large amounts of electronic data, as well as directed denial-of-service attacks overloading operating systems and temporarily shutting them down. However, future attacks could potentially disrupt public infrastructure, with catastrophic consequences. In November 2015, for example, Sweden's air traffic was crippled by cyber-attack at three of its major airports, forcing the cancellation or re-routing of flights to and from Arlanda, Landvetter and Bromma airports.[93] It has also been reported that the Swedish power company Vattenfall may also have been a target in the same cyber-attacks.[94]

Under the auspices of the NATO Cooperative Cyber Defence Centre of Excellence in Estonia, an international group of experts produced what has become the leading authority on the legal regulation of cyber-warfare – the *Tallinn Manual on the International Law Applicable to Cyber Warfare*.[95] The *Tallinn Manual* adopts the general position that international law applies to cyber-warfare as much as it does to kinetic warfare and states have not disputed

---

90 See, for example, Dr John Barrett, "The Internet of Things," TEDxCit Talk, 5 October 2012 at: https://www.youtube.com/watch?v=QaTIt1C5R-M; Jacob Morgan, "A Simple Explanation of the Internet of Things," *Forbes*, 13 May 2014 at: http://www.forbes.com/sites/jacobmorgan/2014/05/13/simple-explanation-internet-things-that-anyone-can-understand/#355e82576828.

91 See, for example, Patrik Maldre, *Global Connections, Regional Implications: An Overview of the Baltic Cyber Threat Landscape*, International Centre for Defence and Security, Estonia (October 2015), 9, citing Symantec's "2015 Internet Security Threat Report." ICSD Analysis available at: https://www.icds.ee/fileadmin/media/icds.ee/failid/Patrik_Maldre_-_Global_Connections__Regional_Implications.pdf.

92 Ibid.

93 See Kjetil Stormark, "Sweden Issued Cyber Attack Alert as its Air Traffic Reeled," *AldriMer*, 12 April 2016 at: https://www.aldrimer.no/sweden-issued-cyber-attack-alert-as-its-air-traffic-reeled.

94 Kjetil Stormark, "Vattenfall Possible Cyber Target," *AldriMer*, 12 April 2016 at: https://www.aldrimer.no/vattenfall-possible-cyber-target.

95 Michael N Schmitt (ed), *Tallinn Manual on the International Law Applicable to Cyber Warfare* (Cambridge, Cambridge University Press, 2013).

this proposition.[96] But war by virtual means is novel and some specific questions arise: can an armed conflict be triggered solely by virtual means and, in particular, can the twin criteria of intensity and organization for a non-international armed conflict[97] be satisfied purely by virtual means? Can a well-coordinated group of hacktivists who have never met each other and may not even know each other's identity be sufficiently "organized" for the existence of a non-international armed conflict? What is the requisite quantity of damage or loss of functionality for a cyber-operation to constitute an "attack" under international humanitarian law? And can electronic data constitute an "object" for these same purposes?

Robotics and unmanned weapons technology has also been developing at a dramatic pace and the use of unmanned aerial vehicles (UAVs), or "drones," to undertake targeted killings is the highest-profile example. The technological capability of remotely piloting an aircraft over Afghanistan or Pakistan, "loitering" over a target for up to 48 hours with live and constant high-resolution imagery, and choosing the optimal moment to launch a precision-guided missile – all literally from the other side of the world (at a US Air Force base in Nevada, for example) – is both incredible and controversial. The deployment of lethal military force by drone has instigated a robust public discussion about the legal and ethical implications of the policy and also about future technological developments. After all, a drone is controlled by a human pilot, but robotics specialists are increasingly developing greater levels of machine autonomy – including the capacity to deploy lethal military force without human intervention.[98]

---

96 See, for example, the US Department of Defense *Law of War Manual* (2015), which states at 996–997 in the chapter on Cyber Operations that: "Specific law of war rules may be applicable to cyber operations, even though these rules were developed long before cyber operations were possible. The law of war affirmatively anticipates technological innovation and contemplates that its existing rules will apply to such innovation, including cyber operations. Law of war rules may apply to new technologies because the rules often are not framed in terms of specific technological means. For example, the rules on conducting attacks do not depend on what type of weapon is used to conduct the attack. Thus, cyber operations may be subject to a variety of law of war rules depending on the rule and the nature of the cyber operation. For example, if the physical consequences of a cyber attack constitute the kind of physical damage that would be caused by dropping a bomb or firing a missile, that cyber attack would equally be subject to the same rules that apply to attacks using bombs or missiles."

97 These two criteria were first articulated in *Prosecutor v Tadić* (Case no. IT-94-1-T, ICTY Trial Chamber, 7 May 1997), para. 562. For a detailed analysis of the *Tadić* formulation and subsequent reiteration and application in international criminal jurisprudence across multiple international criminal courts and tribunals, see Caitlin Dwyer and Tim McCormack, "Conflict Characterisation" in Rain Liivoja and Tim McCormack (eds), *Handbook on the Law of Armed Conflict* (London, Routledge, 2016), 50, at 56–61.

98 See generally Tim McFarland, "Factors Shaping the Legal Implications of Increasingly Autonomous Military Systems" [2016] *International Review of the Red Cross* 1–27, available at: https://www.cambridge.org/core/journals/international-review-of-the-red-cross/article/

Significant levels of autonomy in weapons systems already exist, particularly in anti-missile defence, including, for example:

> "close-in weapon systems" (CIWS) on naval vessels, and their land-based counterparts, C-RAMs (short for "counter rocket, artillery and mortar") ... CIWS and C-RAM are rapid-fire, computer-controlled, radar-guided guns designed to engage automatically and defeat incoming missiles and other close-in threats.[99]

Any attempt to introduce a human operator into a close-in missile defence system will significantly reduce efficacy. The tracking of the speed and trajectory of any incoming missile and the consequent decision to fire to intercept the missile require rapid calculations and almost instantaneous decision-making. Machines are proving to be so much more effective than humans in this specific context, and the legal and ethical implications of the utilization of automation for the deployment of lethal force are relatively uncontroversial. However, the relative lack of controversy in the specific anti-missile defence context evaporates in any general discussion about possible future applications of autonomous robotic capability. It is one thing to develop an anti-missile system that can intercept and destroy an incoming missile – particularly in a maritime environment physically isolated from any possibility of incidental civilian damage – but a different concept altogether to contemplate the deployment of autonomous weapons systems intended to kill enemy combatants without human intervention.

Recurrent questions of concern invariably include whether a robot will be capable of: distinguishing enemy soldiers from civilians; distinguishing an armed enemy soldier from one attempting to surrender; and undertaking a proper proportionality calculation if harm to civilians and damage to civilian property is expected. There is also an ongoing debate about accountability – who will be held responsible if a robot perpetrates a war crime?[100]

Debate about the legal challenges posed by the deployment of sophisticated robotic weapons systems has been largely polarized by two overly simplistic extremes. Some argue in favour of a proactive and comprehensive prohibition on

---

factors-shaping-the-legal-implications-of-increasingly-autonomous-military-systems/9D5E20943ABC778DA20D33DCBB45BE4D.

99 Rain Liivoja, Kobi Leins and Tim McCormack, "Emerging Technologies of Warfare" in Rain Liivoja and Tim McCormack (eds), *Handbook on the Law of Armed Conflict* (London, Routledge, 2016) 609, citing as an example Raytheon, "Phalanx Close-in Weapon System: Last Line of Defense for Air, Land and Sea," available at: www.raytheon.com/capabilities/products/phalanx.

100 See, for example, Tim McFarland and Tim McCormack, "Mind the Gap: Can Developers of Autonomous Weapons Systems Be Liable for War Crimes?" (2014) 90 *International Law Studies* 361–385, available at: https://www.usnwc.edu/getattachment/ed8e80ad-b622-4fad-9a36-9bedd71afebe/Mind-the-Gap--Can-Developers-of-Autonomous-Weapons.aspx.

all lethal autonomous weapons systems,[101] while others assert that international humanitarian law is more than capable of regulating the use of all categories of weapons – including autonomous weapons systems – and that there is no need to be concerned about the adaptability of the law to novel weapons technology.[102] The most appropriate response lies somewhere between these two extremes. It is true that international humanitarian law is adaptable – the principles have been applied to and have proved themselves capable of regulating the use of new weapons technologies for more than 150 years. But it is also true that new technologies sometimes contribute to novel scenarios that the law has never had to deal with previously.

Huge advances in the sophistication of artificial intelligence are a good example. The trend is for "deep learning" – for computational capacity to be so vast as to enable the processing of massive amounts of data and the replication of much greater levels of human thought processes than has previously been possible. There will, of course, be wonderful applications of such technological advances, but there will also be concerns about the utilization of such capacity for nefarious purposes.[103] The capacity of robots to self-learn – to be capable of responding to *in situ* experience and adapting their behaviour in future situations – may not be beyond practical realities at some future stage. The theoretical possibility of an armed robot capable of self-learning from an operational environment and changing its approach to its future use of lethal force options raises all sorts of challenges to the existing framework of international humanitarian law. Such a scenario should raise grave concerns.

Military applications of other emerging technologies will also surely raise their own challenges to international humanitarian law. Nanotechnology – the ability to work with materials at the molecular level – raises the spectre of limitless capacity to manipulate matter, to change the properties of materials and to create substances or effects previously unknown. Advances in the field of bionics – supplementing or duplicating parts of the human body with electronic

---

101 See, for example, Human Rights Watch, *Losing Humanity: The Case against Killer Robots* (2012), available at: https://www.hrw.org/report/2012/11/19/losing-humanity/case-against-killer-robots. See also the Campaign to Stop Killer Robots at: https://www.stopkillerrobots.org.

102 See, for example, William H Boothby, *Weapons and the Law of Armed Conflict* (Oxford, Oxford University Press, 2009) 370; William H Boothby, *Conflict Law: The Influence of New Weapons Technology, Human Rights and Emerging Actors* (The Hague, TMC Asser Press, 2014) 192–194; and Darren Stewart, "Maximising Compliance with IHL and the Utility of Data in an Age of Unlimited Information: Operational Issues" in Dan Saxon (ed), *International Humanitarian Law and the Changing Technology of War* (Leiden, Martinus Nijhoff Publishers, 2013) 180.

103 On the concept of deep learning and advances in artificial intelligence generally, see Robert D Hof, "Deep Learning: With Massive Amounts of Computational Power, Machines Can Now Recognize Objects and Translate Speech in Real Time. Artificial Intelligence is Finally Getting Smart," [2016] *MIT Technology Review*, at: https://www.technologyreview.com/s/513696/deep-learning.

devices and/or mechanical parts – also offers an array of potential military applications and possibly a serious challenge to the demarcation between human and machine. Cyborgs have always been the stuff of science fiction, but developments in bionic enhancement are now much closer to reality and legal challenges will undoubtedly ensue from continuing advances.

4. THE COMPLEXITY OF OPERATIONAL ENVIRONMENTS AND MORE EFFECTIVE IMPLEMENTATION OF INTERNATIONAL HUMANITARIAN LAW

4.1. 1996 CONCERNS: THE COMPLEX BALKANS CONFLICTS

Writing in 1996 on challenges to more effective implementation of international humanitarian law (IHL), I focused on the complex operational environment in the Balkans, as well as on the nature and scale of some of the shocking violations of IHL perpetrated there. I wrote in particular of the UN Commission of Experts' analysis of in excess of 80 distinct parties to the Balkans conflicts, some of whom changed allegiances depending upon the opposition at a particular time.[104] This seemed to me an unprecedented level of complexity necessitating a meticulous unravelling of who was fighting who in any particular region and at any specific moment in time. Many of those parties were organized non-state armed groups and paramilitary forces who had not been involved in either the making of or the development of IHL and so, perhaps understandably, did not necessarily consider themselves bound by this body of law.

I also wrote of a range of appalling violations of IHL throughout the conflicts: the wilful targeting of cultural property – of churches and mosques, of schools, of bridges and of historic towns because they were emblematic of the "other"; the notion of "ethnic cleansing" and of the targeting of civilians of the other group precisely because of their ethnicity; the establishment of rape camps to forcibly impregnate Bosnian Muslim women and to detain them until either they bore their offspring or until their pregnancies reached such a late term that abortion was impossible – all in order to change the ethnic composition of the children born to them and so to compound the humiliation not only of the Muslim mothers of ethnic Serb children but also of the entire Muslim population; the anecdotal evidence of blood-sport enthusiasts travelling over the Austrian border to opportunistically kill civilians in the Balkans with impunity because it would be assumed that the deaths had occurred in the

104 McCormack, *supra* note 1, at 638–642.

course of the armed conflict.[105] I wondered how the ICRC could increase respect for IHL in circumstances where parties to the conflicts were clearly determined to violate the law. The establishment of the ICTY was an important step toward accountability for egregious IHL violations, but any enforcement of the law involves, by definition, an *ex post facto* response. What could the ICRC do to encourage proactive observance of the law?

4.2. TWO DECADES OF DEVELOPMENT: NO ABATEMENT IN THE LEVELS OF COMPLEXITY OR OF ATROCITIES

Surely it is never wise to attempt to relativize the complexities of military operational environments, but it is clear that throughout the last two decades, there has been no abatement in the complexity of contemporary military operations. In the Balkans conflicts, the complexities emanated from the sheer number of distinct parties to multiple conflicts and from a readiness to switch allegiances in pursuit of vested interests. Attempts to characterize the type of armed conflict to determine the applicable law and to sort through who was fighting who at any given moment were rarely straightforward exercises. However, it is also true that throughout the entire period of armed hostilities in the Balkans, the various conflicts were based largely along ethnic lines. Political leaders manipulated and exploited ethnic differences, including religious affiliation, to exacerbate animosities in the region, and distinct parties to specific conflicts largely identified themselves as aligned to one ethnic group or another. Members of armed forces also tended to distinguish themselves from the civilian population, although civilians were deliberately targeted because they represented an ethnic "other."

The emergence of global terror networks and the threats they pose have been a defining characteristic of the past two decades. The attacks on the twin towers of the World Trade Center and the Pentagon on 9/11 heralded a new and terrifying reality for Western states – a reality materializing in subsequent and devastating attacks in London, Madrid, Brussels and Paris. Reportage of terror attacks in major Western cities could create the misapprehension that such attacks are unprecedented. Sadly, however, attacks intended to maximize civilian casualties for some stated political motivation have been all too frequent elsewhere in the world and, in some situations, a tragically ubiquitous feature of life – at various times and often in multiple locations, including, for example, in Afghanistan, Turkey, Yemen, Iraq, Syria, Lebanon, Egypt, Israel and Palestine; in Pakistan, India, Sri Lanka and Bangladesh; in Indonesia, Thailand and the

105 Ibid, 639.

Philippines; in Algeria, Nigeria, the Democratic Republic of the Congo, Kenya and Angola; in Russia; and in Colombia.

Both the legal appropriateness and the relative merits of strategic decisions about the most effective response – declaring a so-called "Global War on Terror" and deploying a military response or characterizing such attack(s) as criminal and implementing a policing operation – are keenly contested.[106] In circumstances where a military response has been preferred, asymmetric conflict usually follows, with one side possessing overwhelmingly superior firepower and technological capability and the other side utilizing all available strategies to minimize, or at least offset, the disparities. A common sentiment among militarily superior forces that "if only these bastards would come out and fight fair, we'd smash them" is undoubtedly true and precisely why the militarily inferior forces do not come out and fight fair. In particular, refusing to wear uniforms and blending in with the local civilian population, locating military objectives within civilian residential areas and using civilian human shields to either minimize the likelihood of attack or to provide potentially damaging public relations propaganda in the event of an attack are all-too-familiar strategies faced by many armed forces.

The Bush administration took its own approach to the applicable law in its self-declared "Global War on Terror." Lawyers for the administration sought to rely on the existence of an armed conflict and the applicability of IHL for the permissive purposes of targeting, the right to detain members of opposing forces and for the utilization of military commissions to try those taking up arms against the United States. However, those same lawyers also sought to distance the application of IHL for the constraining purposes of rights of protection to those held in custody and minimum standards of fair trial. In *Hamdan*, for example, the plurality of the US Supreme Court dismissed the argument that those detained in the War on Terror fell into a gap between Common Article 2 to the Geneva Conventions (international armed conflicts) and Common Article 3 (non-international armed conflicts). The argument was that neither Common Article 2 nor Common Article 3 applied because al-Qaida is not a state, so there was no international armed conflict, and because the conflict with al-Qaida is of an international character taking place on the physical territory

---

106 See, for example: Andrew Majoran, "The Illusion of War: Is Terrorism a Criminal Act or an Act of War?" (2015) 3 *International Politics Reviews* 19–27, at: http://www.palgrave-journals.com/ipr/journal/v3/n1/full/ipr20158a.html; Aziz Z Huq and Christopher Muller, "The War on Crime as Precursor to the War on Terror," (2008) 20 *International Journal of Law, Crime and Justice* 1–15, at: https://www.researchgate.net/publication/270974236_The_War_on_Crime_as_Precursor_to_the_War_on_Terror; Jennifer Elsea, *Terrorism and the Law of War: Trying Terrorists as War Criminals before Military Commissions*, Congressional Research Service Report for Congress, 11 December 2001 at: http://fas.org/irp/crs/RL31191.pdf.

of more than one state, there was also no non-international armed conflict.[107] Instead, the plurality found that the protections of Common Article 3 provide *de minimis* prohibitions which apply in all armed conflicts not covered by the broader protections in the Geneva Conventions.[108] The assault by the Bush administration on the minimum protections of IHL was roundly criticized and extensively discredited.[109]

The past two decades, particularly in the Middle East region, have witnessed the removal of a succession of repressive regimes – the Taliban, Saddam Hussein, Hosni Mubarak, Muammar Gaddafi and the attempted overthrow of the regime of Bashar Al-Assad. The coalition invasion of Iraq in 2003 and the so-called "Arab Spring" of 2011[110] both promised so much for the long-suffering populations of those states previously subjected to protracted dictatorships. But the removal of repressive regimes has not resulted in greater freedoms for respective populations and instead seems to have either unleashed pre-existing animosities along tribal, local or religious lines or created power vacuums which different interest groups have been quick to exploit. Religious minorities in particular have suffered terribly in many parts of the greater Middle East region.

The conflict in Syria, now in its eighth year, has been an unmitigated humanitarian catastrophe. The Syrian Center for Policy Research (SCPR) estimated a death toll of 470,000 and climbing in 2015.[111] Counting of the death toll has since ceased because of a lack of secure access to areas still subject to intense fighting. In addition, the ICRC estimates that eight million Syrians have become internally displaced within their own war-torn country[112] and the United Nations High Commissions for Refugees (UNHCR) reports that now 4.8 million Syrians are registered as refugees – the overwhelming bulk of them in neighbouring Turkey, Lebanon, Jordan and Iraq.[113] The combined total of

---

107 For a detailed analysis of the arguments and the attempt to preclude the application of legal protections to detainees, see Alison Duxbury, "Drawing Lines in the Sand: Characterising Conflicts for the Purposes of Teaching International Humanitarian Law (2007) 8(2) *Melbourne Journal of International Law* 259–287.

108 See *Salim Ahmed Hamdan v. Donald H Rumsfeld, Secretary of Defense*, 548 US __ (2006) 1, 66–67.

109 See, for example, Françoise Bouchet-Saulnier, *The Practical Guide to Humanitarian Law* (Lanham: Rowman and Littlefield, 3rd English language edn, 2014) 430.

110 The Western media have been accredited with coining the term, but the term has also been criticized as overly simplistic. See: http://middleeast.about.com/od/humanrightsdemocracy/a/Definition-Of-The-Arab-Spring.htm for an explanation of the terminology and criticisms of it.

111 *Confronting Fragmentation: Impact of Syrian Crisis Report*, February 2016, 51, available at: http://scpr-syria.org/publications/confronting-fragmentation. For an analysis of the Report's findings, see Priyanka Boghani, "A Staggering New Death Toll for Syria's War: 470,000," *Frontline*, 11 February 2016, available at: http://www.pbs.org/wgbh/frontline/article/a-staggering-new-death-toll-for-syrias-war-470000/.

112 ICRC, *supra* note 2.

113 See UNHCR, *Syrian Regional Refugee Response: Inter-Agency Information Sharing Portal*, at: http://data.unhcr.org/syrianrefugees/regional.php.

Syrians forced to leave their homes and livelihoods is now close to, or in excess of, half the entire population of the country.

Many Syrian cities and towns have been reduced to rubble and despite international efforts to broker ceasefires and to initiate peace talks, hostilities persist. The conflict began in March 2011 with protests against the Assad regime and was quickly followed by a spiralling descent into civil war between rebels and government forces. The structure of the initial conflict was relatively uncomplicated, even though its conduct was brutal. Now, foreign intervening forces have proliferated and the precise number of distinct armed conflicts is difficult to determine. The schism of the conflict along sectarian lines – majority Sunni seeking the overthrow of the minority Alawite Shia loyal to Assad – has drawn in Iran and Hezbollah in support of Assad and al-Qaida and a raft of other Arab states in support of their largely Sunni rebel brethren. ISIS capitalized on a vacuum of law and order and declared its Caliphate in large swathes of Syrian and Iraqi territory, gleefully joining the fight against the Assad regime. Other parties have different non-religious interests in the fight. The Kurds are fighting for control of their region in Syria with support from across the Turkish border and Turkish government forces are engaged in their ongoing struggle against the Kurds. Russia's military campaign against all those fighting against the Assad regime has nothing to do with Shia sympathies and nor does the engagement of the United States and other Western allies in the fight against ISIS. Attempting to unravel the matted web of vested interests, shifting alliances and precisely who is fighting who seems like an academic exercise compared to the comprehensive unravelling of Syrian civil society and the devastation wrought upon the country. One enduring and consistent feature of the entire conflict has been egregious war crimes and a lack of substantive multilateral initiatives to prevent them, with the sole exception of action in response to recurrent use of chemical weapons. Is the complexity of the Syrian conflict, characterized by egregious violations of IHL, really a new reality for future wars?

5. FUTURE CHALLENGES: "THE EROSION OF HUMANITY" AND RECAPTURING THE MOTIVATION FOR INTERNATIONAL HUMANITARIAN LAW

One obvious conclusion from reflections on developments over the past 20 years is that IHL is both robust and capable of adaptation. The existing legal framework for the regulation of armed conflicts has survived the efforts of proponents of the self-declared "Global War on Terror" to portray the law as anachronistic. The general principles of IHL have been declared by the International Court of Justice to apply as much to nuclear weapons as they do to any other category of weapon. The International Group of Experts responsible for drafting the *Tallinn Manual on the International Law Applicable to Cyber Warfare* have also adopted the position that the existing legal framework applies to virtual warfare as much as it does to war by kinetic means and states have only confirmed their agreement with this approach. It is this body of law that remains the objective standard by which the conduct of hostilities is judged, even, or perhaps especially, in the face of egregious violations of it.

A concomitant conclusion is that the effective enforcement of serious violations of IHL is crucial to increasing respect for the law. The establishment of both the ICTY and the ICTR have had a profound impact on the international criminal justice project, and many subsequent developments have flowed from the UN Security Council's initiatives. The ICC and the various other ad hoc international(ized) criminal tribunals owe their existence to the momentum generated by the Security Council in the early 1990s. While there is still much to be done to consolidate the gains, the past two decades have unquestionably arrested the ascendancy of impunity for atrocity – at least in some situations around the world.

However, there are also obvious reasons to pause and take stock. Armed conflicts are still occurring and many of them persist after decades of protracted and debilitating violence. Civilians are still targeted in massive numbers, their homes, villages, towns and cities are still razed, their children are still abused, their personal belongings are still pillaged, their livestock are still slaughtered and rape is still perpetrated by all sides to conflicts and, still to this day, also by UN peace-keepers. The persistent refusal of Russia and China to allow a UN Security Council referral of the Syrian situation to the Prosecutor of the ICC underscores a debilitating limitation to effective global criminal justice in the face of appalling violations of the law. Even when conduct is lawful, or at least cannot be shown to be unlawful, terrible damage is inflicted. Weapons have become increasingly precise and yet hospitals are still attacked, even if by mistake, and civilians still die in large numbers, even if their deaths are lawfully incidental to attacks on legitimate military objectives.

Compliance with IHL would undoubtedly have made massive differences in the conduct of the Syrian conflict and there are obvious challenges to more effective implementation of the law in that particular conflict and in many others around the world. But I also wonder if adherence to the legal rules is really sufficient to staunch the bloodshed. Where is the commitment to serious investment in proactive initiatives to prevent even some armed conflicts from occurring? Since the attacks of 9/11 and subsequent terror attacks in other Western countries, much has been written about different worldviews and relative lack of respect for human life in "other" cultures. Some Western political leaders have been quick to characterize ISIS as barbaric and uncivilized – a "Death Cult." In the rush to dehumanize the other, it becomes easier to justify resort to military force and easier to accept violations of IHL. Dehumanization is insidious and can manifest in: exclusionary asylum seeker and refugee policy; denial of due process rights to "terrorists"; humanitarian aid and relief fatigue; and violations of fundamental human rights.

Those committed to the promotion of understanding of and respect for IHL have a massive challenge to recapture the commitment to humanity that was the driving motivation for the original development of the law. Henri Dunant was driven to action by the human misery he witnessed. We need more like him in spite of the saturation of coverage of human misery in the world and the danger of becoming inured to it. UN Secretary-General Ban Ki-moon called an unprecedented World Humanitarian Summit in May 2016 in Istanbul to challenge what he described as "the erosion of humanity which we see in the world today."[114] The Summit provided an important forum for global leaders to reaffirm their commitment to humanity and to the integrity of the normative legal framework in armed conflict and in peacetime.[115] Statements of intent are important, but states must follow through on the implementation of, and adherence to, the principles they have affirmed. In her various roles, Louise Arbour consistently and persistently challenged the international community to adhere to international legal obligations. I wish we could clone her. A few more Louises in today's world would be awesome.

114 See United Nations Regional Information Centre for Western Europe announcement, 4 April 2016, at: http://www.unric.org/en/latest-un-buzz/30132-we-will-not-accept-the-erosion-of-humanity-which-we-see-in-the-world-today.

115 For texts of statements at the Summit, see: https://www.worldhumanitariansummit.org.

PART III

OF WOMEN AND LEADERSHIP

LEADERSHIP IN THE UNITED NATIONS AND THE CHALLENGE OF COURAGE

Fabrizio Hochschild[1]

At this time of great conflicts … and violent clashes of interests, technological and economic developments have, as never before, brought us together as members of one human family, unified beyond race or creed on a shrinking globe, in face of dangers of our own making.[2]

Sixty-four years ago, Dag Hammarskjöld, then second Secretary-General of the United Nations (UN), spoke these words to students in a commencement address at Johns Hopkins University. What was forward-looking then, in the face of climate change, mass population flows and cross-border terrorism is more self-evident today. There is also greater awareness now that transnational threats require transnational solutions and to achieve these, bold, enlightened leadership with a global, long-term vision is critical.

In this context, many look to the United Nations (UN) for leadership and solutions. Among the many traits that enable international leadership in unsettled, danger-ridden times, Dag Hammarskjöld promoted one as being of particular importance in the same commencement address: courage linked to integrity.

1 This article was written prior to the author taking up his current position in the Office of the Secretary-General of the United Nations. *The opinions expressed in this chapter are those of the author only.* The author is deeply indebted for this chapter to a unique and most exceptionally gifted collaborator, Sabina Stein. Her inspiration and contribution were as invaluable as they were indispensable. The author is also indebted to the patient and insightful help of a wise friend, Naresh Peripanayagam.

2 Hammarskjöld, D., "International service," address at John Hopkins University Commencement Exercise, 14 June 1955.

What is the meaning of courage in leadership? What examples can we find of it in the UN? How is it valued as a quality by those in positions of influence in the UN? What nurtures and constrains it in the organization? What can we learn about courage from the UN leadership of the person to whom this book is dedicated, Louise Arbour? These are the questions this chapter endeavours to explore.

1. ON COURAGE IN LEADERSHIP

The *Oxford English Dictionary* defines courage as "that quality of mind which shows itself in facing danger without fear or shrinking; bravery, boldness, valour."[3] Winston Churchill referred to courage as "the quality that guarantees all others"[4] and it is arguably one of the oldest attributes associated with leadership. In Homer's *Iliad*, the Cretan King Idomeneus describes the courage of his aide Meriones in these words:

> In every ambush you have proven your valor ... you would meet the blow with belly or chest as you charged ahead of the front-most ranks.[5]

This illustrates how courage and leadership go together: the leader is by definition the one who charges into battle first, "ahead of the front-most ranks," not flinching in battle, taking the first blows and not fearing death.

Homer's embodiment of courage is Odysseus. Through bravery, persistence, insight and cunning, he overcomes a ten-year-long series of near-fatal trials before finally making it home to his wife and son. Odysseus illustrates how courage is also linked to perseverance, to caring for those one leads, and to inspired strategic thinking that sees opportunity where others only see threats.

Nearly three thousand years after Homer, the management theorist Simon Sinek, in a TED talk on leadership,[6] uses a modern-day Homeric tale to illustrate the link between leadership, courage and care for others. From a film posted on YouTube taken by soldiers and medics with cameras on their helmets, he describes how in Afghanistan, a Marine captain, Captain William Swenson, entered live fire to rescue an injured comrade, a sergeant, to rush him to a helicopter with blades still spinning for evacuation. The film also showed how, before returning to the battle zone to collect more wounded, Captain Swenson

3 *Oxford English Dictionary*, 1971 edition.

4 Coote, C. (1949) *Maxims and Reflections of the Rt. Hon. Winston S. Churchill*, London: Houghton Mifflin, p. 168.

5 Homer, *The Iliad*, translation. Fagles, R. (1990), New York: Penguin Putnam, Book 13, 276.

6 Sinek, S., "Why good leaders make you feel safe," TED Talk, March 2014. Accessed on 2 September 2015 at: http://www.ted.com/talks/simon_sinek_why_good_leaders_make_you_feel_safe.

was seen gently kissing his wounded sergeant on the forehead. After having retrieved the wounded, the captain remained in the battle zone until he had also recovered the bodies of his dead men.

Sinek uses the story to illustrate how the best leaders place themselves in peril for the safety and wellbeing of others in an organization. In his analysis, courage is an act of sacrifice for others, for making others feel safe:

> We call them leaders, because they go first; we call them leaders, because they take the risk before any one else does; we call them leaders because they will choose to sacrifice so that their people may be safe and protected and may gain.[7]

While Sinek explains the link between leadership, courage and care, another modern-era illustration of the link between courage and perseverance is the story of Sir Ernest Shackleton,[8] the early twentieth-century polar explorer, who met disaster in an attempt to cross Antarctica. After his ship got trapped and crushed in pack ice, he was compelled to lead his men back in a two-year long odyssey, camping on ice flows and sailing over 1,000 kilometres in a flimsy lifeboat. One author[9] ascribed his survival and success to the spirit reflected in his family motto, *Fortitudine Vincimus*, by endurance we conquer.

What Meriones, Odysseus, Captain Swenson and Sir Ernest Shackleton all demonstrate is physical courage, the courage to persevere despite the threat of death. As narratives of leadership and the modern study of it are derived from a context of battle, much focus has been placed on – as the examples thus far illustrate – usually male, physical courage.

In the context of leadership of a norm-based international organization such as the UN, equally or perhaps more relevant than physical courage is its close relative: moral courage. Moral courage is defined by the *Oxford English Dictionary* as "that kind of courage which enables a person to encounter odium, disapproval or contempt rather than depart from what he or she deems the right course."[10] Where physical courage implies a willingness to face the fear of death, moral or political courage implies a willingness to face the fear of social condemnation, of ostracization.

There are many examples of overlap between these two forms of courage, as happens when defending inconvenient, contrarian ideas or values puts one at risk of certain death. At the end of the sixteenth century, Dominican friar Giordano Bruno defended his theological and cosmological theories in front of the Roman Inquisition, refusing to recant despite knowing this would lead to his

---

7 Ibid.

8 See Perkins, D., Holtman, M. et al (2000) *Leading at the Edge: Leadership Lessons from the Extraordinary Saga of Shackleton's Antarctic Expedition*, New York: Amacom.

9 Ibid.

10 *Oxford English Dictionary*, 1971 edition.

death as a heretic.[11] Three hundred and twenty years later, in the Berlin of 1919, socialist leader Rosa Luxembourg was arrested, beaten and shot for upholding workers' rights and democratic ideals.

Moral courage relates to societal battles over principles and values, and when exercised in government and politics, it is also referred to as "political courage." In a classical study,[12] John F. Kennedy argues that greatness in leadership stems not from cultivating popularity, but from "political courage," from showing bravery in upholding integrity and promoting the principles one believes in even when such a course of action makes one unpopular. Kennedy portrays eight US political leaders whose courage he found exemplary because,

> each one's need to maintain his own self respect for himself was more important to him than his popularity with others – because his desire to win or maintain a reputation for integrity and courage was stronger than his desire to maintain his office – because his conscience, his personal standard of ethics, his integrity or morality, call it what you will – was stronger than the pressures of public disapproval – because his faith that his course was the best one, and would ultimately be vindicated, outweighed his fear of public reprisal.[13]

In the same manner that physical courage means showing a willingness to stand up to the threat of death for a higher cause or concern for others, political or moral courage means being willing to face popular condemnation for a higher cause or concern for others. Kennedy goes a step further and suggests that a measure of social isolation and condemnation is inevitable to those who lead on the basis of integrity and courage. In the motto that introduces the book, he quotes from Edmund Burke:

> remember that obloquy is a necessary ingredient in the composition of all true glory; … remember … that calumny and abuse are essential parts of triumph …

Kennedy concludes his book by according the same value to moral or political courage – which he refers to here as the "courage of life" and "the basis of all human morality"[14] – as is accorded to physical courage, courage in the face of death. He also lamented that political courage was not more frequent in his age.

Half a century before observing this, Kennedy's compatriot Mark Twain made a similar observation: "It is curious that physical courage should be so common in the world and moral courage so rare."[15] While the fear of death

---

11 White, M., *The Pope and the Heretic: The True Story of Giordano Bruno, the Man who Dared to Defy the Roman Inquisition*, New York: Harper Perennial, 2002.

12 Kennedy, J.F. (2006) *Profiles in Courage*, New York: Harper Perennial.

13 Ibid, pp. 218–219.

14 Ibid, p. 225.

15 Quoted in de Voto, B. (ed.) (1940) *Mark Twain in Eruption: Hitherto Unpublished Pages about Men and Events*, New York: Harper & Brothers Publishing.

is unambiguous and overcoming it is universally admired, a readiness to be a social outcast, to stand up for what one believes is less consistently admired and therefore occurs more rarely.

The virtue of moral courage at the time it is exercised, if not in hindsight, will often be more debatable than an act of physical courage. The defiance of the fear of death in a manner that upholds a cause or shows concern for others – as in the acts of firemen and police officers – is more straightforward, more broadly recognized, and more celebrated than the defiance of social condemnation to uphold the integrity of a value system. The dominant social values of the time which are being defied by an act of moral or political courage may be seen – at least at the time – as more important than the alternative value system, which is being upheld to reject them.

The complications with the adequate recognition of moral or political courage was the subject of an op-ed in *The New York Times* by Salman Rushdie, entitled "Whither Moral Courage."[16] Rushdie illustrated the ambivalence moral courage can evoke with the example of a provincial governor in Pakistan, Salman Taseer, who had demonstrated moral courage by opposing the dominant values of his constituents and refusing to condemn a Christian woman, accused of blasphemy, to death. As a result, he was murdered by one of his bodyguards and his killer was subsequently celebrated as the true hero. The governor's "courage was obliterated by religious passions" writes Rushdie and, like Mark Twain, he concludes, "we find it easier, in these confused times, to admire physical bravery than moral courage."[17]

As indicated above, what distinguishes moral from physical courage is the nature of the fear stood up to. What is noteworthy is what physical and moral courage have in common as they relate to leadership. Four elements can be identified. The first element that both physical and moral courage have in common is the defining element of leadership: both moral and physical courage are exercised by being out in front, by absorbing blows or criticism ahead of, and on behalf of others, and thus setting an example for others. Both types of courage, and leadership itself, are defined by being the first to face danger; the first to make the way into perilous or unknown territory.

In this regard, it is important to bear in mind that being courageous – whether physically or morally – does not necessarily mean plunging ahead blindly into danger. One contemporary wrote in this regard of Sir Ernest Shackleton:

> He was brave, the bravest man I have seen, but he was never foolhardy. When necessary he would undertake the most dangerous things, and do so fearlessly; but always he would approach them in a thoughtful manner and perform them in the safest way.[18]

---

16 Rushdie, S., "Whither moral courage," *The New York Times*, 27 April 2013.

17 Ibid.

18 Perkins, D. et al (2000), p. 125.

Likewise, in describing political courage, Kennedy is eager to stress that it need not mean blind rigidity in the pursuit of a cause. He writes of the leaders he portrays: "Some demonstrated courage through their unyielding devotion to absolute principle. Others demonstrated courage through their acceptance of compromise, through their advocacy of conciliation, through their willingness to replace conflict with co-operation. Surely their courage was of equal quality, though of a different caliber."[19] He is eager to stress that political courage can incorporate compromise:

> Compromise need not mean cowardice. Indeed it is frequently the compromisers and conciliators who are faced with the severest tests of political courage as they oppose the extremist views of their constituents.[20]

This points to the second element that both physical and moral courage require to make them valuable as a leadership asset: courage needs to be accompanied by a degree of insight and strategic vision that is aware of the threats, but also envisages opportunities. Odysseus overcame his trials thanks to a combination of what his companions described as "courage, counsel and intelligence".[21] Courage has to be informed by an intelligent and convincing vision.

The importance of vision is stressed by all leadership literature. Two well-known leadership researchers formulated its importance as follows: "Envisioning exciting possibilities and enlisting others in a shared view of the future is the attribute that most distinguishes leaders from non-leaders."[22]

This indicates the third critical element that physical and moral courage have in common: the risk-taking is always motivated by care for others or for a cause. As Sinek indicated in the earlier cited TED talk, courageous acts are not carried out in isolation without reference to others, but rather to promote or safeguard the wellbeing of others or of a value system. What the moral philosopher Alasdair MacIntyre writes in this regard applies both to physical and moral courage:

> We hold courage to be a virtue because the care and concern for individuals, communities and causes which is so crucial to so much in practice requires the existence of such a virtue. If someone says that he cares for some individual, community or cause but is unwilling to risk harm or danger on his, her or its own behalf, he puts in question the genuineness of his care and concern. Courage ... has its role in human life because of this connection with care and concern.[23]

---

19 Kennedy (2006), p. 221.

20 Ibid, p. 18.

21 Homer, *The Odyssey*, trans. Fagles, R. (1996), New York: Viking, 12.208–213.

22 Kouzes, J.M. and Posener, B. (2009) "To lead, create a shared vision," *Harvard Business Review*, January 2009, p. 20.

23 MacIntyre, A. (1981) *After Virtue: A Study in Moral Theory*, London: General Duckworth & Co., p. 179.

The fourth element that physical and moral courage share with respect to leadership is the link to perseverance, as illustrated both in the example of Odysseus and John F. Kennedy (Kennedy suffered from almost incapacitating back pain and also withstood recurrent political isolation). The single act of defiance of the threat of death – be it physical or social – is not sufficient for courage in leadership. It requires sustained, persistent countering of threats. A classic author on leadership writes:

> A leader needs courage – not just bravery of the moment but courage over time, not just willingness to risk, but to risk again and again, to function well under prolonged stress, to survive defeat and keep going.[24]

2. ON COURAGE AND UN LEADERSHIP[25]

How do these points and other findings on leadership and courage apply in the context of the work of the UN?

The UN is an organization where courage in leadership, in particular moral courage, is a necessity to safeguard the essence of the organization, to uphold its authority and to promote the realization of its objectives. At the same time, much in the organization's operating environment and culture mitigates against the exercise of courage in leadership.

The work of the UN unfolds in circumstances characterized by a series of opposing tensions. The first relates to tension between its normative base and the transient political interests, which inform its daily work. The organization works on the basis of objectives and principles set out in the UN Charter and international law, supplemented by and elaborated in a broader body of international conventions, which its Member States have voluntarily signed up to. At the same time, however, the UN Secretariat and its agencies are the subject of constant political pressure related less to the normative framework of the organization than to political interests of its individual Member States and other stakeholders. The fourth Secretary-General, Javier Perez de Cuellar, described the tension in these words:

> The idealism and hope of which the Charter is a luminous expression have to confront the narrow dictates of national policies.[26]

---

24 Gardner, J.W. (1990) *On Leadership*, New York: The Free Press, pp. 51–52.

25 The following sections draws heavily from a 2010 study on leadership in the UN by Hochschild, F. "In and above conflict: A study on leadership at the United Nations." Available at: http://www.isn.ethz.ch/Digital-Library/Publications/Detail/?id=120456.

26 Quoted in Cockayne, J. and Malone, D.M. (2007) "Relations with the Security Council" in Chesterman, S. (ed.) (2007), *Secretary or General? The UN Secretary-General in World Politics*, Cambridge: Cambridge University Press, p. 69.

As much as any UN leader may wish to act on the basis of principle and uphold the norms of the organization, he or she will be placed under pressure to act on the basis of more narrow political expedience and to bow to the interests of one or another powerful stakeholder.

A second set of tensions relates to the high expectations placed on the UN by civil society, and the less inspired reality of the dominant culture and work practices within it. The organization is often seen, especially in conflict settings, as bearing the promise of peace, development and respect for human rights, the ideals championed by the UN in speeches and elaborated upon in its normative framework. At the same time, the internal culture and work practices can mean that on a day-to-day basis, the immediate focus is on issues far removed from its aspirational rhetoric.

In its daily work, many other pressing concerns can take precedence over the Charter objectives of promoting peace, social justice and development – for example, the requirements of countless internal processes that govern the UN's work, bureaucratic reporting requirements, the need to respond to the interests of powerful Member States, turf battles with other UN entities or the prioritization of funding. Extraneous concerns also gain dominance because of the weight of the bureaucracy and the organizational culture, which many staff members have described as conservative, overly cautious and more focused on procedure than substance.

In a 2006 reform report,[27] Secretary-General Kofi Annan speaks of "a damaged culture, which is seen as limiting creativity, enterprise, innovation and indeed leadership itself." And more recently in a 2015 article,[28] former UN Deputy Secretary-General Mark Malloch Brown, after praising the virtues of the organization, referred to:

> the heavy bureaucracy, the risk aversion and too often, the apparent abandonment of the exciting founding principles of peace, justice and human development that were intended to animate the UN's activities.

In an environment dominated by these constraints, in situations where there is controversy or there are contradicting views, where potentially unpopular decisions need taking or powerful interests require confronting, much in the

---

27 A/60/692, "Investing in the United Nations: For a stronger organization worldwide," Report of the Secretary-General, United Nations General Assembly, 7 March 2006, p. 20.

28 Brown, M.M, "The UN is an under-funded, bureaucratic labyrinth – and a force for good in the world," *The Telegraph*, 26 June 2015, accessed on 3 September 2015 at: http://www.telegraph.co.uk/news/worldnews/11699243/The-UN-is-an-under-funded-bureaucratic-labyrinth-and-a-force-for-good-in-the-world.html.

organization can gravitate toward passivity or inaction or seek refuge in the safety of established procedures. A recent report on peace operations[29] suggests:

> Too often, the choice is between what makes sense for the mission or what is compliant with unwieldy procedures, and usually the choice is to do what is compliant.

While conservatism and caution can tend to predominate, a number of exceptional UN leaders have emphasized that the organization's political constraints, heavy bureaucracy and conservative organizational culture make the need for more enterprising, more courageous leadership all the more essential.

No other Secretary-General reflected as much on the values that should underpin the work of those in the organization as Dag Hammarskjöld and his words have been used for guidance by every other Secretary-General, as well as inspiring generations of staff members in the UN and beyond.

In the same commencement address referred to at the beginning of this chapter and in other speeches, Hammarskjöld set out a vision of international service. He saw four interrelated core values underpinning the work of the international civil servant: integrity, loyalty to the principles of the UN Charter and independence from any national or regional interests. UN staff, he told a group of Member State representatives "should have only one loyalty in the performance of their duties, and that is to the UN."[30] Finally, he stressed the importance of courage in order to be able to uphold the former three values.

Hammarskjöld considered and explicitly dismissed the notion that international service requires an attitude of unbending neutrality, moral relativism and passivity in the face of opposing ideologies and worldviews. He believed that international service required courageous activism on behalf of the principles set out in the Charter, and their importance as the true reference point for the UN Secretariat could not be overstated for him. He told the Security Council:

> The principles of the Charter are, by far, greater than the Organization in which they are embodied, and the aims which they are to safeguard are holier than the policies of any single nation or people ... The discretion and impartiality required of the Secretary-General may not degenerate into a policy of expedience. He must also be a servant of the principles of the Charter, and its aims must ultimately determine what for him is right and wrong. For that he must stand ...[31]

---

29 "Uniting our strengths for peace – politics, partnership and people," Report of the High Level Independent Panel on United Nations Peace Operations, 16 June 2015, p. 83, para. 289.

30 Quoted in: Urquhart, B. (1994), *Hammarskjöld*, New York: W.W. Norton & Company, p. 523.

31 Security Council Official Records, Eleventh Year, 751st Meeting, 31 October 1956.

Courageous loyalty to the ideals of the Charter and international law was held by Hammarskjöld as a higher value than neutrality.[32] As he pointed out in a speech at Oxford in 1961:

> in the last analysis, this is a question of integrity, and if integrity in the sense of respect for law and respect for truth were to drive (the Secretary-General) in to positions of conflict with this or that interest, then that conflict is a sign of his neutrality and not of his failure to observe neutrality – then it is in line not in conflict, with his duties as an international civil servant.[33]

Hammarskjöld frequently stressed the value of integrity as the indispensable leadership characteristic. He concluded his Johns Hopkins commencement speech with the words: "Those who are called upon to be teachers or leaders may profit from intelligence but can only justify their position by integrity."

It is important to note that integrity was understood by Hammarskjöld in a much broader sense than the narrow definition with which it is predominantly understood in the UN today. Integrity did not merely mean refraining from financial or other professional or personal wrongdoing. It was an active quality, a proven readiness to uphold international law and speak up for the principles set out in the Charter, even where it is uncomfortable and personally disadvantageous to do so. In other words, Hammarskjöld understood integrity as moral courage.

The proactive, principle-based integrity of which Hammarskjöld spoke requires one "to defend what is your conviction even when you are facing the threats of powerful opponents." In his commencement speech at Johns Hopkins, he states:

> International service … will expose us to conflicts. It will not permit us to live lazily under the protection of inherited and conventional ideas. Intellectually and morally, international service therefore requires courage to admit that you, and those you represent, are wrong, when you find them to be wrong, even in the face of a weaker adversary, and courage to defend what is your conviction even when you are facing the threats of powerful opponents.[34]

Hammarskjöld himself demonstrated this courage in responding to an attack against him by Soviet Premier President Khrushchev in the General Assembly

---

32 John F. Kennedy's view on neutrality was also striking. According to a 1963 forward to "Profiles in courage" by his brother Robert (p. xvii), "President Kennedy was fond of quoting Dante that 'the hottest places in Hell are reserved for those who, in a time of great moral crisis, maintain their neutrality.'"

33 From a lecture delivered at Oxford University on 30 May 1961. Quoted in Hammarskjöld, D., *Markings*, trans. Sjoberg, L. and Auden, W.H. (1970), New York: Alfred A Knopf, Inc., p. xix.

34 Hammarskjöld, D., "International service" (1955).

on 3 October 1960. Khrushchev criticized him for his handling of the Congo crisis and called upon him to resign. In his reply, Hammarskjöld insisted – in words that elicited a rare standing ovation – that he would stay on as long as other, less powerful Member States wished him to do so. He noted his responsibility was to all Member States and to the organization as a whole:

> It is not the Soviet Union or, indeed, any other big powers who need the United Nations for their protection; it is all the others. In this sense the Organization is first of all their Organization ... I shall remain in my post during the term of my office as a servant of the Organization in the interests of all those other nations, as long as they wish me to do so. In this context the representative of the Soviet Union spoke of courage. It is very easy to resign; it is not so easy to stay on. It is very easy to bow to the wish of a big power. It is another matter to resist.[35]

Only through integrity or moral courage, drawn from the principles of the Charter, could the Secretary-General withstand the opposing pressures "demanding loyalty to divergent ideas" and "find the will and strength to fight for ideals and interests which we hold dear and to which we are bounden."[36]

In his exercise of UN leadership, Hammarskjöld exemplified the four points previously identified as critical aspects of courage in leadership: a readiness to take blows first, the exercise of courage informed by vision and in the service of a cause and, finally, perseverance.

In responding to Khrushchev, as on many other occasions, he stood up, valiantly faced up to public criticism, and defended those he represented and the principles on which the UN was founded. His courage was not arbitrary bravado, but linked to a well-elaborated vision, which still motivates many in the organization until this day. His vision was informed by an acute awareness of political currents and countercurrents of the time, but did not succumb to them. He transcended political pressures through reference to principle.[37]

Hammarskjöld's courage upheld the cause of the values set out in the UN Charter. He embraced and lived the ideals of the UN in their own right and not under pressure from one or another group. He stood up for them at all times, in particular when it was inconvenient and uncomfortable to do so.

He also showed perseverance. In another commencement address from 1955 at the University of California, he spoke about the need to persist despite

---

35 UN General Assembly, Fifteenth Session, Official Records, 883rd Plenary Meeting, Monday 3 October 1960, p. 332, paras 11 and 12.

36 Ibid.

37 In this respect, he is recalled as saying that an international civil servant should be "politically celibate," but without being a "political virgin." See Ali, A., "The international civil service: The idea and the reality" in AAFI, *Commemorative Report: 90th Anniversary of the Founding of the Civil Service*, December 2009, p. 11.

the inevitable setbacks that occur in the pursuit of any difficult objective: "We need perseverance, of the kind that equips us not to take defeats to heart, in the knowledge that defeats are unavoidable, and that if our efforts do not seem to get results it may be because we have not yet applied the necessary degree of perseverance."[38]

The ideals served by the UN, he said, seldom lend themselves to quick wins. At the end of his Johns Hopkins University commencement address, he stated that "results are determined not by superficial ability but by the consistency of the actors in their efforts and by the validity of their ideals ... Apparently easy successes ... are possible for the juggler, but lasting results are achieved only by the patient builder."[39]

These sentiments are echoed by Hammarskjöld's best-known biographer. In his memoirs, the former UN Under-Secretary-General Brian Urquhart wrote:

> Reason, justice and compassion are small cards to play in the world of politics, whether international, national or tribal, but someone has to go on playing them. If you hold on to your belief in reason and compassion despite all political manoeuvring, your determined effort to do what seems objectively right may in the end produce results.[40]

In addition to the four aspects of courage associated with leadership, in his commencement address at Johns Hopkins University, Hammarskjöld added a fifth: the courage to freely admit mistakes, to show humility: "Courage to admit that you, and those you represent are wrong, when you find them to be wrong." The quality of critical self-reflection and consequent humility is one he practised and elaborated upon in his personal musings, which were posthumously published in a book called *Markings*.[41]

The quality of personal modesty is also one that inspired his successor, U Thant, UN Secretary-General from 1961 to 1971. According to Walter Dorn, a former UN staff member who has written on him, U Thant's integrity and personal humility allowed him to speak out much more forcefully for UN principles than would have been possible had he been a less modest person: "Thant did not receive a strong rebuff from nations for his criticisms ... His sense of morality gave power to his words, but they were spoken with great humility, respect, and sensitivity."[42]

---

38 Hammarskjöld, D., "The world and the nation," commencement address at Stanford University, California, 25 June 1955.

39 Hammarskjöld, D., "International service," (1955).

40 Urquhart, B. (1987), *A Life in Peace and War*, New York: W.W. Norton & Company, p. 196.

41 First published in Sweden as *Vagmarken* in 1963.

42 Dorn, W. (2007), "U Thant" in Kille., K.J. (ed.), *The UN Secretary-General and Moral Authority: Ethics and Religion in International Leadership*, Georgetown: Georgetown University Press, p. 147.

Hammarskjöld, whom John F. Kennedy referred to as "the greatest statesman of our century,"[43] is broadly recognized as an exceptional, exemplary leader, with ethical standards that remain a reference point both for UN staff and for others involved in international service. His example begs the question of how widespread courage in leadership is in the UN.

A number of dramatic failures of courage in leadership in the organization are well known and have been extensively documented in a distinguished series of hard-hitting, self-critical UN reports.[44] In 1994 in Rwanda, the UN failed to react to early warning signs of impending genocide and when it erupted, urged the mission on the ground not to intervene except to assist in the evacuation of third-country nationals. The Security Council ordered troop withdrawals, abandoning civilians who they should have protected. Then barely 15 months later, in Srebrenica in 1995, the UN mission in Bosnia-Herzegovina closed its eyes to the worse mass killing in Europe since World War II. Fourteen years later, in Sri Lanka in 2009, during the final offensive of the Sri Lankan armed forces against the Tamil Tigers, the UN failed to speak up adequately to try and prevent the killing of civilians – an estimated 40,000 – trapped in the north.

These and other failures to uphold the norms underlying the organization have been publicly exposed and fully acknowledged. However, public acknowledgment of the organization's failures has stopped short of those in leadership positions assuming any personal responsibility. An individual assumption of responsibility for failures in the exercise of moral courage has been rare as are resignations on grounds of principle. In the case of Rwanda, for example, there were apologies for the failure to act, but no one thought fit to offer their resignation.

By contrast, some who bore no responsibility for the institutional failure but acted with great courage on the ground suffered grave consequences. General Dallaire, the Canadian commander who remained in charge of the reduced force of UN peace-keepers, paid a high price for his bravery, suffering for many years from post-traumatic stress disorder (PTSD)[45] and associated alcohol abuse. Likewise, after the failure to prevent the round-up and mass executions of Bosnian men in Srebrenica, no one in a senior position resigned. Among the Dutch troops present, however, there was at least one guilt-induced suicide.[46]

---

43 Quoted in Gilmour, A. (2013) "Dag Hammarskjöld: Statesman of the Century," *The Nation*, 19 September 2013.

44 See, for example, Report of the Secretary-General pursuant to General Assembly Resolution 53/35: The fall of Srebrenica [A/54/549], 15 November 1999; Report of the Independent Inquiry into the actions of the United Nations during the 1994 genocide in Rwanda [S/1999/1257], 16 December 1999; Report of the Secretary-General's Internal Review Panel on United Nations Action in Sri Lanka, New York, November 2012.

45 See Dallaire, R. (2003), *Shake Hands with the Devil: The Failure of Humanity in Rwanda*, New York: Avalon.

46 See BBC documentary "UN & Dutch Disaster in Srebrenica." According to the documentary, about 70% of the original "Dutchbat" have left the army and ten have reportedly committed suicide.

There have been some notable exceptions to the general tendency to remain silent in the face of the organization's failures to uphold the principles on which it stands and, in 2015, the Secretary-General, Ban Ki-moon, has stressed the need for senior officials to be accountable for grave human rights abuses on their watch.[47] Between 1998 and 2000, three senior UN officials, Denis Halliday, Hans von Sponeck and Jutta Burghardt, resigned in protest at the economic sanctions imposed on Iraq, in association with the Oil-for-Food program. Hans von Sponeck said that the provisions of food foreseen under the Oil-for-Food program fell short of international standards and were in violation of the Iraqi people's rights under the Universal Declaration of Human Rights. He felt duty-bound as a UN official and as a humanitarian coordinator to speak up despite upsetting major powers by doing so:

> As a UN official, I should not be expected to be silent about that which I recognize as a true human tragedy that needs to be ended.[48]

There are many other instances of where UN officials at all levels have set aside considerations of personal risk and placed themselves in harm's way in defence of the principles the UN was established to aid and protect. Many involve the organization's military personnel and the rare number of women who have occupied senior UN leadership positions.

One of the most inspiring examples is that of Captain Mbaye Diagne, a Senegalese UN Military Observer in Kigali in 1994. When UN troops were withdrawn from Rwanda by the UN Security Council, Captain Mbaye and other UN Military Observers – along with the UN Force Commander General Dallaire and a small UN Ghanaian contingent – refused to evacuate. He organized his colleagues and – armed with only his radio – broke many UN rules to drive around Kigali during the genocide to extract civilians in danger and escort them to safety. What the international community had failed to do, he achieved through a combination of persuasion, coercion, courage and persistence. In mid-1994, while on one of these patrols, he was killed by a stray mortar shell. He was credited by the BBC international journalist in Kigali at the time with saving hundreds of lives.

---

47 The Secretary-General, Ban Ki-moon, said at a press stakeout in New York on 12 August 2015 in the context of the resignation of the SRSG in CAR over allegations of grave abuses committed by peacekeepers on his watch: "I will ask for responsibility of those leaders … when serious human rights violations take place … I have made it quite clear that there should be some accountability on the part of our leaders."

48 Quoted in Marsden, C., "UN aid coordinator for Iraq resigns in protest at 'human tragedy' of sanctions," *World Socialist Website*, 25 February 2000, accessed on 2 September 2015 at: https://www.wsws.org/en/articles/2000/02/iraq-f25.html.

After reflection on the failures of Rwanda and Srebrenica, awareness grew on the need to better protect civilians and, on at least two occasions, UN staff in times of violence and conflict have opened compounds to provide protection for civilians fleeing for their lives. In East Timor in 1999, when violence broke out after the announcement of the vote for independence, the UN team refused to evacuate their compound until all the Timorese who had sought refuge within it could be brought to safety.[49] In South Sudan in 2013, tens of thousands of South Sudanese were offered refuge in UN compounds and were defended by the peace-keepers manning the compounds.[50]

One of the earliest examples of moral courage in the UN is that of Eleanor Roosevelt, the widow of President Franklin D. Roosevelt. She went against the customs of the time and attracted criticism by assuming a public role and championing civil rights and women's issues. After the death of her husband, she was appointed as the US delegate to the newly formed UN General Assembly and led the formulation of the Universal Declaration of Human Rights.

Forty years later, in the early 1990s, Sadako Ogata, the first female UN High Commissioner for Refugees, did what none of her male predecessors had done before her: she courageously defied traditionalists in the refugee organization and among its stakeholders by launching major humanitarian operations in countries in war – in Iraq in 1991 and Bosnia in 1992 – rather than waiting for the victims of conflict to cross borders to become refugees.[51]

Other examples of exceptionally courageous UN women leaders include Nafis Sadik of Pakistan and Thoraya Ahmed Obaid of Saudi Arabia, executive directors of the UN population fund (UNFPA), who opposed the customs and norms of the societies from which they came to become global champions of women's education, health and reproductive rights.

A further example of a UN leader following Hammarskjöld's example of courageously upholding the principles of the Charter and promoting its objectives in the face of objections of a major power was Secretary-General Kofi Annan's 1998 trip to Iraq.[52] He undertook the trip against US advice to make a last-minute pitch for peace prior to the US invasion. Although the trip was not successful, it is still remembered and admired as it affirmed the value of peace over war and upheld the independence of the UN. Furthermore, history has vindicated the soundness of the reasons for which it was undertaken.

The complex political environment in which the organization frequently operates can make those occupying leadership positions often risk-averse.

49 Based on accounts shared with the author during his time in East Timor by survivors.

50 "South Sudan: Number of civilians protected at UN peacekeeping bases is 'swelling,'" UN News Centre, 16 April 2014.

51 From discussions of the author with UNHCR staff involved in the decision-making process.

52 "Annan admits Iraq trip could be last chance for peace," CNN World News, 18 Febuary 1998.

Expedience and political realism are highly valued and considerable emphasis is laid on conserving the goodwill of major or influential powers. Kofi Annan himself stressed:

> The Secretary-General's particular concerns should be to protect the weak against the strong yet he must understand that it is often only by winning and preserving the confidence of the strong that he can hope to do that.[53]

Like all senior officials, Annan was acutely aware of the dependence of the UN on major powers and the limitations this implied on speaking out. Quoting a Ghanian proverb, he explained to one of his senior aides, Shashi Tharoor, "you cannot hit a man on the head when you have your fingers between his teeth."[54]

To uphold the principles and norms of the UN in what are often contrary circumstances, moral courage is required. At the same time, courage has to be exercised with a clear understanding of the political constraints the institution is subjected to. In a morass of frequently conflicting political interests and pressures, advancing the principles and objectives of the UN means following a hazardous, unmarked path, which at times will require moving forward with caution and at other times will demand boldness.

Courage, insight, foresight and judiciousness all need to be applied. Boldness without insight can cause insurmountable blockages to advancing principles or put others at needless risk. An attitude informed only by caution and risk aversion is likely to lead to a loss of credibility of the institution and perceptions of a lack of independence. It also undermines the values and principles from which the organization draws its standing and authority.

3. LOUISE ARBOUR[55] AND CONCLUSIONS ON COURAGE IN UN LEADERSHIP

Dag Hammarskjöld emphasized that pursuing a calling of international service with the required integrity and courage was difficult and demanding: few are able to live up to Hammarskjöld's example. Senior leaders in the UN will often owe their career advancement to their political sensitivities and abilities, but may be less gifted at showing moral or political courage.

---

53 Quoted in Cockayne, J. and Malone, D.M. (2007), p. 69.

54 Quoted in Tharoor, S. (2007) "The most impossible job" in Chesterman, S. (ed.), *Secretary or General? The UN Secretary-General in World Politics*, Cambridge: Cambridge University Press, p. 39.

55 This section was enriched by observations and anecdotes on Louise Arbour from three of her former staff: James Stewart of the ICC; Naresh Perinpanayagam of the UN Secretariat; and Graham Blewitt, now retired, formerly of the ICTY.

One UN leader who was both politically astute and courageous and managed the challenges of her UN positions with exceptional skill is the person to whom this book is dedicated, Louise Arbour. Arbour exhibited many of the values identified thus far as required aspects of courage in leadership.

Arbour served in two leadership roles in the UN from 1996 to 1999 as Chief Prosecutor of the International Criminal Tribunal for the former Yugoslavia (ICTY) and the International Criminal Tribunal for Rwanda (ICTR), and from 2004 to 2008 as the UN High Commissioner for Human Rights. In both roles she gave new relevance to the institutions she led. At the ICTY, she achieved senior-level indictments, including that of President Slobodan Milošević, and ensured the capture of many of those indicted. At the end of her four-year tenure at the Office of the High Commissioner for Human Rights (OHCHR) in 2008, the organization had doubled in size and tripled the number of staff deployed to the field after she personally convinced Member States and UN officials of the merits of both. The Office had embraced the idea of focusing resources and efforts on the implementation of existing rights at the country level. It had grown in confidence in its field operations and was producing an unprecedented number of important public reports on human rights crises across the globe.

In the promotion of the application of international norms and human rights, Arbour combined outstanding integrity with political courage, vision and insight. She was finely attuned to political constraints, but an awareness of constraints did not hinder her from consistently upholding and advancing the principles of the UN. She stressed that political realism need not imply fatalism or resignation: "You have to work with the feasible, but that does not mean that you take the feasible as a given. You have to push the feasible to its limits."[56]

On many occasions, Arbour acted with unusual political courage. In pursuing her mandate, she was ready to take unpopular stances and to confront major powers. As High Commissioner for Human Rights in 2006, she criticized the United States for the use of torture[57] and in early 2007 submitted an *Amicus Curiae* brief arguing that the trials of Saddam Hussein and of his associates had not met international standards.[58] While the efforts to stop the executions failed, she vindicated the independence of her Office and upheld the principle that the standards of fair trial had to be respected, even for the most abusive dictators.[59]

Arbour was not intimidated when her actions provoked strong criticism from Ambassador John Bolton, the US representative to the UN, and others. She was

56 Quoted in Hochschild (2010), p. 84.

57 See e.g. Winning, A. (2008) "UN says waterboarding should be prosecuted as torture," *Reuters*, 8 February 2008, accessed on 2 September 2015 at: http://uk.reuters.com/article/2008/02/08/uk-usa-torture-un-idUKN0852061620080208.

58 Based on author's first-hand knowledge as OHCHR Chief of Field Operations at the time.

59 See e.g. "UN appeals to Iraq on executions," *BBC News*, 4 January 2007, accessed on 2 September 2015 at: http://news.bbc.co.uk/2/hi/middle_east/6227655.stm.

aware of the necessity for those who wish to show integrity in upholding the law to have the moral courage required to face unpopularity. On being appointed to the Supreme Court of Canada, she urged her colleagues not be overly swayed by public opinion:

> It takes courage to stand apart, where the comfort of conformity is withdrawn.[60]

Her courage was exercised in the pursuit of a vision. Both at the ICTY and the OHCHR, she dedicated significant time and resources to revamping the vision of the institutions she led. At the OHCHR, as indicated, she gave new impetus to the institution's field work. At the ICTY, she placed new emphasis on the prosecutorial strategy on getting hitherto hesitant NATO forces to arrest indicted war criminals. She changed the practice of issuing public indictments to issuing sealed indictments and served them to NATO, demanding that the indicted be apprehended and transferred to the ICTY. While admired by many both at the ICTY and OHCHR for her courage, she herself insisted that insight, vision and strategy were as important, if not more so:

> Courage is a lot easier than clarity – a leader must first bring clarity about what to do, then courage falls in place.[61]

Once she and her staff had developed clarity about the direction to take, she was both courageous and relentless in pursuing her objectives. At the ICTY, she faced down considerable pressure from senior leaders in NATO and its Member States not make the indictments public and to back off demands that NATO apprehend indicted war criminals.[62] Much later, she issued a public indictment for President Slobodan Milošević – the first ever for a serving president – at a time when many indicated that this would threaten a peace settlement for Kosovo, fears that ultimately proved unfounded. Many also said that the indictment could never be executed. She argued that patience was required and again time proved her right.[63]

Arbour also had a quality that Hammarskjöld referred to in his Johns Hopkins commencement address as being integral to moral courage: the ability to face up to one's mistakes. In early 2008, a few months before leaving office, on the advice of some of her staff, she issued a statement praising the recently ratified Arab Human Rights Charter. This proved ill-advised as the Charter included the juxtaposition of Zionism and racism and had various

60 Stewart, E. (1999), "Arbour urges courage in courts," *Toronto Star*, 5 October 5 1999, accessed on 2 September 2015 at: http://www.fact.on.ca/newpaper/ts99100a.htm.

61 Quoted in Hochschild (2010), p. 88.

62 Graham Blewitt in an email of 29 August 2015.

63 James Stewart in an email of 17 July 2015.

other flaws. After her statement, Arbour was mercilessly criticized by pro-Israeli interest groups, some of whom urged her to fire whoever was responsible for the statement. When she issued an additional statement highlighting weaknesses in the Charter, she was in turn accused by many ambassadors from Muslim-majority countries of lacking impartiality. She was upset by the tide of criticism from both sides, especially as it cast a shadow over her last months at the OHCHR, but she rationalized it, telling one of those responsible for the mistake:

> I have received and receive much undeserved credit for things others have done, it is balanced out a little if sometimes I receive some undeserved criticism.[64]

Beyond a degree of modesty, Arbour has a rarely rivaled intellect, considerable charm and an irreverent sense of humour. She is approachable and speaks to the great and the meek with the same frankness and engagement. She leads with a rare combination of courage, vision, insight, charisma, integrity and perseverance. Her leadership made greater the impact of the institutions she has headed and her legacy lives on as she continues to be cited as an example and inspiration for UN staff at all levels.

Mary Robinson, a predecessor of Arbour's in the role of UN High Commissioner for Human Rights, once wrote:[65]

> Almost by definition and certainly according to its Charter, the United Nations exists to promote human rights. Somewhere along the way many in the United Nations have lost the plot and allowed their work to answer to other imperatives. That is the root cause of much of the criticism that is levelled at the Organization.

In the same vein, a recent report on UN peace operations refers to the danger of "squandering" the principles of the Charter and calls for a "shift in mind set" among UN staff:

> UN personnel must be at once committed to the purposes and principles of the United Nations and be committed to helping improve the lives of people living in conflict-affected countries whom they have been mandated to serve.[66]

While states depend for their influence largely on resources, power and knowledge, the UN depends for its authority on its moral standing. How well

64 Quoted in Hochschild (2010), p. 97.

65 Robinson, M. (2006) "A personal voice" in Boyle, K. (ed.) (2006) *A Voice for Human Rights: Mary Robinson*, Philadelphia: University of Pennsylvania Press, p. 9.

66 "Uniting our strengths for peace – politics, partnership and people," Report of the High Level Independent Panel on United Nations Peace Operations, 16 June 2015, para. 60.

senior leaders live up to the ideal of ethical leadership in international service, as exemplified by Dag Hammarskjöld, will significantly determine the scope of its impact in furthering the Charter-based objectives of peace, human rights and development. The integrity, skill and courage with which senior leaders pursue the implementation of UN principles is decisive. Where an approach is not perceived to conform with UN values, over time the credibility and influence of the organization are eroded.

The importance of political awareness and of vision are given prominence in training on UN leadership, as well as in writing on leadership in general. The value of political or moral courage linked to integrity nurtured by fundamental principles are not given the same prominence in writings and teachings in recent decades.[67] As Salman Rushdie indicated in the article quoted earlier in this chapter, this is perhaps because where there are conflicting value systems, political or moral courage can be harder to grasp and can take more time to appreciate.

The value of moral courage in leadership is not lessened by the difficulty of recognizing and celebrating it. If anything, its importance is heightened for without it, leadership in the fog of uncertainty and amidst the confusion of contradictory pressures will become paralyzed. In this regard, Arbour once pointed out that "it takes courage to act in the face of uncertainty, when the luxury of being proven right may be forever withheld."[68] Clarity of vision and integrity are essential for leadership, but neither can thrive where the courage to step ahead, to face controversy and to weather unpopularity or condemnation are lacking.

As Hammarskjöld stressed in his Johns Hopkins commencement address, "at this time of great conflicts … in face of dangers of our own making," considerations of the broader global good and a dedication to international service are essential. The lessons of Dag Hammarskjöld, of Louise Arbour and of other exceptional UN leaders on the fundamental importance of leadership with clarity of vision and integrity enlivened by moral courage are therefore now more necessary than ever.

67 A review of the indexes of dozens of books on leadership published in the last two decades showed that 5% include "courage" among the topics considered.

68 Stewart (1999).

THE WORLD BANK AS A HUMAN RIGHTS-FREE ZONE

Philip ALSTON*

This chapter addresses the question of whether the World Bank should engage with issues relating to human rights and, if so, why and how. Although such questions have long been matters of public controversy, they have never been satisfactorily resolved. In addition to the fact that there are strong reasons to revisit them now, they also carry a special resonance in looking back at the many contributions that Louise Arbour has made to the human rights cause in the

* I am very grateful to Christiaan van Veen for his invaluable assistance in the preparation of this chapter. An earlier version was submitted as a report to the United Nations Human General Assembly in my capacity as Special Rapporteur on extreme poverty and human rights, A/70/274, 4 August 2015.

course of her multifaceted and extraordinarily distinguished career. Whether as judge, chief prosecutor, High Commissioner or think-tank president, she distinguished herself by always thinking creatively and challenging established dogmas. She combined compelling logic and analytical skills with intellectual and political courage, along with a marvellous dry sense of humor. Of particular relevance to the topic I have selected for this chapter is the fact that, as United Nations (UN) High Commissioner for Human Rights, she was a tireless promoter of the need to integrate human rights considerations into mainstream activities in fields such as development, security and transitional justice.[1]

1. THE WORLD BANK'S KEY ROLE

No international development agency is more important than the World Bank in terms of its influence on overall development thinking, its shaping of policies to overcome poverty, and its ability to encourage or discourage governments and other key development actors to incorporate human rights considerations into their policies and programs. Some might question this characterization on the grounds that the $61 billion that the Bank provided in loans, grants, equity investments and guarantees to governments and businesses in the fiscal year 2016 represents only a fraction of the total private capital flows to developing countries from all multilateral and national development banks, bilateral donors and private investors. However, in addition to the funding dimension, its research is more voluminous and influential than that of its peers, it remains the key standard-setter in many areas, its knowledge and expertise are often crucial, and its seal of approval frequently encourages the participation of other donors or investors.

This chapter begins by observing that human rights are approached differently depending on which aspect of the World Bank's work is involved. This applies particularly to the areas of legal policy, public relations, policy analysis, operations and safeguards. The chapter then examines the reasons that might explain the World Bank's historical aversion to human rights, argues that a new approach is needed and explores what difference that might make. Finally, consideration is given to what a World Bank policy on human rights might look like.

The thrust of the analysis is that the World Bank's existing approach is incoherent, counter-productive and unsustainable. It is based on outdated legal analysis and shaped by deep misperceptions of what a human rights policy would require. What is needed is a transparent dialogue designed to generate

---

1 See e.g. Louise Arbour, "Economic and social justice for societies in transition," (2007) 40 *New York University Journal of International Law and Politics* 1; and Mac Darrow and Louise Arbour, "The Pillar of Glass: Human Rights in the Development Operations of the United Nations," (2009) 103 *American Journal of International Law* 446.

an informed and nuanced policy that will avoid undoubted perils, while enabling the Bank and its members to make constructive and productive use of the universally accepted human rights framework.

2. THE HUMAN RIGHTS POLICY OF THE WORLD BANK

The World Bank does not have a single comprehensive human rights policy; rather, it has many different and competing approaches to the issue. For the purposes of analysis, we can see that it has adopted different human rights policies in each of the following contexts: legal policy, public relations, policy analysis, operations and safeguards.

2.1. LEGAL POLICY

The Articles of Agreement of the International Bank for Reconstruction and Development (IBRD) contain several provisions commonly referred to as the "political prohibition." Most importantly, Article IV, section 10 provides that: "The Bank and its officers shall not interfere in the political affairs of any member ... Only economic considerations shall be relevant to their decisions." Successive General Counsels of the World Bank have provided legal interpretations that have sought to distinguish legitimate "economic considerations" from inappropriate "political" factors.

In the mid-1960s, the General Assembly characterized the policies of apartheid in southern Africa and the colonial policies of Portugal as violations of the UN Charter and crimes against humanity. It requested UN specialized agencies, including the IBRD and the International Monetary Fund, to deny assistance to those governments. In 1967, the World Bank refused to comply with the relevant resolutions, citing a legal opinion that such action would be political rather than economic.

Beginning in the late 1980s, the General Counsel of the World Bank, Ibrahim Shihata, revisited the human rights issue. In a 1990 opinion, he considered the question of governance,[2] and in 1995, the political prohibition.[3] Although the latter opinion recognized the indivisibility of human rights, it drew a clear distinction between the two sets of rights. The General Counsel argued that although the operations of the Bank already promoted a broad range of

2 Ibrahim Shihata, "Issues of 'Governance' in Borrowing Members: The Extent of their Relevance under the Bank's Articles of Agreement," legal memorandum of the General Counsel of the World Bank Group, 21 December 1990.

3 Legal opinion of the General Counsel of the World Bank Group, 11 July 1995, in Ibrahim Shihata, *The World Bank Legal Papers* (The Hague, Martinus Nijhoff Publishers, 2000).

economic, social and cultural rights, its Articles of Agreement would normally prohibit it from promoting political rights. He left open the possibility of an exception in that latter regard when "an extensive violation of political rights which takes pervasive proportions" had "significant economic effects."[4]

In January 2006, on his last day in office, the then General Counsel, Roberto Dañino, circulated a legal opinion on the World Bank and human rights. Without explicitly claiming that the Bank had human rights obligations, the opinion charted a new approach. First, the Bank could take any type of human rights into account, provided there was economic impact or relevance. Second, where violations or non-fulfilment of human rights obligations had an economic impact, the Bank should take them into account. Third, the Bank might assist member countries to meet their legal obligations regarding human rights and should be broadly supportive of such commitments where they had an economic impact or relevance.[5]

In October 2006, the next General Counsel, Ana Palacio, characterized her predecessor's interpretation as "allowing, but not mandating, action on the part of the Bank in relation to human rights." That is more restrictive than the actual conclusion of Mr Dañino, which was that there are instances in which the World Bank should take human rights into account. Ms Palacio accepted that the Bank had a role in supporting its members to fulfil their human rights obligations. Her analysis began with an affirmative reference to Mr Shihata's approach and she added that "human rights would not be the basis for an increase in Bank conditionalities, nor should they be seen as an agenda that could present an obstacle for disbursement or increase the cost of doing business."[6]

In a letter responding to a suggestion by two UN Human Rights Council Special Procedures mandate holders in 2012 that World Bank financing should support the human rights obligations of states, the then General Counsel, Anne-Marie Leroy, and the Vice-President for the Africa Region, Makhtar Diop, stated that "only economic considerations – meaning those that have a direct and obvious economic effect relevant to the Bank's work – can be taken into account in decisions by the Bank and its officers. Therefore, in our view, your suggestion goes beyond the bounds of the Bank's institutional mandate."[7]

---

4 Ibid.

5 See Roberto Dañino, "The Legal Aspects of the World Bank's Work on Human Rights: Some Preliminary Thoughts" in *Human Rights and Development: Towards Mutual Reinforcement*, Philip Alston and Mary Robinson, eds. (Oxford, Oxford University Press, 2005).

6 Ana Palacio, "The Way Forward: Human Rights and the World Bank," (October 2006) 8(2) *Development Outreach* p. 35.

7 Letter from Anne-Marie Leroy and Makhtar Diop to the Special Rapporteur on the right to food and the Independent Expert on the effects of foreign debt and other international financial obligations of states on the full enjoyment of all human rights, particularly economic, social and cultural rights, 9 October 2012. Available at: http://spdb.ohchr.org/hrdb/22nd/OTH_09.10.12_(7.2012).pdf.

In a subsequent letter, Ms Leroy sought to distance the Bank definitively from Mr Dañino's opinion by noting that it "was neither presented to, nor endorsed by, the Bank's Board of Executive Directors and therefore, at this stage, it should not be represented as Bank policy."[8] In February 2017, Ms Sandie Okoro became Legal Counsel, but she had yet to make a formal pronouncement on human rights policy by the time this chapter was finalized.

As the legal approach of the World Bank to human rights currently stands, the most problematic aspect is that it is based on double standards. On the one hand, successive General Counsels have found convincing rationales to facilitate the wish of the management to work on issues as diverse as corruption, money laundering, terrorist financing, governance and the rule of law, but on the other hand, human rights remains on a very short blacklist, along with support for the military and intelligence services, as issues that are currently classified as being predominantly political and thus prohibited.

The most telling example of this double standard is to be found in a 2012 opinion by the former General Counsel justifying the involvement of the World Bank in the criminal justice sector.[9] It is a carefully argued analysis that invokes Mr Shihata's opinions extensively in order to reach the conclusion that the mandate of the Bank permits it to work in that area "provided that proposed interventions are grounded in an appropriate and objective economic rationale and are structured so as to avoid interference in the political affairs of a member country." Because the issues raised and many of the matters dealt with have so much in common with human rights, it is instructive to examine the methodology and arguments employed and to consider the extent to which they could be applied equally to human rights.

The 2012 opinion relies on a broad range of sources. Previous legal opinions are invoked extensively but selectively. The practice of other multilateral development banks and of multilateral and bilateral development agencies are all considered to be pertinent. Finally, independent scholarship and World Bank research are both cited to bolster the legal arguments made.

The opinion begins with definitions. First, the criminal justice sector is expansively defined, thus potentially enabling the World Bank to undertake wide-ranging activities under that rubric. The definition includes "human rights and ombudsman's offices," but in practice these will presumably fall foul of the political prohibition.

---

8 Letter from Anne-Marie Leroy to the Special Rapporteur on the right to food and the Independent Expert on the effects of foreign debt and other international financial obligations of States, 16 January 2013. Available at: http://spdb.ohchr.org/hrdb/22nd/World_Bank_16.01.13_(7.2012).pdf.

9 Anne-Marie Leroy, "Legal Note on Bank Involvement in the Criminal Justice Sector," 9 February 2012. The quotes in the following pages are all taken from this Legal Note.

Next is the definition of development. In contrast to the notion current over 70 years ago when the Articles of Agreement were adopted, development today is said to encompass "broad areas of human development, social development, education, protection of global public goods, governance and institutions, as well as issues such as inclusion and cohesion, participation, accountability and equity" – but not, apparently, human rights, which are somehow different.

The author of the opinion then seeks to demonstrate that economic considerations demand a focus on criminal justice. It is argued that crime and violence impede economic development, reduce investment and employment growth, and make countries less competitive. They undermine strategies to increase levels of social and human capital, which are key to economic growth, divert funds away from development and other productive activities, weaken the economies of fragile states and can exacerbate conflict. They also disproportionately affect the poor by undermining employment, reducing mobility and hindering access to basic services.

The next step is to demonstrate that criminal justice interventions will not violate the political prohibition. While acknowledging that "most development efforts" have a "political dimension," a narrow interpretation is adopted, according to which the World Bank cannot involve "itself in the partisan politics or ideological disputes that affect its member countries." Inappropriate involvement is said to include "favoring political factions, parties or candidates in elections" or "endorsing or mandating a particular form of government, political bloc or political ideology."

Finally, the author of the opinion acknowledges that there will always be a risk that criminal justice interventions might cross the line into the essentially political realm. A range of methods to manage such risk are thus identified, such as promoting "country ownership" of the activity, including through consultation with non-state stakeholders, avoiding involvement in enforcement on specific cases, undertaking careful risk analysis and setting up a special review mechanism if particular concerns arise.

In effect, although the World Bank's lawyers might be expected to strenuously dispute the proposition, the template just described could be applied in a very similar fashion to justify a human rights policy. Previous legal opinions have left space for the crafting of such a policy, other multilateral development banks and most multilateral and bilateral development agencies have human rights policies, and there has been voluminous scholarly research on these issues. The General Counsel's definition of development for the purposes of interpreting the mandate clearly accommodates human rights. There are innumerable ways in which human rights violations have major economic impacts and the poor are disproportionately affected. And, just as with the criminal justice sector, there will be some aspects of some rights which would fall foul of the political prohibition, thus requiring a series of risk management strategies to avoid such problems.

The adoption of an expansive criminal justice policy, while refusing to engage with human rights, leads to a highly artificial separation of the two issues. One example is the explanation in the opinion of activities that would be inappropriate by reference to "international due process standards," a concept that has little meaning unless interpreted as incorporating human rights standards.

2.2. PUBLIC RELATIONS POLICY

Since the early 1990s, the World Bank has made numerous public relations statements affirming the importance of human rights. It has often observed that human rights and development are inter-related, insisted that its projects contribute to the fulfilment of economic, social and cultural rights, argued that its work on governance contributes to an institutional environment in which human rights can thrive, and claimed that it consistently applies "human rights principles" such as participation in its operations. These claims, however, are usually made in the abstract, without detailed analysis or supporting evidence.[10] While the Nordic Trust Fund, established within the Bank, has succeeded in facilitating a more sophisticated debate, its outputs have yet to bring changes to the actual practice of the Bank.

2.3. POLICY ANALYSES

There are, however, some Bank studies which enter into detail on the issue of human rights, such as those in its annual flagship publication, the World Development Report, which deals with issues such as equity, gender equality, conflict resolution, HIV/AIDS and disability. In 2006, the World Development Report urged that equity should be a central concern in the design and implementation of development policy. It noted that the "international human rights regime testifies to the shared belief that all should have equal rights and be spared extreme deprivation" and acknowledged various other links between human rights and equity.[11] In 2011, the World Development Report focused on conflict, security and development. The message of the report was that strengthening legitimate institutions and governance to provide security, justice and jobs for citizens is crucial to breaking cycles of violence in fragile countries.

---

10 See, for example, Anupama Dokeniya, "Rights and Development," 16 May 2012. Available at: http://blogs.worldbank.org/publicsphere/node/5989.

11 World Bank, *World Development Report 2006: Equity and Development* (Washington, D.C., World Bank, 2005).

Building confidence is a major challenge and one that requires the protection of human rights. Detailed suggestions are explored for achieving that goal.[12]

The main message of the *World Development Report* in 2012 on gender equality and development was that gender equality was both a core development objective and "smart economics." It mattered because "the ability to live the life of one's own choosing and be spared from absolute deprivation is a basic human right." Development is defined as "a process of expanding freedoms equally for all people," and international and regional human rights instruments as crucial in achieving gender equality. The report described the Convention on the Elimination of All Forms of Discrimination against Women as "the primary international vehicle for monitoring and advocating gender equality."[13]

Since 2011, the World Bank has published three major studies on populations at risk of HIV/AIDS. All three take the approach that assisting those vulnerable groups is a human rights imperative. They also contain explicit references to the relevant human rights norms.[14]

In the World Report on Disability, jointly published by the World Bank and the World Health Organization, the leaders of the two organizations stated that the report aimed to "provide the evidence for innovative policies and programs that can improve the lives of people with disabilities, and facilitate implementation of the United Nations Convention on the Rights of Persons with Disabilities … This landmark international treaty reinforced our understanding of disability as a human rights and development priority."[15] The report itself is full of practical guidance about how international human rights law is relevant to dealing with disability issues in development.

A striking example of a publication dealing with human rights is the report, published jointly by the Bank and the Organisation for Economic Co-operation and Development (OECD), entitled *Integrating Human Rights into Development: Donor Approaches, Experiences, and Challenges*. It makes a powerful case for the integration of human rights and development, although, as with most such publications, it includes at the front of the book a caveat that "the findings, interpretations, and conclusions expressed in this work do not necessarily reflect the views of the World Bank, its Board of Executive Directors, or the governments they represent."[16]

---

12 World Bank, *World Development Report 2011: Conflict, Security and Development* (Washington, D.C., World Bank, 2011).

13 World Bank, *World Development Report 2012: Gender Equality and Development* (Washington, D.C., World Bank, 2011).

14 World Bank, *The Global HIV Epidemics among Sex Workers* (2013); *The Global HIV Epidemics among Men Who Have Sex with Men* (2011); and *The Global HIV Epidemics among People Who Inject Drugs* (2013).

15 World Health Organization and World Bank, *World Report on Disability* (Geneva, World Health Organization, 2011).

16 World Bank and OECD, *Integrating Human Rights into Development: Donor Approaches, Experiences, and Challenges* (Washington, D.C., 3rd edition, 2016), iv.

Other valuable research on human rights topics has also been published under World Bank auspices with funds from the Nordic Trust Fund, a fund specially set up for the purpose.[17] I am not, however, aware of any significant internal policy impact resulting from these publications.

2.4. BANK OPERATIONS

Despite the powerful arguments marshalled in World Bank publications for acknowledging the links between human rights and various development objectives, Bank-financed projects and programs go to great lengths to avoid any operational references to human rights. One case study out of many must suffice. It concerns gender-based violence, a phenomenon that is universally recognized as violating human rights.

I analyzed 13 projects on gender-based violence that are part of a major World Bank initiative on the issue and were approved between January 2012 and June 2015. None of the relevant project documents engages substantively with the human rights dimensions of gender-based violence. Passing references can be found to the Convention on the Elimination of All Forms of Discrimination against Women or the Universal Declaration of Human Rights, but no analysis of the relevant rights and obligations is provided and the provisions are not linked to the project at hand.[18] In fact, even the generic terms "human rights" and "rights" are rarely used, and when they are, no elaboration is provided. The intended project beneficiaries are presented not as rights holders, but as clients or service recipients. The borrowing state bears contractual responsibilities toward the Bank, but no reference is made to its international or domestic human rights obligations. No reference is made to responsibility for gender-based violence by state actors, such as police or health-care workers, despite the frequency of such problems, and no reliance is ever placed upon the detailed human rights-based frameworks for tackling gender-based violence drawn up by the Committee on the Elimination of Discrimination against Women and various other international human rights actors, despite the fact that the Convention has been almost universally ratified.

---

17 See, for example, Varun Gauri and Siri Gloppen, "Human Rights-Based Approaches to Development: Concepts, Evidence, and Policy" *Polity* (October 2012) 44(4); Daniel Brinks and Varun Gauri, "The Law's Majestic Equality? The Distributive Impact of Litigating Social and Economic Rights," Policy research working paper No. 5999 (World Bank, 2012); and Salman M.A. Salman and Siobhán McInerney-Lankford, *The Human Right to Water: Legal and Policy Dimensions* (World Bank, 2004).

18 See, for example, projects P130819 (HN safer municipalities), Honduras, approved on 13 December 2012; P132768 (Pernambuco equity and inclusive growth development policy loan), Brazil, approved on 25 June 2013; and P145605 (enhancing fiscal capacity to promote shared prosperity development policy loan), Colombia, approved on 6 September 2013.

The systematic avoidance of human rights language, frameworks and institutions in the context of World Bank projects on gender-based violence is replicated in most other areas of its activities,[19] although there have been some exceptions over recent decades in areas such as HIV/AIDS and some gender-related projects.

2.5. SAFEGUARD POLICIES

One context in which the relevance of human rights might have been expected to be acknowledged is the environmental and social "safeguard" policies of the World Bank. However, the current safeguards contain no explicit human rights policy and the sole reference to human rights occurs in operational policy 4.10 on indigenous peoples.[20] Human rights have sometimes had an indirect influence on the interpretation of the safeguard policies by the World Bank Inspection Panel, but the practice in this regard has been inconsistent and piecemeal.[21]

In 2013, the World Bank began the process of updating its environmental and social safeguards for investment project financing. In late 2014, 28 special procedures mandate holders addressed a lengthy and detailed analysis of the July 2014 draft framework to the World Bank.[22] My own position is adequately summarized in the letter, in which the authors state that "the document seems to go out of its way to avoid any meaningful references to human rights and international human rights law, except for passing references in the vision statement and environmental and social standard (ESS) 7." Unfortunately, the final version of the safeguards, adopted in August 2016, proved to be no improvement in that regard, despite voluminous submissions by large numbers of stakeholders calling upon the Bank to take account of human rights.[23]

---

19 Kirk Herbertson, Kim Thompson and Robert Goodland, *A Roadmap for Integrating Human Rights into the World Bank Group* (Washington D.C., World Resources Institute, 2010); and Galit Sarfaty, *Values in Translation: Human Rights and the Culture of the World Bank* (Stanford, Stanford University Press, 2012).

20 Operational policy 4.10 on indigenous peoples begins by stating that the policy "contributes to the Bank's mission of poverty reduction and sustainable development by ensuring that the development process fully respects the dignity, human rights, economies, and cultures of indigenous peoples".

21 Adam McBeth, *International Economic Actors and Human Rights* (Abingdon, Routledge, 2010).

22 Letter from 28 special procedures mandate holders to the President of the World Bank, 12 December 2014. Available at: www.ohchr.org/Documents/Issues/EPoverty/WorldBank.pdf.

23 For all official documentation on the consultation on the draft framework, see: http://consultations.worldbank.org/consultation/review-and-update-world-bank-safeguard-policies.

3. EXPLAINING THE AVERSION OF THE WORLD BANK TO HUMAN RIGHTS

Before considering why the World Bank should change its approach, it is essential to seek to understand why there is currently such an aversion to human rights within the management of the Bank. Six factors would seem to be especially important.

3.1. INSTITUTIONAL CULTURE

From its creation in 1944, the World Bank has sought to present itself as a functional, technical agency and hence one that is above the political fray. This was deemed essential to avoid the appearance of choosing sides in the aftermath of World War II and subsequently in the fraught climate of the Cold War. This technocratic image is mirrored in the internal culture of the Bank, which is dominated by economists. This in turn affects how institutional goals are shaped and justifications are framed. To become relevant, human rights factors need to be presented in terms of economic impact rather than as matters of values, law or dignity.[24] Just as human rights proponents are uncomfortable with the consequentialism of economics, economists often perceive rights as being rigid, anti-market and overly state-centric. The concern is that the engagement of the Bank with human rights would bring about a radical paradigm shift with unknown consequences.[25]

Another institutional element is the pressure to approve loans or, as a famous World Bank report put it, to "push money out the door."[26] Despite official denials, these pressures continue. In such a setting, it is unsurprising that some see social safeguards and even more so human rights as factors likely to raise costs and delay lending. An internal Bank report observed that management is often uninterested in, or resistant to, work on safeguards and treats it as a box to be checked.[27] However, minimizing safeguard concerns enhances the likelihood of flawed project design, which neglects elements important for success, overlooks

---

24 See, for example, Sarfaty, *Values in Translation*, *supra* note 19; and Nordic Trust Fund and World Bank, "Human Rights and Economics: Tensions and Positive Relationships" (2012).

25 Mac Darrow, "The Millennium Development Goals: Milestones or Millstones? Human Rights Priorities for the post-2015 Development Agenda," (2012) 15(1) *Yale Human Rights and Development Law Journal* 55.

26 W. Wapenhans, "Effective Implementation: Key to Development Impact," report of the Portfolio Management Task Force (Washington, D.C., World Bank, 1992).

27 World Bank Internal Audit Department, "Advisory Review of the Bank's Safeguard Risk Management" (16 June 2014).

likely opposition and resistance, creates ill will and damages the credibility of the Bank. It also assumes, contrary to the findings of a report by the Independent Evaluation Group, that the costs of safeguards outweigh their benefits.[28]

3.2. MISPLACED LEGALISM

The goals and policies of the World Bank have changed radically since 1944. The Articles of Agreement contain no mention of either of its current proclaimed "twin goals" of ending extreme poverty and promoting shared prosperity. The General Counsels have played a key role in the necessarily dynamic interpretation of the Articles required to reflect and justify that evolution.

Interpretation of the Articles is decided by the Executive Directors by a simple majority vote, with the possibility of appeal to the Board of Governors.[29] In practice, legal opinions by the General Counsel have provided the basis for most such interpretations. General Counsels also provide regular advice to the Executive Directors and the President and senior management, including on interpretation of the mandate.[30] The most influential General Counsels have acknowledged the need to adopt a purposive or teleological approach.[31]

The principal exception to this general rule has been the issue of human rights. As theories of development have changed and the World Bank has confronted new challenges, legal counsels have had no difficulty in justifying the engagement of the Bank with issues such as corruption, the rule of law, environmental degradation and other novel issues. Alone among these new issues, human rights is classified as political rather than economic, despite the view of a former General Counsel that "human rights are an intrinsic part of the Bank's mission."[32] Today, it is still the Legal Department that takes the lead in "policing" the human rights taboo within the Bank.[33] This is said to apply even within the discussions in the Executive Board.

It is particularly striking that one of the most complex and contentious issues confronting the World Bank in the twenty-first century, namely a human rights policy, is resolved not on the basis of any detailed legal or empirical analysis, or

28 Independent Evaluation Group, World Bank, *Safeguards and Sustainability Policies in a Changing World: An Independent Evaluation of World Bank Group Experience* (Washington D.C., World Bank, 2010).

29 IBRD Articles of Agreement, Article IX. See also Aron Broches, *Selected Essays: World Bank, ICSID, and Other Subjects of Public and Private International Law* (Dordrecht, Martinus Nijhoff Publishers, 1995).

30 Shihata, *The World Bank Legal Papers*, *supra* note 3.

31 See, for example, Shihata, *The World Bank Legal Papers*, *supra* note 3; and Broches, *Selected Essays*, *supra* note 29.

32 Roberto Dañino, *supra* note 5.

33 See Sarfaty, *Values in Translation*, *supra* note 19.

of transparent debates within the Bank, but on the basis of a legal opinion rooted in the politics of the last century and based on a mode of legal analysis that has long been considered to be unjustified and unsustainable in relation to almost every other issue.

3.3. CULTURAL RELATIVISM

Ironically, given the widespread perception that the World Bank is dominated by Western interests and values, the argument is often heard that the Bank needs to avoid human rights discourse because it may be perceived as imposing Western values on non-Western countries. Thus, the authors of a report on gender and human rights-based approaches in development felt the need to address such concerns in a separate annex.[34] While the debate over cultural relativism is a very vibrant one in both political and scholarly circles, the justifiable issue of concern is not the basic universality of the standards, which has long been reaffirmed, but the degree of cultural appropriateness shown in their application.[35] For the Bank to invoke a relativist justification to refuse all engagement with the universal standards is contrary to international law. Particular interpretations of human rights will always be contested, but so too will definitions of poverty, the rule of law, corruption and a great many other notions which lie at the heart of its work. Avoidance is no substitute for sophisticated and nuanced engagement.

3.4. THE SHADOW OF SANCTIONS

The World Bank has a long, and generally unhappy, history in which human rights concerns have been linked to demands for it to impose sanctions on client states. Such demands have come from many sources, including the General Assembly, the United States and other governments, and a wide range of non-governmental organizations (NGOs). In principle, the Bank has rejected most such calls on the grounds that they involve politics rather than economics. In practice, however, it occasionally succumbed to political pressure and delayed or withheld funds, albeit insisting that its actions did not amount to sanctioning.[36]

---

34 World Bank and Nordic Trust Fund, "Report of Gender and Human Rights-Based Approaches in Development" (2013).

35 In its strongest form, cultural relativism claims "that no transcendent or transcultural ideas of right can be found or agreed on, and hence that no culture or state … is justified in attempting to impose on other cultures or states what must be understood to be ideas associated particularly with it." Philip Alston and Ryan Goodman, *International Human Rights* (Oxford, Oxford University Press, 2012).

36 The best-known cases relate to Chile in 1972, Kenya in 1991 and again in 2006, Indonesia in 1999 and the Russian Federation in 2000.

An especially problematic, if well-intentioned, case was the decision in February 2014 to delay a $90 million health project loan to Uganda after the country adopted a draconian anti-homosexuality act. The World Bank suggested that it had acted only to ensure that the health project would not be adversely affected by the act. However, the President of the Bank explained that he had acted because he was not convinced that the loan would not lead to discrimination or even endangerment of the lesbian, gay, bisexual and transgender community.

The President sought to make the case that serious institutional discrimination had economic costs that the World Bank could legitimately take into account, but the same argument applies to equally problematic forms of discrimination against different groups in a large number of countries in which the Bank continues to operate, and in response to which no action has been taken. No convincing justification was put forward by the Bank as to why Uganda alone was singled out among the various countries that have laws that criminalize homosexuality. No explanation was given as to why discrimination against lesbian, gay, bisexual, transgender and intersex communities was the trigger for action rather than often deeply entrenched official discrimination against various other groups. Nor was the action based on any policy document that had previously been elaborated. And finally, if the Bank itself had been directly implicated in the issue at hand, urgent remedial action would have been much more readily defensible, but it was not.

While it was clearly not intended as such, the most significant impact of the decision was probably to convince an even larger number of countries that the World Bank should indeed be kept away from human rights issues for fear that it would start to apply sanctions more broadly and in an equally unpredictable and ad hoc manner.

The challenge now is to ensure that there is a silver lining to this incident. The World Bank needs to elaborate a nuanced policy which will avoid such incidents in the future, eschew sanctions of that type except in the most extreme and pre-defined situations, and develop a range of policies that can promote respect for human rights in a constructive manner consistent with its overall policy objectives and its mandate.

3.5. TURNING THE WORLD BANK INTO A HUMAN RIGHTS COP

On various occasions, senior World Bank officials have warned of the dire consequences that would follow if the Bank were to become some sort of global policeman, responsible for enforcing respect for human rights by its client governments. Because of the sanctions mentality described above, that fear is not altogether unfounded.

There is a vast difference, however, between having a carefully tailored human rights policy and becoming an enforcer of rights. Many other international organizations have adopted such policies; none of them have become enforcers. The established international human rights regime exists to engage with states that are accused of violations and to find ways to encourage, facilitate and promote compliance with international norms. There is no reason why that task would or should move to the World Bank if it were to acknowledge that human rights are also relevant to its operations. There are many ways in which the Bank can encourage or even assist states to design policies and projects that are consistent with the obligations that those states have voluntarily undertaken through the ratification of binding international treaties. It is especially noteworthy in this respect that the Bank safeguards already require it to take account of the international environmental treaty obligations of a country when undertaking an environmental assessment and it has managed to do that without giving rise to undue controversy.[37]

3.6. COMPETITION WITH OTHER LENDERS

It is often suggested that obliging the World Bank to take human rights into account would place it at a disadvantage to other lenders, which might not do so. In 2006, the then President of the Bank, Paul Wolfowitz, criticized the government and banks of China for not attaching human rights and environmental standards to their loans to Africa. In 2011, China overtook the Bank in terms of the volume of its development lending. The creation of new multilateral investment banks and the growth of national development banks in countries like Brazil and India means ever more competition in the market for lenders. While the World Bank has always downplayed such suggestions, most commentators suggest that these developments have placed it under competitive pressure.

In fact, if the major new banks do not adopt appropriate social protection policies, there would be good reason to assume that the World Bank will be less able to compete in terms of the time taken for project planning, the conditions offered to borrowers and the speed of disbursement. Both the New Development Bank, which proclaims itself "as an alternative to the existing US-dominated World Bank and International Monetary Fund,"[38] and the Asian Infrastructure Investment Bank were set up in 2015. The Articles of Agreement of both banks

---

37 See, for example, operational policies 4.01 and 4.36.

38 See: http://ndbbrics.org/.

reproduce the same political prohibition clause as is contained in the Articles of Agreement of the World Bank.[39] The Asian Infrastructure Investment Bank is committed to addressing environmental and social impacts, but it remains to be seen what type of standards and safeguards will be adopted and how, if at all, human rights will be factored in. These are issues that will warrant the most careful scrutiny going forward.

The immediate question for the World Bank is whether the best strategy is to compete with the new lenders in a race to the bottom or to adopt a principled stance. Despite obvious temptations, there are strong arguments for the latter approach. Strong safeguards, as noted above, ensure sound planning, reduce subsequent problems, facilitate public support, minimize reputational costs for the lender and facilitate better overall outcomes. Loans that are made in secrecy and without such precautions carry with them the seeds of eventual disaster for both the borrower and the lender. The real comparative advantage for the World Bank lies in underwriting high-quality projects and maintaining its role as an innovator rather than in a race to lend more at whatever cost. Of course, none of this means that the Bank should not explore efficiency gains that might be achieved through means other than cutting standards and avoiding human rights considerations.

4. TIME FOR CHANGE: WHY THE WORLD BANK NEEDS A NEW APPROACH TO HUMAN RIGHTS

Based on the preceding review, the following propositions seem to encapsulate the actual practice of the World Bank: (a) pay lip service to human rights in official settings, as long as there are no consequences; (b) acknowledge the theoretical significance of human rights in studies and analyses of issues in relation to which they are incontestably relevant; (c) ensure that, as a general rule, the Bank does not engage with any aspect of human rights in its actual operations and lending; and (d) be prepared to make exceptions when political imperatives require it, even if this involves a high degree of inconsistency.

There are many reasons why a new approach is needed. The following six seem especially compelling.

First, an inconsistent, ad hoc and opaque policy of the type that exists today is in no one's interests. The world has changed dramatically since the 1980s and human rights are an unavoidable feature of national and international policies

[39] See Article 13(e) of the Articles of Agreement of the New Development Bank, available at: http://ndbbrics.org/agreement.html; and Article 31(2) of the Articles of Agreement of the Asian Infrastructure Investment Bank, available at: www.aiibank.org/uploadfile/2015/0629/20150629094900288.pdf.

and debates. It is illusory to believe that the World Bank can be fully effective without any meaningful engagement with that entire field of activity. By treating human rights as a taboo issue, the Bank has ensured that a whole range of issues that are universally acknowledged to be crucial to the development and poverty eradication agendas cannot be openly addressed or factored into its work.[40] As noted below, the valiant effort to rely upon surrogate terms can never be an adequate substitute for engaging with the human rights framework and norms. The result is a staff and management with relatively little understanding of the complexity of the international human rights regime, which in turn results in unfounded fears, avoidance of debates that would otherwise be a matter of course, a poor sense of how to respond when human rights problems force themselves onto the agenda and the absence of a credible Bank voice when these issues are discussed in other settings.

Second, the policies of the World Bank need to reflect the current status of international human rights law rather than the situation in the 1960s or the 1980s, when its existing policies were frozen into place. Even in the late 1980s, international human rights law was in its infancy and remained relatively contested. There were relatively few human rights treaties and many states had ratified none of them. The Cold War dominated and distorted discussions. By contrast, today every country in the world is a party to multiple international human rights treaties and all engage voluntarily in international forums in which they explain and justify their human rights policies and practices. In short, it might have been justified to suggest in the late 1980s that much of the human rights regime was of a political nature. Today this is no longer the case and human rights law is an integral part of the international system.

Third, rather than being an outlier, the World Bank needs to bring its approach into line with that of almost every other major international organization. In the mid-1980s, the Bank was one of many international organizations that were reluctant to engage with the human rights regime. The easiest example to cite is the United Nations Children's Fund (UNICEF), which gradually changed from a policy of ignoring rights issues during the 1980s to become an agency devoted to promoting the provisions of the Convention on the Rights of the Child. The same transition has occurred in many other international organizations, so that by 2013, the Secretary-General could adopt a "Human Rights Up Front" initiative, in which he called upon the UN, its agencies, funds and programs to treat human rights as a system-wide core responsibility.

As of January 2015, the United Nations Development Programme (UNDP) officially recognized "the centrality of human rights to [its goals] … and is committed to supporting 'universal respect for, and observance of, human

40 See Independent Evaluation Group, World Bank, *Results and Performance of the World Bank Group 2014* (Washington, D.C., World Bank, 2015).

rights and fundamental freedoms for all.'" It "shall ... refrain from providing support for activities that may contribute to violations of a State's human rights obligations and the core international human rights treaties." The UNDP policy does, however, contain provisions that seek to limit its human rights obligations. The policy says that it will support state efforts, meet human rights obligations "as requested," notes that the UNDP does not have a human rights "monitoring role" and comments that it will monitor its own compliance with its policies as a matter of "due diligence."[41] This is a formulation that has been carefully crafted both to acknowledge the centrality of human rights, but also to allay any concerns of governments and officials that the organization is in the business of human rights enforcement.

Even in comparison with other multilateral development banks, the World Bank is still an outlier. A recent Bank study concluded that: "Most of the other MDBs refer to 'human rights' in supportive aspirational terms while recognizing the responsibility of clients to respect human rights." The World Bank, it noted, does so solely in relation to indigenous peoples.[42] Thus, while the Bank was in good company in the 1980s in being wary of incorporating human rights standards into its work, it now stands almost alone, along with the International Monetary Fund, in insisting that human rights are matters of politics which it must, as a matter of legal principle, avoid, rather than being an integral part of the international legal order.

Fourth, the World Bank needs to bring its operational policies into line with mainstream development theory, especially its own. In 1999, Amartya Sen published a landmark study entitled *Development as Freedom*, based on lectures given at the Bank. Sen made a powerful case that freedom and the enjoyment of a range of rights were integral to achieving meaningful development. More recently, William Easterly has argued that "the cause of poverty is the absence of political and economic rights, the absence of a free political and economic system that would find the technical solutions to the poor's problems." He dismissed policies that seek to artificially separate human rights from development as technocratic illusions.[43] The Bank itself has often paid lip service to the consensus that has emerged since the end of the Cold War that recognizes that "democracy, development and respect for human rights and fundamental freedoms are interdependent and mutually reinforcing," as proclaimed in the Vienna Declaration and Programme of Action, adopted by consensus by

---

41 UNDP, "Social and Environmental Standards" (New York, 2014), available at: https://consultations.worldbank.org/Data/hub/files/consultation-template/review-and-update-world-bank-safeguard-policies/en/phases/mdb_safeguard_comparison_main_report_and_annexes_may_2015.pdf.

42 World Bank, "Comparative Review of Multilateral Development Bank Safeguard Systems" (May 2015).

43 William Easterly, *The Tyranny of Experts: Economists, Dictators, and the Forgotten Rights of the Poor* (New York, Basic Books, 2013).

171 states in 1993. By staunchly maintaining the technocratic illusion, not in its conceptual work but in its operations where it really matters, the Bank has not only placed itself firmly outside mainstream development thinking and policies formally endorsed by all states, but perhaps more problematically has sent the message that rights and development can, and in its own case must, be kept separate. The knock-on effect of this negative example cannot be underestimated.

Fifth, the Bank needs at least a convincing due diligence policy to enable it to adjust or reject projects that would otherwise lead to, or support, human rights violations. Its safeguard policies have long been referred to as "do-no-harm" policies, but their very limited coverage in terms of the full gamut of the human rights obligations of states has meant that many serious violations are alleged to have occurred in the context of projects funded by the Bank.[44] I am in no position to judge the accuracy of any particular allegations of rights violations and nor is it necessary to do so in the present analysis. Suffice it to note that the Bank's own internal reports have made clear that existing safeguard arrangements have often proved to be inadequate. Reports by the Inspection Panel have highlighted significant problems in specific projects and a report by the Internal Audit Department on resettlement programs has revealed serious systemic deficiencies.[45] To its credit, the Bank responded to the latter by announcing extensive reforms.[46] Nonetheless, these evaluation reports provide powerful evidence of the need for a more sustained and better integrated approach, reflecting the full range of international human rights standards rather than the static list of specific concerns that are currently singled out for monitoring. Integrating human rights into operational policies is necessary to comply with the Bank's aim of doing no harm.

Sixth, by refusing to take account of any information emanating from human rights sources, the World Bank places itself in an artificial bubble, which excludes information that could greatly enrich its understanding of the situations and contexts in which it works. This includes especially the materials generated by human rights treaty bodies, special procedures mandate holders and the universal periodic review process of the Human Rights Council, as well as analyses generated by NGOs. It is striking that the Bank regularly consults

---

44 See International Consortium of Investigative Journalists project, "Evicted and Abandoned: The World Bank's Broken Promise to the Poor," available at: www.icij.org/project/world-bank; and Human Rights Watch, "At Your Own Risk: Reprisals Against Critics of World Bank Group Projects" (June 2015); and "Waiting Here for Death: Displacement and 'Villagization' in Ethiopia's Gambella Region" (2012).

45 See, for example, Inspection Panel, World Bank, report and recommendation, "Republic of Uzbekistan: Second Rural Enterprise Support Project (P109126) and Additional Financing for Second Rural Enterprise Support Project (P126962)" (9 December 2013).

46 World Bank, "Action Plan: Improving the Management of Safeguards and Resettlement Practices and Outcomes" (4 March 2015), available at: http://pubdocs.worldbank.org/pubdocs/publicdoc/ 2015/3/714814254831199332/action-plan-safeguards-resettlement.pdf.

religious leaders, such as the faith-based and religious leaders' round table it held in 2015, but has no comparable meetings with human rights experts.

5. WHAT DIFFERENCE WOULD A HUMAN RIGHTS POLICY MAKE?

The two most common responses heard from World Bank officials in reply to suggestions that it should adopt a human rights policy are in direct contradiction to one another. The first takes various forms, suggesting that such a reform would transform the nature of the Bank's role, open up a Pandora's box, create political havoc or be generally unmanageable. The second is that the Bank already does so much to promote the realization of human rights that a change in policy would make little difference and is thus unnecessary. The argument tends to go something like this: by improving access to goods and services such as health care, education and water, and by lifting people out of poverty, the Bank enhances the enjoyment of human rights in many countries. Its focus on governance improves human rights, its emphasis on consultation enhances people's right to participate and its publications often acknowledge the importance of human rights. At the end of the day, the Bank might use different language from that of human rights law, but its goals are the same.

The last of these claims is reflected in the following statement: "In fact, it has been possible to integrate human rights (using principles derived from the human rights framework) without an explicit approach, as can be seen in the work of some of the international financial institutions." But the very next sentence in the same report provides a compelling rebuttal of that very claim: "A potential shortcoming of such an approach is the risk of 'rhetorical repackaging,' which involves a superficial use of human rights terms in development without a full incorporation of human rights obligations or principles."[47] The third edition of the same publication adjusts this analysis and instead describes "rhetorical repackaging" as occurring "when the distinction between the use of operational principles that might be tangentially related to human rights and interventions specifically grounded in the human rights framework is blurred."[48]

The key question then is whether it actually matters if the World Bank uses the language of human rights or opts instead for surrogate terms which are perceived to be less politically loaded or contentious. After all, if it advocates for gender equality, does it really matter if it uses the language of human rights, or whether any reference is made to UN standards or to the work of bodies such as the Committee on the Elimination of Discrimination against Women?

---

47 World Bank and OECD, *Integrating Human Rights into Development*, *supra* note 16.

48 Ibid, 3rd ed, 2016, p. xxiv.

Or if the Bank works to expand access to water and sanitation, who cares if it characterizes them as human rights or not? Or if the Bank talks about problems relating to inclusion, participation, governance or the rule of law, does it matter if the issues are framed in "Bank speak" rather than in terms of the human rights obligations of the state? Or if the focus is on assisting those living in extreme poverty, why worry if the Bank assiduously stops short of talking about a human right to social protection? Surely, what counts are results, not scoring points for correct language usage?

In fact, however, the use of a human rights framework and discourse actually makes an enormous difference, which is of course precisely why the World Bank is so resistant to using it and so attached to the never-ending search for surrogate language that enables it to get at the same concerns through a different route. Using human rights language provides a context and a detailed and balanced framework; it invokes the specific legal obligations that states have agreed upon in the various human rights treaties; it emphasizes that certain values are non-negotiable; it brings a degree of normative certainty; and it brings into the discussion the carefully negotiated elaborations of the meaning of specific rights that have emerged from decades of reflection, discussion and adjudication. Even more importantly, the language of rights recognizes the dignity and agency of all individuals (regardless of race, gender, social status, age, disability or any other distinguishing factor) and it is intentionally empowering. Whether in the home, the village, the school or workplace, or in the political marketplace of ideas, it makes a difference if one is calling for the realization of agreed human rights to equality or to water rather than merely making a general request or demand, and human rights are inseparable from the notion of accountability. Where rights are ignored or violated, there must be accountability.

This is well illustrated by considering the situation of persons living in poverty. In most societies they continue to be marginalized, stigmatized and the objects of condescension and charity. Recognition of their human rights does not guarantee them food, education or health care, but it does acknowledge their dignity and agency, empower them and their advocates and provide a starting point for a meaningful debate over the allocation of societal resources in contexts in which their interests have been systematically ignored. Indeed, it is, as Easterly observes, a technocratic illusion to assume that those dimensions can be ignored as long as bureaucratically directed projects and policies are well designed by the staff of the World Bank.[49] Similarly, it makes a huge difference if education reforms are premised on the right to education of the beneficiaries, as opposed to the good intentions or largesse of the Bank.

Finally, it is not necessary in the present chapter to repeat the powerful ethical, legal and instrumentalist arguments that have been made in the

49 Easterly, *The Tyranny of Experts*, *supra* note 43.

extensive literature on integrating human rights into development policies and programs. Ironically, nowhere have the arguments been more systematically explored than in the World Bank's own publication on integrating human rights into development, produced in collaboration with the OECD.[50]

6. CONCLUSION

For most purposes, the World Bank is a human rights-free zone. In its operational policies in particular, it treats human rights more like an infectious disease than universal values and obligations. The biggest single obstacle to moving toward an appropriate approach is the anachronistic and inconsistent interpretation of the "political prohibition" contained in its Articles of Agreement. As a result, the Bank is unable to engage meaningfully with the international human rights framework or to assist its member countries in complying with their own human rights obligations. This inhibits its ability to take adequate account of the aspects of its work within countries relating to the social and political economy, and contradicts and undermines the consistent recognition by the international community of the integral relationship between human rights and development. It also prevents the Bank from putting into practice much of its own policy research and analysis, which points to the indispensability of the human rights dimensions of many core development issues.

One of the most striking aspects of the relationship between the World Bank and human rights is how little thought has been given to what a human rights policy might look like in practice. As a result, the prospect has assumed bogeyman status and Bank officials regularly suggest that if there was such a policy in place, truly draconian consequences would follow. While it might be argued that such fears reflect either fear-mongering or a lack of understanding (or both), the real problem is that there has been nothing even vaguely resembling a blueprint on the table. Whether the Bank ultimately maintains, adjusts or changes its existing policy, it is essential that the policy should be principled, compelling and transparent. The key question is what a human rights policy for the Bank could or should look like in practice.

The starting point in providing an answer is to acknowledge that no outsider could prescribe a comprehensive ideal recipe for the World Bank to follow in adopting a human rights policy. There are many options and paths that could reasonably be taken. The Bank is a very special organization and it will need a carefully tailored policy that takes adequate account of the many concerns that will undoubtedly be expressed. Most of all, there needs to be a transparent discussion, based on carefully thought-through proposals.

---

50 World Bank and OECD, *Integrating Human Rights into Development*, *supra* note 16.

In terms of process, the initiative must come from the President and the staff, as has been the case in relation to almost every major policy initiative of this kind. The Executive Board cannot be expected to meaningfully debate an abstract proposition in the absence of a detailed exploratory analysis. At the same time, member countries and especially Executive Board members, need to begin to grapple seriously with what a policy should look like rather than simply saying they are for or against any such policy. Governments especially need to explore ways to ensure that there is policy coherence between the positions they take in human rights forums and those they take in the context of the World Bank.

One of the starting points must be to put on the table the legitimate concerns held by governments, World Bank staff and other stakeholders so that they can be fully discussed and approached creatively and sympathetically. There are certainly hard questions to be addressed. The experience of the many other international organizations which have adopted human rights policies over the past decade or more should greatly help to dispel many of the concerns expressed by Bank officials.

Diverse civil society actors also need to think through in a more systematic and nuanced way what exactly they would like to see from a human rights initiative taken by the World Bank. It is at least debatable whether some of the roles that the Bank has been called upon to undertake in the past are appropriate. The Bank cannot be expected to carry the burden of the expectations of every human rights demand that might be made in a given situation. There are limits to what can reasonably be expected of it and there are legitimate questions related to its mandate and the respective roles that should be played by different actors. Placing unreasonable demands on the Bank merely reinforces the fears of those who are currently resisting change in that area.

The World Bank needs to remove the roadblock that has been erected by its anachronistic, artificial and unjustifiable interpretation of the political prohibition contained in its Articles of Agreement. Admittedly, it is conceivable that the Bank might be tempted to pursue some issues using prohibited political approaches and would need to guard against them. However, positive measures designed to promote respect for obligations based on human rights treaties that are binding upon borrowing states would generally not cross such a line. Of course, much will depend on how the issue is approached, but a blanket prohibition on any such action as being political is wholly unwarranted. Just as the phrase "economic considerations" has been interpreted to accommodate Bank measures to combat corruption and to promote the rule of law and criminal justice reform, so too can the phrase accommodate a policy which takes account of the economic consequences of ignoring or violating human rights in a given project.

The essential foundation for any meaningful policy is to acknowledge that human rights are unavoidably relevant to the World Bank's twin goals. Exactly how this relevance should manifest itself in different situations and policies is a matter to be explored and developed over time. It makes sense in such contexts to move with all deliberate speed. In the longer term, a change of culture within the Bank would be required, as has often been remarked in relation to safeguards and other concerns by internal evaluation mechanisms. When UNICEF adopted a policy grounded in the rights of the child, it took considerable time for the internal culture to change, and the same would apply to the Bank. Training will be an essential component, but if any organization is capable of mastering a new policy direction of this kind, it is the Bank.

Engagement with human rights experts and mechanisms should become routine. A good starting point would be for the Human Rights Council to invite the President of the World Bank to address it and engage in a dialogue with its members. The Bank should also set up a forum in which it could engage human rights leaders on a regular basis, just as it has done with religious and faith leaders.

The overarching policy principle, already accepted in relation to safeguards, is that the World Bank should "do no harm" through its own involvement. How far the Bank can or should go in trying to make government policies more human rights-friendly in relation to policies that have no direct bearing on Bank projects is open to debate. Again, some of the demands made by civil society critics in this respect appear to be both unrealistic and counter-productive. But the Bank should at least have a due diligence policy that spells out some of the circumstances under which it would be unable to continue providing support for a given project. The UN due diligence policy in relation to peace-keeping is of direct relevance here. There is reason to believe that in many cases that subsequently became controversial, the Bank could have promoted relatively minor changes to make some of the projects much less vulnerable to criticism on human rights grounds. As the old aphorism says, a stitch in time saves nine.

All stakeholders need to rethink the approach to "sanctions" imposed upon borrowing states in response to human rights violations. In the past, such policies have too often been arbitrary, inconsistent and even counter-productive. If the World Bank were to sanction every Member State that is accused of a serious human rights violation, it would have very few borrowers and just as few lenders. As long as sanctions are considered to be the main element in a human rights policy, many governments will continue to resist progress in this area. Based on their experience to date, their position is not difficult to understand. The debate needs to move beyond the sanctions mentality and take a far more positive and nuanced turn.

In response to the concern expressed by World Bank officials that any engagement on human rights issues would turn the Bank into a "rights cop," it should be acknowledged that measures to enforce respect for human rights remain the prerogative of the Human Rights Council and of the other appropriate UN political organs, and not of the Bank. But the Bank should nevertheless explore the ways in which it could encourage and assist governments to meet their existing obligations under international law in relation to human rights. Other international organizations explicitly seek to do this and the Bank has long done it in relation to international environmental treaty obligations.

In general, the policies of the World Bank should emphasize the ways in which it can provide positive support, advice and assistance to states in relation to human rights. It could start by establishing a program to assist governments that wish to establish domestic institutional mechanisms to promote the integration of human rights into development policies. In particular, it should adopt a policy addressing economic, social and cultural rights as human rights. Its frequent claims to be almost inadvertently doing this already are not persuasive, but there is much that it could do to promote a basic program in this area, which would add enormous value to what the international community has so far been able to achieve.

COME A LONG WAY AND A LONG WAY TO GO

UNSCR 1325 and Women's Participation in Peace-Making

Antonia Potter Prentice and Camille Marquis Bissonnette

To be powerful and influential, one can argue, requires not just representation but presence, and not just presence, but meaningful, empowered presence. In 2016, there were only ten women serving as heads of states and nine serving as heads of government, and women held only 22% of seats in parliaments around the world. Despite huge effort and promotion, women candidates for the top jobs at the United Nations (UN) and the US Government failed to prevail.[1] Peace processes, in particular, as they "provide key opportunities for major reforms that transform institutions, structures, and relationships in societies affected by conflict or crises,"[2] are instrumental for women's empowerment and for their consideration in the construction of their post-conflict society. According to a study by UN Women based on 31 major peace processes occurring between

1 UN Women, "Facts and Figures: Leadership and Political Participation," available at: <http://www.unwomen.org/en/what-we-do/leadership-and-political-participation/facts-and-figures> accessed 10 November 2016.

2 M. O'Reilly, A. Ó Súilleabháin and T. Paffenholz, *Reimagining Peacemaking: Women's Roles in Peace Processes*, New York, International Peace Institute, 2015, 2.

1992 and 2011, women represented 2.4% of chief mediators (although the UN itself has never appointed a woman as chief mediator),[3] 4% of peace agreement signatories, and 9% of negotiators in formal peace processes.[4] Most of the time, this low representation of women in peace negotiations is the result of passive – as opposed to deliberate – exclusion,[5] but as some feminist writers have clearly underlined, gender-neutrality often corresponds to gender-blindness. Traditionally, women are very much involved in informal peace negotiations at the grassroots level and within civil society initiatives, and in particular in disarmament processes; this contribution is now widely documented and recognized.[6] But as is well known, women's participation in formal peace negotiations remains very marginal. Moreover, even when women are included, their viewpoints are often sidelined,[7] as they are perceived to lack relevant qualifications, credibility or simply power.[8]

Many hypotheses have been proposed to explain the dramatic underrepresentation of women in formal peace processes, starting with a lack of women in the traditional institutional "pipelines" to mediation and negotiation. For example, women are still a minority within governments and armies, and in the military and political wings of armed groups, and yet the belligerents' representatives are generally perceived to be the most crucial actors in peace-making[9] – at least in the prevailing concept of peace-making – to the expense of other groups, mostly civil society. As the UN Secretary-General (UNSG) underlines:

> Many negotiations have focused solely on the military and political parties of conflict and on high-level processes where women remain underrepresented and too few of

---

3 UN Women, *Women's Participation in Peace Negotiations: Connections between Presence and Influence*, 2012, 7.

4 Ibid, 3.

5 T. Paffenholz, *Inclusivity in Peace Processes*, United Nations University, Centre for Policy Research, 2015, 1.

6 E. Rehn and E. Johnson Sirleaf, *Women, War, Peace: The Independent Experts' Assessment on the Impact of Armed Conflict on Women and Women's Role in Peace-Building (Progress of the World's Women 2002, Vol. 1)*, New York, UNIFEM, 2002, available at: <http://www.unwomen.org/fr/digital-library/publications/2002/1/women-war-peace-the-independent-experts-assessment-on-the-impact-of-armed-conflict-on-women-and-women-s-role-in-peace-building-progress-of-the-world-s-women-2002-vol-1> accessed 30 July 2015, 79; UNSG, *Women, Peace and Security: Study Submitted by the Secretary-General Pursuant to Security Council Resolution 1325 (2000)*, UN, 2002, para. 165.

7 UNSG, *Women, Peace and Security*, *supra* note 6, para. 186.

8 Centre for Humanitarian Dialogue, *Women at the Indonesian Peace Table: Enhancing the Contributions of Women to Conflict Resolution*, Report and policy recommendations with the Indonesian Institute of Sciences, Women at the Peace Table, Centre for Humanitarian Dialogue, 2010, 11.

9 Centre for Humanitarian Dialogue, *Experts Meeting: Women at the Peace Table – Asia Pacific Summary Report*, Centre for Humanitarian Dialogue, 2010, 2.

> them are in positions of authority. This has often resulted in further empowering "men with guns" and incentivizing future cycles of violence and impunity.[10]

This analysis is also consistent with a narrow definition of peace process aiming solely at the cessation of hostilities (also called negative peace) rather than the building of a fair and peaceful post-conflict society in all its aspects (the corresponding concept of positive peace).[11] Indeed, social issues in peace negotiations are often considered as "women's concerns" and for the same reason are left unsettled. As Kuhmann recalls, during the peace talks ending World War I, women were denied access to peace negotiations because it was said that they would argue for peace instead of their states' best interests.[12] Peace processes thus often reproduce elites schemes of society (including the society of the so-called "international community") in giving a voice to those who already held power in the pre-conflict society,[13] to which women often lack access,[14] and in failing to widen the discussions to include, for example, structural social problems which may be part of the drivers of conflict. Finally, there are the issues of pragmatic obstacles to women's representation, such as the lack of funding for their preparation and participation, and the tendency to hold official talks away from the conflict zone for security reasons,[15] the cultural limitations related to the perception of women's and men's defined social roles,[16] and the issue of legitimate representation which applies to all groups traditionally excluded from formal peace talks. As such, peace processes, conceived as aiming toward a mere cessation of hostilities, are incomplete in three respects, which all have a bearing on the low participation of women: they most frequently fail to address a reasonable set of the issues relevant to the building of a stable and peaceful

---

10 UNSG, *Report of the Secretary-General on Women and Peace and Security*, UN, 2015, para. 11.

11 C. Bell, *Women and Peace Processes, Negotiations, and Agreements: Operational Opportunities and Challenges*, Policy Brief, Norwegian Peacebuilding Resource Centre, 2013, 2.

12 E. A. Kuhlman, *Reconstructing Patriarchy after the Great War: Women, Gender, and Postwar Reconciliation between Nations*, New York, Palgrave Macmillan, 2008, available at: <http://public.eblib.com/choice/publicfullrecord.aspx?p=433576> accessed 10 August 2015, 111; I. Sharp, "Feminist Peace Activism 1915 and 2010: Are We Nearly There Yet?" (2013) 38(2) *Peace Change*, 162.

13 D. F. Haynes, F. Ni Aolain and N. Cahn, "Gendering Constitutional Design in Post-conflict Societies," (2010) 17 *Wm. & Mary J. Women & L.* 523.

14 B. Woroniuk, *Gender Equality & Peacebuilding: An Operational Framework*, Gender Equality Division and Peacebuilding Unit Canadian International Development Agency (CIDA), 1999, 4; Sharp, "Feminist Peace Activism 1915 and 2010," *supra* note 12, 162.

15 UNSG, *Women, Peace and Security, supra* note 7, para. 168; Centre for Humanitarian Dialogue, *supra* note 8, 12. Bell, *supra* note 11, 2.

16 C. J. Onyejekwe, "Women, War, Peace-Building and Reconstruction" (2005) 184 *International Social Sciences Journal, UNESCO* 279; Centre for Humanitarian Dialogue, *Experts Meeting, supra* note 9, 2.

peace conflict society; they also often neglect to challenge the structures – economic, social and political, including discriminatory gendered attitudes – of the pre-conflict and conflict society; and they finally demonstrate a lack of political will to take any, let alone every measure possible to favour the inclusion in peace-making of representatives of the whole population, both masculine and feminine.

Against this background, UN Security Council Resolution 1325 (2000) ("UNSCR 1325")[17] was adopted in October 2000 to encourage states and non-state actors, the international community and civil society to promote women's participation in peace-making and to recognize their valuable contribution as actors for peace. This chapter aims to assess the impact of UNSCR 1325 on women's representation in peace negotiations. It will first briefly develop on the reasons why women should be involved in peace-making and will then explain what UNSCR 1325 was intended to do, before looking at its achievements and shortcomings. The chapter concludes with recommendations to fast-track the implementation and impact of UNSCR 1325 with regard to women's participation in peace-making.

1. WHY SHOULD WOMEN BE INCLUDED IN PEACE-MAKING?

Perhaps the most obvious answer to the question as to why women should be included in peace-making is and should be that they form 50% of the global population, "the marginalized majority." Thus, the inclusion of women should simply be based on the principle of equality, supported by the human rights obligations of states.[18]

If principle is not enough, it should be underlined that women's experiences of armed conflicts,[19] and their needs arising from it, are distinct from those of men. Moreover, as stated by Pampell: "Whereas most men come to the negotiating table directly from the battlefield, women usually arrive from civil activism

17 UNSC Resolution 1325 (2000), S/RES/1325. See the full text of the resolution in the Appendix.

18 See, for example, International Covenant on Civil and Political Rights Adopted by the General Assembly of the United Nations on 19 December 1966, Article 3; Convention on the Elimination of All Forms of Discrimination against Women, adopted and opened for signature, ratification and accession by General Assembly Resolution 34/180 of 18 December 1979, entry into force 3 September 1981.

19 UNGA, *Further Actions and Initiatives to Implement the Beijing Declaration and Platform for Action*, A/RES/S-23/3, 2000, para. 135; T. Plümper and E. Neumayer, "The Unequal Burden of War: The Effect of Armed Conflict on the Gender Gap in Life Expectancy," (2006) 60(3) *International Organization* 723–754, at 724; C. Chinkin, "Gender, Human Rights, and Peace Agreements" (2002) 18 *Ohio St. J. Disp. Resol.* 873.

and family and community care with a 'finger on the pulse' of the population that must live with conflict and with a peace agreement."[20] This is a part of the reality; however, one must not ignore the fact that there are also a lot of fighters and providers of support of a range of kinds to armed groups or armed forces who are girls and women. In both cases, be they civilians or fighters, women come out of the conflict with views and needs that are distinct from those of men, who experienced similar realities differently. Research has thus shown that women are better able to frame peace negotiations into a broader notion of what post-conflict society should be, in bringing gender-sensitive issues[21] and other societal concerns such as capacity-building, access to loans, land reform,[22] etc. into the talks, rather than focusing solely on the cessation of armed hostilities or the sharing of power.[23] Increasingly, women's organizations posit that the discussion should not be about "power-sharing" but about "responsibility-sharing."[24] However, women's participation is not systematically associated with the inclusion of gender-sensitive concerns and formulations, and this question must be nuanced and treated carefully.[25] Indeed, women's significant participation is not tantamount to a gender-sensitive approach. As will be seen below, there also needs to be adequate preparation and formation of all actors of the peace negotiations, both women and men, and the modalities of women's participation must allow and favour the free expression of any gender-related concern.

Indeed, if we posit that a contemporary peace agreement should be conceived as a "roadmap"[26] for a future society, in which a durable peace is to prevail, and as an opportunity to challenge the prevailing social structures and inequalities,

---

20 C. Pampell, "Institute for Inclusive Security More Than Victims: The Role of Women in Conflict Prevention – Institute for Inclusive Security", available at: <http://www.inclusivesecurity.org/publication/more-than-victims-the-role-of-women-in-conflict-prevention/> accessed 30 July 2015, 23.

21 O'Reilly, Ó Súilleabháin and Paffenholz, *supra* note 2, 11.

22 UNSG, *Women, Peace and Security, supra* note 7, para. 191.

23 A. Potter, "Women and Negotiations with Armed Groups," Policy Brief, *Centre for Humanitarian Dialogue* 2008, 3; M. Preston McGhie and E. Njoki Wamai, "Beyond the Numbers: Women's Participation in the Kenya National Dialogue and Reconciliation," Policy Brief, *Centre for Humanitarian Dialogue* 2011, 10; T. Bouta, G. Frerks and I. Bannon, *Gender, Conflict, and Development*, Washington, D.C., World Bank, 2005, 52.

24 International Civil Society Action Network, "The Better Peace Tool," 2015, available at: <https://static1.squarespace.com/static/561fe570e4b0fcf85503b6ce/t/563a8fa9e4b0d87f0dff2a83/1475519941712/Printable-Better-Peace-Tool.pdf> accessed 18 November 2016, 4.

25 BMZ, *Promoting Women's Participation in Peace Negotiations and Peace Processes*, Berlin, Programme Promoting Gender Equality and Women's Rights, Federal Ministry for Economic Cooperation and Development (BMZ), 2014, 39; Bouta, Frerks and Bannon, *supra* note 23, 53.

26 C. Bell and C. O'Rourke, "Peace Agreements or Pieces of Paper? The Impact of UNSC Resolution 1325 on Peace Processes and their Agreements" (2010) 59 *International and Comparative Law Quarterly* 4, 947.

then we need to recognize that women's exclusion from it can thus lead at least to the perpetuation of discrimination based on gender.[27] As suggested above, it may also mean that issues and perspectives favourable to a durable peace are ignored. Furthermore, studies have shown that lesser discrimination toward women, and increased participation, has a positive influence on the establishment and durability of peace.[28]

In light of a recent groundbreaking study, it has been found that women's participation and effective influence in formal peace processes increase the chances that they will reach a positive outcome.[29] It also improves the chances that the agreement is implemented,[30] as well as its durability. This study thus finds that peace agreements have a 20% greater chance of lasting at least two years, and a 35% greater chance of lasting at least 15 years if women are significantly involved in their negotiation.[31] Moreover, it appears that when involved in the process from the beginning, women are better able to gain corresponding funding for the agreement's implementation,[32] not only but in particular through funding lines linked by donor countries to their National Action Plans on the implementation of UNSCR 1325.[33] In line with this argument, it has also been found that women's involvement in peace processes favours the social acceptance of the resulting peace agreements[34] and that the participation of women's groups has a positive impact of the content of peace agreements, as they increase the consideration of context-specific women's rights and gender issues.[35]

27 Haynes, Ni Aolain and Cahn, *supra* note 13, 525; UN, *Report of the Secretary-General on Women, Peace and Security*, S/2002/1154, UNSG, 2002, para. 29.

28 Woroniuk, *Supra* note 14, 3; UNSG, *Report of the Secretary-General on Women and Peace and Security, supra* note 10, para. 23.

29 O'Reilly, Ó Súilleabháin and Paffenholz, *supra* note 2, 11.

30 Ibid.

31 Ibid, 12.

32 Preston McGhie and Njoki Wamai, *supra* note 23, 8.

33 See, for example, Australian Government, *Australian National Action Plan on Women, Peace and Security 2012–2018*, 2011; FPS Foreign Affairs, Foreign Trade and Development Cooperation, *Women, Peace and Security: Belgian National Action Plan on the Implementation of UN Security Council Resolution 1325, 2009*; Ministry of Foreign Affairs, Ministry of Defense and Danish National Police, *Denmark's National Action Plan for Implementation of UN Security Council Resolution 1325 on Women, Peace and Security 2008–2013*, 2008; Ministry for Foreign Affairs of Finland, *UN Security Council Resolution 1325 (2000) "Women, Peace and Security": Finland's National Action Plan 2012–2016*, 2012; Federal Government, *Action Plan of the Government of the Federal Republic of Germany on the Implementation of United Nations Security Council Resolution 1325 for the Period 2013–2016*, 2012; Department of Foreign Affairs and Trade, *Ireland's National Action Plan for Implementation of UNSCR 1325, 2011–2014*, 2010; Foreign and Commonwealth Office, *UK Government National Action Plan on UNSCR 1325 Women, Peace & Security*, 2012.

34 Bouta, Frerks and Bannon, *supra* note 23, 49.

35 O'Reilly, Ó Súilleabháin and Paffenholz, *supra* note 2, 11.

2. WHAT IS UNSCR 1325 AND WHAT WAS IT MEANT TO BE?

Women's active participation in peace-making and the consistent use of a gendered perspective are key to UNSCR 1325. Its adoption is thus groundbreaking as it contrasts sharply with the traditional language of "women-and-children" and the portrayal of women as victims or as objects of protection in previous UNSC resolutions. The passage of the resolution marked the occasion of the first session entirely dedicated to women's experience in armed conflict and post-conflict. Significantly, it was adopted unanimously by the Council. In the same vein, it also uses peremptory language, as it "urges Member States," "requests the Secretary General" and "calls upon Member States" in expressing several of its conclusions.

2.1. THE CONTEXT OF UNSCR 1325'S ADOPTION

While it was an important innovative step at the Security Council, UNSCR 1325 has a unique history behind it and was built on a strong normative edifice. At the time of its adoption, the 1979 Convention on the Elimination of All Forms of Discrimination against Women (CEDAW)[36] had already laid down women's right to fully and equally participate in public and political life (see e.g. Articles 7 and 8), and its 1999 Optional Protocol[37] even introduced a mechanism to allow individual and group complaints, and provided for the monitoring of states' obligations under the CEDAW. Of great importance in UNSCR 1325's background are also the 1995 Beijing Declaration and Platform for Action[38] and its five-year review in 2000 (Beijing +5) that already called for states to promote equal participation of men and women in peace fora and activities.[39]

UNSCR 1325 was initiated by civil society and women's movements worldwide, whose intent was to make gender a routinely considered component of war and peace, to reinforce protection of women, and to raise the visibility and influence of women's involvement in peace-making and peace-building. As peace activist Cora Weiss puts it, its objective was not to "make war safe for

---

36 Convention on the Elimination of All Forms of Discrimination against Women, *supra* note 18.

37 Optional Protocol to the Convention on the Elimination of All Forms of Discrimination against Women adopted on 6 October 1999.

38 UNGA, *Beijing Declaration and Platform of Action, Adopted at the Fourth World Conference on Women, 27 October 1995, Endorsed by GA Resolution 50/203, 22 December 1995.*

39 See e.g. UN, Report of the Fourth World Conference on Women, A/CONF.177/20/Rev.1,1995; UNGA, *Further Actions and Initiatives to Implement the Beijing Declaration and Platform for Action, supra* note 19.

women," but to change the UNSC approach to peace and security: it was about changing war, not about women's rights. Taken together with the instruments mentioned in the previous paragraph, however, it makes a strong case to link women's equal participation in peace-making with an alternative conception of peace, thus joining an important strand of feminism, which is integrated with pacifism.[40]

2.2. UNSCR 1325'S MESSAGE ON WOMEN'S PARTICIPATION

Women's participation is paramount throughout the resolution. The preamble recognizes that women's participation in peace-making is intertwined with peace and that it is valuable for peace and security. In its opening paragraph, UNSCR 1325 "*[u]rges* Member States to ensure increased representation of women at all decision-making levels in national, regional and international institutions and mechanisms for the prevention, management, and resolution of conflict."[41] It then also addresses women's involvement in peace-making and at other steps of peace-building, as well as within UN personnel, including special representatives and envoys. It also calls for states to take measures to protect women and girls from gender-based violence, to end impunity and to take into account the different needs of female ex-combatants in DDR processes. Importantly, it entwines women and peace processes in two ways: by gender-balance, the increased representation – though not going as far as *equal* representation – of women in peace-making; and by gender-mainstreaming, the inclusion of a gender-sensitive approach and of specific references to women in the content and in the implementation of peace agreements. It is in fact remarkably comprehensive in this regard.

3. HOW UNSCR 1325 HAS AND HASN'T BEEN USED THROUGHOUT THE YEARS

UNSCR 1325 is a seminal piece of international law regarding women's participation in peace-making, but its tangible effects remain mitigated.[42] We argue that is has brought some undeniable successes, but that the bulk of the work on participation is still to be done, and must be accelerated in the face of

40 S. Aroussi, "Women, Peace and Security: Moving beyond Feminist Pacifism," Political Studies Association Annual Conference, 2009, 3.

41 UNSC Resolution 1325 (2000), *supra* note 17, para. 1.

42 UNSG, *Report of the Secretary-General on Women and Peace and Security, supra* note 10, para. 10.

the very many conflicts currently occurring, which threaten peace and security worldwide, a call which was resoundingly echoed in the Open Debate on Women Peace and Security on 25 October 2016 at the UN Security Council.[43]

3.1. SUCCESSES AND HOW UNSCR 1325 HAS BEEN USED

One of the major achievements of UNSCR 1325 was to shift the focus from women as victims to women as agents in armed conflict and post-conflict settings. In this regard, UNSCR 1325 has created soft law. It has thus become an important lever for non-governmental organizations (NGOs) to interact with the UNSC, and other important organs of the UN, on a continuous and sustained basis. It moreover provides a language and instruments to be used in the field by peace-making actors, including mediators, and by civil society. It is therefore used as a tool for peace advocates and for the international community[44] and, if well disseminated, women's organizations and other civil society groups can also use it to push for women's inclusion in formal peace negotiations. Even if the dissemination of UNSCR 1325 remains a challenge to its own effectiveness,[45] it has nevertheless been translated into more than 100 languages[46] and flyers have been made out of it in order for its content to be better known and understood. While the resolution has been criticized as being a Western product[47] – even if the first countries that pushed for it were not Western countries[48] – or that the UN has pushed it too much in certain settings, the overwhelming response of conflict-affected women's civil society is that it is a vital tool. In response to this criticism, efforts have been launched by, for example, the Global Network of Women Peacebuilders to localize the initiatives in response to UNSCR 1325,

---

43 Peace Women, "Security Council Open Debate on Women Peace and Security, October, 2016", available at: <http://www.peacewomen.org/security-council/security-council-open-debate-women-peace-and-security-october-2016> accessed on 16 November 2016.

44 Haynes, Ni Aolain and Cahn, *supra* note 13, 521.

45 Centre for Humanitarian Dialogue, *Women at the Indonesian Peace Table, supra* note 8, 12.

46 Peace Women, "National Action Plans: National Implementation Overview," available at: <http://www.peacewomen.org/pages/about-1325/national-action-plans-naps.> accessed 20 August 2016.

47 B. SPEAKES, "A Gendered Approach to Peacebuilding and Conflict Resolution," *E-International Relations Students*, available at: <http://www.e-ir.info/2013/02/11/a-gendered-approach-to-peacebuilding-and-conflict-resolution> accessed 21 November 2016; R. Santos, S. Roque and T. Moura, "Missed Connections: Representations of Gender, (Armed) Violence and Security in Resolution 1325" (2003) 5 *Revista Critica de Ciêncas Sociais* 5, para. 16.

48 UNGA, "Preventing Conflict, Transforming Justice, Securing the Peace," 2015, available at: <http://www.un.org/pga/70/wp-content/uploads/sites/10/2015/08/2015_October_02_Global-Study-on-the-Implementation-of-the-United-Nations-Security-Council_2.pdf> accessed 18 November 2016, 8.

by way of national action plans, to ensure that language and concepts best fit specific contexts.[49]

Importantly, UNSCR 1325 has allowed a better understanding and documentation of women's valuable contribution to peace-making. This brings with it the disadvantage of supporting an instrumentalist argument for the inclusion of women rather than a rights-based participation. It is worth noting that research into men's contribution to peace has not been demanded or undertaken, and in fact this would be very hard to do, given that men form the overwhelming majority involved in peace processes. It is thus questionable that women's positive impact on negotiations has to be quantitatively demonstrated to favour their participation while men's involvement is (perceived as) natural. Nevertheless, now that such data and analysis exist and are being acknowledged at the highest diplomatic levels, including in the 2015 Global Study on the Implementation of UNSCR 1325 and in the 2015 Secretary-General's Report on Women Peace and Security, it certainly is useful as it gives women and gender peace advocates *additional* tangible arguments to push for their involvement.

UNSCR 1325 has broadly been used to increase the representation of women in the military and to sensitize the armed forces members to gender-based issues, including gender-based violence. For example, the NATO policy for the implementation of UNSCR 1325 provides for the creation of a gender office, of an advisory commission of experts and of a working group to incorporate UNSCR 1325 into operational planning and execution, the hiring of gender advisers at different levels of the military command structure, the specific consideration of recruitment and support of female leaders both in civilian and military structures, and the implementation of gender training programs.[50] The focus on awareness raising and on quantitative changes in the representation of women within the military is also apparent from the national action plans of conflict-affected countries.[51] This may be because focusing on military structures can bring about faster, more quantitative results than political structures, due to the nature and design of those structures. But using the UNSCR 1325 to "feminize the military" is missing the point of the resolution, and the critique of

---

49 The Global Network of Women Peacebuilders, "Inspiring Locally, Implementing Globally: Localization of UNSCR 1325 and 1820", available at: <http://gnwp.org/program/inspiring-locally-implementing-globally-localization-of-unscr-1325-and-1820> accessed 18 November 2016.

50 "NATO/EAPC Policy for the Implementation of UNSCR 1325 on Women, Peace and Security and Related Resolutions," *NATO*, available at: <http://www.nato.int/cps/en/natohq/official_texts_109830.htm> accessed 10 August 2015.

51 See e.g. Bosnia-Herzegovina, Burundi, the DRC, Nigeria, the Philippines and Uganda: ikNOW Politics, "List of National Action Plans for the Implementation of UNSCR 1325," *International Knowledge Network of Women in Politics* (2014), available at: <http://iknowpolitics.org/en/knowledge-library/website-database/list-national-action-plans-implementation-unscr-1325> accessed 10 August 2015.

militarization which for many underpins it.[52] As UN Women puts it in its 2015 Global Study on the Implementation of UNSCR 1325, "the value of the women, peace and security agenda is its potential for transformation, rather than greater representation of women in existing paradigms of militarized response."[53]

Furthermore, UNSCR 1325 allowed the issue of women's participation in peace-making to be mainstreamed within international institutions, in particular within the UN. It is noteworthy that the Friends of Women, Peace and Security, as well as the Taskforce on Women, Peace and Security, a network which gathers most UN agencies, Member States and NGOs to follow-up on UNSCR 1325, have been created.[54] UNSCR 1325 also drove the set-up of a "gender architecture" in peace process support organizations, for example, by the inclusion of gender advisers within UN peace-keeping operations,[55] as well as a gender-sensitive approach in UN Development Program interventions in conflict and post-conflict contexts.[56] It also sensitized NGOs and even private companies involved in peace process to develop mechanisms to deal with gender.[57]

Moreover, UNSCR 1325 inspired the development of tools dealing with women's representation in peace-making by regional organizations. The European Union (EU), the Pacific Islands Forum, the Inter-Governmental Authority on Development and NATO have adopted regional action plans regarding peace, women and security.[58] The latter also created a position for a Special Representative on Women, Peace and Security in 2012.[59] As to the League of Arab States, in 2010 it adopted a strategy on the topic of women, peace and security.[60] For its part, in 2004 the African Union (AU) adopted its Solemn Declaration on Gender Equality in Africa, which specifically builds on UNSCR 1325 and takes over on the commitment to ensure "full and effective participation and representation of women in peace process including the prevention, resolution, management of conflicts and post-conflict reconstruction

52 K. E. Brown, "The Securitisation of Human Rights" in J. Steans and D. Tepe-Belfrage (eds.), *Handbook on Gender in World Politics*, Cheltenham, Edward Elgar, 2016, pp. 255–262.

53 UN Women, *Preventing Conflict, Transforming Justice, Securing the Peace: A Global Study on the Implementation of UNSCR 1325*, 2015, 135.

54 D. Otto, "The Exile of Inclusion: Reflections on Gender Issues in International Law over the Last Decade" (2009) 10 *Melbourne Journal of International Law* 1, 17.

55 Ibid.

56 See e.g. UNDP, *UNDP Gender Equality Strategy 2014–2017*, UN, 2014.

57 See e.g. Chemonics, "Gender Equality and Social Inclusion", available at: <http://www.chemonics.com/OurWork/OurPractices/gender/Pages/default.aspx> accessed 11 August 2015.

58 UNSG, *Report of the Secretary-General on Women and Peace and Security*, *supra* note 10, para. 107.

59 NATO, "NATO Names Norwegian Diplomat as Special Representative for Women, Peace and Security," available at: <http://www.nato.int/cps/en/natohq/news_89583.htm?selectedLocale=en> accessed 18 November 2016.

60 UNSG, *Report of the Secretary-General on Women and Peace and Security*, *supra* note 10, para. 107.

in Africa."[61] In 2014, the AU also launched a five-year Programme on Women, Gender, Peace and Security for 2015–2020[62] and appointed a woman as the AU Special Envoy for Women, Peace and Security.[63]

As an illustration of UNSCR 1325's potential to draw attention on women's participation in peace-making, the fifth goal for sustainable development proposed by the UN Open Working Group on Sustainable Development Goals aims to "achieve gender equality and empower all women and girls," and one of its target is to "ensure women's full and effective participation and equal opportunities for leadership at all levels of decision-making in political, economic, and public life."[64] In addition, the sixteenth goal on the promotion of peaceful and inclusive societies provides that states should "ensure responsive, inclusive, participatory and representative decision-making at all levels."[65]

UNSCR 1325 has thus brought a few concrete and tangible positive results as it pushed changes in the perception of women within peace processes and institutional architectures in particular.

3.2. SHORTCOMINGS AND HOW KEY ACTORS FAILED TO USE UNSCR 1325

These achievements are notable and positive, but for women on the ground and women the future of whose countries is being negotiated at peace tables, the impacts of UNSCR 1325 are still very limited.[66] If women's increased representation has not been fully implemented in any of the spheres covered by UNSCR 1325, it has nonetheless been better achieved in peace-keeping operations and in the humanitarian arena.[67] UNSCR 1325 seems to be more effective "as a focus of mobilization for women outside of peace processes than in securing women's participation within formal peace processes."[68] The resolution has moreover failed to increase the security of human rights defenders, as well as to get more women in leadership roles such as mediators, and even as UN Special Representatives to the Secretary-General, despite

---

61 African Union, *Solemn Declaration on Gender Equality in Africa* (2004).

62 UNSG, *Report of the Secretary-General on Women and Peace and Security, supra* note 10, para. 107.

63 Ibid, para. 111.

64 United Nations Department of Economic and Social Affairs, "Open Working Group Proposal for Sustainable Development Goals," *Sustainable Development: Knowledge Platform*, available at: <https://sustainabledevelopment.un.org/focussdgs.html> accessed 11 August 2015.

65 Ibid.

66 UN Women, *Women's Participation in Peace Negotiations: Connections between Presence and Influence, supra* note 3, 2.

67 UNSG, *Women Peace and Security, supra* note 7, 118.

68 Bell and O'Rourke, *supra* note 26, 969.

increasing evidence that women with relevant skills do exist. It would appear the problem is more on the demand side than on the supply side.

Regarding gender mainstreaming, according to a study lead by Bell and O'Rourke based on peace agreements concluded between 1990 and 2010, only 16% of the peace agreements surveyed reference women, and many of these references are unsubstantial.[69] The authors nonetheless found that this level has increased from 11%, before the adoption of UNSCR 1325, to 27% after its adoption.[70] This is a significant increase, but contemporary peace agreements are very far from systematic inclusion of a gender perspective therein, and even further from systematic inclusion of UNSCR 1325 language portraying women as active agents and change-makers.

As Puechguirbal underlines, even in the subsequent UNSC resolutions dealing with specific peace-making, peace-keeping or peace-building processes, there are still many references to women taking the form of "women-and-children" language or assimilating women with other vulnerable parts of the population in need of protection. She also notes that while most of these resolutions mention UNSCR 1325, they fail to address women's practical involvement in the process and, more generally, in post-conflict society.[71] Indeed, a definition of women based on their reproductive role, which equates them to vulnerability, "is a major hindrance to their empowerment because it apprehends women as weak human beings in need of protection without any control over their own lives."[72] In addition to the still prevalent marginalization of women in peace processes, the international community, including within the UNSC, has consistently failed to analyze conflict and power in a way that takes gender seriously rather than considering it as a "thematic" or "side" issue.

UNSCR 1325 was the first of a series of now eight resolutions on Women, Peace and Security, the latter being passed at the fifteenth anniversary, under the Spanish presidency of the UNSC. One of the major flaws of most of the resolutions that followed UNSCR 1325, namely UNSCR 1820 (2008), 1888 (2009), 1889 (2009), 1960 (2010), 2106 (2013), 2122 (2013) and 2242 (2015), is that they mostly leave UNSCR 1325's dedication to women's empowerment aside and instead go back to the "women-as-victim" language in focusing on sexual violence. There are however two exceptions, as two resolutions following UNSCR 1325 developed on its entire content, including on women's agency. The first of these two resolutions is UNSCR 1889 (2009), which assessed the mixed results of UNSCR 1325 and reaffirmed UNSC's commitment to the

69 Ibid, 968.

70 Ibid, 954.

71 N. Puechguirbal, "Gender and Peace Building in Africa: Analysis of Some Structural Obstacles" in E. Natugunda-Togboa and D. Rodriguez-Montero (eds.), *Gender and Peace-Building in Africa*, University for Peace, Ciudad Colón, Costa Rica, 2005, 3.

72 Ibid, 4.

promotion of women's participation in peace-making. The latter resolution 2122 (2013) also shifts from the focus on sexual violence of the two preceding resolutions to address the issue of women's participation, in line with UNSCR 1325. Whatever one thinks of the content of these resolutions, the fact that they are so numerous, while simultaneously all being passed unanimously and yet so poorly implemented, does suggest that the dynamic to drive implementation has not yet been created by these diplomatic means.

As to the monitoring of UNSCR 1325, the progress on its implementation is accounted for by the UNSG in his annual reports, as requested by the resolution itself.[73] However, Member States are not held to any strict accountability process, unlike for, for example, UNSCR 1612 (2005) on children and armed conflict.[74] Thus, failure to produce results tends to create more urges and pledges, but not necessarily more action or resources on the concrete issues raised by the resolution.

Importantly, one of UNSCR 1325's greatest flaw is the selectivity of the issues addressed in its implementation, and its failure to deal with the root causes of women's scattered participation in peace-making, or even to link it with gender equality. In particular, for Otto, the resolution's omission of the longstanding fight of women for disarmament in its Women, Peace and Security resolutions thus shows an incomplete and conditional commitment to women's full inclusion in peace-making:

> The price of the Council's endorsement of women's participation in peacemaking and peace-building, and its increased accessibility to the NGO Working Group, is the silencing of feminist critiques of militarism and the failure to recognise the "inextricable" link between gender equality and peace.[75]

Furthermore, UNSCR 1325 fails to take into account the multiplicity and complexity of men's and women's identities and to deconstruct the stereotypical perceptions of men and women, an omission that may inhibit both sexes' contributions to peace.

In sum, the scientific community has a growing understanding of socially built men's and women's identities, how they interact and the impacts they have in society. The peace and security community has started to tap into this and can now also benefit from significant research on women's contributions to peace. This all squares nicely with a pile-up of good policy on women, peace and security, mostly within the UN, the implementation of which is patchy and weak, due to the lack of political will, imagination and capacity alluded to above.

73 UNSC, Resolution 1325 (2000), *supra* note 17, para. 17.
74 Otto, *supra* note 54, 22.
75 Ibid, 21.

4. RECOMMENDATIONS: HOW TO UP THE GAME ON UNSCR 1325

The concluding section presented here enumerates some recommendations to improve the implementation of UNSCR 1325 with respect to women's participation in peace-making.

Indeed, it has been demonstrated that women's mere presence is not sufficient for them to have a significant positive impact on peace-making.[76] Presence is also unsatisfactory from a gender equality viewpoint. Thus, policies should focus not only on the number of women present in negotiations, but also on the taking into account of their substantive contribution so their participation is fully effective. Quotas designed, as a temporary measure, to ensure a critical mass of at least 30–40% of women's representation[77] are therefore a valid first step, but since they exclusively address presence without considering influence, they must be accompanied with training, support, mentoring of all peace-making actors, men and women, including members of women's organizations.[78] Quotas alone are not effective in securing gender mainstreaming[79] and are not an accurate indicator of women's involvement in peace processes.[80] What they are is a tool for kick-starting the process and should not therefore be neglected, even by those who are inherently uncomfortable with them, but it should be kept in mind that they do not constitute, on their own, a magical solution to gender inequality in peace processes.

Too much emphasis on numbers may lead to the entrenchment of unhelpful stereotypes, the marginalization of women and the failure to deal adequately with the gendered victimization of men and boys.[81] Thus, we argue that the inclusion

---

76 O'Reilly, Ó Súilleabháin and Paffenholz, *supra* note 2, 11.

77 See E. Rehn and E. Johnson Sirleaf, *Women, War, Peace: The Independent Experts' Assessment on the Impact of Armed Conflict on Women and Women's Role in Peace-Building (Progress of the World's Women 2002, Vol. 1)*, New York, UNIFEM, 2002, available at: <http://www.unwomen.org/fr/digital-library/publications/2002/1/women-war-peace-the-independent-experts-assessment-on-the-impact-of-armed-conflict-on-women-and-women-s-role-in-peace-building-progress-of-the-world-s-women-2002-vol-1> accessed 30 July 2015, 80; A. Potter, "We the Women: Why Conflict Mediation is Not Just a Job for Men," Centre for Humanitarian Dialogue, 2005, 16. Bouta, Frerks and Bannon, *supra* note 23, 62; Centre for Humanitarian Dialogue, *Peacemaking in Asia and the Pacific: Women's Participation, Perspectives and Priorities*, Centre for Humanitarian Dialogue, 2011, 103.

78 See C. Chinkin and H. Charlesworth, "Building Women into Peace: The International Legal Framework" (2006) 27 *Third World Quarterly* 5, 953; *Report of the Secretary-General on Women, Peace and Security*, S/2002/1154, UNSG, 2002, paras. 32, 39; C. Cohn, H. Kinsella and S. Gibbings, "Women, Peace and Security Resolution 1325" (2004) 6 *International Feminist Journal of Politics* 1, 132; Bell and O'Rourke, *supra* note 26, 978.

79 UNSG, *Women, Peace and Security*, *supra* note 7, para. 200.

80 Otto, *supra* note 54, 152.

81 Bell and O'Rourke, *supra* note 26, 945.

of women must be based on gender equality and human rights rather than on femininity. It is vital not to essentialize men's and women's gender identities, and not to simply associate women with the stereotypical vision of pacifism and men with militarism. Indeed, associating women with motherly concerns or biological stereotypes is too simplistic in light of the inherent potential of women's participation.[82] Policies and actors in peace-making must be careful to instead take into account the complexity and multiplicity of their identities.[83]

To be coherent, the inclusion of women must take into account these crucial other aspects of identity – social class, political, religious, ethnic affiliation and so forth,[84] especially when they are related to the conflict. It must not simply reproduce existing power structures in including solely women who were already close to influence before and during the conflict.[85] Moreover, women as well as men should be chosen on the basis of their capacity, leadership, credibility, legitimacy and on representativeness, but without, as we do frequently in the case of men, letting the perfect be the enemy of the good.[86]

It is widely recognized that not only has gender equality and sensitivity a positive impact on the durability of peace, but it also is an important factor in conflict prevention.[87] Markers of gender inequality, including violence against women, are early warning signs of violent conflict in society.[88] In turn, such violence also inhibits women's participation in peace-making,[89] further reinforcing arguments for security, protection, justice and victim support. As such, women's participation in peace processes and other public decision-making institutions may allow for a better understanding and treatment of these concerns,[90] while also favouring women's participation within society *per se*. Besides, attention to structural gender discrimination may also reveal underlying causes and drivers of conflict, and thus contribute further to preventing new or repeated armed conflict.[91] Framing a post-conflict society without addressing the root causes of violence thus hinders the transformative potential of the process in the long term. This underlines how vital and

---

82 Otto, *supra* note 54, 165.

83 Preston McGhie and Njoki Wamai, *supra* note 23, 8.

84 Centre for Humanitarian Dialogue, *Peacemaking in Asia and the Pacific, supra* note 77, 103; Chinkin, *supra* note 18, 876.

85 Otto, *supra* note 54, 151.

86 Centre for Humanitarian Dialogue, *Peacemaking in Asia and the Pacific, supra* note 77, 103; BMZ, *supra* note 25, 24.

87 See F. Hill, "Women's Contribution to Conflict Prevention, Early Warning and Disarmament," (2003) *Women, Men, Peace and Security* 4.

88 UN Women, *Gender-Responsive Early Warning: Overview and How-to Guide* (2012), 5.

89 T. Paffenholz, "Results on Women and Gender from the 'Broader Participation' and 'Civil Society and Peacebuilding' Projects," Policy Brief (2015), The Graduate Institute Geneva: Centre on Conflict, Development and Peacebuilding, 3.

90 Saferworld, Gender and Conflict Early-Warning, Report, Saferworld (2012), 1.

91 Ibid, 2.

appropriate an opportunity a peace process, broadly conceived, can be to address structural causes of discrimination. Policy implementation should thus prioritize those processes in order both to secure women's meaningful and safe participation in peace-making and to favour their meaningful inclusion in the post-conflict society.

With these structural causes of inequality in mind, it may be useful to conceptualize the situation as men's overrepresentation in peace-making rather than women's underrepresentation, and to deal with it accordingly.[92] As Otto rightly puts it:

> Treating "gender" as synonymous with "women" fails to recognize the relational quality of gender representations. If ideas about women are to change, ideas about "men" must also change. This insight must be embraced before the transformative potential of the category of gender will be realized.[93]

Pragmatically, as the previous section underlined, institutional changes within states and institutions regularly involved in peace-making are a prerequisite in order to better secure delivery on UNSCR 1325. Indeed, the resolution needs to be translated and implemented into the daily procedures of all UN organs and other relevant structures, be they international or regional organizations, or NGOs.[94] Gender advisers with peace process technical expertise should also be systematically present at every step of the peace processes to better incentivize and raise awareness on women's representation and gender sensitivity in the process.[95] Similarly, a systematic assessment of peace agreements by an external actor, in light of both gender inclusion and gender mainstreaming, should be undertaken in real time and following the closure of negotiations.[96]

More radically, and in line with a coherent, long-term and all-encompassing approach to women's inclusion in all fora and at all steps of peace-making, room must be given to women in order for them to bring their optimal contribution. They should have the space to challenge the dominant vision of peace-making, both in structural terms of how peace should be framed (e.g. negative or positive, as described above) but also in terms of having a say in the concrete modalities of the process: the allocation of financial resources, the timeframe, the choice of the negotiators invited to join the process, the role of the international community, etc. It is self-evident that in order to encourage and stimulate women's participation in peace processes, they should be given the necessary means to achieve a meaningful involvement, including funding, which is of crucial importance for women to access the relevant fora in order for

92 Cohn, Kinsella and Gibbings, *supra* note 78, 137.
93 Otto, *supra* note 54, 160.
94 Cohn, Kinsella and Gibbings, *supra* note 78, 132; Pampell, *supra* note 20, 9.
95 Bell, *supra* note 11, 4; BMZ, *supra* note 25, 40.
96 Chinkin, *supra* note 18, 884.

their requests and priorities to be heard, and for their safety, political space and access to the spheres of power to be guaranteed. Practical matters like separate meeting, washing, eating and praying places, the location of the negotiations as well as services for elder care and child care, and space for the provision of technical support should be considered. Moreover, as Moghadam puts it, "achieving peace and security for women cannot be guaranteed in the absence of a broader socio-political and economic project that rests on participation and redistribution of resources."[97] Women, if they are to be fully included in peace-making, should be allowed to partially reconceive peace-making instead of just making them fit into the existing mold.[98]

UNSCR 1325 was intended to be transformational, and anything that transforms necessarily confronts an existing status quo. As demonstrated here and elsewhere, the status quo in peace and security still remains to be seriously challenged. This is an urgent problem to be addressed in the context of the current proliferation of armed conflicts, violent extremism and their massive and indiscriminate impact on society, civilians and social institutions. This responsibility lies on all actors involved in peace processes, starting from every individual involved in peace-making and extending to states fighting armed conflicts, international organizations, civil society, the international community at large and even armed groups. In order to create inclusive and durable peace, women must be recognized and empowered as the valuable agents they are in the transformation of societies during and after the occurrence of armed conflicts.

97 V. M. Moghadam, "Peacebuilding and Reconstruction with Women: Reflections on Afghanistan, Iraq and Palestine" (2005) 48 *Development* 3, 70.

98 Bell and O'Rourke, *supra* note 26, 980; Centre for Humanitarian Dialogue, *Peacemaking in Asia and the Pacific*, *supra* note 77, 105; Bell, *supra* note 11, 2; Centre for Humanitarian Dialogue, *Experts Meeting*, *supra* note 9, 5.

APPENDIX

UNITED NATIONS SECURITY COUNCIL RESOLUTION 1325 (2000)

Adopted by the Security Council at its 4213th meeting, on 31 October 2000

The Security Council,

Recalling its resolutions 1261 (1999) of 25 August 1999, 1265 (1999) of 17 September 1999, 1296 (2000) of 19 April 2000 and 1314 (2000) of 11 August 2000, as well as relevant statements of its President, and recalling also the statement of its President to the press on the occasion of the United Nations Day for Women's Rights and International Peace (International Women's Day) of 8 March 2000 (SC/6816),

Recalling also the commitments of the Beijing Declaration and Platform for Action (A/52/231) as well as those contained in the outcome document of the twenty-third Special Session of the United Nations General Assembly entitled "Women 2000: Gender Equality, Development and Peace for the Twenty-First Century" (A/S-23/10/Rev.1), in particular those concerning women and armed conflict,

Bearing in mind the purposes and principles of the Charter of the United Nations and the primary responsibility of the Security Council under the Charter for the maintenance of international peace and security,

Expressing concern that civilians, particularly women and children, account for the vast majority of those adversely affected by armed conflict, including as refugees and internally displaced persons, and increasingly are targeted by combatants and armed elements, and recognizing the consequent impact this has on durable peace and reconciliation,

Reaffirming the important role of women in the prevention and resolution of conflicts and in peace-building, and stressing the importance of their equal participation and full involvement in all efforts for the maintenance and promotion of peace and security, and the need to increase their role in decision-making with regard to conflict prevention and resolution,

Reaffirming also the need to implement fully international humanitarian and human rights law that protects the rights of women and girls during and after conflicts,

Emphasizing the need for all parties to ensure that mine clearance and mine awareness programmes take into account the special needs of women and girls,

Recognizing the urgent need to mainstream a gender perspective into peacekeeping operations, and in this regard noting the Windhoek Declaration and the Namibia Plan of Action on Mainstreaming a Gender Perspective in Multidimensional Peace Support Operations (S/2000/693),

Recognizing also the importance of the recommendation contained in the statement of its President to the press of 8 March 2000 for specialized training for all peacekeeping personnel on the protection, special needs and human rights of women and children in conflict situations,

Recognizing that an understanding of the impact of armed conflict on women and girls, effective institutional arrangements to guarantee their protection and full participation in the peace process can significantly contribute to the maintenance and promotion of international peace and security,

Noting the need to consolidate data on the impact of armed conflict on women and girls,

1. Urges Member States to ensure increased representation of women at all decision-making levels in national, regional and international institutions and mechanisms for the prevention, management, and resolution of conflict;
2. Encourages the Secretary-General to implement his strategic plan of action (A/49/587) calling for an increase in the participation of women at decision-making levels in conflict resolution and peace processes;
3. Urges the Secretary-General to appoint more women as special representatives and envoys to pursue good offices on his behalf, and in this regard calls on Member States to provide candidates to the Secretary-General, for inclusion in a regularly updated centralized roster;
4. Further urges the Secretary-General to seek to expand the role and contribution of women in United Nations field-based operations, and especially among military observers, civilian police, human rights and humanitarian personnel;
5. Expresses its willingness to incorporate a gender perspective into peacekeeping operations, and urges the Secretary-General to ensure that, where appropriate, field operations include a gender component;
6. Requests the Secretary-General to provide to Member States training guidelines and materials on the protection, rights and the particular needs of women, as well as on the importance of involving women in all peacekeeping and peace-building measures, invites Member States to incorporate these elements as well as HIV/AIDS awareness training into their national training programmes for military and civilian police personnel in preparation for deployment, and further requests the Secretary-General to ensure that civilian personnel of peacekeeping operations receive similar training;

7. Urges Member States to increase their voluntary financial, technical and logistical support for gender-sensitive training efforts, including those undertaken by relevant funds and programmes, inter alia, the United Nations Fund for Women and United Nations Children's Fund, and by the Office of the United Nations High Commissioner for Refugees and other relevant bodies;
8. Calls on all actors involved, when negotiating and implementing peace agreements, to adopt a gender perspective, including, inter alia:
   (a) The special needs of women and girls during repatriation and resettlement and for rehabilitation, reintegration and post-conflict reconstruction;
   (b) Measures that support local women's peace initiatives and indigenous processes for conflict resolution, and that involve women in all of the implementation mechanisms of the peace agreements;
   (c) Measures that ensure the protection of and respect for human rights of women and girls, particularly as they relate to the constitution, the electoral system, the police and the judiciary;
9. Calls upon all parties to armed conflict to respect fully international law applicable to the rights and protection of women and girls, especially as civilians, in particular the obligations applicable to them under the Geneva Conventions of 1949 and the Additional Protocols thereto of 1977, the Refugee Convention of 1951 and the Protocol thereto of 1967, the Convention on the Elimination of All Forms of Discrimination against Women of 1979 and the Optional Protocol thereto of 1999 and the United Nations Convention on the Rights of the Child of 1989 and the two Optional Protocols thereto of 25 May 2000, and to bear in mind the relevant provisions of the Rome Statute of the International Criminal Court;
10. Calls on all parties to armed conflict to take special measures to protect women and girls from gender-based violence, particularly rape and other forms of sexual abuse, and all other forms of violence in situations of armed conflict;
11. Emphasizes the responsibility of all States to put an end to impunity and to prosecute those responsible for genocide, crimes against humanity, and war crimes including those relating to sexual and other violence against women and girls, and in this regard stresses the need to exclude these crimes, where feasible from amnesty provisions;
12. Calls upon all parties to armed conflict to respect the civilian and humanitarian character of refugee camps and settlements, and to take into account the particular needs of women and girls, including in their design, and recalls its resolutions 1208 (1998) of 19 November 1998 and 1296 (2000) of 19 April 2000;

13. Encourages all those involved in the planning for disarmament, demobilization and reintegration to consider the different needs of female and male ex-combatants and to take into account the needs of their dependants;
14. Reaffirms its readiness, whenever measures are adopted under Article 41 of the Charter of the United Nations, to give consideration to their potential impact on the civilian population, bearing in mind the special needs of women and girls, in order to consider appropriate humanitarian exemptions;
15. Expresses its willingness to ensure that Security Council missions take into account gender considerations and the rights of women, including through consultation with local and international women's groups;
16. Invites the Secretary-General to carry out a study on the impact of armed conflict on women and girls, the role of women in peace-building and the gender dimensions of peace processes and conflict resolution, and further invites him to submit a report to the Security Council on the results of this study and to make this available to all Member States of the United Nations;
17. Requests the Secretary-General, where appropriate, to include in his reporting to the Security Council progress on gender mainstreaming throughout peacekeeping missions and all other aspects relating to women and girls;
18. Decides to remain actively seized of the matter.

WHY ARE WOMEN CANADA'S FASTEST-GROWING PRISON POPULATION AND WHY SHOULD WE CARE?

Kim PATE

When I first started work with Elizabeth Fry, I actually believed that there was not much difference between the circumstances of men and women prisoners.[1] It only took a couple of months of being in the job to realize how wrong I was. Women's histories of neglect and abuse, poverty, motherhood, isolation and dislocation, and the overwhelming realization that they really were too often simply considered "too few to count" brought their circumstances into sharp relief, and I soon realized that the landscape of women's criminalization and imprisonment stood in stark contrast to any of my preconceived notions. The women and this work have educated and activated me in many ways, as we have journeyed many bumpy and seemingly obscure paths together.

One such seemingly impassable journey and also one of life's turning points for me started on 28 April 1994, the day that I went into the Prison for Women (P4W) in Kingston after the emergency response team had stripped and shackled several women and left them naked or dressed with only a flimsy paper "gown" in the segregation unit. At the end of that long day, when I advocated that they unshackle the one woman who was still restrained and release from segregation all eight of the other women, I was advised that I was misinformed about the circumstances and treatment of the women and that, in fact, there were no women in restraints. When I insisted that I had actually observed the shackles, it was suggested by staff that perhaps it was a reflection from the bars. And when I persisted, I was counselled against being so easily "conned" by the women.

As I exited P4W that evening with my then three-and-a-half-year-old son, I remember standing on the steps and realizing that they must believe that this information would never emerge and that if it did, no one would ever believe it. On that day, I thought, I don't know exactly how to do this, I don't know how

1 For most of the decade preceding my January 1992 appointment with the Canadian Association of Elizabeth Fry Societies (CAEFS), I worked with youth and men in the criminal and penal systems in Canada.

one comes up against a system that has all of the resources and a full government department of lawyers to assist them in that process, but I had better figure out how.

I met and spoke with everyone I could think of, from Members of Parliament to bureaucrats, allies, the media and anyone else who might listen. Thanks to the decision of the Office of the Correctional Investigator (OCI) to replace an ineffectual investigator with a wonderful woman who immediately recognized the importance of investigating and documenting our "allegations," on 15 February 1995, pursuant to s. 193 of the Corrections and Conditional Release Act (CCRA),[2] that office produced its first ever special report to the Solicitor General, Herb Gray.[3]

This report provided detailed documentation of strip-searching, shackling, transfer to a men's prison, Kingston Penitentiary (KP), and prolonged confinement in administrative segregation of the women. The OCI Special Report concluded that the actions of the Correctional Service of Canada (CSC) were "a massive display of force being exercised in the face of virtually no resistance," and that the strip searches and cell extractions were "without question degrading and dehumanizing for those women involved."[4] The Correctional Investigator also criticized the CSC's internal investigations and reporting on the P4W, declaring the CSC Board of Investigation reports as "incomplete, inconclusive and self-serving"[5] and an overall "white wash."[6]

A few weeks later, the CBC's investigative documentary program *The Fifth Estate* obtained and aired portions of the video of the events of 26 April 1994.[7] It shocked Canadians and the world.

Very soon thereafter, Solicitor General Herb Gray and Minister of Justice Allan Rock appointed the Honourable Madam Justice Louise Arbour to conduct a Commission of Inquiry into Certain Events at the Prison for Women in Kingston. This led to my meeting the woman who would become one of the brightest beacons of hope to women in prison and one of my most revered mentors, inspirations and friends.

The first time I saw Louise Arbour walk into the P4W, I was immediately struck by her courage, grace, intelligence, humanity and integrity. With a

---

2 Corrections and Conditional Release Act, SC 1992, c 20.

3 Office of the Correctional Investigator, *Special Report of the Correctional Investigator Concerning the Treatment of Inmates and Following Certain Incidents at the Prison for Women in April 1994 and Thereafter* (Ottawa: Correctional Investigator Canada, 1995).

4 *Ibid* at 5–6.

5 *Ibid* at 2.

6 *Ibid* at 4.

7 CBC's television program *The Fifth Estate* aired an exposé entitled "The Ultimate Response." For the first time, the Canadian public saw for itself what had taken place on 26 April 1994, when portions of the videotaped recordings of the stripping and shackling of the women at the P4W by the Kingston Penitentiary (KP) male Institutional Emergency Response Team (IERT) were broadcast.

wonderful sense of humour and steely determination, she strode into and through a prison and overall system that had been used to having full control over who entered its doors, as well as over all information that exited them.

Louise treated every single person with warmth, compassion and honesty, whether it was a person working in the frontline as a correctional officer, a prisoner in segregation, the Commissioner of Corrections or me – even though I was sporting my "God grant me the authority to change the things I cannot accept" button. The other message she imparted was that every single person who came into that hearing room was treated with respect, humanity and dignity. When they were brought from a segregation cell or maximum-security unit, they came in without shackles or restraints of any kind, and they came and participated without escorting guards, and as such they came in able to stand tall with as much equality as was possible in a very unequal situation.

For years, women talked about the experience of witnessing Gayle Horii walk through the front doors of the P4W with Madam Justice Louise Arbour. Gayle had last been taken out on a stretcher, having almost died during a hunger strike undertaken in her quest for a humanitarian transfer following her husband's heart attack and hospitalization. Gayle walked through those front doors with Louise – as she was encouraged to call her – to the segregation cells and introduced the women there to Madam Justice Arbour. That alone sent two messages: to the women that they were valued and important; and to the staff that everyone is entitled to be treated with humanity, compassion and respect. The resulting change of atmosphere within the P4W was palpable and meaningful, and it continued until it closed in 2000.

Why do I raise these examples? Who does not know of Louise Arbour? In addition to demonstrating how to work with heart, kindness, integrity and without bending to pressure or being cowed by authority, resources, privilege or power, her work and the resulting Commission report raised the profile of issues and concerns regarding the increased criminalization and imprisonment of women in Canada.

The Arbour Commission report highlighted that the cornerstone of any oversight strategy must be accessible and effective judicial review for illegalities and rights violations, and must include remedial sanctions.[8] Justice Arbour

---

8 Canada, Commission of Inquiry into Certain Events at the Prison for Women in Kingston, *Report* (Ottawa: Public Works and Government Services Canada, Cat. No. JS42-73/1996E, 1996). In making her recommendation for judicial oversight to remedy interference with the integrity of the sentence, Justice Arbour addressed the concern that such a remedy would be an undue burden on an already stretched court system. She noted that any additional burden "would only be so in relation to the Correctional Service's non-compliance with the law" (at 184), pointing out that there are ways to control frivolous litigation should such a problem arise.

also underscored the reality that although women – especially Indigenous women and those with disabling mental health issues – are the fastest-growing prison population, there are a relatively small number of women sentenced to federal penitentiaries[9] and they generally pose an extremely low risk to public safety. She urged the government to recognize this as an opportunity to pilot innovative programs and initiatives,[10] and to reduce the number of women who are incarcerated in federal prisons. As she suggested, to do so would "free the resources necessary to ensure that those who are imprisoned are treated in accordance with the law."[11]

More than 20 years after her groundbreaking report, Louise Arbour continues to raise the collective bar and profile the key issues, as exemplified by her recent call for an end to the use of segregation, particularly for women, those with mental health issues and Indigenous prisoners, and a review of the sentences of those who are disproportionately impacted by the resulting conditions of confinement.[12]

As a non-Indigenous woman who lives in Algonquin territory and has the privilege and responsibility of walking with many Indigenous women, men and young people, I consider it a duty to name the negative impact of colonization on all of us. Every day of the more than 37 years that I have spent walking into and out of prisons for youth, men and women, I have been painfully confronted with the genocidal impact of colonization. I have seen first hand the over-representation of Indigenous men, boys, girls and – most especially – women. Indigenous women represent more than 41% of women serving federal sentences and this proportion has increased by 60% over the past decade.[13] The problem is even worse in some provincial and territorial jails and remand centres, where the number of Indigenous women exceeds 50%, 70% and even 80%.[14]

---

9 Provincial and territorial governments administer prisons and sentences for those sentenced to terms of imprisonment of under two years, whereas the federal government administers prison sentences of two years or more.

10 Canada, Commission of Inquiry into Certain Events at the Prison for Women in Kingston, *Report, supra* note 8 at 229.

11 *Ibid* at 184–185.

12 Catharine Tunney, "Louise Arbour, former Supreme Court justice, calls for end of segregation in prisons. Death of an inmate this week leaves former judge 'outraged,'" *CBC News* (9 July 2016). Online: <http://www.cbc.ca/news/politics/louise-arbour-segregation-inquiry-1.3670487>.

13 Howard Sapers, *Annual Report of the Office of the Correctional Investigator: 2016–2017* (Ottawa: Office of the Correctional Investigator, 28 June 2017) at 59. Online: <http://www.oci-bec.gc.ca/cnt/rpt/pdf/annrpt/annrpt20162017-eng.pdf>. See also Statistics Canada, "Study: Women in Canada: Women in the Criminal Justice System" (Ottawa: Statistics Canada, 2017) at 2. Online: <http://www.statcan.gc.ca/daily-quotidien/170606/dq170606a-eng.pdf> (39% of women in federal prison are Indigenous).

14 *Ibid* at 59; See also Nancy Macdonald, "Canada's prisons are the 'new residential schools,'" *MacLean's* (18 February 2016). Online: <http://www.macleans.ca/news/canada/canadas-prisons-are-the-new-residential-schools/>.

The Canadian Association of Elizabeth Fry Societies (CAEFS) has 24 member societies throughout Canada, providing services to marginalized, victimized, criminalized and institutionalized women, especially those who are imprisoned. CAEFS also undertakes policy and law reform initiatives, most of which, these days, are aimed at trying to undo the outrageous injustices being perpetrated at breakneck speed in Ottawa. CAEFS regularly makes submissions to Parliamentary and Senate Committees, in addition to conducting public, legal and other educational and advocacy initiatives.[15] They also make every effort to address the inter-connectedness of economic, social, legal and political decisions that contribute to women being the fastest-growing prison population.[16]

As we see the further erosion of the substantive equality of women, especially those most vulnerable because of multiple intersections of marginalization and discrimination, be it race, sexual orientation, ability – particularly disabling mental health issues – or those escaping violence, we are witnessing the exponential growth of women in prison. Women are the fastest-growing prison population worldwide.[17]

The fact that women are the fastest-growing prison population is not accidental. In Canada, we recognize that our links to the United States have meant that we were amongst the first countries to be impacted by the regressive so-called law and order agenda, which makes prisons the default option for those most significantly impacted by the destruction of social safety nets, and by the evisceration of medical, economic and education standards and services. In fact, people receiving benefits from Ontario's social assistance programs fall well below the poverty line and are living in a greater depth of poverty now than a generation ago.[18]

In too many communities and contexts, prisons are the only "service" that cannot turn people away because of waiting lists, a lack of beds or resources, or lack of mandate. In Ontario, the affordable housing waiting list has been

15 For example, please see this link to a current e-petition with which CAEFS is involved: E-48 (Electoral system). Online: <https://petitions.parl.gc.ca/en/Petition/Details?Petition=e-482>.

16 Canadian Association of Elizabeth Fry Societies, Ottawa. Online:<http://elizabethfry.ca/>.

17 Natasha A. Frost, Judith Greene and Kevin Pranis, *The Punitiveness Report, HARD HIT: The Growth in the Imprisonment of Women, 1977–2004* (New York: Institute on Women and Criminal Justice, 2006) at 7. Online: <http://csdp.org/research/HardHitReport4.pdf>; Rob Allen, *Global Prison Trends 2015* (London: Penal Reform International, 2015) at 12–13. Online: <http://www.penalreform.org/wp-content/uploads/2015/04/PRI-Prisons-global-trends-report-LR.pdf>; Public Safety Canada, *2015 Annual Report: Corrections and Conditional Release Statistical Overview* (Ottawa: Public Works and Government Services Canada, Cat. No. PS1-3E-PDF, February 2016) at 39.

18 Kaylie Tiessen, *Ontario's Social Assistance Poverty Gap* (Ontario: Canadian Centre for Policy Initiatives, May 2016). Online: <https://www.policyalternatives.ca/sites/default/files/uploads/publications/Ontario%20Office/2016/05/CCPA%20ON%20Ontario%27s%20social%20assistance%20poverty%20gap.pdf>.

growing since 2007, and as of 2014 the average wait period was four years.[19] Across Canada, access to therapy for low-income Canadians is severely limited[20] and women seeking safety in shelters are denied beds, most commonly because the shelter is at full capacity. In 2014, on one day alone, 338 women along with 201 children were unable to be accommodated in shelters in Canada.[21]

Imagine if, instead of continuing to cram more people into overcrowded prisons, we limited the number of bed days available for judges to impose as sentences or if we turned women away and would not allow them access to prisons when what they really need is housing, a shelter to escape violence, treatment to deal with past sexual abuse and other forms of trauma, drug and/or alcohol detoxification or treatment to address mental health and/or addiction issues.

In CAEFS, at the national level and amongst its members, they have recognized this reality very concretely by the change of the organization's mission to identify that they work with women who are criminalized versus the historical orientation of working with women who come into conflict with the law.[22] With this reality comes the recognition that it is the laws and policies that are increasingly coming into conflict with peoples' lives, resulting in the virtual inevitability of criminalization rather than the notion that people are the full and consenting authors of their own circumstances.

For instance, in 1996, Canada followed the US lead when the federal government eliminated the Canada Assistance Plan and therefore the essential source of Canadian standards of social, medical and educational resourcing. We then experienced the same sorts of cuts and knee-jerk band-aid responses – all of which normalize the definition of crime and justify criminal justice and penal responses, thereby presuming criminality and perpetuating the problems of the past, be they crime prevention, homelessness, restorative justice or other responses.[23] Another devastating blow was the decision in 2012 to dismantle

---

19 Ontario Non-Profit Housing Association, *2015 Waiting List Survey* (Ontario: Ontario Non-Profit housing Association, 2015). Online: <http://onpha.on.ca/Content/PolicyAndResearch/Waiting_Lists_2015/2015_Waiting_Lists_Survey.aspx?WebsiteKey=49cb1e54-80a5-4daf-85fb-a49e833ec60b>.

20 In Erin Anderssen, "We have the evidence … Why aren't we providing evidence-based care?," *The Globe and Mail* (22 June 2016). Online: <http://www.theglobeandmail.com/life/the-case-for-publicly-funded-therapy/article24567332/>: "Low-income Canadians – who are three times more likely to report poor to fair mental health, and yet are the least likely to be able to afford private psychotherapy – are suffering disproportionately".

21 Sara Beattie and Hope Hutchins, *Shelters for Abused Women in Canada, 2014* (Juristat, Statistics Canada catalogue no. 85-002.X, 6 July 2015). Online: <http://www.statcan.gc.ca/pub/85-002-x/2015001/article/14207-eng.htm>.

22 Canadian Association of Elizabeth Fry Societies, *supra* note 16.

23 Canada, National Council on Welfare, *The 1995 Budget and Block Funding* (Ottawa: Minister of Supply and Services Canada, Spring 1995) at 8. Online: <http://publications.gc.ca/collections/collection_2012/cnb-ncw/H68-37-1995-eng.pdf>.

the National Council of Welfare,[24] a renowned group that offered in-depth information on poverty and provided the poor with a voice. This decision came just one year after the group published a report demonstrating that the federal government could save billions in the long run by investing in tackling poverty head-on.[25]

Over the past several years, we've seen Canada rush to follow the US trend to incarcerate the most dispossessed for longer and more brutalizing periods. Ironically, this was occurring at a time when many US jurisdictions were retreating from the regressive "law and order" agenda.[26] Indeed, in 2008, the same year the Canadian government passed legislation creating more mandatory minimums,[27] a panel of federal judges ordered California to reduce its prison population by 40,000 over the following two years – which roughly reflected a 27% cut from the population of 150,000.[28] Until very recently, Canadian politicians were ignoring their social and fiduciary responsibilities to Canadians by passing laws, seemingly without regard to the human and fiscal costs associated with them. The long list of criminal justice reforms under the Conservative Harper government have raised incarceration rates and sucked resources out of the community. In 2012, the then Parliamentary Budget Officer, Kevin Page, estimated that the government's conditional sentencing bill alone would cost the federal government $8 million and the provincial and territorial governments $137 million.[29] The previous government passed more than 30 new crime laws, many of which still remain to be challenged. The result is that even though the national crime rate has been on the decline since 1998,[30] criminal justice costs have increased by nearly 25% over the past decade.[31]

---

24 Canada Without Poverty, Press Release, "Decision to cut poverty advisory group is wrong, say anti-poverty leaders" (4 April 2012). Online: <http://www.cwp-csp.ca/2012/04/decision-to-cut-national-council-of-welfare-is-wrong/>.

25 National Council of Welfare, *The Dollars and Sense of Solving Poverty* (Ottawa: National Council of Welfare, Volume 130, Autumn 2011). Online: <http://publications.gc.ca/collections/collection_2011/cnb-ncw/HS54-2-2011-eng.pdf>.

26 Todd R. Clear and James Austin, "Reducing mass incarceration: Implications of the Iron Law of prison populations" (2009)3 *Harvard Review of Law and Policy* 307 at 308. Online: <http://www.hlpronline.com/Vol3-2_ClearAustin_HLPR.pdf>.

27 Tackling Violent Crime Act, CS 2008, c 6. Online: <http://laws-lois.justice.gc.ca/eng/annualstatutes/2008_6/page-1.html>.

28 Solomon Moore, "Court orders California to cut prison population," *The New York Times* (10 February 2009) A12.

29 Tolga R. Yalkin and Michael Kirk, *The Fiscal Impact of Changes to Eligibility for Conditional Sentences of Imprisonment in Canada* (Ottawa: Office of the Parliamentary Budget Officer, 28 February 2012). Online: <http://www.parl.gc.ca/PBO-DPB/documents/Conditional_sentencing_EN.pdf>.

30 Public Safety Canada, *2015 Annual Report: Corrections and Conditional Release Statistical Overview, supra* note 17.

31 Howard Sapers, *Annual Report of the Office of the Correctional Investigator: 2014–2015, supra* note 13 at 3.

By imposing criminally low social assistance – formerly known as welfare – rates throughout Canada and even banning receipt of state resources in some jurisdictions, many poor people are immediately relegated to the criminalized underclass. If we were truly interested in addressing fraudulent transactions that harm others rather than resorting to the criminalization of poor women for welfare fraud, drug trafficking or whatever other survival strategies are employed, criminally low welfare rates would result in the criminalization of those who craft, those who pass and those who enforce the laws and policies, not those subjected to them.[32]

We are also seeing the increased feminization of the criminalization of poverty. Welfare fraud is one example of how poor women are increasingly likely to be criminalized. Their attempts to survive poverty too often result in charges ranging from fraud (including welfare fraud), soliciting, pimping, living off the avails of prostitution, or importing and trafficking. As we learned from the *Hamilton* and *Brown* cases, black single mothers are literally recruited to traffic narcotics as they exit meetings with their assistance workers.[33] Women who are trying to make the rent and/or feed their children/families are especially vulnerable. It used to be that we might see women resorting to such means to address extraordinary expenses such as birthdays, Christmas and/or other holidays, child care, summer camp expenses,[34] etc. Increasingly sole support moms are turning to these illicit means just to try to cover basic living costs.[35]

In Ontario, the tragic reality of the life and death of Kim Rogers serves as a stark reminder of these inequalities.[36] Kim was criminalized in the first place because she attended school while she was receiving "Ontario works" (the Ontario government's welfare system) funding. She was charged and convicted of "welfare fraud" and her death was ruled a suicide while under house arrest as a sentence to this "offence." She was faced with this label and subsequent punishment because she attempted to return to school as an adult to obtain an

---

32 Canadian Feminist Alliance for International Action, *No Action, No Progress: Canadian Feminist Alliance for International Action Report on Canada's Progress in Implementing Priority Recommendations Made by the United Nations Committee on the Elimination of Discrimination against Women in 2008* (Ottawa: Canadian Feminist Alliance for International Action, February 2010) at 4–5. Online: <http://www2.ohchr.org/english/bodies/cedaw/docs/ngos/NoActionNoProgress_CanadaFU.pdf>.

33 Cited in Susan C. Boyd, "Representations of Women in the Drug Trade" in Gillian Balfour and Elizabeth Comack (eds), *Criminalizing Women: Gender and (In)justice in Neo-liberal Times* (Halifax: Fernwood, 2006) at 132, 138–139, 147–149.

34 Margaret Little, "The blurring of boundaries: Private and public welfare for single mothers in Ontario" (1995) 47 *Studies in Political Economy* 89.

35 César Amaya Sandino, "Prostitution in the UK (I): Poverty, the driving force," *The Prisma* (15 July 2012). Online: <http://www.theprisma.co.uk/2012/07/15/prostitution-in-the-uk-part-1-poverty-the-driving-force/>.

36 Jennifer Keck, "Remembering Kimberly Rogers" (2002) 23:3/4 Perception 10–11. Online: <http://www.ccsd.ca/perception/2354/kimberly.html>.

education while still on social assistance. As part of the process, she also sought and received student loans. Although it is well documented that it is impossible to live on welfare without some supplemental income/support, to be "caught" doing so means the near-certainty of criminal prosecution. We question why those responsible for the development of such harmful social policies and legislation are not held legally responsible for the human and social costs of criminalizing the most marginalized, vulnerable and oppressed.

In Kim Rogers' circumstances, her death was the result of criminal negligence and complicit political, economic, legal and social policy decisions, yet only she was held accountable. Moreover, after her death, we discovered that she could have been attending school *and* receiving additional benefits had she or, more to the point, her social worker known. She was eligible for disability benefits. Her usual work was waitressing and bar-tending, but her knee surgery made it impossible for her to continue in that work, so she went back to school.

We should all examine the realities regarding who benefits from the discrepancy in monitoring, charging, prosecuting and sentencing of tax evasion, unemployment fraud, Ontario Health Insurance Plan/doctors' over-billing, lawyers dipping in to their trust funds and goods and services tax (GST) fraud versus the demonization of the poor exemplified by the criminalization and pursuit of welfare recipients. We should also question why some behaviour is characterized as almost benign omission versus purposeful, criminally intended, fraud.

During the mid-1990s, all of the provincial, territorial and federal heads of corrections in Canada met and agreed that we needed to reduce reliance on prisons. They opined that as many as 75% of those in prison, either serving sentences or awaiting trial, could be released to the community without any corresponding increase in the risk to public safety. The Correctional Investigator has repeatedly called on the government to address the needs of those with mental health issues in the community rather than continuing to abandon them to prisons.[37]

In the United Kingdom, noted policy leaders such as Pat Carlen[38] and the Howard League[39] are amongst those calling for the criminal justice system to refuse to proceed with criminalizing the young, those escaping violence, those with intellectual disabilities and mental health issues; they are also amongst those calling for more decarceration, community development and social (re)investment. Indeed, many academics, professionals and practitioners on the

37 "Access to Mental Health Services (1A)" in Howard Sapers, *Annual Report of the Office of the Correctional Investigator 2010–2011* (Ottawa: Office of the Correctional Investigator, 29 June 2011) at 10. Online: <http://www.oci-bec.gc.ca/cnt/rpt/pdf/annrpt/annrpt20102011-eng.pdf>.

38 Pat Carlen, *Alternatives to Women's Imprisonment* (Milton Keynes: Open University Press, 1990).

39 Howard League for Penal Reform (2012). Online: <http://howardleague.org>.

front lines have also characterized the push to criminalize the most dispossessed as the present manifestation of race, ability, class and gender bias, and argue that this demands we examine our fundamental beliefs and notions of whose interests and biases are privileged, and at whose expense.[40]

When we know the histories of abuse, poverty and extreme marginalization that is the reality of most of the young women and girls who are criminalized and imprisoned, we begin to realize how ludicrous it is that we continue telling them not to take drugs to dull the pain of abuse, hunger or other devastation; we begin to see the hypocrisy in telling women and girls that they must stop the behaviour that has allowed them to survive poverty, abuse, disabling health – especially mental health – issues, etc. in the face of no current or future prospect of any income, housing, medical, educational or other supports. Surely none of us thinks it benefits anyone to continue to imprison women and girls, and then release them onto the street with little more than psycho-social, cognitive skills or drug abstinence programs, along with the implicit judgment that they are in control of and therefore responsible for their situations, including their own criminalization. We all must rethink, resist and reject such notions.

Indigenous women continue to suffer the shameful and devastating impact of colonization. From residential schools to child welfare seizure and to juvenile and adult detention to being disappeared and murdered, Indigenous women and girls are vastly overrepresented in institutions under state control. Although Indigenous women make up 1–2% of the Canadian population, they account for about 40% of the federal prison population; this number continues to grow each year,[41] despite the Truth and Reconciliation Commission calling upon the federal, provincial and territorial governments to commit to eliminating the overrepresentation of Indigenous peoples in custody.[42]

Further, Indigenous women too often represent the majority of women who are classified as maximum-security prisoners.[43] The consistent overclassification of Indigenous women may be explained, at least in part, by the continued reliance by the CSC on psychological and risk assessment tests, which Justice Phelan of the Federal Court found in 2015 to be susceptible to cultural bias and consequently unreliable when used on Indigenous prisoners.[44] Indigenous women's marginalization is translated into "risk." On appeal, the Supreme Court of Canada agreed with Justice Phelan regarding the unreliability of correctional

---

40 Paul Wright and Tara Herivel (eds), *Prison Profiteers: Who Makes Money from Mass Incarceration* (New York: The New Press, 2008).

41 *Supra* note 13.

42 Truth and Reconciliation Canada, *Calls to Action* (2015). Online: <http://www.trc.ca/websites/trcinstitution/File/2015/Findings/Calls_to_Action_English2.pdf>.

43 Howard Sapers, *Annual Report of the Office of the Correctional Investigator: 2014–2015, supra* note 13 at 51.

44 *Ewert v. Canada*, 2015 FC 1093 (CanLII). Online: <http://www.canlii.org/en/ca/fct/doc/2015/2015fc1093/2015fc1093.html>.

classification tools. Disappointingly, though the Court concluded that CSC places Indigenous prisoners in "clear danger" of systemic discrimination, it declined to find a violation of equality rights or to take notice of significant evidence of the adverse impact of classification tools on federally sentenced women, particularly Indigenous women and those with disabling mental health issues.[45]

Indeed, even as we work to deinstitutionalize and decarcerate, we are seeing that "treatment" is increasingly the colonial control mechanism of choice.[46] In fact, we've seen this issue exemplified in the case of G, a pregnant young Indigenous woman who was institutionalized for forced treatment.[47] This sort of pathologizing and criminalization results in women being institutionalized in what are referred to as transcarceral circumstances.[48]

The focus on foetal alcohol spectrum syndromes and disorders are gendered, classist and racist in approach and we must venture forth very carefully. Consider for a moment the reality that such alphabet soup diagnoses of FAS, FAE, FASD, ARND (alcohol-related neurological disorders), etc. are most prevalent in countries that have high rates of criminalized Indigenous populations. Even though the shopping list of symptoms or characteristics of foetal alcohol labels overlap significantly with other conditions, including inadequate nutrition, oxygen deprivation, learning disabilities, attention deficit, etc., the labels are persistently used in places such as Canada, New Zealand, Australia and the United States. It is not coincidental that these are also countries with high rates of criminalization of racialized Indigenous peoples.[49]

In the European Union, on the other hand, this approach is not seen as particularly helpful – they consider the symptoms and impact of other toxins, be they pollution, bad water, insufficient nutrients, lack of prenatal and postnatal supports, accidental brain injuries, lack of oxygen, etc., as equally important. After all, despite the rhetoric that it is 100% preventable, since many women do not know they are pregnant before the apparently crucial day 17 of gestation, the only way to make it so would be to prohibit the consumption of alcohol by all women of childbearing age.

45 *Ewert v. Canada*, 2018 SCC 30; for application, see e.g. *R v. Ituluk*, 2018 NUCJ 21 at para 7.

46 Howard Sapers, *Annual Report of the Correctional Investigator: 2015–2016* (Ottawa: Office of the Correctional Investigator, 30 June 2016) at 10–11, 14–15, 17–18, 20. Online: <http://www.oci-bec.gc.ca/cnt/rpt/pdf/annrpt/annrpt20152016-eng.pdf>.

47 *Winnipeg Child and Family Services (Northwest Area) v. G. (D.F.)* [1997] 3 SCR 925. Online: <http://csc.lexum.org/en/1997/1997scr3-925/1997scr3-925.html>.

48 Gillian Balfour and Elizabeth Comack (eds), *Criminalizing Women: Gender and (In)justice in Neo-Liberal* Times, *supra* note 33 at 19. Online: <https://fernwoodpublishing.ca/files/criminalizingwomen.pdf>; "Prison watchdog says more than a quarter of federal inmates are aboriginal people," *supra* note 42.

49 "Canada votes 'no' as UN rights native declaration passes," *CBC News* (13 September 2007). Online: <http://www.cbc.ca/news/canada/story/2007/09/13/canada-indigenous.html>.

Moreover, new research is beginning to document the potential negative impact of alcohol use on male sperm,[50] suggesting that prohibitions on drinking should extend to men as well. Obviously, we all want to limit the impact of alcohol and other toxins on foetal development, but we know that criminalizing behaviour is only likely to result in targeting those least able to defend themselves against it. Current access to justice issues being what they are, a focus on foetal alcohol exposure, in isolation, is likely to continue to result in societal judgment and a disproportionate application of the law against poor and racialized women. It is crucial that any FASD (foetal alcohol spectrum disorders) preventative programs are developed in collaboration with Indigenous peoples and delivered in culturally appropriate ways.[51]

How many fewer diagnoses of FASD, etc. would there be if that label meant that the recipients thereof could not be relegated to the most isolating prison conditions? If such a label meant that someone could not be criminalized, but must be found to be in need of community support because their disability renders them incapable of forming criminal intent, we predict that the diagnoses would virtually evaporate. Courageous jurists like Mary Ellen Turpel-Lafond (as she then was) have tried to take on this issue in individual cases.[52] We applaud and encourage such efforts and continue to push for broader, systemic change.

It is no accident who is criminalized or who is imprisoned, nor is it an accident who is not! What if, instead of denying and defending abuse of power and force by police and prison personnel, as well as the neglect and abuse of institutionalized persons, we collectively condemned and stopped such practices?

I used to meet most women who had significant mental health issues kneeling on a cement floor, peering through a meal slot in a solid metal door. For almost three years following the publicity surrounding the death of Ashley Smith,[53] I was denied access to the segregation unit where she died. In order

---

50 Hye Jeong Lee, Jae-Sung Ryu, Na Young Choi, Yo Seph Park, Yong Il Kim, Dong Wook Han, Kisung Ko, Chan Young Shin, Han Sung Hwang, Kyung-Sun Kang and Kinarm Ko, "Transgenerational effects of paternal alcohol exposure in mouse offspring" (2013) 17(6) *Animal Cells and Systems* 429–34. Online: <http://dx.doi.org/10.1080/19768354.2013.865675>.

51 Truth and Reconciliation Canada, *Calls to Action*, 2015, *supra* note 42 at no 33.

52 Maria Morellato, "Success in the face of adversity: First Nations in the legal profession" (2006). Online <http://www.blakes.com/english/view_disc.asp?ID=3209>.

53 Nineteen-year-old Ashley Smith died on 19 October 2007. Initially jailed for breach of probation after being convicted of assault for throwing crab apples at a postal worker, Ashley was serving a cumulative sentence of more than six years, having accumulated more than 100 charges while in prison. She died after tying a ligature around her neck, while under suicide watch in custody at the Grand Valley Prison for Women. Despite guards watching her at her cell door and via video monitors, it was 45 minutes before guards or supervisors entered her cell and confirmed her death. Although initially the guards were charged with criminal negligence causing death, the Crown dropped all charges. The jury examining her death ruled it a homicide.

to meet with women placed in similar circumstances as those faced by Ashley before she died, we must both first "agree" to them being fully shackled, usually handcuffed to the back, isolated behind bulletproof glass, and monitored by two to five correctional officers.

Attempts to address these issues include meetings with judges, prosecutors, the defence bar, correctional authorities and mental health professionals. Mental health and youth workers in particular have lamented the reality that the evisceration of their resources and, combined with the advent of zero tolerance to violence policies, have resulted in policy directives that instruct them to call the police and urge the pursuit of criminal prosecution in cases where those with mental health and/or intellectual disabilities are assaultive or abusive.[54] Behaviour that was previously considered symptomatic of the psychiatric or mental health label attached to the individual is now treated as criminal or "bad" behaviour in the criminal justice context. Reduced resources and priorities mean that mental health professionals are usually without the requisite support to handle the most challenging folks. Further, because there is a long line-up of others in the community who are not criminalized awaiting treatment options, the move to criminalize is seen as legally and ethically justified.

The reflex of corrections services to develop mental health services in prisons sounds positive to many, yet, in reality, it is only serving to exacerbate the trend toward increasingly criminalizing women with mental health issues and intellectual disabilities. Developing such services in prisons at a time when they are increasingly non-existent in the community[55] is resulting in more people receiving federal sentences because of a presumption that there is an ability to access services in prison that are not available in community settings. However, it is vital that we recognize that prisons are not, and cannot be, treatment or healing centres.[56] The tendency of CSC staff, who are generally not extensively trained in the area of mental health,[57] to deal with self-injurious behaviour by placing

---

54 Canadian Nurses Association and Canadian Federation of Nurses Unions, *Joint Position Statement: Workplace Violence* (2008) at 2–3. Online: <http://www.nursesunions.ca/sites/default/files/workplace_violence_position_statement_cna-cfnu_0.pdf>.

55 Erin Anderssen, "We have the evidence ... Why aren't we providing evidence-based care?", *supra* note 20: "Low-income Canadians – who are three times more likely to report poor to fair mental health, and yet are the least likely to be able to afford private psychotherapy – are suffering disproportionately."

56 See Office of the Correctional Investigator, *Risky Business: An Investigation of the Treatment and Management of Chronic Self-Injury among Federally Sentenced Women – Final Report* (Ottawa: Office of the Correctional Investigator, 30 September 2013). Online: <http://www.oci-bec.gc.ca/cnt/rpt/oth-aut/oth-aut20130930-eng.aspx?texthighlight=Kinew#TOC7>; Howard Sapers, *Annual Report of the Office of the Correctional Investigator: 2014–2015, supra* note 13.

57 Elizabeth Bingham and Rebecca Sutton, *Cruel, Inhuman and Degrading? Canada's Treatment of Federally-Sentenced Women with Mental Health Issues* (Toronto: International Human Rights Program, 2012). Online: <http://www.dawncanada.net/main/wp-content/uploads/2013/12/Cruel-and-Inhuman_FINAL_Print.pdf>.

them in segregation in the face of evidence that segregation can actually elevate the risk of suicide is but one example that supports this conclusion.[58]

In fact, those subject to federal terms of imprisonment are too often relegated to the most isolating conditions,[59] almost inevitably accumulating additional charges, and subsequently serving many more years in prison, as a result of behaviour arising largely in response to the conditions of confinement to which they are subjected.[60]

Moreover, this phenomenon is reflected in both Kinew James' and Ashley Smith's cases. Kinew's sentence of six years stretched into 15, six of which she spent in isolation. On 20 January 2013, Kinew died in her maximum-security cell of an apparent heart attack many hours after she first sought medical attention.[61] Ashley Smith was originally sentenced to one month, but ended up spending three years in prison, mostly in segregation, before dying in the segregation cells at the Grand Valley prison for women. At an inquest, her death was ruled a homicide. The jury made a great deal of important recommendations, but the CSC's report in response to these recommendations was far from adequate. Many of the recommendations were addressed only by reference to old CSC policies and many were not addressed

---

58 Office of the Correctional Investigator, *Risky Business: An Investigation of the Treatment and Management of Chronic Self-Injury Among Federally Sentenced Women – Final Report*, *supra* note 56. See also Office of the Correctional Investigator, *Fatal Response: An Investigation into the Preventable Death of Matthew Ryan Hines – Final Report* (15 February 2017). Online: <http://www.oci-bec.gc.ca/cnt/rpt/oth-aut/oth-aut20170215-eng.aspx>. Office of the Correctional Investigator, *A Three Year Review of Federal Inmate Suicides (2011–2014)* (10 September 2014). Online: <http://www.oci-bec.gc.ca/cnt/rpt/oth-aut/oth-aut20140910-eng.aspx#_ftnref3>. Report to the Attorney General, *Public inquiry into the death of Edward Christopher Snowshoe* (4 June 2014). Online: <https://open.alberta.ca/publications/fatality-inquiry-2014-july-8>.

59 *Ibid* at para 59: "It is clear that there are significant differences between CSC and external health providers' management of self-injury incidents. In community psychiatric care settings, the staff that deal with the identification, assessment and management of self-injurious behaviour are nearly always health care professionals … While in CSC facilities, these women spent long periods of time in either clinical seclusion or segregation due to their self-injurious behaviour. In contrast, while at the community psychiatric hospitals, the women often attended work, program or therapy as part of their daily routines." See also Howard Sapers, *Annual Report of the Office of the Correctional Investigator: 2014–2015*, *supra* note 13 at 32. Regardless of how their segregation was characterized by CSC staff, women reported that they saw no difference between administrative segregation, disciplinary segregation, suicide watch or clinical isolation or seclusion, and perceived their placement as punishment for their self-injurious behaviour. Further, segregation was found to be an independent factor that raised the risk of suicide.

60 For further insight into this phenomenon, readers are encouraged to consult Marian Botsford Fraser, "Life on the installment plan," *The Walrus* (12 March 2010) at 1–6. Online: <https://thewalrus.ca/life-on-the-instalment-plan/>.

61 Office of the Correctional Investigator, *Risky Business: An Investigation of the Treatment and Management of Chronic Self-Injury Among Federally Sentenced Women – Final Report*, *supra* note 56.

at all.[62] In the words of Federal Correctional Investigator Howard Sapers, the CSC's response "fails to support core, preventative, oversights and accountability recommendations issued by the jury."[63] Indeed, recommendations to create effective therapeutic interventions and to provide adequate staffing of qualified mental health care providers with experience in treating self-harm were not directly addressed in the CSC's response.[64]

Unlike the sentiment expressed by mental health workers, corrections staff necessarily categorize mental health considerations as secondary. Because they are dealing with people who have been criminalized, the behaviour is generally labelled as bad – manipulative, attention-seeking, capable of control (indeed, within the control of the individual) – and mental health issues almost always take a back seat to security and punitive responses. In fact, a 2013 report from the correctional investigator found that when dealing with self-harm incidents, the "security or control interventions [employed by CSC staff were] generally disproportionate to the risk presented and often inappropriate from a mental health needs perspective."[65]

We need to continually question who benefits from such approaches. The offloading of responsibility without requisite resources, the lack of appreciation by many of the impact of resource cuts and the apparent belief that someone else will address the issues are resulting in the reality that increasingly, social issues are being abandoned to the criminal courts and penal systems to rectify.

The pre-existing lack of trust, connection and communication (too often further exacerbated by literacy and English as a second language issues) between "client" and "counsel" will only serve to further isolate the most marginalized. Despite recent increases in funding to legal aid and the subsequent relaxing of legal aid eligibility, limited access to justice remains a very live issue.[66] Those left standing and/or advocating with and on behalf of the most marginalized

---

62 Ashley Smith Inquest, *Coroner's Inquest Touching the Death of Ashley Smith. Verdict of Coroner's Jury* (Ottawa: Correctional Service Canada, 19 December 2013). Most recently, in what is perhaps best described as an ill-advised and transparent litigation strategy, CSC invoked Ashley's name as justification for introducing Bill C-83, which renames segregation and allows CSC to characterize such segregation placements as s. 29 transfers to mental health intensive intervention units.

63 Office of the Correctional Investigator, *Annual Report of the Office of the Correctional Investigator: 2014–2015, supra* note 13 at 51.

64 *Response to the Coroner's Inquest Toughing on the Death of Ashley Smith* (Ottawa: Correctional Service Canada, December 2014). Online: <http://www.csc-scc.gc.ca/publications/005007-9011-eng.shtml>.

65 Office of the Correctional Investigator, *Risky Business: An Investigation of the Treatment and Management of Chronic Self-Injury Among Federally Sentenced Women – Final Report, supra* note 56 at 16, para 37: "security or control interventions are generally disproportionate to the risk presented and often inappropriate from a mental health needs perspective."

66 Laura Bruneau and Dounia Khali, "Access to justice for the self-represented class member" (January 2013) Western Canadian Class Actions Conference. Online: <http://www.cle.bc.ca/PracticePoints/LIT/13-AccesstoJustice.pdf>.

are generally without adequate support or resources, and continue to be vilified for their inability to make things work.

To sum up, according to Statistics Canada, there has been a steady increase in the numbers of people remanded in custody and, with the exception of a slight increase two years ago, the imprisonment rate for men has been falling for much of the last two decades.[67] It is appropriate that sentences reflect the credited time for pre-trial custody; pre-trial custody is generally warehousing in a maximum security – often very isolated – setting. The lack of community-based resources and the resulting increase in homeless people, those with mental health and addiction issues, as well as those escaping violence are directly contributing to the increased numbers remanded in custody.

Women account for 10–15% of those charged with violent offences, and 45.5% of all property-related charges against women are for "shoplifting."[68] A total of 85% of women in federal custody are serving their first federal term of imprisonment, 58.4% are between 20 and 34 years of age,[69] and 17% are serving life sentences.[70]

It currently costs between $211,000 and upwards of $350,000–$600,000 per annum to jail a woman in the federal system, compared to approximately $35,000 for residency in a funded, supervised community-based setting.[71] Even a few weeks remanded in custody can interfere with housing, employment, social assistance, child custody and so on. Relatively few women receive conditional sentences.[72] Operating expenditures for adult correctional services reached more than $4.6 billion in 2015, which does not even account for

---

67 Linda Porter and Donna Calverley, "Trends in the use of remand in Canada" (May 2011) Juristat Statistics Canada, at 5. Online: <http://www.statcan.gc.ca/pub/85-002-x/2011001/article/11440-eng.htm>.

68 Public Safety Canada, *2015 Annual Report: Corrections and Conditional Release, Statistical Overview*, *supra* note 17.

69 *Ibid.*

70 Canadian Human Rights Commission, *Protecting their Rights: A Systemic Review of Human Rights in Correctional Services for Federally Sentenced Women* (Canadian Human Rights Commission, December 2003) at 5–6. Online: <http://www.caefs.ca/wp-content/uploads/2013/05/fswen.pdf>.

71 Prison Justice, "Statistics for 2004/2005" (July 2007). Online: <http://www.prisonjustice.ca/politics/facts_stats_2007.html>. See also Diana Zlomislic, "Ottawa's prison plan won't work, critics say," *The Star* (7 August 2010). Online: <www.thestar.com/news/canada/article/845272--ottawa-s-prison-plan-won-t-work-critics-say>. Office of the Parliamentary Budget Officer, *The Funding Requirement and Impact of the "Truth in Sentencing Act" on the Correctional System in Canada* (22 June 2010) at 94, Table 12-G. Online: <http://publications.gc.ca/collections/collection_2010/dpb-pbo/YN5-28-2010-eng.pdf>. Office of the Parliamentary Budget Officer, *Update on Costs of Incarceration* (22 March 2018) at 12, Table 3-2, 3-3. Online: <https://www.pbo-dpb.gc.ca/web/default/files/Documents/Reports/2018/Update%20Incarceration%20Costs/Update%20on%20Costs%20of%20Incarceration_EN.pdf>.

72 Robin Maynard, "Criminal (in)justice: An interview with Gillian Balfour," *Briarpatch Magazine* (1 March 2011). Online: <http://briarpatchmagazine.com/articles/view/criminal-injustice>.

policing and court costs.[73] In provincial and territorial jails, custodial services accounted for 80% of all correctional spending. As the Parliamentary Budget Officer reported in June 2010, one new law alone – of the many already passed or in the works – will cost taxpayers $7–10 billion.[74] Rather than addressing the egregious conditions in local lock-ups and remand centres, the government passed a law to eliminate judicial discretion to credit time served for those awaiting trial.[75]

So, where do we go from here?

We want to continue to challenge lawyers and judges to throw out cases that bring the administration of justice into disrepute. How can this not be the case for welfare fraud, for instance? Why have those responsible for the regressive legislative and policy decisions not been called to account? Why do the provincial and federal governments routinely intervene to restrict access to justice to the oppressed rather than assist them by intervening on behalf and in support of progressive laws and policies, for example, cases involving breaches of section 15 of the Canadian Charter of Rights and Freedoms?

We also need to challenge current definitions of *mens rea* and theories regarding definitions of what is a crime. The opportunity for this was explored by the Law Commission of Canada – before it was obliterated – regarding the definition of what is considered to be a crime.[76] Resources are always an issue when it comes to matters of equality and social justice, so we also need to ensure that adequate and flexible resources exist to assist women, Indigenous, anti-poverty and other grassroots groups, and those living the oppression to alleviate – indeed, eliminate – the structural inequity occasioned by current social, economic and legal policies and law reforms.

We need to breathe life into the initiatives proposed by true leaders, women like Louise Arbour, who have called on us to demand a Canada that pushes for human rights that equate with freedom from want.[77] We must push municipal,

---

73 Statistics Canada, *Adult Correctional Services in Canada, 2014/2015* (Ottawa: Statistics Canada, 2016). Online: <http://www.statcan.gc.ca/pub/85-002-x/2016001/article/14318-eng.pdf>.

74 Indeed, the Parliamentary Budget Officer estimated that based upon information available to his office regarding correctional costs, it costs an average of $343,810 per woman per year to imprison women in federal penitentiaries. See Kim Page, *The Funding Requirement and Impact of the "Truth in Sentencing Act" on the Correctional System in Canada* (Ottawa: Office of the Parliamentary Budget Officer, 22 June 2010) at 94; "Sentencing reform could cost $10B over 5 years," *CBC News* (27 April 2010). Online: <http://www.cbc.ca/news/politics/story/2010/04/27/page-budget-estimates-bill-c25.html>.

75 Robin Maynard, "Criminal (in)justice: An interview with Gillian Balfour," *supra* note 73; Ontario Women's Justice Network, "Truth in sentencing: Telling the truth about what the end of 2-for-1 credit means for Aboriginal and racialized women and their communities" (2010).

76 Law Commission of Canada (ed), *What is a Crime?* (Vancouver, B.C.: UBC Press, 2004) at viii–ix. Online: <http://www.ubcpress.ca/books/pdf/chapters/whatisacrime/whatcrime.pdf>.

77 Louise Arbour, "'Freedom from want' – from charity to entitlement" (Lafontaine-Baldwin Lecture 2005 in Quebec City). Online: <http://www.icc-icc.ca/fr/lbs/docs/

provincial and federal governments to restore or develop sorely needed housing, guaranteed liveable incomes, social services, supportive women-directed counselling, educational and advocacy services, and further to facilitate access to these services.

Encouraging and facilitating the access of advocacy groups like CAEFS and others doing feminist, anti-racist, anti-poverty and human rights work to provide women and girls with accurate and accessible information and tools as to how to advocate individually and collectively is yet another strategy. Until very recently, Elizabeth Fry Societies in Ontario were denied access to women in provincial jails, and information booklets regarding their rights were seized and labelled as "contraband" within the prisons.

Another vital need for women in and from prison is access to affordable academic and vocational training opportunities. In a time where governments will be cutting social services in an attempt to balance their books, such cuts are not only fiscally disastrous for all of us, but the diversion of funds into prison systems will further erode the social fabric of Canada. Most of us do not want to have our tax dollars spent on building prisons instead of on social services, schools and hospitals. It costs substantially less to host and maintain community programs than it does to build more prisons.[78] Furthermore, community-based prevention and sentencing options are more effective than prison in promoting public safety.

Some important first steps have already been taken. In the mandate letters to the Ministers of Justice and Public Safety, Prime Minister Justin Trudeau called upon his cabinet to prevent the criminalization and imprisonment, as well as to promote the decarceration of Indigenous peoples and people with mental health issues. He has further signalled that the recommendations of the Ashley Smith inquest jury and the Truth and Reconciliation Commission must be implemented.[79]

We must stand up and object to the current trend to send more people to prison instead of college and university. Penal expansion has far-reaching consequences beyond prison walls, which are extremely damaging to us all.

Much is possible, right now, if we merely have the will to stand together, to collaborate and confront the myths, misconceptions and realities that are our current challenges. One source of hope and further work is presented by the

---

LouiseArbour2005EN.pdf>. See also Canada, Commission of Inquiry into Certain Events at the Prison for Women in Kingston, *Report*, *supra* note 8 at v–viii.

78 Statistics Canada, *Adult Correctional Services in Canada, 2010/2011* (Ottawa: Statistics Canada, 2011) at 10. Online: <http://www.statcan.gc.ca/pub/85-002-x/2012001/article/11715-eng.pdf>. See also Statistics Canada, *Adult Correctional Services in Canada, 2014/2015, supra* note 74 at 5.

79 Prime Minister of Canada, "Minister of Justice and Attorney General of Canada mandate letter". Online: <http://pm.gc.ca/eng/minister-justice-and-attorney-general-canada-mandate-letter>.

government's promise to reinstate the Court Challenges Program.[80] A similar fund to the Court Challenges Fund needs to be established for prisoners, such that the Prisoner Challenge Program funds can be accessed by those who are in prison and who may otherwise not be able to avail themselves of legal representation and assistance in order to ensure that their rights and entitlements are realized.

Crime is a theory.

Name any behaviour and we will be able to identify times when it is considered legal and times when it is not. Law and criminalization are theories and choices made by those to whom we give the authority, as well as by those who take power.

Who among us does not already acknowledge that jails are not the shelters battered women need, that they are not treatment centres or places of healing, that they are not an appropriate substitution for adequate and affordable housing, education or skills development? We know who is and who is not in prison. With few exceptions, the wealthy and most privileged are not jailed. Crime is a theory – defined, monitored and enforced for specific identifiable purposes.

Rather than personalizing the various legal, human rights and social justice struggles and uprisings of prisoners, we are hopeful that increasingly, all will recognize that it is always in our collective interest when the oppressed resist and challenge their oppression. Increasing prisoner access to the justice and equality occasioned by social inclusion will benefit all of us, including our respective communities of interest.

The Association of Elizabeth Fry Societies and others encourage everyone to join the growing worldwide political, economic and social coalition to stop the increased intrusion of the state in terms of surveillance and social control, as well as the retreat of the state in the provision of supportive social, health and educational services.

And, as Lilla Watson, an Indigenous woman in Australia has stressed, we need to work together to correct current injustice. I will conclude with her words, shared with me more than 25 years ago by Gayle Horii:

> If you have come here to help me,
>
> you are wasting our time.
>
> If you have come here because your liberation is bound up with mine,
>
> then let us work together.

---

80 The Court Challenges Program of Canada (CCP) was a non-profit organization established to provide financial assistance for court cases that advance language and equality rights guaranteed under Canada's Constitution. The program was terminated by the government in 2006. The Prime Minister has mandated the Heritage Minister to reinstate the program: see *ibid.*

I dedicate these words to the memory of Terry Baker, Camille Strickland-Murphy, Veronica Park and Kinew James, as well as to Ashley Smith and the far too numerous other men, women and children who have died unnatural and preventable deaths in our prisons. And I offer the foregoing with heartfelt appreciation and gratitude to Louise Arbour for the model and the instruction that she continues to provide to me personally and to so many the world over. I thank her for always being a beacon of hope, integrity, intelligence and brilliance, and for inspiring all of us to do the best that we can and to be the best that we can be in, whatever sphere that we are in, whether we are in prison in a cell, whether we are working with prisoners, or whether we are leading the country or walking into a war zone. We thank her so very much for the countless opportunities she has provided to so many of us to share portions of her amazing journey and we honour her for her exemplary leadership.

Thank you, Louise, for being such a beacon of hope for so many years for so many people. And thank you for demonstrating how you can fundamentally insist on compliance with the law and the rule of law, and for investing in people in the way that you do.

Thank you to all of you for the part you play now and in the future, when you use your legal and other training and life experience to change the world, and try to prevent harm befalling others. And to women with the lived experience and expertise who are my constant allies, agitators, mentors and friends, your strength, courage and perseverance continue to inspire and drive me.

MOVING BEYOND FACIAL EQUALITY

Examining Canadian and French Niqab Bans*

Natasha BAKHT

We should not coerce those we wish to liberate. And it is particularly offensive to advance our fight on the backs of those women who are now among the most marginalized and whose access to the workplace is the best guarantee of both their autonomy and their integration.[1]

Calls by politicians to ban the niqab or burqa[2] have become commonplace. Muslim women who cover themselves using face veils, though relatively small in number, have managed to become front-page news in many jurisdictions and have regularly captured the global imagination. French President Nicolas Sarkozy stated in front of parliamentarians that the burqa is not welcome in France.[3] Canadian Prime Minister Stephen Harper said that the niqab was "anti-women"[4]

* I am grateful for the excellent research assistance provided by Jordan Palmer and the insightful comments of the anonymous peer-reviewers.

1 Louise Arbour, "With the Charter, Quebec risks closing its mind" *The Globe and Mail* (12 February 2014). Online: <https://www.theglobeandmail.com/opinion/with-the-charter-quebec-risks-closing-its-mind/article16823409/>.

2 The burqa is a full-body covering including a mesh over the face while the niqab is a full-face veil that leaves visible an opening for the eyes. *SAS v. France*, No. 43835/11 [2014] ECHR 1, at para 11 [GC].

3 "Nicolas Sarkozy says Islamic veils are not welcome in France" *The Guardian* (22 June 2009). Online: <https://www.theguardian.com/world/2009/jun/22/islamic-veils-sarkozy-speech-france>.

4 Steven Chase, "Niqabs 'rooted in a culture that is anti-women,' Harper says" *The Globe and Mail* (10 March 2015). Online: <https://www.theglobeandmail.com/news/politics/niqabs-rooted-in-a-culture-that-is-anti-women-harper-says/article23395242/>.

and that it was "offensive that someone would hide their identity";[5] "[it's] not the way we do things here."[6] The Australian Prime Minister stated that he found the burqa "a fairly confronting form of attire and frankly I wish it weren't worn."[7] In the United States,[8] Germany[9] and Canada,[10] Muslim women have asked courts to recognize their right to wear the niqab in a variety of contexts. The niqab has been criminalized nationally in eight countries (France, Belgium, Bulgaria, Austria, Denmark, the Netherlands, Chad and the Congo), with partial or regional bans in Canada, Italy, Switzerland, Germany, Spain, Egypt, Syria, China, Cameroon, Niger and Algeria.[11]

This chapter builds on work already written about Muslim women who wear some sort of face veil and the ongoing agitation that has been expressed about them. I have argued elsewhere that the depth of discomfort evoked by

---

5 Morgan Lowrie, "Harper says Ottawa will appeal ruling allowing veil during citizenship oath" *The Globe and Mail* (12 February 2015). Online: <https://www.theglobeandmail.com/news/national/harper-says-ottawa-will-appeal-ruling-allowing-veil-during-citizenship-oath/article22979142/>.

6 Chase, *supra* note 4.

7 Jonathan Pearlman, "Tony Abbott shows support for burqa ban in parliament" *The Telegraph* (1 October 2014). Online: <http://www.telegraph.co.uk/news/worldnews/australiaandthepacific/australia/11132599/Tony-Abbott-shows-support-for-burqa-ban-in-parliament.html>.

8 Robert A. Kahn "The headscarf as threat: A comparison of German and U.S. legal discourses" (2007) 40(2) *V and J of Transnat'l L* 417. See also *Muhammad v. Enterprise Rent-a-Car*, No. 06-41896-GC (Mich 31st Dist Ct Oct 11, 2006).

9 Kahn, *ibid.*

10 *R v. NS*, 2012 SCC 72 [*NS*]; *Ishaq v. Canada* 2015 FC 156. Most recently, see *National Council of Canadian Muslims (NCCM) c. Attorney General of Quebec*, 2017 QCCS 5459, a constitutional challenge to Quebec's Bill 62 which prohibits people wearing face-veils from working in or receiving public services.

11 See Kristin Shorten, "Burqa bans already in place in many countries" *News Corp Australia* (3 October 2014). Online: <http://www.news.com.au/national/burqa-bans-already-in-place-in-many-countries/news-story/e29a9d15c79af75b0e2c6bd0fa98e316>; Angel Krasimirov, "Bulgaria bans full-face veils in public places", *Reuters* (30 September 2016). Online: <https://www.reuters.com/article/us-religion-burqa-bulgaria/bulgaria-bans-full-face-veils-in-public-places-idUSKCN1201FV>; "Austrian full-face veil ban comes into effect", *Deutsche Welle* (1 October 2017). Online: <https://www.dw.com/en/austrian-full-face-veil-ban-comes-into-effect/a-40765541>; Emil Gjerding Nielson & Teis Jensen, "Denmark parliament bans face veils in public spaces", *Global News* (1 June 2018). Online: <https://globalnews.ca/news/4248183/denmark-face-veils-niqab/>; The Associated Press, "Dutch parliament approves limited ban on burqa, niqab", *Daily News* (27 June 2018). Online: <http://www.nydailynews.com/news/world/ny-news-dutch-parliament-ban-burqa-20180627-story.html>; Radhika Sanghani, "Burka bans: The countries where Muslim women can't wear veils", *The Telegraph* (17 August 2017). Online: <https://www.telegraph.co.uk/women/life/burka-bans-the-countries-where-muslim-women-cant-wear-veils/>; "The Islamic veil across Europe", *BBC News* (31 May 2018). Online: <https://www.bbc.co.uk/news/world-europe-13038095>; "Syria bans full face veil at universities", *The Telegraph* (20 July 2010). Online: <https://www.telegraph.co.uk/news/worldnews/middleeast/syria/7899618/Syria-bans-full-face-veil-at-universities.html>. *SAS*, *supra* note 2 at paras 40–42; Bill 62, *infra* note 25; Steven Jiang, "China bans wearing burqa in biggest Muslim city" *CNN* (14 January 2015). Online: <http://www.cnn.com/2015/01/13/world/asia/china-burqa-ban/index.html>.

these women and their outward markers of religiosity have resulted in a wide range of mostly specious rationalizations as to why these items of clothing must be banned.[12] Logic appears not to be a measure used when managing issues involving women who cover their faces. Rather, one sees a predisposition, often unstated, toward linking such modest clothing to radical and violent interpretations of Islam.[13] Where such explanation is implausible, a strident dislike of the niqab manifested as an affront to national values is articulated as though that is explanation enough for the curtailment of rights. No further justification is required. In this chapter, I will examine two incidents where attempts have been made, one successfully and one unsuccessfully, to ban the niqab in certain public contexts using this rationale. I have used *Ishaq v. Canada*[14] and *SAS v. France*[15] as my case studies. Canada and France are both nations that have had a surprising amount of legal and political activity involving Muslim women who cover parts of their bodies, despite the fact that each nation's approach to diverse populations is quite different.[16]

---

12 Natasha Bakht, "Veiled objections: Facing public opposition to the niqab" in Lori G. Beaman, ed, *Reasonable Accommodation: Managing Religious Diversity* (Vancouver: UBC Press, 2012) 70.

13 In the summer of 2016, more than 30 French towns banned a full-length swimsuit, that left the face uncovered, worn by some Muslim women. The prohibition of this modest attire was rationalized using a variety of justifications (to protect Muslim women from enslavement and humiliation, to protect public order and secularism), but the most often articulated reason for banning the so-called "burkini" was the concern and heightened tensions after a series of terror attacks in France. Jim Bitterman, Sheema McKenzie and Catherine E. Shoichet, "French court suspends burkini ban" *CNN News* (26 August, 2016). Online: CNN News <http://edition.cnn.com/2016/08/26/europe/france-burkini-ban-court-ruling/index.html>.

14 *Ishaq*, *supra* note 10.

15 *SAS*, *supra* note 2.

16 Multiculturalism has been described as "A fundamental characteristic of the Canadian heritage and identity." Citizenship and Immigration Canada, "Discover Canada: The rights and responsibilities of citizenship, study guide", (2012) CIC. Online: <http://www.cic.gc.ca/english/pdf/pub/discover.pdf> at 8 (hereinafter "Citizenship guide"). The *Canadian Charter of Rights and Freedoms* makes specific mention of "the preservation and enhancement of the multicultural heritage of Canadians." *Canadian Charter of Rights and Freedoms*, Part I of the Constitution Act, 1982, being Schedule B to the Canada Act 1982 (UK), 1982, c 11 (hereinafter "Charter"), s 27. Linguistic, racial, cultural and religious differences among others are accommodated in Human Rights Acts across the country, including the Canadian Charter of Rights and Freedoms. Canada's citizenship guide notes that: "By the 1960s, one-third of Canadians had origins that were neither British nor French, and *took pride in preserving their distinct culture in the Canadian fabric.* Today, diversity enriches Canadians' lives ...", "Citizenship guide," *supra* at 25 (emphasis added). French law prohibits any special treatment, positive or negative, based on a differentiated appreciation of citizens. The public space is dominated by a discourse of "blind" or "disinterested" policy in relation to different cultural and ethnic identities. Artan Fuga, "Multiculturalism in France: Evolutions and challenges" (2008) Eurosphere Online Working Paper Series. Online: <http://eurospheres.org/files/2010/08/Eurosphere_Working_Paper_12_Fuga.pdf> at 2. Data on religious affiliation is not collected during the census as such concerns are considered private. Adam Taylor, "Map: France's growing Muslim population" *The Washington Post* (9 January 2015). Online: <https://www.washingtonpost.com/news/worldviews/wp/2015/01/09/map-frances-growing-muslim-population/?utm_term=.eae695523bd0>.

In addition to unpacking problematic arguments that insist on prohibiting face veils, this chapter will highlight the salient voices of resistance from niqab-wearing women themselves and their allies, who challenge stereotypes that link agentic choices with oppression. In our progressively multicultural societies, comprising people with diverse and deep commitments, it is imperative that we try to live peacefully together. Such peaceful coexistence requires an understanding of "others," a willingness to hear the voices of those marginalized, and an attempt to set fear and discomfort aside in order to learn about someone else. The stories of Muslim women who cover their faces may offer such a starting point.

1. THE CANADIAN CONTEXT

Although there have not been calls to ban the niqab nationally in the public arena, there has been much contestation of niqab-wearing women in Canada. In particular, there have been four attempts to prohibit the niqab in certain contexts, despite constitutional guarantees that protect religious freedom,[17] uphold respect for minorities[18] and promote multiculturalism.[19]

In 2007, the federal government introduced Bill C-6, *An Act to amend the Canada Elections Act (visual identification of voters)*,[20] to require voters to have their faces uncovered when voting. The bill was supposed to enable election officials to identify voters visually, even though it was permissible under the Canada Elections Act[21] to submit two pieces of non-photo identification in order to vote or indeed to vote by mail. The Bill was apparently an attempt to counter the problem of the multiple-voting veiled Muslim woman, mythical as this phenomenon was.[22] Forcing Muslim women to show their faces would not combat voter fraud; it was merely a measure to target and exclude Muslim women.

In 2010, the province of Quebec introduced Bill 94 (*An Act to establish guidelines governing accommodation requests within the Administration and certain institutions*),[23] which required "un visage découvert" or a "naked face" when providing or receiving public services. Though not specifically mentioning the niqab or Muslim women, the Bill was justified on the basis of state neutrality and gender equality. It effectively curtailed the provincial protections of reasonable accommodation and violated constitutional guarantees against

17 Charter, *ibid*, s 2(a).

18 *Reference re Secession of Quebec* [1998] 2 SCR 217 at para 49.

19 For example, Charter, *supra* note 16, s 27.

20 Bill C-6, *An Act to amend the Canada Elections Act (visual identification of voters)*, 1st Sess, 39th Parl, 2007.

21 Canada Elections Act, SC 2000, c 9.

22 *House of Commons Debates*, 39th Parl, 2nd Sess, No. 016 (14 November 2007) at 873, 875 (Hon. Paul Dewar).

23 Bill 94, *An Act to establish guidelines governing accommodation requests within the Administration and certain institutions*, 1st Sess, 39th Leg, Quebec, 2010.

overbreadth and of religious freedom. In 2013, Bill 60,[24] popularly known as the "Charter of Quebec Values," expanded Bill 94's reach beyond face veils to include all people wearing "conspicuous religious symbols." The Bill would have prevented people wearing certain outward signs of religiosity from working in government, notwithstanding their competence and training simply because of an unproven assertion that they would be unable to perform their jobs neutrally or without religious bias. Niqab-wearing women would also have been prevented from accessing government-run services such as child care, health care and education, despite the contention that Bill 60 was in part about the equality of men and women. Though Bills 94 and 60 never became law, in October 2017, Bill 62, which bans people who cover their faces from working in public service and receiving government services, was adopted.[25] The new law will seriously hinder niqab-wearing women's equality rights and religious freedom by curtailing their mobility, political participation, health, education and work opportunities.

The continuing and vocal dislike of face veils was also evident in a 2012 Supreme Court of Canada decision involving a devout Muslim sexual assault complainant who wished to wear her niqab while testifying in court.[26] The sexual assault context of the case helped to complicate the usual objections to the niqab based on gender equality, that is, the universalist feminist approach that sees the ideal woman as equal to men and thus necessarily unveiled,[27] ignoring intersectional feminist experiences that consider gender along with religion and race among other identities. Rather than focusing abstractly on whether the niqab-wearer is forced to wear the face veil or is under false consciousness in her choice to veil, the circumstances of the case revealed the religious *and* gender bias that would result if the complainant were forced by the state to remove her niqab in court. Given the history of legal and procedural norms that revictimize sexual assault complainants and reinforce their inequality through rape mythologies, many saw the perversity of asking a sexual assault complainant to remove her usual clothing in order to seek justice.[28] The case was

---

24 Bill 60, *Charter affirming the values of State secularism and religious neutrality and of equality between women and men, and providing a framework for accommodation requests*, 1st Sess, 40th Leg, Quebec, 2013.

25 Bill 62, *An Act to foster adherence to State religious neutrality and, in particular, to provide a framework for religious accommodation requests in certain bodies*, 1st Sess, 41st Leg, Quebec, 2015.

26 See in particular, the concurrence in *NS*, *supra* note 10 at paras 58–79.

27 See for example *Şahin v. Turkey*, No. 44774/98, [2005] 41 ECHR 8 at paras 12 and 111 [GC].

28 See, for example, Natasha Bakht, "In your face: Piercing the veil of ignorance about niqab-wearing women" (2015) 3 *Social and Legal Studies* at 7. Online: <http://sls.sagepub.com/cgi/reprint/0964663914552214v1.pdf?ijkey=G1X0XWhGfmxUMLY&keytype=ref>; see also *R v. NS* "Intervener's, Women's Legal Education & Action Fund (LEAF) Factum by Susan S Chapman & Joanne Birenbaum" (17 November 2011), SCC File No. 33989 at para 23. Online: <http://www.leaf.ca/wp-content/uploads/2012/12/NS-SCC.pdf>.

also unique in that it involved, unlike any of the previous examples, an instance of two competing constitutional rights – the accused's right to a fair trial versus the complainant's right to religious freedom and equality.

Importantly, the majority of the Supreme Court left open the possibility that niqab-wearing women can testify in court wearing their usual clothing.[29] The Chief Justice rightly stated that Canada's traditions do not involve leaving one's religious convictions at the courtroom door. This view from the highest court of the land was an important counter-statement defying explicit governmental discrimination against niqab-wearing women.

2. CASE STUDY: *ISHAQ v. CANADA*

The fourth instance involving niqab-wearing women in Canada is also one of the case studies of this chapter. It involves a federal governmental policy to ban face veils during citizenship ceremonies. On 25 October 2008, Zunera Ishaq, a former high school teacher from Pakistan, became a permanent resident of Canada. Ms Ishaq met all of the preconditions for citizenship, including the age and residency requirements, demonstrating sufficient knowledge of one of Canada's official languages, having no criminal prohibitions, and passing a test proving adequate knowledge of the country and the responsibilities and privileges of citizenship. Her application for citizenship was approved; however, in order to be considered a citizen under section 3(1)(c) of the Citizenship Act,[30] she was also required take the oath of citizenship. She was prepared to take the oath, which is a symbolic affirmation of one's allegiance to the Queen and one's readiness to observe the laws of Canada.[31] Her objection was to a new policy that changed the manner in which she was compelled to take the oath.[32]

On 12 December 2011, Immigration Minister Jason Kenney announced a ban of face coverings such as niqabs, worn by some Muslim women, during the taking of the citizenship oath. In his speech introducing the policy, he stated:

> … starting today, my department will require that all those taking the oath do so openly. From today, all persons will be required to show their face when swearing the oath.

---

29 *NS*, *supra* note 10. For an article that analyzes *R v. NS* and argues that the majority decision did not go far enough in protecting niqab-wearing women see Bakht, *ibid.*

30 RSC 1985, c C-29.

31 The words of the Canadian citizenship oath are: "I swear (*or* affirm) that I will be faithful and bear true allegiance to Her Majesty Queen Elizabeth the Second, Queen of Canada, Her Heirs and Successors, and that I will faithfully observe the laws of Canada and fulfill my duties as a Canadian citizen." Schedule to Citizenship Act, *ibid.*

32 *Ishaq*, *supra* note 10 at para 3.

> I have received complaints from members of Parliament, from citizens, from judges of the citizenship court that it is hard to ensure that individuals whose faces are covered are actually reciting the oath. Requiring that all candidates show their faces while reciting the oath allows judges and everyone present to share in the ceremony, to ensure that all citizenship candidates are in fact, reciting the oath as required by our law. This is not simply a practical measure. It is a matter of deep principle that goes to the heart of our identity and our values of openness and equality. The citizenship oath is a quintessentially public act. It is a public declaration that you are joining the Canadian family and it must be taken freely and openly.[33]

Minister Kenney changed the requirement of taking the oath to that of *being seen* to be taking the oath.[34] Apparently, niqab-wearing women could not be trusted to pronounce the words of the oath; one needed to see their mouths moving, even though all new citizens were already required to sign a declaration certifying that they had taken the oath.[35] Ms Ishaq, who wears the niqab, challenged the government's new policy in January 2014.

In February 2015, the Federal Court of Canada rendered a straightforward analysis of the legality of the policy, declaring it inconsistent with the regulations of the Citizenship Act. Section 17(1)(b) of the regulations to the Citizenship Act requires a judge to "administer the oath of citizenship with dignity and solemnity, allowing the *greatest possible freedom* in the religious solemnization or the solemn affirmation thereof."[36] Justice Boswell found that religious solemnization refers to permitting candidates to swear the oath on a holy book of their choice or, in the case of an affirmation, on no book at all. He held that it could also refer to how the oath is administered and the circumstances under which candidates are required to take it. Thus, the new policy, which made it mandatory for judges to ensure that candidates for citizenship recite the oath with their faces uncovered, was invalid as it could not trump the Act or its regulations.[37]

That citizenship judges are required to administer the oath allowing for the "greatest possible freedom" in its solemnization or affirmation is consistent with

---

33 Honourable Jason Kenny, PC MP, Minister of Citizenship, Immigration and Multiculturalism (Speaking Notes delivered in Montreal, Quebec, 12 December 2011). Online: <http://www.cic.gc.ca/english/department/media/speeches/2011/2011-12-12.asp>.

34 According to an official at Citizenship and Immigration Canada (CIC), no accommodations are permitted, such as a private oath-taking with a female official. *Ishaq*, *supra* note 10 at para 47.

35 Canada SOR/93-246, s 21(hereinafter the "Citizenship Regulations").

36 *Ibid*, s 17(1)(b) (emphasis added).

37 Justice Boswell did not consider any of the Charter arguments raised for reasons of judicial restraint and a desire to avoid "unnecessary constitutional pronouncements [that] may prejudice future cases, the implications of which have not been foreseen." *Ishaq*, *supra* note 10 at para 66. The Federal Court of Appeal took the same approach on appeal. See *MCI v. Ishaq*, 2015 FCA 194, at para 5.

Canadian values and principles of multiculturalism and respect for minorities.[38] Indeed, one Toronto-area citizenship judge noted in an interview with CBC radio that: "If [veiled women] don't take the face covering off, there is an opportunity for them to come in front of the judge again after the ceremony and take the oath … they don't have to remove the veil right there in front of all these people."[39] This reasoning is entirely in keeping with human rights legislation that accommodates minorities when "neutral" rules of general application disproportionately burden or exclude them from participating in society.[40]

Despite persistent popular beliefs that niqab-wearing women come to Canada and ask to have certain laws changed for their benefit,[41] the Citizenship Act already contained a provision that endorsed the Canadian tradition of accommodating minority practices. It was the Conservative government that changed the law in a way that targeted Muslim women who wear full-face veils. In fact, the government is shocking in its trivialization of the denial of citizenship, stating: "If the Applicant is opposed to baring her face, then … she should just accept the consequences of not becoming a citizen; she will retain all of the benefits of permanent residence."[42] This not only ignores that citizenship gives one the essential rights to vote and run for political office, but that a citizen is at much less of a risk of being deported.[43] Essentially, the government hoped to relegate niqab-wearing women to second-class status.

In a decision delivered from the bench, the Federal Court of Appeal upheld the Federal Court's judgment striking down the ban on face coverings at Canadian citizenship ceremonies.[44] Importantly, the judges held "that it is in the interests of justice that we not delay in issuing our decision … so as to hopefully leave open the possibility for the respondent to obtain citizenship in time to

38 Charter, *supra* note 16, s 27; *Secession Reference*, *supra* note 19. In *Bruker v. Marcovitz*, 2007 SCC 54 at paras 1–2, the Supreme Court of Canada held that minority practices must be protected where they are compatible with fundamental values.

39 *Ishaq*, *supra* note 10 at para 48.

40 Though the wording of CIC's policy is neutral on its face, the government conceded that it would primarily affect niqab-wearing women. *Ishaq*, *supra* note 10 at para 36.

41 Adam Frisk, "Tory MP apologizes for telling women wearing niqab during ceremony: 'Stay the hell where you came from'" *Global News* (17 March 2015). Online: <http://globalnews.ca/news/1886751/tory-mp-to-women-wearing-niqab-during-ceremony-stay-the-hell-where-you-came-from/>. MP Larry Miller also said: "I'm so sick and tired of people wanting to come here because they know it's a good country and then they want to change things before they really officially become a Canadian."

42 *Ishaq*, *supra* note 10 at para 39.

43 Amendments to the Citizenship Act have granted CIC unprecedented powers to revoke and deny citizenship, while making it harder to appeal such decisions. The amendments specifically target dual nationals, naturalized Canadians and the descendants of immigrants, creating a two-tiered and arguably racialized system of citizenship. For an overview of the amendments, see Voices-Voix, "Canadian Citizenship (Bill C-24)". Online: <http://voices-voix.ca/en/facts/profile/canadian-citizenship-bill-c-24>.

44 *MCI v. Ishaq*, *supra* note 36.

vote in the upcoming federal election."[45] Zunera Ishaq did indeed obtain her Canadian citizenship in a private ceremony on 5 October 2015.[46] She also voted in the federal election that removed the Conservative party from power.

Despite this happy ending for Ishaq and her supporters, it is nonetheless useful to examine the reasons given for requiring removal of the niqab in this context. In his explanation for the new policy, Minister Kenney said: "Allowing a group to hide their faces while they are becoming members of our community is counter to Canada's commitment to openness, equality and social cohesion."[47] Similarly, in vowing to appeal the Federal Court decision, Prime Minister Stephen Harper noted: "I believe and I think most Canadians believe that it is offensive that someone would hide their identity at the very moment where they are committing to join the Canadian family. This is a society that is transparent, open and where people are equal."[48]

Both politicians first referred to niqab-wearing women as hiding. While it is true that these women conceal their faces from general view,[49] they are not in fact hiding their identity as suggested. In Ms Ishaq's case, in accordance with the new policy, she removed her niqab at the citizenship-testing site, in order for a female official to confirm her identity before she wrote the exam.[50] This was not a situation where an imposter could have written the exam for the citizenship candidate under disguise. Similarly, at the oath ceremony, a candidate wearing a face veil would be required to reveal her face in private to a female official in order to compare her face against the documents on file and confirm her

---

45 *Ibid* at para 5.

46 "Zunera Ishaq, who challenged ban on niqab, takes citizenship oath wearing it" *CBC News* (5 October 2015). Online: <http://www.cbc.ca/news/politics/zunera-ishaq-niqab-ban-citizenship-oath-1.3257762>.

47 "Niqabs, burkas must be removed during citizenship ceremonies: Jason Kenney" *National Post* (12 December 2011). Online: <http://nationalpost.com/news/canada/niqabs-burkas-must-be-removed-during-citizenship-ceremonies-jason-kenney/wcm/41d525a2-714e-4d73-93eb-f05fd78ced0e>.

48 Lowrie, *supra* note 5.

49 Ishaq has stated that she "decided to wear the niqab after having done research on the requirement of woman to cover their faces in Islam. To her, the niqab is integral to the modesty that a Muslim woman must show and a fundamental part of her identity." *Ishaq v. Canada*, "Applicant's Memorandum of Law by Lorne Waldman & Marlys A Edwardh" (1 June 2015), FCA File No. A-124-15 at para 10. The applicant in *SAS v. France* wears the niqab in public and in private "but not systematically: she might not wear it, for example, when she visited the doctor, when meeting friends in a public place, or when she wanted to socialize in public. She was thus content not to wear the niqab in public places at all times but wished to be able to wear it when she chose to do so, depending in particular on her spiritual feelings." *SAS v. France*, *supra* note 2 at para 12. For an interesting analysis of the fluidity of religious practice, see Lori G Beaman, "Living together v. living well together: A normative examination of the *SAS* case" (2016) 4(2) *Social Inclusion* 3.

50 *Ishaq*, *supra* note 10 at para 3.

identity. This process is required by the new policy and was likely already in place before its implementation.[51]

Second, both politicians make reference to Canadian society as "open," suggesting that the niqab runs afoul such an ideal. What do they mean by an "open" society? Relying on the concurring judgment of Justice LeBel in *NS*,[52] the government argued "that taking the oath is a public act and it reasonably advances an important objective to expect all candidates to come together and recite the oath openly and equally."[53] However, the openness of Canadian society legally refers to the requirement of a system of open and independent courts where "the public is entitled to know or learn about what goes on before them."[54] This would not be pertinent during a citizenship ceremony. In the terminology of political theory, an open society has a culture in which there is freedom and tolerance of belief and political structures that are flexible and transparent.[55] The government's policy of banning the niqab during citizenship ceremonies is wholly at odds with an open society in that it directly targets a religious group, Muslim women who cover their faces, and insists on erasing public evidence of their Muslim-ness.[56]

A non-legal or popular reading of openness might refer to open or broadmindedness in relation to difference, or a receptiveness and understanding of atypical ways of living. Certainly, the language of section 27 of the Constitution, which states that the "Charter shall be interpreted in a manner consistent with the preservation and enhancement of the multicultural heritage of Canadians,"[57] suggests a broad, respectful approach to heterogeneity rather than the insular and xenophobic interpretation implemented and championed by the Conservative government's policy. Perhaps the reference to openness literally means an "open" or uncovered face, but this begs the following question: to what end? Showing one's face in the context of the oath of citizenship would not confirm identity since, as previously noted, that would have already taken place. It could not

---

51 Section 13.2 of Citizenship and Immigration Canada's policy manual, "CP 15: Guide to Citizenship Ceremonies." Online: <http://www.cic.gc.ca/english/resources/manuals/updates.asp>. This states: "Candidates for citizenship wearing a full or partial face covering must be identified. When dealing with these female candidates it is the responsibility of a citizenship official to confirm the candidate's identity. This should be done in private, by a female citizenship official. The candidate must be asked to reveal her face to allow the CIC official to confirm the identity against the documents on file."

52 Justice LeBel problematically held in *NS* that: "Wearing a niqab … does not facilitate acts of communication. Rather, it restricts them." *NS*, *supra* note 10 at para 77. For a critique of this opinion, see Bakht, *supra* note 26.

53 *Ishaq*, *supra* note 10 at para 37.

54 *NS*, *supra* note 10 at para 75.

55 Karl Popper, *The Open Society and its Enemies* (Princeton, NJ: Princeton University Press, 2013) at 513; Ludwig Kramer, "The open society, its lawyers, and its environment" (1989) 1 *Journal of Environmental Law* 1 at 4.

56 Robert Leckey, "Face to face" (2013) 19(6) *Social Identities* 743 at 744.

57 Charter, *supra* note 16, s 27.

be relied on as a visual confirmation of oath-taking since one could mouth or mumble the words without being detected by lip-reading. It would show that the candidate has a face, but nothing more.

Notably, Harper and Kenney's references to an "open" society are also paired with the idea of equality. Harper's meaning is quite clear: "We do not allow people to cover their faces during citizenship ceremonies. Why would Canadians, contrary to our own values, embrace a practice … that is not transparent, that is not open and frankly is rooted in a culture that is anti-women."[58] "Open and equal" seems to pertain to how women should dress if they are to be viewed as equal. Though most would agree that the state should never dictate how women ought to dress, in reality women are often sent conflicting messages by the state and policy-makers about what and how much to wear or not wear.[59] Muslim women who cover parts of their bodies are told that they must be "suitably dressed"[60] and that they must undress to be free of oppression. Justice Eliana Marengo refused to hear the case of Rania El Alloul because she was wearing a headscarf in a Montreal courtroom.[61] She was judged to be wearing too much. By contrast, a tried and tested tactic in sexual assault trials is to blame the attack on the complainant's manner of dress.[62] In an incident in Toronto, 18-year-old Alexi Halket was urged by her principal to clothe herself when she wore a midriff-baring crop top to school[63] because her shirt was deemed inappropriate and looked too much like a bra. These women are judged to be wearing too

---

58 Chase, *supra* note 4. Minister Kenney also stated about the niqab: "It's a cultural tradition, which I think reflects a certain view about women that we don't accept in Canada. We want women to be full and equal members of Canadian society and certainly when they're taking the citizenship oath, that's the right place to start." Laura Payton, "Face veils banned for citizenship oaths" *CBC News* (12 December 2011). Online: <http://www.cbc.ca/news/politics/face-veils-banned-for-citizenship-oaths-1.1048750>.

59 Lori G Beaman, "Overdressed and underexposed or underdressed and overexposed?" (2013) 19(6) *Social Identities* 723 at 724.

60 Sean Fine, "Quebec Judge's No-Head-Scarf Rule Sparks Outcry" *The Globe and Mail* (28 February 2015) A5.

61 Michael Shulman, "Judge's refusal to hear case of woman in hijab left her in tears" *CTV News* (27 February 2015). Online: <http://www.ctvnews.ca/canada/judge-s-refusal-to-hear-case-of-woman-in-hijab-left-her-in-tears-1.2256718>. See *Muhammad*, *supra* note 8 for an American case where the judge refused to hear a niqab-wearing woman's case.

62 In *R v. Ewanchuk* (1998), 57 Alta LR (3d) 235 at 245, a sexual assault case involving a minor, Justice McLung of the Court of Appeal stated that "it must be pointed out that the complainant did not present herself to Ewanchuk or enter his trailer in a bonnet and crinolines." At the Supreme Court of Canada ([1999] 1 SCR 330 at para 103), Justice McLachlin held: "On appeal, the idea also surfaced that if a woman is not modestly dressed, she is deemed to consent. Such stereotypical assumptions find their roots in many cultures, including our own. They no longer, however, find a place in Canadian law."

63 Liam Casey, "'They were sexualizing my outfit': Toronto students wear crop tops to school after teen told to cover up" *National Post* (28 May 2015). Online: <http://nationalpost.com/news/toronto/they-were-sexualizing-my-outfit-toronto-students-wear-midriff-baring-crop-tops-to-school-to-protest-cover-up-order/wcm/9278e9cb-d3cd-4efb-a7cc-f9bc0ede2f00>.

little and are seen as inviting unprofessional glances or sexual assault. These stark examples reveal that acceptable attire falls within a very particular range of options. Otherwise women's dress, whether they wear too much or too little, is seen as distracting or interfering with the rights of others.

3. THE FRENCH CONTEXT

France has had a precarious relationship with its minority populations and Muslims in particular. Although France has the largest Muslim population in Europe, conflicts with this community have increased dramatically.[64] Politicians have claimed that the presence of certain religious symbols are the key social problem amongst this community,[65] despite the rampant unemployment rates of French North African immigrants, their spatial segregation in housing estates in the suburbs, and the fact that there are few Muslims in the French National Assembly.[66] Muslims are blamed for refusing to integrate into French society when the reality is that France will not allow them to do so.[67]

The now infamous 2004 French law banning female students from wearing headscarves in public schools was justified using the doctrine of *laicité* or secularism, which, grounded in the principles of French Republicanism, discourages the assertion of separate ethnic identities.[68] The problem with relying on secularism[69] to justify banning headscarves is that it favours rigorous

64 Leland Ware, "Color-blind racism in France: Bias against ethnic minority immigrants" (2015) 46 *Washington University Journal of Law & Policy* 185 at 185.

65 Bakht, *supra* note 12 at 77.

66 The only current member of the National Assembly of France of Muslim background is Abdoulatifou Aly ("Muslims in European politics" *Euro-Islam* (blog). Online: <http://www.euro-islam.info/key-issues/political-representation/>). Before Aly was elected in 2012, there were no Muslim members in the National Assembly (Myriam Renaud, "France's incomplete citizens and why some put Islam first" (21 April 2016), University of Chicago Divinity School (blog). Online: <https://divinity.uchicago.edu/sightings/frances-incomplete-citizens-and-why-some-put-islam-first>). In 2005, Azouz Begag became the first French Muslim cabinet member when he was appointed Equal Opportunities Minister (Elaine Ganley, "French Cabinet Minister rejects tokenism" *The Washington Post* (26 October 2006). Online: <http://www.washingtonpost.com/wp-dyn/content/article/2006/10/26/AR2006102600990.html>).

67 Ware, *supra* note 62 at 188.

68 Ellen Wiles, "Headscarves, human rights and harmonious multicultural society: Implications of the French ban for interpretations of equality" (2007) 41(3) *Law & Society Review* 699 at 702. For a detailed history and analysis of this controversy, see John R Bowen, *Why the French Don't Like Headscarves: Islam, the State, and Public Space* (Princeton: Princeton University Press, 2007); and Joan Wallach Scott, *The Politics of the Veil* (Princeton: Princeton University Press, 2007).

69 The 1905 law on the Separation of Church and State that established state secularism once stood against the power of the Catholic Church, which was until 1905 the state religion. *Loi du 9 décembre 1905 concernant la séparation des Eglises et de l'Etat*, JO, 11 December 1905, 7205.

irreligion, though some may prefer to lead a faith-based life. More recently, secularism in France has favoured certain forms of modern religion over other legitimate faiths, thus functioning to promote Christian culture and to scapegoat Muslims.[70] The *Conseil d'Etat*[71] concluded in 2009 that the wearing of religious symbols in public schools, while not incompatible with secularism in principle, would threaten the religious freedom of others if the ostentatious character of the symbol constituted pressure, provocation, proselytism or propaganda, or compromised the health, safety or normal operation of teaching activities.[72] There was in fact no evidence that wearing headscarves interfered with classroom instruction or the daily operation of schools. "A more credible explanation for the ban was [that] the display of an Islamic religious symbol ... offended school officials."[73] President Jacques Chirac called the wearing of headscarves "an act of aggression" and 70% of the French public expressed strong support for the law[74]

It thus came as no surprise when the presence of women wearing niqabs and burqas also became a contentious issue in France. This time, President Sarkozy expressed his disapproval of the burqa, stating that it was a violation of the "French republic's idea of women's dignity," that it was not a sign of religion but subservience and that it was not welcome in France.[75]

A parliamentary commission was subsequently established to investigate the practice of wearing the full-face veil and eventually an opinion from the *Conseil d'Etat* was sought on a potential law prohibiting concealment of one's face in the public arena. Interestingly, the *Conseil d'Etat* did not recommend a general ban of face veils, but suggested a narrower prohibition in certain public spaces if concealing one's face were to pose a substantial safety or security threat to public order, arguing that this would most appropriately be met by bans introduced locally in reaction to specific problems.[76] Secularism could not be used as a justification in this instance because this principle applies to public institutions

---

70 Bakht, *supra* note 12 at 82. Louise Arbour noted in Quebec's "Charter of Secular Values" controversy: "The proponents of the charter will argue that there is no infringement of freedom of religion in the first place as religion is fundamentally a private matter, best kept in the private sphere, and that the right doesn't encompass displays of religious affiliation. This is a very Catholic understanding of religion, which of course cannot be the starting point for defining the contours of religious freedom, particularly in an environment where Catholicism – religious or cultural – is dominant." Arbour, *supra* note 1.

71 The *Conseil d'État* is a body of the French national government that acts both as legal adviser of the executive branch and as the supreme court for administrative justice.

72 Ware, *supra* note 62 at 231.

73 *Ibid* at 231–232.

74 *Ibid* at 233.

75 *Supra* note 2.

76 Daniel Barton "Is the French burka ban compatible with international human rights law standards?" (2012) 9(1) *Essex Human Rights Review* 1 at 8. Online: <http://projects.essex.ac.uk/ehrr/V9N1/BARTON.pdf>.

such as schools and colleges, but cannot be used to restrict the beliefs or practices of individuals at large.[77]

However, this somewhat nuanced position did not prevent the government from presenting and eventually passing a bill that stipulates that no one shall wear a garment that conceals the face in a public space, which is defined as places open to the public or where public services are provided. The law provides some exceptions for garments prescribed by law or justified for health or professional reasons or for the purposes of sports, festivals or artistic or traditional events. Breach of the law is punishable by a fine of up to €150 or a citizenship course, or both.[78] The requirement of a "citizenship course" presumes that the niqab-wearing woman is a foreigner unfamiliar with French ways, when in fact she may have lived her entire life as a French citizen.

Asked by the President of the National Assembly and the President of the Senate to assess the Act prohibiting the concealing of faces in public, the *Conseil constitutionnel*[79] held that the law required only that the scope of the exceptions be expanded to cover the exercise of religious freedom in places of worship that are open to the public.[80] The law came into force in April 2011.

4. CASE STUDY: *SAS v. FRANCE*

In *SAS v. France*, a 24-year-old niqab-wearing French citizen originally from Pakistan challenged the 2011 general ban of face veils as a violation of several provisions of the European Convention on Human Rights.[81] The Grand Chamber of the European Court of Human Rights held that France's ban was valid on the ground that concealing the face created an obstacle to social interaction.

France also argued that the ban was for the purposes of (1) public safety, (2) that it sought to protect women's equality and (3) that it was a matter of respect for human dignity, as those who wore the niqab were erased from public spaces. The Court accepted that public safety was a legitimate aim for the ban, but found that it was not proportionately pursued, since no evidence had been adduced

77 Barton, *ibid* at 20.

78 The law also envisages severe punishments for anyone forcing another to conceal his or her face (a fine of €30,000 and one year of imprisonment; in the case of a minor, a €60,000 fine and two years' imprisonment). *Loi no 2010-1192 du 11 octobre 2010*, JO, 11 October 2010, 18344.

79 The *Conseil constitutionnel* is the highest constitutional authority in France.

80 Cons const, 7 October 2010, 2010-613 DC at para 5.

81 The following are the grounds upon which *SAS* argued that the French ban violated her rights and that the Grand Chamber of the European Court of Human Rights held were admissible: Article 8 (Respect for private life), Article 9 (Freedom of thought conscience and religion; and freedom to manifest one's religion), Article 10 (Freedom of expression) taken separately and together with Article 14 (Prohibition of discrimination): *SAS*, *supra* note 2 at paras 74–75.

that the wearing of niqabs posed a general threat to public safety. On the second argument, the Court held that gender equality could not be invoked by a practice that was explicitly defended by some women as an exercise of their Convention rights. The human dignity argument was also rejected because notions of virtue and decency vary widely when it comes to uncovering the human body and these varied views contribute to pluralism inherent in democracies.[82] That the latter two arguments failed shows some evolving understanding of gender equality and pluralism in the Court's jurisprudence from earlier cases, *Şahin v. Turkey*[83] and *Dahlab v. Switzerland*,[84] where Muslim women were denied the right to wear headscarves in their educational institutions on the grounds that it was contrary to gender equality and incompatible with a tolerant society that respects the rights and freedoms of others.

The Court's acceptance of France's novel argument that the niqab breaches "the right of others to live in a space of socialisation which makes living together easier"[85] has been roundly criticized.[86] Firstly, "living together" is not defined, permitting an extremely broad interpretation that does not allow for the possibility that while some groups may wish to and do live together, others may prefer not to.[87] Deliberately living within one's own cultural community or community of choice must be respected.[88] As the dissent in *SAS* noted, "it can hardly be argued that an individual has a right to enter into contact with other people, in public places, against their will."[89] Second, the assertion that living together becomes "impossible if the full face is not shown" presumes that communication or social interaction requires a visual of the face. Such a perspective is able-ist and disingenuous when one considers the multiple

82 *SAS*, *supra* note 2 at paras 116–121.

83 *Şahin*, *supra* note 25. In *Şahin*, a medical student challenged a Turkish law that banned the wearing of the Islamic headscarf at universities and other educational and state institutions. The European Court of Human Rights upheld the Turkish law. In this case and in *SAS*, the Court has held that the width of the margin of appreciation, or deference to national legislatures, is greater than usual where the relationship between state and religion is at stake. Many have argued that the universal aspirations for the protection of human rights are devalued by the Court's use of the doctrine of margin of appreciation.

84 *Dahlab v. Switzerland*, No. 42393/98 [2001] V ECHR 1. In *Dahlab*, the dismissal of a schoolteacher for wearing a headscarf when teaching was upheld by the European Court of Human Rights.

85 *SAS*, *supra* note 2 para 122.

86 See, for example, Susan S Edwards, "No burqas we're French! The wide margin of appreciation and the ECtHR burqa ruling" (2014) 26 *Denning Law Journal* 246; John Adenitire, "Has the ECHR recognised a legal right to glance at a smile" (2015) 131 *Law Review Quarterly* 43; Daniel Barton, "The ECHR's upholding of the French face-veil ban sets a very worrying precedent for the freedom of religious expression" (24 July 2014), Democratic Audit UK (blog). Online: <http://www.democraticaudit.com/?p=6769>.

87 Edwards, *supra* note 84 at 256.

88 Parekh in Edwards, *ibid* at 257.

89 *SAS*, *supra* note 2, dissent at para 8.

technological advancements that do not require a visual of the face for all sorts of communication. Women in face veils still interact publicly; they just look different doing it.

The Court's reasoning in fact seeks to protect the majority against encounters with the minority on the basis of their subjective feelings of uneasiness with the niqab, where no harm is caused. As the dissent states, the veil "cannot be perceived as aggressive *per se* ... the recurring motives for not tolerating the full-face veil are based on interpretations of its symbolic meaning."[90] The majority essentially endorses the view that women who wear the burqa or niqab are inherently frightening and this value judgment is understood to be compulsory and not something to be unlearned.[91]

The Court's conclusion that the general ban of face veils could be justified on the ground of "living together," which it linked to the protection of the rights and freedoms of others, is a significant legal novelty. The European Convention on Human Rights has a strictly limited list of possible justifications for restricting freedom of religion, and the requirements of "living together" are not listed, nor do they appear in any of the Court's jurisprudence.[92] "Living together" was not only recognized as a legitimate public interest, but a legal right that could be balanced against the applicant's Convention rights.[93] That such a "far-fetched and vague"[94] concept could be used to derogate from freedoms guaranteed in the Convention suggests that the Court was looking for a way to ban face veils publicly, regardless of the reasoning. Indeed, the Court's reasoning encourages a persistent culture of fear promoted by the French Parliament that Muslims who do not look a particular way literally threaten other citizens and, by their mere existence, the social order.

What becomes clear with the justification that the niqab curtails "living together" or, in the words of the Canadian Minister of Immigration, prevents "social cohesion" is that merely making these declarations is enough. No further explanation is required because it is simply well known or taken for granted that covering one's face is necessarily an affront to national values. The majority becomes victimized by the minority's practices, though no evidence of this victimization is provided. Indeed, the fact that the European Convention on Human Rights and the Canadian Charter of Rights and Freedoms are bills of human rights meant to protect minorities from the threat of the tyranny of the majority[95] is ignored. The decision to curb women's choice of clothing reveals a remarkable and unshakable, though unsubstantiated, distrust of Muslims.

90 *Ibid* at para 6.
91 Bakht, *supra* note 12 at 89.
92 *SAS*, *supra* note 2, dissent at para 5; Barton, *supra* note 85.
93 Adenitire, *supra* note 84.
94 *SAS*, *supra* note 2, dissent at para 5.
95 *R v. Big M Drug Mart Ltd*, [1985] 1 SCR 295 at para 96.

That such sweeping and general prohibitions will affect not only the minority's right to religious freedom, but will also impair her right to work, to education, to mobility and to equal protection of the law seems to be of little consequence.[96]

5. RESISTANCE: THE STORIES OF NIQAB-WEARING WOMEN

Perhaps one of the goods gained by these steadfast global controversies regarding the veil has been to finally hear from the women most affected; listening to what they have to say is the next step: "take the time to get to know me, and before you ask me to take [the niqab] off, perchance ask me why I put it on."[97]

In Zunera Ishaq's case, she has eloquently suggested that the niqab is one part of her identity, but also important to comprehend if one were to really know her is that there is more to her than simply the niqab. Ms Ishaq is a 32-year-old mother of five young children who lives in Mississauga, Ontario. She has helped to organize a children's festival, taken part in tree-planting events, helped raise funds for a women's shelter and believes strongly in the right to vote in order to be a fully functioning and engaged member of society.[98] Some of Ishaq's relatives would have like her to just accept the government's policy and get her citizenship while unveiled. She prefers to think for herself. In her words:

> I am not looking for Mr. Harper to approve my life choices or dress. I am certainly not looking for him to speak on my behalf and "save" me from oppression, without ever even having bothered to reach out to me and speak with me ... To me the most important Canadian value is the freedom to be the person of my own choosing. To me, that's more indicative of what it means to be Canadian than what I wear ... And now that Mr. Harper is so busy speaking about me in public, I am looking for him to include me in the discussion.[99]

Opposition to women wearing the niqab has struck an alarmingly popular chord, with polls suggesting that 67% of Canadians agreed with Prime Minister Harper[100] and 82% of the French populace approved of France's burqa ban.[101]

---

96 Amnesty International in *SAS*, *supra* note 2 at para 90.

97 Aysha Luqman-Pandor "My niqab gave me a voice" (19 March 2015). Online: <www.TheTyee.ca>.

98 *Ishaq*, Applicant's Memorandum of Fact and Law, *supra* note 47 at para 9; Zunera Ishaq, "Why I plan to wear a niqab at my citizenship ceremony" *The Toronto Star* (16 March 2015) A11.

99 Ishaq, *ibid.*

100 Andrew Dreschel, "We need more citizens like Zunera Ishaq" *The Hamilton Spectator* (20 March 2015). Online: <https://www.thespec.com/opinion-story/5516517-dreschel-we-need-more-citizens-like-zunera-ishaq/>.

101 Adam Scott Kunz, "Public exposure: Of burqas, secularism, and France's violation of European law" (2012) 44 *George Washington International Law Review* 79 at 80.

The increase in harassment and hate crimes against Muslims generally, but Muslim women in particular,[102] is not surprising but is very troubling. The discriminatory effects of niqab bans include that they increase social isolation, political exclusion and vulnerability to violence and victimization.[103] However, the ubiquitous racist utterances that niqab-wearing women ought to return home[104] have also been met with resistance. One woman retorted: "I know that I'm in Canada, please learn something from me."[105] Others have pointed out that they were in fact born in the countries that have chosen to exclude them. Aysha Luqman-Pandor, a 30-year-old school administrator who has called Canada home since birth, balks at the idea that the niqab does not represent a Canadian identity: "I'm not here to state a ruling on whether the veil is mandatory in my faith or not, I'm here simply to say it is mandatory for me, and I choose to observe it."[106]

The allies of women who wear face veils have also been vocal in their opposition to governmental oppression, including inventing strategies for circumventing niqab prohibitions and mocking politicians for their absurd legislative proclivities. In France, suggestions have been made that niqab-wearers equip themselves with anti-pollution or surgical masks that are exempt from the ban.[107] Moreover, an association was founded with the aim of reimbursing fines imposed on women for wearing a niqab.[108] In Canada, many commentators have delineated the weak legal reasoning behind the citizenship ban.[109] Hundreds of individuals took to Twitter with #DressCodePM to express their consternation with the Prime Minister's comments regarding the dress of Muslim women.[110] These inclusionary assertions of acceptance and support are critical to women

---

102 *SAS*, *supra* note 2 at para 104; Barton, *supra* note 74 at 23; Edwards, *supra* note 84 at 260; Lynda Clarke (2013) "Women in niqab speak: A study of the niqab in Canada," Canadian Council of Muslim Women. Online: <http://ccmw.com/wp-content/uploads/2013/10/WEB_EN_WiNiqab_FINAL.pdf> at v.

103 *Ishaq v. Canada*, "Motion for Leave to Intervene Record of the Barbra Schlifer Commemorative Clinic by Joanna Birenbaum" (27 May 2014), FCA File No. A-124-15 at paras 44–45.

104 *Supra* note 39. See also Ware, *supra* note 62 at 233, describing an incident where a 60-year-old female lawyer ripped a 26-year-old woman's burka off in a clothing shop in France.

105 Clarke, *supra* note 100.

106 Luqman-Pandor, *supra* note 95.

107 Barton, *supra* note 74 at 23.

108 *Ibid.*

109 See, for example, Richard Moon, "The government is sure to lose its appeal in the citizenship oath-niqab case. Maybe that's the point" *The National Post* (17 March 2015); Aaron Wherry, "Larry Miller and the case against the niqab: Parsing the niqab debate" Maclean's Macleans.ca (17 March 2015); Navdeep Bains, "Beware Stephen Harper's crusade against unfamiliar clothing" *The Toronto Star* (24 March 2015).

110 See: <https://twitter.com/search?f=realtime&q=dresscodepm&src=typd>. Some particularly amusing and poignant posts include those by Rob Nickerson: "Need clarification. Does PM Harper need to approve my wife's clothing or can any man do it?" By Canteach: "I am wearing black jeans and a long sleeved black cardigan today. Am I looking oppressed, Mr. Harper?"

who have been increasingly targeted for engaging in public life even as they are demonized for failing to integrate.

I suspect that most people who object to face veils have never actually met and had a conversation with a niqab-wearing woman. Creating a negative image of a group of people is far easier to do when we know nothing about them except what we hear from politicians' intent on fear-mongering. To accept these received ideas of extremism, radicalism, aggression, cruelty and maltreatment[111] about the veil without further questioning is to dehumanize individuals who are complex and who typically just wish to go about their daily lives. Disagreements are to be expected where people from many different walks of life try to live together. But we do a disservice to community relations and discourage dialogue when we succumb to reductive reasoning. Peaceful interactions in our increasingly diverse societies require more of us.

111 Notably, the messages deployed about Muslim women are entirely contradictory. The veiled woman is both threat and threatened. Bakht, *supra* note 26.

SELECT BIBLIOGRAPHY

BOOKS

War Crimes and the Culture of Peace, University of Toronto Press, Toronto, 2002.

CONTRIBUTIONS IN EDITED VOLUMES

'L'inaccessible étoile' in A. CASSESE, P. GAETA and S. ZAPPALÀ (eds.), *The Human Dimension of International Law: Selected Papers of Antonio Cassese*, Oxford University Press, Oxford, 2008.

'Placing Human Rights in the Geneva Consensus' (with S. MAJLESSI) in G.P. SAMPSON (ed.), *WTO and Global Governance: Future Directions*, United Nations University Press, Tokyo-NY-Paris, 2008.

ARTICLES

'The Relationship Between the ICC and the UN Security Council' (2014) 20:2 *Global Governance* 195–201.

'The Pillar of Glass: Human Rights in the Development Operations of the United Nations' (2009) 103:3 *American Journal of International Law* 446–501 (with M. DARROW).

'Without Want of Fear' (2008) 64:8/9 *The World Today* 6–8.

'The Responsibility to Protect as a Duty of Care in International Law and Practice' (2008) 34 *Review of International Studies* 445–458.

'Economic and Social Justice for Societies in Transition' (2007–2008) 40:1 *New York University Journal of International Law and Politics* 1–27.

'Beyond Self-Congratulations: The Charter at 25 in an International Perspective' (2007) 45:2 *Osgoode Hall Law Journal* 239–275 (with F. LAFONTAINE).

'In Our Name and On Our Behalf' (2006) 55 *International and Comparative Law Quarterly* 511–526.

'Legal Professionalism and International Criminal Proceedings' (2006) 4:4 *Journal of International Criminal Justice* 674–685.

'The Crucial Years' (2004) 2:2 *Journal of International Criminal Justice* 396–402.

'Will the ICC Have an Impact on Universal Jurisdiction?' (2003) 1:3 *Journal of International Criminal Justice* 585–588.

'Litigation Before the ICC: Not If and When, But How? (International Criminal Court)' (2001) 40:1 *Columbia Journal of Transnational Law* 1–10.

'The Prosecution of International Crimes: Prospects and Pitfalls' (1999) 1:13 *Washington University Journal of Law and Policy* 13–25.

'The Need for an Independent and Effective Prosecutor in the Permanent International Criminal Court' (1999) 17 *Windsor Yearbook of Access to Justice* 207–220.

REPORTS

'Making Migration Work for All – Report of the Secretary-General' General Assembly, 72nd Session, 12 December 2017 <https://refugeesmigrants.un.org/report-secretary-general-making-migration-work-all-0> accessed 20.09.18.

GLOBAL COMMISSION ON DRUG POLICY. '"On Drugs" – Report of the Global Commission on Drug Policy' June 2011 <http://www.globalcommissionondrugs.org/reports/> accessed 20.09.28.

'Plan of Action Submitted by the United Nations High Commissioner for Human Rights' (summary) (2005) 3:2 *SUR International Journal of Human Rights* 165–167.

'Commission of inquiry into certain events at the Prison for Women in Kingston' (1996) <http://publications.gc.ca/site/eng/9.646174/publication.html> accessed 20.09.18.

SPEECHES

'Women's Rights: Does the Law Matter?' International Conference: Women, Power and Politics – The Road to Sustainable Democracy, Oslo, 14 November 2013 <https://www.crisisgroup.org/global/womens-rights-does-law-matter> accessed 20.09.18.

'Doctrines Derailed?: Internationalism's Uncertain Future' Global Briefing 2013 opening speech, New York, 25 October 2013 <https://www.crisisgroup.org/global/doctrines-derailed-internationalism-s-uncertain-future> accessed 20.09.18.

'Transitional Justice and Colombia's Peace Talks' Universidad Externado de Colombia, Bogotá, 29 August 2013 <https://www.crisisgroup.org/latin-america-caribbean/andes/colombia/speech-transitional-justice-and-colombias-peace-talks> accessed 20.09.18.

'The Rule of Law in a Transitional Democracy' Lahore High Court Bar Association, Lahore, 11 July 2012 <https://www.crisisgroup.org/global/rule-law-transitional-democracy> accessed 20.09.18.

'The Laws of War: Under Siege or Gaining Ground?' Kirby Lecture at the Australian National University, Canberra, 23 June 2011 <https://www.crisisgroup.org/global/laws-war-under-siege-or-gaining-ground> accessed 20.09.18.

'The Rise and Fall of International Human Rights' Sir Joseph Hotung International Human Rights Lecture 2011, London, 27 April 2011 <https://www.crisisgroup.org/global/rise-and-fall-international-human-rights> accessed 20.09.18.

'Self-Determination and Conflict Resolution: From Kosovo to Sudan' Carnegie Council for Ethics in International Affairs, New York, 22 September 2010 <https://www.crisisgroup.org/global/self-determination-and-conflict-resolution-kosovo-sudan> accessed 20.09.18.

'Auschwitz Never Again' Dutch Auschwitz Committee, Royal Tropical Institute, Amsterdam, 27 January 2010 <https://www.crisisgroup.org/global/auschwitz-never-again> accessed 20.09.18.

'L'avenir des opérations de maintien de la paix dans les conflits contemporains' Université de Montréal, Montréal, 7 October 2009 <https://www.crisisgroup.org/fr/global/l-avenir-des-operations-de-maintien-de-la-paix-dans-les-conflits-contemporains> accessed 20.09.28.

'Civil Society and Public Interest Diplomacy' Georgetown University at the 28th Annual Trainor Award for Distinction in the Conduct of Diplomacy, Washington, 30 September 2009 <https://www.crisisgroup.org/global/civil-society-and-public-interest-diplomacy> accessed 20.09.18.

'Freedom From Want – From Charity to Entitlement' LaFontaine-Baldwin Lecture, Toronto, 3 March 2005 <https://newsarchive.ohchr.org/EN/NewsEvents/Pages/DisplayNews.aspx?NewsID=3004&LangID=E> accessed 20.09.18.

'Crimes against Women under International Law' Stefan A. Riesenfeld Symposium, Berkeley, 28 February 2002, published in *Berkeley Journal of International Law* (2003) 21 196–212.

BLOG POSTS

'Managing Migration: Why Leadership Matters' *The Elders*, 22 March 2018 <https://www.theelders.org/article/managing-migration-why-leadership-matters> accessed 20.09.18.

SHULMAN, H. 'Rewriting the Migration Story with Louise Arbour', Podcast, Center for Global Development, 7 June 2018 <https://www.cgdev.org/blog/rewriting-migration-story-louise-arbour-cgd-podcast> accessed 20.09.18.

ON LOUISE ARBOUR

OTTAWA LAW REVIEW. 'An Interview with the Honourable Madam Justice Louise Arbour' (2015) 46:2 *Ottawa Law Review* 383–416.

PLAXTON, M. 'Foucault, Agamben, and Arbour J.'s Dissent in Gosselin' (2008) 21:2 *Canadian Journal of Law & Jurisprudence* 411–428.

RENKE, W. 'Class Rooms, Court Rooms, War Rooms, Cells: Madam Justice Louise Arbour, Canada's Newest Court Justice' (1999) 10:3 *Constitutional Forum* 81–90.

THOMPSON, A. 'Louise Arbour' (2004) 59:3 *International Journal* 681–692.

UNIVERSITY OF TORONTO FACULTY OF LAW REVIEW. 'The Protection of Human Rights Through International Criminal Law – A Conversation with Madam Justice Louise Arbour, Chief Prosecutor for the International Criminal Tribunals for the Former Yugoslavia and Rwanda' (1999) 57:1 *University of Toronto Faculty of Law Review* 83–99.

uOttawa
Faculté de droit
Faculty of Law
Section de common law
Common Law Section

REVUE DE DROIT D'OTTAWA
OTTAWA LAW REVIEW

2014–2015

Volume 46, no 2
Faculté de droit, Section de common law

Volume 46, No 2
Faculty of Law, Common Law Section

An Interview with the Honourable Madam Justice Louise Arbour

L'honorable Louise Arbour a reçu un LL.L. (avec distinction) de l'Université de Montréal en 1970 et est membre des Barreaux du Québec et de l'Ontario. Au cours de sa carriére exceptionnelle, Madame Arbour a occupé différentes fonctions : elle a notamment en- seigné à la Osgoode Hall Law School, œuvré comme juge à trois différents échelons du système judiciaire et été nommée Haut-Commissaire des Nations unies aux droits de l'homme. Plus récemment, Madame Arbour a ajouté la pratique privée au vaste éventail de ses diverses fonctions en se joignant au cabinet juridique Borden Ladner Gervais s.r.l., s.e.n.c.r.l. (BLG) en qualité de juriste en résidence*.

L'équipe de la *Revue de droit d'Ottawa*, composée d'Andrea Kareclas, de Jason Wang, de Julio Paoletti et de Morgan Teeple Hopkins, a rencontré Madame Arbour dans les bureaux de BLG à Montréal au cours de l'automne 2014. Madame Arbour a relaté son par- cours en remontant au tout début de sa formation juridique, elle a généreusement accepté de partager les expériences qu'elle a vécues dans nombre de ses importantes fonctions, en ponctuant son récit de réflexions à propos de différents domaines du droit, et a conclu en nous donnant un aperçu des projets auxquels elle travaille actuellement.

The Honourable Madam Justice Louise Arbour received an LLL (with honours) from the Université de Montréal in 1970 and is a member of both the Québec and Ontario Bars. Over the course of her distinguished career, Louise Arbour has worked in a number of varied positions, including teaching at Osgoode Hall Law School, serving as a judge at three different levels of court and acting as the United Nations High Commissioner for Human Rights. Most recently, Louise Arbour added private practice to her repertoire of diverse positions, joining the law firm Borden Ladner Gervais LLP (BLG) as a jurist in residence.*

The *Ottawa Law Review's* Andrea Kareclas, Jason Wang, Julio Paoletti and Morgan Teeple Hopkins met with Louise Arbour at the Montréal office of BLG in the fall of 2014. Starting right at the beginning of her legal education, Louise Arbour shared her experience in a number of exciting positions, provided her insight on different areas of the law and gave us a glimpse at some of the work she is currently engaged in.

* As a jurist in residence, Louise Arbour mentors younger lawyers and provides strategic advice to BLG's International Trade and Arbitration Group. See Borden Ladner Gervais LLP, "The Honourable Louise Arbour, C.C., G.O.Q.", online: <www.blg.com>.

An Interview with the Honourable Madam Justice Louise Arbour

November 21, 2014

Ottawa Law Review [OLR]: *What initially inspired you to study law?*
Louise Arbour [LA]: Nothing, in short. I was raised here in Montréal and I went to a classical college. In fact, when I started there it was a girls' convent school.[1] So I have a BA with a classical background, and what you did after that, at least what women typically did since I was in an all-girls school until after I finished my BA, was either medicine, law – I don't think anybody ever thought of engineering – and some would do a graduate degree in history or literature and then go and teach. So the avenues were very narrow. I didn't know any lawyers or judges, there were none in my family, and I had no idea what law was really about. But I had eliminated all the other options and so I went into law very much by default, thinking of it as a continuation of my general education with what I thought at the time may lead to a career in either journalism or politics. And then by Christmas of first-year, I knew it was really for me – I thought law was just a perfect fit. And I had done much better in law school than I had done in undergrad. It was a miracle they even accepted me – in those days they were not very discriminating. I was always a good student, but not fabulous, and I was no longer very interested in the girls school environment when I graduated. But law school, no question, it was made for me.

1 Louise Arbour attended Collège Régina Assumpta in Montréal. Collège Régina Assumpta was founded in 1955 as an all-girls school by The Sisters of the Congregation of Notre-Dame. It ceased awarding Bachelor of Arts degrees in 1967. Louise Arbour was a member of the last graduating class. It is now a private secondary school for girls and boys. See Collège Régina Assumpta, "Historique", online: <www2.reginaassumpta.qc.ca>.

OLR: *After law school*[2] *you went on to clerk for Justice Louis-Philippe Pigeon at the Supreme Court of Canada.*[3] *We'd like to hear about your clerking experience, starting with what the hiring process was like for clerks at the time.*
LA: It was actually quite interesting. First of all, I had heard about it from I think a poster in the bar admission course and somebody had told me that a guy named Gérald Tremblay[4] had done it and I think I spoke with him about his experience. I had never been to Ottawa and in fact hadn't had much contact with English Canada in those days. I had been to France a couple of time but never much west of Québec. And I had made applications to do graduate work in a couple of places and somebody said to me, "Well, clerking is like graduate work except it pays, instead of you paying," which was a major attraction. So back then you would send an application to the Chief Justice, not to individual judges, and then you just waited to see if anybody called. And in those days for some peculiar reason, the three Québec judges[5] would only take people who were already called to the bar, while all the other judges from other provinces took students straight out of law school. They had some kind of notion – I think mostly the Chief Justice[6] – that you had to have been sworn to the bar or something, I don't know. So I applied after I finished my bar admission course and I received a call from Justice Pigeon. So I borrowed a car and, I'll never forget, I drove to Ottawa and I thought "no way," I hadn't given it very serious thought as I had a couple of acceptances for graduate work. So I drove there, I got to the court and nobody spoke French – so I didn't think that was looking too good. And then when I got to the interview with Justice Pigeon, he spoke to me entirely in French, and only at the end I think he said something like, "How is your English?," and I said, "Good," which was *not* the truth. And then he said, "Well I'd like to offer you the position." So I said to him, "Well I have to think about it." And he was not pleased. He said, "Well you applied" and I said, "Yes – but," and he interrupts

2 Louise Arbour attended the Faculté de droit, Université de Montréal from 1967 to 1970, and graduated with an LLL (with distinction). See Supreme Court of Canada, "The Honourable Madam Justice Louise Arbour", online: <www.scc-csc.gc.ca> [Supreme Court of Canada Biography, Justice Arbour].

3 Louise Arbour clerked at the Supreme Court of Canada from 1971 to 1972 *(ibid)*.

4 Gérald R. Tremblay is now a partner at McCarthy Tétrault LLP in their Litigation Group in Montréal. Mr. Tremblay was a law clerk at the Supreme Court of Canada from 1967 to 1969. See McCarthy Tétrault LLP, "Gérald R. Tremblay", online: <www.mccarthy.ca>.

5 The Supreme Court of Canada is composed of the Chief Justice and eight puisne judges. Under the *Supreme Court Act*, RSC 1895, c S-26, three of the nine judges must be from Québec. By either convention or established practice, the remaining six are divided between Ontario (3), British Columbia (1), Alberta/Saskatchewan/Manitoba (1) and the Maritime Provinces (1). See Adam Dodek, *The Canadian Constitution* (Toronto: Dundurn Press, 2013) at 122.

6 The Right Honourable Joseph Honoré Gérald Fauteux was named Chief Justice of Canada on March 23, 1970. He served on the Supreme Court for 24 years and retired on December 23, 1973. See Supreme Court of Canada, "The Right Honourable Joseph Honoré Gérald Fauteux, P.C., C.C.", online: <www.scc-csc.gc.ca>.

and said, "You thought you never had a chance." And I said, "Well, yes that's true." And then he made his first mistake – he said, "Because you're a woman." And I thought oh man he hasn't figured out I don't really speak English! And then he went on and explained to me at length that he had been instrumental in the reform of the Québec Civil Code[7] dealing with the status of married women and that given equal competencies he would always give a chance to a woman. I thought this was so cool. I said, "Okay then I'll come." So there I went.

OLR: *Can you describe your experience clerking at the Supreme Court of Canada?*
LA: It was fantastic. First of all, there were just nine of us and we were in this room – in those days just in front of the library – and it had on top of the door that led to the library nine Christmas-like lights, and when your judge wanted you, your light went on. So we'd all be in the same room with a big black telephone and sometimes you'd be reading something and someone would say, "Hey, Louise – *ta lumière est allumée*," and you'd have to put your jacket on and rush down to see the judge. Now you have to imagine, in those days, there was an automatic right of appeal for all cases over just $10,000.[8] So there were very few motions for leave to appeal, because virtually everything was appealable as of right, although there were still some things that you needed leave for. So, there was a little courtroom – it's now the judges' dining room – for the motions that were argued on I think Monday morning, and the caseload was huge, with a significant backlog. The list went from Ontario, Maritimes, West and so on, and we never got beyond the backlog. So you had to fish out the good cases out of this massive non-descript pile. Justice Pigeon, when he interviewed me, asked me what areas of law interested me and I told him criminal law, administrative law, constitutional law – all public law. And he said, "Well that's very interesting because I will not require your services in these areas because since you're interested I take it you will keep up your interest." He said, "You have to understand you're not here to help me, I'm here to help you continue your education, and therefore, I will try to develop your skills in other fields." So the first case he gave me was under the *Canada Shipping Act*,[9] which of course I didn't find very interesting. Oh, and we would do memos handwritten, typed by a legal secretary, with a carbon copy – oh my god – it was quite antique!

---

7 The Honourable Mr. Justice Louis-Philippe Pigeon was a Law Clerk of the Québec Legislature from 1940 to 1944. He also acted as legal adviser to the Premier of Québec, Jean Lesage, from 1960 to 1966. See Supreme Court of Canada, "The Honourable Mr. Justice Louis-Philippe Pigeon", online: <www.scc-csc.gc.ca>.

8 *Supreme Court Act*, RSC 1970, V-vii (1st Supp), c S-19, s 36(a), as it appeared in 1971 [*Supreme Court Act*, 1970].

9 Today, the *Canada Shipping Act, 2001*, is the principal legislation governing safety in marine transportation and recreational boating, as well as protection of the marine environment. It applies to Canadian vessels operating in Canadian waters, including canoes, kayaks, cruise ships and tankers. See *Canada Shipping Act, 2001*, RSC 2001, c 26; Transport Canada, *Canada Shipping Act, 2001 (CSA 2001)*, "Frequently Asked Questions", online: <www.tc.gc.ca>.

OLR: *Did you always agree with Justice Pigeon's decisions?*
LA: Almost never. And he didn't seem to care. And he was not very keen to discuss. I would write him something with my opinion, certainly in criminal cases, all the areas that I liked, and, under the *Canadian Bill of Rights,*[10] he had a very conservative interpretation. Fortunately, Justice Bora Laskin[11] was there. He was a junior judge at the time, so I liked him. Justice Pigeon was a wonderful man and I remained in touch with him subsequently, but in terms of the substance of the work, our opinions would often differ. I remember one day there was an appeal that I worked on and I sent him a note and I said, "I don't think the court has jurisdiction," because it was an insurance claim and there were 12 individual claimants, each one of whom who had a claim under the $10,000 limit, so collectively, the case looked like a $60,000. So I wrote to him and I said, "I looked at the *Supreme Court Act*,[12] and I'm really concerned that there's no jurisdiction here, they should have asked for leave." And I was very keen to see what he would say, so I asked him, "So what do you think?" And he just sort of smiled and didn't say anything. So he goes into court, I'm in the courtroom, the appellant stands up, and before the appellant can open his mouth, Justice Pigeon – who was feared by all litigants, he had a formidable voice – said, "Counsel, can you explain to me on what basis we have jurisdiction?" And the guy had no idea what he was talking about, and I kept thinking, "Just tell him you're going to ask for leave!" And so the appellant was devastated and I think Justice Pigeon dismissed the whole thing. And so afterwards I went to go see him and I said, "Had you noticed that yourself or …?" and he wouldn't tell me, which I thought was very mean.

OLR: *Do you think Justice Pigeon influenced you as judge?*[13]
LA: Well it's difficult to say whether it was Justice Pigeon or just being at the court. For me, the whole clerking experience was a very big thing. First of all, I worked in French with Justice Pigeon but the entire environment was English and it was the first time in my life that I really had to work in English. And, during that year, I also did my Master's courses at the University of Ottawa. I never wrote the thesis, but I took five courses at night during that year, because when I moved there I thought, "I don't know anybody in Ottawa and I won't have

10 *Canadian Bill of Rights*, SC 1960, c 44, reprinted in RSC 1985, App III.

11 The Right Honourable Bora Laskin was appointed to the Supreme Court of Canada on March 19, 1970. He was named Chief Justice of Canada on December 27, 1973 and served on the Supreme Court of Canada for 14 years. See Supreme Court of Canada, "The Right Honourable Bora Laskin, P.C., C.C.", online: <www.scc-csc.gc.ca>.

12 See *Supreme Court Act*, 1970, *supra* note 9.

13 Louise Arbour was appointed to the Supreme Court of Ontario (High Court of Justice) in 1987. She was then appointed to the Court of Appeal for Ontario in 1990 and then to the Supreme Court of Canada in 1999. See Supreme Court of Canada Biography, Justice Arbour, *supra* note 3.

anything to do," looking back I don't know what I was thinking. But, anyway, I was very busy, and the whole year was very important for me, so it's hard to tell how much of that was Justice Pigeon. Justice Pigeon was a very, very rigorous man. His great specialty was statutory interpretation, on which he wrote what was then the reference book. I didn't know that area of law very well, so he drew me into that. And Justice Pigeon was very patient with me. When he decided I had to learn something, he would walk me into the library and show me. It was a great experience – scary – but great.

OLR: *What were your fellow law clerks like? Were there many women?*
LA: There was one other woman, she was also from Québec, but we didn't see very much of her. She was married and I didn't know her very well. As for the others, one of them became the father of my children – so I knew him quite well. He's no longer a part of my life, but he was for 30 years and that in fact triggered my staying in Ontario, teaching at Osgoode and so forth. And I've stayed in touch with several other people I clerked with. When we have law clerk reunions, I see them and, although there are a few with whom I've lost contact, it was a fantastic group; we were all very close. I remember at lunchtime the only place to eat near the Court was the basement at some place I think on Sparks Street. It was a pool hall, it was very big, and it had some 20 billiard tables. The guy who owned it was a great big guy, retired football player, and the clerks always went there, and I would go with them. At the beginning I just sat there – and then one day the owner said to me, "If you come Saturday mornings, I'll teach you how to play." And I did. And I played pool quite competently that year and subsequently.

OLR: *Were there any other reasons you decided to stay in Ontario instead of your home province of Québec?*
LA: Not really, no. Since there were only nine law clerks every year or so, it was a small pool of candidates and the Deans from different law schools would come to the court and try to recruit. The year I was clerking, Harry Arthurs,[14] who was the Dean of Osgoode Hall Law School, asked me to teach and I told him I didn't think I could teach in English at the time. And I didn't right away. I stayed in Ottawa for one year after I clerked. Tony Lamer,[15] who had taught me criminal law and was then the Vice-Chairman of the Law Reform Commission

[14] Harry Arthurs was the Dean of Osgoode Hall Law School from 1972 to 1977 and President of York University from 1985 to 1992. He is a distinguished academic, arbitrator and mediator in labour disputes. See Osgoode Hall Law School, "Harry Arthurs", online: <www.osgoode.yorku.ca>.

[15] Antonio Lamer was appointed Vice-Chairman of the Law Reform Commission of Canada in 1971 and then Chairman of the Commission in 1976. Four years later, he was appointed to the Supreme Court of Canada and became the Chief Justice in 1990. See Supreme Court of Canada, "The Right Honourable Antonio Lamer, P.C., C.C., C.D.", online: <www.scc-csc.gc.ca>.

of Canada, had asked me to come work for the Commission, which was then a full-fledged big enterprise.[16]Another one of my criminal law professors was also there, Jacques Fortin,[17] lots of people – Neil Brooks[18] and so on – so it was a really good place. And so I stayed in Ottawa after the Court for one year and my English got better. And then I moved to Toronto and started teaching, one year part-time and then I got a full time tenure – track appointment at Osgoode Hall Law School.[19]

OLR: *While you were teaching at Osgoode Hall Law School, you were offered a judicial appointment. Can you tell us about the day you received the offer? How did it unfold?*
LA: *Oh mon Dieu*! Well, first of all, in those days you didn't apply. And so I was called to the Bar in Québec in 1971, and then when I started teaching at Osgoode, I got a letter one day from the Law Society[20] saying, "As a tenure-track law professor in Ontario, after two years you're entitled to an academic call to the Bar." And I thought, "I can't practice law here," I thought, "I still don't know about my English and so on." And so then this friend of mine said to me, "You have to go, this is ridiculous. They're giving it to you, you don't even have to write anything; you're going to be a member of the Law Society of Upper Canada. Just go." And I remember, in fact, the call to the Bar in Ontario, because I was pregnant, so I had to borrow a robe, or some gown or something. So anyway, I went and I was called to the Bar and then I carried on teaching. And then

16 The Law Reform Commission of Canada was initially created in 1971 to recommend the improvement, modernization and reform of federal laws. The federal government disbanded the commission in 1993 in an attempt to reduce spending and the federal deficit. The Commission was re-established in 1997 with the objective of keeping federal laws relevant to the changing times. The Commission developed research programs, engaged in public consultation and produced reports to Parliament on recommended law reforms. Although the Commission was permanently disbanded in 2006, law reform commissions continue to exist at the provincial level. See Patricia G Bailey, "Law Reform Commission of Canada" (30 March 2009), online: The Canadian Encyclopedia <www.thecanadianencyclopedia.ca>.

17 Jacques Fortin taught criminal law, criminal procedure and criminal evidence at the Faculté de droit, Université de Montréal. He played a significant role in the work of the Law Reform Commission of Canada and was the Commission's Vice-President when he died in 1985. See Patrick Fitzgerald, ed, *Crime, Justice & Codification: Essays in Commemoration of Jacques Fortin* (Toronto: Carswell, 1986) at vii.

18 Neil Brooks was a Research Officer with the Law Reform Commission of Canada from 1971 to 1973. He is currently the Director of the Graduate Program in Taxation at Osgoode Hall Law School and has taught tax law and policy for over 35 years. See Osgoode Hall Law School, "Neil Brooks", online: <www.osgoode.yorku.ca>.

19 Louise Arbour was a law professor at Osgoode Hall Law School from 1974 to 1987. She and Mary Jane Mossman became the first women to teach as full-time faculty members in the 1976–1977 school year. See Osgoode Hall Law School, "History: 1976" online: <www.osgoode.yorku.ca>.

20 The Law Society of Upper Canada governs the admission of lawyers to the Bar in Ontario. See The Law Society of Upper Canada, "About the Law Society", online: <www.lsuc.on.ca>.

I became the Associate Dean at Osgoode,[21] and every day I would come back to my office with a pile of messages. One day I had a message from someone from Ottawa I didn't know, with no details, and it took me several days to return his call. When I finally, did I said, "Sorry it took so long to get back to you, but it didn't seem urgent, you called me …" And the guy on the phone said, "You obviously have no idea who I am," and I said, "Actually, no." And he said, "I'm the Appointment Secretary to the Minister of Justice, usually people return my call within 10 seconds of my leaving a message!" *[Oh!]* So then he asked me, "Would you consider a judicial appointment? Contrary to what is usually the case with academics, we are thinking of the trial court." [*Gasp*] I had never practiced, and then he said, "We need to clarify one thing: can you confirm the date that you were called to the Bar in Ontario?" I think at the time you had to have been called to the Bar for at least 10 years before you could be a judge in Ontario.[22] So of course I thought, "Oh man, did I make a good move that time." It was 10 years and 1 month, basically. So he said, "That's what we have in our records, we just wanted to be sure. So, we'll let you know, we just want …" – and then I told him, "Listen, I'm teaching, so you cannot appoint me at just any time. This is something I would consider, but it would have to be, either in the summer or between terms. I cannot drop everything midterm." This was in October, I think. And then, when I was supervising my Evidence exam in December – 14th or 16th – my secretary came to the room and she said, "You've just been appointed to the bench" [*Laughs*] Yeah, and then it was done. I mean, when they move, it's done – there's nothing to negotiate and then you have to drop everything. So I had to quit teaching and resign from the Canadian Civil Liberties Association and become a trial judge, which was a big step.

OLR: *How did you manage the transition from being a law professor to a judge, especially considering you had never practiced law before?*
LA: Well, because God is a very kind person. I had volunteered just out of the kindness of my heart the semester I was appointed to teach civil procedure because the Dean was a bit short. And I had taught Criminal Law, Evidence, Criminal Procedure – even some Comparative Law. But Civil Procedure, I had

21 Louise Arbour became the Associate Dean of Osgoode Hall Law School in 1987. See Supreme Court of Canada Biography, Justice Arbour, *supra* note 3.

22 Today, the 10 year call to the bar requirement is still in place for judicial appointments in Ontario. The minimum requirement to apply to be a judge in the Ontario Court of Justice is 10 complete years at the Bar of one of the Provinces or Territories of Canada. To be considered a candidate for a judicial appointment to the Superior Court of Justice, an individual must be a lawyer who has practiced law for at least 10 years. See Ontario Court of Justice, "Judicial Appointments Advisory Committee: Frequently Asked Questions", online: <www.ontariocourts.ca/ocj>; Superior Court of Justice, "About Judges & Judicial Officials", online: <www.ontariocourts.ca/scj>.

never taught that. But the Dean was short for people and I thought, "Well, I'm interested in comparative procedural systems so I'll do it." [*Sigh*] Obviously to teach it, I had to learn it – and I needed to learn it in Ontario in particular because I don't have a common law degree, I have a civil law degree. So at least I figured out *before* my appointment the mechanics of the whole process and costs and all these things that I had long forgotten (I must have taken it in Québec in the Bar Admission Course, but that was a long time ago). So, fortunately, I knew something about it, and I knew *a lot* about Evidence, which unfortunately didn't seem to play very much in the day-to-day – particularly in civil litigation – it doesn't play a very big role ... Now I should say, I've had lots of jobs for which I was completely unqualified, there's no question about it. That's not to suggest that I didn't do well, I think that I did perfectly well, but on paper, every step of the way, I did something – I clerked without speaking English, I started teaching law without, again, not being very good in English, and not having a common law degree. So, I think right from the beginning, I did things that were very challenging. This was [*laughs*] at that point, probably the biggest step, but I only stayed on the trial court two years, and then I went to the Court of Appeal, which is too bad – you know, you can't turn it down – but I would have liked to stay maybe five or six years because I did a lot of things only *once* as a trial judge and then I'd always think, "Oh, if I could just get another wrongful dismissal – I would know how it works!" But then I never got another one. I got lots of new things all the time.

OLR: *Are there any memorable trials or cases that really stand out to you from your time as a trial judge?*
LA: I remember more of my cases in these two years than of all the cases I've had in the Supreme Court of Canada. First of all, because, in some cases, they take longer and you have real people in front of you, so it's like remembering a movie, or something. In the Supreme Court, sometimes I go back and I read something I've written but, if my name was not on it, I'm not sure I would recognize it. I vaguely remember but I can't tell if it's something I've read – maybe an article – and if you just took my name and took the context out, I'd have trouble remembering it. But the things I did as a trial judge – and I was only there two years – I remember. For example, after just five months of being a trial judge, the Chief Justice[23] sent me on a special assignment. He sent me to Windsor, Ontario, on a trial to determine the ownership of the tunnel between Windsor and Detroit. God. [*Laughs*] It was a very big case, which unfortunately only took a few days in court, and then I went back home with about sixty boxes of documents. [*Laughs*] I thought I was going to drown trying to master that case! This one

23 William Dirkens Parker was the Chief Justice of the High Court of Justice from 1985 to 1989. See Ontario Courts, "Former Judges of the Superior Courts", online: <www.ontariocourts.ca>. [Ontario Courts, "Former Judges"].

I remember very well, even though there was not a lot of court time and it was appealed all the way to the Supreme Court.[24] Then I had a very large motor vehicle accident case that I remember very well.[25] It took about thirteen weeks. I remember the people in it; I remember the witnesses. And then I remember the counsel who appeared before me during my trial work much more than the people who have appeared before me on bigger issues on appeal subsequently. It was really, very interesting work.

OLR: *Moving from your time as a trial judge, we'd like to hear about your experience at the Ontario Court of Appeal. Who were some of your colleagues at the time?*
LA: I remember every one of them. But first of all I should tell you, and you may find it strange when I say it, a lot of people don't believe me, but I think it was the best job I've ever had. I've had other jobs that were much more exciting, but for me it was the absolute perfect mix of intellectual challenge, volume of work and space for a collegial, and I would say pretty stress-free, environment. I think it's more stressful to be a trial judge. Anyway, it was a dream – an absolute dream job, I really had a wonderful time. And my colleagues were splendid – all of them. Charles Dubin was the Chief Justice at the time.[26] He was fantastic – very smart, very funny, very engaged, very supportive of me – including when I talked to him about going to prosecute war criminals in The Hague. He never blinked. He also encouraged me to take the Commission of Inquiry in the Prison for Women. Allan Goodman,[27] David Doherty,[28] Coulter Osborne,[29] Jean-Marc Labrosse[30]

---

24 *Windsor (City) v Detroit and Windsor Subway Co* (1988), 66 OR (2d) 353, 3 RPR (2d) 152 (H Ct J), aff'd (1990), 12 RPR (2d) 244, 50 MPLR 225; *Detroit & Windsor Subway Co v Windsor (City)* (1989), 69 OR (2d) 665, 6 RPR (2d) 201 (H Ct J), rev'd (1990), 74 OR (2d) 626, 12 RPR (2d) 240 (Div Ct), aff'd (1995), 26 OR (3d) 737, 87 OAC 187 (CA), leave to appeal to SCC refused, 25149 (26 September 1996).

25 See *Andani Estate v Peel (Regional Municipality)* (1989), 15 ACWS (3d) 99, 1989 CarswellOnt 1646 (WL Can) (H Ct J).

26 Charles Dubin was appointed to the Court of Appeal for Ontario in 1973 and was Chief Justice from 1990 to 1996. See The Law Society of Upper Canada, "In Memoriam: Charles L. Dubin, O.C., O. Ont., Q.C., 1921–2008" *Ontario Lawyers Gazette* (2008) 48, online: <www.lsuc.on.ca/media/olg_winter08_in_memoriam.pdf>.

27 Allan Goodman served on the Court of Appeal for Ontario from 1979 to 1996. See Christopher Moore, *The Court of Appeal for Ontario: Defining the Right of Appeal in Canada, 1792–2013* (Toronto, University of Toronto Press, 2014) at 231.

28 David H. Doherty was appointed to the Court of Appeal for Ontario in September, 1990, and is still at the Court today. See Court of Appeal for Ontario, "Brief Biographical Note of Justice David H. Doherty", online: <www.ontariocourts.ca>.

29 Coulter A. Osborne was appointed to the Court of Appeal for Ontario in 1990 and in 1999 to the position of Associate Chief Justice. Since retiring from the bench in 2001, Mr. Osborne has been engaged in alternative dispute resolution on corporate and commercial matters. See Arbitration Place, "The Honourable Coulter A. Osborne", online: <www.arbitrationplace.com>.

30 Jean-Marc Labrosse was appointed to the Court of Appeal for Ontario in 1990. See Ontario Courts, "Former Judges", *supra* note 24.

and Marc Rosenberg[31] were some of my colleagues, along with older judges and people who came on the court around the same time I did. They were all terrific colleagues and friends with whom I'm still very friendly. Hilda McKinlay[32] was also at the Court of Appeal. She was the second woman appointed to the Ontario Court of Appeal after Bertha Wilson,[33] and I was the third. And Hilda was great. She had been mostly a commercial lawyer – very good company, good friend. It was a very collegial court – very strong both in Criminal Law and Commercial Law. It had a terrific reputation. Sid Robins[34] too, just wonderful people. I could go down the list one by one – it was always a pleasure to work with all of them.

OLR: *What types of cases did you enjoy the most during your time at the Ontario Court of Appeal?*
LA: Everything. It, again, was a very big surprise for me because my background was very much in criminal law and I didn't even have a formal background in common law, I enjoyed it all, including the private law matters. Today it's the same thing. The minute you put something in front of me, I read two paragraphs and I think, "Now wait a minute, that's interesting. How does it work?" [*Laughs*] And the next thing you know, I'm in it. And so I liked a lot of things. Of course, I think I had more to contribute in the fields in which I had a deeper academic understanding – so evidence, criminal law, constitutional issues – but there was nothing I didn't like.

OLR: *Were there any specific cases that really stood out for you at your time at the Court of Appeal?*
LA: There are several. Maybe the one … well I should say first, I think it's very difficult to talk about cases. I think it is bad form for judges to talk about their decisions, but there is this one case that stands out for me, and what I will tell you is on the record. It's called *Eaton v Brant County Board of Education.*[35] The issue was the question of the integration of a severely disabled child into a mainstream public classroom. There was a young child, about 10-years old at the time who

31 Justice Marc Rosenberg was appointed to the Court of Appeal for Ontario in December, 1995, and is still at the Court today. See Court of Appeal for Ontario, "Brief Biographical Note of Justice Marc Rosenberg", online: <www.ontariocourts.ca>.

32 Hilda M. McKinlay served on the Court of Appeal for Ontario from 1987 to 1999. She was honoured by Osgoode Hall Law School with The Award of Excellence in 2003 and is a member of ADR Chambers, a Toronto-based alternative dispute resolution group. See York Media Relations, "Three Distinguished Alumni to Receive Osgoode Award of Excellence" (17 February 2003), online: York University <news.yorku.ca>.

33 Bertha Wilson was appointed to the Ontario Court of Appeal in 1975. She was also the first woman to be appointed to the Supreme Court of Canada in 1982. See Dodek, *supra* note 6 at 130.

34 Sydney Lewis Robins served on the Court of Appeal for Ontario from 1981 to 1998. See The Law Society of Upper Canada, "In Memoriam: Sydney L. Robins, O. Ont, QC, 1923–2014" (13 January 2014), online: <www.lawsocietygazette.ca>.

35 22 OR (3d) 1, 123 DLR (4th) 43 (CA).

had very severe cerebral palsy with no known means of communications, and the Board said that she had to be in a special education classroom with other children with special needs, and her parents insisted that she should be in the general population. Basically, in other words, as I use the expression, not segregated. And I reversed the Board's decision – and my two colleagues agreed with me.[36] I felt very strongly that as a matter of constitutional right basically, the burden was on those who wanted to exclude or segregate the child to make the case. That's the way to approach it, as a matter of law. The decision was then reversed by the Supreme Court of Canada, 9-0 from the Bench.[37] That's in part why I remember it!

OLR: *During your time at the Ontario Court of Appeal, you led the Commission of Inquiry into Certain Events at the Prison for Women in Kingston.*[38] *Is there anything in particular that really stands out to you from that experience?*
LA: There are many things. The first one, which I think is very explicit in my report, is, even for someone like me, who had worked in criminal law most of my career, it just made me realize how the correctional part of it – everything that happens post-sentence is – *occulté* – it's completely obscured in the system. It actually reminded me of how the law was, when I was in law school, about police powers. The incidents didn't happen in court, but the only criminal law part that you saw was the court part; what happened before and after you didn't see. Now, over the decades, we've put a lot of spotlights on investigative powers, supervision of police powers, and the *Charter* required a lot of that. But then when I arrived in this correctional environment, I realized, "This is surreal. I've worked all my life in this field and I know virtually nothing about this environment." So in my report I called for a lot more transparency, openness and judicial oversight. So that was the first thing. The second thing is that it was the first time that I worked on an issue very intensely and in a very concrete way that was totally

---

36 Justice James Joseph Carthy and Justice Jean-Marc Labrosse presided over the case with Louise Arbour.

37 The Supreme Court of Canada held that the decision of the Ontario Special Education Tribunal, which confirmed the child's placement in a special education class contrary to the wishes of her parents, did not contravene the equality provisions of section 15 of the *Charter*. The Court concluded that the Tribunal based its decision on what was in the best interests of the child and therefore no violation of section 15 occurred. The Court refused to consider the issue of the validity of section 8 of the *Education Act*, RSO 1990, c E.2, which authorized the Tribunal to proceed as it did, on the basis that no notice of a constitutional question had been given in accordance with section 109 of the *Courts of Justice Act*. See *Eaton v Brant (County) Board of Education*, [1997] 1 SCR 241, 31 OR (3d) 574.

38 Louise Arbour was appointed Commissioner "to investigate and report on the state and management of that part of the business of the Correctional Service of Canada that pertains to the incidents that occurred at the Prison for Women in Kingston, Ontario, beginning on April 22, 1994." See Canada, Public Works and Government Services Canada, *Commission of Inquiry into Certain Events at the Prison for Women in Kingston* (Ottawa: Public Works and Government Services Canada, 1995) at 2.

gender-specific. It was a women's issue which was, again, very interesting for me, and it's very acute; in this kind of environment – it raises all kinds of questions about the suitability of having, for example, male correctional officers in women's prisons, all these things. And thirdly, it was my first encounter with the specificity of Aboriginal peoples who, across the system, are disproportionately represented in the correctional system and were so in my inquiry.[39] I think of the eight principal women involved, five or six were Aboriginal women. So, for me it was an opening to all kinds of really interesting insights.

OLR: *Also during your time at the Ontario Court of Appeal, you were part of the five-judge panel that confirmed the acquittal of Imre Finta in Canada's first trial of an alleged war criminal.*[40] *Did that experience inform your role as the chief prosecutor for the International Criminal Tribunals for the formerYugoslavia and Rwanda?*

LA: Well, first of all, until the creation of these tribunals, international criminal law did not really exist – I mean, since Nuremburg and Tokyo, there hadn't been any other enforcement of international humanitarian law and the Geneva and Genocide Convention.[41] So when I heard about the creation of these tribunals, I thought, "That has to be the answer," because at least in this country, where there's a constitutional right to a jury trial for serious offenses, domestic criminal law was never developed to go that far back in history. But the tribunals were meant to be contemporaneous to the offences, give-or-take a few years, so you're not reaching back. But, domestic criminal law, at least certainly in common law systems, has been unsuccessful in prosecuting war criminals, particularly when reaching back over long periods of time. For example, all efforts to prosecute Nazi war criminals had been, for the most part, unsuccessful in Australia, in the UK, in Canada. It's been a little bit more successful in civil law jurisdictions such as France – but even here, the rules of evidence, the burden of proof, the methods

39 See e.g. Statistics Canada, *The Incarceration of Aboriginal People in Adult Correctional Services*, vol 29, No 3 by Samuel Perreault (Ottawa: Statistics Canada, July 2009) at 9 (in 2007/2008, aboriginal adults accounted for 17 percent of adults admitted to remand, 18 percent admitted to provincial and territorial custody, 16 percent admitted to probation and 19 percent admitted to a conditional sentence – yet only 3.1 percent of adults over the age of 18 identified themselves as Aboriginal in the 2006 Census).

40 See *R v Finta* (1992), 92 DLR (4th) 1, 73 CCC (3d) 65 (Ont CA). The majority of the Court held that the trial judge was correct in holding that it was the jury and not the trial judge that was required to determine whether the respondent's acts violated the *Criminal Code*, RSC 1985, c C-46, and whether they amounted to war crimes or crimes against humanity.

41 The United Nations Security Council established the International Criminal Tribunals for the former Yugoslavia and Rwanda in May 1993 and November 1994 in order to bring to trial those persons responsible for violations of international humanitarian law (and human rights) before an international jurisdiction. These two tribunals were the first international judicial bodies to be given the responsibility of trying war criminals since the Nuremberg and Tokyo Trials in 1945. See Track Impunity Always, "The International Criminal Tribunal for Rwanda", online: <www.trial-ch.org>.

of introducing evidence, relying a lot on, for instance, eye-witness identification and so on, are just not geared to reaching way, way back in history. In fact, in a lot of places you have statutes of limitations in criminal cases. We don't, but we rarely have to go back, you know, 30 to 40 years. So, the strain on the jury system, I think, meant that the chances of successful historical prosecutions in common law countries were probably not very good, so the creation of these international venues had a better chance in the long run of being contemporaneous, which I thought, was very exciting.

OLR: *How were you appointed to the position of Chief Prosecutor for the International Criminal Tribunals for the formerYugoslavia and Rwanda?*
LA: Well like for most of my positions, I didn't apply! That just shows you what a different generation we are. In my day, for a lot of things you didn't apply. And it's not very helpful when I talk to students for example and all I can say is, "Well, you know, the phone rang." So again here, the way it started was with a phone call from a Canadian judge, whom at that point I had never met, from another province, and he told me that he had agreed to go to a conference in South Africa, but he couldn't go and he asked me if I would replace him. And I had never been to Africa. And I said to him, "I thought we had sanctions against South Africa?" He said, "Yes, but on this one, the government is very keen, it's to start talking to judges and lawyers about the new South Africa when the Apartheid regime will collapse" – it hadn't collapsed then, this was in, I think probably 1990.[42] So I went and I met Richard Goldstone[43] at that conference, who became the first prosecutor of these international tribunals. I was then invited to go back the following year to give a keynote address at the annual meeting of the Bar, I think in Durban. So I went and I met Richard again. And then, a year or so later, he was a judge at the Constitutional Court of South Africa, and I found out, just in the newspaper or something, that he's been appointed the prosecutor for these war crimes in Yugoslavia. And I thought, "That's amazing!" I didn't even know they had started these tribunals. And then he called me and said that he and his wife were coming to Ottawa for a visit, and they'd come to Toronto. We had dinner,

42 In 1990, Nelson Mandela was released from prison after 27 years and began to lead the negotiations with President Frederik Willem de Klerk to end apartheid. In 1994, a new constitution that enfranchised black South Africans and other racial groups took effect and elections that year led to a coalition government with a nonwhite majority, marking the official end of the apartheid system. See A+E Networks Digital, "Apartheid", online: History Canada <www.history.ca>.

43 Justice Richard Goldstone served as Chief Prosecutor of the United Nations International Criminal Tribunals for the former Yugoslavia and Rwanda from August 1994 to September 1996. He was a justice at the Constitutional Court of South Africa from 1994 to 2003. See The Codification Division of the United Nations Office of Legal Affairs, "Justice Richard Goldstone", online: The United Nations Audiovisual Library of International Law <legal.un.org/avl/pdf/ls/Goldstone_bio.pdf>.

and I told him, "This is amazing! Tell me about these war crime tribunals, it's so exciting" and he said "Yeah, but I can't stay. I have to go back. The Constitutional Court has lots of big cases coming up – death penalty, constitutionality of death penalty, and so on. I have to go back." He had been there for about a year, year and a half. And he said, "The Secretary General has asked me for names for my replacements." In the meantime, he had inherited the Tribunal for Rwanda, so they were looking at bilingual people preferably because Rwanda was mostly French. He said, "I'd like to give your name." [*Laughs*] I said, "You're crazy! I mean I'd never set foot in the UN, I don't know anybody in Canada in foreign affairs. I've never worked internationally. But international criminal law? This is ... wow." So I said, "Give my name," absolutely persuaded this would never go anywhere. And I was in the middle of my Commission on the Prison for Women. And then, a month or so later, I got a call from the Canadian Ambassador to the UN, who said "the Secretary General would like to speak to you, he asked me to reach out to you. Can you take his call at four o'clock today?" I said, "Yes." He said, "Do you know why the Secretary General wants to talk to you?" I said, "You should know, you're the Ambassador, you're sitting there." I said, "Well I have an idea." I thought this had to be it. When I spoke to the SG, I said, "Well, you know, I'm a judge in Canada – I would have to know what the Government of Canada thinks of that." And he said, "Well actually, I've just spoken to your Prime Minister, and he's very keen."

OLR: *Was it complicated to amend the Judges Act*[44] *to allow you, as a sitting judge, to hold another paid function?*
LA: It was very complicated. At first I didn't know how it would work. I was on a leave of absence with pay to do the Commission of Inquiry – so I knew how that worked because when I took that on, they explained to me: you know you just keep drawing your salary, you work for the Government of Canada – it's fine. This one, I wasn't too sure until it became perfectly clear that I couldn't do it under the existing circumstances. And so something needed to be done because I was not prepared to resign because I had no idea whether this thing was for real. Richard Goldstone had stayed only a year and a half, even though it was a four-year appointment, renewable once. So, of course, I didn't think I'd be able to come back after eight years to the Court of Appeal and just sit like I'd never left – but, on the other hand, there was no guarantee that I'd even stay six months. I had no idea. I just remember thinking, "Is this serious? Is this credible? Is this workable?" So the government amended the *Judges Act*.

44 *Judges Act*, RSC 1985, c J-1.

OLR: *Did you know that section 56.1*[45] *of the Judges Act is still in force?*
LA: I haven't looked. I suppose it's just part of the historical record.

OLR: *Can you tell us what you found to be the most challenging part of your role as Chief Prosecutor?*
LA: I think the most challenging part is that it was *extremely* operational. When I went, I thought of it as a kind of a laboratory of comparative law – you know, I was going to work with civil law trained lawyers and criminal lawyers and international lawyers and prosecutors – but I didn't realize that in fact in the early years during my time, 90 percent of the work was investigations and arrests. We were barely getting one or two cases into trial. And *that* [investigations and arrests], I didn't know very well. In fact, when the Secretary-General[46] made the proposal to appoint me to the Security Council, the Americans in particular asked a lot of questions – I found out subsequently that they tasked one of their lawyers to read every single decision I've ever written, and I had to meet with them. And then after the Russians found out, I had to meet with them as well. The French didn't care as much; as soon as they figured out I was French-speaking, they were very favourable. And the British I heard, subsequently, weren't very keen to meet with me because they had their own candidate. I didn't know any of that at the time, just the phone rang, and they said, "Yes, it's done". So I admit I didn't really know. I don't know what I thought it would be but, when I got there, we had to run investigations in very challenging circumstances with none of the tools that I was familiar with. We obviously didn't speak the language. We were investigating in a country where I had only been as a tourist – Dubrovnik, Zagreb, Sarajevo – and I had never been to Belgrade. And the investigators came from all over the world, so they didn't speak Serbo-Croatian as it was then called. We didn't know the country; we had no pre-existing network of informants; we didn't have wiretap capacity; we didn't have search warrant capacity. It was *very* challenging. And for me, the body of law was also very new because what we were investigating were crimes against humanity – war crimes, that is Geneva Conventions.[47] And I didn't know anything about the function of

45 *Ibid.* Section 56.1(1) states that, "[n]otwithstanding section 55, Madam Justice Louise Arbour of the Ontario Court of Appeal is authorized to take a leave from her judicial duties to serve as Prosecutor of the International Tribunal for the Prosecution of Persons Responsible for Serious Violations of International Humanitarian Law Committed in the Territory of the Former Yugoslavia and of the International Tribunal for Rwanda."

46 UN Secretary General Boutros Boutros-Ghali invited Louise Arbour to the post of Chief Prosecutor. See Jane Petch, "Louise Arbour at Salt Spring's Forum", *Island Tides* 25:13 (4 July 2013) 8, online: <www.islandtides.com>.

47 The Geneva Conventions comprise four treaties, and three additional protocols that establish the standards of international law for the humanitarian treatment of war. See *Geneva Convention for the Amelioration of the Condition of the Wounded and Sick in Armed Forces in the Field*, 12 August 1949, 75 UNTS 31, Can TS 1965 No 20 [Geneva Convention I];

armies, chains of command – and so that part of it was very hard. The politics were also really brutal. And when I say it was operational, the biggest challenge when I arrived was to get people arrested. There was a lot of pressure from the judges in particular who had nothing to do to amend the statute to make us a court that would try *in absentia* – which I thought, "If they go this way, I'm going home. It's going to just be like an archive, I don't want to do that." So we developed strategies for arrest and initiatives. And I had to, in my own mind, develop a position as to the legality of arrests. Would I sustain a position where we might try to apprehend someone through methods that might not be fully legal? And what position would I take? We had to design all kinds of rules that would work in that unique environment. This is not like a state. In fact, in most cases, the state is on the other side, no wonder it was so hard. We kept asking ourselves that. It was so hard because we were using national rules in a sense to put constraints on the might of the state facing an individual who needs a lot of protection, such as the right to counsel and the presumption of innocence. But in those international cases, very often, the accused was a general or a political leader from a country that was protecting him, sheltering him and not sharing evidence ... so it was operationally and structurally very hard.

OLR: *Can you tell us how you decided to indict Slobodan Milošević*[48] *and what needed to happen for that to take place?*
LA: The statute required that we investigate and prosecute those most responsible for the most serious crimes. So we had determined internally that those most responsible meant up the chain of command and that the low-key perpetrators, even though they may have actually killed hundreds of people, were not the most responsible in a system that didn't have the capacity to try thousands or even hundreds of cases. The original strategy that my predecessor had put in place was very similar to what you would do in a national system in an organized crime type prosecutions – or at least so they say: you start by catching the small fish and you squeeze them by making a deal – give them either some kind of immunity or a very light sentence and then they turn. Well first of all, it doesn't

Geneva Convention for the Amelioration of the Condition of Wounded, Sick and Shipwrecked Members of Armed Forces at Sea, 12 August 1949, 75 UNTS 85, Can TS 1965 No 20 [Geneva Convention II]; *Geneva Convention Relative to the Treatment of Prisoners of War*, 12 August 1949, 75 UNTS 135, Can TS 1965 No 20 [Geneva Convention III]; *Geneva Convention Relative to the Protection of Civilian Persons in Time of War*, 12 August 1949, 75 UNTS 287, Can TS 1965 No 20 [Geneva Convention IV].

48 Slobodan Milošević was President of Serbia from 1990 to 1997 and President of the Federal Republic of Yugoslavia from 1997 to 2000. The International Criminal Tribunal indicted him for crimes carried out against civilians in Kosovo, Croatia, Bosnia and Herzegovina including genocide, deportation, murder and persecutions on political, racial or religious grounds. See International Criminal Tribunal for the former Yugoslavia, "Slobodan Milošević", online: <www.icty.org/x/cases/slobodan_milosevic/cis/en/cis_milosevic_slobodan_en.pdf>.

necessarily work very well in an extremely politicized environment where there are lots of loyalties and where people don't turn because they believe in their cause. More importantly, what kind of deal do you make to someone who is a party to genocide? So when I got there, I thought we now know enough about what happened to select the events that we think, on the basis of what we know so far, are the most likely to bring us up the chain of command. And, in the case of Milošević, this was *very* challenging because most of the crimes that we were looking into had been perpetrated in the territory of Bosnia. Milošević was never the President of Bosnia – in fact, to make an analogy, it's as though you were trying to impute responsibility to the Governor of Arizona for crimes perpetrated by the US Army in Afghanistan. Well, what's the connection? *De jure*, there is no connection. *De facto*, everybody knew he called all the shots. But what everybody knows and what you can bring in a courtroom is a very different thing. So that's why it took *many* years, even after I left, before there was enough evidence to bring charges against him for crimes in Bosnia. What changed, even though we were working on that from the time I got there, was when Milošević started committing crimes in Kosovo, which led to NATO essentially declaring war in January 1999, when it agreed to the use of air strikes and started bombing.[49] At that point, under the Serbian Constitution, Milošević became *de jure*, in law, the Commander of the Army and of all the police forces – so now *in law*, he was imputable. And we would systematically send him letters telling him that we have reasonable grounds to believe that a massacre has been perpetrated, you have a duty to prevent, and a duty to punish, so that he couldn't say, "I didn't know." So it was at this point that the legal case was falling into our hands, we just had to collect the facts, which was challenging enough. So I indicted him in May 1999 for offences committed in the prior three months because finally it was falling into place. But what had become a little easier as a matter of law, had become a lot harder as a matter of politics because NATO was

---

49 Kosovo lies in southern Serbia and has a mixed population, the majority of which being ethnic Albanians. The region enjoyed a high degree of autonomy within the former Yugoslavia until President Milošević altered the status of the region by removing its autonomy and bringing it under the direct control of Belgrade, the Serbian capital. The Kosovar Albanians strenuously opposed the move. In 1998, open conflict between Serbian military and police forces and Kosovar Albanian forces resulted in the deaths of over 1,500 Kosovar Albanians and forced 400,000 people from their homes. The international community became gravely concerned about the escalating conflict, its humanitarian consequences and the risk of it spreading to other countries. President Milošević's disregard for diplomatic efforts aimed at peacefully resolving the crisis became a concern for the North Atlantic Treaty Organization (NATO). In January 1999, NATO agreed to the use of air strikes if required, by issuing a warning to both sides in the conflict. In March 1999, US Ambassador Holbrooke flew to Belgrade in a final attempt to persuade President Milošević to stop attacks on the Kosovar Albanians or face imminent NATO air strikes. Milošević refused to comply and NATO gave the order to commence air strikes (Operation Allied Force) on March 23, 1999. See NATO, "NATO's Role in Relation to the Conflict in Kosovo" (15 July 1999), online: <www.nato.int>.

bombing. This is actually also an interesting little footnote to my appointment as Chief Prosecutor under the *Judges Act*. There had been suggestions that I could go and remain paid by Canada, sort of seconded to the UN, to do that role. And I took the position that this was not realistic – even though Canada was not a party and there was not an immediate appearance of conflict of interest – the statute said that a Prosecutor shall not seek nor receive instruction from any government nor any other source. So the Chief Prosecutor position was a purely independent post and I couldn't be on Canada's payroll. Well, as it turned out, when NATO started bombing Kosovo, Canada fell under my jurisdiction. So had I not insisted on the necessity to have *no links*, I think at that point I would have been in a very difficult position because there would have at least been an appearance of a conflict. Anyway, so the politics then were tense because NATO was conducting war essentially from 35,000 feet – there were no troops on the ground and so no body bags – and they had been bombing for about 70 or 80 days when I brought the indictment and NATO started to be very worried that Milošević was not capitulating and they might have to send ground troops. And so, even though nobody said anything to me, I think the general feeling was that an indictment would not be a good idea because Milošević would feel trapped and he would never surrender, which may require an escalation of the war and a change of methods. Well he did: he surrendered about a week after we indicted him. I can't take credit for that, because there was no way to know how he would react to the indictment.

OLR: *Following your time as Chief Prosecutor, you were then appointed to the Supreme Court of Canada.*[50] *Did you think at that point you would return to a position with the United Nations?*

LA: No – I never expected to have any other job once I was appointed to the Supreme Court. Even though I had a pretty jumpy career, I really thought that this is it. I bought a house, I renovated it and I thought it was going to be my home in perpetuity. That's very much how everybody feels when you go to the Supreme Court. In retrospect, I think I probably would not have stayed until 75. And I look at others who have been appointed after me and I think there is more of a trend now – you know give it a good 10, maybe 15 years, and retire. When you are appointed relatively young I believe you've had a chance to make your mark and say what you have to say in 10 or 15 years. And there is lots of talent in this country, lots of other people who have something to contribute, and so I believe that that's good. But in my case, in none of the jobs that I've had, have I thought about the future. I mean, when I was Chief Prosecutor, I left

---

50 Louise Arbour was appointed to the Supreme Court of Canada on September 15, 1999 and retired from the bench on June 30, 2004. See Supreme Court of Canada Biography, Justice Arbour, *supra* note 3.

after three years because the Prime Minister called – the phone rang – and offered me the Supreme Court, which I felt I had to go. But if I hadn't received that call, I would have completed my four years and gone back to the Court of Appeal. Again because I thought in the longer term: if I'm away for eight years, I'm done with Canada. And my children were still relatively … not young, young, but too young for me to cut my ties completely to Canada and plunge into purely international work. So when I went to the Supreme Court, I was coming home for good.

OLR: *So then what?*
LA: Then the phone rang.

OLR: *And what was it about that phone call that really made you decide to return to the UN?*
LA: First of all, again, it's very surreal how these things happen. I came out of court one day, my secretary told me that there's a message to call the Secretary-General of the UN.[51] So I assumed that he must want a reference to someone and I felt *very* badly because this was in October of 2003 and that August before, his very, very good friend, whom I knew very well, Sérgio Vieira de Mello,[52] had been killed in Baghdad. And I meant to write to the Secretary-General and I knew Sérgio, and I knew they were very close, but it was one of the things – you don't say, you don't do it, you don't write – and I knew as soon as I had him on the phone, I would have to say something about Sérgio and I thought, "This is really painful." So I called them back and before he could say anything, I said, "I want to tell you how sorry I am about Sérgio." And he said, "Well that's the purpose of my call." He said something like, "I'd like you to replace him." And I thought, "You want me to go to Baghdad, you're serious?" And then I had forgotten that Sérgio was the High Commissioner for Human Rights, very briefly, about eight months and then he went on a special assignment in Iraq and was killed. So I'd forgotten that he was actually the High Commissioner for Human Rights. So he said, "I'd like you to come back as the High Commissioner for Human Rights." And I said, "I can't, you don't understand, I'm at the Supreme Court. Nobody quits, I can't. I mean this is my lifetime assignment, in perpetuity!"

51 The Secretary-General of the United Nations at the time was Kofi Annan, who held the position from January 1997 to December 2006. See United Nations, "Former Secretaries-General", online: <www.un.org>.

52 Sérgio Vieira de Mello was appointed to the position of United Nations High Commissioner for Human Rights on September 12, 2002. Shortly after his appointment, he took a leave from the position to serve as Special Representative for Kofi Annan in Iraq. Sérgio Vieira de Mello and 22 colleagues were killed in an attack on the United Nations headquarters in Baghdad on August 19, 2003 at the age of 55. See Office of the High Commissioner for Human Rights, "Sérgio Vieira de Mello", online: United Nations Human Rights: <www.ohchr.org>.

But I also told Kofi Annan "But you know how much I enjoyed working with you, if I can help you in any other way, you know small things that I could do, talk, that's fine. But I can't do that." And I hung up the phone and I didn't tell anybody. But I just kept thinking, "Oh my god, that would be great, human rights." And the Office of the High Commissioner for Human Rights did not have a very good reputation in the UN. It was not very operational, and I thought, "I can move it and make it much more field based – anyway, stop dreaming it won't happen." And then during the Christmas holiday, actually I think New Year's Eve that year, I had a friend from The Hague who used to work with me, Catherine Cisse. We were at a New Year's party and it had been a long time since the call and so I decided to mention it to Catherine and to someone else who was not a lawyer but knows the politics, the UN, *et cetera.* And I said, "You'll never believe who called me this fall – Kofi." And she says, "Oh yeah, what did he want?" And I said, "Oh, he wanted me to become the High Commissioner." And she said "And …?" And I told her, "And I said no." She says, "Are you crazy? There's nine of you on the Supreme Court, you're just a voice in the wilderness, that's the job you must take." And I said, "Well I'm sure they've filled it anyway, so just forget about it." And, well, they hadn't filled it, and the issue got resurrected and they called again and I thought I could do something – especially if Kofi backs me up at the beginning – since this was midway through his second term, his term would expire before mine – I thought, maybe I could do something. So I went.

OLR: *What were some highlights of your time as the UN High Commissioner*[53] *and some of the challenges?*
LA: Well, it's very interesting, because very often the most impact that you can have or the biggest challenges are completely invisible. I think, in that job, in the four years I was there, the work that to me was the most significant is the work I did internally. It's an office that had not been, I think, historically very well managed. So there were lots of employment issues, a lot of the people, like 80 percent of the staff, were on three- to six-month contracts. It was just very messy and very hard then to mobilize people. So for the first almost 18 months I was there, I did a lot of work internally to try to regularize posts. And part of my objective in doing that was to get people out of Geneva and become much more field based. It was a system that was way too geared to servicing member states, servicing the United Nations Commission of Human Rights (UNCHR) as it was then called. Later, it became the United Nations Human Rights Council and, in a sense, too deferential, I think, to states' interest and just addicted to seminars and conferences and so on. I was concerned about the lack of impact and so I tried to reorganize the office and tried to open space for us to work in the field, which

[53] Louise Arbour served as United Nations High Commissioner for Human Rights from 2004 to 2008. See Office of the High Commissioner for Human Rights, "Louise Arbour", online: United Nations Human Rights <www.ohchr.org>.

was *very* hard. I encountered lots of resistance. States saw it exactly the way I did, which is where the impact will be, and therefore many of them were not very keen. And to add insult to injury, if you can imagine the political environment – this was 2004 to 2008, which was during the Bush Administration in the US so the Americans on a good day were absent, and on a bad day, pretty hostile. At a time when they were confronting even the normative basis of the torture convention, resorting to extraordinary rendition and the like, I mean it was a *very* challenging environment politically when you have a country that should be a pillar of support so disengaged and adding duel to the claims of double standards that many countries were advancing to distance themselves from their own human rights obligations. But to me, the biggest thing was to try to get a bigger presence in the field and the one that was the most successful became huge – we opened a very large presence in Nepal. Again, it's not very visible because it never makes the press in countries like Canada, but it had a lot of impact.

OLR: *Following your position as the UN High Commissioner for Human Rights, you then served as the President and Chief Executive Officer for the International Crisis Group.*[54] *Can you tell us some of the priorities of that role, some of the challenges and some of your proudest accomplishments?*

LA: I knew Crisis Group from my work as the Chief Prosecutor in the years that I worked at The Hague and subsequently as the High Commissioner. The Crisis Group was founded in the Balkans and, at the time, I was doing something very narrow, which was investigating war crimes. But Crisis Group was doing contemporary political analysis, which we had no capacity to do internally at ICTY – so I read a lot of their materials and thought it was really good and very helpful. So when I left The Hague and joined the Supreme Court of Canada, they asked me to join their Board. And, after talking to a few of my colleagues, I realized I could probably do that because Crisis Group will never be a litigant before the Court. So I joined the Board. I would go to their meetings; it was my lifeline to international affairs – you know remaining at least knowledgeable. So when I left the post of High Commissioner, again I rejoined, I had resigned because it was incompatible. So I rejoined the Board and then Gareth Evans,[55] who had been the President and CEO for nine years, left they approached me

---

54 The International Crisis group is an independent, non-profit, non-governmental organization that works to prevent and resolve deadly conflict. It conducts field-based research, provides policy prescriptions and engages in global advocacy. See International Crisis Group, "About Crisis Group", online: <www.crisisgroup.org>.

55 The Honourable Gareth Evans was President and Chief Executive Officer of the International Crisis Group from 2000 to 2009. He is recognized internationally for his role in the UN peace plan for Cambodia and was made a Companion of the Order of Australia (AC) in 2012 for his eminent service to international relations, particularly in the Asia-Pacific region. He has been Chancellor of the Australian National University since January 2010. See Personal Website of Gareth Evans, "Summary Biography of Gareth Evans", online: <www.gevans.org>.

and asked me if I'd be interested. At that point, all these stints I made in Europe had been short: I was three years in The Hague, four years in Geneva. It's very hard for me to be away for long periods. And this was based in Brussels. I was not very keen to live abroad again but I loved the organization and I thought the work was very high quality. So I agreed to go, first for three years, and then eventually I stayed five. But it's the longest I've been away. And in this role, it's the farthest I've been away from law. Even as the High Commissioner, it's not all law, but there is a legal framework for international treaties. This was pure political analysis in crisis, conflict prevention and conflict resolution. There were *some* legal issues: we had to deal at times with the effectiveness of the International Criminal Court, the Court of Lebanon – of which we were quite critical – so it was a again a new learning curve for me. Even though I knew the organization a bit, I had not run something that had so little legal content. But the mandate was very clear, the people were very talented, so there was not a big challenge like I found in my prior positions, where you had to build things from scratch at the tribunal or as the High Commissioner and where there had been so many internal challenges and dysfunctions. This was not at all the case at the Crisis Group. So, in a sense, the biggest challenge for me was the challenge of being a generalist leading teams of specialists. It's a very humbling position to in. What remained for me the most difficult part of that kind of work, which I think eventually got the better of me, was the fundraising aspect. Crisis Group has an annual budget of about $20 million. It's an NGO and you have to raise that money. It takes a lot of time and energy, and it's a talent and it's very hard and it's not something I particularly enjoy.

OLR: *Is there one moment or accomplishment that really stands out for you during your time as the President and the CEO of the ICG?*
LA: The biggest project that I oversaw was the work we did in Sri Lanka. Even though it was a little bit at the edge of the organization, we produced a report the first year I was there called "War Crimes in Sri Lanka."[56] Almost nobody else was doing that kind of work, and we were doing it, not from human rights point of view, but from a conflict prevention point of view. We took the position that, unless the government acknowledges and accounts for the slaughter that basically took place when the government finally eradicated the LTTE (Liberation Tigers of Tamil Eelam) in 2009 – unless there's a truthful accounting for that with responsibility visited on the particular government officials responsible for the killing – we estimated 30,000 – subsequently some numbers went up to 40,000 Tamils on the beaches of Sri Lanka – the chances of a sustainable peace in Sri Lanka would disappear and there will eventually be a revival of extremism. So we did it from that perspective but it was very difficult work – taking on a

56 See International Crisis Group, "War Crimes in Sri Lanka, Asia Report N°191" (17 May 2010), online: <www.crisisgroup.org>.

government that is again very hostile and ferociously organized to push back. And not many others were doing that. And, as an NGO, it's pretty remarkable because we published a report and we basically lobbied the United Nations to take it on. And eventually to his credit, Ban Ki-Moon[57] almost personally took an interest, which led to reports by the UN that validated the work we had done and put a lot of pressure. Now, there still hasn't been any prosecutions, but what otherwise would have been buried a long time ago hasn't gone away either. So of all the things during my time with the Crisis Group, this is probably the one in which I was the most directly involved and that I think had quite a substantial impact.

OLR: *What led you to private practice after all your years of work on the international stage?*
LA: Well, I don't feel – even though we are sitting here in this wonderful office – that I'm in private practice in the traditional sense. Although it's hard to tell, whatever comes across my desk I seem to find interesting. But I have kept some of my international commitments. I was appointed to be *ad hoc* judge at the International Court of Justice in the case between Bolivia and Chile.[58] I'm a member of the Global Commission on Drug Policy,[59] which I'm very interested in. I'm going to Geneva tomorrow for the International Commission against the Death Penalty.[60] So I have all kinds of bits and pieces of things

57 Secretary General Ban Ki-Moon is the current Secretary General of the United Nations and has held this position since January 1, 2007. Secretary General Ban Ki-Moon was unanimously re-elected in 2011, and he will continue in this role until December 31, 2016. See United Nations, "Secretary General Ban-Ki Moon: Biography", online: <www.un.org>.

58 Bolivia initiated proceedings against Chile in 2013 over a dispute about Bolivia's sovereign access to the Pacific Ocean. When a state party to proceedings before the International Court of Justice (ICJ) lacks a judge from its country on the ICJ bench, that party may select a judge to sit *ad hoc* on that case. See International Court of Justice, "The Court: Judges *ad hoc*", online: <www.icj-cij.org>; International Court of Justice, Press Release, No 2013/11, "Bolivia Institutes Proceedings Against Chile with Regard to a Dispute Concerning the Obligation of Chile to Negotiate the 'Sovereign Access of Bolivia to the Pacific Ocean'" (24 April 2013), online: <www.icj-cij.org/docket/files/153/ 17340.pdf>.

59 The purpose of the Global Commission on Drug Policy is to bring to the international level an informed and science-based discussion about humane and effective ways to reduce the harm caused by drugs. The Commission's main areas of inquiry include the current international drug control regime; global overview of drug policies and laws; confronting the production and supply chain; criminal justice challenges; demand reduction through prevention, harm reduction and treatment; and the economic and political implications of drug trade and organized crime. See Global Commission on Drug Policy, "What We Do", online: <www.globalcommissionondrugs.org> [Global Commission on Drug Policy].

60 The mandate of the International Commission against the Death Penalty is to support work that aims to abolish the death penalty in all regions of the world. Its objectives include abolishing the death sentence in national legislation, promoting a worldwide moratorium on the death penalty and calling for a stop to executions where International Law restricts the practice. See International Commission against the Death Penalty, "Mandate", online: <www.icomdp.org>.

that I need to do and I need help for that. And maybe because I had drifted quite a bit from the law in my most recent job, I was keen to reconnect with a legal environment. But I thought it would be interesting to, now that I'm back home, to keep involved in these international issues, but re-engage a bit more on domestic matters. So I knew several of the lawyers at this firm who had appeared before me, mostly in fact from the Toronto and Ottawa offices, because that's where most of my career was, but I knew some people in the Montréal office and I was determined to finally come back to Montréal. So it was an easy choice and very good fit for me. And I only started a couple of months ago, so already people come to me with different things. So it's not a very traditional practice, but it suits my interests and I hope it's helpful to some people inside the office.

OLR: *Reflecting back on your career is there anything you would change or do differently? Or do you think everything happened the way it did for a reason?*
LA: I don't know what the reason is so far but there can only be so many coincidences. Why am I so often moved to very different things? Presumably, I must have – I mean I look at some of my colleagues who were appointed to the bench at the same time I was, who are still there having developed very deep expertise. Some of them are still doing murder cases 30 years later, so they know everything there is to know about one thing, and I think some people find their professional comfort in that exquisite amount of specialization. I would not have had this insight into my own makeup at the outset but now, when I look back, I think it's pretty obvious that what I like and crave is that period of uncertainty – that kind of learning curve. It's very clear: I really like that phase where I don't really get it. And it's not that I get bored. In fact, that's the irony of it. After I finally feel a little more comfortable, I'm really interested. I've never walked away from anything I've done – from teaching, trial work, appellate work, international work – because I didn't like it, and even less so because I was bored. There is nothing boring about it. It's just that I seem to have this irresistible attraction to taking on something for which I'm entirely unqualified. There's no other way to put it I think.

OLR: *As a woman who has had so many leadership roles, what work, if any, do you think still needs to be done to increase the number of women in leadership positions in the legal profession?*
LA: I think it's obvious we have to do something because it's just not happening. Women have entered the law schools in unprecedented numbers. They enter the profession in all kinds of different capacities and then they just disappear. I think collectively we have to find an explanation. I know there's a big debate in the literature between different viewpoints. For example, there's Sheryl Sandberg's

perspective who wrote *Lean In*[61] – the idea that women have to learn to be much more aggressive, putting themselves forward and so on. And then there's Anne-Marie Slaughter who published this piece in the Atlantic entitled "Why Women Still Can't Have It All."[62] I tend to be more of that view. I think culturally, legally, politically – it's a question of time management in two ways: first, the 24-hour working day is notoriously unhelpful to women who have, and in our culture continue to have, disproportionate family responsibilities. And by family I mean looking after their small children, looking after their teenagers, looking after their elderly parents. All this. So the 24-hour working day, even with all the technological advances that at some point we thought would be a real revolution like work-at-home and flextime. And so the reality is that, certainly, high-paying jobs, but probably across the marketplace, have either pushed women into poorly paid part-time work or have not opened the space. So the 24-hour day is bad for women. And then the life span of when you're supposed to take off in your career is problematic. It's reasonably egalitarian when women don't have a lot of family responsibilities. So until you're, in our society, in your late twenties where you don't have small children, teenagers or ancient parents, you're at a competitive par with your peers. But the minute these family responsibilities kick in, they just happen to hit you in the decade where you're supposed to be on the jumping pad to great success and that's where it doesn't happen. So I think it's both ways. I think it's not helpful. And I think the reality speaks for itself. It's just not happening. I was talking to a woman I met yesterday about women in the workplace and the glass ceiling and how Hillary Clinton, when she ran, said, "I put 18-million cracks in the highest and hardest glass ceiling" and so on.[63]

61 See Sheryl Sandberg, *Lean In: Women, Work, and the Will to Lead* (New York: Alfred A Knopf, 2013). Sheryl Sandberg is the Chief Operating Officer of Facebook. She holds a BA in Economics from Harvard and an MBA from Harvard Business School. Before joining Facebook, she was the Vice-President of Global Online Sales and Operations at Google and Chief of Staff at the United States Treasury Department.

62 See Anne-Marie Slaughter, "Why Women Still Can't Have It All", *The Atlantic* 310:1 (July/August 2012) 84. In 2012, Princeton Professor Anne-Marie Slaughter wrote a popular article that renewed debate over the professional barriers women face as a result of incompatible work and family obligations. Slaughter drew on her experience as Director of Policy Planning at the State Department to argue that American women today "still can't have it all." She argues that most women are forced to make tough choices between pursuing a successful career and participating fully in family life. In the article, Slaughter criticizes Sandberg's explanation for the lack of women in leadership positions as implicitly blaming women for their under-representation.

63 In 2008, Hillary Clinton gave a speech announcing that she would suspend her campaign for the Democratic presidential nomination. In the speech she said, "[a]lthough we weren't able to shatter that highest, hardest glass ceiling this time, thanks to you, it's got about 18 million cracks in it and the light is shining through like never before, filling us all with the hope and the sure knowledge that the path will be a little easier next time." See "Hilary Clinton Endorses Barack Obama", Transcript, *The New York Times* (7 June 2008) online: <www.nytimes.com>.

So it's a metaphor that is very familiar. And this woman said to me, "I don't think it's quite right." And I said, "Oh no, how is that?" And she said, "Well, when you think of the glass ceiling, it has some features: it's invisible but it's very real and you move on and then one day boom! You just crash and you hit your head and it just shatters or it doesn't shatter, but it shatters you. But it's this hard, invisible thing. But the reality is, we should be thinking of it more as a kind of zone of toxic poison. Like an ozone layer of toxic gas. Also invisible. So you move along and you go to law school and you do your thing. And then one day you don't feel so good. Things are just not coming your way anymore. You don't know it but you've entered this poisonous gas." I like it. I think it's a much better metaphor than the ceiling. It's an invidious toxic thing that has the same effect essentially, but is even more pernicious than the ceiling.

OLR: *If you could give students starting their legal careers one piece of advice, what would it be?*
LA: It's very hard. As I said, I don't have a lot of insights. I did a lot of different things. So I could say, "If you want to be like me ...." But why should I assume anybody wants to be like me? But assuming that's what you think you'd want to do, well then I would say, you have to be able to take risks. The biggest risk I took after having invested years in law school and the Bar admission course was moving to Ontario, which is like moving to Mars. I didn't speak the language. I didn't know the legal system. I was not a member of the Bar. After that everything else was of the same genre. You have to be able to take risks, not fit the mould and not let anybody squeeze you into their expectations of what your career should look like. And it's going to sound completely absurd but also not to be too ambitious. [*Laughs*] How can one look at my career and say oh she was not very ambitious? But I think sometimes ambition can just drive you into making the wrong choices – making conservative choices – you know being worried that you've invested in something and you should stay there. But who am I to say that? What good is it to people who are not like me and who will have a wonderful, happy, professional life in a very different environment, maybe much narrower in a great area of specialty? So in the end, I think the greatest difficulty is the lack of insights we have into our own desires or ambitions or needs. And particularly for you, and for me at least, there were just so many choices ... now you're solicited in so many ways I don't know how you manage this. On the other hand, compared to many people I've met in the rest of the world, how can you complain about having so many choices and options and opportunities? So I would say just trust your instinct. Don't be scared. You could try something and it may not work out. I can't really say that. Things worked out pretty well for me but it wasn't written anywhere that it was going to work out. It just worked. But I don't know if it would work for anybody else.

OLR: *We'd like to shift now and ask you your opinion on a few substantive areas of law drawing on some of judgments. In Gosselin v Québec*[64] *you wrote a dissenting opinion where you held that section 7 of the Charter*[65] *imposes a positive obligation on the state to offer basic protection for the life, liberty and security of its citizens. The majority held that the facts did not compel finding a positive obligation under section 7, but left open the possibility that another factual scenario could support finding a positive obligation on the part of the state to ensure the life, liberty and security of the person for individuals. Do we have any reason to think the Court will ever recognize positive obligations under section 7?*

LA: Quite honestly, I have no reason to think anything about what the Court will do in the future. First of all, I don't know them. I don't read judgments on a systematic basis. I mean I'm not a student of the Court. Even though I sat there for many years, I don't sit around reading all their cases – so I don't have a very good sense of what the current thinking is, whether the Court is very imaginative or not, or what it's doing. And the bottom line is, the Court cannot initiate anything, so a case would have to come up that would have the right set of facts. And the beauty of the law is that of course that you can never anticipate. The good case that comes to you is never a case that you saw coming for the most part and the issues come to you in all kinds of different ways. So I have absolutely no idea whether a case will ever come up that will give an opportunity for the Court to revisit what I thought was its erroneous position and whether the Court at that time would be as enlightened as I thought I was.

OLR: *Having worked in the field of international human rights for several years after Winnipeg Child and Family Services v KLW,*[66] *do you see the balancing*

---

64 *Gosselin v Québec (Attorney General)*, 2002 SCC 84, [2002] 4 SCR 429. Gosselin brought a class action lawsuit challenging the constitutionality of certain provisions of the social assistance scheme in Québec. Gosselin argued that conditions and restrictions on access to social assistance for recipients under the age of 30 violated sections 7 and 15 of the *Canadian Charter of Rights and Freedoms*, Part I of the *Constitution Act, 1982*, being Schedule B to the *Canada Act 1982* (UK), 1982, c 11 [*Charter*]. While the majority of the Court rejected both arguments, Justice Arbour (as she then was) wrote an important dissent recognizing a positive obligation on the state to ensure basic protections for life, liberty and security of the person.

65 *Charter, supra* note 63, s 7. Section 7 provides that "[e]veryone has the right to life, liberty and security of the person and the right not to be deprived thereof except in accordance with the principles of fundamental justice."

66 *Winnipeg Child and Family Services v KLW*, 2000 SCC 48, [2000] 2 SCR 519. This case concerned the constitutionality of a legislative provision allowing for the warrantless apprehension of a child in non-emergency situations. The majority of the Court held that even in non-emergency situations, the risks posed to the child's life and health by the delays associated with a prior hearing outweigh the benefits of requiring a hearing. In a dissenting opinion, Chief Justice McLachlin and Justice Arbour found that a post-apprehension hearing could not justify infringing upon an individual's section 7 rights. The principles of fundamental justice require prior judicial authorization before interfering with the parent's interests in raising one's own child.

act between the rights of the parent and child at the heart of this case any differently now?

LA: Probably not. If I think in the context of, for instance, child-parent relationships they're very different from other contexts because, in most societies, for instance, in developing worlds, what parents crave is more state support or intervention because they have so few resources and that's why economic and social rights are so important. The right to health and the right to education are critical for the actual survival of their children. So, in that sense, the social and political context would sometimes be very different than what in that case was the question of the protection of the child. We must balance intrusive state action and procedural protections to put in place to ensure that in its protective mandate, the state doesn't overstep or shatter the relationship unduly. So the context may be very different. In a sense it comes back maybe to *Gosselin*. I think in lots of developing countries where politically there is always a stronger claim for support for social and economic rights than for civil and political rights. It's in part because of that. Because of what is needed from the state, I think, is much more compatible with the interests the parents have and their children. They just need a lot of help to raise them. But in the end it wouldn't change my sense starting from *Gosselin* that states have a responsibility, not just to their citizens but to all people that fall under their jurisdiction to provide for life, liberty, security, health, education, safety in a family environment. But also that there needs to be a recognition of the parental relationship and the danger I think in societies that have a lot of state capacity of overreach and so on. And that's where the judiciary has to play an important role, whether it's the judiciary or any kind of independent observer. So the context is very different but I think the call … the relationship between the individual and the state with respect to fundamental rights is the same it's just the context that is different.

OLR: *In Sauvé v Canada (2002),*[67] *you wrote for the court that section 51(e) of the Canada Elections Act,*[68] *which denied prisoners the right to vote, was unconstitutional. Over 10 years later, you heard a similar constitutional challenge at the Supreme Court of Canada.*[69] *Was there anything striking about hearing*

67 *Sauvé v Canada* (1992), 7 OR (3d) 481, 89 DLR (4th) 644 (CA). Sauvé challenged the constitutionality of section 51(e) under the *Canadian Elections Act*, which denied the right to vote to all persons undergoing punishment as an inmate in any penal institution for the commission of an offence. Justice Arbour found that the provision infringed section 3 of the *Charter* and was not justified under section 1.

68 *Canada Elections Act*, RSC 1985, c E-2, s 51(e).

69 *Sauvé v Canada (Chief Electoral Officer)*, 2002 SCC 68, [2002] 3 SCR 519. After the Supreme Court found the section prohibiting all inmates from voting in federal elections unconstitutional, Parliament replaced the section with a narrower prohibition on voting for inmates serving sentences of two or more years. See *Canada Elections Act*, SC 2000, c 9, s 4(c).

a case as a Supreme Court judge when you had heard a related case as a Court of Appeal judge?

LA: It was a different case because the *Canada Elections Act* had been amended, and the justification that the government was putting forward for the deprivation of the right to vote for prisoners was very different than the rationale that they advanced at the Ontario Court of Appeal. At the Court of Appeal, the law at that point I think was that you couldn't vote if you were incarcerated on the day of the vote. I mean under *Oakes* you couldn't even pass a rationality test. There was nothing rational about it, particularly when I think the evidence was that, on any given day, as much as a third of the people who are incarcerated were there on a default provision. So it was completely irrational, totally random. I mean if the elections had been the day before or the day after – a lot of people are there for 24 hours or a very short period – they would have been able to vote. But, by the time the case came to the Supreme Court of Canada, the law had changed and the rationale for it was articulated differently. I think you couldn't vote if you'd been convicted of a felony punishable by more than two years or something. And now the government's rationale was that in order to be entitled to exercise your constitutional right to vote, Canada needed an enlightened and decent citizenry – or something like that. So even though the case may look like the same case – it's a prisoners' right to vote case – the entire analysis was very different. What it reveals about the dialogue – I don't know about other areas of the law – but I think it's fair to say on this one the Canadian government was pretty tenacious on its position. They just wouldn't take no for an answer and came back at it in many different ways, which is quite ironic because when the *Charter* came into force in 1982, there were at least two classes of people who were clearly disenfranchised – prisoners and judges – and both challenged it. Of course judges alerted the Minister that they would challenge the constitutionality of that and the Minister caved in right away and said, "Don't worry, we'll change the provision, you're right, this is not constitutional." And then for prisoners, it's like decades of litigation, change the law, and so on. So, if one wants to be a little cynical, this is the kind of issue that is very costly politically. I don't think you lose a lot of votes for resisting giving prisoners the right to vote, nor do you gain many votes by granting them that right. Maybe it's purely ideological.

OLR: *The next question stems from your judgment in R v Khan,*[70] *where, in the context of a murder trial, a lot of faith is placed in the jury's ability to appreciate*

[70] *R v Khan*, 2001 SCC 86, [2001] 3 SCR 823. During a first-degree murder trial, the jury was in-advertently given access to documents with inadmissible evidence that should have been expunged. The jury found the accused guilty of first-degree murder. The trial judge refused to grant defence counsel's motion for a mistrial. Both the Court of Appeal and the Supreme Court upheld this finding. The majority of the Supreme Court found that the trial judge was in the best position to assess the impact of the inadmissible evidence on the jury and that she did not err in refusing to grant a mistrial.

the rules of evidence that govern the relevant materials upon which they are called upon to make a decision. Do you think juries are equally capable of applying the rules of evidence in the civil context?

LA: I've only had I think two civil jury trials when I was a trial judge and, of course, we didn't have that in Québec, so this was very new. I think what's different in the civil cases I did – it's a long time ago, maybe the rules have changed, I don't know. First of all, I think trial judges are best placed to evaluate the jury's capacity to handle the case – and there may be disagreements on that – but many trial judges that I've spoken to, and that I've known over the years, are impressed with a jury's ability to appreciate the rules of evidence, including in some cases where the verdict goes against the expectations of public opinion. And you'd speak to the trial judge and they'd say the jurors were right on it – diligent, attentive. And you know, who are you, as a single judge, to think you know better? Maybe you understand the mechanics of the rules better, but you know, I've had juries who came to a conclusion different than the one I would have taken, but I defer entirely. On their appreciation of the facts, I would have found probably differently, but I defer. They got it right, as far as I'm concerned. So in a civil case, because they answer questions, there is the capacity to get more insight into the jury's thinking. It's a little bit like forcing them to give reasons by unpacking the questions. And when the law is odd and you charge the jury, you say something that you know that they're going to think doesn't make any sense. And you look at them and sure enough, you can just see on their faces, this can't be serious. Like causation, for instance. Say you have a murder case where there's an issue of causation. So, the accused did the initial act but then there were a lot of pre-existing or intervening causes. You have to decide whether they broke the chain of causation so as to exonerate the accused. … Explain that to the jury, and sometimes they look at you, "Seriously?" You can tell. But I've never sensed their reluctance. You know, when you explain to them, "You have to take the law as I give it to you. If I make a mistake it will be fixed, but you can't change that. But on the facts, I'm entitled to give you my opinion. But I won't and if you think you know what I think, don't pay attention to it." I have a lot of trust and confidence in juries. I had a civil case where again I didn't know how the jury would decide – it was an accident in which a child died and I called one of my colleagues and I said I have this intuition that the jury is going to award more damages than the plaintiff asked for – for loss of care, guidance and companionship – and I said, "This was a really sad case and I have a sense they're going to come up with a much larger award". And so they came back with a question: could I give them a range? And in those days, the law was no. Which frankly made no sense. I had to say to them, "All I can tell you is that you have to give something that's not too little, not too much." What is that supposed to mean? Completely unhelpful. Now I think it's changed. Shortly after I rendered the decision, I think now judges are entitled to give a range for these kinds of cases. Anyways, I couldn't give them a range and sure enough they came back with a number way above the range. And I'd asked my colleagues, "What do I do?" So they said, "Well if you have an experienced counsel for the plaintiff, he's going to ask to amend the pleadings. And you say yes, and let the Court of Appeal sort it out. And if he's not very experienced, you look at him and you say, 'Counsel, do you have a motion to amend your pleading?'" Because you have to get a record that's appealable. And he was experienced so he asked to amend and I said "yes" and it was all set.

OLR: *In your dissenting opinion in R v Lévesque,*[71] *you stated that you disagreed with the majority on the admissibility of evidence "on the very particular facts" of the case. You have mentioned in other interviews how important the specific facts of a case are to the study and practice of law. Do you think the importance of the very particular facts is equally true for all cases or are subtle nuances in the facts of a case more important in certain areas of law over others?*

LA: I think it's all about facts. It was the greatest revelation for me going from teaching law to being a trial judge. Having taught law, particularly evidence and so on, it was all rules and systems and so on, and then I walked into court, particularly when I had to sit alone as a trial judge in areas of the law that I didn't really know, and I would think, "Oh, that's going to be so complicated." But after you found the facts, you have the story, the narrative, you just have to look it up and it usually falls into place. The law is not the hard part – it's sorting out contradictory evidence, what is plausible, and then when you have that, I still believe, that if you're honest about. … And unfortunately, in modern litigation, the facts may have become unmanageable – you know when you have discoveries of billions of e-mails and so on, you're buried under a massive amount of factual reconstruction, which I think is. … I don't know how lawyers do it, where I hear about these very large cases where there's so much material to digest. After you've got that, you've got the narrative fully in place, usually, certainly at the trial level, you make all your findings and if the Court of Appeal has the decency not to interfere unless you really miss something very big, then in *some cases*, there is a legal issue where the law is unresolved or has gone in different directions, but that's not the run of the mill case and that's fixable either at the trial level or higher up. I'm still a big believer of the facts.

---

[71] *R v Lévesque*, 2000 SCC 47, [2000] 2 SCR 487. The accused pled guilty to robbery at a residence and was sentenced to 10 years in prison. The accused appealed the sentence and sought to have new evidence admitted. The Court of Appeal allowed the motion to bring new evidence and substituted the sentence for a lesser one. The majority of the Supreme Court overturned this decision, finding that fresh evidence could not be admitted on appeal simply because it provides more detail than evidence brought at trial. In her dissenting opinion, Justice Arbour held that the Court of Appeal was entitled to admit fresh evidence because the trial judge had mischaracterized the crime. As such, the Court of Appeal was within its authority to admit the evidence required to determine the proper sentence for the accused.

OLR: *In your dissenting opinion in R v Malmo-Levine,*[72] *you held that the harm associated with marijuana use did not justify the state's decision to use imprisonment as a sanction against the prohibition of its possession. What informed your opinion in this case?*
LA: I believe that there are restrictions both on the *mens rea* side and on the *actus reus* side to what the state can do through the use of imprisonment or the threat of imprisonment, which I view as the criminal law field. I believe in the state's power to regulate conduct, including by prohibiting certain things, but not under the stigmatization and the employment of measures that are particular to the criminal law. The work I'm doing now on the Global Commission on Drug Policy[73] is really interesting because it's basically the same issue. It's a massive international effort to revisit all the international conventions that have been put in place worldwide – a system for the control of the non-medical use of drugs that is 100 percent repressive based on prohibition. There is no other field – you know nuclear waste – there's no other field that is the subject of total prohibition. Everything is regulated on a scale, including firearms. All kinds of very dangerous things are regulated. And, in fact, if somebody today … if we didn't have 50 years of experience with the war on drugs, and we were today trying to put in place a system, those who would advocate for total prohibition would be seen as radicals, proposing an unmanageable system of repression. So yes, I do believe that the recourse to the criminal law has to be done with great circumspection both on what the mental, moral element of what the crime is and what kind of conduct should be susceptible to that extreme form of state intervention.

OLR: *Drawing on that, has your work on imprisonment issues, such as your work on the Commission of Inquiry in the Prison for Women, informed your opinion the scope of the criminal law power?*
LA: I think imprisonment is a positive act on the part of the state, the deprivation of liberty is pretty fundamental, and so that's why on the correctional side I believe if you deprive people of their ability to look after themselves – when you're in prison you have no capacity to feed yourself, to look after your health, your security, your intellectual needs and so on – it imposes on the state

72 *R v Malmo-Levine; R v Caine*, 2003 SCC 74, [2003] 3 SCR 571. Malmo-Levine operated a non-profit association focused on reducing harm of marijuana use. Police entered the premises and seized 300 grams of marijuana, charging Malmo-Levine with possession of an illegal substance for the purpose of trafficking under the *Narcotic Control Act*. Malmo-Levine challenged the constitutionality of the provision on the grounds that it violated the harm principle. The majority of the Supreme Court rejected this argument, finding that the harm principle is not a principle of fundamental justice. In a dissenting judgment, Justice Arbour held that a law carrying the risk of imprisoning a person whose conduct causes little or no harm to others offends the principles of fundamental justice.
73 See Global Commission on Drug Policy, *supra* note 60.

an enormous obligation because you've put a person in a position of *extreme* vulnerability. But it's not just that: I think the stigma of a criminal conviction is a serious matter, and that's why I think we have a system of safeguards, such as the presumption of innocence, appellate review, *et cetera*, which are entirely appropriate before we take that kind of disposition. But imprisonment is particularly an enormous responsibility on the part of state, which cannot be taken lightly and where I think the state needs to take enormous responsibility, including in the case of wrongful convictions.

OLR: *In order for international law to be effective, do you think there needs to be an enforcement mechanism, such as a tribunal? Are international treaties more effective in certain areas of law over others?*
LA: I think in the field of international human rights law, the absence of an international court of human rights is fatal to the serious enforcement of rights. I think, in all the countries or regions in which human rights have had a real bite, it's been done through courts. It's true in Canada; it's true in countries that have constitutional human rights protection. And then it's true regionally, for example, the European Court of Human Rights and Inter-American Court of Human Rights. And in contrast to that, the absence of national and/or regional, sub-regional mechanisms in Asia, is a blatant explanation as to why these rights are so difficult to enforce. This is not to diminish the importance of the treaty bodies, for instance in the UN system, and the further development of the advancement of doctrines for the development of cultural political acceptance of the boundaries of gender discrimination, racial discrimination for example. At the end of the day, states are duty bearers and we are rights holders, and the system is run by duty bearers for their own benefit. Until you have a court, an adjudicator – you know the human rights council is a marketplace of trade-offs between different interests, of finger-pointing, of positioning, of posturing. But at the end of the day, without an impartial, credible, public, transparent, adjudicative function with enforcement capacity, the progress will be extremely limited. Now, there may be other areas of the law where you can rely on in state-to-state cooperation and don't need that. But when you're dealing with this politically intimate relationship between a state and its citizens, I don't think that a body of state is likely to be the best environment to advance rights. But this will not happen in my lifetime – I mean that's one thing I tried when I was the High Commissioner. I thought I was being very subtle, but not obviously subtle enough: I tried to launch an initiative to merge all the treaty bodies, so you have you know CEDAW (the Committee on the Elimination of Discrimination Against Women), the Committee Against Torture and the Committee on the Rights of the Child – and they all have their individual meetings and they do their own things and they're *completely* invisible as far as I'm concerned. Certainly, when I was a judge in the Supreme Court of Canada, we didn't spend a lot of time reading opinions of the UN Treaty Body System. So I told them,

we should merge all these committees with one big main door – be the door to the treaty bodies. What I could see over the horizon is, if you did all that, that's step one to eventually, possibly, a court. Well I think although I was being very subtle – "No not a court, no no no!" – but I think others could see where that could go – and then of course all the actors have an interest in preserving their own specialty and they're just so special and so much better than the other guys. Anyway, it went absolutely nowhere, but in my mind that was it – it was trying to invest into a movement that could eventually lead to an adjudicative body with enforcement – with coercive capacity.

OLR: *As a final question to wrap up our interview today, in what areas of law do you think we'll see significant changes or advancements in the foreseeable future?*
LA: It's hard to tell. I don't follow enough of the literature or the case law in the courts. On the big picture, I think the big tickets are environmental protection. I think climate change is the defining challenge of our generation and so if there was ever to be an international treaty and so on, I think that this would then lead to national implementation. So that's one possibility. Politically, it still looks slightly out of reach for the time being, but it has to start happening – it's really five minutes to midnight on this one. The work I do on the International Commission on Drug Policy has actually moved somewhat faster than we thought – I mean with the first report of the Commission,[74] all we were hoping for was the capacity in the US, in Canada, in Europe to have conversations about the failure of the war on drugs – just put a little oxygen so you're not denounced for being some kind of hippy every time you want to have a conversation about it. Well, even that we thought would take a decade. But it moved pretty quickly. Now the next chapter is trying to mobilize enough space for countries to be allowed to experiment with different models of regulation, which is what we're talking about. I think it's a mistake to talk about legalization, because people hear – even though that's not what it means – free for all, totally unregulated – which is absurd because there is no area of human conduct that is totally unregulated. So we need to talk about regulation. If this happened, it would again have a significant impact on human health because we want to shift from a repressive model to a public health model. It would have a huge impact on organized crime and violence in countries. You know this initiative came from Latin America, not surprisingly, chaired by President Cardozo of Brazil, all former heads of states in Mexico, Columbia, Guatemala that are trying to mobilize for a change. If this were to happen, it would change organized crime and, therefore, have

74 *War on Drugs: Report of the Global Commission on Drug Policy* (June 2011), online: Global Commission on Drug Policy <www.globalcommissionondrugs.org/wp-content/themes/gcdp_v1/pdf/Global_Commission_Report_English.pdf>.

an influence on corruption issues. But I'm not holding my breath that this is around the corner. These are the areas I know – domestically I don't know what's brewing in the court system that's ripe for change. I just don't follow it enough to know.

OLR: *Thank you for sharing your experiences and insights in such depth with us today.*

IN MEMORIAM

Asma Jahangir
(1952–2018)

On the final page of this book in honour of Louise Arbour, we pay tribute to Ms Asma Jahangir, one of Pakistan's most distinguished and respected human rights advocates. During her decades-long career, Asma devoted her boundless energy, keen intellect and exceptional moral courage to advancing social justice in her country. With her sister Hina Jilani, Asma co-founded Pakistan's first all-female law firm, along with the Human Rights Commission of Pakistan that she also chaired. Asma and Hina worked heroically to defend the rights of women, children and disenfranchised populations. Asma served as President of the Supreme Court Bar Association and UN Special Rapporteur on Human Rights in Iran. Her contributions to democracy and the rule of law in Pakistan and around the world cannot be overstated, and she has received dozens of awards in recognition of her extraordinary service, including, posthumously, Pakistan's highest civilian award, the Nishan-i-Imtiaz.

We were overjoyed when Asma accepted our invitation to contribute to this book in honour of her close and dear friend Louise Arbour. "It would be a privilege to be associated with anything that Louise is", she wrote. Unfortunately, Asma's health deteriorated and it eventually became impossible for her to keep up her usual pace. When it appeared as though Asma's health was improving, she wrote to us saying that she planned to write something along these lines:

> I met Louise after her appointment as Human Rights Commissioner. It was a hugely challenging position but Louise kept her dignity and balance. She resigned when she felt she could not compromise. But it was as President of the Crisis group where I bonded with her. Her wisdom impressed us all and she gradually transformed the Board from being heavily male and western to a more diverse Board. She has an amazing memory and her colleagues in the office looked up to her and yet found a friend in her. Louise is compassionate and very human. She never tried to put up a brave face when [she was] obviously distressed in reaction to personal challenges. But she faced them bravely. Her family has always been as dear to her as her work. Very few people have reached the top of their profession without being ambitious. Louise is an achiever but not ambitious.

Asma passed away on 11 February 2018. We could not imagine publishing this book without her.

www.ingramcontent.com/pod-product-compliance
Ingram Content Group UK Ltd.
Pitfield, Milton Keynes, MK11 3LW, UK
UKHW051918100926
8556IPUK00021B/1242

9 781780 683546